Holistic Nursing

A Handbook for Practice

Second Edition

Barbara Montgomery Dossey, RN, MS, FAAN
Director, Holistic Nursing Consultants
Santa Fe, New Mexico
Co-Director, Bodymind Systems
Temple, Texas

Lynn Keegan, RN, PhD
Associate Professor, University of Texas
Health Science Center at San Antonio
School of Nursing
Co-Director, Bodymind Systems
Temple, Texas

Cathie E. Guzzetta, RN, PhD, FAAN
Director, Holistic Nursing Consultants
Nursing Research Consultant
Parkland Memorial Hospital
Co-Editor
Alternative Therapies in Health and Medicine
Dallas, Texas

Leslie Gooding Kolkmeier, RN, MEd
Private Practice and Consultant
Celeste, Texas

Endorsed by the American Holistic Nurses' Association

An Aspen Publication®
Aspen Publishers, Inc.
Gaithersburg, Maryland
1995

Library of Congress Cataloging-in-Publication Data

Holistic nursing : a handbook for practice / Barbara Montgomery Dossey
. . . [et al.]. — 2nd ed.
p. cm.
"Endorsed by the American Holistic Nurses' Association."
Includes bibliographical references and index.
ISBN 0-8342-0574-2
1. Holistic nursing. I. Dossey, Barbara Montgomery.
II. American Holistic Nurses' Association.
[DNLM: 1. Nursing Care. 2. Holistic Health. WY 86 H7325 1995]
RT42.H65 1995
610.73—dc20
DNLM/DLC
for Library of Congress
94-33099
CIP

The authors have made every effort to ensure the accuracy of the information herein. However, appropriate information sources should be consulted, especially for new or unfamiliar procedures. It is the responsibility of every practitioner to evaluate the appropriateness of a particular opinion in the context of actual clinical situations and with due considerations to new developments. Authors, editors, and the publisher cannot be held responsible for any typographical or other errors found in this book.

Editorial Resources: Ruth Bloom

Library of Catalog Card Number: 94-33099
ISBN: 0-8342-0574-2

Printed in the United States of America

1 2 3 4 5

The burning candle flame symbolizes the human spirit that is at the core of healing. In 1854, Florence Nightingale first made her late night, solitary rounds in a Crimean military hospital with a lamp, caring for wounded soldiers by candlelight. Now, as then, her lamp captures the soul and spirit of healing.

As we strive to meet our modern goal—being nurse healers—we blend the knowledge of technology and the healing arts. The following words remind us of the essence of contemporary nursing:

Nursing is an art; and if it is to be made
an art,
it requires as exclusive a devotion, as hard
a preparation, as any painter's or
sculptor's work;
for what is the having to do with dead
canvas or cold marble,
compared with having to do with the living
spirit—the temple of God's spirit?
It is one of the Fine Arts;
I had almost said,
the finest of Fine Arts.

Florence Nightingale

To Our Colleagues in Nursing:

When a nurse
Encounters another
Something happens
What occurs
Is never a neutral event

A pulse taken
Words exchanged
A touch
A healing moment
Two persons
Are never
The same

Table of Contents

Visions of Healing

Reviewers

Barbara W. Allerton, RN, MSN
Special Lecturer
Department of Nursing
Boise State University
President
Idaho Nurses' Association
Boise, Idaho

Elizabeth Ann Manhart Barrett, RN, PhD, FAAN
Professor and Coordinator
Center for Nursing Research
Hunter-Bellevue School of Nursing
Hunter College of the City University of New York
New York, New York

Genevieve Bartol, RN, EdD
Professor and Chair
Psychosocial Division
The University of North Carolina Greensboro
School of Nursing
Greensboro, North Carolina

Susan Stanwyck Bowman, RN, MN, MEd, PhD(cand.)
Professor
Department of Nursing
Humboldt State University
Arcata, California

Nina M. Coppens, RN, PhD
Professor
Department of Nursing
University of Massachusetts Lowell
Lowell, Massachusetts

Nancy Fleming Courts, RN, PhD, NCC
Assistant Professor
University of North Carolina
Greensboro, North Carolina

Sara Hunt Harper, RN, PhD
Director
Stress Management Center
Plano, Texas

Willie Hayek, RN, MSN
Assistant Professor
University of Texas Health Science Center at San Antonio
School of Nursing
San Antonio, Texas

Terry L. Jones, RN, MS, CCRN
Critical Care Education Coordinator
Parkland Memorial Hospital District
Dallas, Texas

JoEllen Koerner, RN, PhD, FAAN
Vice President Patient Services
Sioux Valley Hospital
Sioux Falls, South Dakota

Maggie McKivergin, RN, MS
Assistant to the Senior Vice President
U.S. Health Corporation
Columbus, Ohio

Tuni Miller, RN, MS
Primary Nurse Provider
Clinical Studies
Carl Clinic Association
Community Nursing Organization
Champaign, Illinois

Gail C. Mornhinweg, RN, PhD
Associate Professor
University of Louisville
School of Nursing
Louisville, Kentucky

Patricia L. Munhall, ARNP, EdD, PsyA, FAAN
Professor
Associate Dean of Graduate Program
Director
Center for Nursing Science
Miami Shores, Florida

Linda Pehl, PhD, RNC
Professor
School of Nursing
University of Mary Hardin-Baylor
Belton, Texas

Barbara L. Rees, RN, PhD
Professor
University of New Mexico
College of Nursing
Albuquerque, New Mexico

JoLynn Reynolds, PhD
Assistant Professor
Texas Woman's University
Denton, Texas

Sally Roach, RN, MSN
Assistant Professor
University of Texas Brownsville
Brownsville, Texas

Bonney Gulino Schaub, RN, MS, CS
Clinical Specialist
Adult Psychiatric-Mental Health Nursing
Co-Director
New York Psychosynthesis Institute and Holistic Nursing Associates
Huntington, New York

Gigi Steele, RN
Oncology Nurse Clinician
Medical City Dallas Hospital
Dallas, Texas

Hilary Straub, RNC, PhD
Assistant Professor of Nursing
Boise State University
Boise, Idaho

Donna Hayes Taliaferro, RN, PhD
Assistant Professor
University of Texas Health Science Center at San Antonio
School of Nursing
San Antonio, Texas

Elizabeth Hahn Winslow, RN, PhD, FAAN
Associate Professor
The University of Texas at Arlington
School of Nursing
Arlington, Texas
Research Consultant
Presbyterian Hospital
Dallas, Texas

Barbara Woods, PhD
Private Practice
Associated Psychological Services
San Antonio, Texas

Kathy B. Wright, RN, MS, CGRN, CS
Specialist (Faculty)
University of Texas at Arlington
School of Nursing
Arlington, Texas

Foreword

The second edition of *Holistic Nursing: A Handbook for Practice* continues the legacy established by Dossey, Guzzetta, Keegan, and Kolkmeier in their earlier work on holistic nursing. Building on the solid foundation that they previously established, they expand the legacy by synthesizing the latest scientific thinking and breakthroughs in bodymind healing arts practices.

As we enter the twenty-first century, there is an inordinate amount of knowledge, technology, and attention placed on learning and practicing in highly specialized inpatient care settings. Indeed, because of the shifting directions in health care, many general hospitals have had to become critical care systems. At the same time, there has been a radical shift to community-based care, managed care, and care that encompasses both ancient and modern healing arts. It is this shift that the second edition of *Holistic Nursing: A Handbook for Practice* is helping to make clear. This work integrates technology, scientific knowledge, and clinical caring-healing modalities into basic and advanced practices of holistic nursing.

By providing both an advanced orientation and advanced knowledge, this work moves holistic nursing beyond the exclusive biomedical focus, beyond the functional techniques and subspecialist knowledge, toward higher level, professional practices that potentiate health and healing. Such dimensions of *Holistic Nursing* bring the latest body-mind-spirit medical and nursing directions related to Era III medicine together with the latest developments in the art and science of nursing.

These Era III bodymind advances, consistent with holistic nursing and transpersonal healing approaches, have the potential to transform our views of the body-mind-spirit whole and the dynamic unity of unbroken wholeness among individuals, environment, and nature. These breakthroughs include notions of an expanding human consciousness that can transcend time and space to affect health and healing outcomes. They include psychophysiology of bodymind; they include values and ethics, and new meanings of human potential.

As holistic nursing experts, these authors are committed to the higher dimensions of nursing, caring, and healing. They practice what they teach in ways that integrate and translate the latest scientific paradigm into concrete nursing actions. In so doing, they bring new meaning to body-mind-spirit wholes, help us to understand the "critical" nature of healing practices and new standards of care with nurse as healer, and provide avenues whereby nurses can be transformative agents for the health care system. Furthermore, these experts point out the need for both an expanded scientific-bodymind-healing approach, as well as an expanded moral approach to general and advanced nursing practice that truly embraces the whole of both the one caring and the one being cared for.

All nursing must be more "holistic," regardless of practice setting or client population. We now see more clearly through these authors that nursing becomes transpersonal and even metaphysical.* When these aspects of nursing are acknowledged and incorporated into our practices, then nursing cultivates access to the intuitive, aesthetic, personal, ethical, and quasi-rational modes of thought, feeling, and action. Thus, there can be greater use of higher self and expanded states of consciousness in engaging in the caring-healing demands of clients and families.

This book translates contemporary nursing theory and practices into understandable nursing actions. The authors both guide and challenge the student, the teacher, the practitioner, and researcher toward more integrative, meaningful practices that

- establish holistic nursing as a paradigm case for all of nursing's caring-healing practices
- demonstrate holistic nursing as a special way of being-knowing-doing
- both apply and generate nursing knowledge and theory

This second edition of *Holistic Nursing* expands and grounds holistic practice through its handbook approach and its descriptions of concrete holistic nursing interventions. All of this translates into new pathways whereby nursing's caring-healing competencies with respect to the

---

*Watson, J. *Nursing: Human Science and Human Care—A Theory of Nursing.* (New York: National League for Nursing Press, 1988).

nurse as healer are made manifest and visible; thus, the nurse as healer approach balances and intersects with the traditional technologic competencies of the modern biomedical milieu. Perhaps more important, this work provides both substance and form for the ancient caring-healing practices of nursing—practices that can now be reclaimed and used in the most modern and demanding setting of today and the future—practices that have relevance to all of nursing.

Jean Watson, RN, PhD, FAAN
Distinguished Professor of Nursing
Director, Center for Human Caring
University of Colorado Health Sciences Center
School of Nursing
Denver, Colorado

Preface

Holistic Nursing: A Handbook for Practice is the essence of contemporary nursing. We define a holistic approach as a body-mind-spirit process for peace in living, as well as for peace in dying. The purpose of our book is threefold: (1) to explore the unity and relatedness of nurses, clients, and others, as well as all aspects of being; (2) to expand the understanding of healing and the nurse as healer; and (3) to develop different strategies to strengthen the whole person.

Not only does our book guide nurses in the art and science of nurse healing, but also it assists nurses in their challenging roles of bringing healing to the forefront of health care and helping to shape health care reform. In 1992, the National Institutes of Health (NIH) responded to the public demand for alternative medicine by creating the Office of Alternative Medicine (OAM) to evaluate bodymind and transpersonal therapies. Among these successful, extremely safe, and cost-effective therapies are relaxation, imagery, biofeedback, meditation, hypnosis, therapeutic touch, expressive therapies (e.g., art, dance, music), and spiritual healing. As nurses, we must contribute our research findings to help with the integration of these modalities into mainstream medicine. Although these approaches may eventually supplant current therapies as the treatment of choice for certain conditions, they should now be considered complements to orthodox medical treatments and not necessarily as replacements for them. We advocate a both/and rather than an either/or approach in interfacing these healing modalities with contemporary medical and surgical therapies.

In the second edition of this book, we have further developed bodymind and transpersonal therapies and have translated healing into action or the knowing-doing-being of healing. We challenge nurses to undertake their own translation of healing by asking three significant questions:

1. What do you know about the meaning of healing?
2. What can you do each day to facilitate healing in yourself?
3. How can you be a nurse healer?

Healing is not just the curing of symptoms. It is the exquisite blending of technology with caring, love, compassion, and creativity. Healing is a lifelong journey into understanding the wholeness of human existence. Along this journey, our lives mesh with those of clients, families, and colleagues, where moments of new meaning and insight emerge in the midst of crisis. Healing occurs when we seek harmony and balance. Healing is learning to open what has been closed so that we can expand our inner potentials. It is the fullest expression of self that is demonstrated by the light and shadow, as well as by the male and female principles that reside within each of us. It is gaining access to what we have forgotten about connections, unity, and interdependence. With a new awareness of these interrelationships, healing becomes possible. A *nurse healer* is one who facilitates another person's growth toward wholeness (body-mind-spirit) or who assists another in the recovery from illness or in the transition to peaceful death.

This holistic approach is developed by incorporating ideas of perennial philosophy, natural systems theory, and a nursing process framework. Thus, the information presented within this book incorporates the following:

- American Holistic Nurses' Association Standards for Holistic Nursing Practice
- nursing diagnoses established by the North American Nursing Diagnosis Association
- guidelines for integration of holistic interventions divided into four areas: before, at the beginning, during, and at the end of the session
- both basic and advanced strategies/interventions
- client case studies in the acute care and outpatient settings
- research and directions for future research

As we have explored new meanings of healing in our work and in our lives, we have interwoven many diverse threads of knowledge from nursing and other disciplines. This has engendered a more vivid, dynamic, and diverse understanding about the nature of holistic healing and its implications for nursing. A Vision of Healing precedes each chapter to encourage the exploration of ideas of healing. Each chapter begins with Nurse Healer Objectives to direct learning in theoretical, clinical, and personal areas. Each chapter has a glossary of definitions for easy reference. Each chapter also includes case studies that illustrate how to use the interventions in clinical practice, as well as how to integrate several interventions. This information is followed by a list of suggested Directions for Future Research. At the end of each chapter, Nurse Healer Reflections are offered to nurture and spark a special self-reflective experience of bodymind and the inward journey toward self-discovery and wellness.

We view persons as co-participants in all phases of care. The challenge is to integrate all concepts in this text in clinical practice and daily life. As clinicians, authors, educators, and researchers, we have successfully used these holistic concepts and interventions from the critical care unit to home health to the classroom.

Our book is divided into five units. Unit I presents the philosophic concepts that help the reader explore what occurs when nurses honor, acknowledge, and deepen their understanding of inner wisdom and healing. Unit II lays the foundation for understanding the psychophysiology of bodymind healing. This unit also provides insight into the ways that people adapt and sustain new health behaviors. It provides information related to wellness, values clarification, and motivation theory. It addresses holistic ethics in both personal and professional arenas. The importance of the nursing process and the use of the unitary person framework to guide holistic assessment and formulation of nursing diagnoses are developed. Guidelines for holistic research are also explored.

Unit III guides the reader in ways to expand concepts relevant to healing and reaching human potential. Some of the specific areas covered are contracts, goal setting, play, laughter, self-reflection, relationships, sexual abuse, deathing and dying in peace. Unit IV provides strategies to assist individuals in ways to establish a healthy life style, such as maintenance of an ideal weight, smoking cessation, and overcoming addictions. Unit V focuses in depth on four holistic modalities—touch, relaxation, imagery, and music therapy.

Our book is intended for students, clinicians, educators, and researchers who desire to expand their knowledge of holism, healing, and spirituality. Because the book contains beginner, intermediate, and advanced concepts and interventions, the reader can approach this book as a guide for learning basic content or for exploring advanced concepts. For example, Units IV and V provide the specific "how tos" for implementing both basic and advanced holistic interventions in clinical practice. Interventions designated as basic are those that the nurse can learn without additional training. Interventions designated as advanced require additional training.

Holistic Nursing: A Handbook for Practice challenges nurses to explore the inward journey toward self-transformation and to identify their growing capacity for change and healing. This effort creates the synergy and the rebirth of a compassionate power to heal ourselves and to facilitate healing within others. This inner healing allows us to return to our roots of nursing where healer and healing were understood.

The radical changes that are occurring in health care reform are very dynamic. Always the rule in health care, change provides us with a greater opportunity to integrate caring and healing into our work, our research, and our lives. We hope that you are as challenged as we are to capture our essence and to emerge as true healers on the doorsteps of the twenty-first century. Best wishes to you in your healing work and life.

Barbara Montgomery Dossey
Lynn Keegan
Cathie E. Guzzetta
Leslie Gooding Kolkmeier

Acknowledgments

Our book flows out of the larger questions that have been raised for us in the health or illness of clients/patients, the professional community with which we have worked, and our families and friends with whom we live and play.

We celebrate with our colleagues in nursing as we explore new meanings of healing in our work and life, as we acknowledge what we have done well, and as we anticipate what we must do better.

Special thanks are due to Jane Garwood, acquisitions editor at Aspen Publishers, who helped us keep our goals in sight and believed in the project; to Ruth Bloom for her attention to editorial details; to Laura Smith for logo, book design, and production details; and to Gail Martin, for helping us keep our writing clear.

Most of all, for their understanding, encouragement, and love in seeing us through one more book, we thank our families—Larry Dossey; Gerald, Catherine, and Genevieve Keegan; Philip, Angela, and Philip C. Guzzetta; and Jim, Catherine, and Jennifer Kolkmeier—who share our interconnectedness.

UNIT I

FOUNDATIONS FOR HEALING AND HOLISM

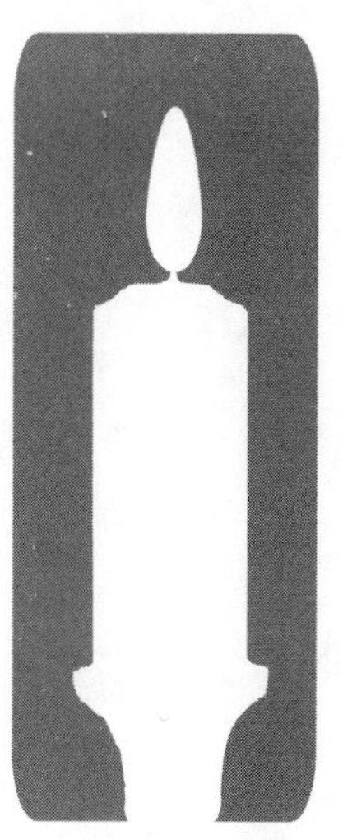

VISION OF HEALING

Exploration of Life's Meaning

Phenomenology is a philosophy that addresses the "phenomenal" question, What does it mean to be human?[1] As you begin exploring holistic ideas in this book, ask yourself, "What does it mean to be a human being? What is meaning? Why should I seek out meaning? What should I do with it? How do I keep it?"

Meaning involves differences, contrasts, novelty, and heterogeneity—and it is necessary for the healthy function of human beings. We seek out meaning because our lives are fuller and richer when they mean something positive. Without an important meaning, life is not worth living. The more we understand about meaning in life, the more we are able to empower ourselves to cope with life effectively. In thus enriching the meaning of our own daily lives, we can become more effective with others as we guide them in searching for the meanings in their lives.

The meanings that a person attaches to symptoms or illness probably have the greatest influence on that person's journey through a crisis. Human beings can view illness from at least eight frames of reference: (1) illness as challenge, (2) illness as enemy, (3) illness as punishment, (4) illness as weakness, (5) illness as relief, (6) illness as strategy, (7) illness as irreparable loss or damage, and (8) illness as value.[2]

Our existence is awash with meaning, and it is only a matter of which meaning we shall choose. The choices are crucial; nowhere is this more apparent than in the area of health and illness. It is clear from the wealth of scientific data that it is impossible to separate the biologic parts from the psychologic, sociologic, and spiritual parts of our being. Therefore, to heal the body-mind-spirit the meaning of symptoms or illness needs to be explored. Meaning is directly linked with mind modulation of all the body systems that influence states of wellness or illness. Because meanings and emotions go hand in hand, is it strange that meanings can affect the body? Or that the body can affect emotions and meanings? These connections are so intimate that we must think of body-mind-spirit as a single integrated unit. What are the lessons here? How can we put meaning in our lives?[3]

- *We need simply to pay more attention to the meanings in life. This is easy to say, but difficult to do. It is much easier to concentrate on the choles-*

terol level, blood pressure, diet, vitamin intake, body weight, and the annual physical examination than on the meanings in life. If we really believed that we could die not only from heart failure, but from "meaning failure," perhaps we would be more attentive to the meanings in our lives.

- *Wellness and illness are vastly more complex than was previously believed. The realization that there is no clear separation between the physical and the mental places much more responsibility on the individual and less on the physician for an individual's health. No prescriptions can be written for meaning; we all have to attend to our own meanings in the way that is best for us. Routinely, we need to assess and evaluate our human potentials to keep meaning in our lives (see Chapter 9).*
- *We need to be leery of anyone who proclaims that any particular problem is "all physical" or "all mental." It is no longer possible to defend these simplistic statements in modern medical science. Those who make such claims cannot even define "the physical" or "the mental," for the dividing line between them has become increasingly thin.*
- *We need to recognize the good news here—positive perceptions and meanings can actually increase the level of our health, all other factors being equal. They can be as therapeutic as a medication or a surgical procedure.*
- *We need to recognize science for the information that it can give us and to understand that the true meaning of wellness and life is in expanding our awareness and potentials.*
- *We need to realize that meanings matter. When the time comes for your next annual physical examination, keep this fact in mind. It is not just the body that needs the checkup; personal life meanings need checkups from time to time, too.*

NOTES

1. P. Munhall, *Revisioning Phenomenology: Nursing and Health Science Research* (New York: National League for Nursing Press, 1994).
2. Z.J. Lipowski, Physical Illness, the Individual and the Coping Process, *Psychiatric Medicine* 1(1970):90.
3. L. Dossey, *Meaning and Medicine: A Doctor's Tales of Breakthrough and Healing* (New York: Bantam Books, 1991).

Chapter 1

Holistic Nursing Practice

Barbara Montgomery Dossey and
Cathie E. Guzzetta

NURSE HEALER OBJECTIVES

Theoretical

- Describe the practice of holistic nursing.
- Synthesize the concepts of natural systems theory.
- Analyze the concept of holism.
- Compare and contrast the different eras of medicine.
- Compare and contrast the allopathic and holistic models of health care delivery.

Clinical

- Explore two ways to integrate a natural systems view into your clinical practice.
- Integrate eras of medicine into clinical practice.
- Determine if you use a bio-psycho-social-spiritual model to guide your clinical practice.
- Integrate the Standards of Holistic Nursing into clinical practice.

Personal

- Determine whether there are areas of fragmentation in your personal life.
- Integrate alternative therapies daily to enhance your well-being.
- Explore the steps that increase your commitment to your holistic developmental process.

DEFINITIONS

Allopathic Approach: the method of combating disease with techniques that produce effects different from those produced by the disease.

Alternative Therapies: interventions that focus on body-mind-spirit integration and evoke healing by an individual, between two individuals, or healing at a distance (e.g., relaxation, imagery, biofeedback, prayer, psychic healing); may be used as complements to conventional medical treatments.

Bio-Psycho-Social-Spiritual Elements: the major elements that give meaning to a person's existence.

Healing: a process of bringing parts of one's self together at a deep level of inner knowledge, resulting in an integrated, balanced whole with each part having equal importance and value; may also be referred to as self-healing or wholeness.

Holism: the view that an integrated whole has a reality independent of and greater than the sum of its parts.

Process: the continual changing and evolution of one's self through life; the reflection of meaning and purpose in living.

Spirituality: values, meaning, and purpose; a turning inward to the human traits of honesty, love, caring, wisdom, imagination, and compassion; the existence of a quality of a higher authority, guiding spirit, or transcendence that is mystical; a flowing dynamic balance that allows and creates healing of body-mind-spirit; sometimes involves organized religion.

Transpersonal: an experience that transcends or goes beyond personal and individual identity; the unification of personal purpose, meaning, and values with universal principles.

HOLISTIC NURSING

As the twenty-first century approaches, two major challenges are emerging in nursing. The first is to integrate the concepts of technology, mind, and spirit into nursing practice; the second is to create models for health care that guide the healing of self and others. Holistic nursing is the most complete way to conceptualize and practice professional nursing. The American Holistic Nurses' Association has described holistic nursing as follows:

Description of Holistic Nursing

Holistic nursing embraces all nursing practice which has healing the whole person as its goal. Holistic nursing recognizes that there are two views regarding holism: that holism involves studying and understanding the interrelationships of the bio-psycho-social-spiritual dimensions of the person, recognizing that the whole is greater than the sum of its parts; and that holism involves understanding the individual as an integrated whole interacting with and being acted upon by both internal and external environments. Holistic nursing accepts both views, believing that the goals of nursing can be achieved within either framework.

Holistic practice draws on nursing knowledge, theories, expertise, and intuition to guide nurses in becoming therapeutic partners with clients in strengthening the clients' responses to facilitate the healing process and achieve wholeness.

Practicing holistic nursing requires nurses to integrate self-care in their own lives. Self-responsibility leads the nurse to a greater awareness of the interconnectedness of all individuals and their relationships to the human and global community, and permits nurses to use this awareness to facilitate healing.[1]

Source: Copyright © American Holistic Nurses' Association, January 1994.

The Association's Standards of Holistic Nursing Practice define and establish the scope of holistic practice (Appendix 1-A). They are based on the philosophy that nursing is an art and a science that has as its primary purpose the provision of services that strengthen individuals and enable them to achieve the wholeness inherent within them. The concepts of holistic nursing then are based on broad and eclectic academic principles. Holistic concepts incorporate a sensitive balance between art and science, intuitive and analytic skills, and the ability and interconnectedness of body, mind, and spirit.

With holism, we consider the integrated whole to understand the person or situation. We view everything in terms of patterns and processes that combine to form a whole, instead of seeing things as fragments, pieces, or parts. Natural systems theory, which is derived primarily from the work of von Bertalanffy,[2] provides a way of comprehending the interconnectedness of natural structures in the universe. The theory is complex, but has relevance for the health care professions (Figure 1–1).

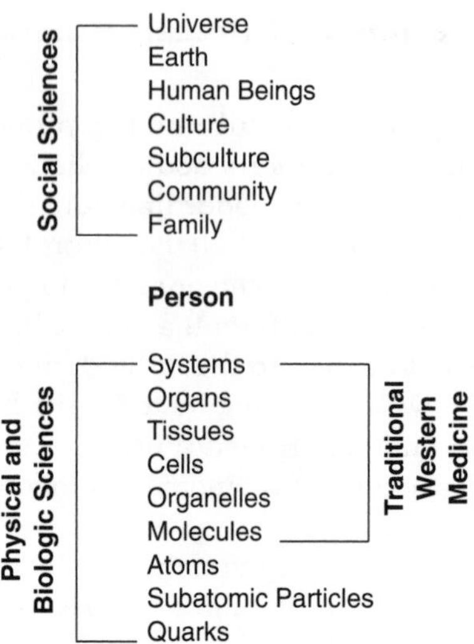

Figure 1–1 Patterns of Natural Systems Components

In brief, natural structures vary in size from the level of subatomic particles to the universe, but each possesses specific characteristics within a structure and is governed by similar principles of organization. Therefore, a change in any one part of the hierarchy affects all the other parts. Changes are occurring in all levels simultaneously; for example, the ripple effect of a pebble thrown in a body of water changes the surface while simultaneously changing the air surface above and the water surface below. As with a kaleidoscope, a slight turn changes the whole configuration.

The traditional western view of disease usually begins at the systems level and stops at the molecule level (see Figure 1–1). The natural systems approach provides a more accurate way of viewing disease, however. Disease can originate in a disturbance at any level from the subatomic to the suprapersonal, and it may result when a force disturbs or disrupts the structure of the natural systems themselves. The goal of health care is to decrease the many different disturbances and stressors caused by a person's illness. These disturbances also have an impact on the family's routine. As the ill person and the family strive to reweave the social fabric of their lives and achieve more harmonious interaction, this moving balance affects all the components of the natural systems hierarchy.

A key characteristic of the hierarchy of natural systems is information flow.[3] Regardless of the point at which it originates, information spreads up and down the components of the hierarchy. Information flow has a domino effect, as it affects the whole system. The magnitude of the problems that may be caused by a disturbance at one level and its impact on the whole hierarchy is clear in any study of the overpopulation of the planet. The result of overpopulation is depletion of natural resources and chaos associated with too many people living in disharmony.

Holism and natural systems theory have important implications for clients' and nurses' views of health and disease, even though medicine's technologic, allopathic focus remains strong today. Those who advocate the allopathic method combat disease with techniques that produce effects different from those produced by the disease; those who advocate the holistic model assert that consciousness is real and is related to all matters of health and illness. Table 1–1 provides a comparison of the allopathic and holistic models.

The Bodymind Dilemma

Data are now available to help health care professionals understand the way that the body and the mind are connected and the way that they communicate. The body approach to treating illness may have missed the mark because it has taken into account neither the profound, devastating effects nor the enormous healing effects of the mind. Treating illness with body-oriented therapies may be only half of the answer. The current awareness that alternative therapies can also be used for healing may provide the missing link in treating clients and patients.

The role of holistic nurses is clear. We need to learn to incorporate mind-oriented therapies in all areas of nursing in order to treat the physiologic, as well as the psychologic and spiritual, sequelae to all illness. In addition, we need to learn to supplement the best of traditional medical therapies with the best of mind therapies to activate inner healing and to augment the effects of drugs, surgery, and technologic therapies. The results may revolutionize the provision of care and may significantly improve not only morbidity and mortality rates, but also the quality of life. Then the essence of real healing may be unveiled.

In 1992, the National Institutes of Health (NIH) created the Office of Alternative Medicine (OAM) to evaluate alternative therapies that capitalize dramatically on bodymind events, to identify the therapies that hold the most promise, and to fund studies on the effectiveness of alternative therapies.[4] The 1993 OAM research budget was $2 million. Alternative

Table 1-1 Assumptions of Allopathic and Holistic Models of Care

Allopathic Model	*Holistic Model*
Treatment of symptoms	Search for patterns, causes
Specialized	Integrated; concerned with the whole patient
Emphasis on efficiency	Emphasis on human values
Professional should be emotionally neutral	Professional's caring is a component of healing
Pain and disease are wholly negative	Pain and disease may be valuable signals of internal conflicts
Primary intervention with drugs, surgery	Minimal intervention with appropriate technology, complemented with a range of noninvasive techniques (psychotechnologies, diet, exercise)
Body seen as a machine in good or bad repair	Body seen as a dynamic system, a complex energy field within fields (family, workplace, environment, culture, life history)
Disease or disability seen as an entity	Disease or disability seen as a process
Emphasis on eliminating symptoms and disease	Emphasis on achieving maximum bodymind health
Patient is dependent	Patient is autonomous
Professional is authority	Professional is therapeutic partner
Body and mind are separate; psychosomatic illnesses seen as mental; may refer (patient) to psychiatrist	Bodymind perspective, psychosomatic illness is the province of all health care professionals
Mind is secondary factor in organic illness	Mind is primary or co-equal factor in all illness
Placebo effect is evidence of power of suggestion	Placebo effect is evidence of mind's role in disease and healing
Primary reliance on quantitative information (charts, tests, and dates)	Primary reliance on qualitative information, including patient reports and professional's intuition; quantitative data an adjunct
"Prevention" seen as largely environmental; vitamins, rest, exercise, immunization, not smoking	"Prevention" synonymous with wholeness: in work, relationships, goals, body-mind-spirit

Source: Reprinted from *Aquarian Conspiracy: Personal and Social Transformation in Our Time*, rev. ed., by M. Ferguson, pp. 246–248, with permission of J.P. Tarcher, © 1987.

therapies targeted for evaluation include bodymind or biobehavioral interventions (e.g., biofeedback, relaxation, imagery, meditation, hypnosis, psychotherapy, prayer, therapeutic touch, distant or psychic healing, art, dance, music), nutritional approaches, traditional and ethnomedicine,

Native American approaches, traditional oriental medicine, structural and energetic therapies (e.g., acupressure, acupuncture, chiropractic, massage, reflexology), pharmacologic and biologic treatments (e.g., antioxidizing agents, cell treatments, metabolic therapy, oxidizing agents such as ozone and hydrogen peroxide), and electromagnetic applications (see Resource List for OAM address).

The ultimate goal of the investigations of alternative medical practices is to integrate validated alternative medical practices with current conventional medical practices. In March 1993, the NIH requested proposals to develop exploratory grants for scientific studies that would evaluate the potential of various types of alternative medical practices to affect the clinical course and outcome of an illness, and/or to increase wellness. By June 1993, the OAM had received more than 460 research proposals. Nurses have the opportunity to play a major role in the future direction and investigation of many of these complementary interventions.

One of the reasons for the OAM's creation was the federal government's recognition that U.S. citizens are pursuing alternative methods of health care with unprecedented enthusiasm. Eisenberg and his colleagues found that approximately one-third of all U.S. adults sought out alternative medicine of some type in 1990.[5] The resulting number of visits to practitioners of alternative medicine, 425 million, exceeded the total number of visits to primary care physicians in the United States. Expenditures for alternative care were $14 billion, most of which was out-of-pocket, unreimbursed by insurance plans.

One of the most interesting findings of Eisenberg's study was that more than 70 percent of the persons who sought alternative care chose not to inform their allopathic physicians that they had done so. This finding may help explain why many allopathic physicians believe that the controversy over alternative measures is a tempest in a teapot; they simply are unaware of what their patients are doing. Skeptics frequently charge that persons interested in alternative medicine are economically deprived, poorly educated, and, thus, easily misled. The Eisenberg study found the opposite to be true, however; consumers of alternative therapies tended to be educated, upper-income whites in the 25 to 49 age group.

Alternative therapies must be considered adjuncts or complements to conventional medical and surgical treatments rather than replacements for them. A "both/and" instead of an "either/or" approach addressing both body and mind takes healing into the health care arena. Many health care professionals and laypersons are asking if healing can take place in our modern hospitals, clinics, rehabilitation programs, and home health care while most parts of the current health care system continue to operate as a disease management industry. Dramatic changes are occurring in health care delivery, however, as health care providers explore the increasing scientific data.

Eras of Medicine

If we delineate three eras of medicine that are operational in Western medicine (Figure 1–2 and Table 1–2), we can better understand how to integrate technology, mind, and spirit.[6] Era I medicine began to take shape in the 1860s, when medicine was striving to become increasingly scientific. The underlying assumption of this approach is that health and illness are completely physical in nature. The focus is on combining drugs, medical treatments, and technology. A person's consciousness is considered a by-product of the chemical, anatomic, and physiologic aspects of the brain and is not considered a major factor in the origins of health or disease.

In the 1950s, Era II therapies began to emerge. These therapies reflect the growing awareness that the actions of a person's mind or consciousness—thoughts, emotions, beliefs, meaning, and attitudes—exert impor-

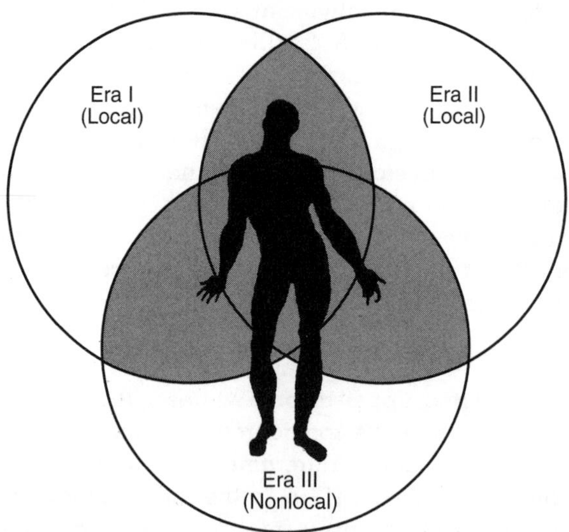

Figure 1–2 Eras of Medicine. *Source:* Reprinted from *Healing Words: The Power of Prayer and the Practice of Medicine* by Larry Dossey, p. 39, Harper San Francisco, with permission of Larry Dossey, © 1993.

Table 1–2 Eras of Medicine

	Era I	*Era II*	*Era III*
Space-Time Characteristic	Local	Local	Nonlocal
Synonym	Mechanical, material, or physical medicine	Mindbody medicine	Nonlocal or transpersonal medicine
Description	Causal, deterministic, describable by classical concepts of space-time and matter-energy. Mind not a factor; "mind" a result of brain mechanisms.	Mind a major factor in healing *within* the single person. Mind has causal power; is thus not fully explainable by classical concepts in physics. Includes but goes beyond Era I.	Mind a factor in healing both *within* and *between* persons. Mind not completely localized to points in space (brains or bodies) or time (present moment or single lifetimes). Mind is unbounded and infinite in space and time—thus omnipresent, eternal, and ultimately unitary or one. Healing at a distance is possible. Not describable by classical concepts of space-time or matter-energy.
Examples	Any form of therapy focusing solely on the effects of *things* on the body are Era I approaches—including techniques such as acupuncture and homeopathy, the use of herbs, etc. Almost all forms of "modern" medicine—drugs, surgery, irradiation, CPR, etc.—are included.	Any therapy emphasizing the effects of consciousness solely within the individual body is an Era II approach. Psychoneuroimmunology, counseling, hypnosis, biofeedback, relaxation therapies, and most types of imagery-based "alternative" therapies are included.	Any therapy in which effects of consciousness bridge between different persons is an Era III approach. All forms of distant healing, intercessory prayer, some types of shamanic healing, diagnosis at a distance, telesomatic events, and probably noncontact therapeutic touch are included.

Source: Reprinted from *Healing Words: The Power of Prayer and the Practice of Medicine* by Larry Dossey, pp. 40–41, Harper San Francisco, with permission of Larry Dossey, © 1993.

tant effects on the behavior of the person's physical body. In both Era I and Era II, a person's consciousness is said to be "local" in nature, that is, confined to a specific location in space (the body itself) and in time (the present moment and a single lifetime).

Era III, the newest and most advanced era, originated in science. Consciousness is said to be nonlocal in that it is not bound to individual bodies. The minds of individuals are spread throughout space and time; they are infinite, immortal, omnipresent, and, ultimately, one. Era III therapies involve any therapy in which the effects of consciousness create bridges between different persons, as with distant healing, intercessory prayer, shamanic healing, so-called miracles, certain emotions (e.g., love, empathy, compassion). Era III approaches involve transpersonal experiences of being. They raise a person above control at a day-to-day, material level to an experience outside his or her local self.

"Doing" and "Being" Therapies

Holistic nurses use both "doing" and "being" therapies (Figure 1–3). Doing therapies include almost all forms of modern medicine, such as medications, procedures, dietary manipulations, radiation, and acupuncture. In contrast, being therapies do not employ things, but utilize states of consciousness, such as imagery, prayer, meditation, and quiet contemplation, as well as the presence and intention of the nurse. These techniques are therapeutic because of the power of the psyche to affect the body. They may be either directed or nondirected.[7] A person who uses a directed mental strategy attaches a specific outcome, such as the regression of disease or the normalization of the blood pressure, to the imagery, for example. In a nondirected approach, however, there is no specific outcome assigned to the strategy. Rather, the person images the best outcome for the situation, but does not try to steer the situation in any particular direction. This reliance on the inherent intelligence within one's self to come forth is a way of acknowledging the intrinsic wisdom and self-correcting capacity within nature.

It is obvious that Era I medicine uses "doing" therapies that are highly directed in their approach. It employs things, such as medication, for a specific goal. Era II medicine is a classic bodymind approach that does not require the use of things except biofeedback instrumentation to increase awareness of bodymind connections. It employs "being" therapies that can be directed or nondirected, depending on the mental strategies selected (e.g., relaxation or meditation). Era III medicine is similar in this regard. It uses being therapies that may be either directed or

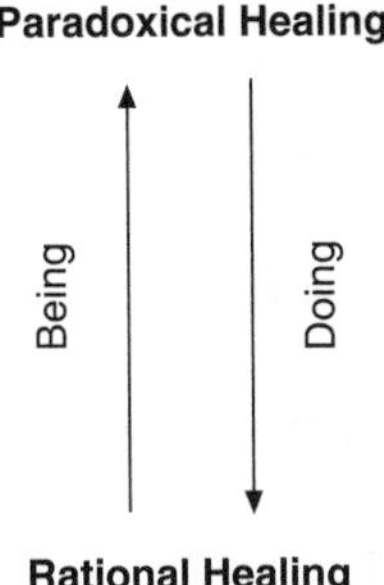

Figure 1–3 "Being" and "Doing" Therapies. *Source:* Reprinted from *Meaning and Medicine: A Doctor's Tales of Breakthrough and Healing* by Larry Dossey, p. 204, Bantam Books, with permission of Larry Dossey, © 1991.

nondirected. It requires a willingness to become aware, moment by moment, of what is true for our inner and outer experience. It is actually a "not-doing" so that we can become conscious of releasing, emptying, trusting, and acknowledging that we have done our best, regardless of the outcome. As the therapeutic potential of the mind becomes increasingly clear, all therapies and all people are seen to have a transcendent quality. The minds of all people, including families and friends, the health care team in close proximity, and those at a distance, flow together as they work to create healing rituals (see Chapter 3). Health and healing are a collective affair.

Rational vs. Paradoxical Healing

All healing experiences or activities can be arranged along a continuum from the rational domain to the paradoxical domain.[8] These domains are determined by the degree of doing and being involved (Figure 1–4).

"Doing" therapies fall into the *rational* healing category, because they make sense to our linear, intellectual thought processes. Based on scientific fact, these strategies conform to our world view of commonsense notions. Often, the professional can follow an algorithm, which may even dictate a step-by-step approach. Examples of rational healing include surgery, irradiation, medications, exercise, and diet.

On the other hand, "being" therapies fall into the paradoxical healing category, because they frequently happen without a scientific explana-

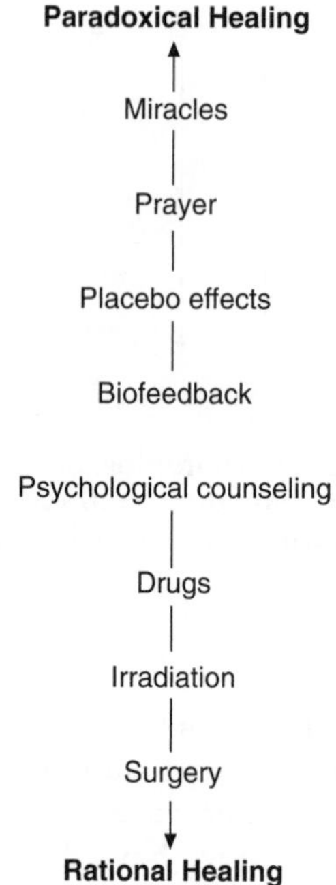

Figure 1-4 Continuum of Rational and Paradoxical Healing. *Source:* Reprinted from *Meaning and Medicine: A Doctor's Tales of Breakthrough and Healing* by Larry Dossey, p. 205, Bantam Books, with permission of Larry Dossey, © 1991.

---

tion. A paradox is a seemingly absurd or contradictory statement or event that is, in fact, true. In psychological counseling, for example, the term *breakthrough* is a paradox. When a patient has a psychologic breakthrough, it is clear that there is a new meaning for a person; there are no clearly delineated steps leading to the breakthrough, however. Such an event is called a breakthrough for the very reason that it is unpredictable—thus, the paradox.

Biofeedback also involves a paradox. In order to reduce their blood pressure or muscle tension, or increase their peripheral blood flow, individuals can enter into a state of "being" or passive volition in which they let it happen. The best way to change these physiologic states in the desired direction is to give up trying and to learn how to be.

Similarly, the phenomenon of placebo is a paradox (see Chapter 8). If an individual has just a little discomfort, a placebo does not work very well. The more pain a person has, however, the more dramatic the response to a placebo medication can be. In addition, a person who does not know that the medication is a placebo responds best. This is referred to as the "paradox of success through ignorance."

Prayer and faith fall into the domain of paradox because there is no rational scientific evidence for their effectiveness. Scientific studies are being conducted, however. In a prayer study done by Byrd, for example, each of 201 patients with acute myocardial infarction was prayed for by 5 to 7 people each day in Protestant and Catholic prayer groups across the United States.[9] Those in a control group of 192 patients also with acute myocardial infarction were not prayed for, although they received the same medical care as the prayed-for group. In this 10-month randomized, prospective double-blind study, the following significant events occurred:

1. Patients in the prayed-for group were 5 times less likely than were those in the control group to require antibiotics (3 patients compared to 16 patients).
2. They were three times less likely to develop pulmonary edema (6 patients compared to 18 patients).
3. None of the prayed-for group required endotracheal intubation, although 12 in the control group required mechanical ventilatory support.
4. Fewer patients in the prayed-for group died (although the difference was not statistically significant).

This study is an example of a nonlocal phenomenon, an Era III approach, because it involves the conscious effort of people praying for others at a distance.

"Miracle cures" are paradoxical because there is no scientific mechanism to explain them. Every nurse has known, heard of, or read about a patient who had a severe illness that was confirmed by laboratory evidence, but disappeared after the patient adopted a "being" approach. Some say that it was the natural course of the illness; some die, and some live. At shrines such as Lourdes in France and Medjugorje in Yugoslavia, however, people who experience a miracle cure are said to be totally immersed in a being state. They do not try to make anything happen. When interviewed, these people report experiencing a different sense of space and time; the flow of time as past, present, and future becomes an "eternal now." Birth and death take on new meaning and are not seen as a beginning and an end. These people go into self and explore the "Not-I" to become empty so that they can understand the meaning of illness or present situations.

HEALING THE SPLIT: BODY-MIND-SPIRIT

Bio-Psycho-Social-Spiritual Model

The most comprehensive model available in mainstream health care is the bio-psycho-social model. In this model, all disease has a psychosomatic component, and biologic, psychologic, and social factors are always involved in a patient's symptoms, disease, or illness. The bio-psycho-social-spiritual model provides an even more complete and holistic understanding of how human beings function, however, and should be integrated into clinical practice, education, and research.[10] As shown in Figure 1–5, all four parameters are interdependent and interrelated. It is necessary to address all these components to achieve optimal therapeutic results. Regardless of the technology, therapy, or treatment used, the human spirit is a major healing force in reversing, stabilizing, and producing remission of disease. The human spirit can make the difference between life and death as well as wellness and illness.

The spiritual dimension in the bio-psycho-social-spiritual model incorporates spirituality in a broad context: values, meaning, and purpose in life. It reflects the human traits of caring, love, honesty, wisdom, and imagination. The concept of spirit implies a quality of transcendence, a guiding force, or something outside the self and beyond the individual nurse or client. It may reflect a belief in the existence of a higher power or a guiding spirit. To some, spirit may suggest a purely mystical feeling or a flowing dynamic quality of unity. It is undefinable, yet it is a vital force profoundly felt by the individual and capable of affecting life and behavior.

Spiritual Elements vs. Psychologic Elements

Spiritual elements differ from psychologic elements.[11] Spiritual elements are those capacities that enable a human being to rise above or transcend the circumstances at hand. These elements include the ability to seek purpose and meaning in life, to love, to forgive, to pray, and to worship. Psychologic elements, on the other hand, include language, perception, cognition, mood, thought, symbolic images, memory, intellect, and the ability to analyze and synthesize data.

It is most unfortunate that spiritual concerns in nursing and medicine have been ignored or confused with religion and personal religious be-

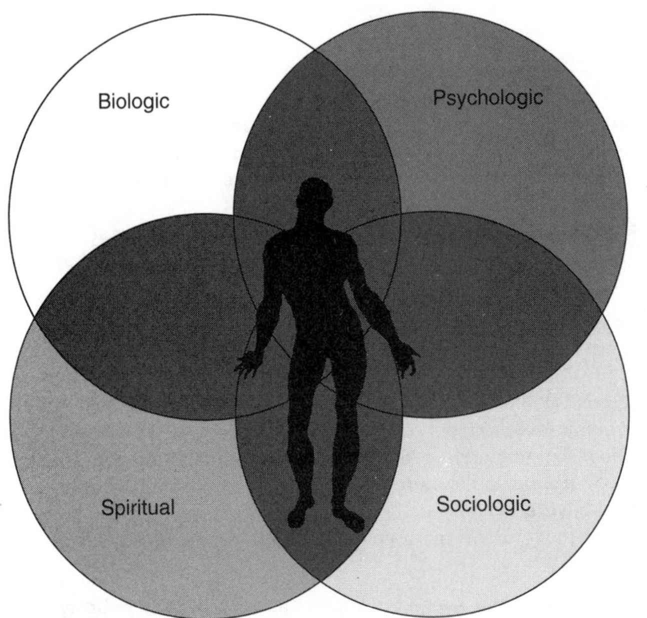

Figure 1-5 The Bio-Psycho-Social-Spiritual Model. *Source:* Reprinted from *Cardiovascular Nursing: Holistic Practice* by C.E. Guzzetta and B.M. Dossey, p. 6, with permission of Mosby Year Book, © 1992.

liefs. Even with technologic advances, however, spiritual factors are crucial in healing. Health care providers must give attention to the role of the human spirit if the treatment plan is to be complete. Nurses must continue to refine, clarify, and develop strategies to heal the human spirit.

Characteristics of Spirituality

In her synthesis of 109 nursing articles and research studies on the concept of spirit and spirituality, Burkhardt found that spirit and spirituality are frequently confused with religiosity.[12] Thus, the use of the participle *spiriting* is more representative of the concept of spirit. This spiriting concept falls into four main categories:

1. spirit/spirituality
2. spiritual dimension
3. spiritual well-being
4. spiritual needs

Exhibit 1–1 Spiritual Assessment Tool

To facilitate the healing process in clients/patients, families, significant others, and yourself, the following reflective questions assist in assessing, evaluating, and increasing awareness of the spiritual process in yourself and others.

MEANING AND PURPOSE These questions assess a person's ability to seek meaning and fulfillment in life, manifest hope, and accept ambiguity and uncertainty.

- What gives your life meaning?
- Do you have a sense of purpose in life?
- Does your illness interfere with your life goals?
- Why do you want to get well?
- How hopeful are you about obtaining a better degree of health?
- Do you feel that you have a responsibility in maintaining your health?
- Will you be able to make changes in your life to maintain your health?
- Are you motivated to get well?
- What is the most important or powerful thing in your life?

INNER STRENGTHS These questions assess a person's ability to manifest joy and recognize strengths, choices, goals, and faith.

- What brings you joy and peace in your life?
- What can you do to feel alive and full of spirit?
- What traits do you like about yourself?
- What are your personal strengths?
- What choices are available to you to enhance your healing?
- What life goals have you set for yourself?
- Do you think that stress in any way caused your illness?
- How aware were you of your body before you became sick?
- What do you believe in?
- Is faith important in your life?
- How has your illness influenced your faith?
- Does faith play a role in regaining your health?

INTERCONNECTIONS These questions assess a person's positive self-concept, self-esteem, and sense of self; sense of belonging in the world with others; capacity to pursue personal interests; and ability to demonstrate love of self and self-forgiveness.

- How do you feel about yourself right now?
- How do you feel when you have a true sense of yourself?
- Do you pursue things of personal interest?
- What do you do to show love for yourself?
- Can you forgive yourself?
- What do you do to heal your spirit?

continues

Exhibit 1–1 continued

These questions assess a person's ability to connect in life-giving ways with family, friends, and social groups and to engage in the forgiveness of others.

- Who are the significant people in your life?
- Do you have friends or family in town who are available to help you?
- Who are the people to whom you are closest?
- Do you belong to any groups?
- Can you ask people for help when you need it?
- Can you share your feelings with others?
- What are some of the most loving things that others have done for you?
- What are the loving things that you do for other people?
- Are you able to forgive others?

These questions assess a person's capacity for finding meaning in worship or religious activities and a connectedness with a divinity or universe.

- Is worship important to you?
- What do you consider the most significant act of worship in your life?
- Do you participate in any religious activities?
- Do you believe in God or a higher power?
- Do you think that prayer is powerful?
- Have you ever tried to empty your mind of all thoughts to see what the experience might be like?
- Do you use relaxation or imagery skills?
- Do you meditate?
- Do you pray?
- What is your prayer?
- How are your prayers answered?
- Do you have a sense of belonging in this world?

These questions assess a person's ability to experience a sense of connection with all of life and nature, an awareness of the effects of the environment on life and well-being, and a capacity or concern for the health of the environment.

- Do you ever feel at some level a connection with the world or universe?
- How does your environment have an impact on your state of well-being?
- What are your environmental stressors at work and at home?
- Do you incorporate strategies to reduce your environmental stressors?
- Do you have any concerns for the state of your immediate environment?
- Are you involved with environmental issues such as recycling environmental resources at home, work, or in your community?
- Are you concerned about the survival of the planet?

Source: Based on Margaret Burkhardt: Spirituality: An analysis of the concept, *Holistic Nursing Practice* 3(3):69. 1989. Reprinted from *Cardiovascular Nursing: Holistic Practice* by C.E. Guzzetta and B.M. Dossey, p. 9, with permission of Mosby Year Book, © 1992.

From these categories, the following three defining characteristics of spirituality evolved: (1) unfolding mystery, (2) inner strengths, and (3) harmonious interconnectedness. Unfolding mystery refers to one's experiences about life's purpose and meaning, uncertainty, and struggles. Inner strengths refer to a sense of awareness, self, consciousness, inner resources, sacred source, unifying force, inner core, and transcendence. Harmonious interconnectedness refers to interconnections and harmony with self, others, higher power/God, and the environment.

Exhibit 1–1 is an assessment tool that is organized by the three defining characteristics of spirituality.[13] It provides reflective questions for assessing, evaluating, and increasing awareness of spirituality in clients/patients, families, and self. These questions can stimulate spontaneous, independent, meaningful initiatives to improve the individual's capacity for recovery and healing. They provide deeper understanding and meaning of body-mind-spirit connections. The use of bio-psycho-social-spiritual tools and integration of alternative therapies also assists nurses in meeting the mandates of the Joint Commission on Accreditation of Healthcare Organizations. For example, the Patient Bill of Rights states that

> care of the patient must include consideration of the psychosocial, spiritual, and cultural variables that influence the perception of illness. The provision of patient care reflects consideration of the patient as an individual with personal value and belief systems that impact upon his/her attitude and response to the care that is provided by the organization.[14]

CONCLUSION

Nurses can reduce the devastating effects of crisis and illness of individuals by using tools for assessing the bio-psycho-social-spiritual human dimensions and integrating alternative therapies with allopathic approaches. These tools and therapies serve as bridges for nurses to understand more fully the emotions and meaning involved in crisis and illness.

DIRECTIONS FOR FUTURE RESEARCH

1. Examine alternative therapies in nursing and medicine that can facilitate healing, and determine which ones are effective for which conditions, and with what results.

2. Explore the value that clients and their families attach to healing modalities and the value that nurses attach to them.
3. Investigate anticipated or actual solutions or complications that result from alternative therapies.

NURSE HEALER REFLECTIONS

After reading this chapter, the nurse healer will be able to answer or begin a process of answering the following questions:

- Do I find meaning in my life?
- How do I define spirituality?
- What have I assessed in a client regarding the meaning of his or her life?
- When I use the words *Guiding Force, Higher Power, God,* or *Absolute,* what kind of link with a universal wholeness do I experience?

NOTES

1. American Holistic Nurses' Association, Description of Holistic Nursing, working description, January 1994.
2. L. von Bertalanffy, *General Systems Theory* (New York: George Braziller, 1972).
3. E. Lazlo, *The Systems View of the World* (New York: George Braziller, 1968).
4. C. Marwick, Alternative Therapies Studies Moves into New Phase, *Journal of the American Medical Association* 268, no. 21 (1992):3040.
5. D.M. Eisenberg et al., Unconventional Medicine in the United States: Prevalence, Costs, and Patterns of Use, *New England Journal of Medicine* 328, no. 4 (1993):246–252.
6. L. Dossey, *Recovering the Soul* (New York: Bantam Books, 1989).
7. L. Dossey, *Meaning and Medicine: A Doctor's Tales of Breakthrough and Healing* (New York: Bantam Books, 1991).
8. L. Dossey, *Healing Words: The Power of Prayer and the Practice of Medicine* (San Francisco: Harper San Francisco, 1993).
9. R. Byrd, Positive Effects of Intercessory Prayer in a Coronary Care Unit Population, *Southern Medical Journal* 81(1988):826.
10. B.M. Dossey and C.E. Guzzetta, Holistic Cardiovascular Nursing, in *Cardiovascular Nursing: Holistic Practice*, ed. C. Guzzetta and B. Dossey (St. Louis: Mosby Year Book, 1992),
11. C. Kuhn, A Spiritual Inventory of the Medically Ill Patient, *Psychiatric Medicine* 6(1988):87.
12. M. Burkhardt, Spirituality: An Analysis of the Concept, *Holistic Nursing Practice* 3, no. 3 (1989):69–77.

13. Dossey and Guzzetta, Holistic Cardiovascular Nursing.
14. Patient Rights, *Accreditation Manual for Hospitals* (Chicago: Joint Commission on Accreditation of Healthcare Organizations, Suppl., 1992).

RESOURCE

National Institutes of Health
Office of Alternative Medicine
6120 Executive Boulevard
Executive Plaza South, Room 450
Rockville, MD 20892-9904
301-496-4000

Appendix 1-A

Standards of Holistic Nursing Practice

CONCEPTS ADDRESSED IN HOLISTIC NURSING PRACTICE

PART 1: NURSE-FOCUSED CONCEPTS

I. Professional Education and Personal Development
II. Community and Global Involvement

PART 2: CLIENT/PATIENT-FOCUSED CONCEPTS

III. Caring for the Whole Client/Patient and Family/Significant Others
IV. Health Education and Mutual Decision Making
V. Cultural Care
VI. Health Promotion
VII. Self-Care
VIII. Spiritual Care
IX. Care of the Environment
X. Research/Theory
XI. Nursing Process (for nurses documenting holistic practice in traditional nursing process format using nursing diagnosis)
XII. Nursing Theory (for nurses documenting holistic practice through a [qualitative] theory-based format).

Source: Based on a working document of the American Holistic Nurses' Association, Copyright © June 1994. The American Holistic Nurses' Association, 4101 Lake Boone Trail, Suite 201, Raleigh, NC 27607, Phone: (919) 787-5181, FAX: (919) 787-4916. Used with permission.

PART 1—NURSE-FOCUSED CONCEPTS

I. Professional Education and Personal Development

Standard of Care:

1. Holistic nurses shall be committed to professional growth.

Standards of Practice:

A. Holistic nurses shall participate in the continuing education of nursing, holistic disciplines and holistic history, philosophy, and theory.
B. Holistic nurses shall support, share, and recognize nursing expertise.
C. Holistic nurses with expertise will mentor others in professional growth (from novice to expert) in areas of holistic development.
D. Holistic nurses shall develop skills to facilitate a sense of sacredness about their work.
E. Holistic nurses shall explore/develop the state of "nurse as healing environment."

Standard of Care:

2. Holistic nurses shall be committed to personal development.

Standards of Practice:

A. Holistic nurses shall continue their own personal development to ensure expertise in holistic nursing practice and interventions.
B. Holistic nurses shall be optimistic that they can participate in improving the client's/patient's situation.
C. Holistic nurses shall have clear intent to care and possess a sense of balance between what they give to self and others.
D. Holistic nurses shall consciously participate in the evolutionary process recognizing that crisis can equal opportunity.
E. Holistic nurses shall mentor and support others in reaching personal goals.

II. Community and Global Involvement

Standard of Care:

1. Holistic nurses shall participate in establishing and promoting conditions in society where holistic health can be achieved.

Standards of Practice:

A. Holistic nurses shall become aware of local, state, national, and international nursing organizations and actively focus on health issues at various levels.

B. Holistic nurses shall become politically active on issues that impact health from a holistic perspective.

Standard of Care:

2. Holistic nurses shall participate in the ethics of care/caring and identify a linkage of caring to public policy.

Standards of Practice:

A. Holistic nurses shall become involved in holistic health care reform and policy development.

B. Holistic nurses shall go beyond advocacy to deal with the pressing issues of health care delivery itself, and to look to the sociocultural world or industry of health care to bring about needed change.

Standards of Care:

3. Holistic nurses shall commit to practices that respect, nurture, and enhance an integral relationship with the earth's functioning.
4. Holistic nurses shall act politically to protect, foster, and advocate for the interspecies of life on the planet.
5. Holistic nurses shall teach, share, and serve as resources in considering the holistic nature of the universe.

Standards of Practice:

A. Holistic nurses shall value and promote mutually enhancing activities, industries, and policies for the human and natural world.

B. Holistic nurses shall advocate for the well-being of the global community's economy, education, and ethical norms.

PART 2—CLIENT/PATIENT-FOCUSED CONCEPTS

III. Caring for the Whole Client/Patient and Family/Significant Others

Standards of Care:

1. Clients/patients and families/significant others experience the presence of the nurse as a shared humanness that includes a sense of connectedness and attention to them as unique persons.

2. Clients/patients and nurse experience a sense of valued interchange (authenticity) between human beings.

Standards of Practice:

A. Holistic nurses shall focus care on the whole client/patient and family/significant others, not merely the current presenting symptoms or tasks to be accomplished.
B. Holistic nurses shall respect the client's/patient's rights and choices and act as an advocate for the client/patient.
C. Holistic nurses shall make decisions about how to proceed with nursing care based on a comprehensive assessment of relevant areas and on holistic understanding of the client/patient and family/significant others.

IV. Health Education and Mutual Decision Making

Standards of Care:

1. Clients/patients and families/significant others possess the knowledge they want and need in order to be involved in decisions about treatment, work, home life, and recreation.
2. Clients/patients and families/significant others receive care based on priorities of care that contribute to desired outcomes.
3. Clients/patients and families/significant others are active partners in health care planning and decision making based on individual desires.

Standards of Practice:

A. Holistic nurses shall use the principles of teaching and learning; they shall provide ongoing assessment, education, and evaluation of clients'/patients' and families'/significant others' knowledge in relation to illness, diagnostic and treatment plans, anticipated outcomes, and self-care activities.
B. Holistic nurses shall collaborate with other health care providers; they shall give timely information related to preparation for procedures and results of tests.
C. Holistic nurses shall engage the client/patient and family/significant others in mutual planning for goals, diagnostic tests, treatments, home care, and follow-up care.
D. Holistic nurses shall be persistent in responding to environmental barriers to the delivery of holistic goal-oriented care; they can take

risks, if necessary, to advocate for the client/patient and family/significant others.

E. Holistic nurses shall support the clients'/patients' sense of personal responsibility and assist clients/patients to achieve desired outcomes.
F. Holistic nurses shall be flexible; they are willing and able to give up control of routines, information, "knowing what is best," and so forth in order to participate in client/patient-centered care.
G. Holistic nurses shall engage clients/patients and families/significant others in problem-solving discussions in relation to living with changes secondary to illness and treatment.

V. Cultural Care

Standard of Care:

1. Clients/patients shall receive care consistent with their cultural backgrounds, health beliefs, and values.
2. Clients'/patients' cultural diversity and its importance to the global community will be respected, protected, and enhanced.

Standards of Practice:

A. Holistic nurses shall gain knowledge of cultural practices of clients/patients and families/significant others in their care, and integrate this knowledge in practice.
B. Holistic nurses shall assess meaning of health, illness, and treatment of each client/patient and family/significant others.
C. Holistic nurses shall make use of appropriate community resources and experts to validate knowledge and practices of different cultural groups.
D. Holistic nurses shall recognize the critical nature of diversity to the global community.

VI. Health Promotion

Standards of Care:

1. Clients/patients and families/significant others shall recognize patterns that place them at risk for health problems, e.g., personal habits, personal and family health history, age-related risk factors.
2. Clients/patients and families/significant others shall practice preventive measures, e.g., immunizations, breast self-exam, fitness/exercise programs, belief practices (prayer).

Standards of Practice:

A. Holistic nurses shall provide and access information to/from clients/patients and families/significant others in relation to primary and secondary prevention.

B. Holistic nurses shall assist and support clients/patients and families/significant others to identify ways to incorporate health promotion in their life styles.

VII. Self-Care

Standards of Care:

1. Clients/patients and families/significant others shall be facilitated and supported in managing self-care to maximize quality of life, e.g., treatments and side effects, activities of daily living, changes in relationships and life style.
2. Clients/patients and families/significant others shall have the information and resources needed for ongoing holistic health care.

Standards of Practice:

A. Holistic nurses shall plan with clients/patients and families/significant others for self-care by assisting with identification and facilitation of their desired level of physical, psychologic, sociologic, and spiritual potential.

B. Holistic nurses shall provide information on nursing and multidisciplinary resources in the clinic, hospital, or community.

C. Holistic nurses shall initiate referrals and facilitate access to health care resources, e.g., clinic appointments, in client/patient admissions, community agencies, schools, financial counselors.

D. Holistic nurses shall provide phone numbers and the name of person(s) to contact with questions/concerns or for urgent/emergent situations that include daytime and after-hours numbers.

E. Holistic nurses shall maintain contact as necessary with clients/patients and families/significant others, and other health team members involved in the client's/patient's care.

VIII. Spiritual Care

Standards of Care:

1. Clients/patients and families/significant others shall receive care that is consistent with their values and beliefs.
2. Clients/patients shall be cared for as whole, spiritual beings.

3. Clients/patients and families/significant others shall receive support for their spiritual growth.

Standards of Practice:

A. Holistic nurses shall assess the client's/patient's values and beliefs, and plan individualized care (see Exhibit 1–1, Spiritual Assessment Tool).
B. Holistic nurses shall provide an environment conducive to reflection, prayer, and spiritual growth.
C. Holistic nurses shall actively support the client's/patient's and family's/significant others' search for meaning and purpose in life, illness, and death.
D. Holistic nurses shall actively support the client's/patient's and family's/significant others' search for relationship with a higher power, with others, and with the environment.

IX. Care of the Environment

Standards of Care:

1. Clients/patients and families/significant others shall receive treatment in an environment that is safe.
2. Clients/patients and families/significant others shall receive treatment in an environment that is respectful and healing.
3. Clients/patients and families/significant others shall be cared for in as healthy an environment as possible, e.g., clean air and water, nutritious food, environmentally "friendly" life sustaining practices.

Standards of Practice:

A. Holistic nurses shall practice according to policies and procedures in relation to environmental safety and emergency preparedness.
B. Holistic nurses shall respect privacy, confidentiality, and environments conducive to experiencing wholeness and harmony.
C. Holistic nurses shall recognize that the well-being of the ecosystem of the planet is a prior determining condition for the well-being of the human.

X. Research/Theory

Standards of Care:

1. Clients/patients and families/significant others shall receive ad-

vice on nursing interventions and holistic therapies based on research findings.

2. Clients/patients and families/significant others receive care by nurses who deliver nursing care grounded in a nursing theory/conceptual model.

Standards of Practice:

A. Holistic nurses shall create an environment conducive to systematic inquiry into clinical problems by engaging in nursing research, and supporting and utilizing the research of others.

B. Holistic nursing interventions and recommendations shall be based on research. Clients/patients and families/significant others shall be told the degree to which information is known or not known regarding all nursing recommendations for treatment.

C. Holistic nursing care shall be grounded in one of the many theories of nursing practice.

XI. Nursing Process (for nurses documenting holistic practice in the nursing process format)

Standard of Care:

1. Clients/patients shall be assessed holistically and continually (see Appendixes 7–A and 7–B).

Standards of Practice:

A. Holistic nurses shall collect data in an organized, systematic fashion to ensure completeness of assessments.

B. Holistic nurses shall utilize appropriate physical examination techniques.

C. Holistic nurses shall demonstrate competency in communication skills.

D. Holistic nurses shall gather pertinent bio-psycho-socio-spiritual data from the client/patient, family/significant others, and other health team members.

E. Holistic nurses shall collect pertinent data from previous client/patient records.

F. Holistic nurses shall use intuition as a means of gathering data from a client/patient and family/significant others. Intuitive knowledge also may be validated with the client/patient and family/significant other.

G. Holistic nurses shall collaborate with other health team members to collect data.

H. Holistic nurses shall review the data base as new information is available.

I. Holistic nurses shall document all pertinent data in the client's/patient's record.

Standard of Care:

2. Client/patient actual and high-risk problems/patterns/needs and opportunities to enhance health, and their priorities shall be identified based upon collected data.

Standards of Practice:

A. Holistic nurses shall utilize collected data to establish a list of actual and high-risk problems/patterns/needs and opportunities to enhance health.

B. Holistic nurses shall collaborate with the client/patient, family/significant others, and health team members in identification of actual and high-risk problems/patterns/needs and opportunities to enhance health.

C. Holistic nurses shall utilize collected data to formulate hypotheses as to the etiologic bases for each identified actual or high-risk problems/patterns/needs and opportunity to enhance health.

D. Holistic nurses shall utilize nursing diagnoses for the actual or high-risk problems/patterns/needs and opportunities to enhance health which nurses, by virtue of education and experience, are able, responsible, and accountable to treat.

E. Holistic nurses shall establish the priority of problems/patterns/needs according to the actual or high risk threats to the client/patient. Opportunities to enhance health shall also be included.

F. Holistic nurses shall reassess the list and priorities as the data base changes.

G. Holistic nurses shall record identified actual or high-risk problems/patterns/needs and opportunities to enhance health and indicate priority in the client's/patient's record.

H. Holistic nurses shall document client/patient situations that provide opportunities to enhance and support growth, development, and movement toward recognizing wholeness.

Standard of Care:

3. Clients'/patients' actual or high-risk problems/patterns/needs or opportunities to enhance health shall have appropriate outcomes specified and revised as appropriate.

Standards of Practice:

A. Holistic nurses shall specify one or more measurable client/patient outcomes for each actual or high-risk problems/patterns/needs or opportunities to enhance health in collaboration with others. Each outcome shall specify something that should or should not occur, the time at which it should occur, and expected results.

B. Holistic nurses shall record outcomes, communicate to others, and revise as needed.

Standard of Care:

4. Clients/patients shall have an appropriate plan of holistic nursing care formulated.

Standards of Practice:

A. Holistic nurses shall develop the plan of care in collaboration with the client/patient, family/significant others, and other health team members.

B. Holistic nurses shall determine nursing interventions for each problem/pattern/need or opportunity to enhance health.

C. Holistic nurses shall incorporate interventions that communicate acceptance of the client's/patient's and family/significant others' values, beliefs, culture, religion, and socioeconomic background.

D. Holistic nurses shall identify areas for education of the client/patient and family/significant others.

E. Holistic nurses shall develop appropriate client/patient goals for each problem/pattern/need or opportunity to enhance health in collaboration with the client/patient, family/significant others, and other health team members.

F. Holistic nurses shall organize the plan to reflect the priority of identified problems/patterns/needs and opportunities to enhance health.

G. Holistic nurses shall revise the plan of care to reflect the client's/patient's current status.

H. Holistic nurses shall communicate the plan to those involved in the client's/patient's care.

I. Holistic nurses shall record the plan of nursing care in the client/patient record.

Standard of Care:

5. Client's/patient's plan of holistic nursing care shall be implemented according to the priority of identified problems/patterns/needs, or opportunities to enhance health.

Standards of Practice:

A. Holistic nurses shall implement the plan of nursing care in collaboration with the client/patient, family/significant others, and other health team members.

B. Holistic nurses shall support and promote client/patient participation in care.

C. Holistic nurses shall participate in care in an organized and compassionate manner.

D. Holistic nurses shall integrate current scientific knowledge with nursing care.

E. Holistic nurses shall integrate the intuitive art of nursing with the scientific knowledge and technical competencies.

F. Holistic nurses shall provide care in such a way as to prevent complications and life-threatening situations.

G. Holistic nurses shall coordinate care delivered by other health team members.

H. Holistic nurses shall document interventions in the record.

Standard of Care:

6. Client's/patient's results of holistic nursing care shall be continuously evaluated.

Standards of Practice:

A. Holistic nurses shall ensure the relevance of nursing interventions to identified client/patient problems/patterns/needs or opportunities to enhance health.

B. Holistic nurses shall collect data for evaluation within an appropriate time interval after intervention.

C. Holistic nurses shall compare the client's/patient's response with expected results.

D. Holistic nurses shall base the evaluation on data from pertinent sources.
E. Holistic nurses shall collaborate with the client/patient, family/significant others, and other health team members in the evaluation process.
F. Holistic nurses shall attempt to determine the cause of any significant deviation between the client's/patient's response and the expected results.
G. Holistic nurses shall review the plan of care and revise it based on the evaluation results.
H. Holistic nurses shall document evaluation and outcomes in the client/patient record.

XII. Nursing Theory (for nurses documenting holistic practice through a [qualitative] theory-based format)

Standard of Care:

1. Nursing theory shall provide the framework for documenting professional nursing practice.

Standards of Practice:

A. Holistic nurses shall identify nursing theory upon which to base their nursing practice.
B. Information relevant to client/patient care shall be gathered according to the theoretical framework.
C. Client/patient problems/patterns/needs or opportunities to enhance health shall be identified based on the theoretical framework.
D. Nursing actions shall be derived from the theory.
E. Care shall be documented and evaluated in the language of the theory.
F. Client/patient records shall be written from within the framework of the theory.

VISION OF HEALING

The Transpersonal Self

The synchronization of mind and body is not a random technique for self-improvement. Rather, the integration of body, mind, and spirit is a basic human goal. In exploring the foundations for healing self and facilitating healing in others, we nurses mature and exercise our human capacity to go beyond individual identity and evolve to our highest potential—the transpersonal self. Yet, knowing the states of the transpersonal self is not an end point, but a continuing process.

*Throughout history, humans have sought to understand why they experience life and what happens after death. This body of knowledge is perennial philosophy—*philosophia perennis. *Roots of perennial philosophy are found in all traditional lore, from the most primitive to the most highly developed cultures. The three major elements of perennial philosophy are*

1. *the metaphysics that recognizes a divine reality substantial to the world of things and lives and minds*
2. *the psychology that finds in the soul something similar to, or even identical with, divine reality*
3. *the ethics that places a human being's final end (death) in the knowledge of the immanent and transcendent ground of all being—the thing is immemorial and universal*[1]

In the writings of perennial philosophy, human beings are described as part of a whole, a part of the totality of the universe. The many levels of human consciousness are referred to as the Great Chain of Being. These levels begin with the physical and move up to the emotional, mental, existential, spiritual, and so on. In order to reach wholeness, humans need to understand the relationship of self with the universe, to come to terms with the finite nature of existence, to accept ego limitations, and to face things as they appear in life.

Each level in the Great Chain transcends, but includes, its predecessor(s).[2] *Just as a three-dimensional sphere includes or contains two-dimensional circles, each higher level in the Great Chain contains functions, capacities, or structures not found on, or explainable solely in terms of, a lower level. The higher level does not violate the principles of the lower level; it simply is not exclusively bound to or explainable by the lower level. All levels are available to us if we allow openness at each level. A person's wholeness and healing are determined by awareness of all levels. Absolute Spirit is that which transcends everything and includes everything.*

The psyche has many layers of consciousness. Early in our personal ego development, self-consciousness is essential for healthy human development. As the self continues to develop and mature, different self-concepts, identifies, and life experiences lead toward the conscious journey of inner understanding. As nurses reflect on the inner dimension of self and ways of being, this conscious journey toward wholeness evolves toward self-transcendence. Moving more inward and seeking inner knowledge along with personal understanding makes it possible to experience the Absolute that is composed of higher ordered wholes and integrations. Basic structures of the psyche are not replaced, but become part of the larger unity. The ultimate part of the journey is awakening, or enlightenment to the knowledge that one is part of the whole.

NOTES

1. A. Huxley, *The Perennial Philosophy* (New York: Harper Colophon Books, 1945), vii.
2. K. Wilbur, *Quantum Questions* (Boston: Shambhala Publications, 1984), 15–16.

Chapter 2

Dynamics of Healing and the Transpersonal Self

Barbara Montgomery Dossey

NURSE HEALER OBJECTIVES

Theoretical

- Define spirituality and transpersonal self.
- Compare and contrast healing versus curing.
- Analyze the dimensions of transpersonal healing and a healing system.

Clinical

- Integrate strategies that facilitate inner healing of self and others.
- Actively listen to individuals' stories, and help them explore the personal meaning within the stories.
- Focus on body-mind-spirit insights in transpersonal healing.

Personal

- Assess self in relationship to levels of being, and describe a plan for learning new skills that can assist you with presence and healing.
- Set aside quality quiet time to recognize your inner wisdom and creativity.
- Learn an imagery exercise that allows images to emerge about the healing qualities that you value most.

DEFINITIONS

Perennial Philosophy: historical recordings of humanity's quest for a divine reality and the universal need to understand why there is human life and what happens after death. Spanning nearly all cultures and ages, this philosophy can be found within all major spiritual traditions.

Spirituality: values, meaning, and purpose; a turning inward to the human traits of honesty, love, caring, wisdom, imagination, and compassion; the existence of a quality of a higher authority, guiding spirit, or transcendence that is mystical; a flowing, dynamic balance that allows and creates healing of body-mind-spirit; sometimes involves organized religion.

Transcend: to raise one's ordinary state of consciousness above control at a lower material level; to be aware, moment by moment, of what is true in both inner and outer experience; to become conscious of one's wholeness, complete in each moment.

Transpersonal Self: the identity that goes beyond the personal individual identity to include purpose, meaning, values, and unification with universal principles.

THE HEALING SYSTEM

Over the last 25 years, health care has focused on curing symptoms in a masculine, allopathic model. Curing has been associated with power, analysis of data, and technology, whereas healing has been largely overlooked. Current information suggests, however, that an integration of curing and healing provides the most effective results. (See Eras of Medicine in Chapter 1.) Many people are now ready to change destructive life style habits that lead to imbalance and illness. Individuals now recognize that both allopathic approaches and healing modalities are needed to stabilize or reverse disease and to improve their quality of life. Nurses also are ready to move forward with new visions of healing.

We must redefine healing.[1] In a lifelong journey into understanding the wholeness of human existence, our lives mesh with those of our clients/patients, their families, and our colleagues, and moments of new meaning and insight emerge in the midst of crisis. Healing occurs when we embrace and transform what we find most frightening or most painful in our lives, when we remember what we have forgotten about connection, unity, and interdependence. Healing is learning to open what has closed so that we can expand our inner human potentials. True healing is entering into a transcendent, timeless connection with a divinity or the universe. It involves creativity, passion, love and learning to trust life. It is seeking and expressing self in its fullness, its light and shadow, its masculine and feminine qualities.

It is time that professionals honor both their masculine and their feminine qualities (Table 2–1). As men and women learn to respect the balance of these qualities, healing will become more prominent in our health care system. We must continue to remember the wisdom of "doing what we know" and "knowing what we do." Nurses have been so buried in the layers of patriarchal learning and conditioning that the doing and knowing have been difficult. Nurses must motivate each other and learn to honor and talk about their healing interactions. (See Chapter 3.) Within the context of community, when nurses honor each other, it is affirming, encouraging, stimulating, and exciting. Nurses are then in a position to share the peace and power about themselves and their healing work.

Table 2–1 Examples of Masculine and Feminine Qualities

Masculine	*Feminine*
Intellect	Intuition
Linear	Nonlinear
How	Why
Knowledge	Wisdom
Power	Compassion
Analysis	Synthesis
Expansive	Contained
Proactive	Reactive
Giving	Receiving
External/public	Internal/private
Technical	Natural
Form	Process
Competition	Collaboration
Objective	Subjective
Doing to	Being with
Curing	Caring
Fixing	Nurturing
Reason	Feelings
Physical world	Invisible world
Decisive	Flexible

Source: Adapted from *Woman as Healer* by J. Achterberg, p. 191, with permission of Shambhala Publications, Inc., © 1990.

Achterberg suggests that a healing system is an interconnected web replete with feminine energy, in contrast to the more common models of linear, hierarchical relationships of masculine thought.[2] This healing system has invisible and nonmaterial bonds among and within levels (Figure 2–1). These bonds are the healing forces of the human spirit—love, compassion, motivation, conscious and unconscious thought, purpose, and will. The challenges are to integrate at each level of the healing system feminine values with masculine standards; to couple flexibility with decisiveness, perspective with focus, synthesis with analysis. As nurses of both genders understand the importance of the feminine voice, spirituality will reawaken in clinical practice. Spirituality is directly related to inner knowing and source of strength reflected in one's being, one's knowing, and one's doing.[3]

This healing system calls for all professionals to acknowledge the inner work that must occur in the spiritual dimension. The wounds of the healers and the wounds of the medical system are very similar in that the reintegration of the feminine principle, the feminine perspective, is a major step in the healing process.[4] We must focus not on curing, but on

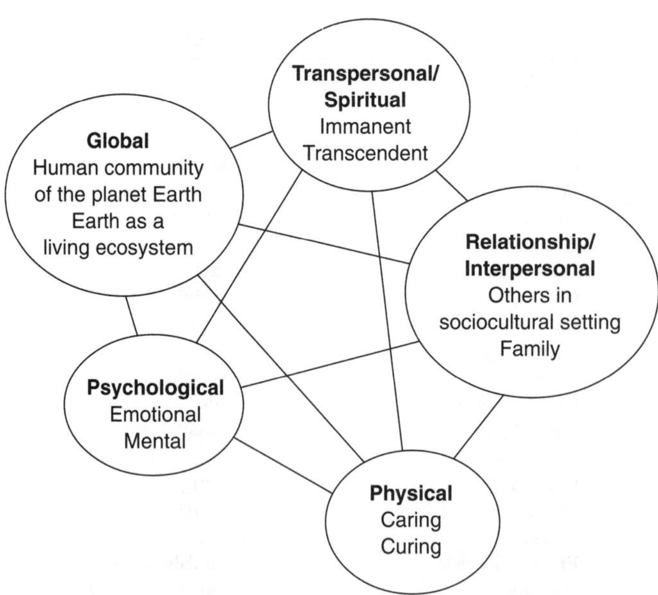

Figure 2–1 Healing System. *Source:* Reprinted from *Woman as Healer* by J. Achterberg, p. 195, with permission of Shambhala Publications, Inc., © 1990.

healing and the laws of healing. This creates a personal transformation that allows the professional to be more available to help others through crisis, transition, and the healing process. Recognizing our "wounded healer" sets us on a healing path that leads to an understanding of the evolving process toward wholeness and healing. The continual process of healing ourselves is the first step in facilitating healing in others.

FOUNDATIONS FOR HEALING

A Human Science

Evoking states of healing and healer establishes a human science. Weber asserts that the universal healing power, not the healer's personal energy, accomplishes healing.[5] The healer is like a channel, passively yet, paradoxically, with discernment permitting the cosmic energy to flow unobstructedly through his or her own energy fields into those of the client. The healer must be aware of the disturbances in the client's wholeness at the higher levels. It is the healer who constitutes the link between the universal and the particular; like an electrical transformer, the healer transforms the prodigious cosmic energy into a form that can be used by the client's body-mind-spirit system.

Watson states that a human science is based on

- a philosophy of human freedom, choices, and responsibility
- a biology and psychology of holism (nonreducible persons connected with others and nature)
- a theory of origins, methods, and limits of knowledge (epistemology) that allows not only for practical experience (empirics) but also for advancement of esthetics, ethical values, intuition, and process discovery
- a branch of metaphysics that deals with the nature of being/reality (ontology) of space and time
- a context of interhuman events, processes, and relationships
- a scientific world view that is open[6]

If we are to establish nursing as a human science, we must understand the concepts of (1) being-in-the-world, (2) the self, and (3) a phenomenal field.[7] A person is viewed as being in the world, possessing the spheres of bodymind spirit. These spheres influence that person's concept of self, the perceptions of "I" and relationships to others. Another level of self is the higher self, the spiritual self that rises above ordinary waking consciousness. A phenomenal field is the individual's frame of reference (i.e., subjective reality). Known only to the person, this phenomenal field influences a person's responses in any given situation. It involves many levels of consciousness, such as awareness, perceptions of self, body sensations, thoughts, values, feelings, intuitive insights, beliefs, and hopes. Thus, when nurse and client come together, two phenomenal fields come together. Both are in a process of being, becoming, and developing transpersonal understanding.

Transpersonal Human Care and Caring Transactions

Watson states that transpersonal human care and caring transactions are the professional, ethical, scientific, esthetic, caring, and personalized giving-receiving behaviors that allow for contact between the subjective world of two people (nurse and other) through physical, mental, and spiritual routes.[8] The nurse and client who come together share a phenomenal field of their individual uniqueness, which creates an event of caring (Figure 2–2). Thus, the human caring process has a transpersonal dimension in which the person of the nurse affects and is affected by the person of the other. Both are fully present in the moment and feel a union with the other. They share a phenomenal field that becomes part of the life history of both. Such an ideal of caring entails an intersubjectivity, in which both persons are involved. This coming together can take place in a mechanical manner in which the nurse or client responds without acknowledging the other or recognizing the other's potentials, or it can occur in an atmosphere of caring that involves actions and choices by both.[9]

Healing and caring have emerged as the essence of nursing. One comparative analysis of conceptualizations and theories of caring resulted in the identification of five major themes: (1) caring as a human trait, (2) caring as a moral imperative, (3) caring as an affect interaction, (4) caring as an interpersonal interaction, and (5) caring as a therapeutic intervention.[10] Outcomes of caring have been categorized as the client's subjective experience, the client's physical response, and the nurse's subjective experience.

The concepts of healing and caring need more scientific investigation, clear definitions, and healthy debate. The levels of knowledge, theory, and research needed in a practice-oriented discipline such as nursing must be considered in relation to different aspects of reality. The expansion of models creates new paradigms that take into account a spectrum of reality from "body" through "mind" to "spirit" and provide a more philosophical basis for understanding multiple modes of inquiry and

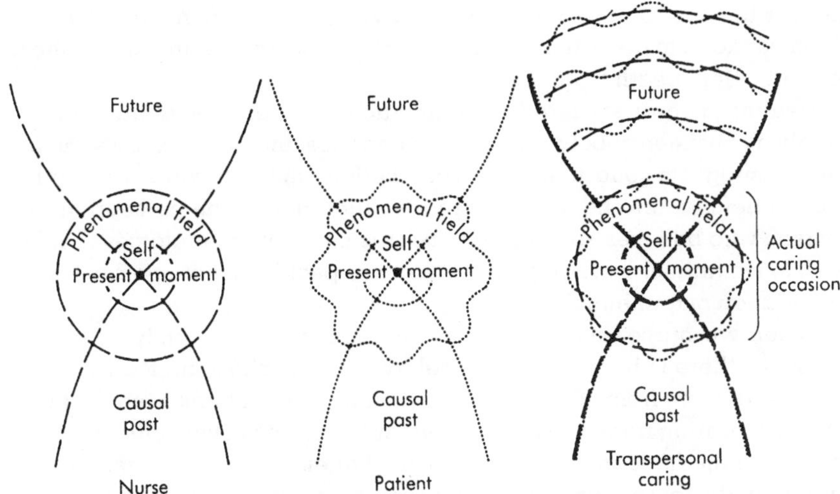

Figure 2-2 Dynamics of the Human Caring Process. *Source:* Reprinted from *Nursing: Human Science and Human Care* by J. Watson, p. 59, with permission of National League for Nursing Press, © 1988. Illustration by Melvin L. Gabel, University of Colorado Health Sciences Center, Biomedical Communications Department.

multiple types of knowledge and theory. This type of thinking makes it possible to see and experience the complementary rather than the competitive or the inherently superior or inferior.[11] This healing presence of caring can evolve as healing awareness increases.

Healing Awareness

Our ability to discipline ourselves to be present in the moment and to understand the meaning of the moment implies that there is a condition of "unknowing" or "openness."[12] This unknowing is the intersubjective experience of two people who come together at moments in time, and it is through this experience that healing emerges. Being present in the moment is a noninterfering attention that allows natural healing to flow.[13] There are several ways to acquire this ability. For example, relaxation, imagery, and various meditative disciplines allow inner silence and inward focusing. These skills can be practiced any place and any time. The message is the same whether delivered by saints, sages, or mystics—whether Hindu, Islamic, Buddhist, or Christian. At the bottom of one's soul is the soul of humanity itself, a divine, transcendent soul, leading from bondage to liberation, from enchantment to awakening, from time to eternity, from death to immortality.[14]

Healing awareness requires authenticity. Not only does authenticity imply a consistency between inner experience and outer expression, but also it suggests congruence between beliefs and behaviors. Perception and beliefs tend to be mutually reinforcing; that is, the perception of a person who believes something to be true selectively reinforces that belief. Much unhealthy living occurs because people do not operate from a foundation of authenticity.

When we nurses model healing awareness, consciously or unconsciously, there is harmony in our behaviors, thoughts, and feelings. Clients learn more from what nurses do than from what nurses teach or say. When operating from a position of authenticity, we act with clear purpose and have the freedom to create choices that empower our lives. Without authenticity, there is an internal conflict that manifests as anxiety, burnout, and confusion about living and may result in illness. When healing awareness is foremost each day in all areas of daily living, we live and practice from our authentic self.

Path toward Transpersonal Healing

General complex factors shape a nurse's world view and influence the nurse's ability to help individuals with spiritual issues:

- pluralism: the vast array of beliefs, values, meaning, and purpose that nurses and clients have
- fear: the nurse's possible confusion about his or her own beliefs and values, ability to handle situations, and invasion of an individual's privacy
- awareness of own spiritual quest: the nurse's contemplation of meaning, purpose, hope, and presence of love in his or her own life
- confusion: the nurse's conflicts between religious and spiritual concepts
- basic attitudes: the nurse's belief system about illness, aging, and suffering[15]

As the nurse becomes more aware of the areas that affect the spiritual dimension, the nurse and client can carry on a dialogue without using traditional religious language to share and express their spiritual dimension (see Exhibit 1–1).[16] Many variables determine the dialogue between the nurse and client, such as each one's position on their inward journey, each one's ability to listen actively and reflect, and the level of trusting relationship that has been established. Our role as nurses is to help individuals explore their human potentials and to go beyond pessimism. Borysenko has described psychologic pessimism as the state of learned helplessness associated with physical illness and mental distress.[17] She believes that psychologic pessimism must be extended to include spiritual pessimism, the idea that our failure to be "good enough" will somehow lead to punishment. This notion is often associated with Judeo-Christian thought and has been referred to as "New Age Guilt."[18] Nurses need to be aware of these issues and help clients shift to spiritual optimism, which presupposes the intrinsic goodness of each person and sees mistakes and problems as learning experiences rather than as evidence of unworthiness. A shift in these fundamental attitudes not only heals the physical body, but also leads to spiritual health.

Physical Health vs. Spiritual Health

There are many flaws in contemporary thinking about the relationship between physical and spiritual health. One of these is equating the two. On the surface it would appear that, since healing and spirituality seem so closely related, those who are highly evolved spiritually would be supremely healthy (Figure 2–3).[19] Both the Eastern and Western mystical literature illustrate that physical health and spiritual attainment do not always correlate, however. Sometimes an inverse correlation seems to occur, for persons with a physical illness may experience a sense of wholeness. It is true that physical illness may disappear as one moves forward on a spiritual path, but such an occurrence seems to be almost a grade or an aside. The inner life of the spirit, not the outer health of the body, is more important in all the great spiritual traditions.

Equating physical and spiritual health is a practice that currently abounds in "holistic" health circles.[20] Common expressions by many individuals are, "If I were really spiritual enough, perfect physical health would follow. My disease would be cured, and I could expect a long and healthy life." These notions do not contain a holistic view, because they separate certain qualities, such as suffering or illness, from the ultimate experience. The resulting dualism is contrary to the principle of wholeness.

Another insidious problem manifests itself in a person's attempt to "be more spiritual" with another agenda in mind—becoming physically healthier. Combining these two goals as if they are one is not always

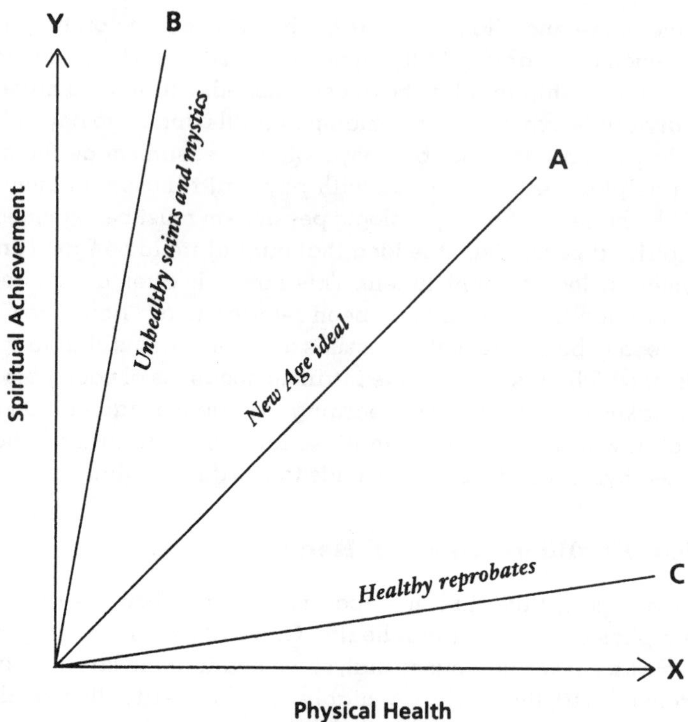

Figure 2–3 Relationship between Physical Health and Spiritual Achievement. The level of spiritual achievement is plotted along the Y axis, and the degree of physical health is plotted along the X axis. The New Age ideal—the notion that spiritual achievement and physical health are always correlated—is illustrated by line A. This notion presupposes that for every gain in spirituality there is a corresponding gain in physical health, without exception—a one-to-one, straight-line, linear, invariant relationship. That this is not the case is illustrated by lines B and C. Line B shows that saints and mystics may be high spiritual achievers but may have poor physical health. Line C illustrates the opposite: people with little spiritual sensitivity—so-called healthy reprobates—can enjoy extremely good physical health. *Source:* Reprinted from *Healing Words: The Power of Prayer and the Practice of Medicine* by Larry Dossey, p. 16, Harper San Francisco, with permission of Larry Dossey, © 1993.

successful, however. For example, meditation with an overt reason in mind simply does not work; intentional, active striving for a particular outcome is doomed to failure. Putting aside personal, results-oriented agendas brings about the real breakthrough. This "passive volition," this "doing nothing," is the key to spiritual awareness necessary for peaceful living and peaceful "deathing." In addition, it is helpful in preventing self-blame if an illness should arise.

Releasing "New Age Guilt"

Certain behaviors can lead to symptoms or illness. Anxiety, panic attacks, headaches, back pain, obesity, hypertension, elevated cholesterol levels, and addictions are obvious examples. These conditions may lead to guilt and self-recrimination; "if I were spiritual enough, I would not have become ill." Persistent disease generates more guilt and self-recrimination; "if I were spiritual enough, I'd be well by now." The appearance of disease in a person who is living a life of spiritual awareness makes it clear that we simply cannot invariably attribute illness to a lack of spiritual awareness, however.

The type of thinking that says, "I can control everything about my body with my thought!" is extremely narcissistic, suggests an impossible omnipotence, and is pathologic.[21] In effect, it holds the entire range of physical expressions and experiences hostage to the inflated ego. The assertive ego (e.g., "*my* feelings, *my* attitudes, *my* emotions, *my* thought") is enshrined as the ruler of everything that can possibly happen and must, therefore, be held accountable when things go wrong. This attitude often creates fear of the shadowy things of life, such as suffering, illness, and death. As long as the ego maintains its narcissistic, omnipotent struggle, the fear will remain. It may descend to the unconscious levels of the mind, however. When this happens, a vicious cycle may ensue; the fear may actually become worse and intensify suffering.

Linking the Physical and Spiritual Domains

Although "the physical" and "the spiritual" domains can be linked, they are not identical and cannot be equated. The meanings of space, time, matter, energy, and causation on the physical level are different from those on the spiritual level. In other words, different "world views" apply to these two levels of being. Both are correct and useful within their respective levels. They are opposite in many ways, but both are necessary to give a full picture of total experience. Realizing this, we can avoid fusing one mode of knowing into another and equating physical health and spiritual health. The lower never includes the higher, but the higher always includes the lower. Just so, the physical cannot account for the spiritual, but is always a part of the spiritual. In the same way, physical and spiritual health can never be the same. Spiritual health is always beyond physical health. It is always transmaterial (beyond the body) and transmental (beyond the individual psyche and the ego).[22]

Integration of Personal and Professional Mission Statements

For healing to take place, personal mission statements and health care mission statements must reflect healing. Furthermore, each must empower the other. Three pioneering programs that integrate personal and professional mission statements and utilize a bio-psycho-social-spiritual approach to helping individuals form healing rituals for living are: (1) the Mind/Body Medical Institute of the New England Deaconness Hospital and Harvard Medical School in Boston, Massachusetts;[23] (2) the Stress Reduction Clinic at the University of Massachusetts Medical Center in Worcester, Massachusetts;[24] and (3) the Center for Human Caring within the University of Colorado School of Nursing in Denver, Colorado.[25]

The transformation of health care from a disease management industry to a healing system requires a paradigm shift of hospitals in order to integrate new frameworks for health care delivery. For example, Riverside Methodist Hospital in Columbus, Ohio, is a huge medical complex with a 1,000-bed capacity where the best of Era I medicine is practiced. Riverside Methodist Hospital administrators, nursing directors, managers, and nursing staff, and the whole hospital system are integrating technology, consciousness, and spirit at all levels including employees, patients, families, and community. Their overall mission statement encompasses healing, wholeness, the providence of God, and care: "We are committed to a partnership for healing and wholeness that integrates with the providence of God, the strengths of patients and their families, the care of the health care team and the service of employees."[26]

As Riverside began its centennial in January 1991, the mission statement for the centennial year was as follows:

> Riverside Methodist Hospital's Centennial Forum will focus on the dynamic relationship between health and the healing process while challenging all employees to assume responsibility for enhancing or initiating new roles in delivering the healing process during the centennial year and beyond.[27]

To place these statements into practice in the centennial year, employees were asked to inform upper management about what they needed to enhance their healing work and to evoke transpersonal human caring and caring transactions. As a result of these efforts, healing rooms have been incorporated into a new 450-bed tower. In addition, courses on therapeutic presence[28] and therapeutic touch are being offered to enhance nurses' skills.

Sioux Valley Hospital is another prototype health care system that has developed an innovative approach. The Healing Web Model guides health care colleagues as they bring together the professional programs in the community to deliver integrated care (Figure 2–4).[29] The model ascribes to core values; collaboration; research; and integration of technology, mind, and spirit. The foundation lines of the web were created by

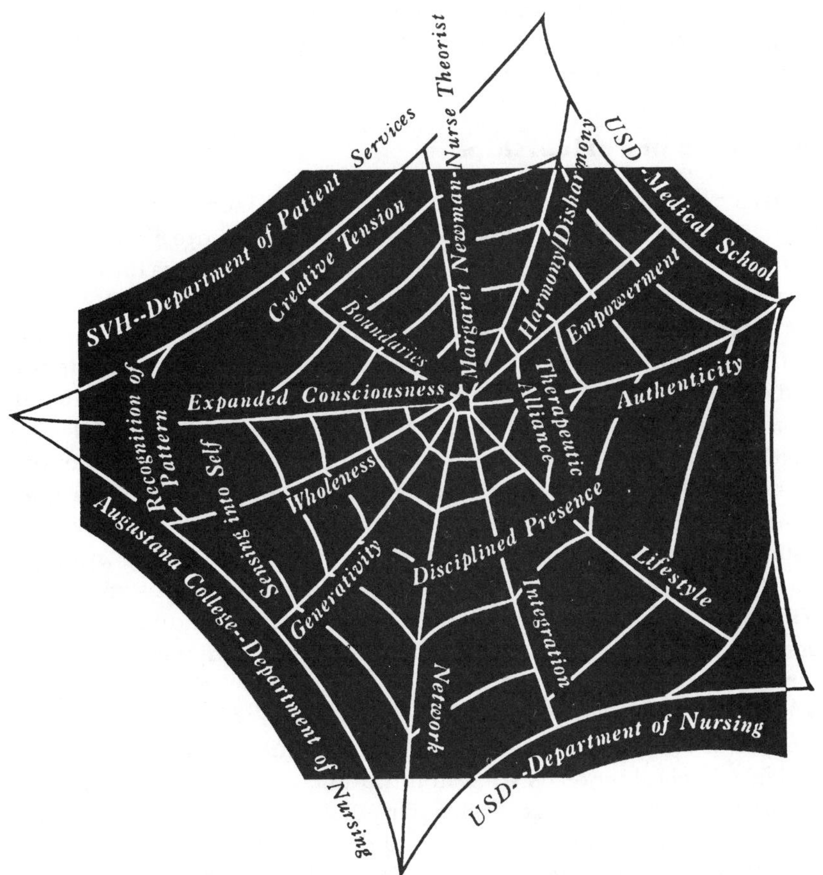

Figure 2–4 Healing Web Model. SVH, Sioux Valley Hospital; USD, University of South Dakota. *Source:* From *Nursing and Health Care* 13(2). Reprinted with permission. Copyright © 1992, National League for Nursing.

bringing together the Augustana College Department of Nursing (baccalaureate degree), the Sioux Valley Hospital Department of Patient Services, and the University of South Dakota Department of Nursing (associate degree) and School of Medicine. Staff of the nursing and medical schools now share grand rounds. The bridge line uses Newman's nursing theory "Health as Expanding Consciousness."[30] The radial lines are the concepts used in developing the curriculum. The spiral lines represent the caring capacities desired as outcomes for the nurses educated in the Healing Web Model. This model originates in the belief that nursing is best understood in terms of the individual nurse-client relationship. As the nurse-client relationship becomes a teacher-learner relationship, both the nurse and the client expand their consciousness so that there is a mutual unfolding of knowledge and caring.

Envisioning of Partnerships

Nurses are challenging the status quo and are incorporating in their caregiving models of partnerships between health care professionals and their clients. If they are to be partners, clients must have the capacity to make decisions about the course of their treatment and about their own lives. Therefore, a partnership is person-centered rather than role-centered. Health care providers are coming to terms with issues such as personal ego or limitations of technology and are accepting open communication with individuals. Remembering that there are usually many ways to reach health care goals, professionals are presenting more than one alternative. They are also encouraging individuals to focus on their strengths and spiritual dimension rather than their limitations.[31] When a person has severe coronary artery disease and no technology will help, for example, the potential for healing and changing different aspects of life style and perceived meaning about the situation remains. As nurses increase their healing awareness and authenticity, major shifts occur in all interactions and outcomes.

We are challenged to go beyond "I" strategies to "we" strategies so that the needs of our clients, patients, and families drive the health care system. Miccolo challenges us with an intriguing model for thinking about the crucial attributes of successful partnerships (Exhibit 2–1).[32] Miccolo believes that each of us is a leader and that we can influence and gain the confidence of our colleagues. She also thinks that each of us is a good follower. The time has come to extend our journey from followship and leadership to partnership, however. A partnership requires close cooperation between parties who have joint rights and responsibilities that all of them clearly understand. We live in an endless array of partnerships with clients, patients, colleagues, spouses, parents, siblings, children, and many more. As we are faced with the stresses of changes in our profession, we need to enhance awareness of nurturing partnerships and envision the multitude of possibilities.

CONCLUSION

Nurse healing is possible when the nurse is attuned every day to the continuous discovery about inner wisdom and awareness of one's being. Nurses must strive to explore and acknowledge inner wisdom as a first step on the journey toward wholeness. The ideas of body-mind-spirit connections are not new, but have been recorded for more than 5,000 years. It is new, however, that science (psychoneuroimmunology and certain areas within biology, physics, engineering, and other fields) is providing data that confirm body-mind-spirit connections.

DIRECTIONS FOR FUTURE RESEARCH

1. Evaluate modes of integrating concepts of transpersonal healing in nursing curriculum, mission statements, in-service education, and seminars.
2. Identify holistic guidelines and therapies to help individuals be in harmony with the changes that occur throughout the life span.
3. Determine whether outcomes achieved in client interactions with nurses who practice self-healing techniques differ from those achieved in interactions with nurses who do not use self-healing techniques.

NURSE HEALER REFLECTIONS

After reading this chapter, the nurse healer will be able to answer or begin a process of answering the following questions:

- How do I feel when I observe transpersonal dimensions in my daily life?
- What occurs when I focus on one new quality of transpersonal healing in clinical practice?
- What is my experience when I allow myself to enter into a natural transpersonal experience through deep relaxation or meditation?

Exhibit 2-1 Effective Partnering

V

ALUES DRIVEN—Partners are driven by values, not by environment, emotions, or circumstances. Do you "walk the talk" of the values you share with your partners?

I

NTERDEPENDENCE—Interdependence involves the "we" of a partnership. We can do it. We can get there. We can create something greater together. Do you partner with a "we" or a "me" focus?

S

HIFTING PARADIGMS—"You can't change the fruit without changing the root." Our paradigms—the models or context in which we do our thinking—frame our attitudes and behaviors. Do you think from the inside out—starting with yourself and putting ethics ahead of personality and popularity? If not, you may need to change your thinking (shift your paradigm). If the fruit is our partnership and the root is how we think, some shifting may be necessary to genuinely achieve your partnership's goals. Are you "root bound"? Do you need to replant your ideas so you can grow better fruit?

I

NTEGRITY—Integrity is the value we place on ourselves. Personal integrity generates trust by keeping us from judging another before checking our perceptions with that person. Integrity stops us from talking behind another's back; from dishonest communication and behaviors; and from self-serving motivation. Are you honest in your communications? Do you participate in conversations about another person without bringing your concerns to that person directly? Do you voice your convictions even if they are unpopular?

RGANIZATIONAL OUTCOMES—Focusing on organizational outcomes is a characteristic of organizational excellence. This holds true for partners, too. When partners focus on outcomes, they gain a shared purpose and direction for progress. Are you focused on outcomes and driven by the ones you share with your partner?

EGOTIATION—In negotiating, partners focus on interests, not positions. A win-win situation is where one partner doesn't succeed at the other's expense. How are your negotiation skills?

Source: Reprinted from Miccolo, M., Effective Partnering, *AACN News*, October 1993, with permission of American Association of Colleges of Nursing, © 1993.

P

RINCIPLE-CENTERED LEADERSHIP—Principles drive every word, action, and priority of effective partners. Are you a principle-centered leader? Do your actions with your partners reflect your values and principles?

A

CCOUNTABILITY—Each of us is accountable to our own effectiveness, for our own happiness, and for most of our circumstances. Are you accountable for your behaviors, words, and priorities in your partnerships?

R

ENEWAL—With renewal, we can replace old patterns of self-defeating and noncollaborative behavior with new patterns of effectiveness, happiness, and trust. What was the most recent thing you did to renew yourself and your partnerships?

T

RUST—Trust nurtures the self-esteem of each partner, enabling him or her to focus on issues rather than personalities and positions. Are you a trustworthy partner? Do you operate above the table at all times?

N

OVELTY—Partnerships are only as much fun and as invigorating as the partners make them. What novel approaches do you use to energize your partnerships?

E

VOLUTION—Evolution happens as partners open up the gates for change. Sometimes this may feel like *revolution*, but it's really a gradual metamorphosis toward interdependence in the partnership. Where are your partnerships now compared to where they began?

R

ESPECT—Only in an environment of mutual respect, where each viewpoint is truly heard, will partners express their most important and truthful thoughts. Are you respectful in your interactions, even in the face of debate and disagreement? Do you listen well without interruption, seeking first to understand before being understood?

S

YNERGY—Synergy happens when the combined actions of people working together create a greater effect than each person can achieve alone. Synergistic partnerships value differences, respect them and build on strengths to compensate for weakness. Do your partnerships focus on the contributions of each partner with the goal of creating a greater good for all?

NOTES

1. J. Achterberg et al., *Rituals of Healing* (New York: Bantam Books, 1994).
2. J. Achterberg, *Woman as Healer* (Boston: Shambhala Publications, 1990).
3. M. Burkhardt and M.G. Nagai-Jacobson, Reawakening Spirit in Clinical Practice, *Journal of Holistic Nursing* 12, no. 1 (1994):9–21.
4. R. Remen, The Eye of an Eagle, the Heart of a Lion, the Hand of a Woman, *The Journal of the Healing Health Care Project* 2, no. 3 (1993):16–19.
5. R. Weber, Philosophical Foundations and Frameworks for Healing, in *Spiritual Aspects of the Healing Arts*, ed. D. Kunz (Wheaton, IL: The Theosophical Publishing House, 1985), 38.
6. J. Watson, *Nursing: Human Science and Human Care* (New York: National League for Nursing Press, 1988), 16.
7. Ibid., 54–55.
8. Ibid., 58.
9. Ibid., 59.
10. J. Morse et al. Comparative Analysis of Conceptualizations and Theories of Caring, *Image* 23, no. 2 (1991):119–126.
11. J. Wolfer, Aspects of "Reality" and Ways of Knowing in Nursing: In Search of an Integrating Paradigm, *Image* 2, no. 2 (1993):141–145.
12. P. Munhall, 'Unknowing': Toward Another Pattern of Knowing in Nursing, *Nursing Outlook* 41, no. 3 (1993):125–128.
13. F. Vaughn, *The Inward Arc* (Boston: Shambhala Publications, 1985).
14. K. Wilbur, *The Spectrum of Consciousness* (Wheaton, IL: The Theosophical Publishing House, 1977).
15. M. Burkhardt, Spirituality: An Analysis of the Concept, *Holistic Nursing Practice* 3, no. 3 (1989):69–77.
16. B. Dossey and C. Guzzetta, Holistic Cardiovascular Nursing, in *Cardiovascular Nursing: Holistic Practice*, ed. C. Guzzetta and B. Dossey (St. Louis: Mosby Year Book, 1992).
17. J. Borysenko, *Guilt Is the Teacher, Love Is the Lesson* (New York: Warner Books, 1990).
18. K. Wilbur, Do We Make Ourselves Sick? *New Age Journal* 6(1988):50.
19. L. Dossey, *Healing Words: The Power of Prayer and the Practice of Medicine* (San Francisco: Harper San Francisco, 1993).
20. L. Dossey, *Meaning and Medicine: A Doctor's Tales of Breakthrough and Healing* (New York: Bantam Books, 1991).
21. L. Dossey, *Recovering the Soul* (New York: Bantam Books, 1989).
22. L. Dossey, *Meaning and Medicine* (New York: Bantam Books, 1991).
23. H. Benson and E. Stuart, *The Wellness Book* (New York: Birch Lane Press Publishing, 1992).
24. J. Kabat Zinn, *Full Catastrophe Living* (New York: Delacorte Press, 1990).
25. Center for Human Caring, University of Colorado Health Science Center and School of Nursing, Denver, Colorado, 1992.

26. T. Wimberly, Riverside Methodist Hospital Mission Statement, Columbus, Ohio, 1991, personal communication.
27. Ibid.
28. M. McKivergin and M.J. Daubenmire, The Essence of Therapeutic Presence, *Journal of Holistic Nursing* 12, no. 1 (1994):65–81.
29. J. Koerner and S. Schmidt Bunkers, The Healing Web: An Expansion of Consciousness, *Journal of Holistic Nursing* 12, no. 4 (1994):51–63.
30. M. Newman, Health As Expanding Consciousness (New York: National League for Nursing, 1994).
31. T. Mansen, The Spiritual Dimension of Individuals: Conceptual Development, *Nursing Diagnosis* 4, no. 4 (1993):140–147.
32. M. Miccolo, Effective Partnering, *AACN News*, October (1993):2.

RESOURCES

For information on American Holistic Nurses' Association, Certificate Program in Holistic Nursing, and Healing Touch Certificate Program contact:

American Holistic Nurses' Association
4101 Lake Boone Trail
Suite #201
Raleigh, North Carolina 27607
(919) 787-5181
(919) 787-4916 FAX

For information on educational video on holistic nursing:

At the Heart of Healing: Experiencing Holistic Nursing
(3½ hours—2 volume set; 15 CEUs)
Kineholistic Foundation
P.O. Box 719
Woodstock, New York 12498

For information on educational video on caring:

A Conversation on Caring with Jean Watson and Janet Quinn
National League for Nursing
350 Hudson Street
New York, NY 10014

Pioneer programs in caring and healing:

Mind Body Medical Institute
New England Deaconness Hospital
185 Pilgrim Road
Boston, MA 02215
(617) 632-9527

Stress Reduction Clinic
University of Massachusetts Medical Center
55 Lake Avenue North
Worcester, MA 01655
(508) 856-2656

Center for Human Caring
University of Colorado School of Nursing
Campus Box C288
4200 East Ninth Avenue
Denver CO 80262
(303) 270-6157

Audio tapes:

The Art of Caring: Holistic Healing with Imagery, Relaxation, Touch, and Music
(set of 4 tapes)—a companion to *Holistic Nursing: A Handbook for Practice, Second Edition.*
Aspen Publishers, Inc.
7201 McKinney Circle
Frederick, Maryland 21701
(800) 638-8437
ISBN: 1-56455-302-7

VISION OF HEALING

Toward the Inward Journey

The root word of healing and healer is hael, which means to facilitate movement toward wholeness or to make whole on all levels—physical, mental, emotional, social, and spiritual. As sophisticated as our modern medical system is, there are no firm criteria by which to evaluate healing. In fact, it often seems that there are two different sets of criteria for the evaluation of healing. One set of criteria focuses on "the numbers" of biologic data; the other set, more subjective, focuses on the client's feeling "stronger" or "better." If we use the root word in the true sense, healing incorporates both sets of criteria. The either/or—that is, either a physical problem or an emotional or spiritual problem—is a false dichotomy. There is no such thing, for the body-mind-spirit is a single integrated entity.

A healer is aware of the importance of understanding the belief systems of self and others. A healer recognizes that consciousness and the human spirit operate not only within a person, but also between and among individuals (e.g., between nurses and clients, as well as among nurses, clients, families, and colleagues). Nurses have the unique opportunity of being present to help people understand the meaning in their lives, whether it be through instruction for wellness, intervention in an acute situational crisis, management of chronic illness, or the transition to a peaceful death. They guide the client in making connections of body-mind-spirit. The clearest way to understand this interaction is through the concept of the nurse as a healer. The fundamental principle of a healer is the skillful bringing together of the inner resources of knowledge and intuition. To do this, the nurse healer must identify his or her own woundedness, the life polarities, and the purposes and meaning in life.

Nurses who live and practice from a holistic perspective recognize that there is no separation between their personal and professional selves. As we expand our consciousness and repattern our lives with healing intention, we take into all aspects of our lives and work a sense of sacredness. When nurses have a sense of sacredness about their work and explore the state of "nurse as healing environment," nurse healing is manifest at the highest level.[1] Studies have shown that, when a group as small as 1 percent of the people in a city's population are practicing transcendental meditation (TM) regularly, the number of negative events, such as crimes, decreases. This is referred to as the "Maharishi effect" since it was predicted by the Maharishi Mahesh Yogi, the founder of TM.[2] With the introduction of the advanced TM-Sidhi program in 1976, the Maharishi proposed that an even smaller proportion, the square root of 1 percent, of the population of a society participating as a group in the practice of the TM and TM-Sidhi programs would create this effect in the entire society.[3,4] Quinn challenges us to imagine what would happen if 1 percent of the nurses in a clinic, hospital, or school began to practice healing modalities.[5] As we challenge ourselves to understand more deeply the sacredness of our work and to perceive ourselves as healing environments, we, too, are healed. We must reawaken our spirit and cultivate it if all the powers of our soul are to act together in perfect balance and harmony. There can never be any real opposition between science and spirituality, for one is the complement of the other. Self-exploration brings us face to face with the mystery of our own being.

NOTES

1. J. Quinn, The Nurse as Healing Environment, *Holistic Nursing Practice* 6, no. 4 (1992): 26–35.
2. L. Dossey, *Recovering the Soul* (New York: Bantam Books, 1989).
3. M. Dilbeck et al., The Transcendental Meditation Program and Crime Rate Changes in a Sample of Forty-Eight States, *Journal of Crime and Justice* 4(1981): 25–45.
4. Maharishi European Research University, *New Horizons in Criminology* (Rheinweiler, Germany: Maharishi European Research University Press, 1979).
5. J. Quinn, The Nurse as Healing Environment.

Chapter 3

Nurse As Healer

Barbara Montgomery Dossey

NURSE HEALER OBJECTIVES

Theoretical

- Compare and contrast patterns of knowing and unknowing.
- Assess your nurse healer characteristics.
- Analyze the personal, interpersonal, and transpersonal dimensions of growth.

Clinical

- Identify real versus pseudo-listening with clients and colleagues.
- Assess your skills as a guide, and decide if there are areas that you wish to improve.
- Identify the qualities that most often allow you to be present with yourself and others.

Personal

- Learn techniques to become more present and integrate these experiences into your daily life.
- Acknowledge your inner feelings when you are fully present with yourself and others.
- Decide on ways to increase rituals of inner healing in your life.

DEFINITIONS

Centeredness: fine-tuned sensitivity to life's inner and outer patterns and processes; a state of balance of self that allows the process of intuition to unfold.

Guide: one who helps others discover and recognize insights and healing awareness about their life journeys.

Healing: a process of bringing parts of one's self (i.e., physical, mental, emotional, spiritual, relational) together at deep levels of inner knowing, leading to an integration and balance, with each part having equal importance and value.

Intention: readiness to allow the natural universal life force to flow and to experience inner calm and peace so that one's work may involve patterns of knowing and unknowing.

Intuition: perceived knowing of things and events without the conscious use of rational processes.

Nowness: the ability to be in the moment.

Nurse Healer: one who facilitates another person's growth and life processes toward wholeness (body-mind-spirit) or who assists with recovery from illness or with transition to peaceful death.

Presence: a state achieved when one moves within oneself to an inner reference of stability of being in the moment.

Polarity: the contrast of opposite qualities or states, such as health and illness, birth and death.

Relationship: joining of one, two, or more people who share interests, successes, and failures; who facilitate and accelerate each other's life potentials.

Transpersonal: going beyond individual and personal uniqueness in a way that involves one's purpose, values, and beliefs.

Transpersonal Self: the sense of self that goes beyond the ego; the "I" that does not identify itself as a single, isolated individual.

Wounded Healer: concept derived from Greek mythology, specifically the myth of Chiron, which suggests that even the greatest healers have inherent weaknesses and fallibility.

PATTERNS OF KNOWING AND UNKNOWING

Contemporary nursing is involved in a "silent" revolution; giving (r)evolution a silent *r* reveals the true meaning. Nurses are broadening their experience of themselves as healers and becoming vocal about what they need to practice the healing arts in all areas of nursing. For example, Carper identified four knowledge patterns essential to professional nursing to empower nurses to recognize their unique qualities.[1] These patterns of knowing—empirical knowledge, personal knowledge, ethical knowledge, and aesthetic knowledge—lead to a form of confidence that is invaluable if new aspects of reality and the true philosophy and science of caring and healing are to emerge.[2] A state of knowing may bring to a halt further exploration of intuition and unknown areas, however. Munhall challenges nurses to a new pattern of knowing called "unknowing."[3] The state of mind and the art of unknowing lead to an openness and authenticity where a nurse can admit to self and another, "I don't know you and your subjective world." This coming together of two people not only creates a phenomenal field (see Chapter 2), but also clearly focuses on the intersubjective space where all sources of human understanding, empathy, and conflict can more easily evolve. In this state of unknowing, the nurse as healer is manifest in the deepest sense. As nurses integrate patterns of both knowing and unknowing, they can demonstrate, not simply proclaim, conceptual frameworks of caring.

Awareness of one's own spirituality and intentionally caring for one's own spirit are important components in the process of integrating spirituality into personal and professional practice.[4,5] Knowing as well as unknowing ourselves leads to more meaningful relationships with others. We are more likely to attune to our life purposes and to the unique qualities that we bring into our work as nurse healers.

Characteristics of a Nurse Healer

- Awareness that self-healing is a continual process
- Familiarity with the terrain of self-development
- Recognition of weaknesses and strengths
- Openness to self-discovery
- Continued effort to develop clarity about life's purposes to avoid mechanical behavior and boredom
- Awareness of present and future steps in personal growth
- Modeling of self-care in order to help self and clients with the inward process
- Awareness that a nurse's presence is as important as technical skills
- Respect and love for clients regardless of who or how they are
- Willingness to offer the client methods for working on life issues
- Ability to guide the client in discovering creative options

- Presumption that the client knows the best life choices
- Active listening
- Empowerment of clients to recognize that they can cope with life processes
- Sharing of insights without imposing personal values and beliefs
- Acceptance of what clients say without judging
- Perception of time with clients as being there to serve and share with them

PURPOSE

As a conscious effort to maximize human potential, purpose in one's life can be increased along two dimensions of growth—the personal and the transpersonal (Figure 3–1).[6] The personal growth is represented by the horizontal axis; the transpersonal growth, by the vertical axis. The wavy line between the two is the interpersonal dimension, or life's path toward transcendence, which is never a straight line. Transcendence, the star in the upper right-hand corner, is the point where individuality (the personal dimension) and universality (the transpersonal dimension) meet. The personal dimension of growth concerns meaning and integration of our personal existence. Involving logical and analytical thought, as well as self-motivation and goal orientation in one's professional and personal life, this personal dimension is more highly valued in Western

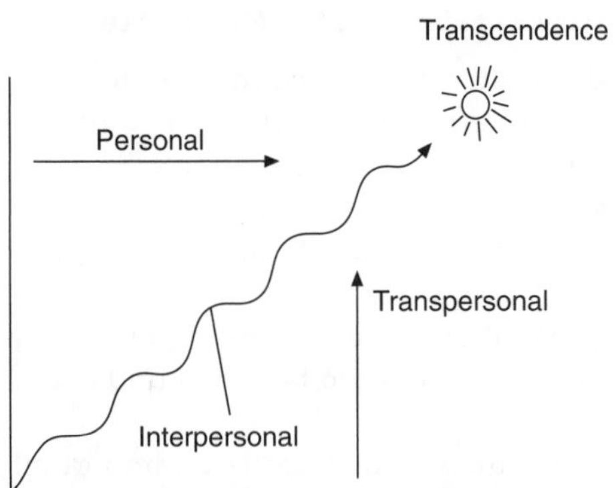

Figure 3–1 Dimension of Individual Growth. *Source:* Adapted from *The Unfolding Self* by M. Brown, p. 21, with permission of Intermountain Associates for Psychosynthesis Press, © 1983.

culture than is the transpersonal dimension. The latter is just as important, however, as it concerns the ultimate meaning and purpose of the universal existence of humanity.

A third dimension of human growth, the interpersonal dimension, is part of the other two dimensions (Table 3–1). In the personal dimension, we develop the basic social skills of communication, courtesy, and friendship that are requisite for survival with others. Then, as we begin to develop along the transpersonal dimension, we become aware of our basic interdependency. The essential merging of these two dimensions with the interpersonal dimension allows us to be more mindful of balanced supportive relationships with family, friends, community, and clients. It also reminds us of the depth necessary in meaningful relationships. Without the interpersonal dimension, our relationships would be, at best, unenlightened and superficial.

As nurses integrate their personal, interpersonal, and transpersonal dimensions, they enlarge their capacity for responsibility and choice in the moment and in life as a whole. They develop a sense of destiny, a meaning, and an overall purpose in life. There is true preference for living in accordance with one's purpose(s) so that different distractions or conflicts are more easily recognized when they arise. Thus, we are more willing to accept the limitations of life and to be in the world just as it is. This awareness gives nurses insight in guiding others in their life processes.

THE ART OF GUIDING

People come to health care professionals in search of healing, but they always bring their healing with them. A nurse healer uses the art of guid-

Table 3–1 Dimensions of Individual Growth

Dimension	*Characteristics*
Personal dimension	Sense of meaning; reasoning skills and logic; self-motivation; goal-oriented focus
Interpersonal dimension	Communication and social skills; friendship and relationships with family and community; development of self-reflection and biobehavioral skills to evoke more transcendental moments that lead to transpersonal understanding
Transpersonal dimension	Understanding of belonging to humanity; acceptance of a universal existence

ing to help others learn new health behaviors, make choices, and discover insights about ways to cope more effectively with daily living. A guide also helps a person explore purpose and meaning in life. Guiding is a special art and a healing intervention that nurses may use at all times.

Healing is easy to evoke when we enter into a state of intention with another to bring to the present moment a person's fullest potential. Being present helps the individual to balance his or her inner resources, to decrease stress, and to direct himself or herself toward harmony. A nurse healer guides the individual in developing all areas of human potential through the inner journey of self-discovery, but the nurse as guide does not presume to know the best course for that individual. Clients must make their own choices. Although nurses know some of the hazards and precautions that occur with life style changes or crisis, they can only suggest new options. Nurses have no way of knowing what each experience holds for a person, for the contrast of polarities (e.g., health and illness, joy and sadness) are always present in one's life. Each nurse and individual are constantly confronted with their woundedness, as portrayed by the Greek mythological figure Chiron.

THE WOUNDED HEALER: THE MYTH OF CHIRON

Chiron was a centaur, half man and half horse, who was skilled in healing. Along with other centaurs, Chiron was invited to the cave of Heracles. Intrigued by the scent of some wine that had been given to Heracles, the other centaurs began to drink. Because they were unaccustomed to drinking, they became intoxicated and began to fight. During the battle, Heracles hit Chiron in the knee with an arrow. Heracles tended the wound by following the instructions of Chiron, the wounded healer. The point of the arrow had been dipped in the poison of the hydra; thus, the wound was incurable. Chiron, an immortal, could not be cured, but neither could he die. From his cave, Chiron taught many heroes his great knowledge of healing. One of his students was Asclepius, who gained knowledge of the healing herbs and the power of acknowledging one's woundedness.

There is a part of all of us that is wounded. No one has total freedom from stress or illness, although many try to hide from it. Yet, the more we hide from our woundedness, the more we become vulnerable to psychophysiologic symptoms that may lead to illness. One of the major obstacles in understanding how both wellness and illness are facts of our existence and how both are necessary is the way in which we perpetuate the myth that the darker side can be ignored.

Life is a matter of polarity, the light and the shadow. Without the shadow we have no concept of the light. Contrast is essential in every aspect of our lives. Particularly in Western culture, the high peaks—the joy, clarity, love, and the sense of the sacred—are emphasized, while the dark night—the shadow—is ignored. The spiritual description of death and rebirth as a "dark night" comes from the writings of the great mystic St. John of the Cross.[7] In an eloquent way, he describes the dark night as a long period of unknowing, loss, uncertainty, and despair that spiritual seekers must traverse in order to empty and humble themselves enough to receive new insight. As we grasp the significance of being in the present moment, we are better able to enter into the darkness in order to gain a powerful part of our being and allow new strengths to be born.

PRESENCE

The concept of presence has significant implications for nursing education, practice, and research. A common recurring definition and use of the word *presence* is "being." *Being* as a noun is commonly defined as "existence" and "actuality."[8] A synonym for *being* is "essence." McKivergin and Daubenmire have delineated three levels of presence (Table 3–2).[9]

1. *Physical presence* is the nurse's "being there" for the client. Many nursing interventions, including the routine tasks that are prescribed for the client, are carried out at this level.
2. *Psychologic presence* is defined as "being with." The nurse uses himself or herself as an intervention tool to create a therapeutic psychologic milieu that meets the client's need for help, comfort, or support.
3. *Therapeutic presence* is the nurse's relating to the client as whole being to whole being, using all of his or her resources of body, mind, emotions, and spirit.

Presence is the state achieved when one moves within oneself to an inner reference of stability. It is a sense of self-relatedness that can be thought of as a place of inner being, a place of quietude within which one can feel truly integrated, unified, and focused. Presence is a personal space apart from either involvement or the consequent reaction to involvement. To be present implies a quality and essence of being in the moment.

Table 3-2 Levels of Therapeutic Presence

Levels of Interaction	*Type of Contact*	*Skills*
Physical presence	Body to body	Seeing, examining, touching, doing, hearing, hugging
Psychologic presence	Mind to mind	Assessment, communicating, active listening, writing, reflecting, counseling, attending to, caring, empathy, being nonjudgmental, accepting
Therapeutic presence	Spirit to spirit Whole being to whole being Centered self to centered self	Centering, meditating, intentionality, at-one-ment, imagery, openness, intuitive knowing, communion, loving, connecting

Source: Reprinted from McKivergin, M., and Daubenmire, J., The Essence of Therapeutic Presence, *Journal of Holistic Nursing*, Vol. 12, No. 1, pp. 65–81, with permission of Sage Publishers, Inc., © 1994.

Presence means daily periods of solitude to quiet the inner dialogue and body simultaneously and to experience sensations in the body-mind-spirit. The practice of various biobehavioral modalities, such as relaxation, imagery, and music or meditative disciplines, can enhance presence. One of the most powerful ways to become present with self and others is through the breath. When we are not in the present moment, our breathing is usually high and shallow in the chest, referred to as the fight-or-flight breathing or "I" (ego)-centered breathing. When we begin to breathe from the abdomen, however, the consciousness changes from "I"-centered to essence-centered breathing.[10] *Presencing* can be defined as the state of awareness where new insight and healing can evolve from any interaction between nurse and client.

Developing the skills and awareness of presence makes us more sensitive to our life patterns and processes. We act more frequently with purposeful intention. We are more willing to experience and face our fears and worries. Presence allows us to devote more time to our inner silence, which helps us understand more of the wisdom that becomes accessible to us when we acknowledge our polarities in life. Our love flows naturally, for we are open to the expressions of nonjudgmental love when we expand our consciousness.[11] Thus, presence makes us more consistently available for meaningful relationships.

Through presence, we can achieve a state of basic vulnerability that allows us to release the outer shell or facade of our role. Ordinarily, we identify the self we know by means of an awareness of our different roles and our constant stream of thoughts and feelings. With inner quietude, we learn to fall into the space between the successive moments of trying to grasp onto ideas and feelings. It is in this space that we open to being with others in a different way.

As presence helps us to enter into the conflicts in our own lives, we become aware of many possible ways to gain new meaning and insights from these conflicts. We can then assist clients in acknowledging the place of conflict in their lives more easily. We are able to see the polarity between conflict and its opposite, which is resolution. We are better able to organize inner energy and balance it with the incoming energy of people and events.

Presence facilitates true healing because the nurse is empty of personal needs, especially the needs to be a good nurse, to have the right technique, or to say the right thing. A nurse's presence in the moment allows the release of the guilt and frustration of "I don't have time to do the important teaching that I should be doing" or "If only I had time to be with the client." Learning the skills of being present allows the nurse to spend 5 to 10 focused minutes with a client and to share ideas that may be a marked turning point in the individual's self-healing. For example, spending a few moments teaching a client breathing and relaxation techniques to decrease anxiety may be the beginning of self-discovery that can awaken the client's own healing potential. This period of focused intention with the person may be as valuable or more valuable than an hour of counseling.

Our basic work as professionals is to become full human beings and to inspire full "human beingness" in other people. When we are present, wholeness vibrates and radiates from us. Being present basically means a spirited presence, an attunement with the situation, and a capacity competently to absorb, process, do, or simply be in the unknowing. It involves a spiritual transcendence where one experiences oneself as a part of a greater force that is a source of energy for caring. It is learning to travel that narrow path between healthy enmeshment with and inappropriate distance from others.[12] The transcendence of ego allows nurses to become deeply involved without succumbing to destructive forms of overinvolvement.

As nurses place a prime value on presence, the clinical environment can change.[13] In many clinical settings, the caring values of nurses have been in opposition to the norms,[14] and nursing has been perceived as a medically driven, delegated workload. A key to transforming this perspective may be in delineating the work that needs to be done in caring for patients. As nurses develop consensual standards of care (e.g., the clinical practice model at Butterworth Hospital, Grand Rapids, Michigan) that focus on independent caring aspects of nursing, presence, and healing are integrated into the realities of clinical practice.[15] In order to sustain a caring-healing practice in all areas, nurses need opportunities for healthy dialogue, time to develop frameworks and standards, and an organizational cultural context that reflects a paradigm shift of caring-healing models and language.[16] For example, a healing room at work can allow us to enter into quietness and be healed at work rather than physically and emotionally drained. Nurses can create visions of healing and urge the administration to establish a Healing Room by considering the following questions:

- Is it possible to convert a room near the unit, in the clinic, or in the school of nursing to be a Healing Room to nourish the staff?
- Is it possible for nurses to sign up each day to go to the Healing Room on or near the unit for 10 or 20 minutes to nourish themselves with a period of relaxation and rest?
- Is it possible to obtain the support of colleagues and administration to go to the Healing Room? Can such a rest period be valued and honored and nurses are encouraged to nourish themselves?
- Is it possible to have a Healing Room with comfortable pillows on a carpeted floor, beautiful pictures hanging on the wall, a few healing objects placed on several low tables for easy viewing, and an audio cassette library with a wide range of music, relaxation, and imagery tapes, headphones, and tape recorders? Can there be a sign on the door that reads, "This Healing Room is for your relaxation and rest. Please enjoy." (For details of establishing an audio cassette relaxation, imagery, music library, refer to Chapter 24.)

It is also important to create a similar kind of space at home so that there is time each day for inner reflection and renewal of the body-mind-spirit.

AFFIRMATIONS OF EXCEPTIONAL QUALITIES

A person selects strong, positive statements to affirm intentions and choices. These affirmations can help an individual clarify goals that direct actions and assist in self-evaluation. They also help to increase a person's responsibility for actions, thoughts, beliefs, and values. If a person's thoughts are hopeful and optimistic, that person's body responds with confidence, energy, and hope. If, on the other hand, negative thoughts and emotions dominate, the body responds with tightness; uneasiness; and increases in respiration, blood pressure, and heart rate, just to name a few physiologic changes. Affirmations can help change perceptions and beliefs. One's mind is constantly engaged in active thought processing, and affirmations selectively reinforce positive thoughts. Since self-dialogue continues into dream states, an important strategy is to make positive affirmations prior to falling asleep. (See image formation, Chapters 4 and 23.)

All nurses have the capability of becoming exceptional. It is helpful to reflect on the following affirmations of exceptional qualities, and experience them as if they already exist:

- I am a critical thinker.
- I take risks.
- I manipulate time and resources wisely.
- I am an advocate for nursing.
- I am assertive.
- I am caring.
- I am future-oriented.
- I am self-aware.

As we learn to recognize our exceptional qualities, we are more likely to help others begin to appreciate their unique qualities.

REAL VERSUS PSEUDO-LISTENING

Any communication process has three components: (1) a sender of the message, (2) a receiver of the message, and (3) the content of the material. In order to understand others, we must listen actively. Simply being quiet while someone else is talking is not real listening, however. The key to real listening is intention, which occurs when we focus with someone in order to understand that person, share that person's joy, learn something from that person, or give help to that person. With such a purpose in our responses and interventions, we can lead others or ourselves toward effective action or personal growth.

Nurses achieve good listening by quieting the inner dialogue. Good listening has an enormous quality of nowness; the listener has the ability to throw away intellectualizations when the client goes off in an unexpected direction. When counseling a client who is intent on telling a part of his or her story, some nurses stop the flow of the story and bring the client back to a certain point; stopping may block the client's insight, however. Nowness helps us to avoid analyzing in our own inner dialogue what we think should be happening and allows the client to move to a state from which an inner wisdom can emerge. Questioning (and listening) that structures the answers only minimally is a great art.

At times, we all lapse into pseudo-listening when we try to meet the needs of others. Some signs of pseudo-listening that indicate a focus on personal needs and a failure to listen actively are:

- remaining silent as you buy time to prepare your next remark
- listening to others so that they will listen to you
- listening only to specific information while deleting the rest
- acting interested when you are not
- partially listening because you do not want to disappoint another person
- listening in order not to be rejected
- searching for a person's weaknesses in order to take advantage of them
- identifying weak points in dialogue so that you can be stronger in your response.

In being with others, the first focus is to learn to listen actively to what is going on with another person. The second focus is to enable the individual to live in what is, not to avoid it, to let it be. Active listening skills promote effective communication in several ways. They clarify the message. The receiver of the message can verify verbal messages through the sender's nonverbal messages, or body language. The receiver can also gather additional information that can help with interventions. Active listening facilitates a greater acceptance of the sender's thoughts and emotions. Thus, the receiver of the message may be better able to choose the most effective behaviors that lead the client toward health and wholeness.

WORKING WITH OTHERS

As we engage in holistic nursing and embark on our inward journey for self-change, everything that we communicate by word, act, attitude, and setting will affect our potential for change.[17] We must be present-oriented and must consciously learn the skills required to stay in the present moment, because change takes place in the present, not in the past or future. Everything—our choice of words, our presence, and our greeting—affects our clients. Every part in the system is connected to every other part, and every part affects every other part. We form a network in which everyone participates. There is no such thing as an independent observer. Nurse and client are always creating change in one another.

Our beliefs affect our self-image, which, in turn, affects our actions and our capacity for self-healing. Furthermore, because clients perceive our beliefs, we must perceive ourselves and the client as a whole. Both the nurse and the client are whole, not a portion of disturbance or pathology. When we focus primarily on disease rather than on the person's healing potential, we encourage pathology. When we perceive the cancer patient as a person with cancer, we release the label.

It is necessary to consider the life patterns and situations that the client is confronting, all the client's life potentials—physical, mental, emotional, spiritual aspects; relationships; and choices.[18] Only when we consider the whole client and his or her significant others do we have a chance to direct the client toward wholeness. We must continue to gain new skills and become self-experienced in all the modalities that we offer to the client. The more we know from experience, the more we know that change is possible.

When we teach from experience, we are in a better position to help the client learn without making judgments. Setting realistic, measurable goals ensures that the client cannot fail. For example, a nurse teaches a person with migraine headaches not to blame himself or herself for the headache symptoms, but to focus on stress management skills to decrease the headache pattern. The client learns that the body is not the problem, but part of the solution. In addition, the client learns to acknowledge all changes, however slight, because each change leads to another and each slight change is progress.

As we teach clients to reframe experiences positively, their internal thoughts create new beliefs that most often lead to new healthier response patterns. Failure that is not reframed leads to more failure. The glass is not half-empty, but half-full. We also encourage the client to involve friends and family in the learning. Learning is an ongoing process and new skills must be practiced, shared, and integrated into all aspects of life.

Laughter, Humor, and Joy

Because joy and sadness pathways cannot operate simultaneously, laughter and humor can reduce daily stress in nursing. These lighter aspects of our human nature serve as healthy ways to relieve tension, help manage pain, and act as distractors. Laughter and humor literally increase our physiologic production of endorphins and shorten the distance between two people. The lighter side of life gives us a sense of being in control; new hope; and alternatives to fear, anger, and grief.

Healing moments of being with yourself and others talking, actively listening, and sharing experiences bring about humor and joy. Laughter and humor can come from telling stories or listening to others' stories. Memories of shared laughter can ease stress long after the story has been told. Often, laughing can break the barriers that prevent nurses from speaking from their hearts. A moment of laughter and humor can be thought of as a "mini-relaxation" strategy, because it has a way of bringing a sense of balance, increasing objectivity, releasing tension, and permitting the expression of emotions. Laughing at a situation allows a person to contact the inner core of joy, to lighten the load of being human.

Sharing Our Healing Stories

In the transformation of our hospitals, clinics, outpatient rehabilitation programs, and schools of nursing into healing environments, sharing our stories, visions, and desires can lead to healthy dialogue and creative action.[19,20] Changes in health care delivery and innovative practice models begin with dialogue. The term *dialogue* is derived from the Greek, with *dia* meaning "through" and *logos* signifying "the word."[21] We cannot change in isolation, but need a dialogue that builds trust and establishes community in the deepest sense. A healthy dialogue means that an individual does not hold a fixed position, but listens to others explore other realities. As we become active listeners and support each other in the change process, our skills and awareness of love, respect, and trust between and among each other will increase. Trust levels can mobilize and enhance our healing journey, while lack of trust creates fear and can paralyze our body-mind-spirit process (Table 3–3).[22]

Most nurses are very modest and take their skills and interactions for granted. They may not even recognize the profound healing that often takes place in ordinariness, such as the way that a nurse touches a client in taking blood pressure or sits with a patient.[23] Common comments by nurses are "Well, that is what I do because I am a nurse," or "It is expected that I help patients." Frequently, nurses do not give themselves credit for healing moments, and this leads to burnout.

Nurses can learn to become open and comfortable in talking about healing. At some major medical centers, nurses have joined together to enhance their healing awareness and incorporate healing modalities. At

Table 3–3 Processes of Trust and Fear

Bodymind Process	*Effects*	*Bodymind Process*	*Effects*
TRUST LEVEL	MOBILIZING LIFE FORCES	FEAR LEVEL	IMPAIRING LIFE FORCES
Motivation	Creates and mobilizes energy, increases strength and focus of motivation	Motivation	Often causes unfocused energy to be channeled into defense with reduced motivation
Consciousness	Unblocks energy flow, expands awareness, makes the unconscious more available	Consciousness	Reduces span of awareness, cuts off threatening areas of near-awareness and unconsciousness
Perception	Increases acuity of perceptions, improves vision and perspective	Perception	Decreases acuity of perceptions, impairs vision and perspective
Emotionality	Frees feelings and emotions to energize all processes of the bodymind	Emotionality	Disrupts feelings and emotions and is often defense oriented and dysfunctional
Cognition	Frees energy to allow focus on thinking and problem solving	Cognition	Possibly causes thinking and problem solving to be unfocused, displaced, defensive, ineffective
Action	Releases person for proactive and spontaneous behavior	Action	Causes reactive, congested, and inhibited behavior because of overconcern for consequences
Synergy	Frees total person for synergistic and holistic integration	Synergy	Causes processes and subsystems to be out of harmony, not synchronistic, and often segmented

Source: Reprinted from Hatcher, M., Transformational and Spiritual Leadership, *Journal of Holistic Nursing*, Vol. 9, No. 1, p. 65, with permission of Sage Publishers, Inc., © 1991.

Beth Israel Hospital in Boston, for example, 21 nurses from 10 different subspecialties in the medical nursing department exchanged healing moments every other Thursday at lunch over pizza.[24] To prepare for each meeting the group wrote up exemplars (i.e., critical patient incidents in which healing had taken place[25,26]) that they had experienced. At each meeting they read two exemplars and discussed them. Broad themes in the discussions were physician-patient interactions, characteristics of novice and experienced nurses and physicians, the system's medical hierarchy, death and dying, advocacy, and patient-focused care. When these themes and concepts were grouped into a set of behaviors, they represented some of the expert nurse's tools that bring about exemplar moments of healing (Table 3–4).

At Maine Medical Center in Portland, a relaxation and imagery committee has been created.[27] Consisting of 12 nurses and a child life specialist, the committee serves as a resource group for staff nurses who are interested in learning to use relaxation and stress reduction techniques with their patients. This group also discusses healing moments with patients, families, and colleagues. Each nursing unit has posted a brochure that clearly states the committee objectives. Information about lectures, discussions, and practice sessions on relaxation, imagery, and stress reduction is also available. Other information includes a list of current audiovisual resource materials, as well as printed material on these topics. In a similar vein, nurses at Riverside Methodist Hospital in Columbus, Ohio teach courses in therapeutic presence and healing touch.[28] They are also currently establishing a pain, comfort, and healing project, and an aromatherapy intervention for patients undergoing magnetic resonance imaging (MRI).

Another way to build trust and share visions among nurses is to adopt a council process.[29,30] Part of a Native American tradition, this process creates a state of focused listening. The group sits in a circle, and one person serves as facilitator for the session. The rules of the council process are simple: speak honestly, be brief, and speak from the heart. Each person is to speak when he or she receives the "talking stick," which can be a stick or any other object with special meaning to the group. The challenge to the council members is to focus on what is being said rather than on what they wish to say later in response. Planning ahead hinders or eliminates much of the spontaneity of speaking from the heart. The council process is transformative and helps build trust. A profound healing experience occurs when a person is silent within and focuses on listening to another person's ideas, visions, or fears.

It is inspiring to join colleagues to carry out a critical analysis about the future of health care, case management, advanced skills, healing interactions, and to identify the essential qualities of healing expertise is inspiring. It also brings together the minds of creative nurse thinkers who have the ability to institute healing practices within nursing.

Table 3-4 Practice Characteristics of Expert Nurses

Characteristics	*Description*
Mobilization of data	Has objective data to spur the medical hierarchy into action, has data to back up intuitive hunches about patient's changing condition
Persistence	Has confidence to keep trying until a patient's needs are met, regardless of being told to quit trying
Good listening skills	Hears what a patient says, is receptive and approachable, builds trust and mobilizes a patient's energy, even when faced with exhaustion, depression, or fear
Ability to create opportunity	Senses precise moment when to act and when to step back, creates space for open dialogue to discuss possible scenarios
Self-disclosure	Develops skills in sharing insight and experience with the patient, family, and colleagues
Incorporation of science into practice	Incorporates a wide range of knowledge into practice, knows the limits of science and when all data do not reflect what the intuitive bodymind feels, incorporates scientific and intuitive ways of knowing, advises novice nurses in incorporating science and intuition
Knowledge of how and when to relinquish control to the patient	Can step aside to reflect on various ways to help a patient reach a goal and recognizes that the patient's solution may be different, but lets it be if the patient needs control and if care and safety are not compromised
Knowledge of the patient	Uses instincts and intuition to help meet human needs while getting to know patient
Responsiveness	Is flexible, changes priorities according to patient's needs, listens to the patient and family to recognize their meanings of the situation
Avoidance of power struggles	Learns the system and how to use it; focuses on outcomes; consciously steers outcomes around the red-tape struggles to get what patients need; interprets, protects, and supports; maneuvers projects through the system and gets to the consumer what is needed—gets to the heart of advocacy and healing

Source: Adapted from Tofias, L., Expert Practice: Trading Examples over Pizza, *American Journal of Nursing*, Vol. 89, No. 9, p. 1193, with permission of American Journal of Nursing Company, © 1989.

RITUALS OF HEALING

An important aspect of inner work in our fast-paced lives is to create a time for rituals. In creating a ritual, there are no absolute rules, although there are a few guidelines. For example, a ritual should have a beginning, a middle, and an end. It helps to plan the details carefully in advance as if a special houseguest were coming. Such details as fresh flowers and books of art or poetry at a bedside create a sacred space in a guest room. A sacred space in which to be alone and reflect on healing awareness deepens our understanding of being connected with self, others, and a higher self. Our anxiety and fears are reduced; feelings of helplessness are lessened. Rituals also help us to understand the meaning of events as well as to assist others as they move through crisis and recovery. Exhibit 3–1 is the first ritual guide to getting well and can be used by the nurse in assisting a person who is faced with symptoms, tests, or decisions about medical or surgical intervention.[31]

The first phase of a ritual, the *separation phase*, is a symbolic act of breaking away from life's busy activities. For example, it may involve going to a quiet room for 15 to 20 minutes, taking shoes off, sitting on a pillow on the floor, putting on the answering machine, and honoring the silence. In this sacred healing place, we may focus on a special object, such as a burning candle or mandala, that brings a sense of calmness.

In the second phase of the ritual, the *transition phase*, we can more easily identify areas in our lives that need attention. It is a time of facing the shadow, the dark, and the difficult as we search for self and for what is real and worthy and in need of healing in the deepest sense. It is the time to go into an unknown terrain across the *limen* (i.e., the meaning threshold), where we leave one way of being to enter another way of participating.

Finally, we enter the last phase of the ritual, the *return phase*, where we reenter real life. This phase allows for a formal release of the old fears, anger, or memories that no longer serve us. We are challenged to integrate a new way of acting, choosing, and relating into our healing awareness so that we can discipline ourselves to be present in the moment and understand the meaning of the moment. This state of being present in the moment results in a noninterfering attention that allows natural healing to flow.

CONCLUSION

Being a nurse healer allows the nurse an opportunity to explore the inner dimensions of personal, interpersonal, and transpersonal growth.

Exhibit 3–1 The First Ritual Guide to Getting Well

This ritual helps you decide what to do if you are diagnosed with the unknowable, the unthinkable, the awful, or the so-called incurable. By doing this, you can better determine how to survive treatment, yourself, your friends and family, and life in general.

1. Find a quiet place, a healing place, and go there. This might be a corner of your favorite room where you have placed gifts, pictures, a candle, or other symbols that signal peace and inner reflection to you. Or it might be in a park, under an old tree, or in a special place known for its spirit, such as high on a sacred mountain or on the cliffs overlooking a coastline or in the quiet magnificence of a forest.
2. Ask questions of your inner self about what your diagnosis or treatment means in your life. How will life change? What are your resources, your strengths, your reasons for staying alive? These deeply philosophical or spiritual issues often come to mind when problems are diagnosed. Listen with as quiet a mind as possible for any answers or messages that come from within, or from your higher source of guidance.
3. Take this time, knowing that very few problems advance so quickly that you must rush into making decisions about them immediately, without first gaining some perspective.
4. Find at least one friend or advocate who can be level-headed when you think you are going crazy; who can be positive for you when you are absolutely certain you are doomed; who can listen when your head is buzzing with uncertainty.
5. Love yourself. Ask yourself moment by moment whether what surrounds you is nurturing and life-giving. If the answer is no, back off from it. Kindly tell all negative-thinking people that you will not be seeing them while you are going through this. You may need never to see them again, and this is your right and obligation to yourself.
6. Assess your belief system. What do you believe? How did you get to believe it in the first place? What is really happening inside you and outside you? How serious is it? What will it take to get you well?
7. Gather information, keeping an open mind. Everyone who offers to treat you or give you advice has their lives invested in what they tell you. Stand back and listen thoughtfully.
8. Now go and hire your healing team. Remember, you hired them—you can fire them. They are in the business of performing a service for you, and you are paying their salaries. Sometimes this relationship gets confused. Make sure they all talk to each other. You are in command. You are the captain of the healing team.
9. Don't let anyone talk you into treatment you don't believe in or don't understand. Keep asking questions. Replace anyone who acts too busy to answer your questions. Chances are, they're also too busy to do their best work for you.

continues

Exhibit 3–1 continued

10. Don't agree on any diagnostic or lab tests unless someone you trust can give you good reasons why they are being ordered. If the tests are not going to change your treatment, they are an expensive and dangerous waste of your time.
11. Sing your own song, write your own story, take your own spiritual journey through a journal or diary. A threat to health and well-being can be a trigger to becoming and doing all those things you've been putting off for the "right" time.
12. Consider these maxims in your journey:
    - Everything cures somebody, and nothing cures everybody.
    - There are no simple answers to complex issues, like why people get sick in the first place.
    - Sometimes disease is inexplicable to mortal minds.
13. You will not be intimidated by the overbearing world of medicine or alternative health know-it-alls but can thoughtfully take the best from several worlds.
14. You can teach gentleness and compassion to the most arrogant doctor and the crankiest nurse. Tell them that you need your mind and soul nurtured, as well as the best medical treatment possible in order to get well. If they are not up to it, you'll find someone someplace who is.

Source: Reprinted from *Rituals of Healing: Using Imagery for Health and Wellness* by J. Achterberg, B. Dossey, and L. Kolkmeier, pp. 32–33, with permission of Bantam Books, © 1994.

True nurse healing requires attention to one's woundedness and the polarities, the purpose, and the meaning in life. Learning to move to a place of centeredness enhances this attention and facilitates presence with intention. Quieting the mind places a nurse in the best position to develop skills of active listening and presence. Learning about the inward journey opens many unique opportunities to be with self and others. The nurse can guide an individual to increase inner awareness, improve self-understanding, and learn new skills that provide great opportunities for reaching one's human potentials. Awareness of healing and healer allows a presence where nurse-client interactions take on new dimensions.

DIRECTIONS FOR FUTURE RESEARCH

1. Conduct studies to examine the interactive variables that evoke the characteristics of nurse healers.
2. Determine whether nurses who practice healing modalities on a regular basis have more empathy, caring, and job satisfaction.

3. Develop guidelines to help nurses increase the skill of active listening.
4. Determine whether client outcomes are better and if clients are more satisfied with nursing care when nurses recognize and integrate the four patterns of knowing and the new pattern of unknowing.

NURSE HEALER REFLECTIONS

After reading this chapter, the nurse healer will be able to answer or will begin a process of answering the following questions:

- How do I feel when I use the word *healer* to describe myself?
- What do I experience when I become present?
- Do I listen actively?
- How do I experience myself as a guide?
- What rituals can I add to my life for healing awareness?

NOTES

1. B. Carper, Fundamental Patterns of Knowing, *Advances in Nursing Science* 1, no. 1 (1978):13–23.
2. J. Wolfer, Aspects of "Reality" and Ways of Knowing in Nursing: In Search of an Integrating Paradigm, *Image* 25, no. 2 (1993):141–146.
3. P. Munhall, 'Unknowing': Toward Another Pattern of Knowing in Nursing, *Nursing Outlook* 41(1993):125–128.
4. M. Burkhardt and M. Nagai-Jacobson, Reawakening Spirit in Clinical Practice, *Journal of Holistic Nursing* 12, no. 1 (1994):9–21.
5. S. Burch, Consciousness: An Analysis of the Concept, *Journal of Holistic Nursing* 12, no. 1 (1994):101–116.
6. M. Brown, *The Unfolding Self* (Los Angeles: Psychosynthesis Press, 1983).
7. E. Peers, *Dark Night of the Soul* (New York: Image Books, 1959).
8. F. Gilje, Being There: An Analysis of the Concept of Presence, in *The Presence of Caring in Nursing*, ed. D. Gaut (New York: National League of Nursing, 1992), 53–67.
9. M. McKivergin and J. Daubenmire, The Essence of Therapeutic Presence, *Journal of Holistic Nursing* 12, no. 1 (1994):65–81.
10. G. Hendricks and K. Hendricks, *At the Speed of Life* (New York: Bantam Books, 1993).
11. M. Newman, *Health as Expanding Consciousness* (St. Louis: Mosby-Year Book, 1986).
12. J. Barnsteiner et al., Defining and Implementing a Standard for Therapeutic Relationships, *Journal of Holistic Nursing* 12, no. 1 (1994):35–49.

13. J. Karl, Being There: Who Do You Bring to Practice, in *The Presence of Caring in Nursing*, ed. D. Gaut (New York: National League of Nursing, 1992), 1–13.
14. C. Montgomery, The Spiritual Connection: Nurses' Perceptions of the Experience of Caring, in *The Presence of Caring in Nursing*, ed. D. Gaut (New York: National League of Nursing, 1992), 39–67.
15. B. Wesorick, Creating an Environment in the Hospital Setting That Supports Caring via a Clinical Practice Model (CPM) in *Caring: the Compassionate Healer*, eds. D. Gaut and M. Leininger (New York: National League for Nursing Press, 1991).
16. S. Kerouac and L. Rouillier, Reflections on the Promotion of Caring with Head Nurses, in *The Presence of Caring in Nursing*, ed. D. Gaut (New York: National League of Nursing, 1992), 89–102.
17. E. Peper and C. Kuskel, A Holistic Merger of Biofeedback and Family Therapy, in *Spiritual Aspects of the Healing Arts*, ed. D. Kunz (Wheaton, IL: The Theosophical Publishing House, 1985).
18. L. Keegan, *Nurse as Healer* (New York: Delmar Publishers, 1994).
19. B. Miller et al., The Experience of Caring in the Acute Care Setting: Patient and Nurse Perspectives, in *The Presence of Caring in Nursing*, ed. D. Gaut (New York: National League of Nursing, 1992), 137–156.
20. M. Sandeloski, We Are the Stories We Tell: Narrative Knowing in Nursing Practice, *Journal of Holistic Nursing* 12, no. 1 (1994):23–33.
21. J. Koerner and S. Bunkers, The Healing Web, *Journal of Holistic Nursing* 12, no. 1 (1994):51–63.
22. M. Hatcher, Transformation and Spiritual Leadership, *Journal of Holistic Nursing* 9(1991):65.
23. B. Taylor, Caring: Being Manifested as Ordinariness in Nursing, in *The Presence of Caring in Nursing*, ed. D. Gaut (New York: National League of Nursing, 1992), 181–200.
24. L. Tofias, Expert Practice: Trading Examples over Pizza, *American Journal of Nursing* 89(1989):1193.
25. P. Benner, *From Novice to Expert* (Menlo Park, CA: Addison-Wesley Publishing Co., 1984).
26. P. Benner and C. Tanner, Clinical Judgement: How Expert Nurses Use Intuition, *American Journal of Nursing* 87(1987):23.
27. J. Thomas, Maine Medical Center, Portland, Maine, Personal communication, 1988.
28. McKivergin and Daubenmire, Essence of Therapeutic Presence.
29. S. Bunkers, The Healing Web, *Nursing and Health Care* 13, no. 2 (1992):68–73.
30. J. Larson, The Healing Web, *Nursing and Health Care* 13, no. 5 (1992):246–252.
31. J. Achterberg et al., *Rituals of Healing* (New York: Bantam Books, 1994).

UNIT II

THEORY AND PRACTICE OF HOLISTIC NURSING

VISION OF HEALING

The Evolving Dance of Life

The dance of human life is an evolving process that can be compared to the natural rhythms of day and night. The shades of light and darkness apply to our lives, with the various shades perceived only in contrasts. Without the light, we have no concept of the darkness. Contrast is essential in every aspect of human life: happiness and sadness, strengths and weaknesses, and wellness and illness. The only way that we can have a concept of personal wellness is to have at some point in our lives a first-hand experience with illness or major life stressors. One of the major obstacles to understanding our wholeness is this inability to recognize and accept these differences. Yet, when we repress these differences, ambiguity is taken into our unconscious and leads to disharmony and psychophysiologic disturbances.

When such major stressors as disaster or illness occur, the tendency is to repress the meaning of these events. Repeated failure to recognize these life situations removes us further from our internal healing resources of hope, strengths, and new insights. At some point, however, we must address these life processes, because they are always present. There is a part of us that always needs healing—the wounded healer—yet we are tempted to ignore this woundedness. We must learn to embrace our limitations, as well as to recognize our strengths. All great healers acknowledge their inherent weaknesses and fallibilities.

When a nurse and a client who come together both deny their woundedness, the outcome of care is mechanical at best. Neither the client nor the nurse is able to use his or her inner wisdom to activate self-healing. Both have devalued this innate potential. Inner healing does not flow from the nurse to the client. The nurse cannot give inner healing to the client, for it already exists within the client. Rather, the nurse facilitates the client's process of inner healing. Healing occurs when the client and the nurse both acknowledge their life processes and use them to move toward balance and harmony.

As the best of both traditional and holistic practices merge, much of the work that remains to be learned is the art of healing. A time for healing reflection can also be a source of creativity and spontaneity. Hence, we need to acknowledge our own stressors in order to open creatively to our clients. Being a healer requires work on the imperfect, fallible self. We must affirm our weaknesses and strengths, and acknowledge our inadequacies. Only then can we know a powerful part of our being and allow new strengths to manifest. The use of self done with intention and presence provides us with our most powerful possibilities for healing.

Chapter 4

The Psychophysiology of Bodymind Healing

Barbara Montgomery Dossey

NURSE HEALER OBJECTIVES

Theoretical

- Discuss information theory.
- Discuss state-dependent learning.
- Explain interconnections of mind modulation and the autonomic, endocrine, immune, and neuropeptide systems.

Clinical

- Acknowledge fragmentation in your clinical practice.
- Choose three health management strategies and use them to decrease stress and tension each day.

Personal

- Assess communication between your body and your mind as expressed in your attitudes, tensions, and images.
- Begin to learn methods to gain access to and reframe state-dependent memory to move toward bodymind healing.

DEFINITIONS

Bodymind: state of integration that includes body, mind, and spirit.

Information Theory: a mathematical model that helps explain many of the connections between consciousness and bodymind healing.

Limbic-Hypothalamic System: the major anatomic modulating link connecting the brain/mind and the autonomic, endocrine, immune, and neuropeptide systems.

Mind Modulation: the natural process by which the brain converts thoughts, feelings, attitudes, and emotions (i.e., neural messages) into neurohormonal "messenger molecules" and communicates them to all body systems (i.e., autonomic, endocrine, immune, and neuropeptide) that evoke states of health or dis-health.

Neuropeptides: messenger molecules produced at various sites throughout the body to transmit bodymind patterns of communication.

Neurotransmitters: chemicals that facilitate nerve transmission in the body.

Receptors: sites on cell surfaces that serve as points of attachment for various types of messenger molecules.

Reframing: identifying behaviors or thoughts and taking the responsibility to add or substitute another more creative alternative for the undesired behavior.

Self-Regulation Theory: a person's ability to learn cognitive processing of information to bring involuntary body responses under voluntary control.

State-Dependent Memory: a person's psychophysiologic state at the time of the experience; all memories are dependent and limited to the state in which they were acquired.

Ultradian Performance Rhythm: widely varying patterns alternating between 90 and 120 minutes of activity with 20 minutes of rejuvenation.

Ultradian Stress Syndrome: physical, psychologic, and spiritual neglect that occurs from overriding the natural ultradian rhythms of rejuvenation.

INFORMATION THEORY

Developed in the late 1940s, information theory is a mathematical model that emerged with modern communications technologies. In 1960,

Black first used information theory as a conceptual base for connecting biologic life and the mind.[1] Information theory appears to be capable of unifying physiologic, psychologic, sociologic, and spiritual phenomena in a framework that helps explain many of the connections between consciousness and bodymind healing.

A person's body-mind-spirit can be seen as an integrated system, a network. The mind is the information flow among all body parts that holds the network together.[2] In this view, the mind is composed of information that has a physical substrate, body and brain, which, in turn, is composed of another immaterial substrate involving information flow, a process we call consciousness.

TRANSDUCTION

The conversion or transformation of information/energy from one form to another is transduction. The mind can be seen as nature's supreme way of receiving, generating, and transducing information. The more improbable an idea or event, the higher its informational value. Those that are new—challenging, intriguing, and mysterious—have the highest information value.[3] New ideas and events evoke bodymind changes; that is, neural pathways and consciousness connect to permit information transduction. For example, a hypertensive client may believe that cold hands are a normal part of her physiology. As she begins to monitor hand temperature on awakening and throughout the day, however, a pattern begins to emerge. Her hands are usually warm on awakening, but become cold in response to daily stressors/activities. As she learns hand-warming techniques, breathing exercises, and other bodymind interventions, the client has a first-hand experience of information transduction. A new understanding of the interconnectedness of body-mind-spirit events evolves, allowing her to control her blood pressure and to decrease her medication and possibly eliminate the need for medication.

Traditionally, health care providers have dealt with the familiar hard sciences and have ignored or devalued consciousness and intuition. Holistic nursing interventions draw on both proven science and intuitive knowledge, however. New information helps individuals to gain access to their inner strengths and to adopt effective coping styles and strategies. These styles and strategies have an influence or effect at the cellular level that stabilizes or even reverses disease, thus improving the quality of life.

Experimental research has demonstrated effective management of many disorders through holistic interventions. In 1990, for example, Ornish published a landmark prospective, randomized, controlled study documenting the reversal of coronary artery disease through life style changes.[4] Patients selected for the study had already undergone technologic interventions with surgery or drugs, but their arteriosclerotic disease was still symptomatic. During the 1-year study, Ornish treated these patients with a noninvasive approach that included the following 4 components: (1) a vegetarian diet of which approximately 10 percent of calories were fat, with a polyunsaturated:saturated ratio greater than 1; (2) exercise at least 3 times a week, with a minimum of 30 minutes per session, with patients exercising within 50 to 80 percent of their target heart rates; (3) stress management through yoga, stretching exercises, breathing, progressive relaxation exercises, imagery, and meditation; and (4) a social support program that involved twice weekly meetings of patients and their families in group sessions led by a clinical psychologist who assisted the group in finding ways to adhere to these new life style patterns and to explore the meaning of their illness. The control group received treatment through a standard medical regimen.

A total of 195 coronary artery lesions were analyzed by quantitative coronary angiography at baseline and following the 1-year intervention in both the experimental and control groups. After 1 year, the experimental group had an average percentage diameter stenosis *regression* from 40 to 37.8 percent, while the control group had an average percent diameter stenosis *progression* from 42.7 to 46.1 percent. Eighty-two percent of the experimental group had an overall change toward *regression*, which means that these patients were able to link their thoughts and behaviors to create changes at the cellular level and reverse supposedly fixed coronary lesions. Until the findings from this study were published, authorities had denied that biobehavioral interventions could reverse fixed lesions, that is, end-stage coronary artery disease, because no researcher had been able to demonstrate such a regression.

The importance of this study is that it integrated the biologic, psychologic, sociologic, and spiritual responses of patients and their families to illness rather than just focusing on symptoms, disease, and technology. It demonstrated the effects possible when the health care team views the patient as a whole person. The Ornish program cost $3,500 for 1 year, compared to the average cost of open heart surgery, which ranges from $35,000 per person to $50,000. Since September 1993, Mutual of Omaha Insurance Company has reimbursed patients who meet certain criteria for participating in a biobehavioral program such as the Ornish program (see Resources at end of chapter).

Nurses have also demonstrated information transduction in studies that focus on reducing the risks of cardiac complications linked to the psychophysiologic results of anxiety. In an experimental study, Guzzetta demonstrated the effectiveness of music therapy and relaxation interventions for 90 patients in a coronary care unit.[5] The experimental groups participated in three sessions over a 2-day period. Stress was evaluated by apical heart rate, peripheral temperature, cardiac complications, and qualitative patient evaluation data. Compared to patients in the control group, patients in the music therapy and relaxation group had lower apical heart rates, higher peripheral skin temperatures, and fewer cardiac complications. Patients also reported feeling more relaxed.

Miller and Perry demonstrated the effectiveness of a relaxation technique taught to patients the night before coronary artery bypass graft surgery.[6] By using the relaxation technique, patients were able to effect significant decreases in blood pressure, heart rate, respiratory rate, and pain. Patients said that the relaxation technique was simple to perform and they would recommend it to others who have postoperative pain.

In another study, Stuart, Decko, and Mandle found that a biobehavioral program can reduce both systolic and diastolic blood pressure in hypertensive patients, with the majority of patients becoming normotensive if they integrate life style changes.[7] At the Mind/Body Medical Institute (MBMI) at New England Deaconness Hospital in Boston, these clinicians teach patients a physiologic and psychophysiologic understanding of cardiovascular disorders and other health-related problems. They integrate stress reduction techniques, cognitive skills, meditation training, and yoga. The MBMI has more than 8,000 patient visits per year. Similarly, Thomas has demonstrated that cardiac patients can reduce tension and cardiac symptoms with transactional psychophysiologic therapy[8] (see Chapter 15). This therapy is a nonpharmacologic, body-centered therapy in which patients learn to recognize their physiologic self through the spoken voice and communication patterns, and their psychospiritual self through cognitive and stress reduction skills and biofeedback, thus facilitating wholeness and healing.

Relaxation and imagery techniques are also helpful during a diagnostic or therapeutic procedure. As nurses guide patients in relaxed abdominal breathing, the auditory nerve perceives the spoken words and sends the message to the motor cortex where it is relayed to the cortical center. The brain then carries out the act of relaxed breathing as soon as it is formulated. This same sequence occurs with all of the senses. Nurses also guide patients in imaging the procedure going well and creating images of increased healing rates.

Imagery as a therapeutic intervention is based on the process of information flow and transduction, that is, transforming the images/ideas into an act of relaxation and physiologic healing (see Chapter 23). By definition, imagery involves information from all the senses—hearing, seeing, touching, tasting, and feeling. The term *visualization* involves primarily the visual sense. A felt sensation such as "butterflies in the stomach" is a kinesthetic sensation that is part of the bodymind imagery information process. A nurse can structure a relaxation and imagery session to allow a patient to incorporate his or her personal images to create a dominant parasympathetic response, or the nurse can guide the patient through a series of images intended to soothe, distract, reduce sympathetic nervous system arousal, or generally enhance relaxation. For example, Achterberg and Kenner taught relaxation and imagery to patients prior to burn dressing changes to decrease pain during the procedure.[9] They also taught biologically correct images of step-by-step burn graft healing over the first 3 days of post-graft. Patients demonstrated a significant decrease in anxiety, pain, and infection, as well as an increase in healing rates.

Information transduction also occurs during biofeedback when specific instrumentation is used to mirror psychophysiologic processes of which the client is normally unaware. As the client thinks and feels relaxed, biofeedback electrodes on his or her body register the transduction of information. The electrodes measure biologic energy in terms of muscle tension, which is then converted to a measurement and displayed on a digital meter; in this way, the patient receives validation of reduced muscle tension. Acosta demonstrated that such biofeedback is helpful in weaning patients from ventilators.[10]

Quinn demonstrated information transduction by exploring time perception (i.e., the sensation of clock time speeding up or slowing down) for both patient and nurse during therapeutic touch.[11] An increased or expanded sense of time for both patient and nurse was demonstrated. This suggests that there is a potential resonance of two individual human fields of consciousness during a healing interaction.

Holistic nursing interventions such as relaxation, imagery, music therapy, and touch therapies work for two reasons. First, they are "novel stimuli," and the bodymind responds to events that have new informational value. Second, they facilitate mind modulation of the autonomic, endocrine, immune, and neuropeptide systems.[12–15]

STATE-DEPENDENT LEARNING AND MEMORY

What is learned and remembered is dependent on a person's psychophysiologic state at the time of the experience and is referred to as state-dependent learning. Our memories are state-dependent because they are limited to the state in which they were acquired.[16] Thoughts that we experience in our daily routines are habitual patterns of state-dependent memories joined together by associative connections.

State-dependent learning plays a major role in bodymind healing and hypnosis, although most learning theories do not integrate memory and bodymind relationships. In his review of the literature between 1855 and 1993, however, Rossi connects state-dependent learning with discoveries of molecular biology and psychoneuroimmunology.[17] He developed four integrated hypotheses about memory and bodymind relationships.

1. The limbic-hypothalamic system is the major anatomic connecting link between body and mind.
2. State-dependent memory, learning, and behavior processes encoded in the limbic-hypothalamic and related systems are the major information transducers between body and mind.
3. All methods of bodymind healing and therapeutic hypnosis operate by gaining access to and reframing the state-dependent learning and memory that encode symptoms and problems.
4. The state-dependent encoding of bodymind symptoms and problems can be reached by psychologic as well as physiologic approaches—and the placebo response is a synergistic interaction of both.

The limbic-hypothalamic system is found within the brain and is biochemically interconnected with all other parts of the body. Within the limbic-hypothalamic system are patterns of both positive and negative emotions. Thus, the mind stores memories of health, as well as painful memories.[18] In the past, it was believed that the mind was contained only within the anatomic structure of the brain. Current thinking holds that memories, thoughts, and behavior processes are stored throughout the body, however. This brain-body network is connected by the information flow at a biochemical and, perhaps, at an energy level. The greatest resistance to these ideas is the holographic notion of the way in which information is received and stored. There are conflicts between the traditional neuroanatomic model and the location of these brain centers.

LOCATION OF THE BRAIN CENTERS

Old models for information transfer were the telegraph/telephone by which a message was sent from one point to another. A more accurate way of understanding brain function, however, is to use the model of a hologram. A specially processed photographic record, a hologram provides a three-dimensional image when a light from a laser is beamed through it. If any part of the hologram should be destroyed, any of the remaining parts is capable of reconstructing the whole image.[19] The brain operates like a hologram. This model does not contradict the traditional model, but it does suggest a new method of considering how information is transmitted, stored, and received.[20]

There are conflicts between the traditional neuroanatomic model and information theory and mind modulation. Current data on brain functioning contradicts the following elements of the traditional neuroanatomic model (brain)[21]:

- Memories do not seem to be stored in any single area, but rather in multiple overlapping areas. Loss of specific memory is related more to the amount of brain damage than to the site of the damage.
- The ability to remember what is lost when the brain is first damaged by gunshot wounds, tumors, or cardiovascular accident (stroke) often returns, even though specific neural regeneration is believed to be impossible.
- Paranormal events, including the transpersonal healing imagery typically related with shamanic work and with psychic or metaphysical healers, involve receiving, processing, and sending information in ways that do not conform to our current understanding of energy transfer and neuroanatomy.
- Such phenomena as phantom limb sensations, persistent phantom pain, and "auras" extending beyond the corporal self call into question the storage of body image, as well as the physical boundaries of the body.
- If the brain processes only one bit of information per second, the current model of memory storage would require 3×10^{10} nerve impulses per second—an inconceivable amount of neural activity.
- The mechanisms of consciousness, or the ability of the brain to consider itself or create or retrieve images, elude description in terms of the sheer knowledge of structures and their function as presented in the anatomic models.

It is important to review these conflicts if we are to use bodymind interventions effectively. Viewing the mind in a holographic manner reveals its omnipotent influence on psychophysiologic function. People who do not believe that they have the conscious ability to effect a physical change with their imagination may never try to do so. They will not sort through memories and patterns of past experience and will continue to respond physically, mentally, and spiritually as they always have in the past.

SELF-REGULATION THEORY

First proposed by Green in 1969, self-regulation theory focuses on the effects of the cognitive processing of information on human behavior.[22] According to this theory, perception (or imagery) elicits mental and emotional responses that generate limbic, hypothalamic, and pituitary biochemical responses; in turn, these biochemical responses bring about physiologic changes that are perceived and responded to, completing a cybernetic feedback loop. Any perception or image can become a schema, a cognitive or mental device that stores and directs the retrieval of the stored information, the focus of attention, and the resulting behaviors and thoughts/images. As bodymind interventions help a client gain access to the raw material of his or her inner memories and internal healing resources, these new imagery patterns become blueprints that can be reinforced or reframed into patterns that may modulate positive changes at biochemical levels within the cells.

The schema or blueprint assists individuals in focusing their attention to produce a desired behavioral response. With attention focused on the objective features of a procedure rather than on the subjective emotional reactions, the person can enhance and use his or her internal healing resources for positive outcome.

ULTRADIAN RHYTHMS

Humans have natural, biologic rhythms. Those that take longer than a day, such as a woman's menstrual cycles, are called infradian rhythms. The circadian rhythms are those that rise and fall once each day, such as our sleep and wake patterns. While awake, we constantly move along a wavelike cycle of activity followed by a short period when the bodymind seeks rest and renewal. In the ultradian performance rhythm, 90 to 120 minutes of activity alternate with 20 minutes of rejuvenation (Figure 4–1).[23] People vary widely in the timing of these rhythms, and individuals can easily shift them with changing demands and daily circumstances.

Over the last two decades, scientists have found that the body periodically gives us important physiologic and psychologic clues about staying healthy, energetic, creative, and productive. These clues are in the ultradian rhythms that cycle many times during a day, such as hunger

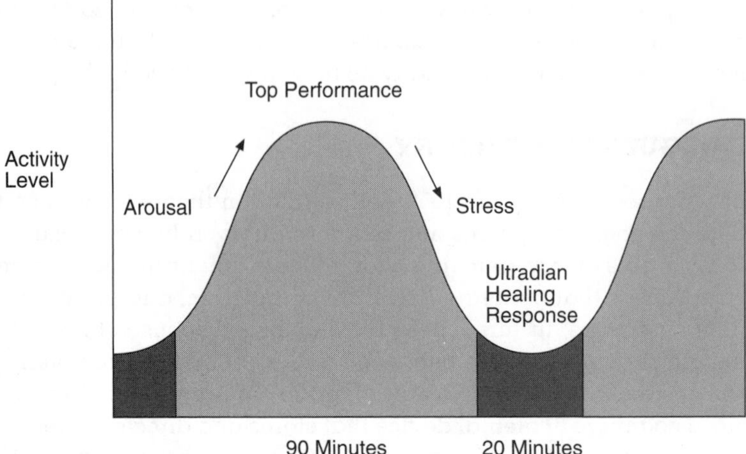

Figure 4–1 Ultradian Performance Rhythm. *Source:* Reprinted by permission of The Putnam Publishing Group/Jeremy P. Tarcher, Inc. from *The 20-Minute Break* by Ernest Rossi and David Nimmons, p. 12. Copyright © 1991 by Ernest Rossi and David Nimmons.

---

and tension cycles. Excessive and chronic overactivity distorts our normal ultradian/circadian rhythms of activity and results in stress and symptoms, the ultradian stress syndrome.[24]

The ultradian healing response, that is, the 20-minute rest period, can ameliorate the ultradian stress syndrome by providing time for our natural bodymind rhythms to normalize themselves. There are three major implications to consider in regard to the ultradian healing response.[25]

1. Ultradian rhythms signal patterns of communication between body and mind that coordinate numerous physiologic and psychologic processes each day.
2. At the peak of each ultradian rhythm, nature has given us a powerful, naturally occurring opportunity to work and feel better if we recognize and utilize this period.
3. Every 90 to 120 minutes, nature has provided us with a 20-minute window to allow our body-mind-spirit to regain balance and health amid the constantly shifting changes and challenges of daily life. We can learn to heed this natural ultradian call for rejuvenation and recovery, transforming ourselves from stress to health, from inefficiency to productivity, and from weakness to strength.

Nurses can use an ultradian performance rhythm diagram to educate clients, patients, and themselves about the importance of integrating the ultradian healing response throughout the day.

MIND MODULATION

Autonomic Nervous System

The mind modulates the biochemical functions within the major organ systems throughout the autonomic nervous system (Figure 4–2). Research has demonstrated that the psychophysiologic stress response causes the stress hormones (e.g., cortisol, epinephrine, norepinephrine) to mediate changes in physiologic and pathologic events, which always produce corresponding psychologic and spiritual events.[26–33] The process of mind modulation of cellular activities by the autonomic nervous system has three stages.[34]

1. Images, thoughts, attitudes, and feelings are generated in the frontal cortex.
2. Images and thoughts are transmitted through state-dependent memory learning and emotional areas of the limbic-hypothalamic system by the neurotransmitters that regulate the organ systems of the autonomic nervous system branches.
3. The neurotransmitters—norepinephrine (sympathetic branch) and acetylcholine (parasympathetic branch)—initiate the information transduction that activates the biochemical changes within the different tissues down to the cellular level. Neurotransmitters act as messenger molecules. They cross the nerve cell junction gap and fit into receptor sites found in cell walls, thus changing the receptor molecule structure. This causes a change in cell wall permeability and a shift of such ions as sodium, potassium, and calcium. The hundreds of complex activations of cell enzymes that are the second messenger system also change the basic metabolism of each cell.

These three stages give us a better understanding of how the different holistic therapies work. When clients learn to use relaxation, imagery, music therapy, or certain types of meditation training, their sympathetic response to stress decreases, and the calming effect of the parasympathetic system takes over—leading to bodymind healing. Everly and Benson have suggested that relaxation and meditation training "retune" the nervous system by dampening the production of adrenergic cat-

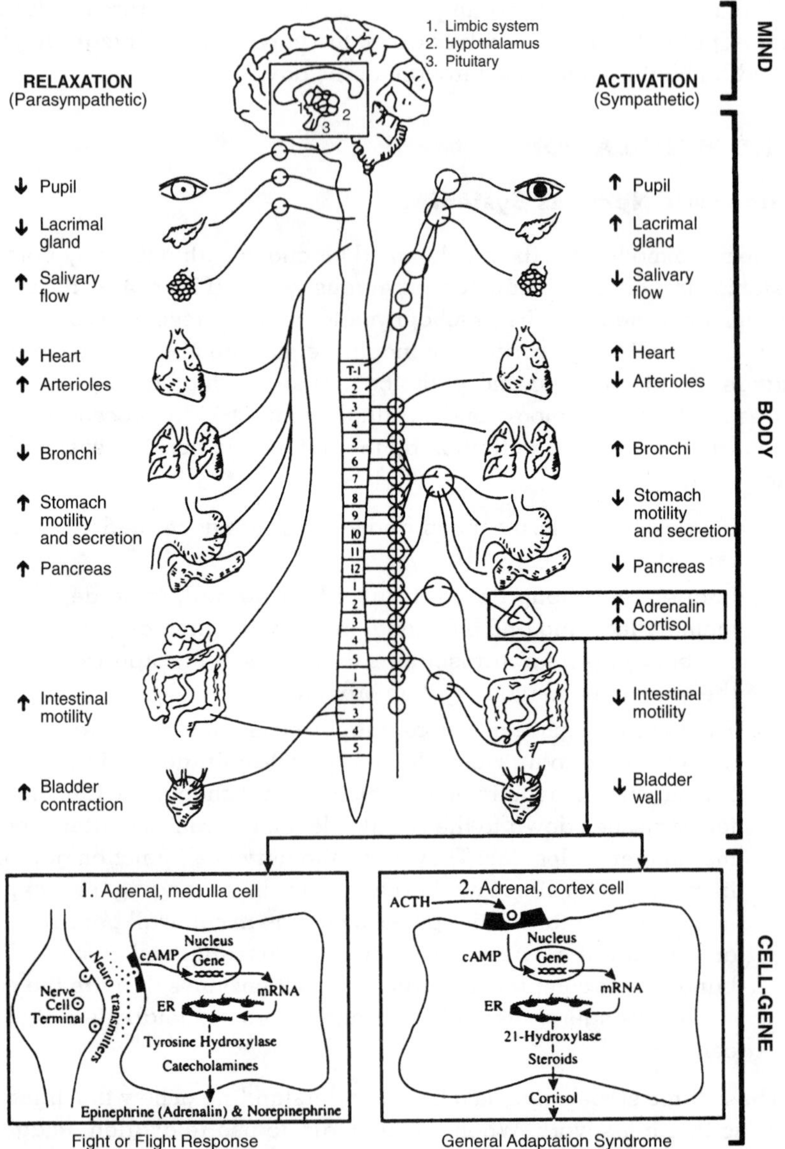

Figure 4–2 Mind Modulation of the Autonomic Nervous System and Its Two Branches. *Source:* Reprinted from *The Psychobiology of Mind-Body Healing: New Concepts of Therapeutic Hypnosis*, Revised Edition, by Ernest Lawrence Rossi, with permission of W.W. Norton & Company, Inc. Copyright © 1993 by Ernest Lawrence Rossi.

echolamines, which stimulate limbic activity.[35] They suggest also that excessive limbic activity may inhibit immune functions. Clients who have learned relaxation, imagery, hypnosis, and biofeedback have been able to change blood flow to various body parts and body cells with the following outcomes[36]:

- warming and cooling different parts of the body for treatment of different types of headaches
- controlling blushing and blanching of the skin
- stimulating the enlargement and apparent breast growth in women
- stimulating sexual excitation and penile erection
- ameliorating bruises
- controlling bleeding in surgery
- curing warts
- minimizing and healing burns
- ameliorating congenital ichthyosis
- producing local skin inflammation similar to previous experienced burns
- aiding coagulation of blood in hemophiliac clients
- ameliorating hypertension and cardiac problems
- ameliorating Raynaud's disease
- enhancing immune function

These changes literally result from connections of clients' images, feelings, emotions, and spirit with their physiology or pathophysiology. Of the actual anatomic locations traced from the limbic system where images and feelings of spirit are formed would correlate with physiologic changes in the brain that follow those nerve pathways down the spinal cord, to then emerge to innervate every organ in the body.[37] There are no exceptions. Furthermore, all these nerves flow from our organ systems back to the brain to our imagery and feeling center in the limbic system.

Endocrine System

As seen in Figure 4–3, the endocrine system is responsible for secreting hormones and regulating these hormones throughout the body. Stimulation of the senses activates specific hormones that modulate the strength of memory of the sensory experience.[38] Central modulating influences on memory in the limbic system interact with influences of the peripheral hormones.

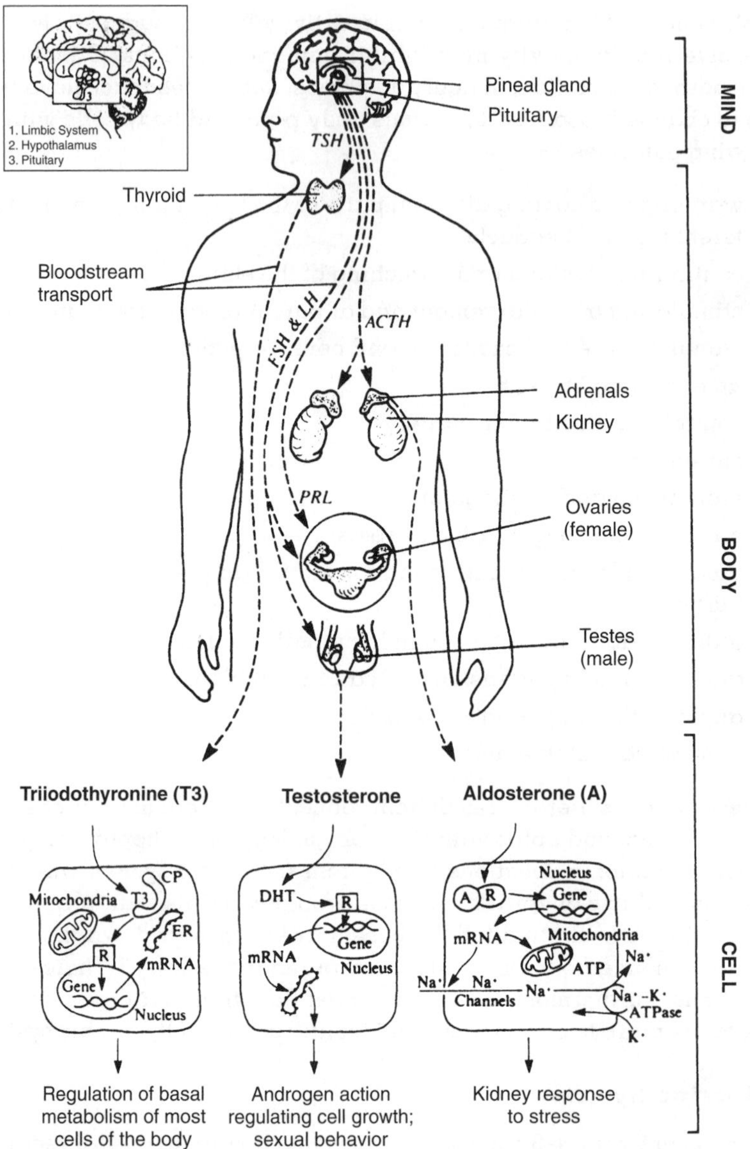

Figure 4–3 Mind-Body Communication via the Endocrine System. *Source:* Reprinted from *The Psychobiology of Mind-Body Healing*: New Concepts of Therapeutic Hypnosis, Revised Edition, by Ernest Lawrence Rossi, with permission of W.W. Norton & Company, Inc. Copyright © 1993 by Ernest Lawrence Rossi.

The central concept of neuroendocrinology is neurosecretion: the transduction of information from the limbic-hypothalamic system into somatic processes of the body via the pituitary and endocrine systems.[39] Thoughts from the limbic system excite or inhibit the neural impulses in the cerebral cortex and these thoughts are converted into pituitary regulation by the neurotransmitter changes of the hypothalamus. This understanding is the basis for the inclusion of psychobiology as a branch of information theory. The endocrinologic discoveries of the pituitary hormones, the endorphins, and the enkephalins (neurotransmitters) show that these hormones influence modulations of stress, pain, perception, addictions, appetite, learning, memory, and sports performances, just to name a few. Some of the hormones that act on the cell receptors of the brain and body are shown in Exhibit 4–1.

Mind-Gene Connection

Genes are in dynamic equilibrium with cellular metabolism. Messenger molecules, hormones, and neurotransmitters modulate changes in the genetic material. The transduction of information in the mind-gene process has three stages[40]:

- Stage 1 involves the frontal cortex. Images and life experiences from the frontal cortex are encoded into the state-dependent memory of the limbic-hypothalamic system.
- Stage 2 involves transduction. The state-dependent memory is transduced by the hypothalamus into the hormone-releasing factors that regulate the pituitary gland. This sets up a cascade of hormones that then affect the entire endocrine system.
- Stage 3 occurs at the cellular level, where hormones are stimulated or pass directly to the cell nucleus that activates the mind-gene process.

The action of the adrenal hormone aldosterone illustrates these three stages. In response to psychophysiologic stress (Stage 1), aldosterone is secreted and acts at many sites. Within the cytoplasm of the renal tubule cells, a specific receptor protein binds with aldosterone, carrying it to the genes to produce new proteins (Stage 2). These new proteins promote sodium reabsorption from the tubules and potassium secretion, referred to as the "sodium-potassium pump," within a brief 45-minute period (Stage 3).

Immune System

The third major regulatory system of the body, the immune system, interacts with all body systems (Figure 4–4). Psychoneuroimmunology fo-

Exhibit 4–1 Hormones That Have Bodymind Function

Corticotropin-Releasing Factor (CRF): A hypothalamic hormone that mediates pituitary release of ACTH, which stimulates the adrenal cortex to release cortisol into the bloodstream.

New Data: Receptor sites for CRF and ACTH in brain cells that can mediate stresslike behaviors and such psychologic variables as attentiveness, memory, and learning have been identified.

Cholecystokinin (CCK): A hormone that is active from the throat to the small intestines, which modulates gall bladder contraction, the pancreatic enzyme, and motility of the gastrointestinal tract.

New Data: CCK receptor sites are found in the brain. This is important information for therapies for obesity because it suggests a psychobiologic route by which mind may modulate appetite. CCK also may mediate the so-called gut feelings.

Insulin: A hormone secreted by the pancreas that affects carbohydrate metabolism by increasing the uptake of glucose by cardiac, muscle, liver, and adipose tissue.

New Data: Insulin receptor sites are located in the brain. This indicates that insulin modulates eating behavior by direct effects on cerebral capillaries.

Gonadotropin-Releasing Hormone (GnRH): A hormone released by the hypothalamus that stimulates the release of pituitary hormones, such as gonadotropin, luteinizing hormone (LH), and follicle-stimulating hormone (FSH), which stimulate growth and regulate sexual processes.

New Data: When receptors in the brain of rats are activated by GnRH, they show sexual posturing.

Vasopressin or Antidiuretic Hormone (ADH): Hormone released from the posterior pituitary when it receives appropriate posterior signals from the hypothalamus. Vasopressin regulates kidney action, water balance, and urine flow.

New Data: ADH also acts as a vasoconstrictor in blood flow regulation, especially the splanchnic circulatory system. With cell receptor stimulation, vasopressin has been found to enhance memory and learning. A relationship has been demonstrated between circadian rhythms and ADH levels in cerebrospinal fluid. Thus, memory and learning may be related to fluctuations in ADH's access to many different types of brain tissue.

Source: Reprinted from *The Psychobiology of Mind-Body Healing: New Concepts of Therapeutic Hypnosis*, Revised Edition, by Ernest Lawrence Rossi, with permission of W.W. Norton & Company, Inc.

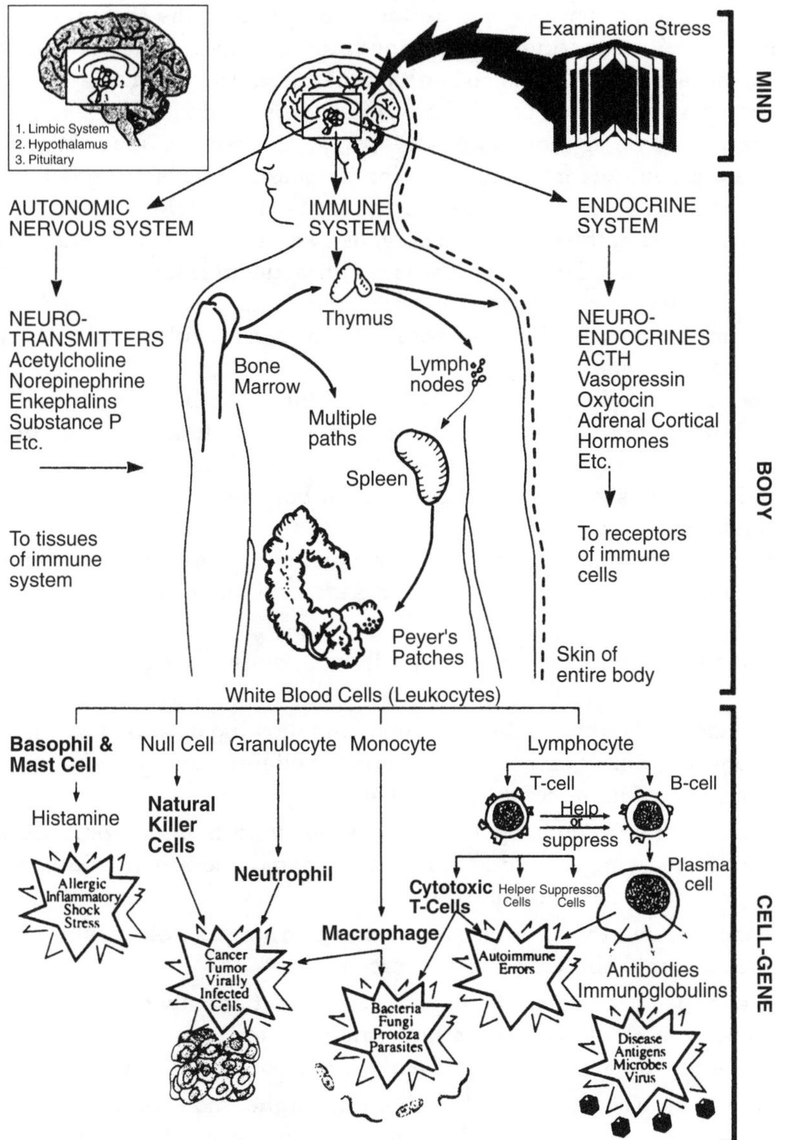

Figure 4–4 Major Communication Loops between the Mind-Brain and the Interacting Networks of the Immune System. *Source:* Reprinted from *The Psychobiology of Mind-Body Healing*: New Concepts of Therapeutic Hypnosis, Revised Edition, by Ernest Lawrence Rossi, with permission of W.W. Norton & Company, Inc. Copyright © 1993 by Ernest Lawrence Rossi.

cuses on interactions of the consciousness (psycho), the central nervous system and endocrine system (neuroendocrine), and the immune (immuno) system to influence health and illness. The brain sends signals along nerves to enhance the body's defenses against infection and to make the body fight more aggressively against disease. None of the body systems is separate from the other, for images and stressors perceived by a client's mind are transduced to the messenger molecules—the neurotransmitters of the autonomic nervous system and the hormones of the endocrine system. Because there is a bidirectional information circuitry operating between the immune system and the autonomic and endocrine systems, the activity of any of these systems can modulate the activity of the other systems.

Receptor sites located on the surface of the T and B lymphocytes have the ability to activate, direct, and modify immune function. They act as locks (the receptors) and keys (neurotransmitters) that open up each system. Research shows a direct correlation between relaxation, imagery, and immunology:

- correlation between various types of leukocytes and components of cancer patient's imagery of the disease, treatment, and immune system[41,42]
- increased phagocytic activity following biofeedback-assisted relaxation[43]
- enhanced natural killer cell function following a relaxation and imagery training procedure for geriatric clients[44] and for adult cancer patients with metastatic disease[45]
- changes in lymphocyte reactivity following hypnotic procedures[46] and following instruction in relaxation and imagery in adult cancer patients with metastatic disease[47]
- altered neutrophil adherence or margination, as well as white blood cell count, following imagery procedures[48]
- changes at the end of a 6-week period statistically associated with the type of imagery procedure employed following training in cell-specific imagery of either T lymphocytes or neutrophils[49]
- increased secretory IgA (significantly higher than control group) following 6 weeks of daily training imaging the location, activity, and morphology of IgA.[50]

Neuropeptide System

Neuropeptides and their receptors are one key to understanding the bodymind interconnections and the ways in which people experience emotions throughout the body (Figure 4–5). Neuropeptides are amino acids produced in the brain, and, when they lock into their receptor sites, they either facilitate or block a cellular response. Approximately 50 neuropeptides have been discovered that are as specific as the first identified neuropeptide, beta-endorphin. These neuropeptides come directly from the body's own DNA. Not only are they located in the brain, but also they circulate throughout the body.

Pert refers to the communication of the neuropeptide system as the informational substrate.[51] The autonomic, endocrine, and immune systems, which form a complex bidirectional network of communication, are the channel carriers for the neuropeptides, the messenger molecules responsible for connecting body and emotions. Pert explains this complex network as follows:

> I am going to suggest that neuropeptides and their receptors form an information network within the body. Perhaps this suggestion sounds fairly innocuous, but its implications are far reaching. I believe that neuropeptides and their receptors are a key to understanding how mind and body are interconnected and how emotions can be manifested throughout the body. Indeed, the more we know about neuropeptides, the harder it is to think in the traditional terms of a mind and a body. It makes more and more sense to speak of a single integrated entity, a "bodymind."[52]

The neuropeptides integrate all of these systems; their receptor sites can be seen as the keys to the biochemistry of emotions. The limbic system, which regulates both the emotions and the body physiology, has 40 times more opiate receptor sites than does any other area of the brain.[53]

Traditionally, it was thought that only glands, not nerve cells, produced hormones. Mapping techniques with radioactive labeling have located the site of neuropeptide action as also in the brain, however. For example, insulin once thought to be produced only by the pancreas and to flow from the pancreas to specific receptor sites is now known to be also produced and stored in the brain. Angiotensin receptors are found not only in the kidney, but also in the brain. The release of the neuropeptide angiotensin leads to behaviors that increase both water consumption and water conservation.[54]

Other receptor sites, called nodal points, have been found throughout the brain. These nodal points are located in places associated with emotional modulation, such as the dorsal horn of the spinal cord. The dorsal horn is where sensory information is transmitted to and processed by the

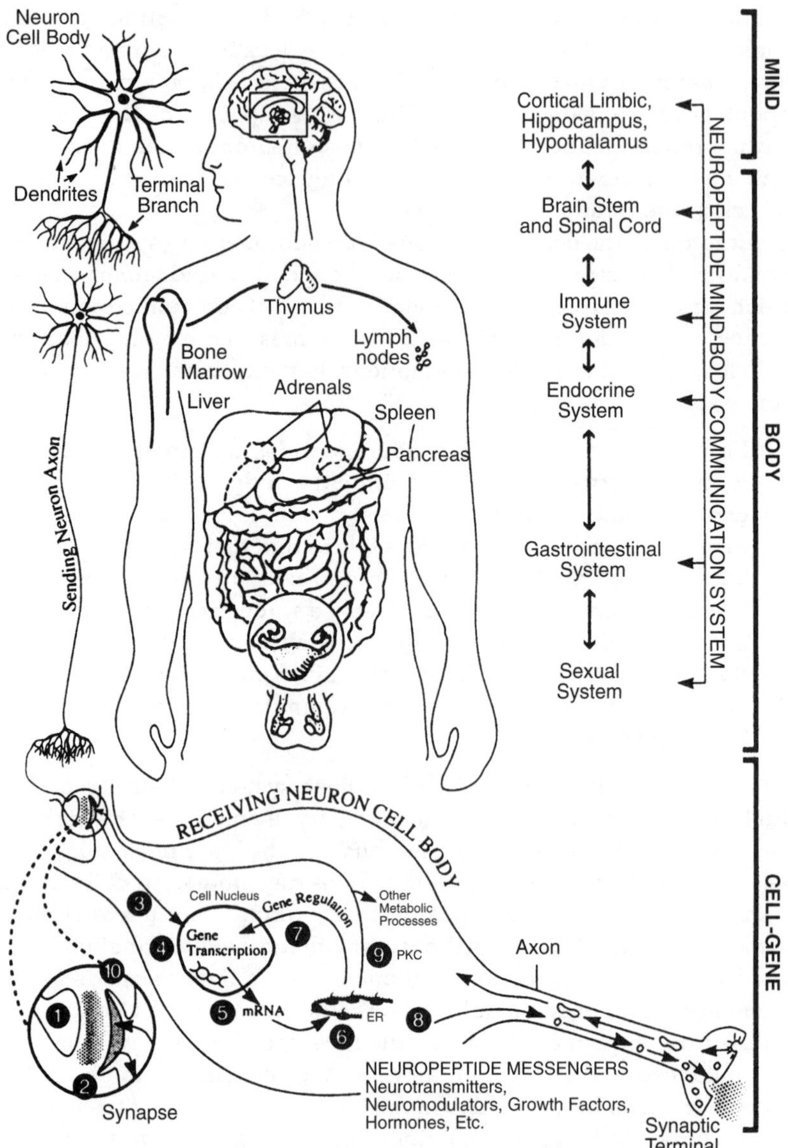

Figure 4–5 Mind-Body-Gene Communication Loop of Neuropeptide System. *Source:* Reprinted from *The Psychobiology of Mind-Body Healing: New Concepts of Therapeutic Hypnosis*, Revised Edition, by Ernest Lawrence Rossi, with permission of W.W. Norton & Company, Inc. Copyright © 1993 by Ernest Lawrence Rossi.

brain. Furthermore, the entire tract from the esophagus to the anus is lined with cells containing neuropeptides and receptor sites.[55] The reality of a "gut feeling" can now be demonstrated.

Neuropeptide research is now focused on six areas: (1) limbic-hypothalamic locus of neuropeptide activity, (2) brain stem and spinal cord locus of neuropeptide activity, (3) immune integration by the neuropeptides, (4) endocrine system integration by the neuropeptides, (5) enteric nervous system, and (6) sexual system and neuropeptide activity.[56]

CLINICAL IMPLICATIONS FOR THE FUTURE

New scientific data continue to emerge rapidly, and we must use this information to guide our theory, diagnoses, clinical practice, and the development of new forms of therapy. It is clear that the autonomic, endocrine, immune, and neuropeptide system within our bodies can communicate with each other. This information helps us understand the reasons that holistic nursing interventions such as relaxation, imagery, music therapy, touch, and meditation are so effective. The therapies are grounded in science. Our challenge is to refine the processes and techniques for specific modulation of bodymind symptoms within nursing practice. This can be done by developing specific courses, both accredited nursing courses[57] and lay public courses in the psychophysiology of bodymind healing. Such courses give students the latest scientific data, as well as experiential sessions, to explore the profound effects of bodymind healing. This way of teaching empowers students to integrate this information in all areas of their lives and to become critical thinkers with new paradigms.

These new data invalidate the Western idea that consciousness resides within the brain. Rather, consciousness can be projected to various body parts—the brain, the glands, and the immune, enteric, and sexual systems. Bidirectional communication exists for each of these areas and their organs. Questions yet to be answered include:

- Can the mind survive the physical death of the brain?
- Where does the information go after the destruction of the molecules and the tissue mass that composed it (e.g., phantom limb pain)?

Pert states that, since matter can neither be created nor destroyed, it is possible that biologic information flow may not disappear at death, but rather may assume another form.[58] No scientist can say that this is impossible, because no mathematical formula has unified gravitational field theory with matter and energy. Although the theoretical and experimental research data have overwhelmingly documented the bodymind interrelationship, nurses must continue to explore effective ways to integrate and evaluate the effects of holistic interventions with clients and their families. In addition, the meaning of a client's illness must be investigated through modules, tools, and experiential techniques that integrate the human spirit with physiologic interventions. L. Dossey states:

> We will never achieve the validation of our spiritual intuitions by scrutinizing monocytes, neuropeptides, and receptor sites. What we will achieve is an expanded view of what it means to be human. The point that we will continue to emphasize is that the physiological and the spiritual are not equivalent, and if we ignore the difference between these two domains it will be at the risk of our spiritual impoverishment. These scientific insights are important signposts pointing to the nonlocal nature of consciousness. They get the mind out of the brain and into the body at large. Any science that helps us toward this understanding—which is contained in the sublimest of the most acute seers of our race—deserves, I would submit, our deepest respects.[59]

CONCLUSION

Information theory, transduction, placebos, self-regulation theory, and mind modulation of the autonomic, endocrine, immune, and neuropeptide systems serve as a theoretical basis for bodymind healing. Nurses can reduce the devastating effects of illness of clients and their families by addressing bio-psycho-social-spiritual human dimensions (see Chapter 1) and integrating holistic interventions. The positive changes that occur evoke healing outcomes for clients and their families, and they allow nurses to understand more fully the emotions and meaning involved in disease/illness.

DIRECTIONS FOR FUTURE RESEARCH

Nurses must continue to document physiologic data of mind modulation of the autonomic, endocrine, immune, and neuropeptide systems along with holistic nursing interventions that can stabilize or reverse disease/illness. The following are important directions for future research:

1. Monitor and evaluate the effect of the "flow of healing intent" in relaxation, imagery, music therapy, and therapeutic touch interventions.

2. Develop valid and reliable tools that measure psychophysiologic responses to specific holistic interventions.
3. Explore the most effective guidelines and therapies that help clients and their families gain access to their spiritual dimensions when faced with illness.
4. Determine whether nurses who use self-regulation interventions have more empathy, caring, and job satisfaction.

NURSE HEALER REFLECTIONS

After reading this chapter, the nurse healer will be able to answer or begin a process of answering the following questions:

- Do I listen to the inner wisdom of my own body-mind-spirit daily?
- When do I allow time for self-reflection in order to increase my creativity and spirituality?
- How can I be aware of and expand my view of what it means to be human?

NOTES

1. S. Black, *Mind and Body* (London: William Kimber, 1969), 1–34.
2. C. Pert, The Wisdom of the Receptors: Neuropeptides, the Emotions, and Bodymind, *Advances* 3, no. 3 (1986):14.
3. E. Rossi, *The Psychobiology of Mind-Body Healing* (New York: W.W. Norton Co., 1993), 23–46.
4. D. Ornish, Can Lifestyle Changes Reverse Coronary Heart Disease? *Lancet* 336 (1990):129–135.
5. C. Guzzetta, Effects of Relaxation and Music Therapy on Patients in a Coronary Care Unit with the Presumptive Diagnosis of Acute Myocardial Infarction, *Heart Lung* 18, no. 6 (1989):609–616.
6. K. Miller and P. Perry, Relaxation Technique and Postoperative Pain in Patients Undergoing Cardiac Surgery, *Heart Lung* 19, no. 2 (1990):136–146.
7. E. Stuart et al., Spirituality in Health and Healing: A Clinical Program, *Holistic Nursing Practice* 3, no. 3 (1989):35–46.
8. S. Thomas et al., Cardiovascular Responses of Patients with Cardiac Disease to Talking and Exercise Stress Testing. *Heart and Lung* 21, no. 1 (1992):64–73.
9. J. Achterberg and C. Kenner, Nonpharmacologic Pain Relief for Burn Patients, *Journal of Mental Imagery* 12, no. 1 (1987):71–88.
10. F. Acosta, Biofeedback and Progressive Relaxation in Weaning the Anxious Patient from the Ventilator: A Brief Report, *Heart Lung* 19, no. 2 (1989):299–300.

11. J. Quinn, Holding Sacred Space: The Nurse as Healing Environment, *Holistic Nursing Practice* 6, no. 4 (1992):26–36.
12. B. Dossey et al., Body-Mind-Spirit, in *Critical Care Nursing: Body-Mind-Spirit*, 3rd ed., ed. B. Dossey et al. (Philadelphia: J.B. Lippincott, 1992), 3–16.
13. A. Roberts, Placebo Therapies. Spark Improvement for 7 in 10, *Brain Mind Bulletin* 18, no. 12 (1993);1.
14. J. Achterberg, *Imagery in Healing* (Boston: Shambhala Publications, 1985).
15. Roberts, Placebo Therapies.
16. Rossi, *The Psychobiology of Mind-Body Healing*, 47–68.
17. Ibid., 67–68.
18. J. Johnson et al., Process of Coping with Radiation Therapy, *Journal of Counseling and Clinical Psychology* 57(1989):358.
19. K. Pribram, *Languages of the Brain* (Monterey, CA: Brooks/Cole Publishing Co., 1971), 5–9.
20. Ibid., 10–11.
21. Achterberg, *Imagery in Healing*, 131–132.
22. E. Green et al., Feedback Technique for Deep Relaxation, *Psychophysiology* 6(1969):371–377.
23. E. Rossi, *The 20-Minute Break* (Los Angeles: J.P. Tarcher, 1991), 11–12.
24. Ibid., 30–46.
25. Ibid., 47–85.
26. C. Freed et al., Blood Pressure, Heart Rate, and Heart Rhythm Changes in Patients with Heart Disease during Talking, *Heart Lung* 18(1989):17–23.
27. Ibid.
28. D. Larson, The Impact of Religion on Men's Blood Pressure, *Journal of Religion and Health* 28(1989):265–268.
29. Ibid.
30. Z. Lipowski, Physical Illness, the Individual and the Coping Process, *Psychiatric Medicine* 1(1970):90–93.
31. C. Thomas, Precursors of Premature Disease and Death, *Annals of Internal Medicine* 301(1976):1249–1253.
32. G. Vaillant, Natural History of Male Psychological Health, *New England Journal of Medicine* 301(1979):1248–1251.
33. B. Dossey et al., Body-Mind-Spirit.
34. Rossi, *The Psychobiology of Mind-Body Healing*, 163–164.
35. G. Everly and H. Benson, Disorders of Arousal and the Relaxation Response, *International Journal of Psychosomatics* 36(1989):15–21.
36. Rossi, *The Psychobiology of Mind-Body Healing*, 168.
37. J. Achterberg et al., *Rituals of Healing* (New York: Bantam Books, 1994).
38. S. Reichlin, Neuroendocrine-immune Interaction, *New England Journal of Medicine* 329, no. 7 (1993):1246–1253.
39. Rossi, *The Psychobiology of Mind-Body Healing*, 190–194.
40. Ibid., 193–194.

41. J. Achterberg and F. Lawlis, Psychological and Blood Chemistry Factors As Predictors of Cancer Progress, *Multivariate Clinical Experimental Research* 3(1977).
42. J. Achterberg and F. Lawlis, A Canonical Relationship between Blood Chemistries and Psychological Variables in Cancer Patients, *Multivariate Clinical Experimental Research* 4(1979).
43. B. Peavey et al., Biofeedback-Assisted Relaxation: Effects of Phagocytic Capacity, *Biofeedback and Self-Regulation* 10, no. 1 (1985):33–47.
44. J. Kiecolt-Glaser et al., Psychosocial Enhancement of Immunocompetence in a Geriatric Population, *Health Psychology* 4(1985):25–41.
45. B. Gruber et al., Immune System and Psychological Changes in Metastatic Cancer Patients Using Relaxation and Guided Imagery: A Pilot Study, *Scandinavian Journal of Behavior Therapy* 17(1988):25–46.
46. H. Hall, Hypnosis and the Immune System, *Journal of Clinical Hypnosis* 25, no. 2–3 (1982–1983):92–93.
47. Gruber et al., Immune System and Psychological Changes in Metastatic Cancer Patients.
48. J. Schneider et al., The Relationship of Mental Imagery to Neutrophil Function, Uncirculated manuscript, Michigan State University, 1983. Republished and abridged with permission in J. Achterberg and F. Lawlis, *Imagery and Disease: Diagnostic Tools* (Champaign, IL: Institute of Personality and Ability Testing, 1984).
49. M. Rider and J. Achterberg, Effect of Music-Assisted Imagery on Neutrophils and Lymphocytes, *Biofeedback and Self-Regulation* 14(1989):3.
50. M. Rider et al., Effect of Immune System Imagery on Secretory IgA, *Biofeedback and Self-Regulation* 15(1990):4.
51. Pert, The Wisdom of the Receptors, 14.
52. Ibid., 16.
53. R. Ader et al., *Psychoneuroimmunology*, 2nd ed., ed. R. Ader et al. (San Diego: Academic Press, 1990).
54. Rossi, *The Psychobiology of Mind-Body Healing.*
55. Ibid.
56. Ibid.
57. G. Bartol and N. Courts, Psychoneuroimmunological Aspects of Nursing, *Journal of Holistic Nursing* 11, no. 4 (1993):332.
58. Pert, The Wisdom of the Receptors, 16.
59. L. Dossey, *Medicine and Meaning* (New York: Bantam Books, 1991).

RESOURCE

For information on Dr. Dean Ornish's **Opening Your Heart Program**, write or call:
Prevention Medicine Research Institute (PMRI)
900 Bridgeway, Suite #2
Sausalito, CA 94965
(415) 332-2525

VISION OF HEALING

Reawakening of the Spirit in Daily Life

Individuals who are psychologically hardy have certain characteristics referred to as the three Cs.[1] First, these individuals feel open and willing to ***change****. They see life events as challenges rather than problems, and they seem to thrive on challenges. Second, they feel a sense of* ***commitment*** *to family, friends, and goals. Third, these individuals have a sense of personal* ***control*** *over life and perceive their body-mind-spirit as an integrative unit. Not only do these characteristics apply to staying healthy, but also they have tremendous usefulness in adopting effective health promotion strategies if chronic illness is present.[2]*

These characteristics of psychologic hardiness assist us in learning more about our human potentials. Change implies flexibility and suggests that life style habits need not be permanent. Changing detrimental habits is essential for well-being. The more we choose effective life style patterns, the better we learn the change process. Often, people who do not change conclude that they do not have the willpower to change. The existence of willpower is a myth that prevents long-lasting life style changes, however. Rather, we should think in terms of "skillpower," which implies new information and abilities that lead to changes in life style patterns. The more we challenge ourselves to change unhealthy life styles, the more consistently we select positive changes because the fear of changing is lessened.

Psychologic hardiness helps us experience a sense of meaning and purpose in our work. This "work spirit" increases effectiveness, productivity, and individual satisfaction, thus contributing to positive results in the workplace. An individual's willingness to take responsibility for changing the course of his or her life and knowledge about maximizing human potentials through such modalities as exercise, nutrition, play, relaxation, and stress management strategies foster work spirit. Also important to work spirit is selflessness, that is, being unself-consciously engrossed in the outcome of work tasks and projects rather than worrying about what others think of the way in which the task is performed. People with work spirit possess the following seven qualities: (1) abundant energy, always appearing to be "on a roll" or "in a flow state"; (2)

sense of purpose; (3) creative and nurturing outlook; (4) different sense of time; (5) sense of higher order and oneness; (6) positive, open state of mind; and (7) full sense of self.[3]

Individuals with work spirit exhibit synergy; they discover common threads when there appear to be only opposites and conflicts in situations.[4] *They work with self and others to produce greater results. They can make frequent shifts in thinking and can release old mind sets. They understand that patterns and processes, rather than isolated parts, create the whole in any project. They value input from colleagues, seek meaningful relationships, and also praise co-workers' talents and resources. They focus on win-win situations.*

Individuals who have low levels of work spirit can create dysergy in the workplace. They focus on an isolated action that promotes one function, but impedes the progress of another person or the group working together.[5] *These individuals tend to work alone or evoke unnecessary insecurity, and they reject meaningful interaction with co-workers. Furthermore, they emphasize win-lose outcomes.*

Organizations can increase individual work spirit by having an identified purpose that workers can share and articulate. When this purpose is clear, supervisors and managers can recognize individual strengths and talents, and they can channel creative energy toward the organizational goals. Those organizations that offer praise and rewards for risk taking and problem solving, while not punishing for mistakes, also increase individual work spirit.

NOTES

1. S. Kobasa et al., Hardiness and Health: A Prospective Study, *Journal of Personality and Social Psychology* 42(1982):168–177.
2. S. Pollack, Human Responses to Chronic Illness: Physiologic and Psychosocial Adaptation, *Nursing Research* 35(1989):90–95.
3. A. McGee-Cooper, *Time Management for Unmanageable People* (Dallas: Bard and Rogers, 1993).
4. Ibid.
5. Ibid.

Chapter 5

Exploring the Process of Change

Barbara Montgomery Dossey and
Cathie E. Guzzetta

NURSE HEALER OBJECTIVES

Theoretical

- Discuss the dialectic relationships of health-wellness-disease-illness.
- Explain the steps in values clarification.
- Analyze the components in the stages of change.

Clinical

- Identify four values that will increase your state of well-being in the workplace.
- Explore with a colleague the cultural variation in human-environmental responses of clients.
- Identify the stages of change with clients, and implement the appropriate strategies to motivate and sustain changed behaviors in these clients.

Personal

- Determine whether you integrate the three steps in values clarification each day.
- Write down two action steps that will guide you in living your personal values.

DEFINITIONS

Motivation: the internal spark or desire necessary for a person to be committed to change, set goals, and succeed.

Self-Image: all the behavioral traits that a person perceives in himself or herself, which may or may not be present, but set the boundaries for what that person can and cannot do.

Self-Responsibility: the ability to respond in order to correct activities, choices, attitudes, and values that lead to integration of body-mind-spirit.

Values Clarification: a process whereby one becomes more aware of how life values are established and how these values control one's life or boundaries to achieve a high degree of well-being.

Well-Being: the process of increasing awareness of reaching human potentials and the journey toward the transpersonal self.

CONCEPTS OF HEALTH-WELLNESS-DISEASE-ILLNESS

The unfolding of events associated with wellness-illness is depicted as a generic paradigm with health, disease, wellness, and illness existing in a dialectic relationship.[1] Such a relationship synthesizes objective and subjective perspectives. Health-disease and wellness-illness are neither mutually exclusive, nor polar opposites, but are part of a process and part of the whole. This perspective makes it easier to understand that the individual is a changing person in a changing world.

The relationship between health-wellness-disease-illness can best be explored by reviewing definitions of each.[2] The term *health* has been defined in many ways, including an ideal state, an integrated balance, and a method of functioning that is oriented toward maximizing the potential of which the individual is capable (see Table 8–1). *Wellness* has been described as a measure of optimal health, an expression of the process of life, and the subjective experience of integrated or congruent functioning. *Disease* has varied definitions, such as the biologic dimensions of nonhealth or breakdown. There are two prevalent views of disease: an ontologic view and a physiologic view.[3] In the ontologic view, diseases are seen as entities in their own right, not as disturbances. In the physiologic view, disease is grounded in the nature of human beings and is believed to occur as the result of deviations from the norm or imbalances. *Illness* is not the absence of health, nor is it identical to disease. It involves the human experience of symptoms and suffering or the state of being in the world; it includes the perceived meaning for the person and how he or she lives within the limitations of symptoms or disability. Thus, health-disease and wellness-illness are both relational and contextual. Health, disease, wellness, and illness are part of the whole, yet distinct.

Wellness-illness is a human experience of actual or perceived function-dysfunction through the interaction of cognitive-affective dimensions.[4] These dimensions affect the patterning of perceptions regarding health-disease, which are reflected in various profiles of meaning that influence the lived experience. Cognitive dimensions of health-disease can be seen as comprehensible/incomprehensible, manageable/unmanageable, and meaningful/meaningless. Affective themes that appear are joy/despair, acceptance/resentment, power/fear, and anticipation/confusion. Nurses must continue to explore the dynamics of health-wellness-disease-illness in order to understand the patterns, meaning, and responses of clients. With more information, nurses can be more effective in facilitating the healing process.

Clients need to receive care within the context of their cultural backgrounds, health beliefs, and values. Cultural beliefs deeply influence the perceived meaning of health and illness for clients and family members. Nurses must continue to gain knowledge of various cultural practices of individuals and integrate this knowledge in nursing interventions. This information should include a client's health-illness beliefs, attitudes, and values; the beliefs about causative agents of symptoms and illness; how healers within the culture diagnose the symptoms or illness; and the recommended treatments by the healers.

Table 5–1 provides knowledge of general patterns of responses for specific cultural and ethnic groups and provides a foundation for further assessment and individualized care.[5] This information serves as a guideline for individualized care. It should never be used as ethnocentric or stereotypic responses by health care providers. Nurses can gain additional information about cultural beliefs from appropriate community resources and experts to validate knowledge and practices of different cultural groups. As nurses continue to identify and utilize ethnic community resources, this will empower clients/families and will effectively bridge between the differing health-illness beliefs and values of individuals.

VALUES CLARIFICATION

The pioneering work of Raths and colleagues explores the complexity and differences in values, beliefs, and attitudes.[6] *Values* are affective dispositions about the worth, truth, or beauty of a thought, object, person, or

Table 5–1 Culture: Human-Environmental Responses

Response Variants	*Cultural Variation in Human-Environmental Responses (Four Examples)*			
	Asian American (Hmong)	*Native American*	*Black American*	*Hispanic*
Communication	Oral tradition. Gender- and age-specific patterns. Group learning. Spiritual link. Taboos guiding topics. Conversation focus to promote harmony. Language barrier—interpreter.	Oral tradition. Storytelling. Group learning. Spiritual foundation of life. Only able to speak for self, nonaggressive. Role of elder.	Black English. Specific dialect. Significance of names/terms. Nonverbal: talk-look at, listening-look away, prolonged eye contact, frequent touch, emotional sharing. Group learning.	Language barrier—interpreter. Verbal: privacy, avoid conflict, emotional expressive. Nonverbal: touch, handshake, avoid prolonged eye contact. Group learning.
Space	Avoid eye contact. Sacred parts of body. Avoid public display of affection and extreme emotions.	Avoid eye contact, limit touch. Negative significance rt handshake.	Often space much closer than "Anglos."	Familial closeness—demonstrative.
Time	Cyclical, present oriented, holistic, fatalistic. Social time vs clock time.	Circular, holistic, present oriented, fatalistic.	Wide variation. Social time vs clock time.	Present-oriented, "Latin Time," Polychronic.
Social Organization	Clan structure. Decision-maker: elder male, clan leader. Family-patrilineal. Male dominant in affairs extending beyond the home. Female more	Clan/family/tribes. Role of elder. Role definition. Social relations-wheel of life. Core values: thanks, harmony, sharing, and hospitality.	Disruptive influence of slavery and discrimination on the family structure. Today variance, a link with social economic status (SES). Lower SES:	"Lafamilia": patrilineal, extended, gender significance. Machismo: decision-maker, protector. Marianismo: nurturer,

continues

Table 5–1 continued

Response Variants	*Asian American (Hmong)*	*Native American*	*Black American*	*Hispanic*
	active role within the home. Clearly defined roles/responsibilities—age and gender. Children indulged until the age of five then more strict discipline—"communal focus."		matrifocused—present focused. Mid/Upper SES: egalitarian. Children—socialized to be in control, independent at earlier age. Importance of extended kinship.	mediator. Respect elders. Children a priority, dependency. Family value: respect, pride, responsibility, spirituality (Catholic).
Environmental Control	Explanatory Model of Health/Illness (H/I): H: Mandate for life, predetermination, maintain harmony. I: Supernatural, soul loss, spiritual, disharmony, imbalance, sins of ancestors, self in relation to others. Curers: Herbalist, Shaman. Tx: foods, maintain harmony with the forces, spiritual divination, massage, herbs, foods, coining, pinching, cupping. Special Tx for certain conditions, e.g., childbirth.	Explanatory Model of Health/Illness (H/I): Beliefs—balance with mother nature, predetermination—Creator. I: lack of harmony, failure to live according to code of life, evil spirits, fear and jealousy of other nations. Curers: Shaman/faithkeeper, Midwiwin, False Face Society, Herb specialist. Tx: herbs, ceremonies, e.g., sweat and medicine lodge, vision quest, talking circle, etc. Significant elements.	Explanatory Model of Health/Illness (H/I): I: an inability to function due to a hex, sins, disharmony, natural or supernatural. Curers: family first, "Old lady" or "Granny," voodoo priest, spiritualist, root doctor. Tx: includes use of teas, cod liver oils, dietary choices, laxatives for purging, wearing of garlic, amulets, copper or silver bracelets. Folk practices include: silver dollar to navel, oil—baby's bath, cradle cap, prayer cloth to diaper, PICA.	Explanatory Model of Health/Illness (H/I): I: Severity rt pain or blood, unable to perform roles/ADLs. Illness: mild or severe, lg of time. Causes: sins, will of God, "evil eye," "nerves," "bad blood"—loss of respect, imbalance of humors or hot and cold. Direct re between certain illnesses—supernatural intervention. Many folk illnesses. Curers: family, curandero herbalist, spiritualist. Tx: prayer, massage, ceremonies rt specific illnesses.

continues

Table 5–1 continued

Response Variants	*Asian American (Hmong)*	*Native American*	*Black American*	*Hispanic*
Biological	Small stature, small bone structure, Mongolian spots, eye. Disease susceptibility: Hepatitis, TB, lactase deficiency, hemoglobinopathies, altered drug metabolism.	Taller, bigger, heavier bone structure. Cheek bones, dark eyes. Disease susceptibility: Diabetes mellitus, ETOH abuse, Tb, SIDS, AIDS. Health Risks: Pneumonia, malnutrition, adolescent suicide, MVA, homicide.	Skin variance: Mongolian spots, keloids, vitiligo, nigra. Heavier/denser bones, shorter trunk, longer legs. Body fat link to economics. Disease susceptibility: TB, Hypertension/CV, sickle cell anemia, enzyme disorders, diabetes. Health Risks: Obesity, ETOH abuse, infant mortality, homicide, AIDS.	Skin color. Susceptibility to disease: Diabetes, TB, AIDS. Health risks: Obesity, alcoholism, adolescent pregnancy.

Source: Used with permission from Kathleen McGlynn Shadick RN, MSN, "A Practice Model for Promoting Cultural Diversity," American Nephrology Nurses Association Annual Conference, Dallas, Texas, 1994.

behavior. Values are important because they influence our decisions, behavior, and our nursing practice. Beliefs and attitudes are closely related to values. *Attitudes* are feelings toward a person, object, or idea that include cognitive, affective, and behavioral elements. *Beliefs* are a subclass of attitudes. The cognitive factors involved in beliefs have less to do with facts and more with feelings; they represent a personal confidence or faith in the validity of some person, object, or idea.

Values give direction and meaning to life and guide behavior and conduct. They provide us with a frame of reference by which to integrate, explain, and evaluate new thoughts, experiences, and relationships, both personally and professionally. Sometimes, personal values are not consistent with professional values. A direct conflict between a strong personal value and a professional value may lead to confusion, frustration, and dissatisfaction. A nurse has the right, however, not to participate in any activity or experience that violates personal values.

Values are more dynamic than are attitudes because, in addition to the cognitive, affective, and behavioral elements, values possess motivational characteristics. Although both values and attitudes influence the outcomes of behaviors, values guide our actions and professional practice. Usually, when confronted with a situation that requires action, we have a variety of alternatives. When choosing among alternative actions, it is important to focus on values in order to choose the best alternative.

Traditionally, values have been transmitted by moralizing, modeling, adopting a laissez-faire attitude, explaining, manipulating, and using a reward/punishment approach. Values clarification is a dynamic process that emphasizes our capacity for intelligent, self-directed behavior. By critical thinking, we find our own answers to a variety of questions or concerns. There is no attempt to create a "correct" set of values, because no one set of values is appropriate for all individuals. Rather, the process of values clarification establishes a closer fit between what we do and what we say.

The process of values clarification has three steps: choosing, prizing, and acting.[7] In the first step, the person chooses the value freely and willingly. The person chooses only after evaluating each alternative and its consequences. The second step is to prize and cherish the decision and to affirm or communicate the choice publicly. The last step in the valuing process is to incorporate the choice into behavior. These steps translate values into a behavioral change that is consistent and repeated over time. They serve as the criteria by which we can determine whether we hold a particular value. A true value passes through all steps although not necessarily in the order discussed.

Many of our beliefs do not meet all the criteria of true values. Such beliefs, which tend to be more numerous than are actual values, are termed value indicators. If the individual is motivated to undergo the values clarification process, a value indicator may become a true value.

Values clarification is a critical component of successful client education.[8] Teaching is not always effective in changing client behaviors, perhaps because we often ignore the important first step of determining what the client values and wants to know. The outcome that the nurse values frequently differs from the outcome that the client values. It may be important, for example, to determine whether a client values a prevention of complications or avoidance of recurrent illness. Nurses can help clients examine their values in terms of their alternatives. They can help clients evaluate the consequences of their choices and choose an alternative behavior that is consistent with their values. Nurses can also support clients in consistently incorporating the valued behavior over time. Health behavior outcomes are then likely to be positive, because the client has made the decision to change based on internally consistent values. The following is an example of values clarification in clinical practice:

> Mr. B.Z. is a 49-year-old man who was admitted to the coronary care unit with a diagnosis of acute myocardial infarction. He was executive vice-president of a large company. Following admission, the patient was stable, and no major complications developed. On the second day of his hospital stay, the patient was found lying in the hospital bed with his briefcase open, surrounded by papers. He was writing a report and requested a telephone in his room. The nurse handled the situation as follows:
>
> *Nurse:* It sure looks like you have a lot of work.
>
> *Patient:* Yes, I have so many deadlines this week, I cannot believe it. I really do not have time to be here. I sure hope my wife brings my fax machine soon.
>
> *Nurse:* It seems that your work is very important to you. I certainly can understand deadline problems. Could we take just a minute to discuss some other things that are important to you right now?
>
> *Patient:* Sure. Getting better and out of here are important to me, and having the energy to deal with the demands of my job. This better not happen to me again.

Nurse: Tell me what you know about preventing another heart attack.

Patient: Well, I know I am going to have to lose some weight and get some regular exercise. I'm not sure how I will fit that into my schedule though.

Nurse: Do you think that the heavy demands of work had anything to do with this illness?

Patient: Well . . . I know a lot of stress can make people sick. I've got to admit that I have had a stressful couple of months at work. Yes, I suppose all of that didn't help.

Nurse: You've told me that your work is important to you. You've also told me that preventing another heart attack is important. You have said that it will be important to lose weight, exercise, and perhaps reduce some of your daily stress. If you were willing to begin to work on one of these areas, which area would you choose?

Patient: I guess learning to deal with stress.

Nurse: That is a great place to start. Many techniques can be used to reduce stress levels. They can have a profound impact on your mind, as well as a positive effect on your body. If you are willing, I'd like to take a few minutes now and guide you in a relaxation technique that can be of help to you right now and later after your discharge. Would you be willing to try this with me?

Patient: Sounds good. I'm willing to try. I suppose I should have thought about this stuff a long time ago.

As nurses apply values clarification in their own lives, they become more aware of the best ways to help clients clarify their values. Clarification is important because values influence our ability to change, our motivation to act, the health services that we choose, and the way that we perceive health concepts.

HEALTH BEHAVIORS

Individuals are beginning to assess their health status to determine if they can change behaviors on their own toward healthier life styles or if they need the help of professionals. People usually undertake preventive behaviors when they are asymptomatic, but wish to enhance their life styles. Changing may or may not be independent of the health care system. Illness behaviors are often associated with symptoms and involve the health care system for evaluation and any necessary treatment.

People who do not adhere to recommended health behaviors are considered noncompliant. Since this term implies client failures in meeting professional expectations, terms such as *engagement* and *lack of engagement* in recommended health behaviors are preferred.[9] Implying that recommendations for health behaviors originate in general theories of behavior, these terms are less judgmental.

Health Belief Model

Three factors that significantly influence a client's motivation to change are his or her health attitudes, beliefs, and social support. The health belief model identifies the specific attitudes and beliefs that influence people to choose preventive health care and to engage in recommended medical regimens. According to this model, the motivation to change behavior comes from the perception that the reward is greater than the perceived cost and the perceived barriers. The major factors in determining engagement include

- the health and willingness of the client to accept medical recommendations
- the client's subjective estimate of his or her susceptibility, vulnerability, and extent of bodily harm
- the extent to which engagement interferes with the client's social roles
- the client's perception of the efficacy and safety of the proposed regimen[10]

Although the health belief model focuses on the perceptions of the client rather than those of the health care worker, it does not predict or screen persons who are at risk for nonengagement. It is known, however, that people who have adequate social support are more likely to choose healthy behaviors and engage in medical regimens. Social support includes the affection, feelings of belonging, emotional support, actual material goods, and all resources provided by other persons. Social support can be assessed in terms of the physical, emotional, and material support that the person receives, as well as the behavioral expectations of the support group in relation to the unhealthy behavior and the newly advised activities. To some degree, an individual's intention to perform a given act depends on that individual's beliefs about what others expect to happen in that situation.

It is possible to identify four categories of individuals according to the relationship of health beliefs, attitudes, and social support to facilitate engagement:

1. individuals who have positive health beliefs and attitudes, as well as adequate social support
2. individuals who have negative health beliefs and attitudes, but adequate social support
3. individuals who have positive health beliefs and attitudes, but little or inadequate social support
4. individuals who have negative health beliefs and attitudes, and little or inadequate social support[11]

The category to which the client belongs determines the choice of strategies to facilitate engagement. In order to identify the category to which the client belongs, the nurse must first assess the client's health beliefs and attitudes regarding high-risk behavior (e.g., smoking, high stress, improper diet, lack of exercise, failure to take hypertensive medication). A thorough assessment includes an evaluation of the following factors:

- the client's general beliefs regarding health
- the client's willingness to seek health care advice
- the client's willingness to accept health care advice
- the client's perception of the seriousness of the high-risk behavior and its consequences
- the client's perception of susceptibility and vulnerability to the consequences of the behavior
- the client's perception of the risks, benefits, and degree of interference that the new behavior will have on current roles[12]

When they become ill, individuals in Category 1 believe that their illness is serious and that their therapy will be helpful. Health care personnel structure their teaching efforts to facilitate affective, cognitive, and psychomotor learning. They match the information that they present to the client's coping style and locus of control. To accommodate different coping styles, those persons who use denial receive basic survival information, whereas those who cope by focusing on the problem receive detailed information. Those persons who are internally controlled (i.e., who believe that what they do will affect the outcome of the illness) receive specific instructions on ways to manage or control the situation; those who are externally controlled (i.e., who believe that others or fate will determine the outcome of the illness) need to have the information presented to them by an authority figure. For individuals with an external locus of control, it is best to discuss the most important points first and then repeat them.

Strategies for individuals in Category 2 (i.e., those who have negative health beliefs and attitudes, but adequate social support) focus on consciousness-raising techniques. After exploring the client's feelings and beliefs regarding behaviors, the nurse can arrange self-help group meetings for the client to meet with other individuals who have similar problems and concerns. Values clarification is useful in exploring alternatives for healthy behaviors. Behavior modification techniques are also helpful with this group of people. Cues that stimulate healthy behavior are recommended, while cues that stimulate unhealthy behaviors are avoided. Small rewards can be suggested to support healthy behaviors. The rewards should follow the behaviors and should be as small as possible, yet still be rewarding (e.g., taking 30 minutes off to read a good book following the daily exercise program). Clients are encouraged to keep a diary and make log entries for several days to identify the cues and consequences of a particular behavior, as well as to identify a list of rewards before attempting the behavior change (see Chapters 10 and 14).

Increased social support and cognitive strengthening are necessary for individuals in Category 3. Providing family and friends with important information and encouraging their involvement with recommended therapy, discussion, or values clarification sessions increase social support. Client involvement with community agencies and self-help groups may also be appropriate. Cognitive strengthening through training in assertiveness, relaxation, imagery, problem solving, and goal setting may enhance coping skills.

The "foot-in-the-door" strategy that requires minimal behavioral change may be effective with clients in Category 4. Although the change is no more than the client can tolerate, it can still produce a positive outcome. Regimens are simplified and basic goals established. Rewards and reinforcement are recommended. A graduated regimen in which complex behaviors are broken into smaller parts is best because clients can master the subparts before moving on to more complex behaviors. Written rather than verbal contracts are recommended for this group of clients.

Stages of Change

Nurses design many excellent action-oriented treatment programs and self-help programs and are very disappointed when only a small percentage of people demonstrate and sustain change of addictive behavior. Modification of addictive behavior involves a progression through five stages of change, however: (1) precontemplation, (2) contemplation, (3) preparation, (4) action, and (5) maintenance.[13]

Precontemplation is the stage at which there is no intention to change behavior in the near future. Individuals in this stage are usually unaware of their problems, although their family, friends, employers, and neighbors are very aware of the problems. If precontemplators agree to therapy, it is usually under pressure from others. Most often, they feel coerced into changing and will demonstrate change only as long as pressure remains.

At the contemplation stage, an individual is aware of the problem and is seriously thinking about overcoming it, but has not yet made a commitment to take action. Serious consideration of the problem solution is the central element of contemplation. The individual knows what action to take, but weighs the pros and cons of the problem and its solution. The struggle to cope with the effort, energy, and loss required to overcome the addiction can last 2 years or longer.

The stage of preparation combines both intention and behavioral criteria. In this stage, individuals plan to take action again within the next month who have unsuccessfully taken action in the past year. Although some action may have reduced the addictive behavior, the criterion for effective action has not been reached.

During the action stage, individuals modify their behaviors, experiences, or environment in order to overcome their addictions. The hallmarks of this action are significant overt efforts and modification of target behaviors to an acceptable criterion. It is in this stage that individuals receive the most external recognition from others. This stage requires an enormous amount of time, energy, and commitment. Individuals are in the action stage if they have successfully altered the addictive behaviors for a period of 1 day to 6 months.

The maintenance stage, in which individuals work to prevent relapse, represents a continuation of change rather than a stop and start of addictive behaviors. The criterion for this stage is that healthy behaviors replace addictive behaviors for longer than 6 months. In reality, this stage extends for 6 months to an indeterminate period past the initial action.

Each stage of change represents a period of time, as well as a set of tasks needed for movement to the next stage. Regardless of whether individuals try to change on their own or seek professional help in changing, they typically recycle through these stages several times before termination of the addiction. Figure 5–1 illustrates the spiral pattern in which

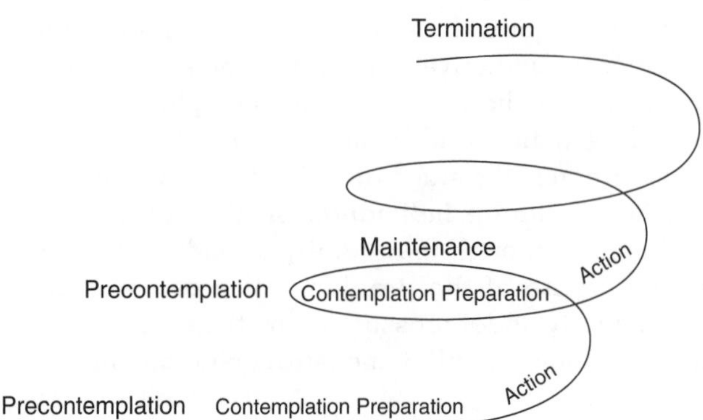

Figure 5–1 A Spiral Model of the Stages of Change. *Source:* Reprinted from Prochaska, J., et al., In Search of How People Change, *American Psychologist* Vol. 47, No. 9, pp. 1102–1114, with permission of American Psychological Association, © 1992.

most people actually move through the stages of change. Individuals may progress from contemplation to preparation to action to maintenance, but most will relapse. The spiral model suggests that most relapsers do not revolve endlessly in circles, nor do they regress all the way back to where they began.[14] Rather, they learn from their mistakes and can try different behaviors the next time that they recycle. The number of successes continues to increase over time; thus, the more action taken, the better the prognosis and success.

To assist individuals with change, the nurse first clearly identifies the person's stage of change. Each stage suggests treatment choices. For example, action-oriented therapies may be effective with individuals in the preparation or action stages, but very ineffective or even detrimental to those in the precontemplation or contemplation stages. The stages of change represent a temporal dimension that guides nurses in understanding when particular shifts in attitudes, intentions, and behaviors occur.

Professionals who counsel individuals with addictions use a transtheoretical approach; they examine recommended change techniques across different theories and then integrate them.[15] Table 5–2 presents ten processes with definitions and examples of interventions for each process. These processes are potent predictors of change for both clients who are self-changers and clients who change with professional therapy.

Table 5–2 Titles, Definitions, and Representative Interventions of the Processes of Change

Process	*Definitions: Interventions*
Consciousness raising	Increasing information about self and problem: observations, confrontations, interpretations, bibliotherapy
Self-reevaluation	Assessing how one feels and thinks about oneself with respect to a problem: value clarification, imagery, corrective emotional experience
Self-liberation	Choosing and commitment to act or belief in ability to change: decision-making therapy, New Year's resolutions, logotherapy techniques, commitment-enhancing techniques
Counterconditioning	Substituting alternatives for problem behaviors: relaxation, desensitization, assertion, positive self-statements
Stimulus control	Avoiding or countering stimuli that elicit problem behaviors: restructuring one's environment (e.g., removing alcohol or fattening foods), avoiding high-risk cues, fading techniques
Reinforcement management	Rewarding one's self or being rewarded by others for making changes: contingency contracts, overt and covert reinforcement, self-reward
Helping relationships	Being open and trusting about problems with someone who cares: therapeutic alliance, social support, self-help groups
Dramatic relief	Experiencing and expressing feelings about one's problems and solutions: psychodrama, grieving losses, role playing
Environmental reevaluation	Assessing how one's problem affects physical environment: empathy training, documentaries
Social liberation	Increasing alternatives for nonproblem behaviors available in society: advocating for rights of repressed, empowering, policy interventions

Source: Reprinted from Prochaska, J., et al., In Search of How People Change, *American Psychologist*, Vol. 47, No. 9, 1102–1114, with permission of the American Psychological Association, © 1992.

One of the most important findings to emerge from the self-change research of Prochaska and colleagues is the integration between the processes and stages of change.[16] Table 5–3 represents this integration from cross-sectional research involving thousands of self-changers at each of the stages of change for smoking cessation and weight loss.[17–22] This research indicates that precontemplators process less information about the problem, devote less time and energy to it, and experience fewer negative reactions to it. Contemplators are more open to consciousness-raising techniques, such as confrontation, observation, and interpretations. As contemplators become more aware of the problem, they evaluate the effect of their behaviors on the people to whom they are the closest. Thus, moving from precontemplation to contemplation increases the use of cognitive, affective, and evaluative processes of change. The research also shows that, during the action stage, people begin to believe that they have the autonomy to change their lives. Like the maintenance stage, the action stage involves high degrees of preparation. In these stages, clients consider what leads to relapse, how to avoid relapse, and what alternative responses are available for effective coping. The important key here for change is the individual's conviction that to maintain change means to operate from a sense of self-value.

Nurses must remember that the underlying structure for change of addictive behaviors is neither technique-oriented nor problem-specific. Efficient self-change or therapy-change depends on doing the right things (processes) at the right time (stages). It is essential that the nurse assess the person's stage of change and tailor the interventions accordingly. Otherwise, outcomes are disappointing.

Table 5–3 Stages of Change in Which Particular Processes of Change Are Emphasized

Precontemplation	*Contemplation*	*Preparation*	*Action*	*Maintenance*
Consciousness raising Dramatic relief Environmental reevaluation				
	Self-reevaluation			
		Self-liberation		
			Reinforcement management Helping relationships Counterconditioning Stimulus control	

Source: Reprinted from Prochaska, J., et al., In Search of How People Change, *American Psychologist*, Vol. 47, No. 9, 1102–1114, with permission of American Psychological Association, © 1992.

WORKPLACE WELLNESS

Many workplace wellness programs are now being developed throughout the United States because of the escalating health care costs of employees, cumulative research findings that document the rising health care costs associated with unhealthy employee behaviors, and employer support of workplace health programs. Generally, workplace wellness programs focus on stress management, nutritional education, weight control, exercise/physical fitness, smoking cessation, management of hypertension, alcohol and drug control, accident prevention, and early cancer detection. Because of their education and holistic focus, nurses are in an ideal position to develop wellness programs within businesses and all areas of the community.[23] Ideally, such nurses should have knowledge of current health care practices, existing workplace wellness programs, and marketing and health care reimbursement. They also need leadership skills.

The first step in developing a wellness program is to conduct a needs assessment of the workplace. Important questions to be addressed include

- What are the costs of health care insurance premiums, disability benefits, and sick leave for this group?
- What are the sociodemographic characteristics of the group (e.g., age, sex, ethnic origin, occupation, education, residence)?
- What conditions or diseases are documented in this group of people? (Gather information related to health, weight, lipid levels, blood sugar levels, blood pressure, and such life style features as diet, exercise, stress, smoking, and use of alcohol and drugs.)
- What kinds of acute and chronic illnesses are being treated in this group?
- What prevention and wellness needs does this group want to consider?
- What kinds of wellness programs does the group believe should be developed?
- What community wellness programs are already available for this group?

When developing wellness programs, nurses find it helpful to include to include clients in the planning process. Family and friends play vital roles in a person's ability to participate in wellness activities, so such programs should include dependents and retired workers. The evaluation of wellness programs should be considered early in the planning stages. Relevant evaluation outcomes are based on the goals and objectives of the program.

Wellness programs must help individuals identify their motivation for change, that is, the spark or desire to improve their present situation. Imagination is a prerequisite of motivation, for it is necessary to answer the question, What do I really want? Discipline and determination must also be engaged. Some of the known circumstances that will block motivated behavior are

- self-doubts and fears of unknown consequences that can override a person's desire to learn new health behaviors
- belief that prior commitments or high-priority projects leave little time for learning or implementing new behaviors
- perception of the person who is learning new skills that the new behaviors are distasteful
- previous failures in changing behavior
- lack of confidence in the ability to implement new strategies
- cultural beliefs that discourage the new behavior
- lack of support from family, co-workers, or other groups[24]

Many people do not recognize to what degree their culture conditions their beliefs, attitudes, and values. They often feel helpless under the burden of their role responsibilities and have a pervasive sense that they can do nothing to change the state of existing problems. Herein lies the challenge for the nurse. As people begin to clarify their values and beliefs, they identify obstacles to change and rename them as challenges. The nurse's effectiveness in motivating clients to see their life challenges depends, in large part, on the degree to which the nurse models wellness and health behaviors.

Increased emphasis on disease prevention and alternative therapies is essential to help reduce skyrocketing health care costs and add to the quality of human life.[25] (See Chapter 1.) Nurses are in a key leadership position to teach healthy life styles and different healing modalities to the public. Nurses across the United States are also placing more emphasis on wellness in their own lives. Not only are they teaching self-care, self-responsibility, and choices that lead toward health, but also they are becoming powerful role models for the message that they bring. As nurses teach clients, they encourage the individual to focus on attention to inner discipline, stamina, and determination. Most people are not able to sustain new health behaviors unless the environment and people with whom they spend most of their time—home, workplace, and community—support them in change.

CONCLUSION

The nurse who is aware of the health-wellness-disease-illness continuum is better positioned to assist an individual in investigating the meaning of an acute crisis or chronic illness. Values clarification, the health belief model, and stages of change explain the complexities that people confront and the reasons for their behavior. These concepts and theories can increase the nurse's awareness of the way in which values and beliefs affect each element of the motivational process and stages of change. People must be motivated before they can begin to change behavior and sustain maintenance behaviors that move them toward well-being. Establishing workplace wellness programs allows nurses to expand their efforts in major health education and implementation.

DIRECTIONS FOR FUTURE RESEARCH

1. Determine whether nurses who understand the health-disease-wellness-illness dialectic relationships among clients utilize holistic therapies more often than those nurses who do not understand and utilize these relationships.
2. Evaluate to what degree client outcomes are enhanced when nurses tailor their interventions to the client's stage of change.
3. Compare and contrast various interventions for specific client groups in which the process and the stages of change are integrated.

NURSE HEALER REFLECTIONS

After reading this chapter, the nurse healer will be able to answer or begin a process of answering the following questions:

- How do I feel when I reflect on my state of well-being?
- What are the inward feelings I acknowledge when I become aware of my motivation?
- What is my self-image?
- What is my current quality of life?
- What are my values regarding well-being?

NOTES

1. L. Jensen and M. Allen, Wellness: The Dialect of Illness, *Image* 25, no. 3 (1993):220–224.
2. Ibid.
3. P. Benner and J. Wrubel, *The Primacy of Caring* (Menlo Park, CA: Addison-Wesley, 1989).
4. Jensen and Allen, Wellness: The Dialect of Illness.
5. K. Shadick, "A Practice Model for Promoting Cultural Diversity." American Nephrology Nurses Association Annual Conference, Dallas, Texas, 1994.
6. L. Raths et al., *Values and Teaching: Working with Values in the Classroom* (Columbus, OH: Charles E. Merrill, 1978).
7. Ibid.
8. J. Havens, The Valuing Process, *Journal of Holistic Nursing* 11, no. 1 (1993):56–63.
9. D. Lauver, A Theory of Care-Seeking Behavior, *Image* 24, no. 4 (1992):281–287.
10. I. Rosenstock, The Health Belief Model: Explaining Health Behavior through Expectancies, in *Health Behavior and Health Education*, ed. K. Glanz and B. Rimer (San Francisco: Jossey-Bass Publishing, 1990), 39–62.
11. Ibid.
12. J. Prochaska et al., In Search of How People Change, *American Psychologist* 47, no. 9 (1992):1102–1114.
13. Ibid.
14. Ibid.
15. Ibid.
16. Ibid.
17. R. Kaplan and H. Simon, Compliance in Medical Care: Reconsideration of Self-Prediction, *Annals of Behavioral Medicine* 12(1990):66–71.
18. L. Beutler and J. Clarkin, *Systematic Treatment Selection* (New York: Brunner/Mazel Publishers, 1990).
19. C. DiClemente, Motivational Interviewing and the Stages of Change, in *Motivational Interviewing: Preparing People for Change*, ed. E. Miller and S. Rollnick (New York: Guilford Press, 1991): 191–202.
20. C. DiClemente and S. Hughes, Stages of Change Profiles in Alcoholism Treatment, *Journal of Substance Abuse* 2(1990):217–235.
21. C. DiClemente et al., The Process of Smoking Cessation: An Analysis of Precontemplation, Contemplation, and Preparation Stages of Change, *Journal of Consulting and Clinical Psychology* 59(1991):295–304.
22. T. Glynn et al., Essential Elements of Self-Help/Minimal Intervention Strategies for Smoking Cessation, *Health Education Quarterly* 17(1990):329–345.
23. J. Dunham-Taylor, Nurses Cut Health Care Costs, *Journal of Holistic Nursing* 11, no. 4 (1993):398–411.
24. J. Achterberg et al., *Rituals of Healing* (New York: Bantam Books, 1994).
25. Ibid.

VISION OF HEALING

Ethics in Our Changing World

Albert Einstein believed that the most important human endeavor is striving for morality in our actions. Our inner balance and even our very existence depend on it. Only morality in our actions can give beauty and dignity to life. Ralph Waldo Emerson relayed a similar message when he said that character is a natural power—light and heat and all nature cooperates with it.

For healing modalities to operate in a natural environment, the disposition of the intellect, will, emotions, and spirit of the healer must be balanced and centered. Such balancing and centering effects are enhanced by knowledge of self. Belief structures and the reasoning behind such belief structures place the individual healer's spirit in a dynamic equilibrium or cybernetic relationship with the powers in the cosmos. It is in this way that conscious evolution proceeds. It is a give and take—a continuous ongoing dialogue between the healer and the cosmic environment that empowers the healer to heal. Healing is a psychophysiologic psychospiritual experience that enables the healer to cooperate with nature and, indeed, exigently coercing nature to cooperate with the healer.

Holistic ethics provides guidelines for the development of this spirit in the healer, and spells out the steps needed to develop the healing attitude. Ethics thus serves as a guide to tap into the wisdom of the cosmos, teaching the individual strategies to release the self to become more participatory in the Greater Self. The participation in the Greater Self forms the linkages between the powers of the cosmos, the healer, and the one to be healed.

Nursing and ethics have been intertwined since the inception of modern nursing. The ethics of nursing encompasses both a bedside ethic and a social ethic, as nurses have always concerned themselves in such matters of public policy as urban slums and tenements, war and disaster, and special needs of the underserved. Recently, the ethics of public policy has also addressed environmental concerns, population issues, human rights, health care delivery, and health promotion. Nurses, both individually and collectively, are directly in the forefront not only of ethical decision making, but also of public policy formation. Many aspects of future health care delivery will be based on the ethi-

cal decisions that we make now. Thus, nurses must examine current and future healing activities from ethical perspectives. All of us must strive to understand the concept and application of ethics.

Chapter 6

Holistic Ethics

Lynn Keegan

NURSE HEALER OBJECTIVES

Theoretical

- Review the classic principles of ethics.
- Synthesize the basic tenets from the work of traditional ethical theorists.
- Explore the new concept of holistic ethics.

Clinical

- Relate ethical theory to clinical situations.
- Gain the knowledge necessary to serve on institutional ethics committees.

Personal

- Begin to see daily choices as opportunities to make a positive impact on your world.
- Clarify your own values and ideas.

DEFINITIONS

Being: the state of existing or living.

Consciousness: a state of knowing or awareness.

Ethical Code: a written list of a profession's values and standards of conduct.

Ethics: the study or discipline concerned with judgments of approval or disapproval, rightness or wrongness, goodness or badness, virtue or vice, and desirability or wisdom of actions, dispositions, ends, objects, or states of affairs; disciplined reflection on the moral choices that people make.

Holistic: concerned with the interrelationship of body, mind, and spirit in an ever-changing environment.

Holistic Ethics: the basic underlying concept of the unity and integral wholeness of all people and of all nature that is identified and pursued by finding unity and wholeness within the self and within humanity. In this framework, acts are not performed for the sake of law, precedent, or social norms, but rather from a desire to do good freely in order to witness, identify, and contribute to unity.

Morals: standards of right and wrong that we learn through socialization.

Nursing Ethics: a code of behavior that influences the way nurses work with those in their care, with one another, and with society.

Personal Ethics: an individual code of thought and behavior that governs each person's actions.

Planetary Ethics: a code of behavior that influences the way in which we individually and collectively interact with our environment and other peoples and animals of the earth.

Values: concepts or ideals that give meaning to life and provide a framework for our decisions and actions.

THE NATURE OF ETHICAL PROBLEMS

Because ethical issues consist of diverse values and perspectives, they are extremely complex. Ethical questions arise from all areas of life. The ramifications of the population explosion, euthanasia, genetic engineering, and allocation of resources, for example, are only a few of a whole host of controversial ethical issues. Furthermore, four specific recent developments in our society have dramatically increased ethical awareness: (1) advanced medical technology, (2) greater recognition of patients' rights, (3) malpractice cases and court-ordered treatment, and (4) scarcity of resources.[1] Jonsen reminds us of the element of mystery intertwined with ethics when he states that, no matter how much we know about antibodies, osmolality, immunoglobulins, or any of the other revealed mysteries of the body, mystery remains at the heart of the science of medicine. The patient also participates in the mystery, for the patient knows himself or herself intimately.[2] Naturally then, mystery adds to the element of complexity.

Unfortunately, ethical dilemmas are usually characterized by the fact that there is no right answer. There are often two or more unsatisfactory answers or conflicting responses. In addition, nurses often find that the expectations of employers, physicians, patients, or other nurses themselves are sources of conflict.[3]

Changes in the knowledge that forms the basis of our values are changing the sources of some of our ethical dilemmas. For example, technologies related to computers and communication have affected patient confidentiality. Improved life support technology has been used to keep patients alive against their wishes. Sophisticated technology has the clear disadvantage of being able to reduce persons to objects.[4] Thus, advances in procedures (e.g., organ transplantation, amniocentesis) and equipment (e.g., respirators, dialysis machines) have opened the doors to new possibilities for extending or prolonging life, but they also prompt the critical ethical question, Does the fact that it *can* be done mean that it *should* be done?[5]

MORALS AND PRINCIPLES

Over the past two decades, biomedical ethicists have identified several moral principles. Three primary principles are (1) respect for persons, (2) beneficence, and (3) justice. Sometimes these principles are stated as obligations; sometimes, as rules. Whether primary or secondary, these principles represent obligations to respect the wishes of competent persons, obligations not to harm others, obligations to benefit others, obligations to produce a net balance of benefits over harm, obligations to distribute benefits and harms fairly, obligations to keep promises and contracts, obligations to be truthful, obligations to disclose information, and obligations to respect privacy and to protect confidential information.[6]

Within natural law ethics, the principle of double effect has special importance for nurses. Oftentimes, nurses are involved in actions that have untoward consequences. For example, administering a drug to relieve a cancer patient's pain may shorten that patient's life. In double effect situations, four conditions must be met before an act can be justified:

1. The act itself must be morally good or at least indifferent.
2. The good effect must not be achieved by means of the bad effect.
3. Only the good effect must be intended, although the bad effect is foreseen and known.
4. The good effect intended must be equal to or greater than the bad effect.[7]

Ethics addresses three types of moral problems: moral uncertainty (unsureness about moral principles or rules that may apply, or the nature of the ethical problem itself); moral dilemma (conflict of moral principles that support different courses of action); and moral distress (inability to take the action known to be right because of external constraints). Ethical debate helps to relieve moral uncertainty by clarifying questions and illuminating the ethical features of the situation. Discussion helps to clarify moral dilemmas by revealing general and specific obligations and values.[8] Milner is concerned that nurses use principles and theory to deal with issues of relationships as well as health care concerns. Moral distress may be reduced when we follow principles rather than emotions or feelings in conflicting situations. Basic ethics that involves how we treat each other as human beings is a necessary first step before we can appropriately deal with broader issues.[9]

TRADITIONAL ETHICAL THEORIES

Many nurse clinicians turn away in frustration when confronted with the details of ethical theories. Perhaps this is because it has been difficult in the past to see how these historical philosophical theories relate to contemporary clinical situations. In order to make these theories meaningful to the work setting, it is helpful to think of situations in which they may apply to current clinical practice.

A number of ethical theories have played a role in Western civilization and have laid the foundation for the development of modern ethics. Aristotelian theory is based on the individual's manifesting specific virtues and developing his or her own character. Aristotle (384–322 B.C.) believed that an individual who practices the virtues of courage, temperance, integrity, justice, honesty, and truthfulness will know almost intuitively what to do in a particular situation or conflict.[10] The system of Emmanuel

Kant (1724–1804) formulated the historical Christian idea of the Golden Rule. "So act in such a way as your act becomes a universal for all mankind."[11] Kant was very much concerned with the "personhood" of human beings and "persons" as moral agents.

Other theories that are helpful in understanding a holistic approach to ethics include the consequentialism theory of Jeremy Bentham (1748–1832) and John Stuart Mill (1806–1873), the natural rights theory of John Locke (1632–1714), and the contractarian theory of Thomas Hobbes (1588–1679). Briefly stated, the consequentialist or utilitarian view of Bentham and Mill is that the consequences of our actions are the primary concern, the means justify the ends, and every human being has a personal concept of good and bad. The natural rights theory of Locke was the forerunner of the U.S. Declaration of Independence, as it included the tenet that individuals have inalienable rights and that other individuals have an obligation to respect those rights. The contractarian theory of Hobbes contends that all morality involves a social contract indicating what we can and cannot do.[12]

Another way of viewing ethics is in terms of the two traditional forms: the deontologic (from a Greek root meaning knowledge of that which is binding and proper) style and the teleologic (from a Greek root meaning knowledge of the ends) style. The former assigns duty or obligation based on the intrinsic aspects of an act rather than its outcome; action is morally defensible on the basis of its intrinsic nature. The latter assigns duty or obligation based on the consequences of the act; action is morally defensible on the basis of its extrinsic value or outcome.

DEVELOPMENT OF HOLISTIC ETHICS

The holistic view of reality reopens vistas of thought that were dominant in the pretechnologic era, times when people were generally closer to their environment and the earth. The allure of new science and technology sidetracked many of us into primarily linear, rational, unidirectional thought. Furthermore, while technology has provided us with conveniences and easy solutions, it has also contributed to our tendency to objectify our universe.

Holistic ethics is a philosophy that couples both reemerging and rapidly evolving concepts of holism and ethics. It involves a basic underlying concept of the unity and integral wholeness of all people and of all nature that is identified and pursued by finding unity and wholeness within the self and within humanity. Within the framework of holistic ethics, acts are not performed for the sake of law, precedent, or social norms, but rather from a desire to do good freely in order to witness, identify, and contribute to unity of the self and of the universe of which the individual is a part. Encompassing traditional ethical views, the holistic view is characterized by the Eastern monad in the yin-yang mode and the Western concept of masculine and feminine. Holistic ethics is not grounded or judged in the act performed or in the distant consequences of the act, but rather in the conscious evolution of an enlightened individual of raised consciousness who performs the act. The primary concern is the effect of the act on the involved individual and his or her larger self.[13]

Presuppositions

Ethics is the study of the paths of practical wisdom. It is concerned with judgments of goodness and badness, rightness and wrongness based on a philosophic view of the nature of the universe. All ethical theories have presuppositions. The following are some of the presuppositions of holistic ethics:

- There is a Being or Spirit who is actively involved with humanity and with the universe and in whose image we are created.
- There is a divine plan. Although modeled on it, the material universe is but an infinitesimal part of the overall plan.
- The Spirit is active in the inner life of individuals.
- Persons (personalities) have a dual existence. One existence is on a material plane (body, mind, and spirit), and another is on the divine plane (soul).
- Humankind has a purpose or task—the evolution of itself and the universe into a more perfect image of its Creator.
- The concept of unity is the key to the path of critical wisdom.
- The matter of which our entire universe (body, mind, and spirit) is comprised is subject to dynamic development under the influence of dialectic laws. These principles operate on a psychologic, as well as a physical, plane.
- The Spirit is operative in the universe. This cosmic view embraces two paths. The first is the scientific or phenomenologic path, which has as its by-product holistic ethics, and the other approach is the theologic path. The two paths intersect at a point called Omega, the apex both of the scientific and of the religious view of nature. According to this concept of time and space, Omega is not only present in the universe, but also represents a different, much larger reality. The symbol of Omega transcends matter.

- There is purposefulness in the universe. All occurrences—the entire range from good to bad, from complex to simple—are in some way part of the divine plan. There is purpose and reason, although oftentimes consciously incomprehensible, for things that happen.[14]

Holistic ethics originates in the individual's own character and in the individual's relationship to the universe. In some way, the universe is present totally in each individual; paradoxically, the person is just a small part of that same universe. Gregorios believes that wisdom is a condition in which the self and the world are in communion with each other within the larger communion with Being in its integrity.[15] A holistic view takes into account the relationship of unity of all being. Albert Einstein, in the course of a serious illness, was asked if he feared death. He replied, "I feel such a sense of solidarity with all living things that it does not matter to me where the individual begins and ends."[16]

An *a priori* belief for a holistic person is probably, I believe in being, or even more simply, I am. In this belief system, no act, principle, or person is independent, but all are interrelated; all are "I." Each and every action is a moral action, either contributing to the unity of being or diminishing it. It is the enlightened and totally expanded "I" that creates a holistic view of ethics.

Moral acts may be judged not solely in terms of their intrinsic nature nor solely in terms of their ends, but in both ways. The act may affect the nature of the person performing the act (the "I") and his or her relationships, as well as the object of the act and the object's relationships. In addition, it can be helpful to explore the relationship of the act to the present and future of humanity. Through use of this construct, holistic ethics is both deontologic and teleologic. Holistic ethics is specifically teleologic in questioning the meaning and quality of life.

As a philosophic design for living, holistic ethics is a system for the individual. It appeals to our emotions, senses, aesthetic appreciation, and the inner self as revealed by meditative techniques. Such techniques may be active (e.g., the body movements of Tai Chi or jogging), passive (e.g., sitting meditative posture), or traditional prayer.

The educative process of holistic ethics is not a matter of memorizing facts or historical perspectives, but is instead a process of developing an attitude of awareness of the sacredness of ourselves and all of nature. It is a process in which there is an expanded view that, for both internal and external transformation, our inner self and the collective greater self have stewardship not only over our bodies, minds, and spirits, but also over our planet and the total universe.[17]

Based upon this emergent ethical theory, the American Holistic Nurses' Association has developed a position statement on holistic nursing ethics (Exhibit 6–1).

Holistic Ethics and Consciousness

The underlying principle in a holistic ethical view is being, and its corollary is consciousness. Being and consciousness can be further defined as having their origin in the spirit.[18] Not only is consciousness accepted in our system as the product of an evolutionary process, but also it is believed to become operative through the effect of the spirit. Our personal will becomes the motivator for continued evolution. In the holistic concept of ethics, moral decisions affect both the spirit of humankind as a whole and our own individual spirits.[19] As each of us evolves our own individual consciousness, we assess and direct the evolution of the consciousness of our species and contemplatively examine our relationship with the universal being.

Holistic ethics is not grounded or judged either in the act performed or in the distant consequences of the act, but rather in the conscious evolution of an enlightened individual who performs the act. The primary concern is the effect of the act on the individual and his or her larger self (that unity of which the individual is a part). Unethical acts are those that degrade or brutalize the individual who performs the act and detract from his or her conscious evolution. The effect of an unethical act is to make us aware of the deprivation of divinity within humanity and of humanity itself. The unethical act dissolves the unity of matter and takes away wholeness. Acts must be judged in this setting to determine whether they promote wholeness and integration of either an individual or the collective whole.[20]

Clearly, it is within the emergence of consciousness that the evolution of ethical action begins. Anthropologist Richard Leakey thinks that consciousness supplied primitive human beings with their first capacity for empathy. For example, when the early human recognized that a particular action would injure the self, that human inferred that a particular action would cause injury to another person (another self). Leakey contends that the mechanism of consciousness (i.e., recognition of self) provided the rudiments of a kind of Golden Rule: "Do not do unto others what you would not have done unto you."[21]

Seshachar describes three levels of consciousness:

1. knowledge and awareness of the external world by exoceptors (e.g., organs of sight, hearing).

Exhibit 6–1 American Holistic Nurses' Association Position Statement on Holistic Nursing Ethics

Code of Ethics for Holistic Nurses

We believe that the fundamental responsibilities of the nurse are to promote health, facilitate healing and alleviate suffering. The need for nursing is universal. Inherent in nursing is the respect for life, dignity and right of all persons. Nursing care is given in a context mindful of the holistic nature of humans, understanding the body-mind-spirit. Nursing care is unrestricted by considerations of nationality, race, creed, color, age, sex, sexual preference, politics or social status. Given that nurses practice in culturally diverse settings, professional nurses must have an understanding of the cultural background of clients in order to provide culturally appropriate interventions.

Nurses render services to clients who can be individuals, families, groups or communities. The client is an active participant in health care and should be included in all nursing care planning decisions.

In order to provide services to others, each nurse has a responsibility toward him/herself. In addition, nurses have defined responsibilities towards the client, co-workers, nursing practice, the profession of nursing, society and the environment.

Nurses and Self

The nurse has a responsibility to model health behaviors. Holistic nurses strive to achieve harmony in their own lives and assist others striving to do the same.

Nurses and the Client

The nurse's primary responsibility is to the client needing nursing care. The nurse strives to see the client as a whole, and provides care which is professionally appropriate and culturally consonant. The nurse holds in confidence all information obtained in professional practice, and uses professional judgment in disclosing such information. The nurse enters into a relationship with the client that is guided by mutual respect and a desire for growth and development.

Nurses and Co-Workers

The nurse maintains cooperative relationships with co-workers in nursing and other fields. Nurses have a responsibility to nurture each other, and to assist nurses to work as a team in the interest of client care. If a client's care is endangered by a co-worker, the nurse must take appropriate action on behalf of the client.

Nurses and Nursing Practice

The nurse carries personal responsibility for practice and for maintaining continued competence. Nurses have the right to utilize all appropriate nursing interventions, and have the obligation to determine the efficacy and safety of all

continues

Exhibit 6–1 continued

nursing actions. Wherever applicable, nurses utilize research findings in directing practice.

Nurses and the Profession

The nurse plays a role in determining and implementing desirable standards of nursing practice and education. Holistic nurses may assume a leadership position to guide the profession toward holism. Nurses support nursing research and the development of holistically oriented nursing theories. The nurse participates in establishing and maintaining equitable social and economic working conditions in nursing.

Nurses and Society

The nurse, along with other citizens, has responsibility for initiating and supporting actions to meet the health and social needs of the public.

Nurses and the Environment

The nurse strives to manipulate the client's environment to become one of peace, harmony, and nurturance so that healing may take place. The nurse considers the health of the ecosystem in relation to the need for health, safety and peace of all persons.

Source: Reprinted from *Position Statement on Holistic Nursing Ethics* with permission of the American Holistic Nurses' Association, 4101 Lake Boone Trail, Raleigh, NC 27607, phone: (919) 787-5181, FAX: (919) 787-4916.

2. inner sensing, not directly derived from sensory data, but triggered by them (e.g., emotions, intentions, memories, dreams, imagination).
3. knowledge of one's self (other than body) characterized by the ability to recognize the present from the information of the past and to project the future, establishing a continuity in one's lifetime. The belief that there is an "I," a self who does the perceiving, makes possible the creation of aesthetic, ethical, and spiritual values that are unique to persons.[22]

Of these three levels, it is possible that only the first is present in lower animals. In some higher mammals, there may be an element of the second. The absence of language, however, makes it difficult for them to express, to compare, and to evaluate these experiences and for us to make a valid assessment of the extent to which this inner sensing has been developed in animals. There is little doubt that the third level of consciousness is exclusive to human beings. Seshachar continues to explain that a fusion of the totality of impressions and experiences makes the consciousness an attribute unique to humans.

Holistic ethics embraces and strives for the fusion between self and others. In the process, it becomes a cosmic ecology, a flowing with the universal tide of events and a co-creator of celestial harmony. All events and ethical decisions become part of the unfolding of a harmonious order and a realization of potentialities. Even tragic events can be analyzed within this harmonious spectrum with full realization of the fusion of relationships. One's own actions can become courageous, truth-full, being-full, beauty-full, assured, detached, and virtuous.[23]

ANALYSIS OF ETHICAL DILEMMAS

We are all confronted daily with the need to make personal and professional ethical decisions. Some decisions are minor, but others are fraught with long-term multifaceted ramifications. In order to make these decisions appropriately, it is necessary, first, to operate from a set of principles and, second, to have some sort of analytical method to help sort out and classify the elements of the problem. When the cases are institutional and patient care–oriented, Jonsen's well established guidelines for analyzing individual cases in ethics may be helpful.[24] Jonsen divides the case analysis process into four components: (1) medical indications, (2) patient preferences, (3) quality of life, and (4) external socioeconomic factors. Present in every clinical ethical case, these four topics are necessary for a thorough analysis. The holistic approach adds questions of relationships: Who am I? What is my relationship to others? What other factors are contributing to my decisions? Am I wise and courageous enough to perceive and respect others' differences and honor them as I would honor my own beliefs?

Medical Indications

The underlying ethical principle in considering medical indications is beneficence: Be of benefit and do no harm. Discussion should focus on discerning the relationship between the pathophysiology and the diagnostic and therapeutic interventions available to remedy the patient's pathologic condition. Questions to be considered in this component are, "What is the overall goal in this case?" and "What should be the goal in cases such as this one?"[25] For the patient who is terminally ill, for example, there may be discussions about the futility of further treatment.

Patient Preferences

In all interventions, the preferences of the patient are relevant. We must ask the questions, What does the patient want? Does the patient comprehend? Is the patient being coerced? In some cases, we will not know, because the patient is incapable of self-expression. Whenever possible, we must ensure the patient's right to self-determination, based on his or her personal values and evaluation of risks and benefits. It is necessary, however, to be clear about what is realistically feasible before considering the patient's wishes.

In the case of a child, we must ask the questions, Do the parents understand the situation? Do the parents appear to have the best interests of the child at heart? Are the parents in agreement or discord?

Quality of Life

A patient enters a health crisis situation with an actual or potential reduction in quality of life, manifested by the signs and symptoms of the illness. The objective of health care interventions is to improve quality of life. In each case, multiple questions surround quality-of-life issues. What does quality of life mean, in general? In particular? How are others responding to their perceptions of it? What levels of quality impose what obligations on providers? This component may be a difficult component of the analysis of clinical problems, but it is indispensable.

External Socioeconomic Factors

Every case has a patient at its center. The persons and institutions that are affected, positively or negatively, by the decisions made about the patient must be specified as far as possible and the relevance of those impacts assessed. The major impacts are psychologic, emotional, financial, legal, scientific, educational, and religious.

ADVANCE MEDICAL DIRECTIVES

The Patient Self-Determination Act, effective December 1, 1991, requires that all individuals receiving medical care also receive written information about their right to accept or refuse medical or surgical treatment and their right to initiate advance directives, such as living wills and durable power of attorney. Advance medical directives are of two types: treatment directives, often referred to as living wills, and appointment directives, often referred to as power of attorney or health proxies. A living will specifies the medical treatment that a patient wishes to refuse in the event that he or she is terminally ill and cannot make those decisions. A durable power of attorney for health care appoints a proxy, which is usually a relative or trusted friend, to make medical decisions on behalf of the patient if he or she can no longer make such decisions. It has broader applications than a living will and can apply to any illness or injury that could leave the patient incapacitated.

An advance directive applies only if a patient is incapacitated. It may not apply if, in the opinion of two physicians, the patient can make decisions. Individuals can cancel advance directives at any time. An advance directive may be as simple or as complex as necessary. Individuals should give a copy of the advance directive to family members and the physician, and should carry a copy if and when hospital admission is necessary.

As part of patient assessment, a nurse may consider asking the following questions:

1. Have you discussed your end-of-life choices with your family and/or designated surrogate and health care team workers?
2. Do you have basic information about advance medical directives, including living wills and durable power of attorney?
3. Do you wish to initiate an advance medical directive?
4. If you have already prepared an advance medical directive, can you provide it now?

CONCLUSION

Holistic ethics embraces both the traditional and the masculine-feminine historical perspectives, but transcends both by taking into account the unity of being. The holistic view of human beings is one of self-actualization, as it places the highest value on the development of the individual to attain higher levels of human awareness and, thus, advances the whole of humanity. Within this framework, a unique moral viewpoint takes its origin. The cybernetic relationship of an act to the universal "I" becomes the new categorical imperative of the holistic person. Evolution and consciousness should be directed toward positive ends. It should be directed toward the "good" of people perceived by a contemplation of the reality of being. The process begins with the individual and his or her own self-realization within a universal context. It is the development of total personality where consciousness shines through with self-luminosity.[26] The best utilization of this theory is to internalize these principles and begin to apply them practically within our own settings.

Many hospitals are developing ethics committees, and soon there may be legislation requiring the participation of these committees in decision-making processes. Ethically knowledgeable nurses are poised to become active participants in ethics committees and decision-making discussions. When those opportunities arise, nurses can begin to articulate a holistic approach that supports the very essence of a comprehensive world ethical view.

DIRECTIONS FOR FUTURE RESEARCH

1. Determine how and where the new theory of holistic ethics fits into the continuum of emerging ethical theories.
2. Develop a process of clinical case analysis based on the process of holistic ethics.
3. Examine specific clinical situations through a process of holistic ethics.
4. Analyze the application of holistic ethics to planetary ethical issues.

NURSE HEALER REFLECTIONS

After reading this chapter, the nurse healer will be able to answer or begin a process of answering the following questions:

- What new insights do I have about the process of ethics?
- How does ethics fit into my clinical practice?
- Do I have the interest and beginning ability to become involved in an institutional ethics committee?
- What role does ethics play in my day-to-day personal life?
- Am I ready to look at planetary issues from a holistic ethical perspective?

NOTES

1. F. Hendrickson and G.L. Deloughery, Ethical Influences on Nursing, in *Issues and Trends in Nursing*, ed. G.L. Deloughery (St. Louis: C.V. Mosby, 1991), 180.
2. A. Jonsen, *The New Medicine and the Old Ethics* (Cambridge, MA: Harvard University Press, 1990), 138.

3. M. Corley and D. Raines, An Ethical Practice Environment as a Caring Environment, *Nursing Administration Quarterly* 17, no. 2 (1993):68–74.
4. Ibid.
5. Hendrickson and Deloughery, Ethical Influences on Nursing.
6. R.M. Veatch, ed. *Medical Ethics* (Boston: Jones & Bartlett, 1989).
7. Hendrickson and Deloughery, Ethical Influences on Nursing, 187.
8. M. Fowler, Ethical Decision Making in Clinical Practice, *Nursing Clinics of North America* 24, no. 4 (1989):955–965.
9. S. Milner, An Ethical Practice Model, *JONA* 23, no. 3 (1993):22–25.
10. H. Sidgwick, *Ethics* (Boston: Beacon Press, 1960), 59–63.
11. Ibid., 273.
12. Ibid., 163–169.
13. L. Keegan and G. Keegan, A Concept of Holistic Ethics for the Health Professional, *Journal of Holistic Nursing* 10, no. 3 (1992):205–217.
14. L. Keegan and G. Keegan, *Holistic Ethics*, unpublished manuscript, 1994.
15. P.M. Gregorios, *Science for Sane Societies* (New York: Paragon House, 1987).
16. M. Born, *Born-Einstein Letters* (New York: Walker, 1971).
17. Keegan and Keegan, Concept of Holistic Ethics.
18. L. Keegan and G. Keegan, Spirituality and the Technological Crisis, *Healing Currents* 11, no. 2 (1987):26–28.
19. D. Singh, The Psychology of Consciousness, in *The Evolution of Consciousness*, ed. K. Gandi (New York: Paragon House, 1983), 68–86.
20. Keegan and Keegan, Concept of Holistic Ethics.
21. Singh, The Psychology of Consciousness.
22. B.R. Seshachar, Biological Foundations of Human Evolution and Consciousness, in *The Evolution of Consciousness*, ed. K. Gandi (New York: Paragon House, 1983), 28.
23. Keegan and Keegan, Concept of Holistic Ethics.
24. A.R. Jonsen, Case Analysis in Clinical Ethics, *Journal of Clinical Ethics* 1, no. 1 (1990):63–65.
25. S.E. Shannon, Living Your Ethics, in *Critical Care: Body-Mind-Spirit*, ed. B. Dossey et al. (Philadelphia: J.B. Lippincott, 1992), 135–141.
26. Seshachar, Biological Foundations.

VISION OF HEALING

Human Care

The human care process between a nurse and another individual is a special, delicate gift to be cherished. The human care transactions make it possible for two individuals to come together and establish contact; one person's body-mind-spirit joins another's body-mind-spirit in a lived moment. The shared moment of the present has the potential to transcend time, space, and the physical world as we generally view it in the traditional nurse-client relationship.[1(p.47)]

* * *

We nurses now find ourselves within a profession that ascribes to the holistic model. Because this model differs philosophically from the traditional biomedical model, it has been called a paradigm shift. Such a philosophic shift has monumental implications that are certain to change the profession forever. Not only does this paradigm make us realize that treating pathophysiologic problems with medical therapy is only half the answer but also it weaves a tapestry of the interconnectedness of all human beings and suggests the presence of an undefined and powerful healing energy that remains to be harnessed. It challenges us to entertain new ideas that may conflict with our logic and science. It forces us to move away from a purely mechanistic view of the way in which human beings function.

Fashioning a new portrait of ourselves and our profession, this new paradigm alters the image of who we are and who we can become. It is also destined to alter the way in which we practice nursing. The challenge is to determine the course of this destiny. The boundaries within which we can assist patients to achieve wellness and help them to realize their own healing potential remain to be defined. Nonetheless, as we help patients facilitate their inner healing, we discover our own—and begin our journey as nurse healers. Each of us, however, must discover the path.[2]

NOTES

1. J. Watson, *Nursing: Human Science and Human Care* (New York: National League for Nursing Press, 1985), 47.
2. C.E. Guzzetta and B.M. Dossey, *Cardiovascular Nursing: Holistic Practice* (St. Louis: Mosby-Year Book, 1992), xvii.

Chapter 7

Holistic Approach to the Nursing Process

Cathie E. Guzzetta

NURSE HEALER OBJECTIVES

Theoretical

- Define the term *nursing process*.
- Outline the steps of the nursing process.
- Discuss the ways in which conceptual models of nursing guide the nursing process.
- Discuss the ways in which standards of care are incorporated into the nursing process.

Clinical

- Analyze the assessment tool that you are using in clinical practice to determine whether the tool is consistent with a holistic nursing point of view.
- Determine whether you are using Taxonomy I for the classification of accepted nursing diagnoses.
- Incorporate wellness diagnoses into your practice.
- Follow the Standards of Holistic Nursing in your practice.

Personal

- Develop and trust your intuitive thinking processes when assessing clients' conditions.
- Evaluate the impact of intuitive thinking in both your professional and personal life.

- Explore your own beliefs and values regarding the concepts of holistic nursing.
- Write down specific examples of holistic nursing at each step of the nursing process.

DEFINITIONS

Intuition: immediately knowing about something without consciously using reason.
Nursing Diagnosis: a clinical judgment about the individual, family, or community responses to actual and potential health problems/life processes.
Nursing Process: steps used to fulfill the purposes of nursing, such as assessment, diagnosis, client outcomes, plans, intervention, and evaluation.
Paradigm: a model for conceptualizing information.
Standards of Care: criteria developed to define and establish the scope of nursing practice.
Taxonomy I: a classification schema for the organization of the accepted list of nursing diagnoses based on the nine human response patterns of the Unitary Person framework.
Unitary Person Framework: a framework created by the North American Nursing Diagnosis Association to guide the identification and development of nursing diagnoses.

NURSING PROCESS

Today, the nursing process has been incorporated into academic and clinical settings throughout the United States. It ensures quality nursing care to maintain the client's health, maximize the client's resources, or return the client to a state of health. The nursing process includes six steps: (1) client assessment, (2) nursing diagnoses, (3) client outcomes, (4) therapeutic care planning, (5) implementation of care, and (6) evaluation. Although each step of the nursing process can be isolated as a distinct component for the purposes of discussion, the nursing process itself is an ongoing, orderly, systematic, and flexible set of actions that cannot be separated in practice.

The nursing process is a client-centered process guided by a holistic framework. For years, leaders of the nursing profession have recommended that a conceptual model of nursing guide the steps of the nursing process.[1] Information relevant to the client's care is gathered according to the theoretical model. Client problems, outcomes, and nursing actions are derived from the theory. Client care is then evaluated and documented in the language of the theory (see Chapter 1, Appendix 1–A, Standards of Holistic Nursing). There are many conceptual models of nursing, such as Roy's adaptation model,[2] Rogers' unitary man model,[3] King's systems model,[4] Orem's self-care model,[5] Watson's human care model,[6] and Newman's health as expanding consciousness model.[7] As nurses become more familiar with these models and test them in clinical practice, they tend to choose a model for their own practice that is realistic, useful, and consistent with their professional values and philosophy of nursing.

The Unitary Person framework, developed by the North American Nursing Diagnosis Association (NANDA),[8] focuses on a person as an open system who interacts with the environment. Within this framework, each person has a unique organization that is manifested by nine human response patterns.

1. **Exchanging:** a human response pattern involving mutual giving and receiving
2. **Communicating:** a human response pattern involving sending messages
3. **Relating:** a human response pattern involving establishing bonds
4. **Valuing:** a human response pattern involving the assigning of relative worth
5. **Choosing:** a human response pattern involving the selection of alternatives
6. **Moving:** a human response pattern involving activity
7. **Perceiving:** a human response pattern involving the reception of information
8. **Knowing:** a human response pattern involving the meaning associated with information
9. **Feeling:** a human response pattern involving subjective awareness of information[9]

These patterns are believed to reflect all parts of the whole person and to indicate the person's state of health. Taxonomy I organizes all NANDA-approved nursing diagnoses according to these nine human response patterns (Exhibit 7–1).[10]

Exhibit 7-1 Taxonomy I—Revised (1992)

Taxonomy I—Revised (1992) includes the nursing diagnoses accepted for clinical testing and use at the tenth conference. The bracketed items and blank spaces found within the Taxonomy represent areas that are yet to be named, described, or voted on.

Approved nursing diagnoses are placed by the Taxonomy Committee based on the following considerations:

1. Level of abstraction
2. Consistency with current theoretic views in nursing
3. Consistency with basic definitions within each pattern area

The order of numbers within a level is determined by the order in which the diagnoses were received, not by priority or importance.

1. Exchanging
  1.1 Altered nutrition
    1.1.1
    1.1.2 [Systemic]
      1.1.2.1 More than body requirements
      1.1.2.2 Less than body requirements
      1.1.2.3 Potential for more than body requirements
  1.2 [Altered physical regulation]
    1.2.1 [Immunologic]
      1.2.1.1 High risk for infection
    1.2.2 [Temperature]
      1.2.2.1 High risk for altered body temperature
      1.2.2.2 Hypothermia
      1.2.2.3 Hyperthermia
      1.2.2.4 Ineffective thermoregulation
    1.2.3 [Neurologic]
      1.2.3.1 Dysreflexia
  1.3 Altered elimination
    1.3.1 Bowel
      1.3.1.1 Constipation
        1.3.1.1.1 Perceived
        1.3.1.1.2 Colonic
      1.3.1.2 Diarrhea
      1.3.1.3 Bowel incontinence
    1.3.2 Urinary
      1.3.2.1 Incontinence
        1.3.2.1.1 Stress
        1.3.2.1.2 Reflex
        1.3.2.1.3 Urge
        1.3.2.1.4 Functional
        1.3.2.1.5 Total
      1.3.2.2 Retention

continues

Exhibit 7–1 continued

- 1.4 [Altered circulation]
  - 1.4.1 [Vascular]
    - 1.4.1.1 Tissue perfusion
      - 1.4.1.1.1 Renal
      - 1.4.1.1.2 Cerebral
      - 1.4.1.1.3 Cardiopulmonary
      - 1.4.1.1.4 Gastrointestinal
      - 1.4.1.1.5 Peripheral
    - 1.4.1.2 Fluid volume
      - 1.4.1.2.1 Excess
      - 1.4.1.2.2 Deficit
        - 1.4.1.2.2.1 Actual (1) Actual (2)
        - 1.4.1.2.2.2 High risk for
  - 1.4.2 [Cardiac]
    - 1.4.2.1 Decreased cardiac output
- 1.5 [Altered oxygenation]
  - 1.5.1 [Respiration]
    - 1.5.1.1 Impaired gas exchange
    - 1.5.1.2 Ineffective airway clearance
    - 1.5.1.3 Ineffective breathing pattern
      - 1.5.1.3.1 Inability to sustain spontaneous ventilation
      - 1.5.1.3.2 Dysfunctional ventilatory weaning response
- 1.6 [Altered physical integrity]
  - 1.6.1 High risk for injury
    - 1.6.1.1 High risk for suffocation
    - 1.6.1.2 High risk for poisoning
    - 1.6.1.3 High risk for trauma
    - 1.6.1.4 High risk for aspiration
    - 1.6.1.5 High risk for disuse syndrome
  - 1.6.2 Altered protection
    - 1.6.2.1 Impaired tissue integrity
      - 1.6.2.1.1 Oral mucous membranes
      - 1.6.2.1.2 Skin integrity
        - 1.6.2.1.2.1 Actual
        - 1.6.2.1.2.2 High risk for impaired

2. Communication
   - 2.1 Altered communication
     - 2.1.1 Verbal
       - 2.1.1.1 Impaired
3. Relating
   - 3.1 [Altered socialization]
     - 3.1.1 Impaired social interaction
     - 3.1.2 Social isolation
   - 3.2 [Altered role]
     - 3.2.1 Altered role performance

continues

Exhibit 7–1 continued

3.2.1.1 Parenting
3.2.1.1.1 Actual
3.2.1.1.2 High risk for
3.2.1.2 Sexual
3.2.1.2.1 Dysfunction
3.2.2 Altered family processes
3.2.2.1 Caregiver role strain
3.2.2.2 High risk for caregiver role strain
3.2.3 [Altered role conflict]
3.2.3.1 Parental role conflict
3.3 Altered sexuality patterns
4. Valuing
4.1 [Altered spiritual state]
4.1.1 Spiritual distress
5. Choosing
5.1 Altered coping
5.1.1 Individual coping
5.1.1.1 Ineffective
5.1.1.1.1 Impaired adjustment
5.1.1.1.2 Defensive coping
5.1.1.1.3 Ineffective denial
5.1.2 Family coping
5.1.2.1 Ineffective
5.1.2.1.1 Disabled
5.1.2.1.2 Compromised
5.1.2.2 Potential for growth
5.2 [Altered participation]
5.2.1 Ineffective management of therapeutic regimen (Individuals)
5.2.1.1 Noncompliance
5.3 [Altered judgment]
5.3.1 [Individual]
5.3.1.1 Decisional conflict (specify)
5.4 Health seeking behaviors (specify)
6. Moving
6.1 [Altered activity]
6.1.1 Physical mobility
6.1.1.1 Impaired
6.1.1.1.1 High risk for peripheral neurovascular dysfunction
6.1.1.2 Activity intolerance
6.1.1.2.1 Fatigue
6.1.1.3 High risk for activity intolerance
6.2 [Altered rest]
6.2.1 Sleep pattern disturbance
6.3 [Altered recreation]
6.3.1 Diversional activity
6.3.1.1 Deficit

continues

Exhibit 7–1 continued

6.4 [Altered ADL]
  6.4.1 Home maintenance management
    6.4.1.1 Impaired
  6.4.2 Altered health maintenance
6.5 Self-care deficit
  6.5.1 Feeding
    6.5.1.1 Impaired swallowing
    6.5.1.2 Ineffective breastfeeding
      6.5.1.2.1 Interrupted breastfeeding
    6.5.1.3 Effective breastfeeding
    6.5.1.4 Ineffective infant feeding pattern
  6.5.2 Bathing/hygiene
  6.5.3 Dressing/grooming
  6.5.4 Toileting
6.6 Altered growth and development
6.7 Relocation stress syndrome
7. Perceiving
  7.1 Altered self-concept
    7.1.1 Body image disturbance
    7.1.2 Self-esteem disturbance
      7.1.2.1 Chronic low self-esteem
      7.1.2.2 Situational low self-esteem
    7.1.3 Personal identity disturbance
  7.2 Altered sensory/perception
    7.2.1 Visual
      7.2.1.1 Unilateral neglect
    7.2.2 Auditory
    7.2.3 Kinesthetic
    7.2.4 Gustatory
    7.2.5 Tactile
    7.2.6 Olfactory
  7.3 [Altered meaningfulness]
    7.3.1 Hopelessness
    7.3.2 Powerlessness
8. Knowing
  8.1 [Altered knowing]
    8.1.1 Knowledge deficit (specify)
  8.2 [xxxxxxxxx]
  8.3 Altered thought processes
9. Feeling
  9.1 Altered comfort
    9.1.1 Pain
      9.1.1.1 Chronic
  9.2 [Altered emotional integrity]
    9.2.1 Grieving
      9.2.1.1 Dysfunctional

continues

Exhibit 7-1 continued

9.2.1.2 Anticipatory
9.2.2 High risk for violence: self-directed or directed at others
9.2.2.1 High risk for self-mutilation
9.2.3 Post-trauma response
9.2.3.1 Rape-trauma syndrome
9.2.3.1.1 Compound reaction
9.2.3.1.2 Silent reaction
9.3 [Altered emotional state]
9.3.1 Anxiety
9.3.2 Fear

Source: North American Nursing Diagnosis Association (1992). *NANDA Nursing Diagnoses: Definitions and Classification 1992–1993.* Philadelphia: NANDA.

Holistic Assessment

An ongoing process, assessment is used to evaluate changes that occur over time. With each client encounter, we incorporate new information that helps to explain interrelationships and validates previously collected data and conclusions. All isolated data are important, but the key to a holistic assessment is to discover the overall pattern of the responses.

At the core of assessment is the nurse-client relationship, which involves an omnidirectional flow of information. In order to be open to this information flow, we must not permit our personal beliefs and prejudices to limit our awareness. Rigidity in our beliefs introduces a barrier to the flow of information and can separate us from our clients. As we transcend beliefs and prejudices, we view the world perceptively and learn to listen with focused intention.

A holistic assessment evaluates the client's total state of being.[11] Assessment of the client's bio-psycho-social-spiritual patterns reveals an overall pattern of interrelationships. Changes in the relationships between and among human response patterns are not isolated events. Viewed within a holistic framework, human response patterns represent the integrated, whole person. Changes in one response pattern always influence changes in other dimensions.

Holistic Nursing Assessment Tool

In a holistic nursing assessment, it is critical that the appropriate data be collected and evaluated. A holistic nursing assessment tool has been developed for use with hospitalized patients to help nurses identify the signs and symptoms that they need to formulate nursing diagnoses (Appendix 7–A). It also can be adapted for use with clients in a wellness or health care clinic setting (Appendix 7–B). Based on the nine human response patterns, it was created so that all parts of the whole person could be assessed.[12] The nine response patterns were rearranged and became the skeleton of the tool.[13] We added the term "transcending" to the valuing pattern and changed the definition of this pattern to one involving spiritual growth because valuing did not thoroughly reflect the spiritual dimension. Three subcategories of transcending (i.e., meaning and purpose in life, inner strengths, and interconnections) were added to this pattern to elicit the necessary information to assess spirituality. (See spiritual assessment tool in Chapter 1). The Standards of Holistic Nursing were incorporated (see Appendix 1–A).[14] Also, specific assessment parameters (signs and symptoms) related to most nursing diagnoses were added to the appropriate nine human response patterns in the tool.[15]

This holistic nursing assessment tool groups parameters for a particular problem so that the nurse can determine whether a specific nursing diagnosis is appropriate. Subjective data are followed by objective data within each major category of the tool. Summary assessment parameters (e.g., "willingness to comply with future health care regimen" under the choosing pattern) help in the evaluation of each nursing diagnosis.

Relevant nursing diagnoses associated with the data appear in the right-hand column of the assessment tool. The diagnoses in the right-hand column may appear in more than one place. They are intended as a guide to focus thinking and direct more detailed attention to the collection of data relative to a possible problem. This column is not meant to be static or absolute.

When assessing signs and symptoms that suggest a particular diagnosis, the nurse circles that diagnosis in the right-hand column. The circled diagnosis does not confirm the presence of that particular problem, but alerts the nurse to a possible problem or alteration. After completing the assessment, the nurse scans the possible problems in the right-hand column visually, synthesizes the data to determine whether other clusters of signs and symptoms also suggest that the problem is present, and formulates a nursing diagnosis.

The benefits of using the holistic nursing assessment tool are multiple. Because the data measure human response patterns, they are pertinent to nursing diagnoses made from a holistic nursing point of view.[16] Furthermore, because the tool permits evaluation of specific signs and symptoms, it assists the nurse in validating the presence of a particular nursing diagnosis. We have found that, when the tool is used in practice, the data are so rich that nursing diagnoses appear to "fall out" after the assessment.[17] Continued use of this tool in various practice settings will be beneficial in easing problems with nursing diagnoses and in refining the Unitary Person framework.

Intuitive Thinking

Assessing the status of clients holistically involves evaluation of data not only from a rational, analytic, and verbal (or left brain) mode, but also from an intuitive, nonverbal (right brain) mode. Unfortunately, we in nursing have not placed much value on "soft" data that cannot be measured and validated through scientific methods. Intuitive perceptions have been seen as opposing the empirical knowledge base of practice.[18] The idea that only quantifiable data are important in science is changing, however (see Chapter 8). In addition to analysis, scientific exploration is now known to involve a qualitative, yet undefinable, process that scientists use to organize fragmented findings into meaningful wholes.[19] This undefinable process is called intuition, the tacit dimension, which is fundamental to all knowing.[20] It is a process whereby we know more than we can explain.

Intuitive perception allows one to know something immediately without consciously using reason.[21] Clinical intuition has been described as a "process by which we know something about a client which cannot be verbalized or is verbalized poorly or for which the source of the knowledge cannot be determined."[22] It is a "gut feeling" that something is wrong or that we should do something, even if there is no real evidence to support that feeling. Some exciting "hard" data indicate that intuitive processes are indeed a valid means of conscious knowing and are necessary and desirable to quality client care. In a qualitative analysis of the intuitive experiences of 15 neonatal intensive care nurses,[23] intuitive thinking was identified in the most experienced and technically proficient nurses. It was enhanced by the feeling, caring, and loving relationship that developed as the nurses provided ongoing care to a particular infant. Intuitive events appeared to emerge when the nurses were open and receptive to the infant's subtle cues, such as color, activity, movement, tone, and posture. These nurses also were able to relate present perceptions to past experiences. They described a kind of *déjà vu* experience whereby they were, at some level, able to link previously experienced events to the present situation.

A study of the intuitive perceptions of 41 female nurses who worked in several agencies revealed that intuition functions both as a process and a product.[24] The intuitive process involves a nurse-client encounter in which cues, feeling, and past experience become integrated with the current event. The intuitive product is a conclusion in the form of knowing something, doing something, or both. In the majority of intuitive incidents, information emanated from "feeling" cues. As 92 percent of the judgments made on the basis of intuition were subsequently categorized as correct, the intuitive cues were useful in deciding on a particular course of action.

Certain conditions or attributes facilitate intuitive thinking.[25] For example, direct client contact and nursing experience have been shown to be associated with intuitive perceptions.[26] In addition, the nurse must be emotionally able and willing to receive information. Personal and emotional problems reduce receptivity. For example, the nurse's energy level influences his or her readiness to receive, perceive, and interpret information. A nurse whose energy level is low, as in times of illness or stress, is less intuitive. Self-confidence also facilitates intuitive thinking by enabling the nurse to believe in the validity of his or her intuition.

Benner's work has been enormously useful in helping us to understand why the novice nurse can never view the world of nursing from the same perspective as the expert.[27] Her work describes a hierarchy of thinking, judgment, behavior, and experience that clearly differentiates the novice from the expert. Novice nurses cling to rules and checklists to guide their practice and often miss the big picture. Because of the richness of their experience, expert nurses have an intuitive grasp of the situation and are able to focus on the real problem.[28] They are able to recognize patterns, understand the problem, and know instinctively when the situation is urgent and warrants immediate action. Moreover, they are skillful in convincing others to change the treatment plan when necessary. Their practice is patient-driven.[29]

Intuitive thinking does not conflict with analytic reasoning.[30] It is simply another dimension of knowing. There are multiple ways of knowing and assessing the status of clients, and intuition is a desirable component of the nursing process.[31] Benner's work makes it clear that intuitive events occur more often in the expert than in the novice.[32,33] Therefore, our expert nurses need to become mentors who help novice nurses cultivate and develop their intuitive skills.[34]

Although it is not possible to teach feelings directly, it is possible to teach the skills necessary to recognize subjective data and to verbalize feelings, cues, and decisions.[35] Nurse educators and clinicians may use various exercises to enhance intuition. Exercises that open a beginner's awareness to intuitive and spiritual experiences include listening to music, participating in physical exercise and progressive relaxation, writing in a journal, and brainstorming and clustering ideas. Exercises to deepen the intuitive process for more advanced intuitive thinkers include meditation, contemplation of harmonic symbols, directed drawing, guided imagery, and dialogue with the transpersonal self.[36] Educators and clinicians can also cultivate intuitive processes by

- emphasizing the value of intuitive thinking combined with analytic thinking in nursing and continuing education (e.g., by including such content as part of nursing articles, textbooks, and conferences)
- encouraging nurses to use their intuition and senses in combination with analytic, objective thinking when assessing patients and clinical situations
- providing inexperienced nurses with subtle, repeated cue patterns that will assist them in recognizing intuitive information, thereby increasing their confidence about interpreting the cues and acting on their decisions
- encouraging nurses to trust their intuition
- using educational strategies that encourage pattern recognition (e.g., case studies, role playing, interactive videos)
- systematically evaluating the usefulness of the cues in making correct decisions
- sharing intuitive experiences with students and colleagues
- supporting nurses who have experienced intuitive events and encouraging them to review and analyze the process
- creating a climate of openness, curiosity, and the yen to discover[37,38]

Nursing Diagnoses

Problem identification was once viewed as the weak link in the nursing process. Now, however, the nursing diagnostic process has become accepted in clinical and academic settings, as well as in our textbooks, journals, standards of care, and nurse practice acts. Even the definition of nursing from the American Nurses' Association (ANA) Congress for Nursing Practice incorporates the concept; it defines nursing as "the diagnosis and treatment of human responses to actual or potential health problems."[39] Thus, problem identification is now a clear and distinct step of the nursing process.

A nursing diagnosis can be defined as a "clinical judgment about the individual, family, or community responses to actual and potential health problems/life processes. Nursing diagnoses provide the basis for selection of nursing interventions to achieve outcomes for which the nurse is accountable."[40] After nursing diagnoses are identified and prioritized, they become the basis for the remaining steps of the nursing process.

North American Nursing Diagnosis Association

Although problem identification has always been an important function of nursing practice, little effort was made to standardize the terminology used until NANDA was formed. By defining, explaining, classifying, and researching summary statements about health problems related to nursing, NANDA has worked to standardize the labels for client problems, facilitate communication, and encourage research so that specific client/patient outcomes and nursing interventions can be developed for each diagnosis.[41] As clinical practice and scientific research continue to validate it, the nursing diagnosis movement has the potential for enhancing the quality of client care and identifying those problems and activities that are unique to nursing.

Types of Nursing Diagnoses

In addition to arranging all approved nursing diagnoses by the relevant human response patterns of Taxonomy I, NANDA has divided nursing diagnoses into three categories: actual nursing diagnoses, high-risk nursing diagnoses, and wellness nursing diagnoses.[42]

Actual Nursing Diagnoses. The description of an individual's actual health problems is the actual nursing diagnosis. These diagnoses describe human responses to health conditions/life processes in an individual, family, or community. Identified from Taxonomy I, the diagnostic label is a "concise phrase or term which represents a pattern of related cues" that defines the diagnosis in practice.[43] The diagnostic qualifiers outlined in Exhibit 7–2 are used with the diagnostic label; other qualifiers can also be used.

Related factors are those "conditions or circumstances that can cause or contribute to the development/maintenance of the actual diagnosis."[44] Related factors can precede, coexist, or be associated with, contribute to, or abet the problem. They help identify what is maintaining the problem and what is preventing improvement. Related factors guide the plan of care, because they convey what the nurse and the client must change so that the client can achieve a state of health.[45]

Exhibit 7–2 Qualifiers for Diagnostic Labels (Suggested/Not Limited To)

Category 1

- *Actual:* Existing at the present moment; existing in reality.
- *Potential:* Can, but has not as yet, come into being; possible.

Category 2

- *Ineffective:* Not producing the desired effect; not capable of performing satisfactorily.
- *Decreased:* Smaller; lessened; diminished; lesser in size, amount, or degree.
- *Increased:* Greater in size, amount, or degree; larger, enlarged.
- *Impaired:* Made worse, weakened; damaged, reduced; deteriorated.
- *Depleted:* Emptied wholly or partially; exhausted of.
- *Deficient:* Inadequate in amount, quality, or degree; defective; not sufficient; incomplete.
- *Excessive:* Characterized by an amount or quantity that is greater than is necessary, desirable, or usable.
- *Dysfunctional:* Abnormal; impaired or incompletely functioning.
- *Disturbed:* Agitated; interrupted, interfered with.
- *Acute:* Severe but of short duration.
- *Chronic:* Lasting a long time; recurring; habitual; constant.
- *Intermittent:* Stopping and starting again at intervals; periodic; cyclic.
- *Potential for Enhanced Use (with wellness diagnoses):* Made greater, to increase in quality or more desired.

Source: North American Nursing Diagnosis Association (1992). *NANDA Nursing Diagnoses: Definitions and Classification, 1992–1993.* Philadelphia: NANDA.

An actual nursing diagnosis and related factors are connected by the phrase "related to," forming a two-part diagnostic statement.[46] For example,

> Knowledge deficit about acute myocardial infarction (AMI) related to newly diagnosed health problem

The phrase "related to" is preferable to the phrase "caused by" or "due to," because cause and effect have not yet been established for most nursing diagnoses.[47] The diagnostic statement should be specific enough to guide the remaining steps of the nursing process.

Before making a specific nursing diagnosis, the nurse assesses the defining characteristics of the diagnosis. Defining characteristics are those behaviors or signs and symptoms (observable cues and inferences) that cluster together as manifestations of the diagnosis.[48] They are necessary to identify the diagnostic entity and to differentiate between various nursing diagnoses. These characteristics, which should be measurable, can be divided into three categories: (1) critical indicators, (2) major defining characteristics, and (3) minor defining characteristics. A critical indicator must be present before the diagnosis can be made. A major defining characteristic is usually present when the diagnosis exists (i.e., it is present in 80 to 100 percent of the clients who experience the condition). A minor defining characteristic provides supporting evidence for the diagnosis, but may not be present in all clients who experience the condition (i.e., it is present in 50 to 79 percent of clients). Although minor defining characteristics are not always present, they help complete the clinical picture.

Partial lists of defining characteristics have been published to assist nurses in verifying a particular nursing diagnosis.[49–51] After assessing a client's condition and formulating the possible nursing diagnoses, a nurse can refer to the list of defining characteristics to determine if the critical indicators actually were observed to confirm the diagnoses. The list of defining characteristics for many nursing diagnoses is not yet complete, however. For many diagnoses, the defining characteristics have not yet been validated by research; for some diagnoses, the defining characteristics have not even been identified. In the clinical setting, this lack of information can be perplexing. Without the defining characteristics for a particular diagnosis, nurses must use their knowledge, education, and experience to determine if the signs and symptoms observed during the nursing assessment are sufficient to confirm the existence of the actual health problem. If the nurse judges that they are, then the nurse makes the diagnosis.

High-Risk Nursing Diagnoses. As of 1992, all NANDA-approved diagnoses that were designated as "potential" were changed to "high-risk for" diagnoses. A high-risk nursing diagnosis is a diagnosis that "describes human responses to health conditions/life processes which may develop in a vulnerable individual, family, or community. High-risk nursing diagnoses are supported by risk factors that contribute to increased vulnerability."[52] The qualifiers listed in Exhibit 7–2 are also used with the high-risk nursing diagnosis.

High-risk nursing diagnoses are associated with risk factors, "environmental factors and physiologic, psychologic, genetic, or chemical elements that increase the vulnerability of an individual, family, or community to an unhealthful event."[53] The risk factors guide nursing interventions to reduce or prevent the occurrence of the problem. The diagnosis and the risk factors are connected by the phrase "related to" and written as a two-part statement; for example,

> High risk for altered nutrition: less than body requirements related to nausea, vomiting, fatigue, and activity intolerance associated with chemotherapy

Specifically stating which clients are at high risk for a particular problem is essential to providing quality nursing care to prevent or reduce the problem in those who are susceptible to it. Moreover, nursing will be better able to demonstrate and document its contribution to desired client outcomes when problems do not occur in clients at risk because of the quality of nursing care. Also the high-risk category is beneficial in justifying allocation of resources and personnel, as well as in obtaining third-party reimbursement.

Wellness Nursing Diagnoses. The North American Nursing Diagnosis Association defines a wellness nursing diagnosis as a diagnosis "that describes human responses to levels of wellness in an individual, family, or community that have a potential for enhancement to a higher state."[54] The diagnoses listed in Taxonomy I are now used together with the phrase "potential for enhanced" to formulate wellness nursing diagnoses. Such diagnoses are written as one-part statements, such as

> Potential for enhanced adjustment to illness

Wellness and health promotion have become national priorities, and wellness nursing diagnoses broaden our perspective from an illness-dominated framework to one that incorporates a positive, wellness orientation. A distinction must be made between the concepts of illness prevention (or risk reduction), health maintenance, and health promotion, however. Illness prevention or risk reduction involves behaviors aimed at actively protecting against or reducing the chances of encountering disease, illness, or accidents.[55,56] The "high risk for" nursing diagnoses are directed toward prevention. Nursing interventions associated with these diagnoses are actively selected to reduce or prevent the particular problem.[57]

Health maintenance focuses on sustaining a neutral state of health. A nursing diagnosis for clients who are unable to identify, manage, or seek help to maintain health would be altered health maintenance (Exhibit 7–3).[58] For these clients, nursing interventions would include activities not only to prevent illness, but also to protect health (e.g., eating a

Exhibit 7-3 Altered Health Maintenance

DEFINITION

Inability to identify, manage, and/or seek out help to maintain health

DEFINING CHARACTERISTICS

Demonstrated lack of knowledge regarding basic health practices
Demonstrated lack of adaptive behaviors to internal/external environmental changes
Reported or observed inability to take responsibility for meeting basic health practices in any or all functional pattern areas
History of lack of health-seeking behavior
Expressed interest in improving health behaviors
Reported or observed lack of equipment, financial, and/or other resources
Reported or observed impairment of personal support systems

RELATED FACTORS

Lack of, or significant alteration in, communication skills (written, verbal, and/or gestural)
Lack of ability to make deliberate and thoughtful judgments
Perceptual/cognitive impairment (complete/partial lack of gross and/or fine motor skills)
Ineffective individual coping
Dysfunctional grieving
Unachieved developmental tasks
Ineffective family coping
Disabling spiritual distress
Lack of material resources

Source: North American Nursing Diagnosis Association (1992). *NANDA Nursing Diagnoses: Definitions and Classification, 1992–1993.* Philadelphia: NANDA.

balanced diet, stopping smoking, having regular medical examinations, sleeping 6 to 8 hours per night).

Health promotion goes beyond illness prevention or health maintenance. Because it involves a personal responsibility for one's health, individuals strive actively to improve their life style to achieve high-level wellness.[59] The diagnosis of health-seeking behaviors (i.e., health-promoting behaviors) is consistent with the concept of health promotion (Exhibit 7–4). Health-seeking behaviors may include such activities as requesting additional information and recipes to enhance a low-cholesterol, low-fat, low-salt, low-sugar, and high-fiber diet; practicing daily relaxation techniques; and participating in aerobic exercises three to

Exhibit 7–4 Health-Seeking Behaviors (Specify)

DEFINITION

A state in which an individual in stable health is actively seeking ways to alter personal health habits and/or the environment in order to move toward a higher level of health*

DEFINING CHARACTERISTICS

Major

Expressed or observed desire to seek a higher level of wellness

Minor

Expressed or observed desire for increased control of health practice
Expression of concern about current environmental conditions on health status
Stated or observed unfamiliarity with wellness community resources
Demonstrated or observed lack of knowledge in health promotion behaviors

*Stable health status is defined as age-appropriate illness-prevention measures achieved, client reports good or excellent health, and signs and symptoms of disease, if present, are controlled.

Source: North American Nursing Diagnosis Association (1992). *NANDA Nursing Diagnoses: Definitions and Classification, 1992–1993.* Philadelphia: NANDA.

five times per week.[60] The new category of wellness nursing diagnoses using Taxonomy I with the qualifier of "potential for enhanced" also addresses health promotion activities and allows the nurse to focus on wellness, facilitate responsibility for self-care, and promote healthy behaviors.

Client Outcomes

Client outcomes direct the plan of care. After nursing diagnoses have been identified, one or more specific and concisely stated client outcomes are written for each diagnosis. A client outcome is a direct statement of the desired end that the client will reach within a specified time frame. It indicates the maximum level of wellness that is realistically attainable for the client.[61] Outcome criteria describe the specific tools, tests, or observations that will be used to determine whether the client outcome has been achieved. Outcome criteria must be measurable and may fall into the following categories:

- circumstances that should or should not occur in the client's status
- the level at which some change should occur
- the client's verbalizations about what the client knows, understands, or feels about the situation
- specific client behaviors or signs/symptoms that are expected to occur as a result of intervention
- specific client behaviors that are expected to occur as a result of adequate management of the environment[62,63]

If outcomes are to be achieved, they must be established by the client with the assistance of the nurse and family. The client must be motivated and want to change in order to establish healthy patterns of behavior.

Plan of Care

During the planning stage, nurses who use the holistic approach to the nursing process help the client and family to identify ways to repattern their behaviors to achieve a healthier state. The planning process reveals interventions that will achieve client outcomes. The plan is developed in terms of nursing prescriptions, which are the specific actions that the nurse performs to help the client solve problems and accomplish outcomes.[64] Nursing prescriptions direct the implementation of care.

A nursing intervention has been defined as "any direct care treatment that a nurse performs on behalf of a client. The treatments include nurse-initiated treatments resulting from nursing diagnoses, physician-initiated treatments resulting from medical diagnoses, and performance of the daily essential functions for the client who cannot do these."[65] During the planning phase, the nurse should generally choose interventions by

- determining whether the intervention will be useful in helping the client achieve the desired outcome
- determining the characteristics of the nursing diagnosis (i.e., whether the intervention is aimed at the etiology, signs/symptoms, or at potential problems)
- evaluating the research base that validates the effectiveness of the intervention, its clinical significance, and the nursing control associated with the intervention
- determining the feasibility of implementing the intervention in terms of the other diagnoses and their respective priorities, and the cost and time involved with the intervention

- evaluating the acceptability of the intervention to the client in terms of his or her own goals and priorities related to the treatment plan
- ensuring the nursing competency necessary to implement the intervention successfully.[66,67]

Efforts have been under way to develop a classification of nursing interventions that parallels the classification of nursing diagnoses. The Iowa Intervention Project has developed a Nursing Interventions Classification that contains an alphabetic list of 336 interventions.[68] Each intervention is listed with a label, a definition, a set of related activities that describe the behaviors of the nurse who implements the intervention, and a short list of background readings. All direct care interventions that nurses perform for patients, both independent and collaborative interventions, are included. Work is continuing to link nursing diagnoses, interventions, and patient outcomes.

Implementation of Care

Nurses who are guided by a holistic framework approach the implementation phase of care with an awareness that (1) clients are active participants in their care; (2) nursing care must be performed with purposeful, focused intention; and (3) a client's humanness is an important factor in implementation. Within the holistic framework, anything that produces a physiologic change causes a corresponding psycho-social-spiritual alteration. Conversely, anything that produces a psychologic change causes a corresponding physiologic-social-spiritual alteration. Thus, a nurse's encounter with a client, be it for the purpose of talking to the client, touching the client, or taking a blood pressure, produces psychophysiologic outcomes. The encounter changes the consciousness and the physiology of both the nurse and the client. Many nurses go through nursing school without ever learning that human emotions can be translated into physiologic responses. Some never learn that the greatest tool/intervention for helping and healing clients is the therapeutic use of self.[69] So often we touch clients or perform some procedure without any conscious awareness of the enormous impact that the event could have on the client if it were a purposeful, centered activity.

Evaluation of Care

Data about the client's bio-psycho-social-spiritual status and responses are continuously collected and recorded throughout the nursing process. The information is related to the nursing diagnoses, the outcome criteria, and the results of the nursing intervention. The goal of evaluation is to determine if client outcomes have been successful and, if so, to what extent. The nurse, client, family, and other members of the health care team all participate in the evaluation process. Together, they synthesize the data from the evaluation to identify successful repatterning behaviors toward wellness. During the evaluation, clients should become more aware of previous patterns, develop insight into the interconnections of all dimensions of their lives, and see the benefits of repatterning behaviors. For example, does the client understand that his or her current job and level of stress have a direct impact on the current illness state? The evaluation of client outcomes must be continuous because of the dynamic nature of human beings and the frequent changes that occur during illness and health. It may be necessary to develop new client outcomes and revise the plan of care. Factors facilitating effective outcomes or preventing solutions to problems must also be explored.

STANDARDS OF HOLISTIC NURSING

The American Holistic Nurses' Association has developed Standards of Holistic Nursing (see Appendix 1–A).[70] These standards define and establish the scope of holistic nursing practice. They are based on the philosophy that nursing is an art and a science that has as its primary purpose the provision of services to help individuals achieve the wholeness inherent within them. Thus, the concepts of holistic nursing are based on broad and eclectic academic principles. Holistic concepts incorporate a sensitive balance between art and science, intuitive and analytic skills, and the ability and knowledge to choose from a wide variety of interventions to promote balance and interconnectedness of body, mind, and spirit.

By definition, holistic nursing can be practiced by any nurse in any setting. The Standards for Holistic Nursing Practice (Appendix 1–A) provide the criteria by which to measure the quality of holistic nursing care rendered to clients. Because these process standards are based on the universal language of the nursing process, they easily may be combined with other more physiologically based standards, such as those for cardiovascular and critical care nursing. Thus, the Standards for Holistic Nursing Practice could be incorporated into all subspecialty standards of care to ensure not only quality physiologic care, but also quality holistic nursing care to these specialty populations.

CONCLUSION

Standards of holistic nursing can be incorporated into each step of the nursing process. To achieve a holistic assessment, it is essential that the appropriate data are collected to evaluate the client's total state of being. The use of wellness diagnoses broadens our nursing practice to help clients assume responsibility for self-care and healthy behaviors. Client outcomes and interventions are selected to assist the clients in achieving their maximal level of wellness. This chapter provides the basis for understanding the nursing process content found within each chapter in Units IV and V and guides the reader in operationalizing the steps involved in providing holistic nursing care.

DIRECTIONS FOR FUTURE RESEARCH

1. Evaluate the correctness of intuitive judgments in terms of their usefulness in making decisions for a variety of client populations.
2. Evaluate the effectiveness of a program designed to enhance intuitive thinking among nurses (i.e., one that includes examining theory, sharing experiences, reviewing and analyzing intuitive events, participating in focusing exercises, providing repeated cue experiences, providing consultation for recognizing and interpreting cues, and building confidence regarding the value of the experience).
3. Determine whether incorporating Standards of Holistic Nursing into practice positively affects subjective and objective client outcomes.
4. Determine whether incorporating Standards of Holistic Nursing into practice improves nurse work satisfaction and turnover.

NURSE HEALER REFLECTIONS

After reading this chapter, the nurse healer will be able to answer or will begin a process of answering the following questions:

- How am I able to remove my life's prejudices regarding traditional methods of healing during the assessment of my clients' conditions?
- Do I value the significance of intuitive thinking?
- Do I feel confident about my intuitive decisions?
- How can I cultivate my intuitive processes?

- How do I react when clients indicate that they are not motivated to change health patterns and behavior?
- How do I feel when I incorporate the principles of holistic nursing into my nursing practice?

NOTES

1. C.E. Guzzetta et al., Cardiovascular Assessment, in *Cardiovascular Nursing: Holistic Practice*, ed. C.E. Guzzetta and B.M. Dossey (St. Louis: Mosby-Year Book, 1992), 40–41.
2. C. Roy, *Introduction to Nursing: An Adaptation Model* (Englewood Cliffs, NJ: Prentice-Hall, 1976).
3. M. Rogers, *Introduction to the Theoretical Basis of Nursing* (New York: Davis, 1969), 39–121.
4. I. King, *Toward a Theory of Nursing* (Boston: Little, Brown and Co., 1981), 10–106.
5. D. Orem, *Nursing Concepts of Practice* (New York: McGraw-Hill, 1980).
6. J. Watson, *Nursing: Human Science and Human Care* (Norwalk, CT: Appleton-Century-Crofts, 1985), 47.
7. M. Newman, *Health as Expanding Consciousness* (St. Louis: C.V. Mosby, 1986), 107–134.
8. C. Roy, Framework for Classification Systems Development: Progress and Issues, in *Classification of Nursing Diagnoses: Proceedings of the Fifth Conference*, ed. M.J. Kim et al. (St. Louis: C.V. Mosby, 1984), 40–45.
9. Ibid.
10. R.M. Carroll-Johnson and M. Paquette, *Classification of Nursing Diagnoses: Proceedings of the Tenth Conference* (Philadelphia: J.B. Lippincott, 1994), 481–483.
11. B. Dossey et al., Nursing Diagnoses Use and Issues: American Holistic Nurses' Association, in *Classification of Nursing Diagnoses: Proceedings of the Tenth Conference*, ed. R.M. Carroll-Johnson and M. Paquette (Philadelphia: J.B. Lippincott, 1994), 160–166.
12. C.E. Guzzetta et al., *Clinical Assessment Tools for Use with Nursing Diagnoses* (St. Louis: Mosby-Year Book, 1989), 1–40.
13. C.E. Guzzetta et al., Unitary Person Assessment Tool: Easing Problems with Nursing Diagnoses, *Focus on Critical Care* 15(1988):12.
14. American Holistic Nurses' Association, Standards of Holistic Nursing (The Association, 1994).
15. North American Nursing Diagnosis Association, *NANDA Nursing Diagnoses: Definitions and Classification, 1992–1993* (St. Louis: The Association, 1992), 11–77.
16. Guzzetta et al., *Clinical Assessment Tools for Use with Nursing Diagnoses*, 1–40.
17. Ibid.
18. C.E. Young, Intuition and Nursing Process, *Holistic Nursing Practice* 1, no. 3 (1987):54.
19. M. Polanyi, *Personal Knowledge* (New York: Harper & Row, 1958).

20. M. Polanyi, *The Tacit Dimension* (New York: Anchor Press, 1966), 4.
21. B.D. Schraeder and D.K. Fisher, Using Intuitive Knowledge in the Neonatal Intensive Care Nursery, *Holistic Nursing Practice* 1, no. 3 (1987):47.
22. Young, Intuition and Nursing Process, 52.
23. Schraeder and Fisher, Using Intuitive Knowledge in the Neonatal Intensive Care Nursery, 45–51.
24. Young, Intuition and Nursing Process, 52–62.
25. Ibid.
26. Schraeder and Fisher, Using Intuitive Knowledge in the Neonatal Intensive Care Nursery, 45–51.
27. P. Benner, *Novice to Expert: Excellence and Power in Clinical Nursing Practice* (Menlo Park, CA: Addison-Wesley, 1985).
28. L.A. Ruth-Sahd, A Modification of Benner's Hierarchy of Clinical Practice: The Development of Clinical Intuition in the Novice Trauma Nurse, *Holistic Nursing Practice* 7, no. 3 (1993):10.
29. P. Benner et al., From Beginner to Expert: Gaining a Differentiated Clinical World in Critical Care Nursing, *Advances in Nursing Science* 14(1992):13–28.
30. C. Jung, *Psychological Types* (New York: Harcourt Brace, 1959), 78.
31. Benner, *Novice to Expert.*
32. Ruth-Sahd, A Modification of Benner's Hierarchy of Clinical Practice, 10.
33. V.E. Slater, Modern Physics, Synchronicity, and Intuition, *Holistic Nursing Practice* 6, no. 4 (1992):20–25.
34. L. Rew, Intuition: Nursing Knowledge and the Spiritual Dimension of Persons, *Holistic Nursing Practice* 3, no. 3 (1989):60.
35. Young, Intuition and Nursing Process, 61.
36. Rew, Intuition: Nursing Knowledge and the Spiritual Dimension of Persons, 61.
37. Young, Intuition and Nursing Process, 61.
38. Ruth-Sahd, A Modification of Benner's Hierarchy of Clinical Practice, 13.
39. American Nurses' Association Congress for Nursing Practice, *Nursing: A Social Policy Statement* (Kansas City, MO: ANA, 1980).
40. North American Nursing Diagnosis Association, *NANDA Nursing Diagnoses: Definitions and Classification, 1992–1993*, 5.
41. A.M. McLane, *Classification of Nursing Diagnosis: Proceedings of the Third and Fourth National Conferences* (New York: McGraw-Hill, 1982), 340.
42. North American Nursing Diagnosis Association, *NANDA Nursing Diagnoses: Definitions and Classification, 1992–1993*, 83–84.
43. Ibid., 83.
44. Ibid., 84.
45. North American Nursing Diagnosis Association, Taxonomy I: Revised 1990 (St. Louis: The Association, 1990).
46. C.E. Guzzetta and B.M. Dossey, Nursing Diagnoses, in *Cardiovascular Nursing: Holistic Practice*, ed. C.E. Guzzetta and B.M. Dossey (St. Louis: Mosby-Year Book, 1992), 80–97.

47. M.D. Mundinger and G. Jauron, Developing a Nursing Diagnosis, *Nursing Outlook* 23(1975):94.
48. North American Nursing Diagnosis Association, *NANDA Nursing Diagnoses: Definitions and Classification, 1992–1993*, 84.
49. M. Gordon, *Manual of Nursing Diagnoses* (New York: McGraw-Hill, 1987).
50. M.J. Kim et al., *Pocket Guide to Nursing Diagnoses* (St. Louis: C.V. Mosby, 1989).
51. North American Nursing Diagnosis Association, *NANDA Nursing Diagnoses: Definitions and Classification, 1992–1993*, 11–77.
52. Ibid., 84.
53. Ibid.
54. Ibid.
55. C.J. Allen, Incorporating a Wellness Perspective for Nursing Diagnosis in Practice, in *Classification of Nursing Diagnoses: Proceedings of the Eighth Conference*, ed. R.M. Carroll-Johnson (Philadelphia: J.B. Lippincott, 1989), 37–42.
56. N.J. Pender, Languaging a Health Perspective for NANDA Taxonomy on Research and Theory, in *Classification of Nursing Diagnoses: Proceedings of the Eighth Conference*, ed. R.M. Carroll-Johnson (Philadelphia: J.B. Lippincott, 1989), 31–36.
57. G.M. Bulechek and J.C. McCloskey, Nursing Interventions: Treatments for Potential Nursing Diagnoses, in *Classification of Nursing Diagnoses: Proceedings of the Eighth Conference*, ed. R.M. Carroll-Johnson (Philadelphia: J.B. Lippincott, 1989), 23–30.
58. S. Tripp and B. Stachowiak, Nursing Diagnosis: Health Seeking Behaviors (Specify), in *Classification of Nursing Diagnoses: Proceedings of the Eighth Conference*, ed. R.M. Carroll-Johnson (Philadelphia: J.B. Lippincott, 1989), 433–436.
59. Ibid.
60. Guzzetta and Dossey, Nursing Diagnoses, 80–97.
61. C.F. Capers and R. Kelly, Neuman Nursing Process: A Model of Holistic Care, *Holistic Nursing Practice* 1, no. 3 (1987):23.
62. G.M. Bulechek and J.C. McCloskey, Nursing Interventions: What They Are and How To Choose Them, *Holistic Nursing Practice* 1, no. 3 (1987):43.
63. Guzzetta and Dossey, Nursing Diagnoses, 86–87.
64. Ibid.
65. J.C. McCloskey and G.M. Bulechek, Classification of Nursing Interventions: Implications for Nursing Diagnoses, in *Classification of Nursing Diagnoses: Proceedings of the Tenth Conference*, ed. R.M. Carroll-Johnson and M. Paquette (Philadelphia: J.B. Lippincott, 1994), 114.
66. Ibid., 116.
67. Bulechek and McCloskey, Nursing Interventions: What They Are and How To Choose Them, 40.
68. Iowa Intervention Project, *Nursing Interventions Classifications* (St. Louis: Mosby-Year Book, 1992).
69. D. Krieger, *Foundation for Holistic Health Nursing Practice* (Philadelphia: J.B. Lippincott, 1981), 201.
70. American Holistic Nurses' Association, Standards of Holistic Nursing.

Appendix 7-A

Holistic Nursing Assessment Tool for Hospitalized Patients

Name: ______________________ Age: ________ Sex: ________
Address: ______________________ Telephone: ______________
Significant other: ______________________ Telephone: ______________
Date of admission: ____________ Medical diagnosis: ______________
Allergies: ______________________ Dyes: ______________

	Nursing Diagnosis (Altered/High Risk for/ Potential for Enhanced)
Communicating—A pattern involving sending messages	
Read, write, understand English (circle) ____________ Other language ____________ Intubated ____________ Speech impaired ____________ Alternate form of communication ____________	Communication Verbal [Nonverbal]
"Valuing/Transcending"—A pattern involving spiritual growth	
Religious preference ____________ Important religious practices ____________ Cultural orientation ____________ Cultural practices ____________ Meaning and purpose in life ____________ Inner strengths ____________ Interconnections (self, others, universe, higher power) ____________	[Spiritual state] Spiritual Well-being Spiritual distress Hopelessness Powerlessness

Source: From Cathie E. Guzzetta, Shelia D. Bunton, Linda A. Prinkey, Anita P. Sherer, and Patricia C. Seifert, *Clinical Assessment Tools for Use with Nursing Diagnoses* (St. Louis: Mosby-Year Book, 1989): pp. 15–22.

	Nursing Diagnosis (Altered/High Risk for/ Potential for Enhanced)
Relating—A pattern involving establishing bonds	
[Alterations in Role]	
Marital status ______	[Role performance]
Age and health of significant other ______	Parenting
______	Sexuality patterns
Number of children ______ Ages ______	
Responsibilities in home ______	
Financial support ______	Family processes
Occupation ______	
Job satisfaction/concerns ______	
Physical/mental energy expenditures ______	
Sexual relationships (satisfactory/unsatisfactory) ______	
Physical difficulties related to sex ______	
______	
[Alterations in Socialization]	
Quality of relationships with others ______	Impaired social interaction
Patient's description ______	
Significant other's description ______	
Staff observations ______	
Verbalizes feelings of being alone ______	Social isolation
Attributed to ______	
Knowing—A pattern involving the meaning associated with information	
Previous hospitalization/surgeries ______	Knowledge deficit
______	
Educational level ______	
History of the following diseases:	
Heart ______	
Lung ______	
Liver ______ Kidney ______	
Cerebrovascular ______ Rheumatic fever ______	
Thyroid ______	
Diabetes ______	
Medication ______	
Current health problems ______	
______	
Current medications ______	
______	

Risk factors	Present	Knowledge of
1. Hypertension	______	______
2. Hyperlipidemia	______	______
3. Smoking	______	______

			Nursing Diagnosis (Altered/High Risk for/ Potential for Enhanced)
Risk factors	Present	Knowledge of	Knowledge deficit
4. Obesity	______	______	
5. Diabetes	______	______	
6. Sedentary living	______	______	
7. Stress	______	______	
8. Alcohol use	______	______	
9. Oral contraceptives	______	______	
10. Family history ______			

Knowledge of planned test/surgery ______

Misconceptions ______

Readiness to learn ______ — [Learning]

Learning impeded by ______ — Thought processes

Feeling—A pattern involving the subjective awareness of information

Alterations in comfort

Pain/discomfort

Onset ______ Duration ______ — Pain

Location ______ Quality______ Radiation ______ — Chronic

Associated factors ______ — [Acute]

Aggravating factors ______ — [Discomfort]

Alleviating factors ______ — Chronic

Acute

Alterations in emotional integrity

Recent stressful life events ______ — Anxiety

Verbalizes feelings of fear or anxiety ______ — Fear

Source ______

Physical manifestations ______

Moving—A pattern involving activity

[Alterations in activity]

History of physical disability ______ — Impaired physical mobility

Limitations in daily activities ______ — Activity intolerance

Exercise habits ______

[Alterations in rest]

Hours slept/night ______ Difficulties ______ — Sleep pattern disturbance

Sleep aids (pillows, medications, food) ______

[Alterations in recreation]

Leisure activities ______ — Deficit in diversional activity

Social activities ______

	Nursing Diagnosis (Altered/High Risk for/ Potential for Enhanced)
[Alterations in activities of daily living]	
Home maintenance management ________	Impaired home maintenance management
Size and arrangement of home (stairs, bathroom) ________________ ________________	
Housekeeping responsibilities ________	
Shopping responsibilities ________	
Health maintenance	
Health insurance ________	Health maintenance
Regular physical check-ups ________	
Alterations in self-care	Self-care
Ability to perform ADL:	Feeding
Independent ______ Dependent ______	Bathing
Specify deficits ________	Dressing
Discharge planning needs ________	Toileting
Perceiving—A pattern involving the reception of information	
Alterations in self-concept	
Patient's description of himself/herself ________	Body image
Effects of illness/surgery on self-concept ________ ________________	Self-esteem Personal identity
Sensory/perceptual alterations	
Vision impaired ______ Glasses ______	Visual
Visual examination ________	
Auditory impaired ______ Hearing aid ______	Auditory
Auditory examination ________	
Kinesthetics impaired______ Romberg ______	Kinesthetic
Gustatory impaired ________	Gustatory
Tactile impaired______ Examination ______	Tactile
Olfactory impaired______ Examination ______	Olfactory
Reflexes: Biceps R ____ L ____ Triceps R ____ L ____	Reflexes
Brachio-radialis R ____ L ____ Knee R ____ L ____	
Ankle R ____ L ____ Plantar R ____ L ____	
Exchanging—A pattern involving mutual giving and receiving	
Alterations in nutrition	
Teeth, gums, lesions ________	Oral mucous membrane
Dentures ________	
Ideal body weight ________	More than body requirements
Height ________ Weight ______	
Eating patterns	
Number of meals per day ________	
Special diet ________	Less than body requirements
Where eaten ________	
Food preferences/intolerances ________	

Nursing Diagnosis
(Altered/High Risk for/ Potential for Enhanced)

Food allergies ______
Caffeine intake (coffee, tea, soft drinks)
______
Appetite changes ______
Presence of nausea/vomiting ______
Current therapy
NPO ______ NG suction ______
Tube feeding ______
TPN ______
Laboratory results
Na ____ K ____ Cl ____ Glucose ______
Cholesterol ______ Triglycerides ______ Fasting ____

[Alterations in physical regulation]
[Immune]
Lymph nodes enlarged______ Location______ — Infection
WBC count ______ Differential______ — Hypothermia
Alteration in body temperature — Hyperthermia
Temperature______ Route______ — Ineffective thermoregulation

[Alterations in physical integrity]
Skin integrity ____ Rashes ______ Lesions ______ — Impaired skin integrity
Petechiae______ Surgical incision ______ — Impaired tissue integrity
Bruising______ Abrasions ______

[Alterations in circulation]
Cerebral (circle appropriate response) — Cerebral tissue perfusion

Pupils	Eye opening
L 2 3 4 5 6 mm	None (1)
R 2 3 4 5 6 mm	To pain (2)
Reaction: Brisk ______	To speech (3)
Sluggish ______	Spontaneous (4)
Nonreactive ______	

Fluid volume
Deficit
Excess

Best verbal	Best motor
Intubated (0)	Flaccid (1)
Mute (1)	Extensor response (2)
Incomprehensible sound (2)	Flexor response (3)
Inappropriate words (3)	Semipurposeful (4)
Confused conversation (4)	Localized to pain (5)
Oriented (5)	Obeys commands (6)

Cardiac output

Glasgow coma scale total
______
Neurological changes/ symptoms ______
[Cardiac]
Apical rate and rhythm ______ — Cardiopulmonary tissue perfusion
PMI ______

Heart sounds/
murmurs ______________________________
Dysrhythmias ___________________________
Pacemaker__________

BP: Sitting Lying Standing
R _____ L _____ R _____ L _____ R _____ L _____

A-Line reading ___________________________
Cardiac index ___________ Cardiac output __________
CVP ___________ PAP ___________ PCWP __________
IV fluids ________________________________
IV cardiac medications ______________________
____
Serum enzymes ___________________________

Peripheral
Pulses: A = absent B = bruits D = Doppler
+ 3 = bounding + 2 = palpable + 1 = faintly palpable
Carotid R ____ L ____ Popliteal R ____ L ____
Brachial R ____ L ____ Posterior tibial R ____ L ____
Radial R ____ L ____ Dorsalis pedis R ____ L ____
Femoral R ____ L ____
Jugular venous distention R ____ L ____
Skin temperature__________ Color______________
Edema ___________ Capillary refill______________
Clubbing __________ Claudication ______________

Gastrointestinal
Liver: Enlarged ____________ Ascites ___________

Renal
Urine output: 24 hour ______ Average hourly _______
BUN _____ Creatinine _____ Specific gravity _____
Urine studies ___________________________

[Alterations in oxygenation]
Rate __________ Rhythm __________ Depth ___________
Labored/unlabored (circle) Chest expansion ________
Use of accessory muscles ____________________
Orthopnea _______________________________
Breath sounds ____________________________
Complaints of dyspnea ______ Precipitated by ______
Cough: Productive/nonproductive _______________
Sputum: Color ______ Amount _____ Consistency ______
LOC _________________ Splinting ______________
Arterial blood gases ________________________
Oxygen percent and device ___________________
Ventilator ________________________________

Nursing Diagnosis
(Altered/High Risk for/
Potential for Enhanced)

Fluid volume
Deficit
Excess

Cardiac output

Peripheral tissue
perfusion
Peripheral
neurovascular
dysfunction
Fluid volume
Deficit
Excess

Cardiac output

GI tissue perfusion

Renal tissue perfusion

Fluid volume
Cardiac output

Ineffective airway
clearance
Ineffective breathing
patterns
Ineffective gas exchange
Inability to sustain
spontaneous
ventilation

Dysfunctional
ventilatory weaning
response

	Nursing Diagnosis (Altered/High Risk for/ Potential for Enhanced)
Alterations in elimination	
Bowel	Bowel Patterns
Abdominal physical examination ______	Constipation
Usual bowel habits ______	Diarrhea
Alterations from normal ______	Incontinence
Urinary	Urinary Patterns
Bladder distention ______	Incontinence
Color ______ Catheter ______	Retention
Usual urinary pattern ______	
Alteration from normal ______	
Choosing—A pattern involving the selection of alternatives	
Alterations in coping	
Patient's usual problem solving methods ______	Ineffective individual coping
Family's usual problem solving methods ______	Ineffective family coping
Patient's method of dealing with stress ______	
Family's method of dealing with stress ______	
Patient's affect ______	
Physical manifestations ______	
[Alterations in participation]	
Compliance with past/current health care regimen ______	Noncompliance Ineffective management of therapeutic regimen
Willingness to comply with future health care regimen ______	

ADL = activities of daily living; A-line = arterial line; BP = blood pressure; BUN = blood urea nitrogen; CVP = central venous pressure; GI = gastrointestinal; IV = intravenous; LOC = level of consciousness; NG = nasogastric; NPO = nothing by mouth; PAP = pulmonary artery pressure; PCWP = pulmonary capillary wedge pressure; PMI = point of maximal impulse; TPN = total parenteral nutrition

Appendix 7-B

Holistic Nursing Assessment Tool for Outpatients

Name ______________________________ Date of Birth ______________ Sex ________
Address ____ Telephone ________________
Significant Others _______________________________ Telephone ________________
Date ________ Education ______________ Employment ___________________________
Medical Diagnosis ____
Reason for Seeking Holistic Nursing Care ______________________________________
____
Height _______ Weight _______ B/P _______ T _______ P _______ R _______

	Nursing Diagnosis (Altered/High Risk for/ Potential for Enhanced)
Communicating—A pattern involving sending messages	
Verbal: ______________________________ Nonverbal: ___________________________	[Communication, altered] Verbal Nonverbal
"Valuing/Transcending"—A pattern involving spiritual growth	
Meaning and purpose in life: ______________ Inner Strengths: __________________________ Interconnections (self, others, universe, higher power): ____	[Spiritual State] Spiritual well-being Spiritual distress Hopelessness Powerlessness

Note: Holistic Nursing Assessment Tool: Developed by Pamela Potter Hughes, RN, BSN, MA, and adapted by Barbara M. Dossey, RN, MS, FAAN, and Noreen Frish, RN, PhD.

Source: Adapted from Cathie E. Guzzetta, Shelia D. Bunton, Linda A. Prinkey, Anita P. Sherer, and Patricia C. Seifert, *Clinical Assessment Tools for Use with Nursing Diagnoses* (St. Louis: C.V. Mosby), 1989.

	Nursing Diagnosis (Altered/High Risk for/ Potential for Enhanced)
Relating—A pattern involving establishing bonds	
Role (marital status, children, parents): ______	Role performance, altered Parenting, altered Parental role conflict [Work] Sexual dysfunction
Occupation: ______	Family process, altered
Sexual Relationships: ______	Sexuality patterns, altered
Socialization: ______	[Socialization, altered] Social interaction, impaired Social isolation
Knowing—A pattern involving the meaning associated with information	
Orientation: ______	Thought processes, altered [Orientation] [Confusion]
Memory: ______	[Memory]
Previous Illnesses/Hospitalizations/Surgeries: ______	
Identified Health Problems (Present/History): ______	
Current Medications (Medication Allergies): ______	
Risk Factors (Smoking, Family History, etc.): ______	
Perception/Knowledge of Health/Illness: ______	Knowledge deficit (Specify)
Expectations of Holistic Health Intervention: ______	
Readiness to Learn (Ready, Willing, Able): ______	[Learning]
Feeling—A pattern involving the subjective awareness of information	
Comfort: ______	[Comfort, altered] Pain, chronic Pain, acute [Discomfort, chronic] [Discomfort, acute]

	Nursing Diagnosis (Altered/High Risk for/ Potential for Enhanced)
Emotional Integrity States: ____	[Grieving] Anticipatory Dysfunctional Anxiety Fear [Anger] [Guilt] [Shame] [Sadness] Post-Trauma Response

Moving—A pattern involving activity

Activity (Physical Mobility Limitations): ____	[Activity, altered] Activity Intolerance Impaired physical mobility Fatigue
Rest: ____	Sleep Pattern disturbance [Hypersomnia] [Insomnia] [Nightmares]
Recreation: ____	Diversional activity deficit
Environmental Maintenance: ____	Impaired home maintenance management [Safety Hazards]
Health Maintenance: ____	Health maintenance, altered
Self-Care: ____	Bathing/hygiene deficit Dressing/grooming deficit Feeding deficit Toileting deficit

Perceiving—A pattern involving the reception of information

Sensory Perception: ____	[Sensory Perception, altered] Visual Auditory

	Nursing Diagnosis (Altered/High Risk for/ Potential for Enhanced)
	Kinesthetic Gustatory Tactile Olfactory Unilateral Neglect
Self-Concept:	[Self-Concept, altered] Body image disturbance Personal identity disturbance Self-Esteem disturbance —Chronic low —Situational
Exchanging—A pattern involving mutual giving and receiving	
Nutrition:	[Nutrition, altered] [Nutritional deficit] < or > Body Requirements Oral mucus membranes, impaired
Elimination:	[Bowel elimination, altered] Bowel incontinence Constipation: colonic Constipation: perceived Diarrhea GI tissue perfusion
Renal/Urinary:	[Urinary elimination, altered] Incontinence (specify) Retention [Enuresis] Renal tissue perfusion
Physical/Tissue Integrity:	[Tissue integrity, impaired] Impaired skin integrity [Injury: Risk] Aspiration

	Nursing Diagnosis (Altered/High Risk for/ Potential for Enhanced)
______	Disuse syndrome
______	Poisoning
______	Suffocation
______	Trauma
Physical Regulation: ______	[Physical regulation, altered]
Immune: ______	Infection: risk
______	Altered protection
______	Thermoregulation, ineffective
______	—Hypothermia
______	—Hyperthermia
Circulation: ______	Cardiac output, decreased
______	[Tissue perfusion, altered]
______	Cardiopulmonary
______	Cerebral
______	Peripheral
______	[Fluid volume, altered]
______	Deficit
______	Deficit: risk
______	Excess
Oxygenation: ______	[Respiration, altered]
______	Airway clearance, ineffective
______	Breathing pattern, ineffective
______	Gas exchange, impaired
Hormonal/Metabolic Patterns: ______	[Menstrual Patterns]
______	[Premenstrual syndrome]

Choosing—A pattern involving the selection of alternatives

Coping: ______	Individual coping, ineffective
______	Adjustment: impaired
Judgment/Decisions: ______	Conflict: decisional
______	Coping: defensive
______	Denial: impaired

	Nursing Diagnosis (Altered/High Risk for/ Potential for Enhanced)
Participation: ______________	Noncompliance
Family Coping: ______________	[Family Coping, ineffective] Compromised Disabled

ADDITIONAL COMMENTS:

____

Goals

1. ______________________________
2. ______________________________
3. ______________________________
4. ______________________________
5. ______________________________

Prioritized Nursing Diagnosis/Problem List/Theory-Based Plan of Care **Date**

1. ______________________________ __________
2. ______________________________ __________
3. ______________________________ __________
4. ______________________________ __________
5. ______________________________ __________

Signature ______________________ Date __________

Holistic Nursing Care Plan

Name: ______________________________

Date: ____________

Client Goals:

1. ______________________________
2. ______________________________
3. ______________________________
4. ______________________________

Nursing Diagnosis and Related Factors	*Client/Patient Outcomes Outcome Criteria*	*Therapeutic Intervention*	*Evaluation*

Client Signature ____________________

DATE ______________________________

VISION OF HEALING

Questioning the Rules of Science

Nothing is more important about the quantum physics principle than this, that it destroys the concepts of the world as "sitting out there," with the observer safely separated from it. . . . To describe what has happened, one has to cross out that old word "observer," and put in its place the new word "participator." In some strange sense the Universe is a participatory universe.[1]

* * *

Nurses traditionally have relied on accumulated practice experience as though it were synonymous with knowledge. Nothing is more effective in shaking this belief system loose than a confrontation with the fact that not everyone's experience leads to the same conclusion.[2]

* * *

We are a peculiar people, we European/North Americans. We often demand to know why and how something works before we ask if it does. It isn't enough for us to experience something and to accept it. We can't accept something of value until we are convinced that it is logical, that the system fits within some preconceived mechanism or that it has been "proven" (by someone else) to work. We have even developed a unique system, the scientific method, to prove things. Science has become one of the special religions of our culture: it both regulates and comforts us.[3]

* * *

Great discoveries have been made by means of experiments devised with complete disregard for well-accepted beliefs.[4]

NOTES

1. J.A. Wheeler, Not Consciousness but Distinction between the Probe and the Probed as Central to the Elemental Quantum Level of Observations, in *Role of Consciousness in the Physical World*, ed. R. Jahn (Boulder, CO: Westview Press, 1981), 87–111.
2. F.S. Downs, Relationship of Findings of Clinical Research and Development of Criteria: A Researcher's Perspective, *Nursing Research* 29(1980):94–97.
3. S. Eabry, *Massage* 47(1994):36.
4. W.I.B. Beveridge, *The Art of Scientific Investigation* (New York: Vintage Books, 1957).

Chapter 8

Nursing Research and Its Holistic Applications

Cathie E. Guzzetta

NURSE HEALER OBJECTIVES

Theoretical

- Discuss ways in which the wellness model has redirected priorities in nursing research.
- Compare and contrast qualitative and quantitative research methods.
- Read a qualitative research study in one of the nursing research journals, and identify the holistic implications (see references 16 and 52 at the end of this chapter).

Clinical

- Collect data from various clients who are participating in some form of alternative therapy to determine their subjective evaluation of their outcomes.
- Discuss the holistic applications of nursing research with a nurse researcher.
- Design a holistic research study based on one of the questions found in the section, "Directions for Future Research," at the end of this chapter.

Personal

- Read a research study on the effects of an alternative therapy (see references 18, 49, and 50 at the end of this chapter; also see Chapter 24's reference list).

- Set aside some time to learn more about research methods.
- Attend a research conference.

DEFINITIONS

Heisenberg's Uncertainty Principle: the idea that one cannot look at a physical object without changing it.

Placebo: a medically inert medication, preparation, treatment, technique, or ritual that has no specific effects on the body and is intended to have no therapeutic value.

Qualitative Research: a systematic, subjective form of research that is used to describe life experiences and give them meaning. Qualitative research focuses on understanding the whole, which is consistent with the philosophy of holistic nursing.

Quantitative Research: a systematic, formal, objective form of research in which numerical data are used to obtain information about the world. Quantitative research embodies the principles of the scientific method and is used to describe variables, examine relationships among variables, and determine cause-and-effect interactions between variables.

Reductionism: the approach of breaking down phenomena to their smallest possible parts.

Research: a diligent, systematic inquiry or investigation to validate and refine existing knowledge and generate new knowledge.

WELLNESS MODEL

The framework of client/patient nursing research is shifting from an illness to a wellness model of health care. The wellness model views individuals holistically as bio-psycho-social-spiritual units who assume responsibility for their own health. It emphasizes the enormous potential that each individual has in healing his or her own body-mind-spirit.

A significant body of research provides evidence of the enormous effects of consciousness on both health and illness. Investigations have shown that alternative therapies have the exciting potential to prevent illness and maintain high-level wellness. In addition, such research has been instrumental in guiding the development of humanistic and holistic approaches to health care. The challenge for nursing is to apply these findings in our nursing practice.[1]

HOLISTIC RESEARCH METHODS

Research can be defined as a diligent, systematic inquiry or investigation to validate and refine existing knowledge, as well as to generate new knowledge.[2] Descartes' teachings in the seventeenth century did much to advance the use of the scientific method in medical research as we know it today.[3] His notion of reductionism in research—the idea of breaking down every question to its smallest possible parts—has been immensely beneficial in isolating those factors responsible for disease. For example, the physiologic part of a human being can be divided into organs, cells, and biochemical substances, then into molecular, atomic, and subatomic levels. Such an approach is useful for identifying the etiology of disease (e.g., the finding that a virus causes acquired immunodeficiency syndrome [AIDS]) and offers direction for studying the cures of disease (e.g., the use of antibodies to kill the bacteria associated with endocarditis).

Quantitative research is a systematic, formal, objective process in which numerical data are used to obtain information about the world. Embodying the principles of the scientific method, this type of research involves descriptions of variables, relationships among variables, and determinations of cause-and-effect interactions between variables.[4] It is the most commonly used method of scientific inquiry.

Quantitative research is classified into four categories: (1) descriptive research, used to describe phenomena; (2) correlational research, used to examine relationships between and among variables; (3) quasi-experimental research, used to explain relationships, examine causal relationships, and clarify the reasons for events; and (4) experimental research, used to examine cause-and-effect relationships.[5] The quantitative method makes it possible to generalize the results obtained in one study to other, similar client populations and to replicate the results in similar studies. The key issue of the quantitative method is its ability to predict and control outcomes.

Biomedical research using quantitative methods abounds as scientists seek to identify unknown causes and cures for physiologic (and sometimes psychologic) illnesses. Efforts to find answers at the molecular level to such problems as the common cold, heart disease, cancer, AIDS, and essential hypertension, to name only a few, have consumed enormous numbers of personnel and dollars. Statistical analyses of isolated parts and group comparisons have indeed validated cause and effect in many cases. The quantitative method, however, does not take into account (1) the responses of the whole human being to variables, (2) the characteristics of one individual's pathway to a particular problem, and (3), the unique patterns and interacting variables of one individual.[6] Historically, these issues have been deemed irrelevant because they have not been priority concerns in the biomedical paradigm.[7]

Current bodymind researchers have challenged the very roots of the biomedical paradigm. The field of psychoneuroimmunology has generated astounding research findings to support the interactive nature of psychophysiologic variables. There is conclusive evidence that thoughts and emotions affect the neurologic, endocrine, and immune systems at the cellular and subcellular levels. As a result, nurses have come to realize that the fit between quantitative methods and holistic nursing practice is not always an ideal one.

Because quantitative methods seek only to find answers to parts of the whole and the central tenet underlying the holistic framework is that the whole is greater than the sum of its parts, nurses have looked to alternative philosophies of science and research methods that are compatible with investigations of humanistic and holistic phenomena.[8,9] Termed qualitative research, this approach is a systematic, subjective form of research that is used to describe and promote an understanding of human experiences such as health, caring, loneliness, pain, and comfort.[10] It is used to study phenomena by investigating the context and meaning of observed patterns. Qualitative research focuses on understanding the whole, which is consistent with the philosophy of holistic nursing.[11–14]

There are six types of qualitative research: (1) phenomenologic research, used to describe an experience as the whole person lives it; (2) grounded theory research, used to uncover the problems in a social situation and the way in which the persons involved handle them; (3) ethnographic research, used to study a culture and the people within the culture; (4) philosophic inquiry, used to analyze meanings, identify values and ethics, and study the nature of knowledge; (5) historical research, used to describe or analyze the events that occurred in the past to understand our present situation better; and (6) critical social theory, used to discern ways in which people communicate with one another and the development of symbolic meanings in society.[15]

For example, Parse, Coyne, and Smith used the phenomenologic research approach to describe the experience of health. They conducted a study to discover a definition of health as people live and experience it in everyday life. They asked the question, What are the common elements in a feeling of health among several different age groups?[16] One hundred subjects between 20 and 45 years old wrote a description of an episode during which they felt healthy and described their feelings, thoughts, and perceptions of the experience. The researchers used the subjects' actual words when reporting the findings. From the data collected, 30 descriptive expressions of health were identified (Table 8–1). From these 30 descriptors, three central themes were recognized: spirited intensity, fulfilling inventiveness, and symphonic integrity. Based on these central themes, the researchers then formulated the following definition: "health is symphonic integrity manifested in the spirited intensity of fulfilling inventiveness."[17] The descriptors in the table are so rich that they give us a clear understanding of the lived experience of health and make it possible to develop a definition of health that is fuller and much more holistic than the traditional biomedical view of health defined as the "absence of disease."

Table 8–1 The Experience of Health—Descriptive Expressions from Participants in a Phenomenological Study

Spirited Intensity	*Fulfilling Inventiveness*	*Symphonic Integrity*
1. Being enthusiastic	1. Finishing a project that takes up time	1. Being at ease
2. Catching a second wind	2. Accomplishment	2. Feeling of worth
3. Exercising and walking	3. Winning the game of life	3. Enjoying own space at that moment
4. Feel in peak condition	4. Trying some new endeavor	4. Peaceful feeling inside while bicycling
5. Positive outlook on life	5. Feeling something enriching my life	5. A "just right" feeling about everything
6. Feeling of refreshment	6. Doing what I struggled for	6. Drinking in the beauty of the day
7. Feeling full of energy	7. Pushing a little extra	7. Peaceful attitude
8. A glowing light of energy burning brightly in my eyes	8. Feel successful as a person	8. Rhythmical, easy, warm
9. A whip the world feeling	9. Ability to extend to limits of endurance	9. Glowing and good inside
10. A surge of energy	10. Accomplishing something	10. Feeling loved

Source: Reprinted from *Nursing Research: Qualitative Methods* by R.R. Parse, A.B. Coyne, and M.J. Smith, p. 32, with permission of Appleton and Lange, © 1985.

Likewise, quantitative intervention studies can be approached more holistically by taking into consideration the interactive nature of the patient's body-mind-spirit. In 1990, Dr. Dean Ornish, a cardiologist, took a giant step in this direction. He published a landmark, prospective, controlled, randomized study to determine the effects of a holistic, comprehensive, life style change intervention program for patients with coronary artery disease.[18] The intervention included all the current state-of-the-art knowledge on preventing heart disease related to diet, exercise, support groups, and stress reduction (see Chapter 4 for details of the intervention). Subjects in the control group were treated with traditional medical approaches. Both groups were followed for one year and were similar at the start of the study regarding age and other demographic characteristics, diet, and life style characteristics, functional status, cardiac history, and risk factors. Also, both groups did not differ at baseline regarding the severity of their coronary artery disease. The outcome of the study was objective—the size of coronary artery lesions of both the experimental and control groups was measured angiographically before and after the one-year intervention.

The results were astonishing. Patients in the experimental group demonstrated significant regression of their coronary artery disease whereas the control group demonstrated a significant progression of their disease. Moreover, the greatest improvement in regression of coronary lesions was found in those experimental group patients who had the most severely stenosed coronary lesions. Even a small amount of regression in a severely stenosed coronary lesion can have a clinically significant effect on myocardial perfusion and hence on functional status since perfusion is a fourth-power function of coronary artery diameter.

Until this study, researchers had been unable to demonstrate regression of coronary artery lesions. Why was this study so successful? It was successful because the intervention took into consideration the interactive nature of each patient's biologic, psychologic, sociologic, and spiritual patterns. It did not try to isolate the effects of one part of the intervention. It used an intervention that addressed the whole. We know diet helps, exercise is important, support groups work, and stress reduction makes a difference. Ornish put these together in a holistic intervention package. But which part of the intervention was most effective? We do not know for sure. Could it be that the interactive nature of the interventions was more powerful than any one of the interventions alone in helping patients to repattern their pathways toward wellness? It appears that such holistic, comprehensive, and interactive interventions were responsible for reversing an outcome that had never been changed before.

Qualitative vs. Quantitative Research

It has taken centuries to generate convincing data that refute the idea of a separation between the body and the mind. Many health care professionals remain tied to the biomedical model and perceive holistic principles and their corresponding research approaches as unscientific. They have doubted the psychophysiologic link between health and illness because the primary evidence of the link has been provided in the form of anecdotes or personal testimonials. "Hard core" researchers who embrace the quantitative method have not placed much value on the "softer" data obtained from qualitative studies. Even when quantitative studies support the link, questions arise about their retrospective designs, methodologic problems, or lack of measurement tools with psychometric properties.[19]

It is clear that, before the bodymind link is universally accepted, additional research is necessary. By virtue of their day-to-day care of clients, nurses are in a unique position to observe, document, quantify, and analyze the interactive relationship of variables in health and illness. The value of qualitative research methods will undoubtedly increase as important bodymind variables are discovered. The respectability of qualitative research findings will also increase as the authors of nursing research texts dedicate more attention to this content area, as research journal editors accept more qualitative studies for publication, and as more qualitative studies attract federal funding.[20] Moreover, the results of qualitative studies are supplying quantitative researchers with a plethora of potential research hypotheses.

Qualitative and quantitative methods should not be viewed from an either/or perspective. Both methodologies are needed in holistic research.[21] Both are important in scientific investigation (Tables 8–2 and 8–3).

Objectivity in Scientific Investigation

Most researchers accept the universal principle that objectivity must govern scientific inquiry. Heisenberg, who studied information obtained from an electron, has shaken this belief, however. His uncertainty principle, which states that it is impossible to look at a physical object without changing it,[22] suggests that objects and clients change when we observe them. The holistic researcher realizes the enormous implications of this principle: the researcher does not stand apart from the research or research subject, but rather is part of the research. We are not objective observers of the world, but rather participants in that world. This partici-

Table 8-2 Quantitative and Qualitative Research Characteristics

Quantitative Research	*Qualitative Research*
Hard science	Soft science
Focus: concise and narrow	Focus: complex and broad
Reductionistic	Holistic
Objective	Subjective
Reasoning: logistic, deductive	Reasoning: dialectic, inductive
Basis of knowing: cause-and-effect relationships	Basis of knowing: meaning, discovery
Tests theory	Develops theory
Control	Shared interpretation
Instruments	Communication and observation
Basic element of analysis: numbers	Basic element of analysis: words
Statistical analysis	Individual interpretation
Generalization	Uniqueness

Source: Reprinted from *The Practice of Nursing Research: Conduct, Critique and Utilization* by N. Burns and S.K. Grove, p. 27, with permission of W.B. Saunders, © 1993.

pation, in turn, affects the results that we obtain through research. Our participation may be a word, an action, a touch, an observation, or simply our presence. The researcher becomes an integral part of the experiment and its outcomes. The term *nonparticipant observer* in research is, therefore, meaningless.

Heisenberg also postulates that it is not possible to obtain a complete description of a physical object because, when we describe it, we change it. Thus, it is impossible to obtain all the data that describe an object; some information will always be unknown.[23] Observations verify research effects, but, if it is impossible to obtain a complete description of a physical object, some outcomes will be unknown. It is misleading to suggest that research can always be validated in terms of testable or observable effects. The effects of a certain experiment, whether they are observable or not, will ultimately affect the subject.[24]

Certain phenomena related to holistic research may not be accessible to scientific investigation. The individual who experiences certain effects while using alternative therapies, for example, may be unable to conceptualize or express them or unable to translate or communicate these effects to another. Likewise, the researcher may be unable to interpret the effects because he or she lacks experience with these effects or because our language is inadequate for describing and communicating these phenomena.

Table 8–3 Investigating an Apple: A Qualitative vs. a Quantitative Approach

Quantitative Approach

A **quantitative** researcher might examine an apple by
- Inspecting the apple closely
- Carefully weighing it
- Cutting into it
- Separating the skin from the meat and
  - Weighing each
  - Analyzing each for sugar, salt, water, fiber, calories, vitamins, and then statistically analyzing the differences between the skin and the meat
- Counting the seeds and examining the inside of the seeds

Qualitative Approach

A **qualitative** researcher might examine an apple by
- Looking at the apple from all sides, top, and bottom
- Feeling it
- Smelling it
- Shining it
- Rolling it
- Appreciating its wholeness
- Biting into it, eating it, and enjoying it, noting its
  - Sound
  - Taste
  - Texture
  - Temperature
- Planting its seeds to determine what they might produce

Note: The author wishes to thank Elizabeth H. Winslow, PhD, RN, FAAN, for sharing this example.

The Placebo Response

Scientists have often viewed the placebo response as a nuisance and an unreliable factor that distorts the research results. Many have assumed that a placebo is effective only when the illness is somehow unreal. Recently, however, we have begun to understand the power of the placebo effect and the mechanisms involved.[25]

Placebo means "I will please." The term refers to a medically inert preparation or treatment that has no specific effects on the body and is intended to have no therapeutic benefit. Yet, this medically inert substance or treatment can evoke a placebo response, relieving pain or dramatically affecting the patient's symptoms or disease. The placebo effect can activate the production of endorphins, peptide hormones produced and secreted by the brain with opiate properties, that are exponentially more potent than morphine. It is thought that endorphins can modify or inhibit the transmission of pain stimuli throughout the central nervous system.[26]

In an analysis of 15 double-blind studies, placebo medications were found to be effective in pain relief for 35 percent of patients with postoperative pain.[27] An analysis of 11 more recent double-blind studies in which 36 percent of the patients received at least 50 percent pain relief from placebos confirmed these findings.[28] In addition, the worse the pain or the more stressful the situation, the more effective the placebo.[29] The placebo effect may be even higher than these findings indicate. A recent study found that approximately 70 percent of patients in preliminary trials of five new promising medical treatments (for asthma, ulcers, and herpes) showed improvements,[30] although treatments later proved useless. This more than doubles the "one in three" rule of thumb governing placebo effectiveness. Thus, it appears that, for more than one-third of clients, and probably for even more, the pharmacologically inert placebo is able to activate bodymind healing mechanisms.[31,32]

The placebo response has also been found to be present in all of the following conditions and therapeutic procedures, demonstrating the mind's ability to produce neurohormonal messenger molecules that alter the autonomic, endocrine, and immune systems[33]:

- hypertension, stress, cardiac pain, blood cell counts, headaches, pupillary dilation (suggesting the mind's ability to alter the autonomic nervous system)
- adrenal gland secretion, diabetes, ulcers, gastric secretion and motility, colitis, oral contraceptive use, menstrual pain, thyrotoxicosis (suggesting the mind's ability to alter the endocrine system)
- the common cold, fever, vaccinations, asthma, multiple sclerosis, rheumatoid arthritis, warts, cancer (suggesting the mind's ability to alter the immune system)
- surgical treatments (e.g., for angina pectoris)
- biofeedback instrumentation and various medical devices
- psychologic treatments, such as conditioning (systematic desensitization) and perhaps all forms of psychotherapy
- making an appointment to see a physician

Thus, the placebo response, also called the general healing response, is a common general mechanism that occurs because of a communication link between the body and the mind that is probably present in all clinical situations.[34] Furthermore, the placebo response probably exists, more or less, in each one of us.[35]

It is known that how a drug is given or how a procedure is performed and by whom can affect the intensity of the placebo response. Therefore, the faith that the client has in the caregiver and the client's expectation that the drug or therapy will work greatly influence the placebo response.[36] Likewise, the faith that the caregiver conveys to the client regarding the drug or therapy, as well as the trust and rapport established between the two, affects the placebo response.[37,38]

It is time to recognize the powerful effects of the placebo. We must learn to incorporate the placebo response in our research and our clinical practice to maximize its potential. To enhance the placebo response when administering medications, for example, we can discuss with our clients the medication's known potency and effectiveness. When patients receive morphine intravenously for chest pain, we can ask them to visualize the molecules of this powerful, pain-killing medicine traveling through their veins to the source of the chest pain. We can suggest that they work to enhance the medication's effectiveness by allowing the relaxed, warm, and comfortable feeling associated with the morphine to flow throughout their bodies.[39,40]

The essence of the placebo response involves positive attitudes and emotions.[41] Many alternative therapies, such as imagery, music therapy, relaxation, and exercise, increase endorphin production. When clients believe that they are doing something to enhance healing, their endorphin levels can rise.[42] Therefore, clients can influence the course of their own illnesses and their responses to therapy by using their own consciousness.[43] Because basic nursing interventions, such as touching, giving back rubs, teaching, positioning, and distracting, all have the potential to raise endorphin levels, it is critical that we discuss with our clients the possible therapeutic benefits of each therapy as a part of our research protocols and in our practice. When we realize that what we say to clients can augment the placebo response, we will develop new communication skills to enhance our clients' healing responses and maximize the benefits of our nursing care.

EVALUATION OF ALTERNATIVE THERAPIES

Many alternative therapies have been used to treat a variety of problems in diverse settings, but their appropriateness and adequacy in various populations and settings have not been investigated fully. Early evaluation studies often focused on discovering whether such interventions "worked" and, as a result, employed an experimental group and a control group to identify differences. Today, we need to be asking a more sophisticated question related to these interventions: Under what conditions is the alternative therapy the treatment of choice, for which particular client/patient, and with what type of clinical problem?[44] Comparative outcome studies are needed to determine the usefulness, indications, contraindications, and dangers of alternative therapies.[45] Moreover, these interventions need to be evaluated for their effectiveness not only in treating various illnesses, but also in promoting high-level wellness and preventing illness.

Office of Alternative Medicine

With the 1992 creation of the Office of Alternative Medicine at the National Institutes of Health (see Chapter 1), many alternative therapies are undergoing scientific evaluation to determine whether they affect the clinical course and outcomes of an illness or whether they enhance wellness.[46] Some traditional researchers are not happy that federal monies are being used to support this kind of research, but we now know that one in every three U.S. citizens uses some form of alternative therapy.[47] These individuals are spending enormous amounts of out-of-pocket money on visits to alternative practitioners. It appears that the public is looking for something more in health care. They are looking for humanistic, holistic approaches that address their body-mind-spirit needs. For these reasons, the time has come to determine which alternative therapies are beneficial, and that is what the Office of Alternative Medicine is trying to do.

To date, the Office of Alternative Medicine has funded 30 studies to evaluate such therapies as acupressure, message therapy, electrochemical treatment, hypnosis, music therapy, guided imagery, biofeedback, prayer, and administration of antioxidants. Major health conditions such as cancer, AIDS, asthma, and women's health issues have been targeted for evaluation. The results of these studies will provide the scientific basis for determining which alternative therapies work, which ones do not work, which ones are harmful, and, most important, which ones improve patient outcomes.[48]

Holistic Measurement Tools

The holistic researcher will quickly discover inherent difficulties when developing outcome studies for alternative therapies. For example, there is a lack of holistic instruments to measure the effects of alternative therapies. If an alternative therapy affects an individual's body-mind-spirit, however, it is reasonable to believe that we should be able to measure these effects. Too often, we have studied body effects and mind effects, but rarely have we studied the interaction and relationship between the two.

The various physiologic instruments available to study the effects of alternative therapies are often used in combination to develop a physiologic profile of observed outcomes. Researchers tend to use psychologic instruments with less confidence, however, viewing them as less reliable and less valid than their physiologic counterparts. Many of the psychologic instruments currently available are not sensitive enough to demonstrate the subtle yet significant psychologic changes that occur with alternative therapies. The finding that a psychologic indicator is not significant does not necessarily disprove the existence of a significant psychologic effect. It may indicate that (1) the wrong variable was studied, or (2) the psychologic tool used was not sufficiently sensitive to measure the effect.

Alternative therapies influence many psychophysiologic parameters, but they do not necessarily influence the same variables in different individuals. Thus, a number of parameters must be used to evaluate the outcomes of these interventions satisfactorily.[49] It is clear that additional tools must be developed to measure the outcomes of alternative therapies. Psychologic and physiologic outcomes should be used in combination and their effects correlated as a means of increasing the validity of the findings and discovering bodymind links. In addition, psychologic and physiologic measurements should be combined in developing psychophysiologic tools.

Like Morse and associates,[50] Curtis and Wessberg found no physiologic changes when they evaluated various forms of self-regulation therapies, but their subjects reported positive evaluations of these therapies.[51] Thus, a rich, promising, and holistic source of data lies within the subjects' own estimates of their behavior and outcomes. Meaning and quality of life are essential tenets of the holistic model, and qualitative methods are well suited to tapping this subjective source of data.[52]

Subjective phenomena such as anxiety, pain, and comfort can be studied by means of quantitative approaches as well as qualitative approaches. Moreover, quantitative studies of holistic phenomena are appearing in the literature with more frequency. For example, the outcome of comfort has been operationalized by total and subscale scores on a holistic instrument that measures a client's physical, psychologic, environmental, and social comfort.[53] Likewise, the Duke–UNC [University of North Carolina] Health Profile has been used to assess the impact of medical interventions on the daily functioning of clients in four areas: symptom experiences, physical function, emotional function, and social function.[54] A variety of visual analog scales, diaries, logs, and graphs are also being used with increasing frequency to capture the holistic, longitudinal, and individualized perceptions of patient experiences.[55]

A current research mandate is to develop instruments that facilitate assessment, diagnosis, and selection of nursing interventions, as well as measure the effectiveness of interventions designed to enhance body-mind-spirit outcomes.[56] Nurses have the knowledge and ability to contribute significantly to this task by using both quantitative and qualitative research methodologies.

CONCLUSION

Nurses have come to realize that the fit between traditional research methods and holistic nursing principles is not always a good one. The shift to the wellness model has caused us to take a new look at our research priorities, methodologies, and findings. We have discovered that the time-honored, quantitative scientific method is not the only valid way to investigate human phenomena.

DIRECTIONS FOR FUTURE RESEARCH

1. Evaluate which alternative therapies promote wellness behaviors in specific client populations.
2. Determine whether alternative therapies can be combined to augment their effectiveness in achieving desired client outcomes (e.g., combining relaxation with biofeedback or music therapy with imagery and progressive relaxation).
3. Determine the most effective way to combine alternative therapies with traditional modes of therapy to achieve optimal client outcomes.
4. Identify the alternative therapies that are most effective for individuals with a specific problem or illness.

NURSE HEALER REFLECTIONS

After reading this chapter, the nurse healer will be able to answer or will begin a process of answering the following questions:

- How do I feel about the importance of research in advancing holistic nursing practice?
- What is my role in nursing research?
- How do I feel when I realize that some intervention outcomes can never be measured?

NOTES

1. P. Flynn, *Holistic Health: The Art and Science of Care* (Bowie, MD: Brady Co., 1980), 1–8.
2. N. Burns and S.K. Grove, *The Practice of Nursing Research: Conduct, Critique, and Utilization*, 2nd ed. (Philadelphia: W.B. Saunders, 1993), 3.
3. L. Dossey, *Space, Time, and Medicine* (Boston: Shambhala Publications, 1982), 12–14.
4. Burns and Grove, *The Practice of Nursing Research*, 26.
5. Ibid., 29–30.
6. D.F. Bockmon and D.J. Riemen, Qualitative versus Quantitative Nursing Research, *Holistic Nursing Practice* 2, no. 1 (1987):71–75.
7. C.C. Clark, *Wellness Nursing: Concepts, Theory, Research, and Practice* (New York: Spring Publishing, 1986), 318.
8. M.A. Newman, *Health as Expanding Consciousness* (St. Louis: C.V. Mosby, 1986), 91–96.
9. M.C. Silva and D. Rothbart, An Analysis of Changing Trends in Philosophies of Science on Nursing Theory Development and Testing, *Advances in Nursing Science* 6, no. 2 (1984):1–13.
10. Burns and Grove, *The Practice of Nursing Research*, 27.
11. Ibid., 26–39.
12. M. Sandelowski, Rigor or Rigor Mortis: The Problem of Rigor in Qualitative Research Revisited, *Advances in Nursing Science* 16, no. 2 (1993):1–8.
13. L. Mehl, *Mind and Matter: Foundations for Holistic Health* (Berkeley, CA: Mindbody Press, 1981), 74.
14. Clark, *Wellness Nursing*, 318.
15. Burns and Grove, *The Practice of Nursing Research*, 30–31.
16. R.R. Parse et al., The Lived Experience of Health: A Phenomenological Study, in *Nursing Research: Qualitative Methods*, ed. R.R. Parse et al. (East Norwalk, CT: Appleton & Lange, 1985), 27.
17. Ibid., 31.
18. D. Ornish, Can Lifestyle Changes Reverse Coronary Heart Disease, *Lancet* 336 (1990):129.
19. C.E. Guzzetta, The Human Factor and the Ailing Heart: Folklore or Fact? (Editorial), *Journal of Intensive Care Medicine* 2, no. 1 (1987):3–5.
20. Bockmon and Riemen, Qualitative versus Quantitative Nursing Research, 71–74.

21. L.C. Dzurec and I.L. Abraham, The Nature of Inquiry: Linking Quantitative and Qualitative Research, *Advances in Nursing Science* 16, no. 1 (1993):73–79.
22. W. Heisenberg, *Physics and Philosophy* (New York: Harper & Row, 1978), 42.
23. G. Zukav, *The Dancing Wu Li Masters: An Overview of the New Physics* (New York: William Morrow, 1979), 111–114.
24. C. Tart, *States of Consciousness* (New York: E.P. Dutton and Co., 1975), 207–228.
25. C.E. Guzzetta and B.M. Dossey, *Cardiovascular Nursing: Holistic Practice* (St. Louis: Mosby-Year Book, 1992), 392–393.
26. A. West, Understanding Endorphins: Our Natural Pain Relief System, *Nursing '81* 2(1981):50.
27. H. Beecher, The Powerful Placebo, *Journal of the American Medical Association* 159(1955):1602.
28. F. Evans, Expectancy, Therapeutic Instructions, and the Placebo Response, in *Placebo: Theory, Research, and Mechanism*, ed. L. White et al. (New York: Guilford Press, 1985).
29. L. Dossey, *Space, Time, and Medicine*.
30. A. Roberts, Placebo Therapies Spark "Improvement" for 7 of 10, *Brain Mind Bulletin* 18, no. 12 (1993):1.
31. J. Frank, Mind-Body Relationships in Illness and Healing, *Journal of Internal Academic Preventative Medicine* 2(1975):46.
32. E. Rossi, *The Psychobiology of Mind-Body Healing*, rev. ed. (New York: W.W. Norton Co., 1993), 15.
33. Ibid.
34. Ibid., 16.
35. S. Perry and G. Heidrich, Placebo Response: Myth and Matter, *American Journal of Nursing* 81(1981):720.
36. R. Sandroff, The Potent Placebo, *RN* (April 1980):35.
37. J. Frank, Mind-Body Relationships in Illness and Healing, 46.
38. L. Dossey, *Healing Words: The Power of Prayer and the Practice of Medicine* (San Francisco: HarperCollins, 1993), 134–135.
39. Perry and Heidrich, Placebo Response: Myth and Matter, 720.
40. Sandroff, The Potent Placebo, 35.
41. E. Rossi, *The Psychobiology of Mind-Body Healing*, 11–22.
42. R. Wilson and B. Elmassion, Endorphins, *American Journal of Nursing* 81(1981):722.
43. L. Dossey, *Space, Time, and Medicine*, 36.
44. D.H. Shapiro, Overview: Clinical and Physiological Comparison of Meditation with Other Self-Control Strategies, *American Journal of Psychiatry* 139(1982):267.
45. American Psychiatric Association, Position Statement on Meditation, *American Journal of Psychiatry* 134(1977):720.
46. T. Cron, It's the Law: There Is an Office of Alternative Medicine, *Alternative Medicine Newsletter* 1, no. 1 (1993):1.
47. D. Eisenberg, Unconventional Medicine in the United States: Prevalence, Costs, and Patterns of Use, *New England Journal of Medicine* 328(1993):246–252.

48. R. Cron, OAM Awards 30 Exploratory Grants in First Round, *Alternative Medicine Newsletter* 1, no. 2 (1993):1.
49. P. Bohachick, Progressive Relaxation Training in Cardiac Rehabilitation: Effects of Psychologic Variables, *Nursing Research* 33(1984):283–287.
50. D.R. Morse et al., A Physiological and Subjective Evaluation of Meditation, Hypnosis, and Relaxation, *Psychosomatic Medicine* 39(1977):304.
51. W.D. Curtis and H.W. Wessberg, A Comparison of Heart Rate, Respiration, and Galvanic Skin Response among Meditators, Relaxers, and Controls, *Journal of Altered States of Consciousness* 2(1975/76):319.
52. C.O. Boyd and P.C. Munhall, A Qualitative Investigation of Reassurance, *Holistic Nursing Practice* 4, no. 1 (1989):61–69.
53. K.Y. Kolcaba, Holistic Comfort: Operationalizing the Construct as a Nurse-Sensitive Outcome, *Advances in Nursing Science* 15, no. 1 (1992):1–10.
54. G.R. Parkerson et al., The Duke-UNC Health Profile: An Adult Health Status Instrument for Primary Care, *Medical Care* 19, no. 8 (1981):805–823.
55. E.R. Giardino and Z.R. Wolf, Symptoms: Evidence and Experience, *Advances in Nursing Science* 7, no. 2 (1993):1–12.
56. Kolcaba, Holistic Comfort, 2.

UNIT III

MAXIMIZING HUMAN POTENTIAL

VISION OF HEALING

Actualization of Human Potentials

Each of us has the ability to achieve a balanced integration of human potentials: physical, mental, emotions, relationships, choices, and spirit. Effective self-care and self-healing depend on taking all these potentials into account. We are challenged to gain access to our inner wisdom and intuition and apply it in our daily lives. As we take responsibility for making effective choices and changes in our lives, we place ourselves in a better position to clarify our life patterns, purposes, and processes.

There are several ways to recognize and validate the healing work that we nurses do each day with our colleagues. After the beginning of shift report each day, for example, it may be possible to take a few minutes to share with each other different personal concerns that are in need of healing. One person may say, "When you think of me today, send me energy, because my sister is ill and I'm worried about her"; or "I'm grieving over Sarah's death last week, and my heart still aches." Another idea is to establish a certain time every other week to discuss healing moments that each person has experienced. Someone may have taught a patient a relaxation exercise that significantly reduced her anxiety; someone else may have learned a new technique to manage stress in the workplace. This time together can validate skills, as well as intuition, build trust, and develop a mutual appreciation that will facilitate the healing process in self and others.

An in-service education committee may develop a questionnaire to establish nurses' desires and needs to learn about specific skills necessary to promote healing. Some classes may be on self-nurturing, learning ways to increase skills of presence to serve and share with intention, therapeutic touch, or empowerment sessions.

Actualizing human potentials means first recognizing and then accepting all the potentials of our being, even those we wish to change. Developing our potentials requires a willingness to assess our position in life, to develop an action plan for change, and then to evaluate our new position in a lifelong process.

Chapter 9

Self-Assessments: Facilitating Healing in Self and Others

Barbara Montgomery Dossey and Lynn Keegan

NURSE HEALER OBJECTIVES

Theoretical

- List the six parts of the circle of human potential.
- Define biodance.

Clinical

- Identify specific areas in each potential that can help you increase and maximize your effectiveness in clinical practice.
- Seek ways to increase your conscious attention to recognizing feelings, environment, relationships, life patterns, and processes in your practice.
- Use the self-assessment and the circle of human potential as interventions with clients.

Personal

- Tabulate your self-assessment score to determine if you are maximizing your human potential.
- Establish areas you wish to focus on in order to create changes and choices that lead to new health behaviors.
- Increase your awareness of ways to gain access to your inner healing.

DEFINITIONS

Healing: a process of bringing all parts of one's self together at deep levels of inner knowing, leading toward an integration and balance, with each part having equal importance and value; also referred to as self-healing or wholeness.

Healing Awareness: conscious recognition and focusing of attention on sensations, feelings, conditions, and facts dealing with needs of self or clients.

Nurse Healer: one who facilitates another person's growth and life process toward wholeness (body-mind-spirit connections) or who assists with recovery from illness or transition to peaceful death.

Process: the continual changing and evolution of one's self through life; the reflection of meaning and purpose in living.

Transpersonal Self: the self that transcends or goes beyond personal individual identity and meaning to include purpose, meaning, values, and unification with universal principles.

Transpersonal View: the state that occurs with a person's life maturity whereby the sense of self expands.

CIRCLE OF HUMAN POTENTIAL

The circle is an ancient symbol of wholeness. As seen in Figure 9–1, the circle of human potential has six areas: physical, mental, emotions, relationships, choices, and spirit. All are important parts of the self that are constantly interacting. When any one part is incomplete, the entire circle loses its completeness because all parts create the whole. It is when we become aware of our strengths, as well as our weaknesses, that we begin to move to our highest capabilities and live in accordance with our philosophy of life. The area of choices is surrounded by an inner and outer dotted circle to represent the idea that our continually evolving spiritual development guides what we consciously/unconsciously choose. Spirit is placed in the outer circle to show that it transcends all the other dimensions and assists us in maximizing our human potentials.

All people are complex feedback loops. As we learn about these feedback loops, we are able to understand our body-mind-spirit connections. Our bodies are in a constant state of change of which we are unaware. Life is a biodance, the endless exchange of all living things with the earth in which all living organisms participate. It exists not only as we live, but also as we die. We do not wait until death to make an exchange

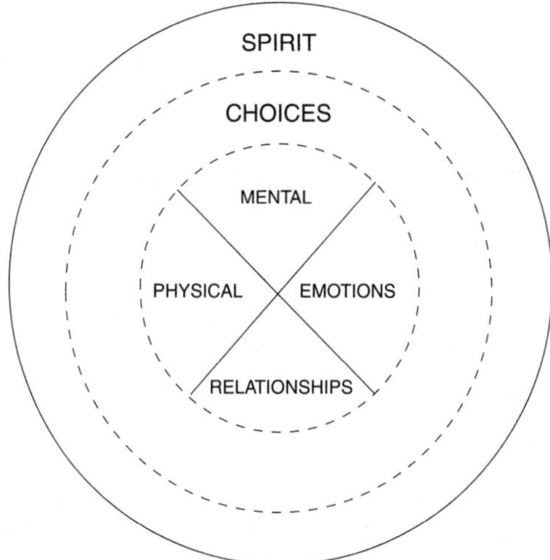

Figure 9–1 Circle of Human Potential.

with the earth, for we are constantly returning to the universe while alive. In every living moment, a portion of the 10^{28} atoms in our body return to the world outside. This is another idea of wholeness, which explains why the notion of "boundary" begins to seem an arbitrary idea, rather than a physical reality.[1]

Assessing our human potential attunes us to our healing awareness; it is the innate quality with which all people are born. It must be developed in order to be actualized to the fullest. Healing is recognizing our feelings, attitudes, and emotions, which are not isolated, but are literally translated into body changes. Images cause internal events through mind modulation that simultaneously affects the autonomic, endocrine, immune, and neuropeptide systems (see Chapter 4). Everyone has the potential and choice to tap into this innate healing potential. When we acknowledge our body-mind-spirit relationships, true healing can occur. Times of stress and crisis in our daily routine can block self-healing. Therefore, it is necessary for us continually to assess and reassess our wholeness.

SELF-ASSESSMENTS

In order to maximize our human potentials, it is important to assess each aspect of our being: physical status, mental status, emotions, relationships, choices, and spirit. The self-assessments in Figures 9–2 through 9–7 help us more clearly identify our current positions in each of these areas.[2] Exhibit 9–1 explains the scoring.

DEVELOPMENT OF HUMAN POTENTIALS

Physical Potential

All humans share the common biologic experiences of birth, gender, growth, aging, and death. Once each person's basic biologic needs for food, shelter, and clothing have been met, there are many ways to seek wholeness of physical potential. Many elements influence physical potential; the major ones are physical awareness of proper nutrition, exercise, relaxation, and balance between work and play. Many people have become obsessed with these elements, but have failed to recognize that they are not separate from or more important than the other potentials. Health is more than the absence of pain and symptoms; it is present when there is a balance. As we assess biologic needs, we must also take into consideration our perceptions of these areas. Many illnesses have been documented as stress-related, because our consciousness is known to play a major role in health and physical potential.

Our body is a gift to nurture and respect. As we nurture ourselves, we increase our uniqueness in energy, sexuality, vitality, and capacity for language and connection with our other potentials. This nurturance strengthens our self-image, which causes several things to happen. First, our body-mind-spirit responds in a positive and integrated fashion. Second, we become a role model with a positive influence on others. Finally, we actually enhance our general feeling of well-being. It is impossible to gain such strengths or empowerment without these changes being manifest and influencing the lives of other people.

Mental Potential

Early in our lives, we have various role models who influence our thoughts, behaviors, and values. As we mature and gain life experience, shifts occur in our thinking, our behavior, and our values. Conflicts develop when we do not take the time to examine our new perceptions and discard old beliefs and values that no longer fit.

Our challenge is to create accurate perceptions of the world through our mental potential. Through both our logical and our nonlogical mental processes, we become interested in a broad range of subjects and expand our full appreciation of the many great pleasures in life. We should increase our awareness of how we use both logical and intuitive thought and increase our skills to create better simultaneous integration of both ways of knowing.

With such interventions as relaxation and imagery, we learn to be present in the moment. It is during these moments that we release our critical inner voice that is constantly judging and in self-dialogue. These are the moments when we expand our mental knowing. As we increase our openness and receptivity to information and suggestions, mental growth can occur. Every aspect of our life is a learning experience and becomes part of a lesson in changing.

Emotions Potential

Involved in our emotions potential are our willingness to acknowledge the presence of feelings and value them as important, and the ability to express them. Emotional health implies that we have the choice and freedom to express love, joy, guilt, fear, and anger. The expression of these emotions can give us immediate feedback about our inner state, which may be crying out for a new way of being.[3]

Emotions are responses to the events in our lives. True healing occurs when we confront both positive and negative intense emotions. Various degrees of chronic anxiety, depression, worry, fear, guilt, anger, denial, or repression result from our failure to confront our emotions. One of the greatest challenges we have is to acknowledge, own, express, and understand our emotions. We are living systems who constantly make exchanges with our environment. All life events affect our emotions and general well-being.

As we become more balanced in living, we allow our humanness to develop. We reach out and ask for human dialogue that is meaningful. Increasing the emotions potential allows spontaneity and a positive, healthy zest for living to emerge. We must be aware of and take responsibility for expression that allows spirit and intuition to flower. It is important to have a consistent harmony between thought processes and emotions, as disharmony causes dissonance.

Emotions are gifts. Frequently, a first step toward releasing a burden in a relationship is to share deep feelings with another. There is no such thing as a good or bad emotion; each is part of the human condition. Emotions exist as the light and shadow of the self; thus, we must acknowledge all of them. They create the dance of life, the polarity of living. The only reason that we can identify the light is that we know its opposite, the

PHYSICAL

Where I Am Now	Almost Always	Some-times	Almost Never	How I Want It To Be
Assess my general health daily	2	1	0	
Exercise 3 to 5 times a week for 20 minutes	2	1	0	
Eat nutritious foods daily	2	1	0	
Play without guilt	2	1	0	
Practice relaxation daily	2	1	0	
Energy level is effective for daily activities	2	1	0	
Do not smoke	2	1	0	
Drink in moderation	2	1	0	
Have regular physical and dental checkups	2	1	0	
Balance my work life with personal life	2	1	0	
Physical Score				

Figure 9–2 Physical Self-Assessment. *Source:* Reprinted from *Self Care: A Program To Improve Your Life*. L. Keegan and B. Dossey with permission of Bodymind Systems, © 1987.

MENTAL

Where I Am Now	Almost Always	Some-times	Almost Never	How I Want It To Be
Am open and receptive to new ideas and life patterns	2	1	0	
Read a broad range of subjects	2	1	0	
Am interested in and knowledgeable about many topics	2	1	0	
Use my imagination in considering new choices or possibilities	2	1	0	
Prioritize my work and set realistic goals	2	1	0	
Enjoy developing new skills and talents	2	1	0	
Ask for suggestions and help when I need it	2	1	0	
Mental Score				

Figure 9–3 Mental Self-Assessment. *Source:* Reprinted from *Self Care: A Program To Improve Your Life.* L. Keegan and B. Dossey with permission of Bodymind Systems, © 1987.

EMOTIONS

Where I Am Now	Almost Always	Some-times	Almost Never	How I Want It To Be
Assess and recognize my own feelings	2	1	0	
Have a nonjudgmental attitude	2	1	0	
Express my feelings in appropriate ways	2	1	0	
Include my feelings when making decisions	2	1	0	
Can remember and acknowledge most events of my childhood including painful as well as happy ones	2	1	0	
Listen and respect the feelings of others	2	1	0	
Recognize my intuition	2	1	0	
Listen to inner self-talk	2	1	0	
Emotions Score				

Figure 9–4 Self-Assessment of Emotions. *Source:* Reprinted from *Self Care: A Program To Improve Your Life*. L. Keegan and B. Dossey with permission of Bodymind Systems, © 1987.

RELATIONSHIPS

Where I Am Now	**Almost Always**	**Some- times**	**Almost Never**	**How I Want It To Be**
I share my opinions and feelings without seeking the approval of others or fearing outcomes	2	1	0	
Create and participate in satisfying relationships	2	1	0	
Sexuality is part of my relationship	2	1	0	
Have a balance between my work and family life	2	1	0	
Am clear in expressing my needs and desires	2	1	0	
Am open and honest with people without fearing the consequences	2	1	0	
Do my part in establishing and maintaining relationships	2	1	0	
Focus on positive topics in relationships	2	1	0	
Relationships Score				

Figure 9–5 Self-Assessment of Relationships. *Source:* Reprinted from *Self Care: A Program To Improve Your Life*. L. Keegan and B. Dossey with permission of Bodymind Systems, © 1987.

CHOICES

Where I Am Now	Almost Always	Some-times	Almost Never	How I Want It To Be
Manage my time to meet my personal goals	2	1	0	
Am committed and disciplined whenever I take on new projects	2	1	0	
Follow through and work on decisions with clarity and action steps	2	1	0	
Am usually clear on decisions	2	1	0	
Take risks	2	1	0	
Can accept circumstances that are beyond my control	2	1	0	
Take on no more new tasks than I can successfully handle	2	1	0	
Recognize shortcomings of people and events for what they are	2	1	0	
Choices Score				

Figure 9–6 Self-Assessment of Choices. *Source:* Reprinted from *Self Care: A Program To Improve Your Life.* L. Keegan and B. Dossey with permission of Bodymind Systems, © 1987.

SPIRIT

Where I Am Now	Almost Always	Some-times	Almost Never	How I Want It To Be
Operate from the perspective that life has value, meaning, and direction	2	1	0	
Know at some level a connection with the universe	2	1	0	
Know some Power greater than myself	2	1	0	
Feel a part of life and living frequently	2	1	0	
Recognize that the different roles of my life are expressions of my true self	2	1	0	
Know how to create balance and feel a sense of connectedness	2	1	0	
Know that life is important, and I make a difference	2	1	0	
Spirit Score				

Figure 9–7 Spirit Self-Assessment. *Source:* Reprinted from *Self Care: A Program To Improve Your Life*. L. Keegan and B. Dossey with permission of Bodymind Systems, © 1987.

Exhibit 9–1 Meaning of the Tallied Scores

Scores of 14 to 20

Congratulations! Your score shows that you are aware of the important areas of your life. You are using your knowledge to work for you by practicing good life patterns that reflect health and balance. As long as you continue with high scores, you will be maximizing your human potential. You are a good model of health to family and friends. Since your score is high in this area move to other areas where your scores are low and identify areas for improvement.

Scores of 10 to 13

Your life patterns in this area are good, but there is room for improvement. Reflect on the "Sometimes or Almost Never," answers. What could you do to change your score? Even the slightest change can make a difference to improve the quality of your life.

Scores of 6 to 9

Your life stressors are showing. You need more information about these important life areas and what changes you can make. Read on to obtain guidance.

Scores of 0 to 5

Your life is full of unnecessary stress. You are not taking good care of yourself. You need to take some time and learn the principles of self-care.

When you finish this exercise you have a composite picture not only of where you are now, but where you want to go. ENJOY THE JOURNEY!

Source: Self Care: A Program To Improve Your Life (3-Part Guided Program: 100-page book, 40-minute relaxation and imagery audiocassette tape, and affirmation cards containing 47 affirmations). All in a deluxe bookshelf binder. Excellent program for professionals and clients. Write Bodymind Systems, 910 Dakota Drive, Temple, Texas 76504.

shadow. When we see the value in both types of emotions, we are in a position of new insight and new understanding, and we can make more effective choices. As we increase our attention to body-mind-spirit interrelationships, we can focus on the emotions that move us toward wholeness and inner understanding.

Relationships Potential

Healthy people live in intricate networks of relationships and are always in search of new, unifying concepts of the universe and social order.

Human beings need to explore and develop meaningful relationships. A healthy person simply cannot live in isolation. In a given day, we interact with many people—immediate family, extended family, colleagues at work, neighbors in the community, and numerous people in organizations. Because we spend at least half of our awake time with colleagues at work, we must support and nourish these relationships. We must also extend our networks to include our nation and planet Earth. Each of us must take an active role in developing local networks of relationships that can have a ripple effect on global concerns.

Relationships have different levels of meaning—from the superficial to the deeply connected. The challenge in relationships is to extend ourselves and to learn to exchange feelings of honesty, trust, intimacy, compassion, openness, and harmony. Sharing life processes requires a true interchange between self and others. Only when we increase our awareness and intention can we promote such interchanges with our family, friends, work colleagues, clients, and community at large. As we increase our network from one person to another, the fact that one contact leads to many more extends our boundaries even further.

It is essential that we identify the cohesiveness in our relationships, as well as the disharmony. We must be aware of the impact that we have on clients, family, and friends. Something always happens when people come together, for life is never a neutral event. Our attitudes, healing awareness, and concern for self and others have a direct effect on the outcome of all our encounters.

Choices Potential

People have an enormous capacity for both conscious and unconscious choices in their lives. Conscious choices involve awareness and skills, such as discipline, persistence, goal setting, priorities, action steps, knowledge of options, and recognition of perceptions. We can enhance our awareness, knowledge, and new skills for living and be active participants in daily living, not passive observers who hope that life will be good to us.

The unconscious also plays a major role in our choices.[4] Jung conceived of the unconscious as a series of layers. Those closest to our awareness are more or less capable of becoming known; those farthest away are, in principle, inaccessible to our awareness and operate autonomously. Jung saw the unconscious as the home of timeless psychic forces that he called archetypes, which generally are invariant throughout all cultures and eras. He felt that every psychic force has its opposite in the unconsciousness—the force of light is always counterposed with that of darkness, good with evil, love with hate, life with death, etc. Jung believed that any psychic energy could become unbalanced and that life's greatest challenge was to achieve a dynamic balance of the innate opposites and to make this balancing process as conscious as possible.

Each of us is responsible for assessing our own values and desires. No one else can make decisions for us. When we do not exercise our ability to make choices, the values of others are imposed on us, and we never reach our highest potential. Choice involves taking risks. We may make some mistakes along the way, but we also gain experience.

Continuing to develop clarity in life enables us to meet goals. A simple process for changing behavior is to learn to change perception. Changing all the "shoulds" in our thoughts and actions to "I could, and I have a choice" is a good place to start. For example, "I should be more loving" can become "I could be more loving, and I have a choice." We create more effective choices when we take the time not to be judgmental and to release fears and guilt. We can all change, and it is a skill of awareness to acknowledge that we are worth the effort.

Spirit Potential

Throughout history, there has been a quest to understand the purpose of human life experience. Humankind is incomplete unless the human condition for transcendence evolves (see Chapters 1 through 3). Spirit comes from our roots—the universal need to understand the human experience of life on earth. It is the vital element and the driving force in how we live our lives. It impacts every aspect of our life choices and the degree to which we develop our human potentials. Spirit involves the development of our higher self, also referred to as the transpersonal self. A transpersonal experience or transcendence is described as a feeling of oneness, inner peace, harmony, and wholeness and connection with the universe.[5–10] The meaning and joy that flow from developing this aspect of our human potential allow us to have a transpersonal view. Some of the ways we may come to know this transcendence are through prayer, meditation, organized religion, philosophy, science, poetry, music, inspired friends, and group work.

Like the other potentials, spirit potential does not develop without some attention. Every day, with each of our experiences, we need to acknowledge that our spirit potential is essential to the development of a healthy value system. We shape our perception of the world through our value system, and our perceptions will influence whether we have positive or negative experiences. Even through the pain of a negative experience, we have the ability to learn. Pain can be a great teacher. On the other side of the experience is new wisdom, self-discovery, and the chance for making new choices based on wisdom.

AFFIRMATIONS

As strong, positive statements acknowledging that something is already so, affirmations can help us change our perceptions and beliefs. If we believe an affirmation to be true, our perceptions selectively reinforce it because we change our self-talk. Our mind is constantly engaged in dialogue with ourselves; in fact, the person we talk to the most in a day is the self. Self-talk even operates in our unconscious through dreams while we sleep. Thus, an important way to influence our unconscious is to focus on positive images and affirmations before we drift to sleep and immediately on awakening. Positive images and affirmations also reinforce those things that have meaning and value. They help us in our spiritual development because they move into the deep layers of the unconscious, become part of our myths, and influence our daily lives.

If our thoughts are hopeful and optimistic, our body responds with confidence, energy, and hope. If negative thoughts dominate, however, our body responds with tightness, uneasiness, and an increase in breathing, blood pressure, and heart rate. Affirmations are statements we select to affirm our intentions and choices; they can help us

- identify what is true for us so that the truth can manifest itself in behavior and more options
- clarify goals, take actions, and conduct self-evaluations
- assume more responsibility for our actions, thoughts, beliefs, and values
- envision a new way of being

CONCLUSION

Each of our human potentials affects our whole being. Our challenge in all aspects of our personal and professional lives is to strive to integrate all our human potentials. When we assess our human potentials and decide how we want our lives to be, we evoke meaning and purpose in life. If one area of our human potential is left undeveloped, things do not seem to be as good as they could be. When one strives to develop all areas, however, a sense of wholeness emerges, one's self-worth increases, and

PHYSICAL

- I assess my general health daily.
- I exercise three to five times a week for 20 minutes.
- I eat nutritious food daily.
- I play without guilt.
- I practice relaxation daily.
- I have energy levels effective for daily activities.
- I do not smoke.
- I drink in moderation.
- I have regular physical and dental check-ups.
- I balance my work life with my personal life.

MENTAL

- I am open and receptive to new ideas and life patterns.
- I read a broad range of subjects.
- I am interested in and knowledgeable about many topics.
- I use my imagination in considering new choices or possibilities.
- I prioritize my work and set realistic goals.
- I enjoy developing new skills and talents.
- I ask for suggestions and help when I need it.

EMOTIONS

- I assess and recognize my own feelings.
- I have a nonjudgmental attitude.
- I express my feelings in appropriate ways.
- I consider my feelings when making decisions.
- I acknowledge both happy and painful memories.
- I listen and respect the feelings of others.
- I recognize my intuition.
- I listen to inner self-talk.

RELATIONSHIPS

- I share my opinions and feelings without seeking the approval of others or fearing outcomes.
- I create and participate in satisfying relationships.
- I allow sexuality to be a part of my relationships.
- I have a balance between my work and my family life.
- I am clear in expressing my needs and desires.
- I am open and honest with people without fearing the consequences.
- I do my part in establishing and maintaining relationships.
- I focus on positive topics in relationships.

CHOICES

- I manage time to meet my personal goals.
- I am committed and disciplined whenever I take on new projects.
- I follow through and work on decisions with clarity and action steps.
- I am usually clear on decisions.
- I take risks.
- I can accept circumstances beyond my control.
- I take on no more new tasks than I can successfully handle.

SPIRIT

- I operate from the perspective that life has value, meaning, and direction.
- I know, at some level, a connection with the universe.
- I know some power greater than myself.
- I feel a part of life and living frequently.
- I recognize that the different roles of my life are expressions of my true self.
- I know how to create balance and a sense of connectedness.

life goals are actualized. Being alive becomes more exciting, rewarding, and fulfilling. Even when frustrations arise, the whole person is able to recognize choices and decrease the barriers to maximizing human potentials.

DIRECTIONS FOR FUTURE RESEARCH

1. Determine if the percentage of desired client outcomes increases when the nurse uses the circle of human potential as an assessment tool and a nursing intervention.
2. Determine if the nurse's self-esteem increases when the concepts of the circle of human potential and affirmations are integrated each day.
3. Determine if the client's self-esteem increases when the concepts of the circle of human potential and affirmations are taught.
4. Evaluate changes in behavior and perceived quality of life when clients learn awareness skills in regard to their human potentials.

NURSE HEALER REFLECTIONS

After reading this chapter, the nurse healer will be able to answer or begin a process of answering the following questions:

- What is my process when I assess my circle of human potentials?
- Am I consciously aware of the daily opportunity to manifest my own human potentials?
- What can I do to increase my conscious awareness of fully participating in living?
- How do I feel when I use the word *healer* to describe myself?
- What is my inner awareness when I acknowledge my healing potential?

NOTES

1. L. Dossey, *Space, Time and Medicine* (Boston: Shambhala Publications, 1982).
2. L. Keegan and B. Dossey, *Self Care: A Program To Improve Your Life* (Temple, TX: Bodymind Systems, 1987).
3. L. Keegan, *Nurse As Healer* (New York: Delmar Publishers, 1994).
4. L. Dossey, *Healing Words: The Power of Prayer and the Practice of Medicine* (San

Francisco: Harper, 1993).

5. J. Achterberg et al., *Rituals of Healing: Using Imagery for Health and Wellness* (New York: Bantam Books, 1994).
6. T. Moore, *Care of the Soul* (New York: HarperCollins, 1992).
7. P. Burkhardt and M. Nagai-Jacobson, Reawakening Spirit in Clinical Practice, *Journal of Holistic Nursing* 12, no. 1 (1994):9–21.
8. J. Kornfield, *A Path with Heart* (New York: Bantam Books, 1993).
9. L. Dossey, *Recovering the Soul: A Scientific and Spiritual Search* (New York: Bantam Books, 1989).
10. L. Dossey, *Meaning and Medicine: Lessons from a Doctor's Tales of Breakthrough and Healing* (New York: Bantam Books, 1991).

VISION OF HEALING

Changing Outcomes

Whatever we focus on expands.

Glenda Lippman[1]

Because our thinking influences the way that we interpret our world, changing our thoughts can change our physical and emotional interaction with society. As clients share their inner dialogue and interpretation of events with nurses, we are allowed glimpses into their distinctive world view.

Our inner conversation forms a backdrop against which our lives unfold; if it is optimistic and affirmative, our actions and attitudes take on a positive tone. If, on the other hand, the inner conversation is negative and bleak, so follows our behavior, and in some cases, our mental and physical health. Gently helping clients identify discrepancies between their thoughts and reality allows them to bring the world into a clearer focus. By examining the silent dialogue that accompanies every interaction with the outer world, identifying false assumptions, distortions, and misinterpretations, clients can choose to make healthy changes. Sensitive questions, frequent restatement of clients' accounts of their perceptions, and requests for clarification will help guide the nurses and clients on the road to accurate interpretation of events, thoughts, and feelings.

Caregivers should proceed into the inner world of the clients' minds with reverence and respect. We are only guests in that world and must facilitate healthy redirection with regard for the multitude of unknown stories that contribute to the wholeness of our clients.

NOTE

1. Personal communication.

Chapter 10

Cognitive Therapy

Leslie Gooding Kolkmeier

NURSE HEALER OBJECTIVES

Theoretical

- Identify the components of a successful client contract.
- Describe seven cognitive errors, and give examples of each.
- Determine the differences and similarities between client-generated and nurse-generated goals.

Clinical

- Identify a client's cognitive distortions, and reflect those distortions in a nonthreatening, therapeutic manner.
- Enter into a contract for change with a client; review and renegotiate that contract over the period necessary for both participants to agree on successful completion.

Personal

- Keep a notebook of your cognitive distortions for 1 week. Correct those distortions, and record the bodymind shifts that accompany the corrections.
- Identify a personal behavior that you wish to change, and write a contract with someone you respect. Monitor your progress as you reevaluate the contract over a 1-month period.
- Develop a list of meaningful personal rewards.

DEFINITIONS

Cognitive Distortions: distortions of thinking; irrational thoughts.

Cognitive Restructuring: examining and reframing one's interpretation of the meaning of an event.

Contract: a written or verbal formalization of an agreement between two people, such as a nurse and client, client and family member, or client and friend.

THEORY AND RESEARCH

Thoughts enter our consciousness uninvited and unplanned, but they wield a great influence over our bodymind. Both positive and negative thoughts and images can affect our immune system, hormone levels, endocrine activity, and physical and mental activity levels and expectations. With the help of nursing interventions, clients can determine their thought patterns, identify the emotional and behavioral consequences of those thoughts, and then choose concrete ways of challenging and changing those thoughts and behaviors.

Cognitive therapy came on the mental health scene in the early 1960s. First used in the treatment of depression, it is now used in the treatment of anxiety and phobias, obsessive-compulsive disorders, and others as well. Cognitive therapy focuses on a client's thoughts in response to his or her interpretation of an event and the meaning attributed to that event.

Goal setting and contracting have been natural outgrowths of the cognitive therapy movement. Although goal setting has been a part of nursing care plans for years, only recently has the client become an integral part of the health care team both in setting goals and in finding ways to implement the care plan. Cognitive restructuring, goal setting, and contracting are means to help clients change their behavior in a health-promoting direction.

It can be crucial to help clients, particularly those who are ill, verbalize their unspoken thoughts and help them correct distortions or fallacies. The health care system may be foreign territory to clients, with its own rules, language, and customs. They can easily misinterpret this unfamiliar land, often to the detriment of their health.

Since the 1970s, nurses have used contracting for a variety of reasons. For examples, contracting has been useful in managing blood sugar levels in diabetic clients, reducing blood pressure, maintaining potassium levels in dialysis clients, increasing use of contraceptives, promoting medication compliance, and dealing with relationship difficulties.[1,2] Contingency contracts are based on the principle of positive reinforcement; they differ from treatment contracts, frequently used in counseling settings, which focus on the therapeutic issues to be covered by the therapist and the client.

Cognitive Restructuring

The stress of life changes or illness frequently leads to errors of thought; conversely, errors of thought increase the stress of daily events and crises. There are various types of irrational or erroneous thoughts.[3,4]

- *assignment of blame:* "If you would come straight home, I wouldn't be so lonely." Other people and events are seen as responsible for the person's happiness.
- *catastrophizing:* "I got a lousy grade on that test. I'll probably have to drop out of school, and I won't be able to find a decent job and have to move back in with my folks." Images of disaster replace reality.
- *discounting:* "You're just saying that because you have to." The person is unable to accept praise.
- *fallacy of fairness:* "It's not fair that she won; my project was a whole lot better." There is an assumption that life is fair and that we all agree on standards of fairness.
- *global labeling:* "She's a blond; what an airhead!" An illogical leap is made from one characteristic to a category that includes many characteristics.
- *mind reading:* "Jimmy went off to bed without saying anything. He's angry with me for overcooking the vegetables." Assumptions are made about thoughts and behavior without validation. Jimmy was preoccupied with problems at work.
- *overgeneralization:* "Fixing my car cost twice what they said it would. All mechanics are dishonest." A general conclusion is made from one or two examples.
- *personalization:* "If Bob and Mary start dating, I'll be left out in the cold." The person sees events only in relation to himself or herself.
- *polarized thinking:* "He didn't call back. Obviously, he doesn't love me." Everything is black or white; there are no grey areas.
- *should statements:* "Good employees should always get to the office early and work until after quitting time." Rigid rules are applied to a wide variety of circumstances.

Cognitive restructuring is a technique used to help clients reappraise or reassess their thinking and thinking errors and choose healthier alternatives. Thus, cognitive therapy seeks to

- identify cognitions relevant to the presenting problem
- recognize connections among cognitions, affects, and behaviors
- examine the evidence for and against key beliefs
- encourage the client to try alternative conceptualizations
- teach the client to carry out the cognitive restructuring process independently[5]

Goal Setting

At the same time as the financial resources available for health care are redirected to expensive equipment and heroic care at both the beginning and the end of the life span, the hospital stay is shortened for many clients. The client and family or home care nurses assume more responsibility for care after discharge. Much of the implementation of a long-term care plan becomes the responsibility of the client and/or family, for example.

Research has shown that clients are more likely to accomplish goals if they have been the major source of planning for those goals.[6] As the population assumes more responsibility for health and moves into a more active partnership with health care providers, we must honor their input in order to achieve successful outcomes.

Contracting

Not only is contracting a way to increase the quality of communication between the client and nurse, but also it can help a client become a more willing participant in self-care through negotiations about numerous aspects of his or her own health care. Successful completion of a contract deepens self-esteem and the client-nurse bond. Failure to comply with the terms of a contract opens the door to frank discussion of the reasons that compliance is a problem and ways in which the situation can be adjusted to achieve a mutually acceptable goal.[7]

The contracting process has five steps.[8]

1. problem identification and priority ranking: mutual agreement on the problem to be resolved
2. contract development: a description of the responsibilities and actions of both the client and the clinician

3. contract implementation: a focus on the carrying out of the individual responsibilities
4. contract evaluation: joint assessment of the outcome of the contract, including a renegotiation of the terms, if necessary
5. contract termination: target date for successful completion of the contract

NURSING PROCESS

Assessment

In preparing to use cognitive restructuring, goal setting, or contracting, assess the following parameters:

- the client's ability to monitor inner dialogue and communicate
- the client's perception of the problem and the degree to which the client wishes to change a thought or behavior
- the client's level of experience with each of the interventions to be used

Nursing Diagnoses

The following nursing diagnoses compatible with cognitive therapy and that are related to the human response patterns of Unitary Person (see Chapter 7) are as follows:

• Communicating:	Altered verbal/nonverbal communications
• Relating:	Altered, actual or potential Impaired social interaction Social isolation Parenting
• Choosing:	Coping, ineffective individual and family
• Perceiving:	Altered self-concept Disturbance in self-esteem, body image, role performance, personal identity Powerlessness
• Knowing:	Altered thought processes
• Feeling:	Anxiety, fear

Client Outcomes

Table 10–1 guides the nurse in client outcomes, nursing prescriptions, and evaluation for the use of cognitive restructuring, goal setting, and contracting in nursing interventions.

Plan and Interventions

Before the Session

- Create a space in which you and the client can feel physically and emotionally safe—a space that is open, pleasant, and comfortable—in order to establish a therapeutic relationship and to facilitate conversation with the client.
- Provide materials for recording cognitive distortions and alternative rational thoughts and statements, goals, or contracts (e.g., paper and pen, blackboard, preprinted forms).

Table 10–1 Nursing Interventions: Cognitive Restructuring, Goal Setting, and Contracting

Client Outcomes	*Nursing Prescriptions*	*Evaluation*
The client will demonstrate the ability to recognize cognitive distortions and correct them.	Guide the client in recording cognitive distortions and irrational thoughts.	The client recorded the positive bodymind shifts that accompany clear thinking. The client reported decreased anxiety, fears, depression, and somatic complaints and an elevation in self-esteem after correcting cognitive distortions.
The client will set a goal, complete a contract for change, and follow through to completion and reward.	Guide the client in setting a reasonable goal, negotiating adequate time and resources for the change, and following through with the co-signer of the contract.	The client shared with the health care provider a sense of self-reliance, increased self-esteem, and an ability to choose further rational goals and rewards. The client chose and participated in appropriate reward.

- Prepare handouts or worksheets to give to the client.
- Center yourself; clear your mind of personal or professional issues in order to be fully present for the client.

At the Beginning of the Session

- Assess the client's level of anxiety, discomfort, or relaxation.
- Review homework from previous session.

During the Session

- Guide and support the client as he or she reports on any events that may have an impact on the session.
- Determine, with the help of the client, which issues need to be addressed.
- Listen with focused intention and provide appropriate feedback, clarification, support, or interpretation.

At the End of the Session

- Have the client identify and verbalize changes that have occurred during the session.
- Assign homework to be done for the next session.
- Use the client outcomes that were established before the session (see Table 10–1) and the client's subjective experiences (Exhibit 10–2) to evaluate the session.
- Schedule a follow-up session.

Specific Interventions

Identification of Cognitive Distortions (Basic to Advanced). Identifying and correcting distorted or irrational thoughts begin with helping the client to understand that these thoughts are automatic; they emerge from the unconscious into the conscious mind in response to a situation that causes discomfort. These thoughts must be captured, examined, refuted, and replaced with healthy, rational alternatives. Clients may have difficulty finding the words to describe their thoughts, and a good rapport between client and nurse is vital so that the client feels safe and free enough to verbalize what may seem to be foolish or embarrassing inner conversation. Role playing or the nurse's sharing a personal incident may help open the way to productive disclosure.

Once the client is able to verbalize thoughts, they must be recorded and examined. Some clients prefer to use a diary; others may prefer a more structured format. For example, the client may use a five-column format to record the following:

1. situation
2. feelings experienced
3. thoughts
4. errors in those thoughts
5. rational alternatives to the thoughts

Early in therapy, it may be necessary for this exploration to take place within the session so that the nurse can help. After gaining more experience and insight, however, the client can do more work outside the session as homework. Eventually, the client will be able to abandon the paperwork, recognize distorted thoughts when they arise, and correct them with rational thinking.

Successful Goal Setting (Basic). Although useful with all clients, goal setting is particularly important in determining the limits of a contract. Goals, time frame, evaluation, and rewards should be primarily client-generated. A nurse cannot know a client well enough to decide the goals toward which that client should strive. On the other hand, the client may have unreasonable ideas about what reasonable goals are, and the nurse must make available all pertinent information needed to arrive at a mutually satisfactory goal. Goals should be specific, concrete, and measurable; in addition, they should offer a good chance of successful completion.

It is important to help clients establish beliefs that will allow them to dictate their own lives and their own experience. Setting goals facilitates this because it serves as a reminder that they have the power to create new experiences in their lives. Nurses may make such suggestions as the following to help clients set goals[9]:

- Examine the rewards or secondary gains that you get from lacking health awareness or from being sick. Set a goal that will allow you to get that same reward from health, not sickness.
- Look at activities you have always wanted to do, but have not because of a lack of time, money, or whatever. Encouraging yourself to do these things can put more meaning in your life.
- Use the 2×-50 rule of goal setting. After stating the goal as it first comes to mind, double the amount of time allowed to accomplish it, or reduce its difficulty by 50 percent. For example, "I will lose 10 pounds in the next month" is an unreasonable goal; "I will lose 10

pounds in the next 2 months" or "I will lose 5 pounds in the next month" is a reasonable goal. Either is within reach and, therefore, more likely to be attained, give the client a sense of achievement, build self-esteem, and foster the enthusiasm to set further goals.

Rewards for Achievement (Basic). It is often difficult for a client to determine what rewards are appropriate for the successful completion of a contract. Many people feel uncomfortable rewarding themselves and fail to realize that rewards are important in learning and maintaining new behavior patterns. The nurse can help the client keep in mind that rewards need not cost money or even be tangible in order to maintain enthusiasm for reaching the agreed upon goal.

The following are responses from a group of health care workers to the question, "How do you reward yourself for accomplishing a goal?"

1. Take a picnic to the country (or to a city park).
2. Buy a new record, tape, or CD.
3. Browse in a bookstore or hardware store.
4. Take a bubble bath and stay in 30 minutes longer than usual.
5. Work on a hobby or project.
6. Buy an item for my craft or hobby.
7. Spend time alone with a special friend.
8. Go to a movie or rent a videotape.
9. Take time alone just to sit and think.
10. Go to a free concert or play in the park.
11. Take a half-day off to go fishing.
12. Cook a special meal or go out for a special dinner.
13. Read in the bathtub.
14. Start a new project.
15. Walk on the beach.
16. Treat myself to a manicure or pedicure.
17. Make a phone call to an old friend.
18. Take a continuing education short course in something new.
19. Take a nap.

Under some circumstances, the nurse may provide reinforcers to reward the client for the completion of a goal. Reinforcers such as candy, small toys, tokens to be used as trade, or special privileges are especially useful with children or others in residential settings who have difficulty establishing rewards and taking responsibility for dispensing these rewards. Like all rewards, reinforcers must be congruent with the difficulty of the goal achieved and need not be time-consuming or expensive. Ideally, clients learn to self-reward as they internalize the new cognitions.

Negotiation of Contracts (Basic to Advanced). When introducing the concept of making a contract to a client, a nurse may ask the following questions[10]:

- What would you most like to change about your life right now?
- How can you begin the first step in that change?
- On what date would you like to achieve that goal?
- How can you reward yourself for success?
- How will your life be different when you succeed?
- How can I help?

Contracts may be verbal, but all parties are more likely to take written contracts seriously. If the contracts are written, both the client and the nurse should sign them. Contracts should always contain these key elements:

1. a specific, realistic, measurable goal to be reached
2. a time limit for completion, as well as specific times to evaluate progress
3. a statement of the responsibilities of both parties (e.g., client and nurse, client and spouse)
4. a clear reward for accomplishing the stated goal

In our era of litigation, clients may find the word *contract* threatening or uncomfortable. If so, the contract may be referred to as an agreement or bargain. When helping a client draft a contract, the nurse assumes the role of facilitator rather than originator. After presenting the concept of contracting and pointing out some of the reasons that such an approach may be valid in the client's particular circumstances, the nurse may try to limit his or her further involvement to guidance and support. The greater the client input, the greater the client compliance with the terms of the contract. Furthermore, the smaller the steps needed to comply with the contract, the more likely the client's success in reaching the desired goal. It is better to construct a series of contracts, each with a high probability of success, than to expect a client to accomplish a difficult goal in one leap.

Exhibit 10–1 Sample Contract

Starting today, August 18, I will not use a salt shaker at the table for 2 consecutive weeks. At the end of those 2 weeks, I will reward myself by taking my boys fishing for the afternoon. The following Monday I will telephone my nurse, and we will write a new contract based on my blood pressure readings and my goals for the month of September.

Signed: Angela Smith

Signed: Robert Long, RN

Source: Adapted from *Journal of Holistic Nursing*, Vol. 2, No. 1, pp. 21–23, with permission of American Holistic Nurses Association, © 1987.

Exhibit 10–1 shows a contract agreed upon by Mrs. Smith and her nurse. Mrs. Smith was having difficulty following a low-salt diet. After discussing with the nurse the use of contracts in cases similar to hers, she wrote up and signed the contract, stayed within its guidelines, and began to make significant changes in her eating behavior. This intervention helped her reach her goal, gain insight into her behavior, and become an active participant in her health care.

Case Study

Setting: Clinic with stress management program

Client: S.M., a 46-year-old nurse

Nursing Diagnoses:
1. Powerlessness
2. Altered health maintenance
3. Knowledge deficit
4. Self-care deficit: all related to the perceived stress of her job and the responsibility of being the single parent of a teen-aged son.

S.M. had recognized that she sometimes "thought crazy thoughts" and also understood that her physiologic changes were symptoms of a physical illness but rather responses to the things that she was thinking. In spite of her intellectual understanding, she still suffered from palpitations, occasional shortness of breath, and frequent insomnia. Her symptoms lessened somewhat when she learned relaxation skills in her stress management course and improved dramatically within a few weeks after she learned to reframe her irrational thought patterns. She brought the following five-column record into class the week after the instructor explained cognitive restructuring to the group:

1. *situation:* 11:30 P.M., Johnny not home from a date, curfew was 11 P.M.
2. *feelings experienced:* fear, dread, anger.
3. *thoughts:* "Something terrible must have happened to him. He must have been in an accident. I shouldn't have let him take the car. He's too young to be dating. I'm a terrible mother. I shouldn't have divorced his father. I need help raising a son."
4. *errors in those thoughts:* catastrophizing, "should" statements, global labeling, polarized thinking.
5. *rational alternatives to the thoughts:* "The game probably ran late. If he had been in an accident, the police would have called. He is a good driver and has had his license for over a year without any problems. He is old enough to take responsibility for dating and is learning good social skills and responsibilities. Staying with his alcoholic father would have done the whole family harm. I'm doing a good job raising him."

When her son arrived 20 minutes later, he explained that he had been unable to call her to let her know the game had run into overtime because long lines of kids were waiting to use the telephone. He had headed home as soon as he took his date home, but a mile from the house, he had a flat tire. Rather than risk walking alone that late at night, he had quickly changed the tire and driven home. He apologized for worrying her, but explained that he had looked at the alternatives and chosen what he thought she would have wanted him to do.

S.M. continued to monitor and correct her irrational thoughts and was soon able to do most of the corrections mentally. She applied her skill to stress-producing thoughts both at work and in her personal life and enjoyed having control over how she felt both physically and emotionally.

Evaluation

With the client, the nurse determines whether the client outcomes for cognitive restructuring, goal setting, and contracting (see Table 10–1) were successfully achieved. To evaluate the session further, the nurse may again explore the subjective effects of the experience with the client based on the evaluation questions in Exhibit 10–2.

Exhibit 10–2 Evaluating the Client's Subjective Experience with Cognitive Restructuring, Goal Setting, and Contracting

1. Did this experience produce any feelings or emotions? Can you describe them?
2. Did the experience change your thoughts concerning life events?
3. Can you put words on your inner conversation during this experience?
4. Do you feel more confident about your ability to recognize thinking errors and choose healthier alternatives?
5. Can you see yourself choosing a goal, breaking it down into manageable parts, and identifying an appropriate reward for reaching that goal?
6. Can you identify any thoughts or behaviors that you might want to change in the future?
7. Would you like to try this again?
8. What would make this a better experience for you?
9. What is your next step (or your plan) to integrate this experience into your life on an as-needed basis?

Completion of a contract or other intervention may take an extended period of time; therefore, continuing support, feedback, and review may be necessary. Nurses use several techniques to help clients shift their inner focus and experience the joy of changing unhealthy behaviors and thought processes. Overcoming lifelong behaviors can be challenging, but with careful choices of interventions and support from others, health-affirming change can take place.

DIRECTIONS FOR FUTURE RESEARCH

1. Measure the effectiveness of various rewards and reinforcers in client contracts.
2. Determine what cognitive distortions are most common among clients with acute conditions and among those with chronic conditions.
3. Determine the degree of satisfaction and compliance in clients who have input into goal setting as opposed to those clients who have little or no input into goal setting.

NURSE HEALER REFLECTIONS

After reading this chapter, the nurse healer will be able to answer or begin the process of answering the following questions:

- What distortions am I aware of in my thinking?
- What internal or external factors seem to influence the degree to which I experience cognitive distortions?
- How successful am I at positively influencing my thought processes?
- What changes do I experience in my work or home life when I actively set and accomplish goals for myself?
- How do I feel when the goals that clients set for themselves differ from the goals that I would have set for them?

NOTES

1. S. Boehm, Patient Contracting, in *Annual Review of Nursing Research*, ed. J. Fitzpatrick et al. (New York: Springer Publishing Co., 1989), 143–154.
2. T. Keane et al., Spouse Contracting To Increase Antabuse Compliance in Alcoholic Veterans, *Journal of Clinical Psychology* 40, no. 1 (1984):341–344.
3. A. Beck, *Cognitive Therapy* (New York: New American Library, 1979).
4. D. Schuyler, *A Practical Guide to Cognitive Therapy* (New York: W.W. Norton, 1991).
5. Ibid., 29.
6. M. Maves, Mutual Goal Setting, in *Nursing Interventions: Essential Nursing Treatments*, ed. G. Bulechek and J. McClosky (Philadelphia: W.B. Saunders, 1992).
7. L. Kolkmeier, Contracting in an Outpatient Setting, *Journal of Holistic Nursing* 2, no. 1 (1987):21–23.
8. G. Bulechek and J. McClosky, *Nursing Interventions* (Philadelphia: W.B. Saunders, 1985), 94.
9. C.E. Guzzetta and B.M. Dossey, *Cardiovascular Nursing: Holistic Practice* (St. Louis: Mosby-Year Book, 1992), 29.
10. Kolkmeier, Contracting.

SUGGESTED READING

D. Burns, *Feeling Good: The New Mood Therapy* (New York: New American Library, 1990).

M. McKay et al., *Thoughts and Feelings: The Art of Cognitive Stress Intervention* (Richmond, CA: New Harbinger Publications, 1981).

VISION OF HEALING

Nourishing the Bodymind

In large measure, joy and vitality can come from eating well, exercising regularly, and moving creatively to the rhythm of life. A wise nurse endeavors to maximize and develop the best of nutrition, exercise, and movement skills both for the self as well as for the client. As we approach the twenty-first century, the ancient Greek ideal of a sound mind in a strong, able body is once again in fashion. A healthy physical body can indeed be the temple for the mind/spirit. The way in which we care for and nourish our body not only affects our general physical well-being, but also increases our mental and spiritual capacities.

Nutrition and exercise work synergistically to promote high-level wellness behavior. Foods have power. Foods transfer their power to human beings when we digest and assimilate them. One of the basic premises behind the ability of food to heal is that food is comprised of organic chemicals just as we are. As physical organisms, we are composed of millions of biochemicals. Their daily replacement in the form of healthy nutrients is critical to our optimal functioning. Food consumption and physical activity have a direct effect on the body, mind, and spirit. Unlike medicines, healthy eating and active movement enables us to build up or tear down the actual tissues of our bodies. When we eat well and exercise, we build strong, healthy bodies, but when diets and movement are defective, we deprive our bodies. In general, the feeling of well-being that comes from physical health permeates each and every individual activity, enabling the quickest mental thoughts, permitting a better night's sleep, and perhaps facilitating spiritual direction.

The lack of proper nutrition, exercise, and movement contributes to major risk factors for disease, such as hypertension, hypercholesterolemia, and obesity. Eating habits affect exercise abilities and vice versa. The exciting fact is that both nutrition and exercise patterns are modifiable when individuals make the decision to move toward wellness. For those who are nutritionally compromised or physically weakened because of illness and disease or because of mental, emotional, or spiritual ennui, the good news is that anyone with knowledge and motivation can use the principles of healing nutrition and exercise to activate and renourish the bodymind.

As we round out this century, each of us has the capacity to become increasingly aware of acquiring information, not only to prevent disease, but to maximize a vital, productive life. The nurse can increase his or her own vigor and vitality and then use the same guidelines to assist the client. As a collective whole, nurses can join with other health professionals to meet the objective of increased health and vitality for all peoples.

Chapter 11

Nutrition, Exercise, and Movement

Lynn Keegan

NURSE HEALER OBJECTIVES

Theoretical

- Learn the definitions of terms in this chapter.
- List the recommended goals set by the U.S. Senate Subcommittee on Nutrition.
- Understand the new guidelines for nutrition under the food pyramid.
- Differentiate among exercise, fitness, and movement.
- Develop a plan that combines good nutrition, exercise, and ideal weight.
- Learn the benefits of exercise in both illness and in health.

Clinical

- Assess the level of nutrition that increases or depletes your energy level at work.
- Develop an awareness of body mechanics during both clinical physical activity and desk work.
- Employ strategies to improve nutrition, exercise, and movement in your workplace.
- Consider the ways in which a nurse serves as a role model during the workday.
- Learn the value of becoming an exercise leader in the clinical setting.

Personal

- Spend time becoming aware of your current eating habits, exercise patterns, and movement activity.
- Assess your habits in each of the areas, recognizing strengths and weaknesses.
- Begin to experiment with new patterns in each area.
- Become increasingly sensitive to nuances of feeling as you gradually refine skills in each area.

DEFINITIONS

Nutrition

HDL: high-density lipoprotein form of cholesterol associated with reduced risk of atherosclerosis.

LDH: low-density lipoprotein form of cholesterol strongly associated with increased risk of atherosclerosis.

Mineral: an inorganic element or compound necessary for human life.

Vitamin: an organic substance necessary for normal growth, metabolism, and development of the body; important in energy transformations, usually acting as co-enzyme in enzymatic systems.

Exercise and Movement

Aerobic Exercise: sustained muscle activity within the target heart range that challenges the cardiovascular system to meet the muscles' needs for oxygen.

Endurance: the period of time that the body can sustain exercise or movement.

Fitness: the ability to carry out daily tasks with vigor and alertness, without undue fatigue, and with ample reserve to enjoy leisure pursuits; the ability to respond to physical and emotional stress without an excessive increase in heart rate and blood pressure.

Flexibility: the ability to use a joint throughout its full range of motion and to maintain some degree of elasticity of major muscle groups.

Maximal Heart Rate: the rate of the heart when the body is engaged in intense physical activity.

Movement: changes in the spatial configuration of the body and its parts, such as in breathing, eating, speaking, gesturing, and exercising; motion away from mental, physical, emotional, or spiritual stasis.

Resting Heart Rate: the rate of the heart when the body is in deep rest.
Strength: the power of muscle groups.
Target Heart Rate: the safe range for the heart during exercise.

THEORY AND RESEARCH

Nutrition

During the past two decades, nutrition has moved into the forefront as a prominent component in health promotion and disease prevention. Most of us are now probably well aware of the correlation between what we eat and how we feel, how the bodymind functions, and whether diseases develop. The primary impetus for the increased public interest and concomitant change came in 1977 from the U.S. Senate Select Committee on Nutrition in the United States. Appointed to study the nutritional habits of U.S. citizens and to make recommendations for improvement, the committee reported that nutrition was the number one public health problem in the United States. The general population consumed an unbalanced supply of calories and nutrients, which contributed to disease and multiple minor ailments. The committee adopted seven dietary recommendations[1]:

1. To avoid becoming overweight, consume only as much energy (calories) as expended. Decrease energy intake and increase exercise if overweight.
2. Increase consumption of fresh fruits and vegetables and whole grains to 48 percent of food intake.
3. Reduce consumption of refined and processed sugars to 10 percent of daily intake.
4. Reduce fat consumption to 30 percent of daily intake.
5. Reduce intake of saturated fat to 10 percent of daily intake; take in 10 percent of calories in polyunsaturated fats and another 10 percent in monounsaturated fats.
6. Reduce cholesterol consumption to 300 grams per day.
7. Limit intake of salt to 5 grams per day.

It was in the 1950s that the U.S. Department of Agriculture introduced the four basic food groups. The newest version of the best foods to eat emerged in 1992 in the form of a food pyramid (Figure 11–1).[2] Like the original system, the pyramid system divides foods into groups rich in certain nutrients. The new pyramid is made up of six groups instead of four, however, and people are advised to eat most from the bottom at the widest part.[3] Part of the impetus to create this guide was the need to urge the public to eat more plant food and reduce fat intake, which is known to contribute to obesity, coronary artery disease, and certain forms of cancer.[4] The heavy emphasis on fruits and vegetables encourages a greater intake of vitamin C, beta carotene, and fiber—food components that are now believed to offer some protection against coronary artery disease, diabetes, and cancer.[5] The small portion of fats, oils, and sweets at the apex of the pyramid emphasizes the need to limit the intake of foods that have the fewest vitamins and minerals and the most fats and calories.

The most recent and still controversial plan to emerge is the Mediterranean Diet Pyramid. The creators of the new Mediterranean diet proposal are a team of nutritionists and epidemiologists from the World Health Organization (WHO) and Harvard's school of public health. The proposal features its own pyramid along with recommendations for daily wine in moderation (one or two glasses a day) and physical activity. See Figure 11–2. Because of the still hotly debated issue of alcohol intake, a footnote to the proposal adds: "From a contemporary public health perspective, wine should be considered optional."[6] The new plan was introduced to the U.S. public and was the focus of attention during the summer of 1994.

Chronic Disease and Food

Cardiovascular Disease. Nutrition is the leading public health problem in the United States, and heart disease is the leading cause of death. In 1987, some 2 million U.S. citizens suffered from heart or vessel disease; 1,500,000 had a myocardial infarction; and approximately 550,000 died from cardiovascular disease.[7] The statistics for 1995 are similar.

Cardiovascular diseases are among the best documented examples of the way in which nutritional intake affects health. It is well established that plaque, a major culprit in cardiovascular disease, progressively builds up on arterial walls in large measure because of poor eating patterns. There are no early warning signs of plaque buildup. Often, the first symptom is a myocardial infarction or cerebral vascular accident. We now know that proper diet and a prescriptive exercise program can prevent plaque buildup in many people. New evidence continues to link what we eat to our risk for heart disease.

Extensive studies have been done on the relationship between atherosclerosis and elevated blood cholesterol levels.[8] Many clinicians believe that an appropriate nutritional program can lower blood cholesterol levels and optimize the ratio of high-density lipoproteins (HDLs) to low-den-

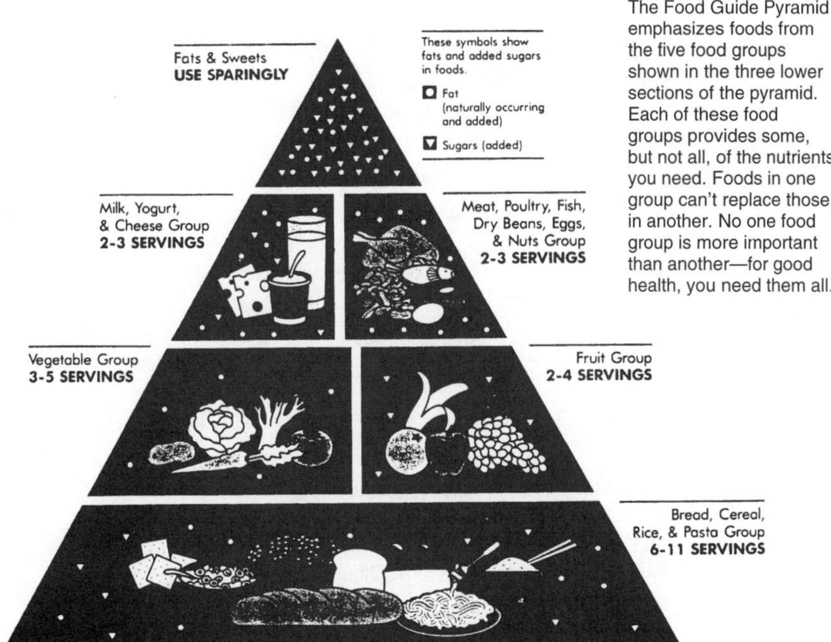
Fats & Sweets
USE SPARINGLY
These symbols show fats and added sugars in foods.
Fat (naturally occurring and added)
Sugars (added)
Milk, Yogurt, & Cheese Group
2-3 SERVINGS
Meat, Poultry, Fish, Dry Beans, Eggs, & Nuts Group
2-3 SERVINGS
Vegetable Group
3-5 SERVINGS
Fruit Group
2-4 SERVINGS
Bread, Cereal, Rice, & Pasta Group
6-11 SERVINGS
The Food Guide Pyramid emphasizes foods from the five food groups shown in the three lower sections of the pyramid. Each of these food groups provides some, but not all, of the nutrients you need. Foods in one group can't replace those in another. No one food group is more important than another—for good health, you need them all.

Figure 11-1 Food Guide Pyramid. *Source:* U.S. Department of Agriculture and the U.S. Department of Health and Human Services, provided by the Education Department of the National Live Stock and Meat Board.

sity lipoproteins (LDLs), thereby reducing the risk of cardiovascular disease. The goal of this nutritional program is to achieve and maintain total cholesterol levels in a range of 160 mg/dL% to 180 mg/dL%, rather than the current adult average of 235 mg/dL%.

Cancer. To some degree, cancers of the colon, breast, lung, mouth, throat, and cervix may all be linked to food consumption. The sluggish bowel syndrome caused by a high-fat, low-fiber diet allows waste products to sit in the colon and break down into potential carcinogens. A high-fat diet has been related to breast cancer, and alcohol intake has been related to cancers of the throat and mouth. Women with dysplasia—precancerous cervical cell changes—are more likely to have low blood levels of vitamin C, beta carotene, and folate than are women without dysplasia.[9]

Figure 11-2 Mediterranean Diet Pyramid. *Source:* Oldways Preservation & Exchange Trust. *Source:* M.W. Miller, Call for a Daily Dose of Wine Ferments Critics, pp. B1–2, June 17, 1994. Reprinted by permission from *The Wall Street Journal*, © 1994, Dow Jones & Company, Inc. All rights reserved worldwide.

Osteoporosis. Twenty million women in the United States have osteoporosis. By the age of 65, one of every four women will have a compression fracture of the spinal vertebrae. To a large extent, this disease and the associated complications are due to the decalcification of bones in postmenopausal women. A high-calcium diet is often helpful for these women.

Populations with Special Needs

Pregnant Adolescents. The nutritional needs of pregnant adolescents are greatest at a time when they are least psychologically interested in meeting them. Dieting, skipping meals, consuming fast foods, and trying unconventional diets are common eating behaviors among adolescents. Busy schedules, search for self-identity, peer influence, group conformity, and body image dissatisfaction also detract young girls from healthy eating. Because of their poor dietary habits, most usually enter pregnancy with reduced nutrient stores and an increased risk of nutritional deficiencies. Consequently, all pregnant teens should have a dietary habit assessment along with special dietary counseling.[10]

Older Adults. Energy expenditure and caloric intake typically decline with age. Unless nutrient and caloric intake improves, a parallel decline in vitamin and mineral intake is inevitable.[11] In addition, there is strong evidence that aging affects the requirements for certain vitamins. The 1989 recommended daily allowances appear to be too low for elderly people for vitamin D, riboflavin, vitamin B_6, and vitamin B_{12}, and too high for vitamin A.[12] Deficiencies or suboptimal intakes of water-soluble vitamins, vitamin D, calcium, zinc, copper, chromium, and water are reported in groups of older adults. Marginal nutrient deficiencies in this population may easily go undetected and contribute to morbidity.[13] Recommendations for these people should aim at correcting or preventing deficiencies by use of supplementary and complementary nutritional products.[14]

Many elderly people live alone and often do not bother to cook for themselves. They may find eating or swallowing difficult because of tooth pain or ill-fitting dentures. Many live on low or fixed incomes, and some take medications that cause adverse nutrient interactions. Reduced appetite or functional disabilities such as impaired taste and smell and other chronic diseases can all affect nutrition in the older adult.

Athletes. The nutritional requirements of athletes differ from those of nonathletes. A balanced diet for athletes consists of 60 percent of calories from carbohydrates, 15 percent from protein, and 25 percent from fat. It is also important to consider the adequacy of mineral and fluid intake.[15] The energy needs of ultraendurance athletes during training vary widely, depending on the duration, intensity, and type of exercise training. It is not known whether ultraendurance athletes have increased protein needs as a result of extended exercise training. Micronutrient needs may be altered for these athletes,, while dietary intake is generally greater than the recommended daily allowance because of high caloric intake. Prior to competition, ultraendurance athletes should consider glycogen supercompensation and a meal eaten 4 hours before the race as a means of improving performance.[16] Most athletes do not have dietary deficiencies, but those who restrict their food intake in order to maintain body weight may be deficient in folate, as well as in vitamins B_6, B_{12}, and

E. Some female athletes' diets are low in calcium, iron, and zinc. A low-calcium diet may reduce peak bone mass in young women.[17]

Healing Foods

In order to follow the dietary goals established by the U.S. Senate Select Committee on Nutrition, several approaches that simply modify the usual food consumption patterns are recommended (Table 11–1). Foods should be as free as possible of chemicals, additives, preservatives, and toxins. The healthiest foods are those subjected to the least processing, such as raw vegetables and fruits, living sprouts, whole grain breads and cereals, brown rice, dry peas and beans, raw unroasted seeds and nuts, and whole soy products. These products also increase the fiber in the diet. Egg yolks and high-fat dairy products should be taken in moderation. Foods are best eaten raw, poached, steamed, or grilled. Whenever possible, high-fat and fried foods should be avoided.

Most people consume 60 percent of their calories from sugar, fat, and alcohol, which contain almost no vitamins or minerals. Fat reduction is a major thrust of healthy eating. A nurse can use the following suggestions to guide the client in ways to substitute low-fat for high-fat foods:

- Because many major diseases are linked to high-fat diets, always choose the leanest cuts of meat.
- Trim all fat from meat, and take the skin off poultry and fish.
- Use meat more as a condiment than as a main course.
- Broil, poach, or steam instead of frying foods.
- Use vegetable oils in moderation.
- Use the nonfat and low-fat varieties of dairy products.

Nontraditional Foods

Today, new foods are available that both satisfy the palate and meet nutritional goals. Yogurt, a traditional Middle Eastern food, is becoming increasingly popular. It is high in B vitamins and low in calories. The best yogurt is the low-fat nonsweetened variety that contains live bacteria cultures. The *Lactobacillus acidophilus* seems to aid in digestion and is reported to replace the intestinal flora lost with the long-term use of antibiotics.

Tofu, which is made by curding the milky part of the soybean, is one of the most versatile protein foods in the world. It has been a high-protein

Table 11-1 Dietary Goals and Recommendations

Dietary Goal	*Food Group*	*Recommendation*
Reduce fat	Meat, fish, and poultry	No high-fat meats Trim fat edges from meats Remove skin from poultry
	Eggs	Two egg yolks or fewer per week, egg whites as desired
	Dairy products	Skim milk, low-fat yogurt, cottage cheese, and sherbet
	Fats and oils	Corn, safflower, or sunflower oils and margarines
	Commercial, processed, and fast foods	Limit to 1–2 times/week Buy with nutritional awareness and savvy
Reduce sugar	Soft drinks	Limit or eliminate soft drink consumption
	Fruits and vegetables	Eat fresh fruit or fresh or frozen vegetables
Reduce and maintain ideal body weight to ± 10%	Calories	Consume calories and expend calories to attain and maintain ideal weight
Increase complex carbohydrates (CHO)	Complex CHO—fiber	Increase use of lentils, dried peas, beans, whole grains products, nuts, and seeds
Reduce salt	Salt	Lower use of salt in cooking Eliminate processed foods high in salt
Reduce caffeine	Caffeine	Reduce coffee, tea, and diet sodas to under 2 cups per day
Reduce alcohol	Alcohol	1 ounce or less per day

staple in parts of Asia for more than 2,000 years. It is low in calories, fats, and carbohydrates, and it contains no cholesterol. Tofu can be prepared and served as a substitute for traditional protein in every kind of food, from entrée to dessert. Tofu cookbooks are appearing in the marketplace, and once the taste buds are reeducated, the prepared meals taste as good or even better than traditional high-fat meals.

Another protein food source introduced from Asia is miso, a fermented soybean paste with a texture resembling that of smooth peanut butter or cottage cheese. Like yogurt, it is a living food that contains *Lactobacillus* and other healthful microorganisms.

Another Asian custom recently introduced to the United States is the eating of sprouted seeds. In 2939 B.C., the Emperor of China recorded the use of "health giving sprouts." Although high in protein, vitamins, and minerals, sprouts are low in calories. The importance of plant seed sprouts will increase in the future as the population grows and the area of arable land decreases. When the seed harvest is sprouted, an acre of land will yield the maximum amount of edible plant food. For example, an acre of land can produce as much as 385 pounds of alfalfa seed from one pound of seed. If 384 pounds were sprouted for food, the yield would be approximately 3,180 pounds of consumable sprouts. It is important to be cognizant not only of individual food needs, but also of the food needs of all people of the earth and the needs of the planet itself.

Vitamins and Minerals

Vitamins are as necessary for our health as food and water. Whether or not we obtain all the necessary nutrients from even optimal food consumption patterns is a controversial topic. There are arguments both for and against supplementation. Therefore, nurses need to continue exploring new advances and controversies in vitamin and mineral therapy and supplementation.

Vitamins. Essential for healthy growth and development, as well as optimal daily function, vitamins differ from proteins, carbohydrates, and fats in that they are noncaloric nutrients. Most vitamins serve as helpers, or co-enzymes, in the metabolism of foods. Vitamins are divided into two basic groups: fat-soluble and water-soluble. Vitamins A, D, E, and K are soluble only in fats and, therefore, are absorbed into the blood together with dietary fats. Since they are insoluble in water, they are transported by the lymphatic vessels or the blood only after they have attached to a protein carrier. They are stored in the body adipose and liver tissues. Water-soluble vitamins, such as B complex and ascorbic acid (vitamin C), are easily absorbed into blood. Because excessive quantities are excreted rather than stored, water-soluble vitamins are seldom associated with toxicity problems. Table 11–2 provides basic information about the benefits and recommended daily allowances of the most common vitamins.

Vitamins C, E, and beta carotene are recognized as antioxidants. The essence of the antioxidants' work is controlling harmful "free radical" molecules. Recent findings indicate that certain doses of antioxidants can reduce the risk of myocardial infarction and other harmful diseases.

Table 11-2 Overview of Fat- and Water-Soluble Vitamins

Vitamin	*Function*	*Adult, Current Recommended Daily Allowance*	*Food Source*
Fat-Soluble Vitamins			
Vitamin A	Maintenance of mucous membranes Growth and development of bones	800 μg	Liver, milk products Dark leafy greens Orange fruit
Vitamin D	Bone growth	5 μg	Eggs, liver, milk
Vitamin E	Antioxidant	8 μg	Vegetable oils
Vitamin K	Blood clotting	80 μg	Egg yolk, liver, milk Leafy green vegetables
Water-Soluble Vitamins			
Vitamin B_1 (Thiamin)	Co-enzyme in oxidation of glucose	1.1 mg	Pork, beef, liver, fish, eggs Grains, legumes
Vitamin B_2 (Riboflavin)	Aid in release of energy from food	1.3 mg	Milk, cereals, bread Green vegetables
Vitamin B_6 (Pyridoxine)	Synthesis of nonessential amino acids	1.6 mg	Pork, milk, eggs Cereals, legumes
Vitamin B_{12}	Synthesis of red blood cells	2.0 μg	Seafood, meat, eggs, milk
Niacin (Nicotinic acid)	Transfer of hydrogen for synthesis of adenosine triphosphate	13 mg	Milk, eggs, fish, poultry
Vitamin C	Wound healing Collagen formation Prevention of scurvy Release of stress hormones Absorption of iron	60 mg	Citrus fruits, tomatoes Brussels sprouts, potatoes Broccoli

Minerals. Also necessary for human growth, development, and optimal function, minerals fulfill nine functions. They

1. are the essential constituents of all cells
2. form the greater portion of the hard parts of the body (i.e., bone, teeth, and nails)
3. are essential components of respiratory enzymes and enzyme systems
4. regulate the permeability of cell membranes and capillaries
5. regulate the excitability of muscular and nervous tissue
6. are essential for regulation of osmotic pressure equilibrium
7. are necessary for maintenance of proper acid-base balance
8. are essential constituents of secretions of glands
9. play an important role in water metabolism and regulation of blood volume

Minerals are divided into two categories: macrominerals, which are needed in relatively large quantities, and trace elements, which are required only in small amounts. Table 11–3 lists the functions, recommended daily allowances, and food sources of both macrominerals and trace elements.

Exercise

Traditionally, regular exercise programs were thought to be necessary only for athletes in training. We now know that vigorous aerobic exercise is good for everyone. Today, less than 1 percent of all the energy used in factories, workshops, and farms comes from human muscles. During the next few years, there will continue to be growth in information and technology occupations that are increasingly sedentary and, hence, potentially unhealthy.

Exercise is a form of movement that ranges from active physical exercise to subtle motions that are only slightly perceptible. In a review of national surveys, one study found that approximately 20 percent of adults exercise with the intensity and frequency necessary for cardiovascular benefit, 40 percent are moderately active, and 40 percent are basically sedentary.[18] Thus, even though the number of adults who exercise regularly is increasing, most are not exercising at the intensity or frequency necessary to obtain maximal health benefits.

Physical activity is positively associated with a vigorous life. A variety of clinical trials support the contention that regular participation in

Table 11-3 Macrominerals and Trace Elements

Mineral	*Function*	*Current Recommended Daily Allowance*	*Food Sources*
Calcium	Key building blocks for bones and teeth; aid in transmission of nerve messages to the brain, muscle movement, and blood clotting	800 mg	Skim or low-fat milk, low-fat yogurt, sardines, salmon, tofu, broccoli
Sodium	Works with potassium to regulate body fluids; necessary for nerve and muscle function	Not established	Table salt and most processed foods
Potassium	Works with sodium to regulate body fluids; necessary for nerve and muscle function	800 mg	Apricots, blackstrap molasses, broccoli, brussels sprouts, dates, figs, bananas, potatoes, sunflower seeds
Chloride	Aid in regulation of muscle movement	Not established	Seafood, skim milk, lean meat, eggs
Magnesium	Acid-alkaline balance, blood sugar metabolism, protein structuring	300 mg	Bananas, roasted peanuts, low-fat milk, yogurt, brown rice, bone meal, bran
Phosphorus	Bone/tooth formation, cell growth and repair, RNA and DNA involvement	800 mg	Lentils, liver, yogurt, milk, dark-meat poultry
Iron	Hemoglobin production, stress and disease resistance, growth in children	18 mg	Cream of wheat, liver, oysters, red meat, tuna, oatmeal, raisins
Zinc	Burn and wound healing, carbohydrate digestion, prostate gland function, reproductive organ growth and development	15 mg	Oysters, low-fat yogurt, grains, dark-meat poultry, liver, red meat, Brewer's yeast, fish, wheat germ

continues

Table 11-3 continued

Mineral	*Function*	*Current Recommended Daily Allowance*	*Food Sources*
Fluoride	Strong bones and teeth, prevention of caries by guarding against demineralization of teeth	Not established	6–8 glasses of fluoridated water daily
Copper	Bone formation, hair and skin color, healing processes, hemoglobin and red blood cell formation, mental processes, and emotional states	2–3 mg	Oysters, lobster, liver, grains, avocado, cauliflower, legumes, liver, molasses, nuts, organ meats, raisins
Chromium	Blood sugar level, glucose metabolism	50–200 µg	Black pepper, cheeses, corn oil
Selenium	Antioxidant, DNA and protein synthesis, immune response, membrane integrity	50–200 µg	Poultry, lean beef, Brewer's yeast, broccoli, fish, onion, tomatoes
Manganese	Enzyme activation, reproduction and growth, sex hormone production	2.5 mg	Bananas, bran, buckwheat, celery, green leafy vegetables, liver, nuts
Iodine	Energy production, body temperature, and growth	150 µg	Iodized salt, seafood, bread, dairy products

physical activity either delays the onset or reduces the severity of several chronic diseases, including obesity and coronary heart disease.[19]

Exercise Needs in Special Situations

Cardiovascular Effects. In acute heart failure, rest is a useful adjunct to pharmacologic treatment. In chronic heart failure, however, avoiding exercise can lead to deconditioning changes in skeletal muscle and in the peripheral circulation that may actually impair exercise tolerance. Although there is still some controversy as to whether training has a beneficial prognostic effect in patients with chronic heart failure and how soon after myocardial infarction it is safe for them to commence training, exercise seems increasingly set to become a popular and useful adjunct in the care of patients with chronic heart disease.[20]

The cardiovascular effects of aerobic exercise include a decrease in the resting heart rate and the heart rate response to submaximal exercise, an increase in resting and exercise stroke volume, an increase in maximal cardiac output, an increase in maximum oxygen consumption, and an increase in arteriovenous oxygen difference. These effects of cardiovascular fitness beneficially alter the coronary artery disease risk profile. An inverse relationship exists between physical fitness and resting heart rate; body weight; percent body fat; serum levels of cholesterol, triglycerides, and glucose; and systolic blood pressure. In addition, exercise increases the HDL fraction of total cholesterol. In order to develop and maintain cardiovascular fitness, an individual should do aerobic exercise 3 to 5 days per week at an intensity of 60 to 90 percent heart rate maximum or 50 to 85 percent heart rate maximum reserve, for 20 to 60 minutes.[21]

The results of one study suggest that clinically stable, aerobically trained cardiac patients may perform moderate to heavy resistance exercises without experiencing complications.[22] A carefully supervised, long-term program of low-resistance strength training appears to be safe with regard to blood pressure and beneficial in terms of strength gain.[23] Age does not seem to be a variable in the effects of cardiac rehabilitation programs. One study found that improvements in exercise capacity, obesity indexes, and lipid levels were very similar in older and younger patients enrolled in cardiac rehabilitation and exercise programs.[24] Because nurses play a key role in the development and implementation of these programs, it behooves them to be aware of research findings in this area so that they can personalize programs for different types of patients.[25]

Neuromuscular Conditions. A 12-week moderate resistance exercise program was performed by 27 patients with slowly progressive neuromuscular diseases and 14 control subjects in order to determine the safety and efficacy of a strengthening program. Results provided evidence that a submaximal strength training program is practical and safe for these individuals and produces moderate improvement in measured strength.[26]

Asthma. Sixty-seven asthmatic adults randomly assigned to a deep diaphragmatic breathing training group, a physical exercise training group, or a waiting list control group participated in a 16-week program.

Deep diaphragmatic training produced significant reductions both in medication use and in the intensity of asthmatic symptoms. Importantly, diaphragmatic training also made possible a nearly 300 percent increase in time spent in physical activities.[27]

Cystic Fibrosis. One study sought to determine whether substituting regular exercise, which also promotes coughing, for two of three daily bronchial hygiene treatments would affect the expected improvements in pulmonary function and exercise response in patients hospitalized with cystic fibrosis. Results indicate that, in some cystic fibrosis patients, exercise therapy is an effective substitute for at least part of the standard protocol of bronchial hygiene therapy.[28]

Low Back Pain. To determine whether graded physical exercise restored occupational function in industrial blue-collar workers who were sick-listed for 8 weeks because of subacute, nonspecified, mechanical low back pain, 103 subjects were randomly assigned to either an activity group or a control group. Subjects in the graded activity group became occupationally functional again, as measured by their earlier return to work, and their long-term sick leave was significantly reduced.[29] Another group of researchers explored the effect of a weekly exercise program on short-term sick leave (50 days) attributable to back pain and the possible correlation between changes in absenteeism and changes in cardiovascular fitness. They found that the number of episodes of back pain and the number of sick leave days attributable to back pain in the intervention period decreased by more than 50 percent in the exercise group.[30] Spinal flexion exercises have been found to increase sagittal mobility more than do extension exercises.[31]

Acquired Immunodeficiency Syndrome (AIDS). The results of a study to determine if progressive resistance exercise improves muscle function and increases body dimensions and mass in AIDS patients show that the experimental group who engaged in such exercise three times a week for 6 weeks significantly improved in 13 of 15 study variables. During the nonacute stage of AIDS, therefore, the physiologic adaptation that occurred in these patients improved muscle function and increased body dimensions and mass.[32]

Psychiatric Conditions. The effects of exercise on clients in a psychiatric rehabilitation program were investigated in three studies. Results indicate that the higher the level of aerobic fitness, the lower the level of self-reported depression.[33,34] Nurses may want to act on such data by establishing exercise programs in psychiatric settings.

Older Adults and Exercise

Loss of lower extremity strength increases the risk of falls in older persons.[35] One exercise program study in elderly male nursing home residents demonstrated that an appropriately designed high-intensity exercise program can result in significant, although limited, improvements in clinical mobility scores, strength, muscular endurance, and certain gait parameters.[36] In another study, a 12-week randomized clinical trial exercise program that focused on strength and balance achieved a clinically significant improvement in gait velocity.[37] Exercise was also found to improve balance in elderly women.[38]

Exercise can also be beneficial for clients with osteoporosis, always a concern for the older woman. In short-term (7 month) programs, exercise with intensity above the anaerobic threshold was found to be safe and effective in preventing postmenopausal bone loss.[39] Other data suggest that adherence to a low-frequency training program can elicit additional positive physiologic changes in elderly women. Furthermore, increased habitual activity patterns are likely to improve functional ability, life style, and independence.[40]

Movement

Various aspects of movement, such as dance, theater, and sport, have been used in ritual, celebration, and healing rites since humans were first organized into collective tribes and families. For thousands of years, Eastern cultures and philosophic thought have considered symbolic physical motion to be essential for physical and mental well-being. Yoga and Tai Chi, for example, are two ancient physical movement forms that are still practiced today to enhance overall health. Tai Chi, a traditional Chinese exercise, is a series of individual dancelike movements linked together in a continuous, smooth-flowing sequence. Movements within such disciplines are based on concepts of total concentration, strength, relaxation, and symbolic motion.

Movement ranges from the rapid motions of active dance or acrobatics to the subtle rhythm characterized by breathing or the slow careful movements of Tai Chi. It includes the way that individuals hold and carry their bodies (i.e., posture) and the way that groups communicate nonverbally (i.e., body language). In Western culture, movement includes dancing, swimming, and sports. Exercise is the form of movement to which we give attention because of its known benefits to health maintenance. In health care, movement is used for a number of therapeutic purposes, including range-of-motion exercises, water exercises, and specific physical therapy movements for a variety of rehabilitative programs.

In one study to determine the potential value of Tai Chi in promoting postural control of the well elderly, performance on five balance tests of nine Tai Chi practitioners was compared to the performance of nine nonpractitioners. Statistical results demonstrated that, in three of the tests, the Tai Chi practitioners had significantly better postural control than did the sedentary nonpractitioners. Men performed significantly better than did women in both the practitioner and nonpractitioner groups on the same three tests.[41] Tai Chi has also been found to be a safe movement therapy for clients with rheumatoid arthritis.[42]

Because we all use movement continually, we usually take it for granted. For many who are handicapped, disabled, or in rehabilitative programs, however, the design of creative movement plans can make the difference between a partial and a full development of their physical potential. Although the occupational or physical therapist often designs and teaches movement programs, new types of therapists have emerged with the increased emphasis on wellness programs. Dance therapists and Tai Chi instructors are now more widely consulted, particularly by those seeking high-level wellness. Creative movement programs are taught in group sessions, at wellness centers, or in continuing education classes.

Creative movements, including dance, Tai Chi, and other expressive movements, are health-promoting behaviors that are appropriate for a variety of populations and age groups. Movement can be a nursing intervention with independent, active people, as well as with those with mobility deficits.[43] Dance, which is one of the major movement therapies, places emphasis on the holism of human beings. In dance, one can externalize concepts created in the mind, thus making another bodymind experience possible.

NURSING PROCESS

Assessment

In preparing to use nutrition, exercise, and movement interventions, assess the following parameters:

- the client's current eating habits, food preferences, and nutritional needs

- the client's alcohol, caffeine, and fat consumption
- the client's financial and religious restrictions, as well as habit patterns formed during childhood
- the client's nonverbal movement patterns and known movement limitations
- the client's desirable body weight and caloric needs
- the client's motivation, desire, and ability to make the necessary life style changes in the areas of nutrition, exercise, and movement

Nursing Diagnoses

The following nursing diagnoses compatible with nutrition, exercise, and movement interventions and that are related to the human response patterns of Unitary Person (see Chapter 7) are as follows:

- Exchanging: Altered nutrition
Altered circulation
Altered oxygenation
- Choosing: Altered coping
- Moving: Altered physical mobility
Sleep pattern disturbance
Altered activities of daily living
- Perceiving: Disturbance in body image
Disturbance in self-esteem
Potential hopelessness
Potential powerlessness
- Knowing: Knowledge deficit
- Feeling: Pain
Anxiety
Grieving

Client Outcomes

Table 11–4 guides the nurse in client outcomes, nursing prescriptions, and evaluation for the use of nutrition, exercise, and movement as nursing interventions.

Table 11-4 Nursing Interventions: Nutrition, Exercise, and Movement

Client Outcomes	*Nursing Prescriptions*	*Evaluation*
The client will be motivated to improve nutrition, exercise, and/or movement.	Assist the client in a personal self-assessment. Encourage the client to participate with the nurse to develop goals and action plans. Prepare the client to follow through with the nurse on evaluation and formulation of new goals.	The client completed a self-assessment form. The client participated with the nurse to develop a personalized program. The client met with the nurse for program evaluation.
The client will demonstrate knowledge of healthful nutrition, exercise, and movement programs.	Motivate the client to contribute to discussions about his or her program. Encourage the client to learn more about healthful behaviors as he or she works with the nurse.	The client participated in the session discussion. The client demonstrated new knowledge.

Plan and Intervention

Before the Session

- Create an environment in which the client feels comfortable discussing the needs of his or her physical body from a nutritional and physical movement perspective.
- Clear your mind of other client or personal encounters in order to be fully present when meeting with the client.
- Gather input data forms and teaching charts.
- Prepare all necessary assessment equipment.
- Prepare handouts or between-session worksheets to give to the client during the session.

At the Beginning of the Session

- Take and record the necessary physical assessment data (e.g., height, weight, skin fold thickness measurements, body contour measurements, blood pressure).
- Guide the client as he or she discloses past habit patterns that affect eating or exercise behavior.

- Have the client write down the foods typically consumed and consumption patterns, or review the food diary that the client brought to the session.

During the Session

- Review with the client current weekly exercise patterns.
- Be alert to psychologic clues that may relate to overeating behavior or extremes (anorexia and bulimia).
- Following data collection, work with the client to develop an individualized nutrition, exercise, and movement program.
- Make certain that teaching is at the client's intellectual and emotional level.

At the End of the Session

- Have the client identify the options that you have presented that best fit with his or her own life style.
- Work together to write down goals and target dates.
- Give the client specific affirmations to use to support these goals.
- Give the client handout material to reinforce the teaching.
- Use the client outcomes that were established before the session (see Table 11–4) and the client's subjective experiences (Exhibit 11–1) to evaluate the session.
- Schedule a follow-up session.

Specific Interventions

Nutrition (Basic). Several chronic diseases, notably coronary artery disease and certain types of cancer, have been associated with nutritionally induced metabolic overload. Some experts are calling for an "optimal" diet and believe that this goal for effective disease prevention is within reach with the appropriate support of an informed public and a cooperative food industry. The "optimal" diet is called the 25/25 diet because 25 percent of calories come from fat and 25 grams per day come from fiber.[44]

Nurses can employ intervention teaching in almost every area of nursing care. Clients who are hospitalized because of acute illness are often interested in anything that they can do to prevent a recurrence. Consequently, the hospital stay is often an excellent time to begin simple nutritional teaching. A registered dietitian can provide detailed information on the client's specific nutritional needs, but the nurse reinforces the specifics and provides the following general information on decreasing cholesterol levels and increasing calcium intake. The six-point program of the cholesterol-lowering diet is as follows[45]:

1. Increase dietary fiber. Cholesterol levels can decrease when the intake of fruits and vegetables increases.
2. Add fish oils to the diet. Ongoing research seems to confirm that eicosapentaenoic acid (EPA) and docosasehexaenoic acid (DHA) do, in fact, lower cardiovascular disease rates. Studies indicate that regular consumption of fish oils may reduce blood lipid levels significantly.
3. Include lecithin, the biologically active form of choline, in the diet. Supplementation with 2 to 10 grams of soy-derived lecithin has been found to reduce the serum cholesterol level.
4. Increase intake of vitamin C, which is necessary for the conversion of cholesterol to bile needed for the digestion of fats. Doses of 1 to 3 grams daily may lower cholesterol.
5. Add alfalfa to the diet. Both animal and human studies have demonstrated that eating alfalfa can reduce blood cholesterol levels and atherosclerotic plaques in the coronary arteries. In humans give 10 teaspoons of alfalfa powdered seed per day, reductions of as much as 20 percent in blood cholesterol levels were seen.
6. Increase intake of garlic. The beneficial effects of garlic are probably due to the sulfur compound, allicin, which reduces serum cholesterol levels by inhibiting cholesterol synthesis. Clinical studies have indicated that approximately 10 grams of garlic per day significantly reduce blood cholesterol and triglyceride levels and improve the HDL-LDL ratio.

For optimal health, an individual should follow a high-calcium diet from early childhood, as about 85 percent of the bone mass is formed by the age of 18 and the remainder by age 35.[46] A high-calcium diet during the growing years increases the bone mass as the skeleton matures and may reduce the risk of fractures later in life.

Several factors influence the use of calcium. For example, a diet high in phosphorus inhibits calcium utilization, and large quantities of phosphorus are found in red meats, some fibers, and carbonated soft drinks. The high consumption of carbonated soft drinks by women in the United States predisposes them to a decreased calcium level and contributes to the prevalence of osteoporosis. The optimum diet should include twice as much calcium as phosphorus. Similarly, a high sodium intake forces the

Table 11-5 Old and New Fitness Paradigms

Old Fitness Paradigm	*New Fitness Paradigm*
Emphasis exclusively physical	A bodymind integration
Compared self with others	Noncomparative
Regulated calisthenics	Aerobic dance to motivational music; individually paced; build up with technology and feedback machines; motivation and subliminal tapes for individual challenge
Competition with others	Competition with self
Rigorous and punitive	Exhilarating and fun
Muscle building	Health building

kidneys to excrete more sodium and, in the process, more calcium, thus contributing to osteoporosis. Cigarette smoking and excessive alcohol intake are also associated with low bone mass and may increase calcium loss. The best natural sources of calcium are oysters, clams, sardines, salmon, dairy products, leafy green vegetables, and legumes. Children and young adults should consume 1,000 to 1,200 milligrams daily, pregnant or breastfeeding women should have an additional 500 milligrams, and postmenopausal women need 1,500 milligrams daily.

Exercise (Basic). A new paradigm of fitness is emerging. Its orientation is broader and focuses more on enjoyment. As the new paradigm gains strength, there will probably be a continuing increase both in the numbers of people exercising and in those exercising at the level of vigor necessary to achieve a cardiovascular benefit. Table 11–5 depicts the old and new fitness paradigms.

The primary purpose of exercise is to produce fitness. The basic components of fitness are

1. flexibility: the ability to use a joint throughout its full range of motion and to maintain some degree of elasticity of major muscle groups. It is important because
   - it provides increased resistance to muscle and joint injury
   - it helps prevent mild muscle soreness if done before and after vigorous activity

2. muscle strength: the contracting power of a muscle. It is important because
   - daily activities become less strenuous as muscles become stronger
   - strong abdominal and lower back muscles help prevent lower back problems
   - appearance improves as muscles become firmer
3. cardiorespiratory endurance: the ability of the circulatory and respiratory systems to maintain blood and oxygen delivery to the exercising muscles. It is important because
   - it increases resistance to cardiovascular diseases
   - it improves the ability to maintain activity levels
   - it allows for a high energy return for daily activities

Beginning the regimen in a disciplined manner increases the chances of maintaining the program. Thus, before beginning an exercise program, an individual should be encouraged to follow these basic guidelines:

- Learn about the different types of exercise programs available in your area.
- Consult your physician or exercise authority. If you are over 35, have never seriously exercised, or have a handicap or chronic illness, obtain guidance to avoid injuries or complications.
- Establish an exercise routine. Choose exercises or sports you will enjoy. Decide on a place and time of day to exercise. Ask a friend to join you or meet some new people at the jogging trail or health club. Create or join an exercise class before, during, or after work. There are endless possibilities.
- Warm up and cool down. Stretching exercises are essential before and after each exercise period.
- Set realistic goals and work toward them. Some benefits of exercise may not be quickly apparent. Be patient. Build up slowly to your long-term goals.
- Evaluate the program periodically. Determine if you are making progress. If you want to go further, set new goals.
- Create competition for yourself only if it benefits you. If you have allowed too much competition, exercise may become more of a burden than a joy.

Many rewards of exercise and physical activity begin immediately. Mental and spiritual improvements include beneficial changes in

- mental attitude toward your work, yourself, and life in general
- ability to cope with stress
- ability to avoid or control mild depression
- sleep patterns
- strength and endurance
- eating habits
- appearance and vitality
- posture
- physical stamina as you age

To reduce risks associated with exercise, it is necessary to know not only how often and how long to exercise, but also how vigorously to exercise. Although the target pulse range allows for a heart rate within 60 to 80 percent of maximal capacity, the American Heart Association guidelines state that regular exercise of moderate capacity, or from 50 to 75 percent of maximal capacity, appears to be sufficient. Thus, maintaining the target pulse rate during physical exercise for 15 to 30 minutes three to five times per week reduces the risk of overexertion, enhances enjoyment, and results in cardiovascular fitness. Because uncontrolled exercising may result in injury, it is wise to follow these guidelines.

- Always warm up for a minimum of 10 to 20 minutes.
- If you are tired, stop.
- If something hurts, stop.
- If you feel dizzy or nauseated, stop.
- Take your pulse at regular intervals.
- Cool down after exercising.

To ease your heart rate into the training range, begin with 10 minutes of low-intensity warm-up exercise. To cool down, do 10 minutes of the same slow activity.

Adherence rates for nurse-led exercise programs are considerably higher than are those for other programs. Women tested at 3- and 6-month intervals after exercise intervention stated that they tried many fitness clubs and spas in the area, but could find no exercise programs that were tailored to their age and fitness level or that took into consideration their individual health needs. Nurses interested and knowledgeable about the changes of aging are in an ideal position to develop and lead exercise programs for older individuals, particularly those with chronic, nondisabling physical problems.[47] Technologic advances that may help in the provision of educational services include videocassettes and computer interactive programs.[48]

Movement (Basic). There are four components of creative movement: centering, warm-up, exploration of surrounding space, and stretching.[49]

1. Centering is the inward focusing on one's own physical reality. The duration of this process varies, but it usually lasts 3 to 10 minutes.
2. The stretching, breathing warm-up exercises follow the centering exercise and are designed to "wake up" the muscles while maintaining the harmonious integration of psyche and soma that was begun through centering.
   - Musical accompaniment has a positive effect on one's ability to perform. Music seems to bypass the psychologic feedback of the sensations of exertion and fatigue and instead produces feelings of exuberance and strength.
   - Exercises are done to synchronize breathing and symbolic imagery slowly and rhythmically. The individual uses images in concert with motion.
   - Social involvement during warm-up adds another dimension to creative movement. Initially, people may be shy with one another, but relaxation and enjoyment increase as the movement accelerates.
   - Additional warm-up techniques allow people to delve deeper into their own personal inward life before proceeding further into group activities, if they wish.
3. Exploration of surrounding space occurs as movement proceeds and there is an awakened sense of self-awareness. With this discovery of new physical capacities comes increased kinetic and spatial awareness. During this time, there may be swinging, swaying, and laughter.
4. Stretching concludes a dance movement, allowing for relaxation as it brings the individual to a resting state. At the conclusion, one should savor the feeling of energetic relaxation.

Case Study

Setting: A nurse-based wellness center

Client: B.V., a 40-year-old married woman who seeks counseling for weight loss

Nursing Diagnoses:
1. Altered nutrition (more than body requirements) related to improper eating and lack of exercise
2. Altered self-esteem related to obesity
3. Ineffective reversal/prevention of coronary artery disease risk factors (hypertension, hypercholesterolemia, obesity) related to stress and low self-esteem

B.V. came to the wellness center after having a physical examination by a physician and being told for the sixth straight year that she needs to lose weight. Her total cholesterol is 340 mg/dL, blood pressure 180/100, height 5′7″, and weight 220 pounds. She is a nurse and seeks help from a nurse colleague at the wellness center because her elevated cholesterol level has finally motivated her to lose weight. Her husband has been encouraging this for years, but she just cannot seem to make it happen.

During the initial session, the nurse takes an eating and diet history. Like most self-referrals for weight loss, B.V. is knowledgeable about various diet programs and has tried different plans for several years. She has a pattern of losing and then regaining up to 50 pounds on each attempt. At this point, she is willing to try anything. The nurse discovers during the interview that B.V. has been on numerous antihypertensive drugs for 10 years without attaining consistent control. The assessment shows that, in general, B.V. is physically out of shape and emotionally depressed and discouraged. She is a fellow health care professional who has reached burnout.

After establishing 6-week and 6-month goals, B.V. and the nurse schedule weekly sessions. B.V. is given a standard form of a weekly diet, exercise, and emotion and attitude recording sheet. She is instructed to write down everything she eats, as well as the feeling that she has before, during, and after the eating periods during the next week.

In the second session, B.V. and the nurse review the eating/feeling diary and discuss where significant relationships between feelings and eating are observed. During this and subsequent sessions, it is important to examine and try to understand the client's feelings, for they are closely tied to the eating behavior. In addition, the physical parameters of weight and body fat calibration measurements are recorded.

Goals that are too difficult to achieve can discourage the client altogether. Therefore, during each session, several small attainable goals are set for the following week. Both exercise and eating patterns gradually improve.

B.V. meets with the nurse on a regular basis for 6 months. During that time, she reduces her weight to 160 pounds, works out in a regular aerobic exercise program four times a week, and increases her knowledge and interest in healthful food consumption. At the end of this period, B.V. and the nurse agree to move to monthly visits for the next three sessions and plan for termination of the appointments at that time.

Evaluation

The nurse determines with the client whether the client outcomes for nutrition, exercise, and movement (Table 11–4) were successfully achieved. To evaluate the session further, the nurse may again explore the subjective effects of the experience with the client based on the evaluation questions in Exhibit 11–1.

Exhibit 11–1 Evaluating the Client's Subjective Experience with Nutrition, Exercise, and Movement

1. Is this the first time you have considered the effects of healing nutrition from a holistic perspective?
2. Have you discovered ways you can eat for increased vitality and vibrant living?
3. Do you think there are any links between your food intake and the potential for development of a chronic disease in your life?
4. Is your life filled with healing foods? Do you want it to be?
5. Do you enjoy the sense of release experienced during physical exertion?
6. Has your vitality increased since you embarked on an exercise regimen?
7. Does physical exercise reduce stress in your life?
8. Do you integrate periods of movement throughout your day? If not, would you feel better if you did?
9. What support systems would help you develop and adhere to a life style that includes healing foods and physical exercise?
10. Can you think of anything else that would help you to maintain a routine that includes healing nutrition and exercise?
11. What is your next step (or your plan) to integrate these experiences on a daily basis?

Nurses should chart the information that they impart to the client, as well as the evaluation of the session. When the nurse works in an inpatient facility, other staff need to be apprised of the program and the progress. Nurses who work in wellness centers, independent practice, or other areas in which counseling sessions are done as the primary care modality should keep records for each client that state the nursing diagnosis, type of counseling employed, and the effectiveness of each session.

Attention to nutrition, exercise, and movement can lead to a general improvement of health, as well as decrease the risk factors of major diseases. The nurse is in a prime position to model the effects of healthy nutrition, exercise, and movement behaviors.

DIRECTIONS FOR FUTURE RESEARCH

1. Investigate the hypothesis that those who exercise and eat a nutritionally balanced diet feel better and live longer.
2. Continue the investigations into the ways in which the life style behaviors of nutrition, exercise, and movement affect a person's general sense of well-being.
3. Study the relationship of vitamin and mineral supplementation to disease prevention and high-level wellness.
4. Investigate the determinants that allow or encourage exercise in unstructured or spontaneous situations.
5. Study the specific factors that are important in tailoring exercise programs to ethnic and cultural groups.

NURSE HEALER REFLECTIONS

After reading this chapter, the nurse healer will be able to answer or begin a process of answering the following questions:

- What sensations accompany my physical well-being because of my improved nutritional, exercise, and movement status?
- How should I feel when I am physically fit?
- What comprises healthy eating both for myself and for my clients?
- What exercise and movement regimens can I incorporate to improve my flexibility and aerobic capacity now?
- How can I model healthy nutrition, exercise, and movement?

NOTES

1. U.S. Senate Select Committee on Nutrition and Human Needs, *Dietary Goals for the United States* (Washington, DC: U.S. Government Printing Office, 1977).
2. Government Gives New Shape to Eating Right, *Tufts University Diet and Nutrition Letter* (July 1992): 2.
3. P.L. Cerrato, Goodbye Four Food Groups, *RN* 55, no. 12 (1992):61–62.
4. Food and Nutrition Board, *Recommended Dietary Allowances*, 5th ed. (Washington, D.C.: National Academy of Sciences—National Research Council, 1989).
5. Ibid.
6. M.W. Miller, Call for a Daily Dose of Wine Ferments Critics, *The Wall Street Journal*, June 17, 1994, pp. B1–2.
7. F. Gaev, Optimal Heart Health for Your Clients, *Nutrition and Dietary Consultant* (April 1986):5.
8. Ibid.
9. G. Maleskey, Food Factors That Stop Cancer: Best News, Best Bets, *Prevention* 39, no. 10 (1987):88–109.
10. Y. Gutierrez and J.C. King, Nutrition during Teenage Pregnancy, *Pediatric Annals* 22, no. 2 (1993):99–108.
11. J.E. Kerstetter et al., Nutrition and Nutritional Requirements for the Older Adult, *Dysphagia* 8, no. 1 (1993):51–58.
12. R.M. Russell and P.M. Suter, Vitamin Requirements of Elderly People: An Update, *American Journal of Clinical Nutrition* 58, no. 1 (1993):4–14.
13. J.E. Kerstetter et al., Nutrition and Nutritional Requirements for the Older Adult.
14. B. Vellas et al., Dietary Intake Recommended for Elderly Persons, *Presse Medicale* 21, no. 12 (1992):574–579.
15. W.S. Holt, Nutrition and Athletes, *American Family Physician* 47, no. 8 (1993):1757–1764.
16. E.A. Applegate, Nutritional Considerations for Ultraendurance Performance, *International Journal of Sports Nutrition* 1, no. 2 (1991):118–126.
17. E.M. Haymes, Vitamin and Mineral Supplementation to Athletes, *International Journal of Sports Nutrition* 1, no. 2 (1991):146–169.
18. T. Stephens et al., A Description of Leisure Time Physical Activity, *Public Health Reports* 100(1985):147–157.
19. W.L. Haskett, Overview: Health Benefits of Exercise, in *Behavioral Health: A Handbook of Health Enhancement and Disease Prevention*, ed. J.D. Matarazzo et al. (New York: John Wiley & Sons, 1984).
20. A.J. Coats, Exercise Rehabilitation in Chronic Heart Failure, *Journal of the American College of Cardiology* 22, no. 4 (1993):172A–177A.
21. L.T. Braun, Exercise Physiology and Cardiovascular Fitness, *Nursing Clinics of North America* 26, no. 1 (1991):135–147.
22. A.D. Faigenbaum et al., Physiologic and Symptomatic Responses of Cardiac Patients to Resistance Exercise, *Archives of Physical Medicine and Rehabilitation* 71, no. 6 (1990):395–398.

23. P.B. Sparling et al., Strength Training in a Cardiac Rehabilitation Program: A Six-Month Follow-up, *Archives of Physical Medicine and Rehabilitation* 71, no. 2 (1990):148–152.

24. C.J. Lavie et al., Benefits of Cardiac Rehabilitation and Exercise Training in Secondary Coronary Prevention in the Elderly, *Journal of the American College of Cardiology* 22, no. 3 (1993):678–683.

25. M.A. Parchert and J.M. Simon, The Role of Exercise in Cardiac Rehabilitation: A Nursing Perspective, *Rehabilitation Nursing* 13, no. 1 (1988):11–14.

26. S.G. Aitkens et al., Moderate Resistance Exercise Program: Its Effect in Slowly Progressive Neuromuscular Disease, *Archives of Physical Medicine and Rehabilitation* 74, no. 7 (1993):711–715.

27. M. Girodo et al., Deep Diaphragmatic Breathing: Rehabilitation Exercises for the Asthmatic Patient, *Archives of Physical Medicine and Rehabilitation* 73, no. 8 (1992):717–720.

28. F.J. Cerny, Relative Effects of Bronchial Drainage and Exercise for In-Hospital Care of Patients with Cystic Fibrosis, *Physical Therapy* 69, no. 8 (1989):633–639.

29. I. Lindstrom et al., The Effect of Graded Activity on Patients with Subacute Low Back Pain: A Randomized Prospective Clinical Study with an Operant-Conditioning Behavioral Approach, *Physical Therapy* 72, no. 4 (1992):279–293.

30. K.M. Kellett et al., Effects of an Exercise Program on Sick Leave due to Back Pain, *Physical Therapy* 71, no. 4 (1991):283–291.

31. I.M. Elnaggar, The Effects of Spinal Flexion and Extension Exercises on Low Back Pain Severity and Spinal Mobility in Chronic Mechanical Low Back Pain (Ph.D. diss., New York University, 1988).

32. D.W. Spence et al., Progressive Resistance Exercise: Effect on Muscle Function and Anthropometry of Select AIDS Population, *Archives of Physical Medicine and Rehabilitation* 71, no. 9 (1990):644–648.

33. T.W. Pelham et al., The Effects of Exercise Therapy on Clients in a Psychiatric Rehabilitation Program, *Psychosocial Rehabilitation Journal* 16, no. 4 (1993):75–84.

34. T.W. Pelham and P.D. Campagna, Benefits of Exercise in Psychiatric Rehabilitation of Persons with Schizophrenia, *Canadian Journal of Rehabilitation* 4, no. 3 (1991):159–168.

35. J.O. Judge et al., Balance Improvements in Older Women: Effects of Exercise Training, *Physical Therapy* 73, no. 4 (1993):254–265.

36. L.R. Sauvage et al., A Clinical Trial of Strengthening and Aerobic Exercise To Improve Gait and Balance in Elderly Male Nursing Home Residents, *American Journal of Physical Medicine and Rehabilitation* 71, no. 6 (1992):333–342.

37. J.O. Judge et al., Exercise To Improve Gait Velocity in Older Persons, *Archives of Physical Medicine and Rehabilitation* 74, no. 4 (1993):400–406.

38. M.J. Lichtenstein et al., Exercise and Balance in Aged Women: A Pilot Controlled Clinical Trial, *Archives of Physical Medicine and Rehabilitation* 70, no. 2 (1989):138–143.

39. M. Hatori et al., The Effects of Walking at the Anaerobic Threshold Level on Vertebral Bone Loss in Postmenopausal Women, *Calcified Tissue International* 562, no. 6 (1993):411–414.

40. P.A. Hamdorf et al., Physical Training Effects on the Fitness and Habitual Activity Patterns of Elderly Women, *Archives of Physical Medicine and Rehabilitation* 73, no. 7 (1992):603–608.

41. S. Tse and D.M. Baily, T'ai Chi and Postural Controls in the Well Elderly, *American Journal of Occupational Therapy* 46, no. 4 (1992):295–300.

42. A.E. Kirsteins et al., Evaluating the Safety and Potential Use of a Weight Bearing Exercise, Tai Chi Chuan, for Rheumatoid Arthritis Patients, *American Journal of Physical Medicine and Rehabilitation* 70, no. 3 (1991):136–141.

43. S. Boots and C. Hogan, Creative Movement and Health, *Topics in Clinical Nursing* 3, no. 2 (1981):21–31.

44. E.L. Wynder and J.H. Weisburger, Nutrition: The Need To Define "Optimal" Intake as a Basis for Public Policy Decisions, *American Journal of Public Health* 82, no. 3 (1992):346–350.

45. Gaev, Optimal Heart Health for Your Clients.

46. E.J. Kozora, ed., *Nutritional Guidelines* (Seattle: American Holistic Medical Association, 1987).

47. P.A. Gillett et al., The Nurse as Exercise Leader, *Geriatric Nursing* 14, no. 3 (1993):133–137.

48. N.K. Wenger, Modern Coronary Rehabilitation, *Postgraduate Medicine* 94, no. 2 (1993):131–136, 141.

49. Boots and Hogan, Creative Movement and Health, 21–31.

VISION OF HEALING

Building a Healthy Environment

The use of the environment has become one of the foremost issues of the 1990s. Nurses have risen to the occasion by proactively forming national organizations and sponsoring conferences to address environmental concerns. For example, Nurses for the Environment, an organization dedicated entirely to nursing-related environmental issues, addresses topics such as recycling, consciousness raising, personal environments, and workplace concerns.[1] The American Holistic Nurses' Association (AHNA) has developed and propagates a statement on environmental issues.

American Holistic Nurses' Association Position Statement
in Support of a Healthful Environment

The philosophy of the American Holistic Nurses' Association includes the belief that "health involves the harmonious balance of body, mind, and spirit in an ever-changing environment."

The environment involves both our immediate as well as global surroundings. Many of us are aware of a need to expand our consciousness regarding environmental issues and believe that this can have an effect on our own personal and community well-being.

Our concerns come from a reverence for the beauty and integrity of the earth which sustains us and is our home, our Mother Earth. Relevant environmental issues include preserving the integrity of the air, soil, and water as well as issues such as global warming, acid rain and other equally challenging situations. We believe as holistic nurses, we have a responsibility for increasing awareness regarding these issues in others, through role modeling and educating within our communities.

The AHNA encourages self-responsible behavior as well as participation in socially responsible environmental groups, to protect and support improvement of the health of our environment.[2]

The reason that politicians, nurses, and most other segments of society are becoming involved in environmental issues is the growing awareness of the relationship between our physical reality and the earth. This century, and even more so, this decade, has witnessed two dramatic events: a sudden, startling surge in human population and an abrupt acceleration of the scientific and technologic revolution.

From the beginning of humanity's appearance on earth to 1945, it took more than 10,000 generations to reach a world population of 2 billion people. Now, in the course of one human lifetime, the world population is increasing from 2 to more than 9 billion people.[3] *All of us working with computers and hospital equipment can attest to the exponential explosion of technology during our careers. These factors and others have magnified our power to affect the world around us by burning, cutting, digging, moving, and transforming the physical matter that makes up the earth. As a society, we are straining under the burden of a burgeoning population that is demanding not only the fulfillment of basic needs, but also access to health care and space age technology. In trying to meet the ever increasing demands, we have contaminated our air, soil, and waters with by-products, and we have attenuated our foods with herbicides, pesticides, and overprocessing. Urban and suburban areas reverberate with noise and violence, and frustrations mount as increasing numbers crowd into congested living areas.*

Nurses are seeking to discover the best ways to utilize the environment to maximize the overall healing effort. All of us must aspire to develop global ecologic skills if we are to endure. Environmental scientists and nurses can cooperate in unique ways to promote a global healing ethic.[4]

On an individual level, the way in which people use their personal space affects not only the way that they feel, but also, in today's shrinking world, the space around others. For example, when we play our stereos or radios, the broadcast should fill only the short space between us and the speaker, not blare so loud that it reaches into the personal space of others who may not want to hear the program. In increasingly congested areas, we must take care to honor each person's right for quiet space. All of us need to work together to find individual and community solutions to the serious environmental issues that face us as we race toward the twenty-first century.

NOTES

1. Nurses for the Environment: P.O. Box 22118, Juneau, AK 99802-2118.
2. Reprinted from *Environmental Philosophy* with the permission of the American Holistic Nurses' Association, 4101 Lake Boone Trail, Raleigh, NC 27607, phone: (919) 787-5181, FAX (919) 787-4916.
3. A. Gore, *Earth in the Balance: Ecology and the Human Spirit* (New York: Plume, 1993), p. 31.
4. J. Case, The Biosphere and the Healing Arts, *Holistic Nursing Practice* 6, no. 4 (1992): 10–19.

Chapter 12

Environment: Protecting Our Personal and Planetary Home

Lynn Keegan

NURSE HEALER OBJECTIVES

Theoretical

- Learn six definitions specific to the environment.
- Examine the theories and research about the environment.
- Increase your awareness of environmental hazards, and commit yourself to reducing these hazards.

Clinical

- Train yourself to become sensitive to the environmental space in your home, institution, health agency, or clinic.
- Choose several different environmental activities, and use them in clinical practice.
- Consider using some specific environmental interventions in your workplace.

Personal

- Make positive changes in your own environmental space.
- Create time to spend in natural environments.
- Attempt to follow the natural schedule of setting your biologic clock to the rise and set of the sun rather than to a mechanical alarm clock.
- Whenever possible, eliminate negative aspects of your personal environment (e.g., stale air, inadequate lighting, subliminal noises).

- Experiment with healing colors, scents, textures, sound, and lighting in your personal environment.

DEFINITIONS

Ambience: an environment or its distinct atmosphere; the totality of feeling that one experiences from a particular environment.

Ecominnea: the concept of an ecologically sound society.

Environment: everything that surrounds an individual or group of people—physical, social, psychologic, cultural, or spiritual characteristics; external and internal features; animate and inanimate objects; seen and unseen vibrations; and frequencies, climate, and not yet understood energy patterns.

Ergonomics: the study of and realization of the importance of human factors in engineering.

Harmonic Environment: the melodious music or sounds that gently fill an individual's personal space.

Personal Space: the area around an individual that should be under the control of that individual, including air, light, temperature, sound, scent, and color.

Toxic Substance: a substance that can cause harm to a person through either short- or long-term exposure, as by (1) inhalation; (2) ingestion into the body in the form of vapors, gases, fumes, dusts, solids, liquids, or mists; or (3) skin absorption.

THEORY AND RESEARCH

Attempts To Document the Modern Dilemma

One of the reasons that it is difficult to study the link between environmental conditions and illness or disease is that there are so many intervening variables. Hundreds of substances and life style factors are involved. Although not all toxic substances and environmental conditions induce immediate untoward reactions, many toxins seem to cause disease later, perhaps years after the period of exposure. Breathing asbestos fibers, for example, seldom causes immediate symptoms, but has often resulted in serious chronic disease many years later. Other environmental elements now known to be hazardous include lead, cigarette smoke, silica, benzene, mercury, chlorine, poor lighting, stress, and noise.[1]

Since the 1970s, national attention has focused on efforts to clean up the nation's environment and ensure workers' safety. Two federal agencies—the Environmental Protection Agency (EPA) and the Occupational Safety and Health Administration (OSHA)—were formed to monitor environmental concerns. In the 1980s, several states enacted "right to know laws" that require employers to notify employees of health hazards; to provide formal education regarding safe use of toxic substances; and to keep medical records of those workers routinely exposed to specific toxic substances.[2] In 1991, the Ecological Society of America published the Sustainable Biosphere Initiative (SBI), calling for a coordination of ecologic research, environmental education, and policy making. The project focuses on global change, loss of biodiversity, and sustainability. Its purpose is to gain a full understanding of the interactions of the biotic and the abiotic worlds in space and time.[3]

Internationally, the England Health and Safety Executive launched a huge campaign in 1991 to peak British awareness of health concerns at work. Called Lighten the Load, one program is designed to raise awareness of work-related musculoskeletal disorders and encourage employers to adopt programs that will reduce the frequency with which these disorders occur. Occupational health nurses play a major part in implementing this program, which includes assessment, intervention, evaluation, and prevention of stresses emanating from environmental working conditions.[4]

As we near the twenty-first century, environmental concerns range from eating contaminated poultry, hormone-fed beef, and irradiated fruits and vegetables to living near high-voltage power lines, understanding the Antarctic atmospheric ozone hole, and coping with other new high-technology hazards that we are only now recognizing (Figure 12–1). Noise, lighting, air quality, space allocation, and workplace toxins have gained increasing attention as chronic stressors.

Noise

Although its danger is still for the most part unrecognized, noise pollution may be the most common modern health hazard. Studies have repeatedly demonstrated that a high noise level is the single most important factor in diminishing office productivity.[5] Yet, more than 20 million workers in the United States are exposed to hazardous levels of noise every year, and the majority of them are in the white-collar work environ-

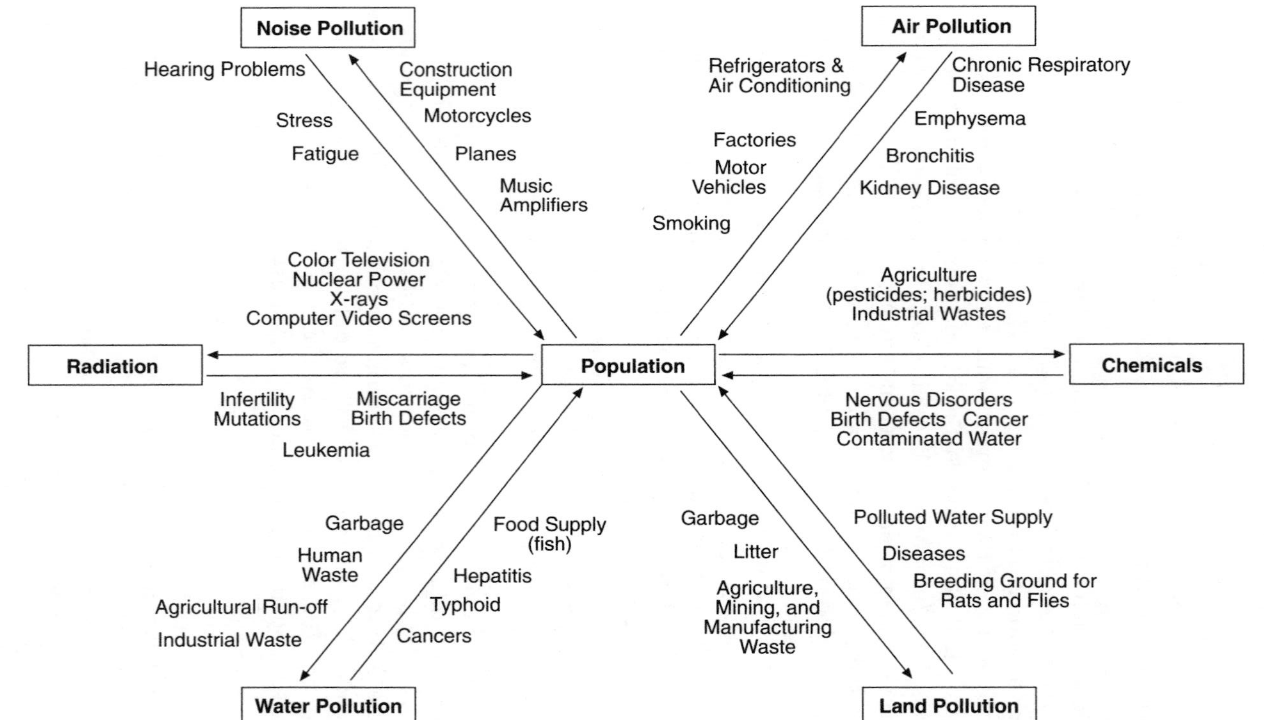

Figure 12–1 Current Environmental Concerns. *Source:* Reprinted with permission from *Health Education*, August/September 1986, pp. 26–27. *Health Education* is a publication of the American Alliance for Health, Physical Education, Recreation and Dance, 1900 Association Drive, Reston, VA 22091.

ment. Other studies here and in Europe have shown that high noise levels constrict blood vessels; increase blood pressure, pulse, and respiration rates; and release extra fats into the bloodstream.[6]

The danger posed by noise pollution is a function of the volume of sound heard over a period of time. Sound and its intensity are measured in decibels, abbreviated dB (Table 12–1). Because the scale is logarithmic, rather than linear, each 10-dB increase is equivalent to multiplying the intensity by 10. The arbitrary zero is the weakest sound that a young, sensitive human ear can hear. Humans begin to perceive irritation around 50 to 90 dB and actually feel pain around 120 dB. At levels above 70 dB, the autonomic nervous system can become aroused, often without the person's awareness. When exposed for 8 hours to noise at 70 dB, which is the sound level of many typing pools or cafeterias, people may become irritable, distracted, or tense.[7] With prolonged exposure to noise levels higher than 75 dB, gradual hearing loss can occur.

People are disturbed not only by loud sound, but also by dissonant or inharmonic sound.[8] Random, unstructured noises, even those below the threshold of awareness, can foster an irritating tension. In most hospitals and health care settings, the "quiet" areas are actually flooded with ran-

Table 12–1 Decibel Levels of Various Sounds

Decibel Level (dB)	*Generating Sound*
120–140	Jet engine at take-off Amplified rock band at close range
100–110	Power lawn mower Oncoming subway train Chain saw Jackhammer
80–100	Alarm clock Screaming child Truck traffic at close range Cocktail party
60–80	Electric kitchen aids Washing machine
40–60	Normal conversation Refrigerator hum
20–40	A cat's purr
0–10	Threshold of hearing

dom noises and subtle, tension-promoting sounds that interfere with restfulness. Varied patterns of auditory input are more restful than quiet ambience. Healthy subjects who were confined to bed in a varied harmonic environment perceived themselves to be more rested than did those subjects confined in a quiet ambient environment.[9] This finding supports the concept that it is better to pattern the auditory input for those confined to bed.

To study the effect of noise exposure on vasoconstriction, Dengerlink and associates measured plasma concentrations of the vasoconstrictor angiotensin II in subjects before and after either rest or exposure to 100-dB white noise (noise with no discernible language or music, with sounds that are a cross between static and a waterfall).[10] Plasma angiotensin II concentrations decreased for subjects in the no-noise condition, but remained high for those in the noise condition, suggesting that noise may stimulate the production of angiotensin II. Elevated levels of angiotensin II may be partially responsible for the reported vasoconstriction and blood pressure increases that appear to accompany noise exposure.

An Australian group monitored noise levels in six intensive care units.[11] The measuring instruments included a Brugel and Kjaer microphone and measuring amplifier. After noting the high baseline or ambient noise level, the researchers found that there were three primary sources of noise: people (i.e., patients, staff, and visitors), equipment, and furniture. People-generated noise was in the range of 70 to 76 dB. The variety of noises generated from equipment included the random beeping alarms. Noise levels were as high as 80 dB when plastic chairs were being moved and 85 dB when garbage was removed. Noise from other routine tasks, such as disposing of used needles, tearing paper from monitors, and wheeling in stretchers, were commonly 10 to 20 dB above the baseline noise levels of the continuously operating machinery.

Considerable empirical evidence supports the claim that advances in hospital technology have led to increased sound levels in the critical care unit. In one study, 70 patients were randomly assigned to a noise or quiet controlled environment while attempting to sleep overnight in a simulated critical care unit. Researchers sought to determine if the sound levels suppress rapid eye movement (REM) sleep. Subjects in the noise group heard an audiotape recording of critical care unit nighttime sounds. These subjects showed poorer REM sleep on 7 of 10 measures. Thus, there appears to be a causal relationship between critical care units and suppression of REM sleep.[12] In a related study of 105 females, a comparison with subjects in quiet environments showed that subjects in noise-simulated conditions had statistically significantly poorer sleep efficiency, more difficulty falling and staying asleep, more intrasleep awakenings, and less time in REM.[13]

Hospital noise has been associated with sleep deprivation, sensory overload, increased perception of postoperative pain, and intensive care unit psychosis.[14] A controlled study of 28 surgical intensive care unit patients indicated that noise not only was disturbing, but also caused heart rate acceleration.[15] A degree of hearing loss has occurred in newborns placed in incubators with ultrasonic nebulizers.[16] In addition, there is concern about the impact of the nursery environment on developing low-birth-weight infants. In contrast to the uterine environment, the neonatal intensive care unit is characterized by bright, often continuous lighting; loud, sharp, unpredictable sound; limited, unpredictable, and often noxious tactile stimulation; and severe limitations on mobility. It has been suggested that such an environment, which differs markedly from the expected, may irrevocably alter neonatal development in ways not yet clearly understood.[17]

Food Irradiation

The stated purpose of food irradiation in plants is to kill larval infestation, thereby (1) increasing the shelf-life of foods; (2) eliminating insects, bacteria, and other organisms; and (3) preventing sprouting. Even though the Food and Drug Administration (FDA) has pronounced it safe, this new technique has been controversial from the time of its first use.

Irradiation raises controversy for three reasons. First, it partially depletes nutrients from the food, with vitamins C, A, B complex, and E being the most vulnerable. In several studies, Temple oranges lost up to 28 percent of their ascorbic acid, corn lost up to 29 percent of its ascorbic acid and 44 percent of its carotene, and whole milk lost up to 61 percent of its vitamin E.[18] The transportation of highly radioactive materials (cobalt-60 and cesium-137) through communities for use in irradiation has also raised concern. Finally, the process creates radioactive products in the form of trace chemicals in the irradiated food product.

Meat irradiation is also controversial, causing *The Wall Street Journal* to print the following:

Meat Irradiation Facts

- What Is It: Short bursts of gamma rays from the radioactive isotopes cobalt-60 or cesium-137, or from electron beams.
- What It Does: Removes almost all traces of *E. coli* in beef, *Salmonella* in poultry, cholera in fish, trichinosis in pork and bacteria that spoil produce.

- Proponents of Beef Irradiation: The National Food Processors Association, the American Medical Association, the World Health Organization, and the American Meat Institute. All say beef irradiation will help reduce deaths from *E. coli*.
- Critics of Beef Irradiation: Food and Water, Inc. They say nutrients are lost in the process, and not enough is known about the stray molecules that result from it.[19(p.B1)]

A study by the U.S. Army found that irradiated beef contained 65 volatile trace chemicals that had not been present before irradiation. Some nuclear chemists contend that the radiolytic particles and substances may be carcinogenic.[20] Although the safety of irradiation is still under investigation, nurses need to be aware of the debate and stay abreast of the issues.

Meat and Poultry Supplementation

For a number of years, cows, pigs, and chickens have been treated with both hormones and antibiotics. The purposes of these treatments are to increase the size and weight of the animal and to prevent *Salmonella* contamination. In 1993, after 9 years of scrutiny, the FDA approved the use of bovine somatotropin (BST). This hormone became commercially available in February 1994. The FDA concluded that the drug, which boosts milk production by more than 10 percent, is safe despite its association with an increase in udder infection common among lactating cows.[21] Like irradiation, supplementation has raised safety concerns among critics because it introduces a new element of pharmacologic intervention into a population that was previously free of disease. Its long-range effects are yet to be determined.

Passive Smoking

We are all aware of the health hazards related to smoking tobacco products, but a new at-risk population has been identified—nonsmokers. Exposure to tobacco smoke produced by others, referred to as passive smoking, places individuals at the same risk for illnesses as their smoking counterparts.[22] In fact, new studies reveal that sidestream smoke contains higher concentrations of carcinogens and other toxic substances than does mainstream smoke.[23] Nonsmokers who are chronically exposed to the pollutants in tobacco smoke scored lower on tests of small airway function than did nonsmokers who had not been exposed.[24] Nonsmoking women exposed to their husbands' smoking are now showing a 2:1 increase in mortality from lung cancer as compared to control groups.[25] Such data should alert nurses and other health care professionals to the continual unfolding of new hazards to public environmental health and safety.

Violence, Dehumanization, and the Technologic Age

Life in the modern age has built-in inherent environmental dangers. For many, the very act of getting to and from the workplace is an encounter with smog, noise, congestion, stench, and debris. In addition, many people spend numerous hours a week in front of television screens, vicariously engaging in violence and corruption. Being exposed to constant news and commercial programming may in part shift our focus to deploring the negative aspects of our world rather than creating a more positive environment for ourselves or for those with whom we live and work.

In the past, people and their environments were harmoniously intertwined. When people worked, they walked from their dwelling to their field, toiled with the elements, and directly reaped the benefits of their labors. In today's technologic era, however, the nature of our relationship with the environment has changed to one of use rather than an exchange with the elements. We have become increasingly alienated from the natural world. The artificial environment of the technologic society has replaced nature as the all-encompassing environment. The technologic society unconsciously evokes from us the emotions of fascination and dread that nature once did.[26] Searching for security, fulfillment, and meaning from our technologic civilization, we unconsciously surrender our freedom and autonomy and replace it with efficiency. For many, the result is dehumanization, demoralization, and victimization. For those who are knowledgeable and able to make choices effectively, the technologic age can heighten the positive effects of the environment and thereby enhance the overall quality of life. In either case, there are specific interventions that the individual nurse can do.

Nurses' Working Environment

Over the past three decades, a growing body of literature has indicated that nursing is a stressful profession. Improved technology and a greater turnover of acutely ill patients are two factors that have increased nurses' work pressure.[27] The constant caring for acutely ill patients with a myriad of physical and emotional needs occurs within an often complex organizatonal system.[28] Hospital work environment stressors include limited control of tasks, ongoing job changes, and continual technologic change.[29] Based on this and additional data, many nurses are proactively addressing this issue. For example, nurses at Kaiser Permanente in California designed a program to create a better work environment for their staff. Before strategic changes were implemented, only 32 percent of the staff felt the hospital did a good job of making nurses feel important. After restructuring management and adopting a more participative decision-making style, 62 percent felt that they had an opportunity to influence decisions about their professional practice environment.[30]

Rationales for the workplace as a primary site for environmental health promotion activities include the large amount of time spent there by the majority of the population, the economic and other incentives for employers to invest in employee health promotion, the opportunity to mobilize peer pressure to help employees make desirable changes in health habits, and the many reports of workplace success in making health promotion changes.[31]

NURSING PROCESS

Assessment

In preparing to exercise environmental control, assess the following parameters:

- the client's personal space for comfort, lighting, noise, ventilation, and privacy
- the client's environment for people or objects that induce anxiety
- the client's awareness that environmental concerns affect individual and family coping skills
- the client's awareness of objects or other environmental factors in the physical space that induce comfort or discomfort
- the client's environmental concerns, as well as the family's environmental concerns
- the client's possible environmental fears (e.g., a feeling of claustrophobia from being confined to a hospital intensive care bed or intravenous lines, or a fear of death because the patient in the next bed just died)
- the client's grief and its relationship to environmental factors (e.g., Is the client in the same home atmosphere in which the spouse just

died? Are others around the client sad and depressed? Are the colors in the environment dark and heavy?)

- the client's personal health maintenance in relation to environmental factors (e.g., Can the client easily reach self-care hygiene items? Are throw rugs anchored? Are sunglasses worn outside to prevent glare?)
- the client's ability to maintain and manage his or her own home
- the client's risk of injury associated with factors in the environment
- the client's activity deficits as a result of environmental factors
- the client's home environment for its potential impact on effective parenting
- the client's potential noncompliance because of environmental factors
- the client's risk of impairment in physical activity because of environmental factors
- the client's risk of impairment in respiratory function because of environmental factors, such as feather pillows, polluted or stale air, cigarette smoking, known or suspected allergens, or overexertion with chronic respiratory conditions
- the client's possible sleep deficit because of agents in the environment, such as lighting, noise, overstimulation, overcrowding, or allergenic pillows
- the client's alterations in thought processes that may be influenced by environmental factors, such as sensory bombardment with noise, lack of sleep, and transient living patterns

Nursing Diagnoses

The following nursing diagnoses compatible with environmental interventions and that are related to the human response patterns of Unitary Person (see Chapter 7) are as follows:

- Exchanging: All diagnoses
- Choosing: Potential for ineffective choices
- Moving: Altered self-care
Altered growth and development
- Perceiving: Potential for sensory/perceptual alteration
- Knowing: Potential for knowledge deficit
- Feeling: Altered comfort

Client Outcomes

Table 12–2 guides the nurse in client outcomes, nursing prescriptions, and evaluation for the use of the environment as a nursing intervention.

Plan and Interventions

Before the Session

- Become aware of personal thoughts, behaviors, and actions that may contribute to the teaching, counseling, or caring environment.
- Prepare the physical environment for optimal lighting, seating, air quality, and noise control.
- Consider your internal environment. Is it calm, centered, and ready to interact with others?
- Clear your mind of other matters or personal encounters in order to be fully present when meeting with the client.

Beginning the Session

- Allow the client to express specific environmental concerns.
- Guide the client to consider changes that would improve his or her personal and employment environment.
- Encourage the client to write down areas of concern or improvement.

During the Session

- Encourage the client to initiate specific intervention ideas in his or her personal or professional work environment.
- Suggest to clients that they can serve on their place of employment, environmental control committee, or if their agency does not have one, that they volunteer to form one.
- Urge clients to consider the areas of sound (noise, music, machinery, etc.), air (quality, smell, circulation, etc.), and aesthetics (art, color, design, and texture), as well as other topics specific to the overall environment.
- Educate hospitalized clients about the deleterious effects of too much noise.
- Encourage hospitalized clients to limit the time spent watching television and instead listen to their own personal cassette players with headphones.
- Create mechanisms whereby music, imagery, relaxation, color, aromas, and the like can be introduced into the workplace settings.

Table 12–2 Nursing Interventions: Environment

Client Outcomes	*Nursing Prescriptions*	*Evaluation*
The client will demonstrate awareness of environment.	Assist the client in shaping his or her own personal space environment.	The client personalized his or her own environment.
	Assist the client with choices that contribute to a positive, safe environment for those who share his or her personal and community space.	The client monitored and controlled the noise that he or she contributed to the surrounding area. The client respected the rights of others by not polluting air, water, and public places with wastes. The client did not violate the personal space of others with tobacco smoke.
	Provide the client with information that helps in expanding concern for the concept of a healthy global environment.	The client participated in discussions, committees, or programs to work for a safe global environment.
The client will avoid contact and exposure to toxic substances and/or hazardous materials.	Give the client ideas for how to participate in safety education programs at his or her place of employment.	The client participated in his or her workplace offerings of environmental safety programs.
	Teach the client importance of not handling unnecessary toxic substances.	The client did not handle unnecessary toxic substances and educated himself or herself about the dangers of hazardous materials.

At the End of the Session

- Be aware that you function as a role model. As such modulate your voice. Speak audibly, but softly during the session.
- Help clients learn practical ways to cope with hazards in the environment (see Table 12–3).

- Work together to write down goals and target dates.
- Give handout material to support established goals.
- Schedule follow-up sessions.

Specific Interventions

Personal Environment (Basic). Strategies to heal our environment abound on both a personal and a professional level. Personally, we begin to modify our own internal environment. The ability to regulate our state of consciousness, thought patterns, and reactive behaviors gives us the power to move smoothly through external crises both at work and at leisure. Approaching a hectic external environment with internal composure and tranquility makes it possible to transform crises into manageable situations. Clean, clear internal environments can influence all the external environments in which we work and live.

As we develop the optimal workplaces and living areas to foster self-actualizing conditions and maximize bodymind responses, we must be aware of the impact of all aspects of the environment on human health. Many nurses find that the following exercise increases their sensitivity to the environment and its impact:

> At different times during the day, close your eyes, and take a few moments to listen carefully to all the sounds in your environment.
>
> - Jot down the many different sounds you hear, noting which are pleasant and which are distracting or disturbing noises.
> - Become aware of all the sounds that you ordinarily hear, such as the air conditioner, radios and televisions, the hum of fluorescent lights, the beeping and buzzing of hospital machinery, or the incessant MUSAK that some institutions play over the speaker system.
> - Notice new smells, feelings of temperature, etc. There will be many sounds, smells, and sensations of which you may not have previously been aware.

Workplace Noise (Basic). Noise seems to be a major area of environmental concern that nurses can control for the most part. It is the accumulation of noises that adds up in decibels and adds up to stress. By becoming increasingly sensitive to all potential environmental stressors, the nurse becomes more attuned to the opportunities for specific interventions.

Table 12-3 Coping with Environmental Hazards

Problem	*Solution*
Too much noise	1. Turn off radios and televisions. 2. Lower your voice. 3. Ask your colleagues to quiet down. 4. Ask to serve on the agency's environmental control committee.
Inadequate lighting	1. Add more lights. 2. Use incandescent bulbs instead of fluorescent tubes whenever possible. 3. Open curtains and blinds whenever possible. 4. Go outdoors for full-spectrum light breaks, rather than taking cafeteria coffee breaks.
Stale air	1. Make sure agency ventilation systems work. 2. When doing home health visits, open the doors and windows and get fresh air in the home when appropriate. 3. Request that broad-leaf green plants be stationed in the workplace. They are aesthetically pleasing and give off oxygen. 4. Wear masks or protective gear if there is any risk of toxic inhalants.
Long periods at computer video display terminal	1. Use a shield that cuts down glare and radiation and grounds the field of electrostatic charge. 2. Learn some relaxation exercises to do at your desk. 3. Ask your institution or agency to have minimassage available on the premises. 4. Take frequent eye and movement breaks away from the screen. 5. Use properly designed chairs.
Space allocation	1. Try to find some personal space in the workplace. 2. Respect others' personal space. Ask before entering the client's room, closet, or dresser. 3. Make the space you are allocated as pleasant as possible. Decorate with colorful objects, soothing scents, and aesthetic objects.

One researcher taught progressive muscle relaxation to coronary care unit patients who were disturbed by hospital noise. This technique significantly decreased noise sensitivity in these patients.[32] We may generalize from this study that we want not only to eliminate noise whenever possible, but also to use creative ways to help our patients to deal with noise when we cannot remove its source.

Some specific recommendations to reduce workplace noise include

- developing staff education programs about noises, their source, and ways to quiet them
- setting telephones and alarms to low volumes or replacing sound devices with flashing lights
- installing buffers in open space areas to minimize impact noise
- closing the patient's door whenever feasible
- using bedside chairs with wheels in patient rooms with hard floors
- choosing quieter equipment
- placing computer printers away from patient rooms, and/or installing soundproof covers
- giving patients headphones to listen to television or radio so that they do not disturb others
- lowering our voices when we speak

Planetary Consciousness (Basic). Schuster believes that there is an impetus and underlying reason for our developing environmental consciousness. She suggests that we are all hoping to foster and sustain our fullest conscious participation in the ongoing web of interrelationships.[33] Three points emerge as most salient within the context of nursing, in general, and holistic practice, in particular.

1. It is important to address the nature of being human and, in our Western mode, the pervasive influence of the self-other dichotomy.
2. We must be aware that we have viable choices of how we want to be and how we represent ourselves in the world.
3. An integration of items 1 and 2 develops a personal orientation to all environmental concerns. With such an orientation, we can act from internal conviction, relatedness, rather than from institutional directives.[34]

The most enduring and far-reaching environmental work originates with individuals as consumers and practitioners, not with organizations, however enlightened.[35] Thus, it is up to each of us to develop an environmental sensitivity in our daily lives and become increasingly cognizant of our opportunities to institute positive change.

Case Study

Setting: Outpatient clinic, or private visit

Client: A.B., a 55-year-old married man

Nursing Diagnoses: 1. Altered comfort related to recurrent headaches
2. Ineffective individual coping related to environmental stress

A.B. visited the occupational health nurse because of recurrent headaches and chronic fatigue. A physical examination and laboratory tests revealed no pathology or disease, but his subjective declaration of feeling stress in the workplace warranted a closer examination of his workplace environment. A detailed history of his work hours, commuting travel, and work setting yielded evidence of environmental imbalance. A.B. began his day with a 45-minute automobile commute through a suburban area to the inner city; he finished the day the same way. He had made this commute for years, but the traffic had lately increased and road repairs frequently slowed his pace. When he arrived at work, he went to his office, an interior room with no windows and fluorescent ceiling lights. The office walls were the standard institutional beige color; A.B. had done nothing to decorate or personalize his office. Instead of a secretary outside his office, he now had his own computer inside his office. During the company's modernization process, middle managers had been taught computer skills, and many secretarial positions had been eliminated. Each manager was now responsible for developing reports and interacting with others via personal computer terminals. A.B.'s work routine had little variation. It consisted of meetings, telephone work, and online computer time.

This information suggested that A.B. was experiencing environment-related stress, and the nurse worked with him to develop a five-step plan of action:

1. Vary the commuting time. Begin the commute 15 minutes earlier to decrease the rushed feeling of getting to work on time. Join a health club in the city, and stay after work to exercise. The traffic would be considerably less 1 hour later, and the commute time would then be only 30 minutes. Total morning and evening commute time would remain the same as before, but more would have been accomplished with less environmental stress.
2. Implement and practice computer protection skills (see Table 12–3).
3. Mount a shoulder rest on the telephone to prevent neck strain after long periods on the telephone.
4. Personalize the office with soft soothing colors. Add a wall picture of a mountain valley and stream that had a personal significance.

5. Put an incandescent lamp on the desk, and use that rather than the overhead fluorescent lights for desk work.

A copy of this plan was posted in a prominent place in A.B.'s home. Along with a plan for exercise and weight management (see Chapters 11 and 18) and a plan for the development of relaxation and imagery skills (see Chapters 22 and 23), this program incorporated A.B.'s need for motivation, life style change, and values clarification as described in Chapter 5.

When A.B. returned for his follow-up visit 2 months later, his headaches had abated, and he had made some progress toward his weight loss. He and his wife had redecorated his office, and on his own he had added a small cassette player to play his favorite classical music.

Six months later, A.B. was free of headaches. He had spearheaded a no-smoking policy for his workplace and asked the company director to install full-spectrum lights on all ceiling overhead panels. He felt he had regained some sense of control over his environment and was working on improvement in the other areas for which he and the nurse had developed plans.

Evaluation

Each environmental intervention should be measured. The nurse can evaluate with the client the outcomes established before the implementation of any interventions (see Table 12–2). To evaluate the results further, the nurse can explore the subjective effects of the experience with the client, based on the evaluation questions in Exhibit 12–1.

Nurses have always been sensitive to environmental issues. Historically, nurses have been the health care providers primarily concerned with health promotion, sanitation, and improvement in the quality of life for all people. Our technologic society has raised new issues and concerns, ranging from the use of increasingly toxic substances to high-technology machinery. Last year's methods of handling laboratory specimens and chemotherapy preparations, for example, may be outdated next year. Nurses keep abreast of the changing face of the environment in order to equip themselves with the newest strategies to counteract hazards. Future nurses would be well advised to remember and recall some of the basic nursing tenets of yesteryear that are still most relevant today. These interventions include fresh air, control for a comfortable climate, cheerful colors and sights, and noise reduction.

Much of how we relate to and what we do about environmental issues is based on the development of our personal philosophy. We continue to

Exhibit 12–1 Evaluating the Client's Subjective Experience with Environmental Concerns

1. Were you aware that noise, lighting, air quality, space allocation, and workplace toxins could be chronic stressors?
2. Are there any of these potential stressors in your environment? If so, can you do anything to reduce or remove them?
3. Do you realize that you can contribute to a healthier planet by virtue of changing elements in your own personal space?
4. Do you have an environmental sensitivity group at your workplace? If one existed, would you like to be a part of it?
5. Do you feel empowered to be the person who initiates change in your work setting?
6. What are some specific things that you would like to do to create a healthier environment in your personal space or work setting?
7. What is your next step (or your plan) to integrate these changes in your life?

become increasingly aware that each of the small things that we do for or against the environment has short- and long-term ramifications. Nurses want to be alert for ways to contribute to positive environmental changes for their own lives, their clients' lives, and the overall health of the planet. Environmental concerns are important to all of us, and one person's actions can have a ripple effect on many other lives. Nurses can be key agents to ensure that the environment is held sacred, supported, and tended as it supports and gives life to all of the earth's people.

DIRECTIONS FOR FUTURE RESEARCH

1. Study the perception of quality of rest by subjects with different types of auditory stimulation.
2. Study the relationship between environmental hazards (e.g., artificial lighting, working on video display terminals, unventilated air, shift work, high noise levels) and the rise in infertility rates, conditions affecting unborn fetuses, and neonate abnormalities.
3. Investigate the use of tactile, auditory, and/or olfactory stimuli on wound healing, decreased complications, rate of recovery, etc.
4. Study the effect of the environment on the reduction of stress and/or anxiety in ambulatory clients.

NURSE HEALER REFLECTIONS

After reading this chapter, the nurse healer will be able to answer or begin a process of answering the following questions:

- How does the environment affect my job satisfaction?
- What are the environmental stressors at work and at home?
- What strategies can I incorporate in my environment to be healthier?
- What things can I do to improve my own personal and workplace environment?
- How can I be involved with environmental issues at work and in my community?

NOTES

1. B. Thomson, Health Hazards in the Workplace, *East West* 17, no. 1 (1987):35.
2. K. Doxsey, Toxic Substances in the Hospital Environment, *Journal of Nursing Staff Development* 3 (1987):41–42.
3. J. Lubchenco et al., The Sustainable Biosphere Initiative: An Ecological Research Agenda, *Ecology* 72, no. 2 (1991):371–412.
4. C. Meusz, The Nurse's Role in Workplace Assessment, *Nursing Standard* 6, no. 49 (1992):29–32.
5. K. Pelletier, The Hidden Hazards of the Modern Office, *Holistic Medicine Newsletter*, 1(1987):13.
6. Thomson, Health Hazards in the Workplace.
7. Pelletier, The Hidden Hazards of the Modern Office.
8. S. Halpern and L. Savary, *Sound Health* (San Francisco: Harper & Row, 1985), 3–9.
9. M. Smith, Human-Environment Process: A Test of Rogers' Principle of Integrality, *Advances in Nursing Science* 9, no. 1 (1986):21–28.
10. J. Dengerlink et al., Changes in Plasma Angiotensin II with Noise Exposure and Their Relationship to TTS, *Journal of the Acoustical Society of America* 72(1982):276–278.
11. A. White and M. Burgess, Strategies for Reduction of Noise Levels in ICUs, *The Australian Journal of Advanced Nursing* 10, no. 2 (1992–1993):22–26.
12. M. Topf and J. Davis, Critical Care Unit Noise and Rapid Eye Movement (REM). *Heart and Lung* 22(1993):252–258.
13. M. Topf, Effects of Personal Control over Hospital Noise on Sleep, *Research in Nursing and Health*, 15, no. 1 (1992):19–28.
14. J.P. Griffin, The Impact of Noise on Critically Ill People, *Holistic Nursing Practice* 6, no. 4 (1992):53–56.
15. C. Baker, Discomfort to Environmental Noise, *Critical Care Nursing Quarterly* 15, no. 2 (1992):75–90.
16. R.W. Beckham and S.C. Mishoe, Sound Levels inside Incubators and Oxygen Hoods Used with Nebulizers and Humidifiers, *Respiratory Care* 35, no. 12 (1990):1272–1279.

17. M.J. Lotas, Effects of Light and Sound in the Neonatal Intensive Care Unit Environment on the Low-Birth-Weight Infant, *NAACOG's Clinical Issues in Perinatal & Women's Health Nursing* 3, no. 1 (1992):34–44.

18. G. Harrington, The Nuclear Pantry, *New Age Journal* (November/December 1987): 25–30.

19. R. Gibson, *The Wall Street Journal*, February 4, 1994: B1.

20. Harrington, The Nuclear Pantry, 30.

21. *Temple Daily Telegram*, February 4, 1994: 6C.

22. N. Schlapman, Concerns about Passive Smoking, *Nursing Success Today* 3, no. 6 (1986):26–28.

23. T. Hirayama, Passive Smoking and Lung Cancer: Consistency of Association, *Lancet* 2(1983):1425–1426.

24. J.R. White and H.F. Froeb, Small Airways Dysfunction in Nonsmokers Chronically Exposed to Tobacco Smoke, *New England Journal of Medicine* 13(1980):720–723.

25. P. Correa et al., Passive Smoking and Lung Cancer, *Lancet* 2(1983):595–596.

26. J. Ellul, *The Technological Society* (New York: Alfred A. Knopf, 1964), ix.

27. G.A. Baker et al., The Work Environment Scale: A Comparison of British and North American Nurses, *Journal of Advanced Nursing* 17(1992):692–698.

28. N.R. Tommasini, The Impact of a Staff Support Group on the Work Environment of a Specialty Unit, *Archives of Psychiatric Nursing* 6, no. 1 (1992):40–47.

29. G. Thomas, Working Can Be Harmful to Your Health, *Canadian Nurse* 89, no. 6 (1993):35–38.

30. M.B. Townsend, Creating a Better Work Environment, *Journal of Nursing Administration* 21, no. 1 (1991):11–14.

31. J.E. Fielding and P.V. Piserchia, Frequency of Worksite Health Promotion Activities, *American Journal of Public Health* 79, no. 1 (1989):16–20.

32. J.P. Griffin, The Effect of Progressive Muscular Relaxation on Subjectively Reported Disturbance Due to Hospital Noise (Ph.D. diss., New York University, 1988).

33. E. Schuster, Earth Dwelling, *Holistic Nursing Practice* 6, no. 4 (1992):1–9.

34. Ibid.

35. Ibid.

VISION OF HEALING

Releasing the Energy of the Playful Child

The joy of playing and playfulness is a gift that we may lose as we grow out of childhood to take on the responsibilities of the adult. Illness may further deplete our ability to see the lighter side of life and take advantage of healthy hilarity. We must search out ways to reconnect with the joyful child within and use that energy to move to a higher level of wellness. When we laugh, our perception shifts. We release feelings of judgment, blame, and self-pity to embrace a more extended knowing of ourselves and others. Deliberately taking the time to amuse and be amused allows us to endure a great deal of change that would otherwise be overwhelming.[1]

Play is part of the richness of life; it enables us to live and grow. As infants and children, we play to learn. As adults, we play to relax, to enjoy interaction with others, to grow, and to gain a different perspective on our lives. Our play can be a variety of activities, from the simple experience of skipping or dancing for the joy of movement, to the excitement of "playing to win" in a tournament or game.

Most animals play for at least some portion of their lives. The animals that play are those that can benefit from experience, those that can learn both step-by-step and on occasion by leaps of the imagination. The ones that play are those that must learn by discovery and practice, acquiring through trial and error (and trial and success) the skills they need to survive.[2]

> *There is more honest "belly laughter" in a Zen monastery than surely in any other religious institution on earth. To laugh is a sign of sanity; and the comic is deliberately used to break up concepts, to release tensions and to teach what cannot be taught in words. Nonsense is used to point to the beyond of rational sense.*
>
> Christmas Humphries[3]

NOTES

1. J. Segal, *Feeling Great* (Van Nuys, CA: Newcastle Publishing Company, 1981), 68.

2. M. Piers and G. Landau, *The Gift of Play* (New York: Walker and Co., 1980), 19.
3. T. Quereau and T. Zimmerman, *The New Game Plan for Recovery: Rediscovering the Positive Power of Play* (New York: Ballantine Books, 1992), 261.

Chapter 13

Play and Laughter: Moving toward Harmony

Leslie Gooding Kolkmeier

NURSE HEALER OBJECTIVES

Theoretical

- Read and understand the definitions and types of play and humor.
- Understand the differences and advantages of both physical and mental play.
- List the psychophysiologic responses to play and laughter.

Clinical

- Integrate preparatory play in your clinical practice.
- Document the psychophysiologic changes that occur in clients when they allow themselves to be playful.
- Begin to build a library of humorous stories, jokes, games, cartoons, comedy videotapes, or audiocassettes suitable for use in your area of nursing practice.

Personal

- Identify times during the day when you are playing, with a sense of freedom and without guilt, rather than competing.
- Learn to use playfulness and humor to reduce tension, anxiety, and fatigue in the middle of difficult days at work and home.
- Heighten your awareness of your psychophysiologic shifts that come with play, such as increased energy and alertness, decreased

heart rate after play, and a change in perception of pain or discomfort.

- Learn to laugh out loud, practicing alone until you are comfortable with a deep, clear "belly laugh."

DEFINITIONS

Humor: "the quality that appeals to a sense of the comical or the absurdly incongruous"[1]; the mental faculty of discovering, expressing, or appreciating wit or comedy. Humor can be kindly and gentle, or sarcastic and bitter; it can be intellectual and witty, or broad, slapstick, and visual. The acknowledgment of humor leads to laughter.

Laughter: "the coordinated contraction of 15 facial muscles in a stereotyped pattern and accompanied by altered breathing. Laughter is the loaded latency given us by nature as part of our native equipment to break up the stalemates of our lives and urge us on to deeper and more complex forms of knowing."[2]

Play: "a voluntary activity at once invigorating and relaxing, challenging and rewarding, unpredictable yet unthreatening, and above all a process we enjoy."[3]

Preparatory Play: play specifically structured to prepare clients for procedures and interventions; activities designed to allow clients to come into imaginary contact with specific people and equipment in a playful, nonthreatening manner before the event. Preparatory play includes playing with models, actual pieces of equipment, and instruments, as well as imitating the anticipated procedure on dolls, stuffed animals, or other figures that simulate the procedure.

THEORY AND RESEARCH

One of our major survival skills since earliest times, laughter is a natural extension of the activity of playing or being playful. The "ability to laugh is one of the most characteristic and deep-seated features of man. Many psychologists and philosophers have even argued that man is the only creature who laughs or has a sense of humor."[4]

The role of play in our lives is evident in the way it pervades our language; we "toy with ideas" and "play with the possibilities." Even in school and work environments, we learn to "play by the rules" in order to advance. In the language, the play concept has even eroded into conscious or unconscious attempts at manipulation, as in "the games people play."

Play in Ancient Cultures

Playing is as old as humankind, as evidenced by the remains of toys found in the ancient ruins of Egypt, Babylonia, China, and Aztec civilizations.[5] Toys have been buried with the remains of both children and adults, indicating the ancient belief in the need for play not only in this world, but also in the next.

The ancient Greeks wrote on the value of play and toys for the development of children. Plato wrote of the need for play opportunities for children. He felt that children would invent games and playthings naturally, especially when left to play among themselves.[6] According to Erikson,

> Plato saw the model of true playfulness in the need of all young creatures, animal and human, to leap. To truly leap, you must learn how to use the ground as a springboard, and how to land resiliently and safely. It means to test the leeway allowed by given limits; to outdo and yet not escape gravity. Thus, wherever playfulness prevails, there is always a surprising element, surpassing mere repetition or habituation, and at its best suggesting some virgin chance conquered, some divine leeway shared.[7]

Play in Today's Society

Child labor laws, a shortened work week, summer vacations from school, an increase in leisure time, and a rise in average family incomes have all made it possible for more people to participate in play and recreational activities. As play has become more accepted for both children and adults, teams and competitive sports have replaced simpler forms of play. The emphasis has been on winning, however, rather than on the joys of physical and mental activity.

"Pure play" is entirely different from the concept of "winning." When we play to win, we are competing, not simply having fun. When we count points scored or try to beat our best time when running, the activity has slipped from the play category into the category of competition. Bettelheim feels that children quickly recognize that play is an opportunity for pure enjoyment, whereas games may involve considerable stress. He wrote of one 4-year-old who, when confronted with an unfamiliar play situation, asked, "Is this a fun game or a winning game?" It was clear that his attitude toward the activity depended on the answer he was given.[8]

We need to approach daily life without regard for winning or losing, but only with the idea of having fun. We must relearn the skill and excitement of participating, whether in quiet, solitary play or in cooperative active games. According to Quereau and Zimmerman, play is about *process* rather than *product*. When we play as children, our forts are never done, and the end of one game is accompanied by cries for "just one more game."[9]

Play is universally felt to be a vital part of a well-rounded life style, although its positive effects on our physical and emotional well-being are only now being researched and scientifically evaluated. The value that play and laughter impart to our lives along the wellness-illness continuum cannot be overestimated.

Bodymind Connections: Play and Laughter

Play and its natural outcome, laughter, produce a number of psychophysiologic effects. They exercise major body systems, including the cardiovascular system. They are thought to stimulate the release of endorphins, which alter mood and help reduce pain perception.[10] Hearty laughter decreases muscle tonus, thus reducing the anxiety that leads to muscle tightness and tension.[11] Furthermore, laughter has positive effects on heart rate, breathing rate, peripheral vascular flow, and self-esteem.[12] The psychophysiologic basis of the smile is thought to be a process of tension relaxation.[13]

In one study, subjects received the stimulant epinephrine, normal saline, or the tranquilizer chlorpromazine. They then watched a humorous film and rated how funny the film was. Those who were physiologically aroused by the injection of epinephrine rated the movie as very funny; those who received the saline rated it as moderately funny; and those who received the tranquilizer did not see any humor at all in the film. "The most intriguing implication of these findings is that even humor, something we generally regard as being so clearly psychological and emotional in basis, has a profound connection with physiological states of the body."[14]

According to Cousins, 10 minutes of belly laughs induced by watching films of Candid Camera and old Marx Brothers movies frequently gave him respite from the pain of his severe ankylosing spondylitis and 2 hours of sound sleep.[15] His description of this experience, together with an understanding of the role played by the neuropeptide–immune-hormone network (see Chapter 4), makes clear the beneficial effects on the bodymind of the positive emotions generated by play and laughter. When we play and laugh, not only do we feel better emotionally, but also we have positively influenced the basis of our physical well-being.

Laughter and Humor As Coping Responses

Laughter eases tensions and may facilitate discussions of more serious matters. The humorist Borge has said, "Laughter is the shortest distance between two people." A gentle joke or funny comment often makes a smooth introduction to a difficult discussion.

The ability to laugh at ourselves permits us to forgive ourselves for imperfections, mistakes, and failures. This removes the incredible burden of striving to be perfect, which demands a degree of self-involvement so high that it stifles the ability to be amused. Timing and appropriateness are vital in these situations and must be carefully assessed before jokes or funny comments are verbalized. If one is hurt physically or emotionally, play must stop until the wound is tended. Play must feel safe; if participants have doubts about their safety, worth, or competence, the concept of play has been misrepresented.[16]

Clients who are disfigured or otherwise visibly handicapped may adapt to their situation by using a sense of humor to put others at ease and overcome awkward moments. Having a repertoire of one liners to introduce themselves or help extricate others from embarrassing situations helps these clients cope with their disability in a healthy manner.[17]

Play and the Adult

When we truly play, we seek to impress no one, and we produce no product; we just enjoy being in the moment. These are not attributes for which we receive external rewards, and nurses and clients may seem to have allowed the skill to atrophy and, in some cases, to die. We should ask our clients what they do *just for fun* and when they last enjoyed that activity. When did they last swing on a porch swing, make a snow angel, or attempt to juggle rolled up socks when folding the laundry?

As we grow older, our ability to "take the leap," as described by Plato, becomes constrained and reserved both literally and figuratively. A serious attention to the business at hand may replace our willingness to laugh and play, subsequently reducing our health-promoting behaviors. Conversely, clients may become less inhibited when they reach a point of maturity that allows them to stop judging and simply enjoy the pleasures of their childhood. For example, the presence of a grandchild may loosen the bonds of "correctness" and give reign to the joys of playfulness.

Much like relaxation, playing is a skill that many adults must relearn. Play and playfulness are often only faint memories for nurses and adult clients. Sometimes, it is difficult to incorporate playing into our lives again because it does not always fit our image of what is necessary and proper for an adult human. Erikson notes that

> What seems to become of play as we grow older depends very much on our changing conceptions of the relationship of childhood to adulthood and, or course, of play to work. Some adults, through the ages, have been inclined to judge play to be neither serious nor useful, and thus unrelated to the center of human tasks and motives, from which the adult, in fact, seeks "recreation" when he plays. Such a division may make life simpler and permit adults to avoid the often awesome suggestion that playfulness—and, thus, indeterminate chance—may occur in the vital center of adult concerns, as it does in the center of those of children.[18]

We nurses have the opportunity to help clients re-create the joyfulness and play of childhood both through instruction and through role modeling. It may be useful to help patients and clients identify the self-talk that inhibits play. Such self-statements as "act your age," "don't be foolish," or "grow up," for example, stand in the way of health-promoting play and laughter.

It is necessary to reinforce play behaviors in the face of life style changes, such as those brought about by retirement, recuperation from an illness, or hospitalization. Clients who are able to be playful while adapting to new circumstances are most likely to survive change. There is a psychophysiologic basis for this effect:

> When we laugh we dramatically alter our existence on the grid of space and time. At the height of laughter, the universe is flung into a kaleidoscope of new possibilities. High comedy, and the laughter that ensues, is an evolutionary event. Together they evoke a biological response that drives the organism to higher levels of organization and integration.[19]

Playfulness in the Work Environment

The activity that you choose does not determine whether you are working or playing; it's your attitude toward it that counts. No matter how gratifying, sustained effort toward a goal depletes one's energy after a while if it isn't balanced by freedom, spontaneous feeling, and laughter. Work drains one's battery; play charges it.

The presence of small toys in the work environment not only personalizes the space, but also gives the bodymind an opportunity to pause occasionally, reduce stress levels, and allow the spark of creativity to flourish. An egg of Silly Putty, a smooth touchstone in a pocket, or a kaleidoscope disguised as a pen may provide just the play break necessary to see a problem from a new angle or allow the solution to a perplexing problem to bubble up from the unconscious.

Nurses turn to humor to defuse the stress of the life-and-death situations that they face on a daily basis. Although humor can relieve tension and stabilize high-stress situations, it must be used with caution. It can be dangerous and destructive if used carelessly. Health care providers should always presume that a patient can hear their comments, even if he or she appears to be comatose. Hearing is the sense that is maintained longest.

The Game of Games

Leonard, a New Games enthusiast, reminds us of what it is like to become a player in the game of living instead of a spectator.

> An athlete in the Game of Games is one who plays life intensely, with heightened awareness of this endeavor. An Athlete is one who can perceive discord and harmony both, who can accept contradiction as the very stuff of play while not losing sight of the ultimate harmony. An athlete in this Game plays voluntarily and wholeheartedly, even while realizing that this Game is not all that is; knows the rules and limitations of play, and sees beauty in the order thus imposed; seeks to expand any frontier available and yet is not unmindful of ethical imperatives and the needs of others. This athlete contends in a game for a prize, and the prize is play itself, a life fully experienced and examined.
>
> The athlete in the Game of Games may be a musician or a carpenter, a householder or a yogi, an Olympic runner or a

> farmer. No one can be excluded merely because of occupational specialty, and differences between the purely physical and nonphysical begin to fade. It is only through a heresy in Western thought that we could consider any aspect of life as "nonphysical." The body is always involved, even in what we call the most cerebral pursuit. Einstein tells us that the Special or Restricted Theory of Relativity came from a feeling in his muscles. Surely he was a great athlete of the Game of Games, in which we are all embodied. Embodiment is indeed the primary condition of play. When Western philosophy and theology attempted to cut away the body from the Higher Life, the Life of the Mind, the attempt failed. The body, unacknowledged, remained a part of every formulation. To the precise extent that it has been ignored, Western thought has become fragmentary and misleading.
>
> Spirit in flesh, flesh in spirit. Abstractions in the muscles, visions in the bones. We can no longer deny the conditions of embodiment—nor can we ever entirely explain them. However far we pursue the mystery, it finally eludes us. The "answer" lies in the unsayable statement, the unprovable proposition that prevents paradox and foreclosure. There are no closed systems. The body opens us to wonders in this and other worlds. Its movements through space and time can launch us on a timeless voyage to a place beyond place.[20]

NURSING PROCESS

Assessment

In preparing to use play and laughter interventions, assess the following parameters:

- the client's ability and willingness to smile and laugh
- the client's sense of humor and laughter, as well as their appropriateness
- the client's attitude toward the ideas of play and laughter
- the client's awareness of the kinds of humor he or she has enjoyed in the past
- the client's ability to read humorous books or watch humorous videotapes
- the client's physical limitations that would influence his or her ability to engage in play activities

- the client's previous experience with play
- the client's frequency of engaging in playful activities

Nursing Diagnoses

The following nursing diagnoses compatible with play interventions can be related to the human response patterns of the unitary person (see Chapter 7):

• Relating:	Altered parenting, actual or potential
	Social isolation
• Choosing:	Ineffective individual and family coping
• Moving:	Activity intolerance, actual or potential
	Deficit in diversional activity
	Impaired physical mobility
• Perceiving:	Powerlessness
	Disturbance in self-concept
	Altered self-esteem, role performance, personal identity
• Sensory-perceptual:	Altered visual, auditory, kinesthetic, gustatory, tactile, olfactory
• Knowing:	Altered thought processes
• Feeling:	Anxiety
	Comfort, altered: pain
	Fear
	Violence, potential for self-directed or directed at others

Client Outcomes

Table 13–1 guides the nurse in client outcomes, nursing prescriptions, and evaluation for the use of play as a nursing intervention.

Plan and Interventions

Before the Session

- Practice smiling and laughing out loud in front of a mirror or on a videotape until you are comfortable with your ability to do so.
- Gain experience with the techniques that you intend to employ in order to know which to use and how best to use them.

Table 13-1 Nursing Interventions: Play and Laughter

Client Outcomes	*Nursing Prescriptions*	*Evaluation*
The client will engage in playful activities.	Guide the client in playful activities; help the client identify amusing puns, jokes, stories, riddles, or other forms of humor.	The client played cards with a family member during evening visiting hours. The client requested two comedy films from the unit library in 1 week. The client greeted afternoon shift nurse with corny "knock-knock" joke.
The client will exhibit appropriate spontaneous laughter.	Model appropriate smiling and laughter for the client. Reflect pleasure when the client spontaneously laughs or smiles appropriately when presented with humorous greeting cards, comedy films, audiotapes, jokes, stories, etc.	The client laughed in response to a comedy audiocassette loaned from the unit library. The client laughed when describing learning to eat soup with her nondominant, uninjured hand.
The client will have a decrease in subjective severity of target symptom as a result of the play/laughter intervention.	Guide the client in grading the severity of a symptom on a 1 to 10 scale before and after the intervention.	The client graded pain level at 6 before playing the video game and graded pain level at 3 (on 1 to 10 scale) after playing the game.

- Center yourself before making contact with the client.
- Sense your own needs and evaluate your own stress load.
- Review the client's chart or consult with others to become familiar with any changes in the client's situation since you last met.
- Have supplies (e.g., tape recorder, books, drawings, cartoons, videotapes) on hand in working condition.

At the Beginning of the Session

- Assess the client's status according to the assessment parameters.

- Record vital signs and ask the client to assess pain, anxiety, or tension level on a numerical scale (e.g., "My pain level right now is a 6 on a 1 (no pain) to 10 (extreme pain) scale").
- Describe to the client the benefits and psychophysiologic changes that may be expected from the intervention.
- Provide the client with appropriate materials and instruction.

During the Session

- Use all interventions with empathy and sensitivity to the client.
- Provide support for the client in terms of your physical presence, encouragement, or time alone if the client wants to read or watch a videotape of humorous material.
- Remember that humor is contagious and social. The intervention may be most effective if used with a group, rather than individually.
- Remember that humor and play are spontaneous and, therefore, are most successful when not precisely planned.
- Continue to evaluate the mood and response of the client, and adapt to the client's perceived needs.

At the End of the Session

- Record vital signs and have the client reevaluate pain or discomfort level on a 1 to 10 scale.
- Discuss the intervention with the client and obtain feedback for future sessions.
- Answer any questions that the client may have.
- Encourage further work on an individual basis.
- Use the client outcomes that were established before the session (see Table 13–1) and the client's subjective experiences (Exhibit 13–1) to evaluate the session.
- Schedule a follow-up session.

Specific Interventions: Play

Cultivating Spontaneous Silliness (Basic). Some nurses and clients may have difficulty employing and participating in what they perceive as "silly" behavior. It may be easiest to begin simply by doing a familiar activity in a different way:

- parting hair on the opposite side
- eating with the nondominant hand

- putting socks on last
- going to therapy by a different route
- pretending to be someone else.

Clients may enjoy remembering youthful tricks, such as pretending to be asleep, moving food around on a plate to give the impression that most of it has been eaten, or identifying images in cloud formations. The nurse may ask clients how old they would be if they did not know their age. The nurse may encourage visualization with humor, such as picturing a disagreeable teacher as an animal or a forbidding authority figure dressed only in underwear. Helping a client deal with difficult people in humorous ways gives the client a sense of control and perspective.

Toys and games can feel good while producing measurable therapeutic progress. For example, Koosh and Nerf balls not only stimulate the sense of touch, but also provide safe projectiles for increasing strength and coordination, playing catch, or playing trashcan basketball.

Playing Games (Basic to Advanced). Games are a form of play on which we have imposed rules and rituals. Because they usually involve an element of competition, they can easily lose some of the spontaneity of pure play. Games may require less physical activity than do some other forms of play, however, so they may be appropriate for the client who is confined to bed or whose physical abilities are decreased.

Cards, board games, puzzles, and word games are appropriate for clients with decreased mobility and may encourage them to socialize. Such activities can take place in a particular area of an inpatient facility, outdoors, or in a client's room. Nurses or hospital volunteers may maintain and distribute game materials to clients from a central location, or each nursing area may have a game drawer or shelf with supplies.

For clients who are more physically active, the nurse is encouraged to learn about New Games. According to its founders,

> New Games is an attitude that encourages people to play together. To learn only the form and not the essence would be to miss the lifeline that gives rise to that attitude. Solely for the purpose of having fun, we can be free and foolish in the arena of New Games and let the spirit carry us.[21]

Various New Games are appropriate for two to several dozen players. They combine physical activity with spontaneity (i.e., a person who does not like the rules is encouraged to change them), develop physical and social skills, and incur very little risk of injury.

Collecting Cartoons (Basic). The value of humor in coping with the tension of hospitalization and illness is obvious in the selection of funny greeting cards displayed in patients' rooms. Keeping a scrapbook of cartoons or jokes related to hospital life can help pass time for both patients and families. Encouraging staff members, we as well as patients and families, to add to the collection helps develop a sense of camaraderie. Some patients may choose to draw their own cartoons based on their hospital experiences.

As with all play and laughter interventions, great care and sensitivity are necessary when using cartoons with patients and families. This is particularly important during an acute event when there may be great uncertainty and concern for the outcome. It is essential to evaluate the emotional status of the patient or family member carefully before suggesting any playful intervention.

Using Humorous Books, Audiotapes, and Videotapes (Basic to Advanced). Because humor is a very individual experience, it is appropriate to have a large choice of materials to offer to the client who chooses to take part in a play and laughter intervention. Audiotapes and videotapes lend themselves to use with groups, increasing clients' opportunity to interact with one another and build upon a framework of common appreciation and experiences. Cassette tapes are available that contain nothing but 20 minutes of laughter. Listening to them can be a delightful way to help a group relearn the joy of being silly.

Case Studies

Case Study No. 1

Setting: Outpatient clinic

Client: J.B., a 45-year-old woman

Nursing Diagnoses:
1. Activity intolerance
2. Anxiety
3. Breathing pattern, ineffective
4. Fear
5. Powerlessness: all related to adult-onset intrinsic asthma

J.B. had visited the clinic for treatment of her asthma over a period of several months. Her bronchodilator medications had been adjusted, she was using a cool mist to thin secretions, her activity level had increased, and she had returned to full-time employment.

In the process of teaching her breathing techniques, the nurse noted that J.B. had difficulty in maintaining prolonged exhalation. She was able to lengthen her expiratory time between attacks, but would forget the intervention when under the stress of wheezing and shortness of breath.

She arrived at the clinic in mild distress after using an inhaler to open her airways with only partial success. After sitting J.B. in a straight chair, the nurse began coaching her breathing pattern while applying gentle pressure on her shoulders with each exhalation. As her breathing became easier, the nurse opened a bottle of bubble solution and invited J.B. to blow bubbles. Although J.B. felt that this was a rather nontraditional approach to her condition, she agreed to participate.

In order to blow bubbles successfully, one must exhale slowly and for a long period of time. J.B. remembered this from her own childhood and from playing with her children. She was soon blowing long streams of fragile bubbles, and her wheezing disappeared as she did so. As the attack eased, the nurse coached J.B. to visualize the bubbles as carrying her tension triggers away. J.B. expressed her delight with her new application of an old skill. Her tension decreased, and she returned to work confident in her ability to apply her skill during stressful situations. Linking the skill with an unusual and playful activity made the breathing strategy stand out in her memory and easier to recall under stress.

Case Study No. 2

Setting: Pediatric oncology unit

Client: F.W., a 7-year-old boy

Nursing Diagnoses:
1. Anxiety
2. Coping, ineffective individual
3. Diversional activity, deficit
4. Fear
5. Powerlessness
6. Social isolation: all related to acute illness

F.W. had received a diagnosis of acute lymphocytic leukemia only a few days before his first contact with the play group organized for pediatric patients on the oncology service. His diagnostic work-up had been prolonged and frightening for him, and he had become more withdrawn, tearful, and frightened as the days went by. Knowing that F.W. was to begin a course of chemotherapy shortly and aware of his terror response to needles and intravenous set-ups, the nurse invited the boy and his mother to join her and several children in the playroom.

F.W. clung to his mother, but was able to sit on her lap at the periphery of the group as the children began to play with stuffed dolls, intravenous bags of water, tape, and, under close supervision, intravenous needles. He listened and watched intently as the nurse helped the children start intravenous lines in the dolls' arms and hands, and he soon began to venture closer to the group. On the second day, F.W. began to take part in the activities. He played with the tubing and needles and talked encouragingly to his doll as he rehearsed the chemotherapy procedure, coached by the nurse and the other children.

During his first chemotherapy treatment, F.W. took his rehearsal doll with him into the treatment room. He cried quietly, but sat still on his mother's lap and even corrected the nurse's technique when she began to tape the intravenous needle in a way that differed somewhat from the way that F.W. had rehearsed with his doll.

As his therapy progressed, F.W. became more confident and began to participate actively in the playroom. He was still frightened of his chemotherapy sessions, but endured them without his original terror. Within a week of his first encounter with the preparatory play dolls and equipment, he was explaining the process to a new patient.

Evaluation

With the client, the nurse determines whether the client outcomes for play and laughter (see Table 13–1) were successfully achieved. To evaluate the session further, the nurse may again explore the subjective effects of the experience with the client (see Exhibit 13–1). Some of the interventions may take place over days or weeks and, therefore, must be periodically reviewed and reevaluated. The process of developing playfulness and a sense of humor in a client takes time, and continued support and feedback are necessary.

Whether helping a client through a difficult procedure or strengthening our own ability to move smoothly through a shift assignment, humor and playfulness help keep us centered and whole. Humor can help us tap into the spiritual and evolutionary possibilities inherent in all events.

DIRECTIONS FOR FUTURE RESEARCH

1. Determine the physiologic changes that occur with the use of play and laughter.

Exhibit 13–1 Evaluating the Client's Subjective Experience with Play and Laughter

1. Was this a new experience for you? Can you describe it?
2. Can you describe any physical or emotional shift that occurred during the exercise?
3. Were there any distractions during the exercise?
4. How long has it been since you had this kind of experience?
5. How was this exercise different for you from the last time you took part in it or one similar?
6. Would you like to try this again?
7. How could the experience be made more meaningful for you?
8. What are your plans to integrate this exercise into your daily life?

2. Develop toys and games as interventions for specific nursing diagnoses.
3. Evaluate the decrease in anxiety when preparatory play is used.

NURSE HEALER REFLECTIONS

After reading this chapter, the nurse healer will be able to answer or begin a process of answering the following questions:

- Can I recall the kinesthetic imagery of weightlessness and timelessness at the top of a wonderful, tall swing?
- What is my inner sense of joy when I hear myself or another laugh out loud?
- Do I nurture my ability and the ability of my clients to be playful?
- Can I play with a sense of freedom and without guilt, even when my work is not yet finished?
- Do I play without competing or feeling that I must accomplish a particular goal?

NOTES

1. *Webster's New Collegiate Dictionary* (Springfield, MA: G. and C. Merriam Co., 1951), 403.
2. J. Houston, *The Possible Human* (Los Angeles: Jeremy P. Tarcher, 1982), 119.

3. T. Quereau and T. Zimmerman, *The New Game Plan for Recovery: Rediscovering the Positive Power of Play* (New York: Ballantine Books, 1992), 131.
4. R. Moody, *Laugh after Laugh* (Jacksonville, FL: Headwaters Press, 1978), xiii.
5. L. Frankel, Play, in *The World Book Encyclopedia* (Chicago: Field Enterprises Educational Corp., 1975), 506.
6. F. Caplan and T. Caplan, *The Power of Play* (New York: Anchor Press/Doubleday, 1973), 256.
7. E. Erikson, *Toys and Reasons* (New York: W.W. Norton, 1977) 17.
8. B. Bettleheim, The Importance of Play, *Atlantic Monthly*, 259, no. 3 (1987):37.
9. Quereau and Zimmerman, *The New Game Plan for Recovery*, 15.
10. L. Hill and N. Smith, *Self-Care Nursing* (Englewood Cliffs, NJ: Prentice-Hall, 1985), 228.
11. Moody, *Laugh after Laugh*, 5.
12. B. Woods, Mirthful Laughter and Directed Relaxation: A Comparison of Physiological Responses (Ph.D. diss., North Texas State University, Denton, 1986).
13. C. Garvey, *Play* (Cambridge, MA: Harvard University Press, 1977), 20.
14. Moody, *Laugh after Laugh*, 8.
15. N. Cousins, *Anatomy of an Illness as Perceived by the Patient* (New York; W.W. Norton, 1979), 39–40.
16. Quereau and Zimmerman, *The New Game Plan for Recovery*, 107.
17. Moody, *Laugh after Laugh*, 26.
18. Erikson, *Toys and Reasons*, 18.
19. Houston, *The Possible Human*, 119.
20. A. Fluegleman, ed., *The New Games Book* (Garden City, NY: Dolphin Books/ Doubleday, 1976), 188.
21. Ibid.

SUGGESTED READING

G. Asakawa and L. Rucker, *The Toy Book* (New York: Alfred A. Knopf, 1991).

J. Carse, *Finite and Infinite Games* (New York: The Free Press, 1986).

M. Csikszentmihalyi, *Flow: The Psychology of Optimal Experience* (New York: Harper & Row, 1990).

C. Hagaseth, *A Laughing Place: The Art and Psychology of Positive Humor in Love and Adversity* (Ft. Collins, CO: Berwicle Publishing Co., 1988).

R.A. Harg, Therapeutic Uses of Humor, *American Journal of Psychotherapy* 408, no. 4 (1986):543–553.

J. Pearce, *Magical Child* (New York: E.P. Dutton, 1977).

J. Pearce, *Magical Child Matures* (New York: E.P. Dutton, 1985).

M.J. Watson, Facilitate Learning with Humor, *Journal of Nursing Education* 27, no. 2 (1988):89–90.

RESOURCES

American Association for Therapeutic Humor
9040 Forestview Rd
Skokie, IL 60203-1913
312-679-2593

Healing through Laughter and Play Conferences
Institute for the Advancement of Human Behavior
P.O. Box 7226
Stanford, CA 94309
415-851-8411

VISION OF HEALING

Healthy Disclosure

Diaries, journals, logs, reviews, stories, and letters enable us to keep track of and enhance the patterns of our lives. Research shows that, in addition to helping us find meaning and depth in our life experiences, writing about occurrences such as trauma or illness improves our health.[1] *Writing may also help us make the experience our own and explore its meaning for us, the way that we come to possess it, and, ultimately, the way that we can release it.*[2]

As adolescents, we may have written in a diary, entering into it both the mundane and the deeply moving events of our days. With the transition into adulthood, we may well have reduced these diary entries to lists of things to do, appointments, chores, and dates. We find time only to jot short notes on a calendar or in a blank book, making longer entries in a loose-leaf notebook or perhaps putting into a box scraps of paper that contain ideas, thoughts, bits of poetry, and plans for a golden tomorrow. Even these abbreviated records provide a skeletal reflection of our lives, which can be filled out and given form by memories.

As nurses, we can refresh our own self-reflection techniques and perfect new ones to help us record and grow from our experiences, intuitions, and connections. We can learn to help ourselves and our clients tap into the spiritual and self-healing aspects of the complex and beautiful web of our existence. Self-reflection helps us evoke more trust and truth in daily living.

> As the Gods created the universe, they discussed where they should hide Truth so that human beings would not find it right away. They wanted to prolong the adventure of the search.
>
> "Let's put Truth on top of the highest mountain," said one of the gods. "Certainly it will be hard to find there."
>
> "Let's put it on the farthest star," said another. "Let's hide it in the darkest and deepest of abysses."
>
> "Let's conceal it on the secret side of the moon."
>
> At the end, the wisest and most ancient god said, "No, we will hide Truth inside the very heart of human beings. In this way they will look for it all over the Universe, without being aware of having it inside themselves all the time."[3]

NOTES

1. J. Pennebaker, *Opening Up: The Healing Power of Confiding in Others* (New York: Avon Books, 1990).
2. M. Crichton, *Travels* (New York: Ballantine Books, 1988), xi.
3. P. Ferrucci, *What We May Be* (Los Angeles: Jeremy P. Tarcher, 1982), 143.

Chapter 14

Self-Reflection: Consulting the Truth Within

Leslie Gooding Kolkmeier

NURSE HEALER OBJECTIVES

Theoretical

- Define the types of self-reflection tools.
- Discuss the theories of adult learning that describe the ability and readiness of a client to use and benefit from the tools.
- Discuss ways in which the right brain activity of intuiting information can be used and applied to the left brain analysis of clinical data.

Clinical

- Implement one of the interventions with a client in whose care you are involved.
- Keep an intuition log for 1 week, recording all instances of intuitive thought concerning your clients.
- Make a list of opening questions or statements to help initiate the life review process with clients.

Personal

- Use self-reflection on your life as a healing intervention in order to tap into intuitive knowledge.
- Choose one intervention with which you are less familiar and spend 1 month increasing your expertise.

- Practice interpreting your intuitions and dreams in order to become more adept and confident in your daily life decisions.

DEFINITIONS

Clustering: a visual representation of an information web; a group of ideas starting from a core word and branching outward.

Diaries and Journals: records that are kept on a periodic or regular basis and contain factual material and subjective interpretations of events, thoughts, feelings, and plans.

Dreams: unself-conscious reflections of the psyche; imagery that occurs just before sleep (i.e., hypnagogic), immediately on awakening (i.e., hypnopompic), or during the rapid eye movement sleep period.

Letters: a simple way of talking in written words to another (e.g., new or old friends, family, body parts, or acquaintances who are alive or deceased).

Life Review or Reminiscence Therapy: the remembering of significant past events that enables an older person, in Eriksonian terms, to reintegrate past issues and experiences in the present for the purpose of achieving a sense of meaning and ego integrity.[1]

THEORY AND RESEARCH

Self-reflection interventions are teaching tools, but they differ from most client education modules in that the learning comes from inner knowledge and is primarily client-generated. The nurse is involved principally as a facilitator.

Adults, unlike children, are voluntary learners, but they need satisfying learning experiences in order to succeed. Educators have identified four ways in which an adult's learning differs from a child's learning.

1. An adult's self-concept has shifted from that of a person who is dependent to that of a person who is capable of self-direction.
2. An adult has a large data base of life experience to use as a resource for learning.
3. An adult's motivation for learning is oriented toward problem solving rather than learning for its own sake.
4. An adult's time perspective has changed in that an adult desires immediate applicability of the knowledge gained.[2]

Self-Concept

The adult self-concept is based on independence and self-sufficiency. When illness or injury threatens self-concept, self-reflection tools that are judiciously presented bolster self-concept and self-esteem and help restore the client to former feelings of independence. Such techniques as clustering of strengths and possibilities or writing journal entries about the feelings that surround an illness or injury can help the client reintegrate a shaken self-image and actually speed physical and emotional healing.

Experience

Adults base many of their coping skills on those that were successful in the past. Because serious illness or injury is not usually a part of becoming an adult, few clients can cope with it by calling up past experiences.

The greater the amount of information that nurses can provide concerning the illness or injury, the faster the pace with which the client can move toward healing. In the acute phase of an illness or injury, the information provided addresses short-term goals, such as anxiety reduction, environmental information, and details of nursing and medical procedures. As clients incorporate this knowledge into their experience base, they can move to somewhat longer term goals, such as behavior change. Using a diary and writing letters to family and friends help the client integrate the health care experience into the "whole story" and, thus, remove barriers to further learning and healing.

Problem Solving

Adults learn new information and life skills primarily through the identification of problems that need to be solved in daily life. Nurses can become discouraged if their teaching focuses on areas in which the client fails to see a problem. The use of clustering or lists may help the client identify related problems and become open to learning new ways to deal with them. Dream logs may help point out areas of conflict that are more unconscious in nature.

Applicability of Knowledge

Children are accustomed to learning material that appears to them to have little application to their daily lives. Adults, however, need to be able to see a direct application of their learning to a perceived problem.

In order to help a client apply self-reflection techniques successfully, the nurse must make clear the connection between the techniques and the alleviation of an identified problem.

BODYMIND CONNECTIONS

Self-reflection acts as an intermediary between the various aspects and expressions of the bodymind. Each of the interventions becomes a tool for exploring thoughts, feelings, and emotions. As these are brought to consciousness, they stimulate shifts in the endocrine, neuropeptide, immune, and hormonal systems (see Chapter 4).

We are all familiar with our body's response when we think of anxiety-laden events. Simply telling or writing about emotionally charged material or a time of physical pain triggers activity in the hypothalamus and pituitary gland: the heart and respiratory rates increase, palms sweat, and the entire General Adaptation Syndrome becomes active. The bodymind connection is immediate and uncomfortable. The connections are just as strong, although perhaps more subtle, when we process thoughts and memories of a less troubling nature. We are still participating in an electrical, chemical, and spiritual dance each time we examine our life process and patterns through the use of a self-reflection intervention.

Self-reflection skills utilize the left hemispheric abilities of logical analytic organization of data, in addition to the right hemispheric skills of intuitive, feeling, nonlogical ways of knowing (see Chapter 8). By incorporating and blending these styles of gathering and organizing information, the nurse and the client build levels of self-esteem, confidence, and feelings of connection within themselves and as members of a larger group.

Progoff calls the interventions that follow transpsychologic; that is, they bring about therapeutic effects not by means of traditional therapy, but by means of active techniques that enable an individual to call up inner strengths and inherent resources for becoming a whole person.[3]

Reconnecting with Life Events

Self-reflection interventions help a client reconnect with events, reinterpret the actions and emotions connected with those events, and reframe their physiologic and emotional implications. These interventions help the client assign *meaning* to significant happenings. Whether the client is reminiscing about an episode in childhood or listing the pros and cons of an anticipated life style change, thinking, talking, or writing about such events elicits a psychophysiologic response. Calling up and examining an event in a relaxed and open manner makes it possible for the client to reframe and modify the event in a safe and receptive environment. Previously frightening, upsetting, or threatening occurrences and their attendant internal responses are seen in a clearer, more realistic light.

Diaries and Journals

With the dawn of the twentieth century came the recognition of the subconscious and the importance of self-reflection. As we enter the twenty-first century, diary and journal keeping are becoming valid tools for growth. They are "personal book(s) in which creativity, play, and self-therapy interweave, foster, and complement each other."[4] They become safe places in which to explore thoughts, ideas, and feelings.

In the words of the great diarist, Anais Nin, the diary allows us to

> discover a voice for reaching the deep sources of metaphysical and numinous qualities contained in human beings . . . the ultimate instrument for explorations of new forms of consciousness and ecstasy . . . a way of opening vision into experience, deepening understanding of others; as a way to touch and reach the depths of human beings; as nourishment; as a means of linking the content of the dream to our actions so that they become harmonious and interactive.[5]

Introducing his reasons and methods of maintaining a journal, Progoff states:

> Many persons have already had experiences in which they have sensed the presence of an underlying reality in life, a reality which they have recognized as a personal source of meaning and strength. It may have come to them in a brief, spontaneous moment of spiritual exaltation, or it may have come as a flash of awareness in the midst of darkness and pain. They came very close then to the deep, unifying contact, but it slipped away from them because they had no means of holding it and sustaining the relationship.[6]

When the nurse or the client feels the need for a structure or a place to express immediate feelings and concerns freely—whether they are coming from a moment of exaltation or a moment of pain—diaries and journals are ideal. Pennebaker's studies support the claims that writing provides catharsis, insight, and illness prevention. Expressing feelings in writing or verbally promotes health and speeds recovery from traumatic events, even those events that occurred years before the opportunity arose to write about them.[7]

Letters

Writing letters to friends and relatives during a time of hospitalization, illness, or approaching death is a way of maintaining and renewing relationships. Writing letters to yourself or to body parts may facilitate the expression of emotions, thoughts, and feelings. The nurse should encourage both clients and their family members and friends to write letters. Receiving letters can also aid the healing process of wholeness.

A letter is a safe vehicle to express anger, fear, and other intense emotions. Writing a letter to express one's feelings about being mistreated or abused and the effect of that mistreatment or abuse on one's life can release long held emotions. Such a letter need never be sent, but sharing it with a trusted other, with a group, or simply reading the letter onto videotape and then watching the tape can help a client move past traumas and back into the productive expenditure of energies.

Drawing on Intuition

Not only do self-reflection techniques enhance self-esteem and understanding, but also they lead to increased confidence in and use of inner, intuitive knowledge and self-healing. They bring the client to higher levels of physical, mental, emotional, and spiritual wellness.

The word *intuition* comes from the Latin *intueri*, which means to look inward or to know from within. "Like sensation, feeling, and thinking, intuition is a way of knowing. When we know something intuitively, it invariably has the ring of truth; yet often we do not know how we know what we know."[8] Frequently, we add elements of intuitive insight to our clinical decision making, but we seldom consciously acknowledge the existence of the rather "fuzzy" processes.

Rational and intuitive aspects of human beings are "complementary modes of knowing."[9] By developing and integrating these two, we move to a wholeness greater than the sum of the parts. Thus, nurses who learn to acknowledge the existence of their intuitive wisdom and add it to their rational, linear ways of caring for clients broaden the base on which their practice rests. Nurses need to begin to process the intuitive leaps, that is, to explain and translate intuition into operational and functional knowledge.[10] By listening closely to inner knowing, we can sharpen our ability to recognize the validity of subtle knowledge and become confident employing this intuition with our clients.

It is not necessary for the nurse to have all the answers to the questions that will surface with the use of self-reflection interventions. Posing reflective questions or asking for more information (e.g., What do you think that means? Can you tell me more about that? Can you put words on the feeling that you are having right now?) keeps the lines of communication open without placing the nurse's interpretation on the client's material. With experience, the nurse becomes more comfortable offering thoughts for the client's consideration. The client alone is the one living the event, however, and is the one who will eventually recognize the personal meaning of that experience.

Understanding Dreams

Jung writes that "the general function of dreams is to try to restore our psychological balance by producing dream material that re-establishes, in a subtle way, the total psychic equilibrium."[11] Dreams, whether experienced during the day or during the rapid eye movement stage of sleep, are one of our richest sources of inner information. Dreams are "the imagistic formulations of what one knows intuitively."[12]

Most adults dream for approximately 100 minutes during an 8-hour night's sleep. They frequently remember only small disconnected portions of the dreams that occur in the later part of the sleep segment, although some people claim never to remember their dreams.[13] Intuitive flashes of insight and symbolic images may be especially accessible during hypnagogic and hypnopompic sleep, the few moments as we drift into or out of sleep.[14]

In ancient Greece and Turkey, the use of dreams as diagnostic and healing tools reached a fine art. Medical practitioners of the day used the time immediately before falling asleep, during which our altered state of consciousness experiences hypnagogic sleep, to stimulate the inner healing of their clients.

The Christian churches, particularly those in England, have used this technique of incubation sleep or "divine sleep of the saints" for diagnosis and treatment from the second century A.D. to the present. Churches dedicated to Saints Cosmas and Damian, patron saints of Western healing, employed healing imagery and dream states based on the techniques of the early Greeks in caring for the sick.[15]

People of various cultures use dreams to find information concerning life goals, to identify the source and cure of illnesses, and to look into the inner world. The Senoi people of Malaya, noted for the peaceful and cooperative nature of their society, use dreams on a daily basis for guidance in personal and social affairs. Children are taught to share their dreams at breakfast and to control their dreams by lucid dreaming. One of their basic rules is always to confront and conquer danger or threatening figures in dreams instead of running away from them.[16]

Telling Stories

Stories are entwined in the fabric of our lives: fairy tales, myths, mystery novels, movies, family anecdotes, religious stories and remembrances. "Sacred stories (are) powerful, imaginative vehicles that tell us about ourselves, thereby transforming us, and they connect us to our fellow human beings, whether our contemporaries or our ancestors."[17]

Healing stories are powerful avenues to the unconscious and can help us all draw on the deep truths of the unconscious. Estes, who calls stories "soul vitamins," entwines storytelling and healing as follows:

> the flow of images in stories is medicine—similar medicine to listening to the ocean or gazing at sunrises . . . stories act like an antibiotic that finds the source of the infection and concentrates there. The story helps make that part of the psyche clear and strong again.[18]

Reminiscing and Embarking on a Life Review

On many occasions, we think, write, or talk about our successes, disappointments, failures, sources of pride, plans, and goals. This is an especially important activity when we are ill or as death approaches. During these periods of reminiscence and life review, we organize our past experiences and imagine future outcomes. Reviewing these past events and future outcomes allows us to experience and integrate the accompanying emotions.

Reminiscence has three components: memory, experience, and social interaction.[19] The client's values, hope, and openness to the review process affect memories. More than a simple inner remembering, memories take on new meaning when related to a concerned other, whether a family member, friend, nurse, or therapist. Small gestures of social interaction, such as a touch or a comment, do much to improve the quality and quantity of the memories.

Guiding clients through the life review process is a skill that nurses develop only when they have integrated the disciplines of reflection and meditation into their own lives. The guide must be balanced in order to facilitate questions and comments from a place of compassion and intention. The guide's responses must be based on a felt sense of the direction that the process is taking. The guide may ask questions about significant people in the client's life or personal objects or pictures of friends or family in the client's room.

Most investigators feel that guided and supported life review helps clients adapt to changes in life style brought about by illness and aging. It can also increase the level of wellness as indicated by higher survival rates than those with life-threatening illnesses who did not participate in life review. Improved coping skills, enhanced levels of self-esteem, better socialization skills, and a sense of belonging in the world are also frequent outcomes of using the life review process.[20]

The use of reminiscence or life review should not be confined to the elderly, as it can also be effective with preteens, adolescents, and adults who are experiencing life-threatening illness or death. Recalling and sharing holidays, vacations, and special events with family or school friends allows young people to see that they have made a difference in the lives of others and that they are part of a larger community, even though their time may not be of the quality or quantity that they would have wished.

NURSING PROCESS

Assessment

In preparing to use self-reflection interventions, the nurse assesses the following parameters:

- the client's ability to read and write. If the client cannot read or write, the techniques can be simply modified by using audiotape recordings or by asking a family member, friend, or member of the health care team to transcribe information from the client.
- the client's goals and level of interest in reaching those goals.
- the client's level of experience with each of the techniques to be used.
- the client's understanding that the purpose of the intervention is to enhance self-esteem, review and interpret recurrent themes, increase creativity, and integrate new information into the life process—not to invade the client's privacy in any way.
- the client's belief system to ensure that the planned intervention is congruent with the client's reality and values.
- the client's homework done during or since previous sessions.

Nursing Diagnoses

The following nursing diagnoses compatible with self-reflection techniques and that are related to the human response patterns of Unitary Person (see Chapter 7) are as follows:

- Communicating: Impaired verbal communication
- Relating: Impaired social interaction
  Altered family process
  Social isolation
- Valuing: Spiritual distress
- Choosing: Impaired adjustment
  Ineffective family coping
  Ineffective individual coping
- Moving: Diversional activity, deficit
- Perceiving: Disturbance in self-concept
  Powerlessness
- Knowing: Altered thought process
- Feeling: Anxiety
  Grieving, anticipatory and dysfunctional

Client Outcomes

Table 14–1 guides the nurse in client outcomes, nursing prescriptions, and evaluation for the use of self-reflection as a nursing intervention.

Plan and Interventions

The nurse experienced with self-reflection tools will find it easy to determine which should be employed. Many of the writing processes are similar to meditation, and the same preparations need to be taken (see Chapter 22).

Before the Session

- Learn to trust and cultivate your intuition; self-reflection is intuitive.
- Center yourself before the session. For example, before entering a client's room, hesitate, take a deep breath and let it out, feeling your relaxation. As you use this technique, notice how you enhance the quality of your client contact.

Table 14–1 Nursing Interventions: Self-Reflection

Client Outcomes	*Nursing Prescriptions*	*Evaluation*
The client will demonstrate increased effective individual and family coping skills.	Guide the client in self-reflection skills to increase individual and family coping skills. Choose letters, dreamwork, clustering, journal keeping, or intuition logs to identify and reinforce appropriate behaviors and interactions with others.	The client demonstrated increased communication with staff and family and decreased dependence on food, drugs, alcohol, and arguments.
The client will demonstrate feelings of self-worth generated by insights gained through diary and journal keeping.	Guide the client in tapping into inner resources through diary or journal keeping. Encourage recording of thoughts and feelings without regard to self-censoring of information. Be open to need for privacy vs. need to share; be available for feedback, if requested.	The client pointed out successes, increased verbalization of self-pride, increased assertive behavior, and increased participation in self-care and other activities.
The client will verbalize feelings of continuity and belonging to a larger group as identified by life review.	Guide the client in the life review process, individually or within a group setting, using discussion of personal items, photographs, historical references, and relationships with family members.	The client verbalized feelings of belonging through discussion of personal items, family members, and a sense of community. The client increased participation in group activities.
The client will demonstrate an ability to move through a previously difficult situation, thought process, or memory by using clustering strategies.	Teach the client the skill of clustering ideas, skills, alternatives, and possible outcomes. Assist with feedback, allowing the client to make final decisions.	The client increased positive verbalization, had a healthful sleep pattern, and expressed emotion appropriately after work with clustering strategy.

- Become personally familiar with the strategy that you plan to present to the client.
- Finish all necessary medical or nursing care so that the client will be able to work for the period of time required to complete the intervention.
- Ensure the client's physical comfort, such as encouraging the client to empty the bladder and adjusting the room temperature, if necessary.
- Explain the purpose of the intervention in light of the client's perceived needs at the moment.
- Enlist the client's cooperation in determining goals for the session.
- Provide for privacy if the client wishes it.
- Have pencil, pen, crayons, markers, paper, and other supplies for writing and drawing on hand.
- Have a tape recorder with fresh batteries and music tapes available.

At the Beginning of the Session

- Describe to the client the intervention that you feel is appropriate and what the client may expect to achieve by utilizing the strategy.
- Provide the client with appropriate materials and instruction.
- Guide the client through a relaxation exercise as necessary to decrease anxiety and facilitate inner work.
- Discuss the completed homework from any previous session.
- Determine the client's needs based on the client's input and any previous sessions.

During the Session

- Support the client by your physical presence and encouragement if the intervention is oral or by time alone if the intervention is written and the client desires solitude.
- Reassess at intervals the client's understanding of both the strategy and the expected outcome.
- Allow yourself to be used as a sounding board for questions and insights that arise from the process.
- Allow adequate time for the comfortable completion of the process or for the client to reach a point where the process can continue without your involvement until the next session. Some techniques, such as journal entries, are ongoing and the client need only be given

materials, instruction, and time alone to work until a scheduled follow-up session. Most sessions require 20 to 60 minutes.

At the End of the Session

- Gently bring the client's attention back to the room. Reorient, if necessary, to time and place.
- Discuss the work that has been accomplished if the client is comfortable doing so, or provide privacy, if needed, for the client's work.
- Answer any questions that the client may have and assist in interpretation of the work if invited to do so.
- Encourage further work on an individual basis.
- Use the client outcomes (see Table 14–1) that were established before the session and the client's subjective experience (Exhibit 14–3) to evaluate the session.
- Schedule a follow-up session.

Specific Interventions

Keeping Diaries and Journals (Basic to Advanced). There is no right way (and therefore no wrong way) to keep diaries or journals. They may be single sheets of paper or more elaborate notebooks with a variety of categories and divisions, such as those used by participants in Progoff's journal workshops (advanced work):

- Period Log
- Daily Log
- Dialogue Dimension: Special Personal Section
- Dialogue with Persons
- Dialogue with Works
- Dialogue with Society, Group Experiences
- Dialogue with Events, Situations and Circumstances
- Dialogue with the Body
- Death Dimension, Ways of Symbolic Contact
- Dream Log, Description, Context, Associations
- Dream Enlargements
- Twilight Imagery Log
- Imagery Extensions
- Inner Wisdom Dialogue

- Life/Time Dimension, Inner Perspectives
- Life History Log, Recapitulations, and Rememberings
- Stepping Stones
- Intersections, Roads Taken and Not Taken
- Now, the Open Moment[21]

Writing in a book or notebook is preferable to writing on loose pieces of paper. A book can be selected for its visual and tactile appeal, as well as for its ease of use. A beautifully bound blank book makes the ritual of the record keeping seem more important than does a loose-leaf notebook filled with school paper. If the client is confined to bed, perhaps even supine in a critical care unit, allowances must be made for ease of use. A simple stenographic pad is useful in these circumstances; it is lightweight, small, and easy to hold, and it has a firm backing to support the hand. The writing instrument, like the diary itself, should combine utilitarian features with visual and sensual pleasures.

Private time is necessary to quiet the mind and the spirit and allow inner material to surface. If privacy for the document is an issue for the writer, a secure location is essential. Most of us are able to find a secure location for our diaries. Privacy for the hospitalized patient may be more difficult to find, but it is certainly not impossible. Many hospitalized patients wish to share their diaries with significant people in their lives and feel no need for privacy. Rather than creating their records alone, some dictate their thoughts to a loved one or even record them on audiotapes.

Diaries can help us determine our individual rhythms so that we can modify schedules, treatments, and activities to nurture these rhythms. A diary developed at the Institute of Living, a Hartford psychiatric hospital, uncovered patterns of recovery and drug reactions that had never before been noticed in hospital patients.[22] The diligent use of diaries, perhaps with computer-aided interpretation, may help us predict the appropriate timing of certain medications, surgical procedures, and other interventions.[23]

Structured diaries, when used in a clinical setting, become a place to record symptom frequency and severity, the client's inner reactions to them, and the efficacy of various relief modalities (Exhibits 14–1 and 14–2). They become a treasure of patterns and possibilities.

The diary is an excellent place to explore the feelings surrounding illness, the fears associated with a perceived or real loss of independence or power, and, in the case of family members, the financial and physical responsibilities of caring for an ill or disabled relative. If a client allows these concerns to flow onto a piece of paper and visualizes them, he or

Exhibit 14–1 Symptom Chart

This diary of a client with migraine headaches shows symptom severity rated on the 1 to 5 scale, hand temperatures before and after relaxation-imagery practice (an indication of the depth of relaxation achieved, see Chapter 22), medications taken, and some general comments on the day's activities.

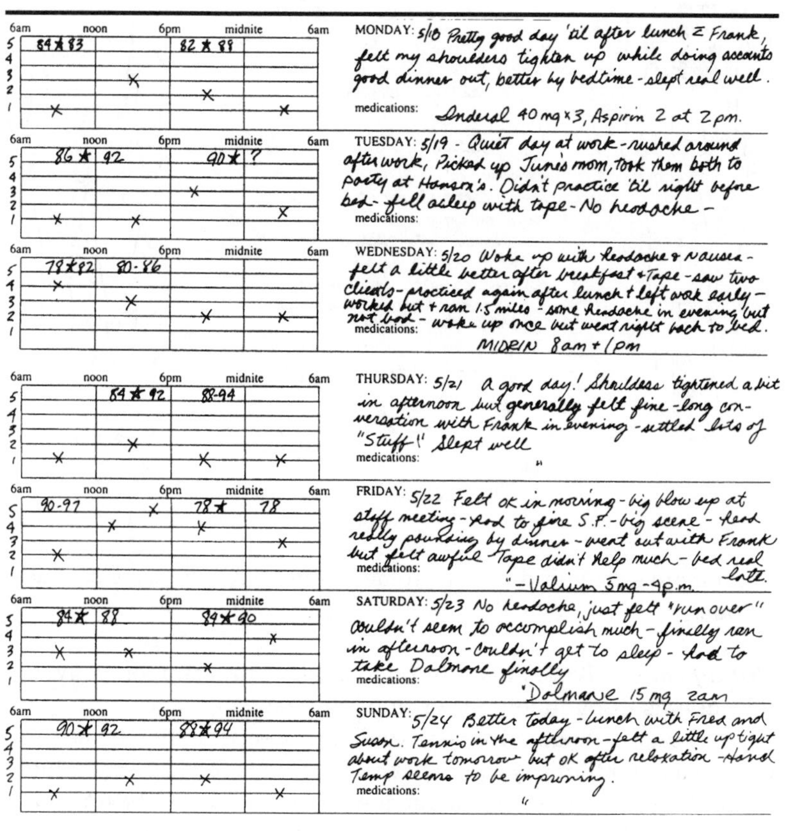

Rate the degree to which you experience your symptom (pain, anxiety, etc.) at least four times during the day. Chart the times you listen to your tape or practice your relaxation exercises, and your hand temperature before and after practice.

Symptom severity range: 1 = absent or very mild
2 = present but can be ignored
3 = moderate, can't be ignored
4 = severe and interfering
5 = incapacitating

MONDAY: 5/18 Pretty good day 'til after lunch c̄ Frank, felt my shoulders tighten up while doing accounts good dinner out, better by bedtime - slept real well.
medications: Inderal 40 mg×3, Aspirin 2 at 2pm.

TUESDAY: 5/19 - Quiet day at work - rushed around after work, Picked up June's mom, took them both to party at Hanson's. Didn't practice 'til right before bed - fell asleep with tape - No headache -
medications:

WEDNESDAY: 5/20 Woke up with headache & nausea - felt a little better after breakfast + Tape - saw two clients - practiced again after lunch + left work early - worked out + ran 1.5 miles - some headache in evening but not bad - woke up once but went right back to bed.
medications: MIDRIN 8am + 1pm

THURSDAY: 5/21 A good day! Shoulders tightened a bit in afternoon but generally felt fine - long conversation with Frank in evening - settled lots of "Stuff!" Slept well
medications: "

FRIDAY: 5/22 Felt OK in morning - big blow up at staff meeting - had to fire S.F. - big scene - head really pounding by dinner - went out with Frank but felt awful - Tape didn't help much - bed real late.
medications: " - Valium 5mg - 4p.m.

SATURDAY: 5/23 No headache, just felt "run over" couldn't seem to accomplish much - finally ran in afternoon - couldn't get to sleep - had to take Dalmane finally
medications: "Dalmane 15mg 2am

SUNDAY: 5/24 Better today - lunch with Fred and Susan. Tennis in the afternoon - felt a little uptight about work tomorrow but OK after relaxation - Hand Temp seems to be improving.
medications: "

Exhibit 14-2 Diary Sheet

This diary sheet shows the client's comments concerning her symptoms and interventions during the week. The shaded-in areas on the human figures indicates areas of perceived muscle tension throughout the week.

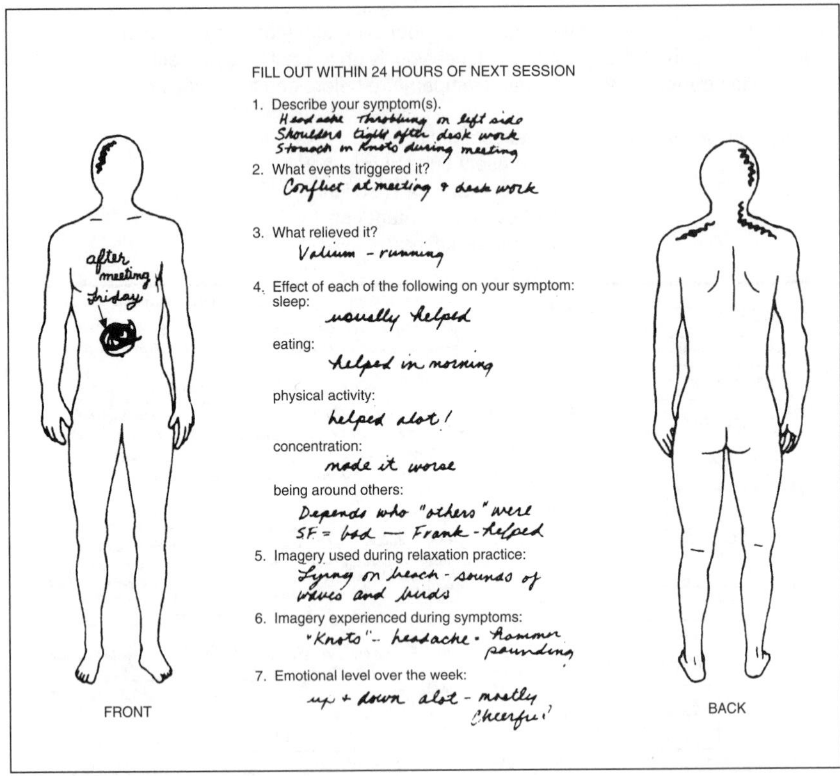
FILL OUT WITHIN 24 HOURS OF NEXT SESSION

1. Describe your symptom(s).
   Headache Throbbing on left side
   Shoulders tight after desk work
   Stomach in Knots during meeting
2. What events triggered it?
   Conflict at meeting & desk work
3. What relieved it?
   Valium - running
4. Effect of each of the following on your symptom:
   sleep: usually helped
   eating: helped in morning
   physical activity: helped alot!
   concentration: made it worse
   being around others: Depends who "others" were
   SF = bad — Frank - helped
5. Imagery used during relaxation practice:
   Lying on beach - sounds of waves and birds
6. Imagery experienced during symptoms:
   "Knots" - headache - hammer pounding
7. Emotional level over the week:
   up & down alot - mostly cheerful

she can more easily understand some of the unknown fears and deeper emotions.

Writing Letters (Basic). In addition to the love and support conveyed to and by clients through letters, writing letters may be a cathartic process to express anger, disappointment, and other deep emotions. The process of writing a letter that says on paper all the things that the individual has kept inside—in some cases, for decades—can finally heal even old emotional wounds. The client keeps the letter for a period of time and rereads it until he or she feels that the emotions have quieted. Then the client may choose to keep it, tear it up, burn it, bury it, or otherwise dispose of it in an appropriately ceremonial ritual. Letters can help a client achieve a sense of peace within a difficult, unresolved situation.

Beginning an Intuition Log (Basic). Clients may find it helpful to begin an intuition log in a small notebook that they carry around with them. Each time they have a flash of insight; hear a small, quiet, inner voice; or sense a vague impression or feeling, they record it in the log. The nurse encourages them to let the intuitions flow and record them without judging their correctness.

Keeping an intuition log and answering questions concerning the information gathered from intuitions can strengthen their intuitive skills.[24] These questions cover what the intuition contained, how it appeared, and what the client was doing just before its appearance. These logs are similar to dream interpretation logs; in fact, the logs may be modified to fit both dreams and intuitions.

Over a period of weeks, clients become more confident in their ability to differentiate the form and feeling of intuitions that are likely to be true from those more likely to be false. As with any skill, accuracy increases with practice. With validation of their increasing skill level, clients will become comfortable acting on intuitive insights in many day-to-day decisions.

The following are excerpts from a nurse's intuition log:

> On the way to work I kept feeling that I had left the house without everything I needed for the day. When I got to the hospital, I found I had left my stethoscope on the dresser. . . . Felt uneasy about leaving Mrs. R. alone with her son-in-law. When I returned to her room, they were arguing and her frequency of PVCs [premature ventricular contractions] had gone up from 2 per minute to over 10 per minute. . . . Before leaving I just knew I had to say good night to Sam and tell him what a good job he had done during the resuscitation. I found him in the break room where he confessed he had been concerned and was really relieved to know he had done well.

All the entries concern nonverbal, right hemisphere descriptions, using such words as "felt" and "knew." By listening to and acting on information from both sides of the brain, we move closer to a whole brain model of the nursing world. Many of our holistic nursing interventions have one foot planted firmly on intuitive ground. Far from abandoning traditional nursing skills, we are bringing them with us into a new era of balanced, whole nursing practice.

Learning from Dreams (Basic to Advanced). Clients can learn to use dreams as self-reflection interventions. The basic skill of recording one's dreams can become more advanced with the application of various interpretation skills.

Sleep and dream researchers have developed techniques to help dreamers become more involved and in control of their dream state.[25] Some dreamers, called lucid dreamers, are actually aware that they are dreaming and are able to direct the "story line" and outcomes of their dreams to some extent. The techniques of lucid dreaming may be used to enhance self-confidence, promote personal growth, and improve both physical and emotional health. As an extension of guided imagery, lucid dreaming may be helpful in gathering inner knowledge and enhancing creativity. LaBerge's lucid dreaming guidelines include the following:

- Pause frequently during the day to ask yourself if you are awake or dreaming
- Test your reality. Look around you for anything out of the ordinary that might indicate you are dreaming.
- When going to sleep, tell yourself that you will have a lucid dream, look forward to it; but be willing to allow it to happen in good time.
- If you awaken at night, imagine returning to your dream immediately.
- Recall your dream in as much detail as possible on awakening. Keep a dream journal.[26]

Dreams, combined with nonsleep imagery, are powerful sources of inner knowledge that facilitates the interpretation of feelings and symptoms. Like the intuition log, a dream log can be a storehouse of information to be interpreted by the client alone or with the help of a nurse or therapist. Looking at a dream log with an eye for people, animals, locations, color, patterns, associated feeling, and repetitive themes helps the client begin to explore meanings and interpretations. Some dream images seem to speak for themselves, whereas others are more obscure in their meaning. Vaughan's questions concerning dream content may help with interpretation and clarification.

- What is an appropriate title for this particular dream? Is there an obvious message to this dream? Is there a particular message that might have some relevance to your life at present?

- What is the predominant feeling tone of this dream?
- What are the principal qualities of the different characters in the dream? Are you aware of these qualities in yourself?
- Can you view the dream from the point of view of one of the other characters in the dream?
- Is this dream a recurring dream? Is the theme familiar, or does it seem entirely new?
- Does this dream seem to be a "big dream" or does it seem to be an ordinary dream?
- If you were to make an affirmation for yourself from this dream, what would it be?
- Is there any particular action you would like to undertake as a result of what you have learned from this dream?
- Would you like to continue this dream in your imagination?
- Would you like to give this dream a different ending?
- If you could redream this dream, how would you change it?[27]

(See Chapter 23 for further imagery interpretation and symbols that may be applied to dreams.)

To make use of the hypnopompic state of consciousness, it is useful to record affirmations on an audiocassette tape that switches on at a predetermined time. Then, positive self-statements drift into the conscious mind as one awakens and affect the self-image throughout the day. (See Chapter 9 for affirmations.)

Building Mind Maps and Clusters (Basic). Clustering of thoughts and ideas, referred to as mind mapping by some authors, is similar to free association.[28] It is an excellent tool to begin a flow of ideas that makes it possible to visualize the interconnections between people, problems, or solutions. Whenever the nurse or a client becomes "stuck," this intervention may reveal the multitude of possibilities and patterns offered by any situation. It requires large sheets of newsprint pads, construction paper, or even typing paper, depending on whether the client is bedridden or ambulatory. Some clients even do clustering on small scraps of paper, but the visual impact and creativity flowing from large pieces of paper are greater.

After a few moments for inner quieting and centering, the nurse or the client writes in the middle of a large piece of paper a central word or theme statement concerning the problem or situation and circles it. This theme word may be a name; a symptom; a short statement of the problem;

a desired outcome; a perceived block; or an image, symbol, or metaphor. As associated words and ideas arise, they are written around the central word, circled, and connected to the center and/or each other with appropriate lines. This and several other chapters of this book began as a single key word. Figure 14–1 shows how a single word grew into a meaningful web of ideas to form this chapter.

Clustering should proceed like a brainstorming session in that nothing should be censored and no idea or connection should be ignored. In as little as a few minutes, the weblike grouping of key words will begin to point to unexpected relationships and possibilities. The shift from a nebulous, indeterminate form to a focus on pattern and relationships, called the trial web shift, occurs during any creative act. The trial web is "your first awareness of a tentative vision, an idea of what you want to say."[29] From seemingly disconnected random words and thoughts, there

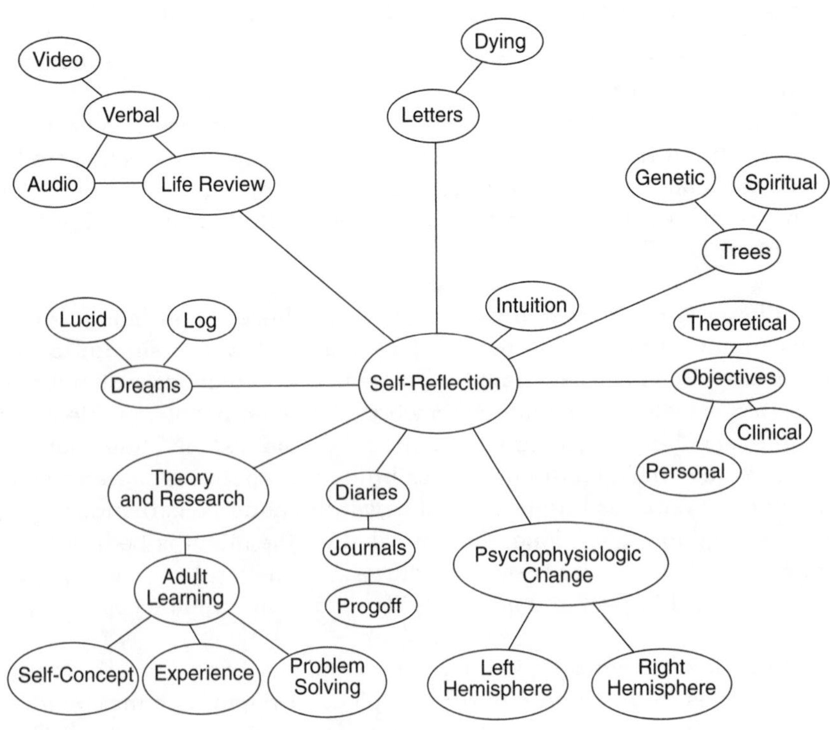

Figure 14–1 Process of Clustering

suddenly emerges a direction, a clarity of purpose, that may lead a person out of the dark and into a solution.

As the clustering project begins to feel complete, the nurse or the client may wish to take another few moments to center and to enjoy the visual and felt pleasure of what has been created. The cluster may be discussed as soon as it is complete or kept for further refinement over a period of several days or weeks. This process frequently opens a period of insight and creativity that can last for the entire length of a project, therapeutic intervention, hospitalization, or relationship.

Sharing Stories (Basic to Advanced). Nurses and clients may find it helpful to share stories with each other. Nurses may choose to share personal anecdotes, "once-upon-a-time" stories, or histories of prior clients who have been working through similar circumstances. Sharing stories helps build the human bond and empowers other forms of healing, traditional or adjunctive. Stories of the power of a new medicine or procedure evoke the belief of the client *and* the response of the client's endocrine, neuropeptide, immune, and hormonal systems, much as a ghost story around a campfire raises chills, or a story of cycles and renewal empowers our belief in something beyond our present suffering.

Children are particularly receptive to stories and delight in telling their own stories. Being able to recount over and over the details of an accident, medical or surgical procedure, or other emotionally charged event helps children (and adults) recover more quickly from that trauma. Stories can engage, teach, and empower children in a format that is more familiar than is a formal relaxation imagery exercise.

Stories can be read, written down, or recorded, but seem most powerful when told simply from the heart and adapted to the individual situation at hand.

Using Reminiscence and Life Review (Basic to Advanced). The basic life review process is the simple recounting of past events to a friend, family member, or interested health care provider. It can progress into more complex levels of transpersonal focusing and inward reflection if the client wishes to explore those levels. Support and skill in dealing with the advanced strategies come with training and clinical experience. Nurses begin with the basic strategies and, as their skills and interest develop, move into the more advanced interventions.

Life review may be oral, for example, occurring in the small time periods while the client is receiving nursing care. Journal keeping and letter writing may also be useful for life review. Some clients and families prefer the more complete and personal record of audio or video recording of reminiscence sessions.

Family members can bring in old photographs to be discussed and identified or to make a scrapbook of treasures. Asking open-ended questions about personal items or photos in a client's room often stimulates discussion and elicits information that will help the nurse provide more personal and meaningful care. For example, such comments as "This is a lovely picture of your wedding. Could you tell me something special you remember about that day?" may open new vistas of understanding for both the nurse and the client. If questions elicit memories of stressful events, the nurse helps the client determine how stressful events have been worked through in the past.

The life review process may involve one session or many sessions that vary in length, depending on the client and the areas to be explored. The intervention cannot be rushed, for the process is one of unfolding and opening.

To facilitate the life review process, the nurse may do the following:

- Encourage self-expression by the client.
- Involve family members and friends.
- Keep the information and process confidential.
- Begin the process when the client has sufficient physical strength and a mood of openness.
- Listen with focused attention.
- Use touch, when appropriate.
- Allow the client periods of silence and a time to retreat, if needed.

Life review is an active imagery process that uses the creativity of both client and nurse. The client may focus on certain sense modalities and may need help bringing forth and describing the sounds, fragrances, or textures of the past. One client described her grieving after the death of her husband in sensory terms. She would go into his clothes closet and enfold herself in his suits, feeling the smooth linings and deeply inhaling the "smell of him." Various articles of clothing brought up memories that helped her fix his life in her memory; eventually, she reached a point where she was able to give away many of his clothes.

Group therapy sessions with a creative guide can also open doors to the past. Discussions of the "old days," first jobs, war experiences, public figures, personal and national losses, and triumphs lead to many insights for both clients and guides. Having clients bring items from their past, such as old quilts, newspaper clippings, photographs, and letters, will stimulate lively discussions.[30] It is important to be alert for members of a group who need to be silent with their own thoughts and to come to them individually to help them explore their memories when they are ready.

Dealing with Death. We have begun to be more open about dying and more aware that it can truly be a transformation—a time of remembering, growth, and peaceful completion of this life. When a client is in the end stages of this life, the life review process begins as at any other stage. The needs of the client and family are assessed, outcomes determined, and the intervention begun with frequent evaluations. The nurse helps the client review the important memories of the past and rehearse events coming in the future. Not only does this intervention ease the potential feelings of psychologic isolation common to the dying, but also it helps the client deal with unresolved conflicts, maintain self-esteem, gain insight into past and present relationships, and focus on the positive aspects of his or her life.

The client should review decisions over which he or she still has some control. Such decisions may concern medications, treatments, daily routines, special requests about a funeral, a will, and the distribution of certain personal belongings. The client may also be helped to deal with unresolved dilemmas, such as questions concerning an afterlife, higher guiding powers, or connections with others.

When death is an inevitable outcome of the current situation, clients may need to take time to prepare themselves and their family members. Unfortunately, many have not dealt with the emotional or physical details of the process and require assistance to do so. As Levine says,

> In a way, it seems strange that we are so unprepared for death, considering how many opportunities we have to be open to what is unexpected or even disagreeable. Each time we don't feel well, each time we have the flu or a kidney stone, or a pain and stiffness in the back, we have the opportunity to see that sooner or later some pain or illness is going to arise that won't diminish but will increase until it displaces us from the body. We can use each situation as an extraordinary opportunity to practice the death chant, to practice Gandhi's closeness with God. We are reminded again and again of the process we are. Continually opportunities arise to practice letting go of this solidness, to tune to the ongoing process, to sense the spaciousness in which it's all unfolding.[31]

Numerous relaxation imagery exercises are appropriate for helping a client practice "letting go of this solidness." The ability to let go of pain, both physical and emotional, eases the client through difficult procedures and conflicts with friends and family and into a sense of calm and self-direction. (See Chapter 17 for exercises to help clients experience death with peace and dignity.)

As death approaches, self-reflection may take on more immediate forms, such as talking or simply maintaining physical touch with a loved one or nurse. The barriers that prevented communication earlier may lift as the client lays aside the burden of the ego. Some clients wish to contact those with whom they have had misunderstandings in the past in order to let go of life and relationships with a sense of closure and peace. Facilitating this need by arranging nursing care in blocks and allowing the client to spend time alone with particular friends and family members—while also helping to set limits on the demands of others, according to the client's wishes—is a vital advocacy role of the nurse as the end of life approaches.

Case Studies

Case Study No. 1

Setting: Client's home

Client: Aldie Hine, a 59-year-old

Nursing Diagnoses:
1. Anticipatory grieving
2. Spiritual distress
3. Powerlessness
4. Social isolation: all related to terminal lung cancer

Through letters, personal contact, and telephone calls, Aldie and his family built a spiritual network to help carry them through his final days. The opening letter, sent to the "biologic family, nonkin family, close friends, and a few concerned professional colleagues," reads as follows:

> We propose to organize ourselves to tap the healing energy-force by coming together each day at 5:00 P.M. for 10 or 15 minutes by ourselves or with anyone who is moved to come here at this time. In silence we will concentrate our love and thoughts on these ideas and hopes. . . . We ask anyone, anywhere, who wants to join us in thought to do the same thing, perhaps at the

> same time of day if this is fitting. We will be sitting near a little fountain lined with stone which we built together during the last 2 months. We recognize the power of symbolic acts and objects. We have each put a pebble in the lower pool to remind us daily of our commitment to a power beyond ourselves. We ask that anyone who wants to join us in our faith in life send us a pebble or small stone from some place you have loved. Each day at the joining time, Aldie will put into the pool any pebbles that have come, and the name of its sender will be in our hearts with gratitude. Each pebble will be to us a symbol of the love and concern people have expressed for us, and we know already how strengthening this has been.[32]

Life review can also be an important aid in the process of going peacefully into death. As Aldie Hine approached the last few days of his life, he lay in his bed and reminisced with his wife and family. "He experienced a very moving sense of 'laying aside the burden of the ego' as he put it. 'I might have come to this without illness . . . but the prospect of death spurs the sense of letting go. The process of dying speeds up the transformation.' "[33]

Aldie Hine died at home, 15 months after the initial diagnosis of lung cancer, but he did so surrounded in body, mind, and spirit by a far-flung web of love and support; in a multitude of ways, he died the "good death."

Case Study No. 2

Setting:	Cancer support group
Client:	S.C., a 29-year-old woman
Nursing Diagnoses:	1. Grieving 2. Spiritual distress 3. Altered comfort 4. Powerlessness: chemotherapy for ovarian cancer

J. had been married for 2 years. She and her husband were planning to start a family when a routine visit to her gynecologist revealed her cancer. In addition to dealing with her diagnosis and an uncertain future, she and her husband were grieving because they would never be able to have a biologic family.

The group decided to conduct two ceremonies during their next two sessions. All group members felt that, although they were working hard to maintain a positive attitude, it was difficult to ignore the "doomsayers." The negative predictions would sneak up on them during quiet moments and undermine their carefully tended, hopeful, optimistic thoughts. Therefore, they focused their first ceremony on the pessimistic comments of friends and family members when they talked about cancer. Everyone wrote his or her collection of fatalistic comments on sheets of paper. Then the group members read them out loud and added to their lists as the words of one person brought back memories of other dire predictions. When they each had collected several pages of negativity, the group leader brought out a paper shredder and each participant shredded the pages of pessimistic comments into confetti. J. gathered up her shreds and took them home. That night, she and her husband carefully fed them into a blazing fire in the fireplace.

In their second ceremony, which was held the following week, the group cut small strips from beautifully patterned handmade paper. On these strips, the group members wrote affirmations. J. wrote short affirmations to the biologic children that she would never have. She wrote about her hopes that these children would be born into loving and caring homes, that their parents would rock them to sleep and treasure them every day. Finally, she wrote out her hope that one day she and her husband would be able to adopt a child who needed a loving home. The group put each of the affirmation strips into a pastel balloon, inflated the balloons with helium, released the balloons in a field next to the building where they met, and watched their hopes ascend into a clear summer sky. These ceremonies helped J. and other members of her group put words on their innermost fears and hopes and then symbolically release them.

Evaluation

With the client, the nurse determines whether the client outcomes for self-reflection interventions (see Table 14–1) were successfully achieved. To evaluate the session further the nurse may again explore the subjective effects of the experience with the client (Exhibit 14–3).

Interventions for self-reflection, for the most part, take place over fairly long periods of time, such as weeks or months. For this reason, they must be periodically reviewed and reevaluated, even though they are not yet felt to be completed. Continued support and feedback are necessary.

We have seen that a variety of tools and interventions can give us access to inner awareness and healing. By using these ourselves and offering them to our clients, we can all reach for higher levels of wellness and understanding of the life process. Each self-reflection intervention can be

Exhibit 14-3 Evaluating the Client's Subjective Experience of Self-Reflection

1. Was this a new experience for you? Can you describe it?
2. Did you have any physical or emotional responses to the experience? Can you describe them?
3. Were there any distractions?
4. Did this exercise change the way you see yourself or your experiences?
5. Did the experience help you recall any memories or details of your life?
6. What are your thoughts and feelings when you review your journal, diary, log, or other self-reflection tool?
7. Would you like to try this again?
8. What would make this experience more meaningful for you?
9. Do you see yourself using this exercise on a regular basis in your life?

successfully woven into the fabric of our nursing practice and experience for our mutual enrichment.

DIRECTIONS FOR FUTURE RESEARCH

1. Develop and test evaluation tools to measure reliably the psychophysiologic effects of self-reflection techniques.
2. Develop guidelines for the interpretation of material from dreams and clustering techniques.
3. Explore changes in behavior, perceived quality of life, and social interaction during and after reminiscence therapy.
4. Determine whether the life review process and conscious dying techniques decrease client and family anxiety and fear around death.

NURSE HEALER REFLECTIONS

After reading this chapter, the nurse healer will be able to answer or begin the process of answering the following questions:

- What inner knowledge, as well as factual records, can I create by keeping a journal?
- How can I facilitate new health behaviors in my clients by using diaries?
- What do I experience about my imagery and creativity when I use clustering techniques?

- How can I ease the emotional pain of death for my clients with the life review process?
- What can I learn from becoming an active participant in my dreams?

NOTES

1. E. Sherman, *Reminiscence and the Self in Old Age* (New York: Springer Publishing Co., 1991), 29.
2. D. Bille, Patient/Family Teaching in Critical Care, in *Critical Care Nursing: Body-Mind-Spirit* (Philadelphia: J.B. Lippincott, 1992), 143.
3. I. Progoff, *At a Journal Workshop* (New York: Dialogue House Library, 1975), 9.
4. T. Rainer, *The New Diary* (Los Angeles: Jeremy P. Tarcher, 1978), 17.
5. Ibid., 9.
6. Progoff, *At a Journal Workshop*, 10.
7. J. Pennebaker, *Opening Up: The Healing Power of Confiding in Others* (New York: Avon Books, 1990).
8. F. Vaughan, *Awakening Intuition* (Garden City, NY: Anchor Books, 1979), 9.
9. Ibid., 51.
10. P. Gerrity, Perception in Nursing: The Value of Intuition, *Holistic Nursing Practice* 1, no. 3 (1987):70.
11. C. Jung, *Man and His Symbols* (Garden City, NY: Doubleday, 1964), 50.
12. Vaughan, *Awakening Intuition*, 119.
13. E. Hartmann, Dream, in *World Book Encyclopedia* (Chicago: Field Enterprises Educational Corp., 1975), 276.
14. J. Ennamorato, *Intuition Success Strategies* (Toronto: NC Press, 1986), 112.
15. J. Achterberg, *Imagery in Healing* (Boston: New Science Library, 1985), 54.
16. Vaughan, *Awakening Intuition*, 144.
17. A. Simpkinson, Sacred Stories, *Common Boundary* (1993):26.
18. Simpkinson, Sacred Stories, 28.
19. D. Hamilton, Reminiscence Therapy, in *Nursing Interventions: Treatments for Nursing Diagnoses*, ed. G. Bulechek and J. McCloskey (Philadelphia: W.B. Saunders, 1985), 139–151.
20. E. Sherman, *Reminiscence and the Self in Old Age*.
21. Progoff, *At a Journal Workshop*, 301–320.
22. G. Luce, Body Time, in *Ways of Health*, ed. David Sobel (San Diego: Harcourt, Brace, Jovanovich, 1979), 405.
23. L. Kaiser, The Next Medical Frontier: Computer and Robotic-Enhanced Health Care, *Group Practice Journal* 35(1986):5–11.
24. P. Goldberg, *The Intuitive Edge* (Los Angeles: Jeremy P. Tarcher, 1983), 209–210.
25. J. Gackenbach & J. Bosveld, *Control Your Dreams* (New York: HarperCollins, 1989).

26. S. LaBerge and H. Rheingold, *Exploring the World of Lucid Dreaming* (New York: Ballantine Books, 1990).
27. Reprinted from *The Inward Arc* by Frances Vaughan, pp. 175–176, with permission of Shambhala Publications, Inc., © 1986.
28. G. Rico, *Writing the Natural Way* (Los Angeles: Jeremy P. Tarcher, 1983), 90.
29. Ibid.
30. Hamilton, Reminiscence Therapy, 145.
31. S. Levine, *Who Dies?* (Garden City, NY: Anchor Press, Doubleday, 1982), 32.
32. V. Hine, *Last Letter to the Pebble People* (Mars Hill, NC: St. Alden's in the Woods, 1977), 28.
33. Hine, *Last Letter to the Pebble People*, 74.

SUGGESTED READING

K.L. Hagan, *Internal Affairs: A Journalkeeping Workbook for Self-Intimacy* (New York: Harper/Perennial, 1990).

VISION OF HEALING

Accepting Ourselves and Others

Wholeness and healing can exist only when we have meaningful relationships. The extent to which we are willing to accept ourselves determines the quality of our relationships, however. If we are unable to accept ourselves, then we are unable to accept others. Without self-acceptance, relationships with an intimate other, family, or community may be confined to the fulfillment of social role obligations and expectations. When we remember that each moment with another is an opportunity to heal and be healed and to share love and forgiveness, we may learn to heal and be healed in a relationship.[1]

Habits, beliefs, assumptions, expectations, judgments, and misconceptions can be major obstacles in relationships. They create conflicts and barriers that block effective communication and sharing of perceptions. The following ten reflective questions are suggested to increase an awareness of patterns in relationships so that the process of healing can occur[2]*:*

1. *Do the important relationships in your life satisfy you? Are your needs met? What do you bring to your relationships? What are the predominant qualities that you experience in your relationships? Do you feel competitive, manipulative, victimized, or rejected? Do you experience joy, vitality, synergy, love, and shared purpose?*
2. *What are the patterns of your relationships? Do you consistently feel misunderstood or mistreated? Do you think you give more than you receive? Do you experience the universal Self as the source and context of relationships?*
3. *What beliefs and assumptions do you hold about relationships? After taking an inventory of beliefs, do you recognize any restricted patterns? Did you become aware of any areas that you are unwilling to address?*
4. *What do you identify with as your true self? Is it your physical, mental, emotional, or spiritual potential, or are all of these areas combined? Are you authentic in your relationships? Do you find that when you are honest with yourself, your relationships are more satisfying?*
5. *What is the purpose of your important relationships?*
6. *What relationships in your life have had the most meaning?*

7. *If you were about to die, would you have any regrets concerning the qualities of relationships in your life? Is there anything that you would have changed?*
8. *If you could change your relationships unilaterally, what qualities would you want to cultivate in your relationships?*
9. *Which of your relationships are in need of healing right now? What are you willing to do to bring about that healing?*
10. *Are you willing to forgive? What part of yourself do you have trouble forgiving?*

Relationships help us understand at a profound level our interconnectedness with people, nature, and the universe. When we are in healthy relationships, we exhibit mutual love, sharing, and the ability to forgive ourselves and others. All our lives we search for answers to questions about living and dying. Our relationships can provide us with many aspects of these answers, for they help us recognize blind spots within ourselves. A relationship is healing if it nurtures expression of feeling, needs, and desires and if it helps remove barriers to love.

NOTES

1. J. Achterberg et al., *Rituals of Healing* (New York: Bantam Books, 1994).
2. F. Vaughan, *The Inward Arc* (Boston: Shambhala Publications, 1986).

Chapter 15

Relationships: Learning the Patterns and Processes

Barbara Montgomery Dossey

NURSE HEALER OBJECTIVES

Theoretical

- Analyze relationship patterns in a family system.
- Identify the characteristics of open and closed systems.
- Discuss six major defense mechanisms that individuals use in relationship conflicts.

Clinical

- Identify the core elements that a nurse needs in order to establish a therapeutic relationship.
- Analyze common counseling strategies.
- Identify three nursing interventions to assist others with relationship conflicts.

Personal

- Identify at least one person whom you are close to and share some special feelings with that person about your relationship.
- Increase your use of the word "I" instead of "you" to enhance sharing of feelings.
- Choose specific times to be alone to reflect on your relationships.

DEFINITIONS

Aloneness: being by oneself for solitude and self-reflection.

Counseling: an interactive therapeutic process between nurse and client/family characterized by the qualities of acceptance, authenticity, and empathy; use of a variety of interventions that focus on the feelings, needs, problems, and challenges of the client that interfere with the client's adaptive behavior.

Crisis: any sharp or decisive change for which old patterns of behavior are inadequate, leading to disorganization and degrees of dysfunction.

Forgiveness: cancellation of our expectations of perfection in ourselves and others.

Intimacy: a relationship that involves trust and the ability to share deepest levels of the self, including hurts.

Loneliness: a melancholy state that results from the absence of significant relationships or our lack of ability to engage in them.

Love: the human quality of being open to feelings that allow understanding and awareness of caring; perception of goodness; and forgiveness of self, others, and all living/nonliving things.

Relationship (Healthy): a state in which there are two or more nonjudgmental people who can share hurts, failures, successes, interests, and excitements, and who enhance each other's life potentials.

Resources: facts, basic options, means, and opportunities available to people whereby they can improve and help themselves and others.

Self-Validation: one's capacity to express one's personal self-worth.

Spontaneity: flexibility and action in accordance with a natural, unstaged feeling.

Stressor (Negative): a situation, event, or change for which a person has had little or no prior preparation or cannot effectively cope.

Stressor (Positive): an event or change that motivates a person to work toward life potentials.

THEORY AND RESEARCH

Patterns in Family Systems and Relationships

In order to view the client as a whole person, it is necessary to consider the client's family or significant relationships. No person can live in constant or perpetual isolation and be healthy. The sequences, patterns, simultaneous events, and circular reactions that occur within families and relationships are often referred to as the family system.[1] A change in the behavior of any family member automatically interrupts the system in either a positive or negative direction. Continuous actions, reactions, and actions of people in response to actions produce a state referred to as a "reverberating feedback loop."[2] For example, a family may be in chaos because family members did not sit together to talk about a stressful event. Instead, there are a number of individual reactions, each based on a knowledge of only a small portion of the event. If family members would sit together to hear each other's perception of the event, there would be a greater chance of working as a cohesive family unit rather than continuing in a state of chaos. Each member would be better able to interpret the experience, as well as listen to the other family members' experience. The same patterns and sequences are seen in all close relationships.

Each family unit has a set of many relationships. In a family where daughter Ann lives with her father, mother, and brother, for example, forming a complete picture of Ann as a family member requires an examination of the way that she experiences and behaves in all of the following individual, dyad, and triad situations:

1. Ann alone
2. Ann with her mother
3. Ann with her father
4. Ann with her brother
5. Ann with her mother and father
6. Ann with her mother and brother
7. Ann with her father and brother
8. Ann with her mother, father, and brother

As shown with this small family, Ann is part of eight different relationships; furthermore, each other family member also has eight different relationships. It is easy to see how family scenarios can become complex. Such dyads and triads are multiplied after a divorce when parents remarry and an individual has more siblings, step-siblings, grandparents, step-grandparents, aunts, uncles, and cousins, and so on. Patterns and characteristics of family systems and personal relationships are extremely changeable and fluid.

Characteristics of Systems

In order to apply systems theory to the family and any other relationship, the nurse should recognize the following family or relationship system characteristics[3]:

- change: a shift of components or relationships within a system (first-order change) or the entrance of new information into the system from outside the system's boundaries (second-order change).
- viability: the ability of the system to change and reform, regulate itself, and adjust collectively to encountered stress.
- entropy: increased randomness and increased disorder within the system.
- open system: a system that allows a constant influx of new information and the constant succession of necessary adjustments to unending changing inputs.
- closed system: a system that rearranges present structure without incorporating new information from outside the system. The only change within this system is first-order, and only according to rigid, inflexible rules.
- boundaries: a continuum of permeable to impermeable borders that acts as a filter to separate the people within the system from the elements of the environment outside. In open systems, some boundaries are flexible and become blurred as they merge with another. In closed systems, boundaries are rigid, inflexible, and totally closed off from one another.
- homeodynamic: relating to a system's ability to scan itself to bring about balance at all times.
- feedback: information that a system receives about itself that is used to maintain or regain homeostasis.
- interconnectivity: the interlocking network of a system whereby a structure is able to endure under stress because of the collective strength of the whole.
- enmeshment: an interlocking network that allows for no new input, thereby becoming entangled and deeply involved in an unhealthy manner, adding to the confusion of the system.
- individuation: the ability of a system to encourage an individual to develop unique style and characteristics and be accepted by the system.

As indicated, an open family system is able to change and reform. Like a bay that allows tidewaters to flow in and out to refresh itself, an open family system can create new conditions while at the same maintaining the boundaries that make it a system. There are stated and unstated rules that allow the system to maintain openness to new ideas and to adjust collectively both to the first-order changes and to the second-order changes that occur within the system. There is also flexibility. Family members feel free to pursue individuality, role versatility, and new roles. Open family systems also allow interconnection between and among members, and individual boundaries become blurred without overinvolvement. In times of stress, family members band together to strengthen the family unit.[4]

Open family systems provide a strong social network and help individuals manage stress. Individuals who are exposed to high levels of stress and who have a poor social network are most susceptible to illness. Strong social networks can act as stress buffers by helping a person cope more effectively with a crisis or a new challenge, such as a job promotion or returning to school. There is no doubt that, when people nurture relationships, their social networks can have a significant health-maintaining influence across the life span.

A closed family system tends to isolate itself from the community. Members do not become involved in the community or with each other. In fact, there may be spoken or unspoken rules that forbid input and output of information. Rigidity, inflexibility, adherence to roles, and discouragement of individuality are characteristics of the closed family system. This enmeshment leads to pathology.

A closed family system responds to stress in a rigid way. If family members lack the resources to deal with a stressful situation, they do not look outside the system for new alternatives. Over time, the family either disintegrates, with its healthier members breaking away from the system, or begins to show signs of significant pathology. Often, enmeshed family members under stress form alliances and work against other family members, rather than all bonding together for a more cohesive system.

Defenses in Relationships

Learned at an early age, defenses are a way of protecting our self-image. They are used so routinely and unconsciously that they hinder authenticity in our communication with the important people in our lives. The degree with which defenses are used determines the obstacles within relationships.[5] The major defenses include:

- denial: a refusal to acknowledge or see what one does not wish to see or cope with; for example, refusing to acknowledge that a friend or mate is drinking too much.
- projection: shifting blame onto others or shifting one's own feelings onto another; for example, calling work colleagues competitive and aggressive when, in fact, one's own behavior reflects these characteristics.
- rationalization: the process whereby one explains and justifies feelings, thoughts, and actions that one has previously thought to be unacceptable; for example, explaining in great detail why an angry outburst was totally appropriate toward a mate when anger is typically avoided at all costs.
- reaction formation: the process whereby one becomes or exhibits that which one fears or wants to avoid; for example, a person who has a strong desire to smoke represses that desire and becomes fanatical about others who smoke.
- repression: the process of selectively forgetting unpleasant memories or tasks to be done; for example, repressing uncomfortable events in one's past.
- regression: the process of reverting to an earlier level of behavior or stage of development to avoid anxiety, fear, and responsibility; for example, returning home after a divorce to have one's parents fulfill basic needs for an indefinite period of time. (If the return is only on a temporary basis, it would not be considered a defense mechanism, but a supportive family relationship.)

The Ultradian Family

A family unit has many complex and demanding issues, activities, and decisions to deal with each day. We speak of a family unit, but it is more accurate to speak of interacting individuals, each moving in his or her own rhythmic patterns. Some rhythms are referred to as infradian rhythms. The best known infradian rhythm is a woman's menstrual cycle. Our daily cycles between waking and sleeping are called the circadian rhythms. The most frequent rhythms are the ultradian rhythms, the 90- to 120-minute cycles that occur more than a dozen times a day, every day of a person's life.[6] For example, families may spend 1 or 2 hours together eating, working at household chores, doing yardwork, watching television, playing games, doing homework, or reading together.

As discussed in Chapter 4, the basic rest-activity cycle modulates many of the key systems of the body, mind, and spirit. A family's fluctuating states and changes of consciousness reflect a rich tapestry of unique ultradian rhythms. Each family has its own rhythms. When families acknowledge each individual's ultradian rhythms and encourage the integration of an ultradian healing response of 20 minutes for rejuvenation every 90 to 120 minutes throughout the day, synchrony within the family unit is increased. The application of current knowledge about family ultradian rhythms to family systems theory makes it possible to recognize and cope with many common family dynamics and to improve bonding between family members. The major links of ultradian rhythms to family harmony can be summarized as follows[7]:

- Sharing ultradian synchrony with family members can enhance familial unity and harmony. The greater the synchrony of family members' ultradian rhythms, the more harmonious and stable the home environment.
- Reducing each person's ultradian stress is an important factor in healing the dysfunctional family. Thus, an ultradian healing response allows for relaxation and helps to restore individuals so that they not only perform better at work, but also become more sensitive parents, siblings, and family members.

A family's lack of ultradian synchrony frequently manifests itself as difficulties, misunderstandings, and squabbles that can lead to abuse. When an individual does not honor his or her ultradian rhythm during the day, the ultradian stress response is likely to increase when the family comes together and conflict may arise. The three key steps for happier and more positive relationships are (1) to entrain circadian and ultradian rhythms together, (2) to become aware of one another's body-mind-spirit cues of ultradian stress, and (3) to recognize whenever an individual is headed toward a breaking point. Ultradian rhythms can also be enhanced by developing the three phases of rituals (see Chapter 3) with creative activities that are particularly significant to the family.[8]

NURSING PROCESS

Assessment

In preparing to use relationship interventions, the nurse assesses the following parameters:

- the client's perception of the problem/situation with a person or specific relationship, including who is doing what (that presents a problem), to whom, and how the behavior constitutes a problem.
- the client's current approach to the problem.
- the client's minimal goals in regard to the perceived problem.
- the client's position in the relationship/current problem.
- the client's body and verbal language as the situation is being described.
- the client's reason for seeking help at this time and the duration of the problem.
- the client's perception of all the people involved in the situation. If appropriate, the nurse may ask to meet the people involved.
- the client's desired behaviors and preferred situation.

Nursing Diagnoses

The following nursing diagnoses compatible with relationship interventions and that are related to the nine response patterns of Unitary Person (see Chapter 7) are as follows:

- Relating: Altered parenting
  Altered sexual dysfunction
- Valuing: Spiritual distress
- Choosing: Coping, ineffective individual or family
  Altered family process
- Moving: Self-care deficit
  Self-care dysfunction
- Feeling: Anxiety
  Grieving
  Violence
  Fear
  Rape-trauma

Client Outcomes

Table 15–1 guides the nurse in client outcomes, nursing prescriptions, and evaluations for nursing interventions in relationships.

Table 15-1 Nursing Interventions: Relationships

Client Outcomes	*Nursing Prescriptions*	*Evaluation*
The client will recognize family and relationship systems patterns.	Help the client verbalize the dynamics within the family and relationships.	The client verbalized the dynamics that occurred within the family and relationships.
	Assist the client in recognizing the difference between open and closed relationships.	The client stated the differences between open and closed relationships.
	Assist the client in recognizing the stressors and resources in living.	The client recognized the stressors and resources in living.
	Assist the client in becoming aware of the effects of relationships on health and illness.	The client became aware of the effects of relationships on health and illness.
	Help the client identify the human needs that are fulfilled by quality relationships.	The client identified the human needs that are fulfilled by quality relationships.
	Help the client recognize body-mind-spirit responses to stress and human dialogue.	The client recognized the body-mind-spirit responses to stress and to human dialogue.
	Help the client identify personal, family, and relationship priorities.	The client identified personal, family, and relationship priorities.
	Help the client engage in awareness exercises to increase intimacy.	The client engaged in awareness exercises to increase intimacy.
	Assist the client in recognizing defenses in relationships that block effective communication.	The client recognized defenses that occurred in relationships that blocked effective communication.
The client will demonstrate awareness of the effect of human dialogue on the body-mind-spirit.	Assist the client with skills to improve the effective expression of feelings with others.	The client learned skills to improve the effective expression of feelings with others.
The client will learn new strategies to improve the quality of relationships.	Provide the client with techniques to improve relationships, such as self-reflection exercises, storytelling, intimacy exercises, "I" statements, stem phrase questions, focusing, empty chair exercises.	The client learned techniques to improve relationships.

Plan and Interventions

Before the Session

- No matter how long or short the session is expected to be, control the environment as much as possible to create a space conducive to a therapeutic relationship. The environment must be safe, both emotionally and physically.
- Clear your mind of other clients and personal issues in order to be present with the client and the perceived problem/situation.
- Spend a few moments centering yourself before counseling the client.

At the Beginning of the Session

- Greet the client in a relaxed manner and assess the client's degree of tension or relaxation.
- Listen actively to the client as the problem/story unfolds.
- Determine whether the client tells one or two sides to the problem.
- Help the client continue to share feelings and hurts that are relevant to the situation.
- Following the assessment, decide which interventions are most appropriate for the client.
- Explain those interventions that you believe will benefit the client and obtain his or her agreement to try the interventions during the session.

During the Session

- Help the client gain insight about the situation part by part and then put the parts together.
- Help the client identify the strengths and the weaknesses within the situation.
- Help the client identify personal strengths, for they are the basis for changing behavior.
- Have the client describe options as you discuss the situation.
- Time and pace your comments in accordance with the client's responses.
- Reassess the way in which the client is receiving new insights.
- Avoid using qualifying language if the client wants you to agree on how a particular person might act. For example, a client may say,

"Don't you think my wife is being unfair?" A "yes" by the nurse validates the client's viewpoint. A "no" can set up an argument. A non-committal response is, "I have not met your wife. Is it possible that your wife. . . ."

- Use qualifying language that can lead toward positive outcomes.
- Continue to encourage the client to be specific about his or her emotions while talking about the situation and to recognize any body sensations that are felt as the emotions are discussed.

At the End of the Session

- Formulate specific steps with the client to move in the direction of the desired outcomes.
- Have the client identify alternatives.
- Have the client choose the most realistic and promising course of action.
- Once choices have been identified, have the client affirm the choice to increase his or her awareness of the energy and actions required to resolve the situation.
- Make a concrete plan to proceed with change, but recognize that this plan can be changed.
- Have the client rehearse in the imagination the course of action.
- Determine whether the situation has been reframed since the start of the session.
- Help the client formulate new goals.
- Use the client outcomes (see Table 15–1) that were established before the session and the client's subjective experiences (Exhibit 15–2) to evaluate the session.
- Schedule a follow-up session.

Specific Interventions

Counseling and Psychotherapy (Basic to Advanced). A client who exhibits normative behavior may seek counseling that focuses on coping behaviors.[9] Counseling may involve assistance with smoking cessation or weight reduction, for example. Psychotherapy provides more in-depth interventions, such as working with clients in the struggles and challenges of life roles, individual/family priorities, intimacy, or changing relationship patterns in a marriage. Psychotherapy is definitely indicated when a client exhibits severe personality disorders or pathologic behaviors, although a client need not demonstrate pathologic behavior to begin psychotherapy.

By demonstrating acceptance of the client's intrinsic worth and dignity, the nurse conveys empathy to the client and facilitates the client's disclosure of personal information. Genuineness and congruency convey the nurse's honesty and personal caring to the client. The counseling process has three overlapping stages.[10]

1. Initial phase. A therapeutic relationship is established, goals developed, and the length of sessions discussed.
2. Working or maintenance phase. The focus is on the client's self-understanding and self-regulation, as well as on learning alternative health behaviors through active and passive counseling techniques and strategies (Table 15–2).
3. Closure and termination. The client is using new behaviors in daily living and, with the nurse, decides to terminate counseling.

Counseling techniques can be incorporated into all areas of nursing, although some of the advanced techniques lend themselves better to individual counseling. Even so, the nurse who is aware of the techniques can integrate various levels of the techniques in the acute care setting.

Storytelling (Basic to Advanced). Stories reveal the importance that we assign to our experiences in life and our perceptions of the world.[11] Storytelling technique becomes advanced when parables and metaphors are used. Such imagery acts as a type of double-exposure to the actual process being described (see Sharing Stories in Chapter 14 and Empowering the Spoken Word in Chapter 23).

All stories may be a means of building double descriptions and enabling the perception of higher order patterns.[12] Because we can take our stories from one situation to the next, we establish different contexts and structures for those stories. This creates the potential for opening new dialogue with the self, which can also contain new purpose and meaning. An additional way to enhance storytelling is to incorporate relaxation, imagery, music, life review, and self-reflective interventions.

Nurses are always listening to clients' stories. If they listen with focused attention, they hear stories about stories. These stories are the therapy; they are the basis for the healing event. We should see therapy as conversation, rather than always classifying it in medical terms. The following guidelines enhance the use of stories as therapy.

- Listen for the themes that bridge one story to the next; listen for the threads of information that also weave through one story to the next.

Table 15-2 Common Counseling Strategies

Strategies	*Description*	*Uses*
Active listening	An attitude of total attentiveness focusing on the client's expression of both verbal and nonverbal behavior	Most effective tool to communicate counselor empathy with the client To provide cues to the client's inner experience To minimize the counselor's tendency to make premature judgment
Questioning	Inquiring or asking for more information in the form of a question	To clarify a matter which is open to discussion; to minimize doubt or uncertainty To facilitate client exploration of a problem or situation
Reflecting	Restating or rephrasing the content or feeling of a client's statement (one type of active listening)	To understand the meaning of what the client is trying to express in either behavior or speech
Clarifying or interpreting	Stating the client's message with additional feedback or explanation	To increase the clearness of communication between counselor and client
Providing information or feedback	Using professional expertise to transmit pertinent information into facts, data, responses	To add to current knowledge or relate new knowledge to prior understanding
Selecting or weighing alternatives	Assisting the client to list and prioritize all possible alternatives to a problem	To aid in expanding options and narrowing choices May facilitate the client's experimentation with unfamiliar options in a nonthreatening setting
Confrontation	Verbalizing the discrepancy between the client's feelings and behaviors (between real and ideal self)	To focus the client's awareness on actions that are incongruent with self-image and actual behavior
Tests and appraisal tools	Using psychological paper and pencil tests or other appraisal tools which the counselor can administer and interpret	To help increase client self-awareness To add to the counselor's data base about the client (Examples: self-inventory of cardiac risk factors or the Holmes and Rahe Social Readjustment Rating Scales)
Self-disclosure	Revealing selected aspects of one's own experiences or personality	To foster genuineness and trust in the counseling situation when used appropriately

Source: Reprinted from *Nursing Interventions: Essential Nursing Treatments*, 2nd ed., by G. Bulechek and J. McClosky, p. 287, with permission of W.B. Saunders Company, © 1992.

- Train yourself to determine if a client is telling only one side of a story.
- Get the client to talk about what the two sides of any story may be, because clients frequently perceive only one side of a story. Viewing the other side gives new meaning and context, however, and enables one to create double descriptions of stories. For example, it is very easy to identify things and events that are wrong in one's life, but it is more valuable to find the strengths in the current situation and the underlying meaning or message of the present situation.
- Become aware of the importance of the stories that you construct from the client's stories. While listening to a client's stories, the nurse is also constructing a story that guides the therapy. When the nurse tell these stories to the client, the exchange of stories allows the client to see or hear new patterns and relationships. With this feedback, the client gains new information and can construct a new way of viewing life. All stories are a means of building double descriptions that facilitate change.

Intimacy Awareness (Basic). Intimacy is a skill from which all can benefit. The following questions can be used in counseling sessions or as reflective exercises between sessions to increase the skills and awareness of intimacy.

- *Love-Intimacy*
  1. What does intimacy mean to you?
  2. What does sharing mean to you?
  3. What hurts are you able to share with family and friends?
  4. What sense of self do you experience when you share with self and others?
- *Love-Caring*
  1. What is love?
  2. What is caring?
  3. How do you show love for yourself and others?
- *Love-Forgiveness*
  1. What is the meaning of forgiveness to you?
  2. How do you forgive yourself?
  3. How do you forgive others?
  4. What do you experience when you forgive yourself and others?

These self-reflective questions can also be shared with family and special friends.[13] The client may focus on one or all aspects of increasing intimacy by using these questions to express feelings with others, and check out his or her inner response in the actual conversation.

"I" Statements (Basic). Many people open dialogues with the use of the pronoun "you" instead of "I." This practice masks the expression of feelings and can be extremely hurtful in family relationships. Increasing clients' awareness of the use of "I" statements increases the sharing of feelings and emotions. Grouped into different categories of self, marriage or life partner, children, friends, work, and play, these statements can be used by the nurse when counseling a client. The client can also use them as reflective exercises between sessions (Exhibit 15–1). The client should be encouraged to share these self-reflective statements with family, special friends, and work colleagues.

Stem Phrase Completion (Advanced). A form of active imagination, stem phrase completion is most helpful when clients are masking (hiding) feelings or are reluctant to share feelings. Stem phrases are vague stimuli that facilitate a client's search for answers from within (Exhibit 15–1). The nurse can invent phrases that seem appropriate for the situation at hand. This nursing intervention lends variety to the usual way of conducting an individual or group session and is a way to increase client participation. It is effective with clients on a one-to-one basis, as well as with families or groups that are dealing with the same condition, such as grief, cancer, or cardiac dysfunction.

By completing stem phrases, a client shares both conscious and unconscious perceptions about events, people, and environment. The answers from the client's realms of consciousness begin to form patterns and processes. Most clients are fascinated by their own answers. They begin to put the pieces of the puzzle together about their own lives. Stem phrase completion is a novel approach to listening to one's self, as well as listening to another. The new stimuli require clients to go beyond their habitual communication patterns.

The nurse can introduce the intervention by saying, "I am going to give you a series of open-ended phrases for which there are no right or wrong answers. Be spontaneous with your answers, allowing the first thought that surfaces to be spoken." If working with two people, the nurse may say, "I will take turns giving each of you a phrase. Let the person to whom I give the phrase respond. You may be tempted to respond to the phrase for the other person, or you may want to correct the other person's re-

Exhibit 15–1 "I" Statements and Stem Questions

"I" Statements

Self
I . . .
I love . . .
I hurt . . .
I fear . . .
I like it when . . .

Partner
I . . .
I love . . .
I hurt . . .
I fear . . .
I like it when . . .

Children
I . . .
I love . . .
I hurt . . .
I fear . . .
I like it when . . .

Friends
I . . .
I love . . .
I hurt . . .
I fear . . .
I like it when . . .

Work
I . . .
I love . . .
I hurt . . .
I fear . . .
I like it when . . .

Play
I . . .
I love . . .
I enjoy . . .
I like . . .

Stem Questions

I can . . .
I will . . .
I must . . .
I am clear about . . .
I get angry . . .
I am most excited about . . .
I get angry when . . .
I wish I could . . .
I want . . .
I must learn to . . .
I feel important when . . .
If I could change . . .
I have the wisdom to change . . .
If you knew me, you would say . . .
The thing that I am most excited about now is . . .
The person I love most . . .
The person who is a guiding force in my life is . . .

sponse, but let their response be. When the phrase comes around again, you can change your response at that time. Do you have any questions?"

The nurse uses intuition and listens carefully to the client's answer, as this can become the stem for the next question. For example, "*I must learn to* be more assertive" can lead to "*An assertive person must* . . ." In addition, some answers are very profound, and encouraging the client to repeat them can provide valuable insight. (See Case Study No. 1 for an example of this intervention.)

When working with family members, the nurse can introduce this technique as a way to increase healthy communication. People should sit so that they have direct eye contact with the nurse or each other. If this is a group intervention, people can work in pairs, taking turns completing stem phrases provided by the nurse facilitator. It is most effective if one member of the dyad first takes the lead and asks all the questions to the other and then the two switch roles.

Development of Spiritual Understanding (Basic). Individuals must recognize that they are the spiritual experts about their lives, that the journey of wholeness and healing requires spiritual understanding, and that this understanding is a developing process.[14–18] Burkhardt and Nagai-Jacobson suggest that, if spirituality is a given and is the essence of one's being, it is useful for individuals to acknowledge their innate qualities.[19] When a person gives these qualities names and tends to them, the qualities are more likely to become healing tools. Ways to increase clients' awareness of opening to their healing potentials include the following:

- connecting: connecting with self, others, higher power, universe; allows individuals to experience being grounded.
- disconnecting: opening to new creative techniques, such as relaxation, imagery, dance, and laughter.
- empowering: challenging one's mind to learn things other than the day-to-day work; exploring personal wisdom; taking a class of a new interest; consulting friends, family, or a therapist when necessary.
- purifying: washing away, not only with water; sitting quietly by a roaring fire or out in nature in the sunshine; "playing in the dirt" without transforming the garden; taking a long bath or shower.
- journeying: traveling in one's imagination; reading a good book; walking or taking a leisurely drive; writing in a journal.
- transforming: using raw materials to restore order and create something new; painting, weaving, needlepoint, or other craft; gardening or creative cooking; cleaning a closet, drawers, or desk.

Ways To Work through Fear (Basic). Individuals often have difficulty making change within the family or in other life situations because of fear. Jeffers suggests that, as individuals learn to identify levels of fear, it becomes much easier to make change and that the best way through the fear is "dare to feel the fear . . . and do it anyway."[20] Fear can be broken down into three levels. Level 1 fears have two subsets—fears of things that happen and fears of things that require action. Things that happen include aging, illness, retirement, being alone, loss of financial security, change, and dying; things that require action include making decisions, changing a career, making or ending friendships, losing weight, going back to school, being interviewed, or giving a speech. Level 1 fears translate into statements such as "I can't handle illness."

In contrast, Level 2 fears are not situation-oriented. These fears involve the ego and have to do with a sense of self and one's ability to handle life's situations. For example, an individual may fear success, failure, rejection, vulnerability, helplessness, loss of image, or disapproval. Level 2 fears translate into such statements as "I can't handle failure."

Level 3 fears keep a person stuck. The biggest fear of all is that the individual will be unable to handle whatever life may bring. Level 3 fears translate into "I can't handle it!" What underlies this level of fear is an individual's idea that, if he or she could handle anything that came their way, what would there be to fear? The answer is, Nothing.

In counseling people who are fearful, the strategy is to help them develop more trust in their own ability to handle whatever comes their way. All people feel the different levels of fear many times in life, even when we realize that there is nothing to fear. Awareness of the following five truths helps individuals to diminish their levels of fear[21]:

Truth 1. The fear will never go away as long as I continue to grow.

Truth 2. The only way to get rid of the fear of doing something is to go out and do it anyway.

Truth 3. The only way to feel better about myself is to go out . . . and do it.

Truth 4. Not only am I going to experience fear whenever I'm on unfamiliar territory, but so is everyone else.

Truth 5. Pushing through fear is less frightening than living with the underlying fear that comes from a feeling of helplessness.

Improved Communication (Basic to Advanced). Communication patterns have a direct impact on mind modulation of the autonomic, immune, endocrine, and neuropeptide systems. Because our relationships evoke every conceivable emotion and communication pattern, they have a significant impact on our physiologic state.

Nurses can help clients improve communication patterns by teaching an awareness of the psychophysiologic response that occurs with communication. With an increased awareness of the direct link between body and emotions, the client can learn to recognize and increase healthy dialogue. As a result, there will be more sharing and owning of emotions, and relationships will be healthier.

Communication involves state-dependent learning (Chapter 4) and the imagery process (Chapter 23), so there are an enormous number of variables in communication interventions. Because they facilitate the incorporation of relaxation skills and awareness of bodymind responses with all dialogue, these interventions are helpful for all nurses and clients.

Advanced communication interventions incorporate in-depth psychophysiologic therapy and biofeedback training.

Lynch and Thomas developed transactional psychophysiologic therapy during more than 30 years of working with clients who exhibited psychophysiologic symptoms and with patients who were in critical care.[22] The basic premise of this approach is that people with stress-linked physical disorders have in common certain interpersonal struggles that lead to health or to illness. For example, it is difficult to control increased cardiovascular responses, such as increased blood pressure, heart rate, and respirations, during stressful dialogue. A person can learn to modulate the magnitude of these cardiovascular changes, however, by such techniques as slowing the rate of speech, doing deep breathing, releasing muscle tension, practicing nondefensive attending to others, and learning to use relaxation techniques. The purpose of the therapy is (1) to teach a variety of physical maneuvers to modulate the significant changes in blood pressure and heart rate during stressful dialogue, (2) to observe vascular reactions to one's interpersonal world, (3) to link the cardiovascular system with human dialogue and an awareness of human feelings, (4) to view all relationships as essential aspects of transactional psychophysiologic dialogue, and (5) to learn to feel and modulate cardiovascular reactions when relating to others. The therapeutic process follows six steps to increase healthy dialogue:[23]

1. Obtain a psychophysiologic assessment focusing on relationships and the client in dialogue. This can be done when client is responding to simple to more complex questions about relationships.
2. Teach the client to observe vascular responses as dynamic, not static. In this way, the client learns to own his or her personal bodymind responses to dialogue and becomes more aware of the cardiovascular system's sensitivity to interpersonal interactions. If equipment is available for continuous blood pressure monitoring or biofeedback, clients learn the techniques quickly and dramatically; however, one can teach these techniques by instructing the client in self-awareness and self-monitoring skills.
3. Teach the client how the cardiovascular system responds to human communication. Changes in blood pressure and heart rate are linked to fast talking; listening, talking, and human dialogue; breathing and relaxing while talking; emotional content of speech; language as a cry; and language as communication. Rapid rates of speech and breathing significantly increase the cardiovascular response, producing an increase in such parameters as blood pres-

sure and heart rate. While listening to others, the client can learn to use relaxed breathing to reduce the increased cardiovascular responses. The client learns the difference between talking in an inarticulate manner (e.g., holding back and not sharing emotions) and expressing oneself in an articulate manner. The client who has known cardiovascular responses/symptoms can learn to estimate blood pressure and pulse before participating in a stressful or emotional charged dialogue.

4. Teach the client to be aware of the link between human feelings and the cardiovascular system. Instruct the client to notice body responses that occur with dialogue, such as a change in heart rate, breathing patterns, or temperature of the face, torso, hands, and feet. Help the client to recognize the physiologic changes and to correlate them with emotions. Emphasize the importance of getting in touch with feelings, rather than controlling them; make it clear that there is no such thing as a good or bad response.
5. Teach clients that our bodymind responds to the presence of people. The cardiovascular responses are a rich source of beingness that must not be denied. All our emotions, thoughts, and feelings are translated into physiologic changes. It is our responsibility to decide what the interpersonal awareness means to each of us.
6. Teach the client to increase awareness of cardiovascular changes when alone and when relating to others. Encourage the practice of these skills in daily living, such as when talking on the telephone or working. The end result is that the client learns to engage in dialogue, sharing more honest feelings by recognizing cardiovascular responses and even becoming more capable of stressful dialogue without drastic changes in cardiovascular response.

Focusing (Advanced). Through the intervention called focusing, a person learns to identify and change the way that personal problems actually manifest themselves in the body.[24] Nurses can teach focusing as a basic way to recognize the subtle body changes that are related to stressful situations. Focusing is a good strategy to increase skills of intuition, for it helps an individual learn to listen to the body wisdom of the felt sense—the marked shift in sensations within the body as a result of the release of tension. Focusing helps guide a person in learning to be more aware of bodymind. At this level of connection answers to many of our life questions and conflicts can be found.

In order to use focusing successfully, the nurse must practice and become familiar with the felt shift from personal experience. The five skills and the five steps to focusing are seen in Figure 15–1.[25,26] To learn the skill, the nurse records the focusing questions on a tape, leaving space to answer the questions silently at a later time. The nurse then listens and critiques the tape. Is the pace appropriate? Is there enough time to answer the questions? In places where it moves too fast, the nurse records the material again until the technique is so refined that the nurse experiences the body change, the felt shift. With practice, it is possible literally to feel body sensations. The personal experience gives the nurse confidence in the technique's usefulness for problem solving. The technique is best used after the client has learned basic relaxation and imagery exercises and trusts the benefit and power of these self-reflective techniques. The nurse guides the client in a general relaxation or imagery script and then ask the focusing questions. (See Chapters 22 and 23 for general relaxation and imagery scripts.)

Script: *What I will ask you to do in a moment is to increase your relaxation. With your eyes closed, begin to focus on the silence and sensations within your body. Let yourself answer the questions silently to yourself. As you answer in silence to yourself, you are better able to focus and stay with the sensations that you feel within your body. After the exercise, we will discuss your experience. There is no particular way to answer to yourself. Just trust any feelings or answers that come as right for now. Stay with the feelings, and try to let go of any judging or analyzing. Do you have any questions? So . . . let yourself begin to close your eyes . . . and relax. All right—inside you, I would like you to pay attention inwardly, in your body, somewhere within your body and. . . .*

1. *Bring an Awareness into Your Body*
   - *How are you? What's between you and feeling fine?*
   - *Don't answer; let what comes in your body do the answering.*
   - *Don't go into anything.*
   - *Greet each concern that comes. Put each aside for a while, next to you.*
   - *Except for that, are you fine?*
2. *Finding or Inviting a Felt Sense*
   - *Pick one problem to focus on.*

The Five Skills

Finding a Relationship

Being Like a Friend

Acknowledging

Resonating

Receiving

The Five Steps

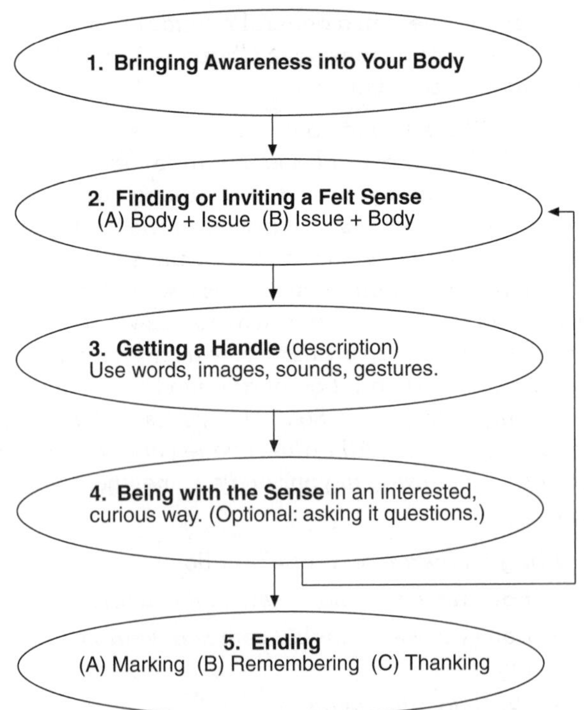

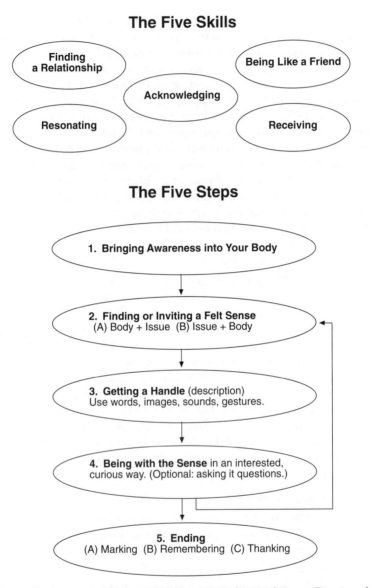

Figure 15–1 Focusing: Five Skills and Five Steps. *Source:* Reprinted from *The Focusing Student's Manual*, 3rd ed. by Ann Weiser-Cornell, with permission of Focusing Resources, Berkeley, Calif. © 1994. For more information, write Student and Guide Focusing Manuals, Workshops, and Newsletters, Ann Weiser-Cornell, PhD, 2625 Alcatraz Ave. #202, Berkeley, CA 94705-2702; (510) 654-4819.

- *Don't go into the problem. What do you sense in your body when you recall the whole of that problem? Sense all of that, the sense of the whole thing, the murky discomfort or the unclear body-sense of it.*

3. *Getting a Handle (description)*
   - *What is the quality of the felt sense?*
   - *What one word, phrase, or image describes this felt sense?*
   - *What quality or word would fit it best?*
4. *Being with the Sense*
   - *Go back and forth between the word (or image) and the felt sense. Is that right?*
   - *If they match, feel the sensation of matching the word and felt sense several times.*
   - *If the felt sense changes, follow it with your attention.*
   - *When you get a perfect match, the words (images) being just right for this feeling, let yourself feel that for a minute.*
5. *Ending*

(Marking and Remembering)

- *What is it, about the whole problem, that makes me so—?*
- *When stuck, ask questions.*
- *What is the worst part of this feeling?*
- *What's really so bad about this?*
- *What does it need?*
- *What should happen?*
- *Don't answer; wait for the feeling to stir and give you an answer.*
- *What would it feel like if it was all OK? Let the body answer: What is in the way of that?*

(Thanking)

- *Welcome what came. Be glad it spoke.*
- *It is only one step on this problem, not the last step.*
- *Now that you know where it is, you can leave it and come back to it later.*
- *Protect it from critical voices that interrupt.*

Does your body want another round of focusing, or is this a good stopping place?

At this point, the client will nod yes or no to another round of focusing. Finish the session with a brief relaxation script and gradually bring the client back into an alert state and allow a period of silence before discussion about the focusing session.

The Empty Chair (Advanced). Popularized by Perls,[27] the empty chair intervention helps people get in touch with and own "parts" of the self that have not been integrated into the whole self. The purpose of the exercise is to get a person to own feelings and beliefs that he or she is projecting onto another person. Such a projection can distort reality within a family or group system. In groups, the empty chair intervention is helpful in exploring issues of lack of assertiveness or not sharing of feelings, a well as in guiding staff or students when there is conflict among group members. The technique becomes an advanced technique when used in one-to-one intensive psychotherapy sessions that focus on feelings and life issues in depth.

To implement this intervention, the nurse positions a client across from an empty chair. The client then places, in imagination, the person with whom he or she has a conflict on the empty chair. The client begins a dialogue with the empty chair, imagining that the person is physically in the chair. The client is instructed to say anything that he or she wishes to this person. When finished, the client switches to the other chair and responds as he or she thinks that the imagined person would respond. The nurse may interject statements or paraphrase what the client appears to be experiencing (e.g., "You mean you are very angry and you want to yell at him"), or the nurse may assume the role of the alter ego and succinctly express what the client seems to be experiencing (refer to Case Study No. 2).

Case Studies

Case Study No. 1

Setting:	Cardiac Rehabilitation Unit
Client:	W.B., a 59-year-old man, after triple bypass graft surgery, in second week of outpatient cardiac rehabilitation. His wife is present at this session.
Nursing Diagnoses:	1. Anxiety related to fear of death 2. Potential for lack of engagement related to new health behaviors after open heart surgery

The cardiac rehabilitation nurse determined that W.B. and his wife were experiencing conflict over perceived meaning in recovery. They were not listening to each other. The nurse took the opportunity to invite the two into her office. This session, her second encounter with the couple, took 20 minutes.

After hearing both sides of the conflict, with each interrupting the other to correct the other's statements, the nurse said, "I see and hear two people who love each other very much who are not listening to each other. I value what each of you is concerned about, and I believe that, if each of you really listens to what the other is saying, you can gain some new insight about the other." The nurse explained the stem phrase completion exercise, and they both agreed to participate. The nurse gave the stem, and then each had a turn to complete the phrase. The couple sat face to face, smiling because the nurse had set the stage to avoid competition. The atmosphere conveyed that the nurse's caring about the couple was genuine.

Nurse (to Husband): Why don't you start? Complete this phrase in whatever way seems right to you just now. *If I weren't so angry. . . .*

Husband: If I weren't so angry, I might listen to you.

Wife: If I weren't so angry, I might quit nagging.

Husband: I am angry for not making faster progress after surgery.

Wife: I am angry because you are not doing what the doctors tell you to do.

Husband: I am clear about I am having a tough time with recovery (*tears in his eyes*).

Wife: I am clear about I feel frustrated because I don't know how to help you.

Husband: If I could change, I would learn how to relax.

Wife: If I could change, I would quit being so afraid

As the nurse listens, the best stem comes from the wife's last completion.

Husband: The thing that I am most afraid of is dying.

Wife: The thing that I am most afraid of is your dying.

Again, the best stem comes from the intuitive feeling that the nurse gained from the wife's last answer, which allowed the nurse to generate this next stem spontaneously.

Husband: The person that I love the most is you.

Wife: The person that I love the most is you.

The nurse concluded the exercise at this point to lead into a discussion of death and spiritual concerns. (See Chapter 1, Exhibit 1-1, and Chapter 17.) The couple was given a teaching sheet with guidelines on integrating relaxation techniques, along with a relaxation tape to begin practicing the skills. This brief session concluded with the couple being deeply grateful for the special attention that they had received from the nurse. Some tears were shed, and tension levels between the couple decreased.

Case Study No. 2

Setting:	Biofeedback department
Client:	A.C., a divorced 42-year-old woman with severe migraine headaches and anxiety, who was frustrated with her 16-year-old son Ron
Nursing Diagnoses:	1. Altered comfort related to incapacitating pain with recurrent weekly migraine headaches 2. Ineffective individual coping related to anxiety, stress of headaches and parenting, and frequent outbursts of aggression toward son

A.C. was having weekly migraines and felt "like I am in quicksand sinking very fast." She described her son as exceptionally aggressive and belligerent. She perceived herself as "acting like things in her life are very much in order." At this particular session, she had only a slight headache. The nurse guided her in a relaxation and guided imagery exercise to increase her skills in biofeedback training. She was successful in relaxing the specific muscle groups that were being monitored by biofeedback. She said, "I am so proud of myself. I wish my son were here right now so I could finish a conversation with him while I am free of my headache." The nurse took the cue and said, "That is a wonderful idea!" The client abruptly said, "What do you mean?"

Nurse: A., could you please imagine your son in this empty chair? (*A. nods.*) Would you tell him what you are feeling just now and how he makes you feel?

A.: Ron, you don't give a damn about me. It seems like you are always doing things to hurt me. I try to please you, but you are so disappointing; you are just walking trouble.

Nurse: Now, sit in this other chair, and give Ron a voice. Let him speak to you in this chair (*the chair that A. has just left*).

A. (As Ron): That's right, I hate you! Did it ever occur to you that you always want me to do things that I don't want to do? I'm sick of hearing you say that this or that will be good for me.

Nurse (As Ron's alter ego): And so I fight you even more because I want to decide for myself what is best. You never give me a chance to prove to you that I can do something that is right by your standards. I'm sick and tired of your nagging me. You never let up. Give me a break.

Nurse: A., now go back to Mom's chair and speak to Ron.

A.: You make me have to constantly try to guide you because you are always doing the wrong thing.

Nurse: Go back to Ron's chair and speak for Ron.

A. (As Ron): I can never do anything to please you. (*With tears, to the nurse*) That's the way it was with my mother. I could never do anything to please her. It would make me so mad, I would want to do things out of spite, but I just worked harder to please her and it still didn't work.

Nurse: Is the problem that your mother was angry and aggressive toward you, now you are always angry toward your son, and your son becomes angry with you and defies you instead of trying to please you as you did with your mother?

A.: It seems that way. I really had not realized that I was doing the same thing with my son that my mother did to me.

Nurse: Imagine that your mother is in that chair and speak to her. Tell her how angry you are with her.

The intervention is the same, but the person in the empty chair is now A.'s mother. When a client deals with family problems, the issues and values in the family of origin frequently surface. The nurse helped A. begin to integrate her past feelings of powerlessness with her mother. By integrating her own aggression, she can be more successful in dealing with the aggression of her son.

Case Study No. 3

Setting:	Biofeedback department with a biofeedback nurse therapist
Client:	L.C., a 42-year-old woman with severe temporomandibular joint (TMJ) dysfunction and tension headaches
Nursing Diagnoses:	1. Altered comfort related to TMJ dysfunctions and tension headaches 2. Ineffective individual coping related to enabling behavior of client with family members

L.C. was referred for biofeedback training because of continued clenching following disk implants for severe TMJ dysfunction. With sobbing tears, she told the nurse that she could not remember a time over the last 20 years when she was free of headaches or pain in her jaws. The nurse asked L. what her pain level was on a scale of 1 (no pain) to 10 (incapacitating pain). Her response was a 20.

Intuitively feeling that the drawing experience could facilitate a breakthrough in perception, the nurse handed L. crayons and paper and asked her to draw her pain (Figure 15–2). The client cried during the entire drawing period, which lasted 30 minutes. The nurse sat at her side as she was drawing, encouraging L. to stay with what she was feeling and to continue her silent inner self-talk. At times, L. would stop crying, but then she would burst into tears again and continue to draw her pain by retracing areas of greater pain. The nurse asked L. what her favorite kind of music was, and she chose to play classical music softly in the background. The nurse asked for no explanations, but sat silently and on occasion encouraged L. to feel the release of pain with the tears. When L.

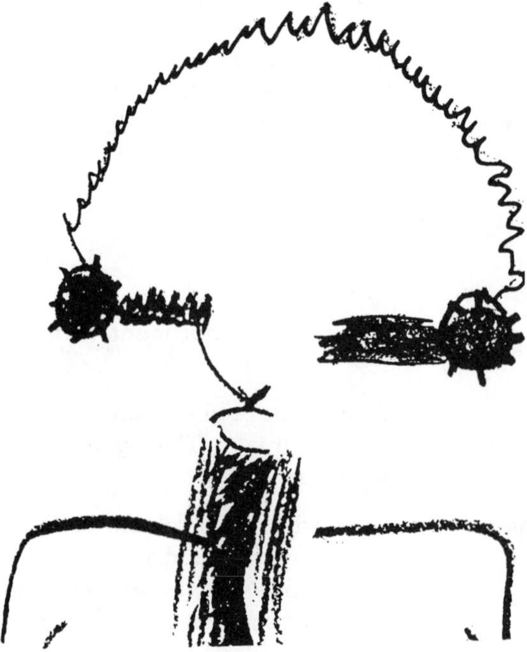

Figure 15–2 Drawing of a Client with Severe Temporomandibular Joint (TMJ) Dysfunction following Disk Implants

was crying intensely, the nurse would reach out and touch her arm. When L. put down the crayons and said, "This is my pain," the nurse with focused attention asked the client to share the meaning of the drawing.

As can be seen in Figure 15–2, there is no face and only details of pain. The new disk implants are drawn in bright red. The client said that "they feel like they are on fire." The lines on the left (also red) indicate the postsurgical numbness that she felt from the jaw through half of her tongue. The pain even flowed down to her throat and chest (bright pink) where she had frequent pain due to continuous tension and anxiety. The line (bright yellow) on the right side showed the bone degeneration that had occurred as a result of her TMJ problem. The zig-zag line (bright blue) across the top is the constant headache that had been present for 20 years.

Following the detailed description of the pain, the nurse asked L. to imagine herself with less pain or without pain altogether. She said that she could imagine a smiling face, free of headache and pain (Figure 15–3). Her disks became blue fluffy clouds, and she frosted her hair and

Figure 15–3 Drawing of Client with Freedom from TMJ Pain

had a new permanent. She even laughed as she did this drawing, which took only a few minutes. She was astounded that she could actually create a spontaneous image of happiness. This exercise helped her become more aware that she was focusing on pain.

Before the end of the first session, the nurse guided L. with a pain assessment script (Chapter 23). She felt immediate, dramatic pain relief. She was instructed to recognize negative images and to focus on a new image of being pain-free. She was encouraged to practice basic rhythmic breathing, to do a pain body scan frequently during the day, and to breathe relaxation into the pain on the inhale and release the pain on the exhale. At the end of this talking session, L. reported her pain level as a 6 on the pain scale.

The second session focused on L.'s ineffective coping related to family members. She perceived herself as helpless, without any means of changing. The nurse introduced her to the concept of enabling behavior, and L. gained understanding about her role in the ineffective family structure. The nurse asked L. to draw her family and the special people in her life (Figure 15–4). She was to write her name in the center of the paper, place the names of family members around her name, and draw arrows to the members who ask her for help and from those members who helped her. (This is another version of a mind map or clustering technique de-

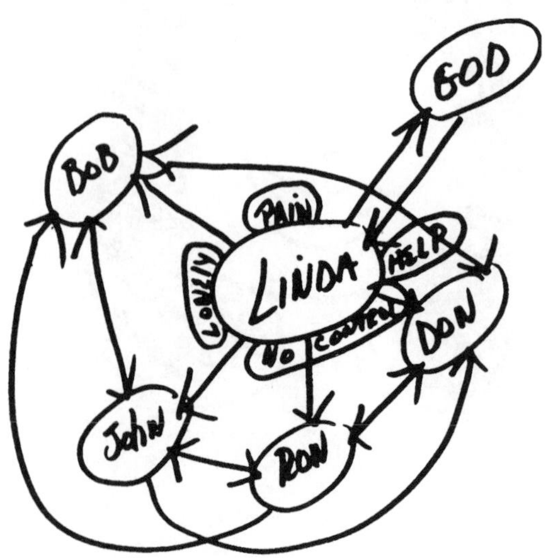

Figure 15–4 Mind Map of a Dysfunctional Family

scribed in Chapter 14.) All the arrows from L.'s name went out to other family members; no arrows returned to her name. It appeared that she gave, but did not receive help from the others. There were arrows to and from God. God was a significant force in her life. She said that God gave her answers during her prayers, but she rarely followed through on the wisdom that she gained through prayer.

Bob, L.'s husband, was unemployed as a result of a back injury. The three sons (John, Ron, and Don), aged 17, 19, and 21, were living at home, were always fighting, and were in and out of work. The oldest two were again using drugs, although they had participated in a drug rehabilitation program. She allowed the adult sons to live at home because they had no money and she feared that they might be worse off on the streets. L. did all the cooking, cleaning, and errands for them.

This woman was in counseling for 10 sessions. During this period, she made significant strides in learning biofeedback skills, managing stress, setting goals, asking for help from the family, and establishing house rules. As she became stronger, she came to understand her victim role and the enabling behavior in which she had been participating. As she grew healthier, she insisted that the two older sons move out because they were not adhering to the basic house rules. The nurse encouraged her to join a women's support group, which she did. She was in the support group for 1 year.

One year after therapy, she divorced and started college. Before the divorce, her husband had always told her she was "smart enough and didn't need book learning." He said that, if she went to college, he would leave her. She decided that she was receiving nothing from her marriage, and she left him. At the 1-year follow-up visit, L. felt the freedom and strengths that she had known before her marriage. Her pain was minimal, and her headaches were infrequent.

Evaluation

With the client, the nurse determines whether the client outcomes for relationship interventions (see Table 15–1) were successfully achieved. To evaluate the session further, the nurse may again explore the subjective effects of the experience with the client (Exhibit 15–2). Healthy relationships increase health and wholeness. As the client becomes more aware of the value of open family and relationship patterns, the client moves in the direction of increased health and healing within the context of relationships.

Exhibit 15–2 Evaluating the Client's Subjective Experience with Relationship Interventions

1. Can you continue to identify and be aware of the relationship that is troublesome to you?
2. What was it like to get in touch with your grievances and resentments in this relationship during the session?
3. Is it possible for you to continue to be clear about your wants and expectations in this relationship?
4. Can you continue to recognize and to work through your fears with respect to this relationship?
5. Is it possible for you to communicate any strengths in this relationship?
6. Can you imagine this relationship if it were healed?
7. What would a healed relationship be like?
8. How would you feel if the relationship was healed?
9. Can you say what you must do to move in this direction?
10. What interventions are most helpful to you to move toward healing this relationship?
11. Do you have any questions about any of the new strategies that you have learned for healing this relationship?
12. What is your next step?

DIRECTIONS FOR FUTURE RESEARCH

1. Develop valid and reliable tools to help nurses measure relationship stressors.
2. Evaluate the tools that are most effective in measuring functional and dysfunctional relationships.
3. Determine which nursing interventions are the most effective in relationship counseling when time is limited.
4. Formulate studies to determine if client teaching sheets with guidelines about enhancing relationships affect the quality of relationships.

NURSE HEALER REFLECTIONS

After reading this chapter, the nurse healer will be able to answer or begin a process of answering the following questions:

- Do I relate to my family and friends in an open manner?
- Am I able to identify the stressors in my relationships?
- What defenses surface in my relationships?

- What are my inner feelings when I share my love?
- Am I able to share my personal hurt with myself and others?
- Can I forgive myself, my family, and friends?
- Am I aware of using "I" statements in order to share more of my feelings and emotions?
- What choices are available to me now to improve my relationships?

NOTES

1. J. Barnsteiner and J. Gillis-Donovan, Being Related and Separate: A Standard for Therapeutic Relationships, *Maternal Child Nursing* 15, no. 4 (1990):223–228.
2. E. Watchel and P. Watchel, *Family Dynamics in Individual Psychotherapy: A Guide to Clinical Strategies* (New York: Guildford Press, 1986), 43–64.
3. Ibid., 50–58.
4. E. Sieberg, *Family Communications: An Integrated Systems Approach* (New York: Gardner Press, 1985), 32–55.
5. Watchel and Watchel, *Family Dynamics in Individual Psychotherapy*, 50–58.
6. E. Rossi, *The 20 Minute Break* (Los Angeles: Jeremy P. Tarcher, 1991), 141–159.
7. Ibid., 147–148.
8. J. Achterberg et al., *Rituals of Healing* (New York: Bantam Books, 1994), 1–33.
9. L. Banks, Counseling, in *Nursing Interventions: Essential Nursing Treatments*, 2nd ed., ed. J. Bulechek and J. McCloskey (Philadelphia: W.B. Saunders, 1992), 279–291.
10. Ibid., 280.
11. M. Sandelowski, We Are the Stories That We Tell, *Journal of Holistic Nursing* 12, no. 1 (1994):23–33.
12. Ibid.
13. F. Vaughan, *The Inward Arc* (Boston: Shambhala Publications, 1986).
14. J. Welwood, *Ordinary Magic: Everyday Life as a Spiritual Path* (Boston: Shambhala Publications, 1992).
15. J. Kornfield, *Path with Heart* (New York: Bantam Books, 1992).
16. M. McKivergin and M.J. Daubenmire, The Healing Process of Presence, *Journal of Holistic Nursing* 12, no. 1 (1994):65–81.
17. M. Burkhardt and M.G. Nagai-Jacobson, Reawakening Spirit in Clinical Practice, *Journal of Holistic Nursing* 12, no. 2 (1994):9–21.
18. G. Hendricks and K. Hendricks, *At the Speed of Life* (New York: Bantam Books, 1993).
19. M. Burkhardt and M.G. Nagai-Jacobson, Spirituality: The Cornerstone of Holistic Nursing Practice, *Holistic Nursing Practice* 3, no. 3 (1989):18–26.
20. S. Jeffers, *Feel the Fear and Do It Anyway* (New York: Fawcett Columbine, 1987), 11–18.
21. Ibid., 20–21.
22. J. Lynch, *The Language of the Heart* (New York: Basic Books, 1985), 311.

23. S. Thomas, Spirituality: An Essential Dimension in the Treatment of Hypertension, *Holistic Nursing Practice* 3, no. 3 (1989):47–55.
24. E. Gendlin, *Focusing* (New York: Bantam Books, 1981).
25. A. Weiser-Cornell, *The Focusing Guide's Manual*, 3rd ed. (Berkeley, CA: Focusing Resources, 1993).
26. A. Weiser-Cornell, *The Focusing Student's Manual*, 3rd ed. (Berkeley, CA: Focusing Resources, 1994).
27. F. Perls, *Gestalt Therapy* (New York: Julian Press, 1951), 1–21.

VISION OF HEALING

Recovering and Maintaining the Self

> The great majority of us are required to live a life of constant, systematic duplicity. Your health is bound to be affected if, day after day, you say the opposite of what you feel, if you grovel before what you dislike and rejoice at what brings you nothing but misfortune. Our nervous system isn't just a fiction, it's a part of our physical body, and our soul exists in space and is inside us, like the teeth in our mouth. It can't be forever violated with impunity.[1]

The client who has endured abuse or violence has had to live a life of distortion and lies. The choice to move beyond the duplicity and into the truth impacts the physical and emotional health of the individual as well as the family system. The journey toward healthy relationships may expose secrets whose effects ripple out into the client's present family as well as back through generations of abuse.

Working with survivors of abuse and violence is one of the most difficult nursing experiences, but it is also one of the most rewarding. Because of a reluctance to inquire, it is possible to work with a client over a long period of time without knowing that he or she has been or may even still be involved in a violent situation. At the other end of the continuum, a nurse may be called upon to provide immediate care for a rape victim in an emergency room. In addition to caring for the client, the nurse must be sure to stay grounded and clear about his or her own needs and issues.

Survivors of abuse may move in and out of the medical-psychologic care system over a period of several years as they process the effects of their abuse. The recovery of the self moves in cycles and layers. Both client and caregiver must be prepared for this circuitous journey to wholeness, taking each new stage as reassurance of progress.

NOTE

1. B. Pasternak, *Doctor Zhivago* (New York: Pantheon, 1958), p. 483.

Chapter 16

Sexual Abuse: Healing the Wounds

Leslie Gooding Kolkmeier

NURSE HEALER OBJECTIVES

Theoretical

- Discuss the phenomenon of repressed memories and ways to avoid imposing one's suspicions of abuse on a client's memory gaps.
- Discuss the possible physical, emotional, and behavioral consequences of childhood abuse.

Clinical

- Incorporate direct questions concerning abuse into your client interview format.
- Identify counselors, support groups, and referral sources for survivors and perpetrators of abuse in your community.
- Review or develop policies and procedures for dealing with the emotional and physical needs of victims of abuse in emergency situations.

Personal

- Prepare a family record and note the presence of any perpetrators or victims of violence, or members with substance abuse problems or eating disorders.
- Develop a personal style of anger management that allows you to express anger without injury to yourself or others.
- Identify any personal experiences of abuse and seek resolution with a trained counselor.

DEFINITIONS

Backlash: the emotional distress and negative self-talk experienced in response to a move forward in understanding the origin and/or meaning of an abusive trauma.

Body Memories: the physical sensations that occur in either the presence or absence of mental images.

Bodywork: therapeutic massage.

Dissociation: the experience of one's mind temporarily splitting off from one's body; a feeling of separation from the body.[1]

Flashback: a vivid reexperiencing of the original abuse; pieces of memory, described by a survivor as "like a slide compared to a film."[2]

Grounding: staying oriented in the present rather than being engulfed by memory.

Incest: sexual activity between a person and a close relative, whether this relationship is consanguineous, by marriage, or by adoption.[3]

Sexual Abuse: exploitative psychosexual activity that goes beyond the developmental level of the child, to which the child is unable to give informed consent, and that violates social taboos regarding roles and relationships.

Trigger: an image, word, fragrance, or sensation that provokes a memory.

Video Therapy: the review of videotaped sessions, stories, confrontations, or other therapeutic activity by the client, client and nurse or therapist, client and family, or client and perpetrator.

THEORY AND RESEARCH*

Precautions When Working with Survivors

Adult survivors of childhood sexual abuse are coming forward in increasing numbers as counseling professionals and society become

*This chapter focuses on the therapeutic interventions for survivors of sexual abuse, yet the concepts may be modified for use with clients who have been victims of any type of abuse. To eliminate awkward wording and in deference to the number of female victims, clients in this chapter are referred to as "she." We recognize, however, that a significant portion of males are also survivors of sexual, emotional, or physical abuse.

more open to hearing the stories and helping the survivors deal with the emotional and physical ramifications of the survivors' experiences.[4] Survivors of sexual abuse may seek care many different times as their stress level and life change events trigger new memories or precipitate new manifestations of physical and emotional pain. Abuse buried in traumatic amnesia may begin to surface when the survivor's child reaches the age of the survivor at the time the abuse began; when the perpetrator dies, removing the possibility of retribution; when the survivor is finally in a safe and loving relationship; or when the survivor leaves home and fears that the perpetrator will transfer the abuse to a younger sibling. It is vital to refrain from imposing one's suspicions of abuse on a client who has not recovered memories. All interventions must remain open-ended and ambiguous; facts, memories, and details must arise in the client, not the nurse therapist.

Data from one study indicate that there was a history of childhood sexual abuse in nearly 4 percent of all psychiatric cases within the studied population.[5] Female survivors outnumber males in all studies, but averages are 71 percent female and 29 percent male. Some authorities speculate that males are abused as often as females; they believe that the numbers do not reflect the reality because males may be more reluctant to report their abuse and because professionals are not as attuned to asking about abuse in male clients.[6,7] There are minor differences in the treatment of male survivors, but the therapeutic strategies remain very similar.[8]

Bodymind Responses

Post-traumatic stress disorder provides a model for the symptoms of sexual abuse and approaches to treatment. Intense recall of information and affect replace amnesia, denial, and emotional numbing as the survivor works through the sexual abuse.[9] Autonomic nervous system hyperarousal, including hypervigilance and exaggerated startle response, may be accompanied by somatic disorders such as headaches, ulcers, irritable bowel syndrome, reproductive difficulties, and urinary tract disorders. Psychologic manifestations of abuse may include depression, recurrent disturbing dreams, thoughts of suicide, outbursts of anger, sleep difficulties, feelings of detachment from others, and inability to experience feelings of trust or love.[10]

The TRIADs Assessment Tool*

At the University of Pennsylvania School of Nursing, Burgess developed an assessment tool, using the acronym TRIADs, to evaluate sexual abuse. It is also applicable to other types of abuse, including domestic violence, ethnic/gay/hate assaults, child abuse, and cult torture. Because the tool is useful for determining the severity of abuse, it helps direct treatment strategies.[11]

I. **T**ype of Abuse
   1. Physical abuse
   2. Sexual abuse
   3. Psychologic abuse

II. **R**ole Relationship of Victim to Offender
   1. Intrafamilial
   2. Extrafamilial
   3. Authority of abuse

III. **I**ntensity of Abuse
   1. Number of acts
   2. Number of abuses

IV. **A**ffective State
   1. Expressed style (anxious, angry, sad)
   2. Controlled style (blank, calm, denial)

V. **D**uration
   1. Length of time

VI. **S**tyle of Abuse
   1. Blitz style of abuse
   2. Repetitive/patterned abuse
   3. Ritualistic/ceremonial abuse

Moving through the Memories

Traditional therapeutic interventions include individual and group counseling and support groups.[12] Emerging adjunctive interventions incorporate expressive arts, such as drawing and psychodrama, bibliotherapy (i.e., asking the client to read specific books relating to her symptoms or history) and journal keeping, anger expression and man-

---

Source: Reprinted from *Counseling Victims of Violence* by Sandra Brown, p. 6, Copyright © 1991, American Counseling Association. Reprinted with permission. No further reproduction authorized without written permission of the American Counseling Association.

agement, body awareness exercises, and the re-creation of positive intimacy experiences.[13]

Therapy has focused on recalling and retelling the stories of abuse ("telling the secret"), connecting with and expressing situation-congruent affect, assigning appropriate responsibility, grieving for the loss of innocence, correcting distortions, and moving on to self-determination and healthy behavioral changes.[14,15] As nurses and counselors gain more experience with adult survivors of abuse, they are developing programs, strategies, and techniques to move the client safely and more quickly to a new level of understanding and inner peace.

NURSING PROCESS

Assessment

In preparing to use abuse interventions, the nurse assesses the following parameters:

- the client's experiences with flashbacks. Fragments of memory may intrude on the consciousness without warning, perhaps triggered by a physical touch, fragrance, or tone of voice, or perhaps for no apparent reason.
- the client's body memories. Physical examinations, surgical procedures involving general anesthesia, or any other medical interventions that deprive the client of a measure of control may trigger memories, flashbacks, fears, or anger that is out of proportion to the event. Body memories may be general and nebulous (e.g., physical pain with no explanation, twitches, nausea), or they may be very specific (e.g., hemorrhoids or vaginal infections in young children, or vaginismus or sexual difficulties in adults).
- the client's experiences with dissociation, especially when undergoing physical examinations, being touched (e.g., during a bed bath or massage), or dealing with traumatic memories. Memories of the abuse may intrude when abuse survivors are undergoing some sort of physical contact that may or may not duplicate elements of the original abuse (e.g., finding oneself "trapped" by traction equipment, intravenous lines, respirators, or other pieces of equipment; undergoing dental work; being strapped down on a surgical cart; having a vaginal examination or a massage; even engaging in "safe" sexual activity with a previously trusted partner). Identifying

these triggers helps the survivor either avoid these situations or work on changing the negative associations.[16]

- the client's present level of physical and emotional safety. The client may not recognize or easily share the fact that abuse is ongoing. She may need help removing herself from the abusive situation and obtaining social services such as alternative housing.
- the client's current period of safety (i.e., the length of time since the client has been abused).
- the client's previous experiences with the intervention planned.
- the client's use of any medications that may influence her ability to participate fully in the intervention.

Nursing Diagnoses

The following nursing diagnoses compatible with abuse interventions and that are related to the human response patterns of Unitary Person (see Chapter 7) are as follows:

- Relating: Impaired social interaction
  Social isolation
  Sexual dysfunction
  Altered sexuality patterns
- Valuing: Altered spiritual state
  Distress
- Choosing: Ineffective individual coping
  Impaired adjustment
  Ineffective family coping
  Altered participation in family and community
- Knowing: Altered self-concept
  Disturbance in body image, self-esteem, and personal identity
  Hopelessness
  Powerlessness
- Feeling: Acute and chronic pain
  Anxiety
  Grieving
  Fear
  Post-trauma syndrome

Client Outcomes

Table 16–1 guides the nurse in client outcomes, nursing prescriptions, and evaluation of abuse interventions.

Table 16–1 Nursing Interventions: Abuse

Client Outcomes	*Nursing Prescriptions*	*Evaluation*
The client will exhibit decreased startle response and other manifestations of hypervigilance, somatic and emotional distress.	Guide the client in performing grounding exercises; verbalizing her story; identifying and expressing her feelings of anger, pain, and loss of innocence.	The client exhibited decreased hypervigilance, somatic and emotional distress as evidenced by normal vital signs; an increase in normal, unmedicated sleep; warm hands; and decreased headaches, abdominal discomfort, anxiety, depression, and suicidal thoughts.
The client will demonstrate an ability to identify dissociation and specific techniques to return to a grounded state.	Teach the client to notice when she is dissociating by asking frequently if she is grounded and calling her attention to dissociated behaviors. Guide her in identifying and using grounding cues, rewarding her for staying "in the present" while talking about her experience or listening to others.	The client demonstrated an ability to stay grounded as evidenced by a. maintenance of eye contact b. decrease in frequency and severity of flashbacks c. decrease in frequency and severity of body memories d. continued orientation to time and place The client used her watch as a talisman for staying grounded. She stayed grounded during group therapy sessions and helped others in the group identify when they were dissociated.

Plan and Interventions

Before the Session

- Develop the skill of identifying signs of dissociation, such as losing one's train of thought; stopping in the middle of a sentence; staring into space; keeping the body still; prolonging verbal response time; exhibiting a flattened affect, a lessened emotional response to highly charged material, or dilated pupils.[17]
- Review grounding techniques and ways that the client can communicate when she is becoming uncomfortable with the material being discussed.
- Spend a few moments centering yourself.

At the Beginning of the Session

- Teach the client grounding skills to help her stay anchored in the present rather than feeling engulfed and swept into a memory. For example, have the client make eye contact or keep her eyes moving, looking around the room or at other people present in the room, to help her stay oriented to the present time and place. Stating aloud the day and place, saying the names of the people around her, and repeating "I am safe" helps the client separate the memory from the present reality.[18]
- Encourage the client to move her feet and reassure her that she is free to move around or even leave the room, if necessary. This empowers her to loosen the ties to a previous time when she may have been trapped and unable to escape.
- Review this information if the session is not the first with this client.

During the Session

- Continue to evaluate the client's state of mind for dissociation.
- Help the client recognize and refute self-destructive statements or negative programming by the abuser. Call attention to negative comments (e.g., "It was all my fault," "I'm worthless," "I'm damaged goods"), and help the client recognize the source of these distortions.
- Assist the client in reframing negative statements: "I was only a child, there was nothing else I could do," "I'm a worthwhile person who was hurt by someone who was older and stronger than I was." (See Chapters 4 and 23.)

At the End of the Session

- Ensure that the client is not dissociated.
- Provide time and supplies, such as pen and paper, crayons, or modeling clay, should the client need to process further the material raised during the session.
- Evaluate client's state of mind for suicidal feelings, and have her verbalize her activity plans until the next session.
- Use the client outcomes (see Table 16–1) that were established before the session and the client's subjective experiences (Exhibit 16–1) to evaluate the session.
- Schedule a follow-up session.

Specific Interventions

Several interventions for sexual abuse require special training, and nurses are encouraged to obtain that training through a formal program or apprenticeship. Some states require certification or licensure for interventions such as biofeedback, hypnosis, or bodywork. It is essential for nurses to refer to the standards of their state nursing practice act.

Grounding Skills (Basic). Grounding helps abuse survivors stay anchored in the present rather than feeling overwhelmed by a memory. Clients often develop their own tools to keep themselves from dissociating, and sharing their most effective grounding techniques can be an excellent icebreaker to welcome new members into a support or therapy group. The use of a talisman, for example, to establish feelings of safety and connection with the present combats anxiety, fear, and dissociation. A ring or other piece of jewelry or any small object that can be touched, held, worn, or carried in a pocket or purse is ideal.[19]

Dissociation may prevent survivors from recognizing dangerous or abusive situations, making them vulnerable to further victimization.[20] The survivor's ability to dissociate or become "numb" in the face of danger may keep her from recognizing abuse and acting to protect herself or her children. The children may then become victims of abuse. This may be one way that sexual abuse becomes a transgenerational problem. Learning to stay grounded and to identify danger signals empowers the survivor and helps prevent recurrences of abuse. It not only helps a survivor, but also may actually protect her children from neglect or abuse.[21]

Relaxation (Basic). Survivors of abuse may need coaching and encouragement to take part in relaxation exercises. Confusing relaxation with laziness or idleness, they may feel that they do not deserve to take time out from the hard work of recovery. Disturbing flashbacks and body memories can surface when the physical armor of tension is quieted. Clients may equate relaxation with vulnerability, which conflicts with their hypervigilance. Thus, survivors of sexual abuse may need to relearn the skill of relaxation in terms of both recreation and physical "letting go." Flashbacks, body memories, and hypervigilance all conspire to make relaxation frightening. The resulting physical and mental tension makes restful sleep, clear thought processes, and pleasant physical sensations difficult or impossible to achieve.

Progressive relaxation, the controlled tensing and relaxing of specific muscle groups, can be very effective with abuse survivors. It allows the client to feel more fully in control of her body and helps alleviate the perceived helplessness or vulnerability of simply relaxing overly tense muscles. Coupled with a systematic desensitization hierarchy, progressive relaxation encourages a client to gain control of both physical and emotional reactions to anxiety-provoking people or events.[22] Slow, deep, abdominal breathing reduces a client's anxiety, encourages grounding, and prevents dissociation. (See Chapter 22 for in-depth relaxation strategies.)

Imagery (Basic to Advanced). Although images may arise spontaneously from a deeply relaxed state, as in the case of memory retrieval, they may also result from the nurse's guidance, as in the case of guided relaxation scenes. An effective guided imagery technique can help an abuse survivor connect with the suppressed emotions surrounding her abuse experience.[23] Once the client has relaxed and has achieved an altered state of consciousness, the nurse asks her to close her eyes and imagine the face of the person with whom she is struggling emotionally. To provide some protection from overwhelming emotion, the nurse may suggest that the client imagine the face on a television screen, a technique called dissociative reviewing.[24] The client then describes the facial expression that she is imaging and her somatic response to it. The somatic response may be "a knot in my stomach" or "a tightness in my chest." The somatic response is a gauge of the intensity of the emotion connected to the person in the image.

Asked what the face represents, the client then interprets the image. She reports on the intensity of the somatic response, which at this point is usually increased. Next, the nurse asks the client to verbalize what the face is saying while identifying her somatic response. By monitoring this response, the client can maintain control over, or pace, the process. The nurse may choose to help the client deepen the altered or trance state and allow the emotional reaction to occur. The final step is to provide the survivor with an opportunity to respond to the abuser by releasing her suppressed emotions. This process allows the client to experience repressed emotions in a safe, structured environment and move beyond the pain. The somatic reaction indicates not only the depth to which the emotions have been buried, but also the progress that the survivor has made. As the "knot" loosens or the tightness in the chest eases, so, too, does the emotional bondage to the person in the image.

Variations of this imagery process help clients connect with long-buried feelings of pain, anger, sadness, pleasure, relaxation, safety, and strength. If clients cannot recall ever feeling safe or nurtured, imagery is a powerful tool to construct a mental stage on which to present the possibility of those feelings. Knowing that acting "as if" produces much the same biochemical changes as the actual happening, we can help clients get in touch with emotions and sensations that they have either forgotten or have never fully experienced.[25] (See Chapter 23 for more information on imagery.)

Biofeedback (Advanced). For many years, biofeedback has helped clients connect with body sensations and gain control over physiologic responses. Combining biofeedback with relaxation and imagery techniques allows both client and nurse to be aware of the effectiveness of a variety of approaches to the goal of deep relaxation.[26]

Hand and foot temperature decreases in the sympathetic or "fight or flight" response of the autonomic nervous system. Thus, the client, partner, or therapist can use hand temperature to monitor comfort level. If a survivor of abuse has cold hands while doing anger work, the anger may still be tied into the fear of being abused in the presence of an angry perpetrator. The use of inexpensive sweat response monitors to evaluate anxiety levels during intimacy exercises allows both survivor and partner to be aware of changes in the survivor's perceived level of safety.

Care must be taken when using biofeedback with survivors of cult abuse. A full explanation of the procedure and reassurance that the client may stop at any time will help overcome any fears of being "wired up" or harmed by the electronic equipment. Medications to reduce anxiety, depression, or other symptoms may affect the responses monitored by the biofeedback equipment, and the nurse should take this into consideration when interpreting the responses to the client.

Hypnosis and Self-Hypnosis (Advanced). Some survivors of childhood sexual abuse find hypnosis or self-hypnosis useful as a way to relax or to retrieve repressed memories.[27] Only professionals with specific training in dealing with the issues that are likely to arise should perform hypnosis, however, and there is some hesitance among professionals toward using hypnosis for memory retrieval. Feeling that the memories are submerged in the unconscious in order to protect the individual from pain that he or she not is not yet ready to handle, some therapists wait for the memories to arise spontaneously when the psyche is strong enough to deal with the associated affect. Powerful recovery work can be done before specific memories surface or even in the face of incomplete memories.[28,29]

Hypnosis for memory retrieval is a structured process of relaxation designed to produce a state of dissociation that facilitates an individual's ability to get in touch with unconscious parts of the self, such as feelings, awareness, or memories.[30] Clients must feel safe in the presence of the hypnotherapist, as the process may put them in a very vulnerable condition. Furthermore, a client must feel in charge of the progress of the session and must feel free to stop at any time.[31] Both client and therapist must have confidence in the client's ability to return to a safe present when faced with overpowering negative feelings.

Safety precautions may include suggesting to the client during induction and while hypnotized that she will go only as far as she feels safe and she may choose to forget anything that she is not ready to handle. Suggestions such as "Place the memories in a safe container, and walk back into the present moment," or "Leave the information safe in the subconscious, knowing that it will be there for you when you are ready," allow the client to deal with the information in safe, manageable doses. Incorporating a sense of distance from the action by suggesting, for example, that the client view a scene as if she were watching a black and white television program that she can turn on or off can provide a feeling of safety and control.[32] Maintaining an adult perspective and adult coping skills while separating themselves from the affect engendered by the memories allows clients to regain repressed memories without feeling retraumatized.[33] Some clients may choose to videotape hypnosis sessions to reassure themselves later about what actually occurred during a session; others may have a trusted friend present to help them stay anchored to a supportive present while exploring a traumatic past.[34]

Bodywork (Basic to Advanced). Not only do bodywork techniques, such as massage, offer survivors an avenue to reconnecting with healthy body feelings, but also they may provide a path to the retrieval of memories. When offered in an environment that is conducive to processing feelings as they arise (e.g., an inpatient unit or a multimodal private practice), bodywork may speed the retrieval of memories and the recovery of body sensation.

Prior to treatment, sexual abuse survivors may sexualize and misinterpret nonsexual touch. Authorities on the subject of bodywork and trauma recovery emphasize the survivor's need to remain in control of the process, to set limits and boundaries on what parts of the body are touched, and to determine how they are touched. Surrendering sufficient control over one's body to allow it to be touched does not mean allowing it to be abused.[35] The client needs to feel all the feelings associated with being touched and to process those feelings rather than succumbing to the easier and more likely defense of shutting down or becoming numb to the sensations. The survivor can learn that she deserves to do something nice for herself, the body is worth it, the body deserves to feel good.

Craniosacral therapy is an outgrowth of osteopathy. It is an extremely gentle manipulation of the bones of the skull and of the spine, as well as the connective tissue.[36] The client remains clothed during craniosacral therapy, which offers an additional feeling of safety to abused clients.

Feldenkrais bodywork, another "safe" way of getting in touch with the body, is generally done in groups and is always done with the clients fully clothed. The movements are gentle and nonthreatening. The general intention of all Feldenkrais work is "to increase awareness, interrupt habitual behavior and gain control over the central nervous system, which, in turn, informs muscular-skeletal motion."[37] Feldenkrais, like many forms of bodywork, can release feelings and memories that traditional talk therapies cannot. (See Chapter 21 for other touch therapies.)

Writing (Basic). Clients who are having difficulty talking about their trauma or connecting with the emotions appropriate to the event may be able to link affect to memory through writing. Because of the sensitive nature of the memories and feelings, privacy for writing and security for the written material are critical. Keeping a diary or journal as therapy evolves can help clients see improvements in their mood and thought processes. Reviewing diary entries can remind them of strategies that helped them through earlier difficult times. Writing poetry or writing in a journal or diary to music may help evoke emotions and help tap into the creative side of the self with use of self-reflection, imagery, and music. (See Chapters 14, 22, and 23 for more information on therapeutic writing.)

Fredrickson calls the journal "a 24-hour therapist" who is always on call when a client is working on a memory fragment or dream.[38] This "avenue to the unconscious" can also be a place to record intuitions, hunches, and questions. Journal keeping is particularly useful for inpatients whose therapy sessions may be more frequent than those of outpatients, leaving little time for processing.

As survivors move through the healing process, there may be a risk of self-mutilation or even suicide. The nurse can encourage the client to write notes to herself, listing things to do that are not self-destructive and leaving the notes where she will find them when overcome by self-destructive urges. Suggestions may include playing an instrument, cleaning out a drawer, calling a supportive friend, going outside, painting, drawing, or writing about the feelings. Seeing the suggestions in her own handwriting seems to make more of an impact on a client than reading the printed words in a book or article.[39]

Writing with the nondominant hand, which "may be more laborious and therefore more compelling than writing in her usual way," is a strategy recommended for anchoring in positive self-statements.[40] Nondominant handwriting may also help the client gain access to unconscious material when the nurse asks her simply to watch what that hand is writing, rather than directing the hand to record conscious thought.[41]

Courtois recommends autobiography writing to guard against "reforgetting" traumatic material.[42] Creating a visual representation of her life (e.g., a time line) can help an abuse survivor see patterns of behavior and perhaps make some sense of her abuse history. The client begins with events that occurred shortly before her birth on the left end of a line drawn horizontally along the length of a large piece of paper to represent time. The client marks meaningful events such as births, deaths, marriages, divorces, starting school, moving, illnesses, instances of abuse, and other significant memories along the time line, sometimes even choosing to color code them in some way.[43]

Many authorities encourage clients to write letters to parents, perpetrators of abuse, or others, even if they never send the letters. Letters can be a powerful way to express feelings toward abusers or others who are dead. The first letter should be uncensored, written with the clear understanding that it is *not* to be sent. After working with the letter and sharing it with the nurse, therapist, or fellow group members, the client can rework it until it is suitable to send if that is what she wishes to do. The client may choose to keep the letter for a period of time until the emotions have quieted. She can then do with the letter as she wishes. She may keep it, tear it up, burn it, bury it, or otherwise dispose of it in an appropriately ceremonial ritual signifying completion.

Quickly finishing a paragraph that begins "once upon a time" or writing a list of five to ten things that she remembers about a family member or an event may help a client make sense of fragments of memory. Working under time pressure forces the mind to rely more on experience than imagination and may help fill in blanks in the client's memory.[44]

Art Therapy (Basic to Advanced). Creative, right brain techniques that permit the sharing of information and the expression of feelings may be at the root of many artistic endeavors. Survivors of abuse may choose a variety of ways to express their feelings of anger, shame, guilt, fear, and hope, as well as to communicate nonverbally the depth and extent of their abuse experience. Collages showing how they felt as a child, how they are feeling now, and what they hope to be experiencing in the future put concrete expression to feelings. A series of paintings or other art forms (e.g., masks, sculptures, photographs, videotapes, clay figures) can help the survivor trace her healing progress; moreover, she may be able to tap into deep feelings and understanding that are inaccessible to the verbal realm alone.[45]

The interpretation of art work can be a collaborative effort. Specialists in art therapy may read much more into a piece of art work, but even those without special training can obtain ample information by examining a client's art work. Color and content may indicate overall mood, and specifics such as proportion and completeness of human images can give a sense of body awareness and feelings of control over the environment.[46] The presence of recurring themes, symbols, or objects may give clues to memory fragments or thoughts that are not yet safe to put into words.[47]

Videotherapy (Basic to Advanced). Therapists are now beginning to videotape their sessions with adult survivors of abuse. Many courts permit the use of videotaped testimony from children so that a child must tell his or her story only once.[48] One danger of the use of videotape is that copies of the tape may fall into the wrong hands. For this reason, some therapists make only one tape and require the client to be responsible for the tape at all times, avoiding concerns about confidentiality and safe storage.[49]

The use of videotape permits an adult client to correct any distortions that she may have about the impact of the abuse on her life and the effect of her disclosure on others, either those who are present at the time of the taping or those who view the tape later. Watching herself talk about her abuse allows her to develop empathy for herself. Videotape offers a client an opportunity to practice either disclosure or confrontation. Being able to stop the tape and ground herself before going on—or even to begin again—puts control of the situation in the hands of the survivor.

The following five-stage process of video disclosure has been suggested[50]:

1. *Stage One* begins with the survivor's decision to make a tape. Because the perpetrator may have threatened the survivor with harm if she "tells," the survivor must have reached a point in therapy where she trusts the therapist and herself to proceed with recorded disclosure. Some clients may choose to tape within the context of a supportive group; others feel more comfortable speaking only to the camera and the therapist.
2. *Stage Two* begins with informed consent, preferably recorded on the tape as well as in writing. The interview is structured around three questions: What happened to you as a child? What have been the consequences in your life? What do you expect will happen when this tape is shown to significant people in your life?
3. *Stage Three* begins with the survivor's viewing of the finished tape, with support from the therapist. The client remains in control of how much of the tape she watches at a time, what happens to the tape, and what changes, if any, are made in the content of the tape. Many clients experience severe backlash at this stage, and care must be taken to evaluate the possibility of self-destructive acts. Access to a protective inpatient environment is a must at this stage.
4. *Stage Four* consists of assembling a support "team" of family and friends and asking them to watch the tape. The client always has the therapist or a member of this support team present when someone new sees the tape for the first time.
5. *Stage Five* involves showing the tape to the offender in the presence of as many members of the support team as possible. If the offender can watch the tape and accept its content, therapy can proceed with the abuser. Even if the abuser refuses to accept the content as true, voices no remorse, or does not offer to make amends, the process of speaking out on tape and sharing her experience with others is therapeutic for the abuse survivor.

Many variations of this five-stage taping process are being used successfully in both inpatient and outpatient group and individual therapy settings, but controlled studies of its efficacy remain to be done.

According to Courtois, approximately half of all incest victims made an attempt at disclosure at the time of the abuse, but most responses were unfavorable.[51] The victim was threatened, accused of lying and abuse may have escalated. Being able to view a videotaped disclosure or confrontation meeting over and over again can reassure the survivor that she was clear about what happened and can allow her to notice many different aspects of the behavior of everyone present at the meeting. Body language and placement of family members relative to each other, tone of voice, and eye contact all help affirm the reality of the meeting and of participants' reactions to the disclosure. Many times, family members ask to see the video again in order to see and hear more clearly what happened in a very emotional meeting. With permission from all participants, the therapist may videotape family sessions to provide the survivor and her family evidence of change and progress. The therapist can validate change within the family and help them voice plans for continued change and growth.[52]

Anger Expression and Management (Basic to Advanced). In most families in which abuse occurs, only the perpetrator is allowed to express anger. Any expression of anger by another member of the family may result in abuse. The abused child quickly learns to equate the expression (or possession) of anger with power. The perpetrator has power, while the child does not.[53]

Abuse survivors have difficulty in recognizing or acknowledging their own anger and, once they recognize it, may associate it so closely with fear that they cannot express it. The internalized anger may lead to headaches, colitis, ulcers, or other stress-related disorders.[54] Anger may be evident in passive aggressive or manipulative behavior, self-mutilation, depression, or anxiety.[55] Once the survivors can express anger in a safe environment, their physical symptoms subside and behavior modification may take place.

Male survivors may link anger with a male perpetrator, be unable to express the anger, and, therefore, feel a diminished sense of masculinity. On the other hand, the male survivor may feel and act constantly angry as a way of asserting his power. This keeps perpetrators away, but it also keeps everyone else away, leaving him angry *and* isolated.[56]

Abuse survivors can learn that anger and rage are appropriate feelings in the face of abuse. They learn that anger is simply one of the many emotions that they are allowing themselves to feel. "Dosing" (i.e., expressing anger in small, manageable amounts) gives the survivor a sense of control over what may be a very new feeling. Time-limiting anger work by using 30-second to 3-minute timers allows the survivor to experiment with expressing feelings for a "safe" amount of time.[57]

Clients may express their anger verbally onto an audiotape, recording additional material as they connect with more angry feelings or memories over time. Playing the tape back in the presence of their nurse, therapist, or a supportive friend helps validate the reality and justification for the anger. Like written material, the tape may be kept for future reference or disposed of in a ceremonial manner.

Exercises to help express anger in safe, time-limited circumstances include throwing balls of clay at a wall; hitting a punching bag with lengths of plastic pipe, a bataca (padded bat used for hitting in controlled settings such as psychiatric units or group therapy), or a baseball bat; hitting sofa cushions, or rugs hung on a clothesline with a tennis racquet. Physical exertion such as running or other aerobic exercises can reduce anger as well. Verbal expressions of anger should always be directed at the perpetrator, even though the survivor may be "mad at myself."[58] Survivors working in group therapy can help each other come up with "anger workouts" appropriate to their life styles and individual comfort levels.

The expression of anger, no matter how subdued, may feel like raging out of control or "flying apart" to the survivor of sexual abuse. By allowing the survivor to be a "neutral observer" of her anger work, videotherapy makes it possible for her to correct distortions about how much anger is being expressed, compared to how much is felt internally. A survivor who subsequently finds herself reacting with anger out of proportion to the intensity of the situation that triggered the anger can learn to stop and identify the way in which this situation resembles a time when she was victimized or abused.[59] Dealing with the original abuse and its resulting anger aids in keeping present day anger-provoking situations in perspective.

Case Study

Setting:	Outpatient family therapy clinic
Client:	J.W., a 32-year-old married mother
Nursing Diagnoses:	1. Anxiety, pain, and potential for violence 2. Altered social isolation 3. Ineffective coping 4. Powerlessness: all related to increasing pain and anger around her menstrual period

J.'s symptoms had been getting progressively worse over the past several years. Now she was missing work at least 1 day a month because of severe menstrual cramping. She resented having to use her allowance of "personal days" to sit at home curled up around a heating pad and was afraid something was terribly wrong with her body and her mind. Her family was beginning to suffer from her unpredictable outbursts of rage, which appeared to be completely out of proportion to the event that triggered them. She felt edgy and anxious for many days prior to her period and felt some relief only after her period started. She had decreased the amount of caffeine in her diet and added regular exercise to her daily routine. Her gynecologist had prescribed several different birth control pills in an attempt to decrease her pain and moodiness, but the medications had caused a variety of side effects, such as breast tenderness and nausea.

As her symptoms escalated and her output at work deteriorated, J.'s boss suggested that she consult the company employee assistance plan counselor. The intake questionnaire that J. filled out for her first appointment covered her history of physical symptoms; previous treatment; her relationship with her family of origin and present family; any experience with physical, emotional, or sexual abuse; and her past and present use of alcohol and drugs. The therapist noticed that J. had answered several of the questions rather briefly and had not answered the abuse questions at all.

On questioning, the therapist discovered that J. had been raped as an 18-year-old university student, but had never reported it for fear her parents would find out and insist that she return home to attend a local community college. Her father had opposed her going out of state to school and, she feared, would have been very angry if he had found out that she had been walking home from the library alone late at night. She had no idea how he would respond if he learned that she had been raped. J. also stated that she did not consider this incident "sexual abuse," because it had happened only once and she thought abuse meant something that went on over a period of time. Shortly after the rape, she had begun to experiment with marijuana. Although she no longer used marijuana, she did admit to drinking more than she should.

J.'s therapist referred her to an intensive 2-week group program for people who had been sexually abused and saw her twice a week for individual sessions. During the daily 3-hour group sessions, the members talked about their sexual trauma, its effect on their lives, and their present feelings. J. began to understand the severity of her trauma and the danger of not being able to talk about what had happened to her. She learned about body memories and the physical pain that may result from unexpressed emotions. She began to express the fear, anger, and sadness that she had about her rape. She talked about it and wrote about it in her journal. She videotaped herself talking about the rape and watched the tape with her therapist, noticing when she was able to connect with her feelings, when she talked about it as if it had happened to someone else, and when she minimized the impact that it had on her.

For J., the portion of the program that had the most benefit was learning to do anger work. In her own words,

> I had no idea how not allowing myself to express my feelings was continuing to cause me problems, years after I thought I was "over" the rape. Doing anger work was the ritual that saved me. In my family, only my Dad ever expressed any real anger; the rest of us just kept it inside and believed that it was "unladylike" to show any outward expression of anger. In group I learned several ways to get the anger out without hurting myself or anyone else. Each session I took a few moments to breathe deeply and then put on baseball gloves, took an aluminum baseball bat and hit a tethered punching bag as hard as I could for 30 seconds. Sometimes I shouted, "No!" or "It wasn't my fault!" as I hit the bag, and sometimes I just focused on the energy I felt in my body. I was too terrified to move or speak when I was raped, and this ritual seemed to liberate all the feelings I had stuffed into my body over the years. After I hit the bag, I talked with the group about what had happened and how I felt and wrote about it in my journal that night. Frequently I started out feeling sad and then got angry about how that unknown rapist was causing me pain after all these years.
>
> As the program continued and my period approached, I realized that my physical and emotional symptoms were much less than they had been. After the group sessions were over, I continued to do the anger work at home. I found that, if I didn't, I would lash out at my kids or begin to feel depressed again. My family helped me come up with some pretty creative ways to express my anger, from throwing ice cubes at the outside brick wall to throwing balls of clay against an old tarp we nailed to the back of the garage. I think this could feel out of control and crazy if I wasn't very attentive to the ritual aspects of it. I always take time to get centered, always use the right equipment to keep from hurting myself, time-limit myself to 30 to 60 seconds, and

> stay focused on what I'm angry about. Taking time afterward to either talk or write about my feelings gives me an opportunity to ease back into my daily routine with a much better sense of myself.

After the intensive program, J. continued to see her therapist to process the rape and to counteract its indirect impact on her family life and work activities. Her cramping and moodiness progressively lessened. She now gets through her monthly period with a minimum of discomfort.

Evaluation

With the client, the nurse determines whether the client outcomes for sexual abuse interventions (see Table 16–1) were successfully achieved. To evaluate the session further, the nurse may again explore the subjective effects of the experience with the client (Exhibit 16–1).

Many strategies for dealing with sexual abuse have yet to be examined in a controlled fashion. Most nurses and therapists who use them do so because of an intuitive sense of their safety and the rewards of seeing their clients do well when these strategies are judiciously employed.

Professionals who work with survivors of violence or abuse in hospitals, private practices, or agencies; with individuals or groups; with inpatients or outpatients need openness and creativity. Candid communication and a spirit of sharing both our successes and our failures with other

---

Exhibit 16–1 Evaluating the Client's Subjective Experience of Sexual Abuse Interventions

1. Was this intervention a new experience for you? Can you describe it?
2. Can you describe any shift in physical or emotional experience after the intervention?
3. Did the experience bring up new information for you concerning your abuse?
4. Did the experience change in any way how you think and feel about your past?
5. Did you stay grounded throughout the intervention? If not, what triggered your dissociation?
6. Did you feel safe during the experience?
7. What would you change about this experience to make it more meaningful for you?
8. Would you like to try this again?
9. What is your next step (or your plan) to integrate this on a daily basis?

nurses and counselors will help our profession embrace the best and discard the less than effective approaches.

DIRECTIONS FOR FUTURE RESEARCH

1. Determine if clients who retrieve repressed memories by using hypnosis and imagery heal faster than those clients who do not use these interventions.
2. Measure the effectiveness of videotaping the disclosure of abuse to help clients develop empathy for themselves and move beyond blocked emotions.
3. Determine the possible beneficial effects of biofeedback for mirroring both activities that increase and activities that decrease anxiety. Quantify the effect of learning that one has control over one's body and its responses.
4. Evaluate the degree to which the use of these strategies reduces the time a client spends in therapy.

NURSE HEALER REFLECTIONS

After reading this chapter, the nurse healer will be able to answer or begin a process of answering the following questions:

- What feelings come up for me when I am working with a client who has been sexually, physically, or emotionally abused?
- Am I comfortable working with clients who may be expressing deep feelings of sadness, anger, or loss?
- How does this work affect my relationships with my co-workers, immediate family, and extended family?

NOTES

1. W. Maltz, *The Sexual Healing Journey: A Guide for Survivors of Sexual Abuse* (New York: Harper Perennial, 1991).
2. E. Bass and L. Davis, *The Courage To Heal* (New York: Harper Perennial, 1988), 73.
3. K. Meiselman, *Resolving the Trauma of Incest: Reintegration Therapy with Survivors* (San Francisco: Jossey-Bass, 1990).
4. S. Sgroi, *Vulnerable Populations: Evaluation and Treatment of Sexually Abused Children and Adult Survivors* (New York: Free Press, 1988).
5. K. Scott, Childhood Sexual Abuse: Impact on a Community's Mental Health Status, *Child Abuse and Neglect* 16(1992):285–295.

6. D. Finkelhor, *A Sourcebook on Child Sexual Abuse* (Newbury Park, CA: Sage Publications, 1986).
7. Sgroi, *Vulnerable Populations.*
8. D.F. Bruckner and P.E. Johnson, Treatment for Adult Male Victims of Childhood Sexual Abuse, *Social Casework: The Journal of Contemporary Social Work* 68 (1987):81–88.
9. Meiselman, *Resolving the Trauma of Incest.*
10. S. Brown, *Counseling Victims of Violence* (Alexandria, VA: American Association for Counseling and Development, 1991), 22.
11. Ibid., 6.
12. C. Courtois, *Healing the Incest Wound: Adult Survivors in Therapy* (New York: W.W. Norton, 1988).
13. Maltz, *The Sexual Healing Journey.*
14. Courtois, *Healing the Incest Wound.*
15. K. Kunzman, *The Healing Way: Adult Recovery from Childhood Sexual Abuse* (New York: Harper & Row, 1990).
16. Maltz, *The Sexual Healing Journey.*
17. Y. Dolen, *Resolving Sexual Abuse: Solution Focused Therapy and Eriksonian Hypnosis for Adult Survivors* (New York: W.W. Norton, 1991).
18. Courtois, *Healing the Incest Wound.*
19. Maltz, *The Sexual Healing Journey.*
20. Dolen, *Resolving Sexual Abuse.*
21. Ibid.
22. E. Westerlund, *Women's Sexuality after Childhood Incest* (New York: W.W. Norton, 1992).
23. D. Siegal and C. Romig, Treatment of Adult Survivors of Childhood Sexual Assault: Imagery within a Systemic Framework, *American Journal of Family Therapy* 16 (1988):229–241.
24. S. Lankton and C. Lankton, *The Answer Within: A Clinical Framework of Eriksonian Hypnotherapy* (New York: Brunner/Mazel, 1983).
25. A. Toufexis, Dr. Jacobs' Alternative Mission, *Time*, March 1, 1993, 43–44.
26. K. Gaarder and P. Montgomery, *Clinical Biofeedback: A Procedural Manual* (Baltimore: Williams & Wilkins, 1977).
27. Maltz, *The Sexual Healing Journey.*
28. Meiselman, *Resolving the Trauma of Incest.*
29. D. Siegal and C. Romig, Memory Retrieval in Treating Adult Survivors of Sexual Abuse, *American Journal of Family Therapy* 18, no. 3 (1990):246–256.
30. R. Fredrickson, *Repressed Memories: A Journey to Recovery from Sexual Abuse* (New York: Simon & Schuster, 1992).
31. Kunzman, *The Healing Way.*
32. Courtois, *Healing the Incest Wound.*
33. Siegal and Romig, Treatment of Adult Survivors.
34. Dolen, *Resolving Sexual Abuse.*
35. M. Lew, *Victims No Longer: Men Recovering from Incest and Other Sexual Abuse* (New York: Harper & Row, 1988).

36. Ibid.
37. S. Martin, *Body and Soul: Physical Therapies for Everyone* (London: Penguin Books, 1989), 87.
38. Fredrickson, *Repressed Memories.*
39. Dolen, *Resolving Sexual Abuse.*
40. Ibid.
41. Fredrickson, *Repressed Memories.*
42. Courtois, *Healing the Incest Wound.*
43. Dolen, *Resolving Sexual Abuse.*
44. Fredrickson, *Repressed Memories.*
45. Dolen, *Resolving Sexual Abuse.*
46. L. Powell and S. Faherty, Treating Sexually Abused Latency Age Girls: A 20 Session Treatment Plan Utilizing Group Process and the Creative Arts Therapies, *The Arts in Psychotherapy* 17(1990):35–47.
47. Fredrickson, *Repressed Memories.*
48. I. Colby and D. Colby, Videotaping the Child Sexual Abuse Victim. *Social Casework: The Journal of Contemporary Social Work* 68(1987):117–121.
49. M. Watson and Y. Hulgus, *Videotherapy with Survivors of Childhood Sexual Abuse*, Unpublished manuscript, 1993.
50. T. Roesler, Network Therapy Using Videotape Disclosures for Adult Sexual Abuse Survivors. *Child Abuse and Neglect*, 16(1992):572–583.
51. Courtois, *Healing the Incest Wound.*
52. T. Trepper and M. Barrett, *Systemic Treatment of Incest: A Therapeutic Handbook* (New York: Brunner/Mazel, 1989).
53. Lew, *Victims No Longer.*
54. J. Cooney, *Coping with Sexual Abuse* (New York: Risen, 1987).
55. Courtois, *Healing the Incest Wound.*
56. Lew, *Victims No Longer.*
57. M. Watson, Personal communication, September 9, 1992.
58. Fredrickson, *Repressed Memories.*
59. Ibid.

SUGGESTED READING

E. Bass and L. Davis, *The Courage To Heal: A Guide for Women Survivors of Child Sexual Abuse* (New York: Harper Perennial, 1988).

L. Davis, *Allies in Healing: When the Person You Love Was Sexually Abused as a Child* (New York: Harper Perennial, 1991).

W. Maltz, *The Sexual Healing Journey: A Guide for Survivors of Sexual Abuse* (New York: Harper Perennial, 1991).

J. Pennebaker, *Opening Up: The Healing Power of Confiding in Others* (New York: Avon Books, 1990).

VISION OF HEALING

Releasing Attachment

Nothing prepares us completely for our own death or for the death of a loved one. Although everyone knows that we will all die, most people have become so accustomed to their bodies that they fear death or view it as a tragedy. Much emphasis in modern culture is placed on extending life. Medicine's highest duty has become to preserve life at all costs, often despite pain and suffering. When we choose to prolong life, however, we deny death. One's soul may literally die in agony before the physical body dies.

The most common sense of time is that it is the same for everybody—that real time flows in a linear sequence and is divisible into past, present, and future. Despite the notion that life is a series of episodic events from birth to death, it has been proven that time is very different from this classic Newtonian model. We are dependent on an external reality when we think of these events in a linear fashion, but the only way we can experience birth, health, illness, and death is by our senses, by our own internal experience. Thus, our meaning in life determines our sense of time.[1] *Thoughts of death often evoke words such as desperate, panic, final, always, ending, or forever. These words create a constricted sense of time and inflict fear and urgency on our experiences. Because our experience of time is bound to our senses, we can learn to expand time, not constrict it with fear and worries.*

We can also gain insight from the Eastern world view, which approaches life and death as complementary dimensions of the same unified experience. Death is always present and everywhere with life. To experience one is simultaneously to experience the other. The deathing process begins with the little daily deaths that prepare us for the death moment.[2] *These little deaths include disappointments at work or with family and friends, goals not accomplished, or temporary illnesses (e.g., allergies, ulcers, infection). These little deaths can also occur as realizations that we should release old behaviors and relationships that no longer serve us in order to allow room for new behaviors, relationships, and possibilities.*

True healing and dying in peace come from releasing our attachment to the physical body.[3] *We must learn to open our body-mind-spirit to healing, which comes from within. The paradox is that, although this healing awareness may seem to be rare, it is a very ordinary and natural event available to each of us at all times. As we practice living in peace, we enter a healing state in which our questions about the complementary nature of living and dying are answered. The insight comes from our own inner wisdom and strength.*

Many fears surrounding death have to do with our ego, the separate individual I-ness, our identifying with personal mental images of objects, desires, wants, and needs.[4] *The will to live is very strong, and it is hard to give up our individual personalities and bodies with which we so identify. The ego keeps us separate from the grander scheme of totality—of beingness, connectedness, and wholeness. We can learn to tap our human capacity to step aside, listen to our inner voice, and experience our thoughts, feelings, and images without attachment, however. Going to the core of true listening to our inner wisdom breaks the ego attachment as we move toward the death moment and know that death is near.*

NOTES

1. L. Dossey, *Recovering the Soul* (New York: Bantam Books, 1989).
2. A. Sheikh and K. Sheikh, *Death Imagery* (Milwaukee, WI: American Imagery Institute, 1991).
3. S. Levine, *A Gradual Awakening* (New York: Anchor Press, 1979).
4. K. Wilbur, *Grace and Grit* (Boston: Shambhala Publications, 1991).

Chapter 17

Peaceful Deathing and Death

Barbara Montgomery Dossey

NURSE HEALER OBJECTIVES

Theoretical

- Analyze the five-stage program to create empowering mythologies that will evoke courage in deathing.
- Discuss with colleagues difficult issues surrounding the care of dying people.
- Interview patients who have experienced near death awareness.

Clinical

- Develop a co-meditation class that includes demonstration and experiential sessions.
- Explore personal myths and beliefs about death with colleagues.

Personal

- Plan your ideal death.
- Record several imagery scripts and experience the letting go with these exercises.

DEFINITIONS

Death: a moment in time.
Deathing: the conscious preparation for the moment of death.[1]

Nearing Death Awareness: the dying person's knowledge of death and attempts to describe this other world to health care providers, family, and friends.

THEORY AND RESEARCH

Myths and Beliefs

Myths are our storylines, values, beliefs, and images; they are our personal manual about the meaning and the journey of the human spirit.[2] Myths help us seek the unfolding mystery in life. In seeking life's meaning and purpose, personal myths help us manifest hope, learn to accept life's struggles and challenges, and deal with life's ambiguity and uncertainty. Myths help us recognize strengths, choices, goals, and faith. They also help us to assess our self-world, to recognize our capacity to pursue personal interests, and to demonstrate love of self and self-forgiveness. Myths provide a sense of connection with a divinity, the universe, and a sense of oneness with all of life and nature.

Throughout life we create many myths; some serve us well, while others hinder our healing journey. From their work on rituals for living and dying, Feinstein and Mayo suggest a five-stage program to create empowering mythologies that will evoke courage in deathing and, thus, toward peaceful death.[3] Each of the five stages has a specific purpose and corresponds with one of the phases in the natural development of personal myths. The first stage deals with recognizing our deepest fears about death. The second stage helps us search for counterforces to our fear of death. The third stage attempts to resolve the natural conflict between the prevailing myth identified in the first stage and the emerging countermyth identified in the second stage by integrating the best of each side into a renewed mythology. In the fourth stage, the deeper solutions to inner conflicts are further articulated, expanded, and anchored in our being. The task in the fifth stage is to weave our renewed mythology into daily life involving three personal rituals: (1) attending to that which will survive us, (2) creating ceremony for the final hour and beyond, and (3) establishing peaceful moments with what we do between now and the final hour.

In 1979, the Senior Actualization and Growth Exploration (SAGE) study began to question society's beliefs about older people and their potential.[4] The researchers taught seniors deep relaxation, biofeedback, breathing exercises, meditation, yoga, and ways to expand creativity through movement, music, art, education, and group discussion. This project not only helped the participants reshape their "declining years" to concepts and life styles of healthy aging, but also gave them new, practical ways to cope with personal problems and a new self-image. With healthier life styles, most people can add a vital 30 or more years to their lifespan. We also have more time to practice a new way of living so that dying in peace can be possible.

Nearing Death Awareness

During their many years of hospice nursing, Callanan and Kelly have identified several recurring themes in the stories of dying patients and their families.[5] Messages about death awareness from dying persons fall into two categories: (1) attempts to describe what they are experiencing while dying and (2) requests for something that they need for a peaceful death. This awareness is not to be confused with near death experiences that happen as a result of cardiac arrest, drowning, or trauma in which a person suddenly leaves this life, but quickly returns. In a state of near death awareness, a person's dying is slower, often because of a progressive illness such as acquired immunodeficiency syndrome (AIDS), cancer, or heart or lung disease. The person remains inside the body, but at the same time becomes aware of a dimension that lies beyond, a drifting between this world and another. The slower dying process allows the dying person to have more time to assess his or her life and to determine what remains to be finished before death. Some dying patients try to describe being in two places at once, or somewhere in between. It is a time for a caregiver to respond to their wishes and needs, and to listen to what death is like for them. This is also a final gift to prepare each of us for what may happen in our deathing.

There is a difference between the dying statements of individuals who are tired of living but do not believe that it is time to die, and the dying statements of those who are truly ready to depart. The clarity with which the words are spoken, the look from their eyes, or their touch are like no other statements, looks, or touches that have been made before or during the deathing process.

Healing Loss and Grief

A necessary process in deathing and death is grief. The more bonded and intimate two people have been, the more severe the grief. Mayo states that appropriate grief work has three characteristics.[6] First, it furthers the healthy grieving process by encouraging ventilation, planning, and insight. Second, it does not exploit others; the mourner has a healing team to provide comfort, but does not act as a parasite who feeds on another's energy. Transactions are caring and clear. The mourner continues to recognize the importance of one's inner work. Third, appropriate grief work cannot be rushed. It takes time to believe genuinely that death has occurred.

NURSING PROCESS

Assessment

In preparing to use interventions for deathing in peace, the nurse assesses the following parameters:

- the different emotions that surface during deathing:
  1. guilt: blame of self and others over management of the dying person; distress over inability to decrease pain.
  2. anger: toward God, disease, family/significant others, doctors, neglect, or survivors; over inability to "fix things" physically, emotionally, and spiritually.
  3. laughter: the shortest distance between two people; relationship between comedy and tragedy (joy and sadness pathways cannot operate simultaneously).
  4. love: an essential element in deathing; a state of self-giving and presence of beingness of a person, where openness and willingness exist for self or another; the network that brings and weaves families/significant others together to work through deathing and move into total acceptance of death.
  5. fear: often evocation of separateness and aloneness, but can become a path leading deeper into the present moment; useful in that it reveals areas of resistance; return to unconditional love after release of fear.
  6. forgiveness: essential element for inner peace; an exercise in compassion that is both a process and an attitude.
  7. faith: the larger vision of existence, which is different for each person; help to harness energy to evoke healing resources and power; understanding that death changes nothing—death is merely a change of worlds.
  8. hope: support of patient or family/significant others during death's darkness; hope for decreased pain and increased physical and spiritual comfort, for a miracle, for peace of mind, for a

remission, for peaceful death transition, and for acceptance of a shorter life than expected or the death of a loved one.

- the patient's interactions with others and the effect of the patient's emotions on these interactions

Nursing Diagnoses

The following nursing diagnoses compatible with the interventions for deathing in peace and that are related to the nine human response patterns of Unitary Person (see Chapter 7) are as follows:

- Exchanging: Altered circulation
  Altered oxygenation
  Altered body systems
- Communicating: Altered communication
  Effective communication (see nearing death awareness)
- Valuing: Spiritual distress
  Spiritual well-being (see nearing death awareness)
- Choosing: Ineffective individual/family coping
- Moving: Self-care deficit
- Perceiving: Body image disturbance
  Powerlessness
  Hopelessness
- Feeling: Pain
  Anxiety
  Grieving
  Fear

Patient Outcomes

Table 17–1 guides the nurse in patient outcomes, nursing prescriptions, and evaluation for assisting patients and their families/significant others in deathing and death.

Plan and Interventions

The following guidelines are appropriate for both the dying person and the caregivers, whether family, friends, or nurse. They are helpful in all settings.

Table 17–1 Nursing Interventions: Deathing in Peace

Patient Outcomes	*Nursing Prescriptions*	*Evaluation*
The patient will demonstrate an understanding of reasons for ongoing assessment and management of anxiety, including • quiet environment • explanations of all personnel, procedures, and equipment • touch and reassurance by nurse • relaxation skills	Continue to reassess states of anxiety and provide ways to decrease anxiety. • Provide quiet environment. • Explain all interventions. • Offer reassurance. • Teach relaxation and imagery skills.	The patient demonstrated an understanding of the reasons for assessment and management of anxiety.
The patient will verbalize feelings of anxiety and will talk spontaneously about fears. (If the patient is intubated, the patient and the nurse use specific communication codes.)	Provide quality time for the patient to share worries and fears. Use common symbols for communication if the patient is intubated.	The patient verbalized anxiety and fears.
The patient will use effective coping mechanisms during course of illness.	Focus on the patient's strengths.	The patient used effective coping mechanisms during the course of illness. (List specific examples.)
The family will communicate stressors associated with the patient's illness to staff.	Allow time for the family to express worries and fears.	The family/significant others communicated stressors to staff.
The patient will verbalize fears of death.	Be present with the patient and allow time for the patient to talk about fears of dying.	The patient talked of death.
The family/significant others will verbalize fears that the patient may die.	If death seems imminent, be with the patient and family to assist them through the death.	The patient's family/significant others acknowledged the impending death and shared feelings about death.
The family/significant others will receive support from nurses and clergy.	Provide spiritual support for the patient through presence, life review, prayer, talking, and handholding. Allow the family to be with the patient. Call clergy for assistance, if requested.	The family/significant others received spiritual support and talked to nurses and clergy.

continues

Table 17-1 continued

Patient Outcomes	*Nursing Prescriptions*	*Evaluation*
The patient, family, and significant others will express fears and other feelings associated with dying and death.	Assist the patient and family to focus on what has been accomplished in life. Provide as much privacy as possible.	The patient and the patient's family focused on life accomplishments.
The patient will experience closure on matters of daily living.	Provide the opportunity to complete "unfinished business." Fulfill the patient's requests to see a member of the family, lawyer, member of the clergy, or a physician.	The patient and the family completed unfinished business.
The patient will be comfortable and participative until death occurs.	Evaluate the procedures and treatments that can be discontinued to make the patient more comfortable. Make provisions for someone to remain with the patient all the time if so desired by the patient.	Procedures and treatments were used for comfort only.

Before the Deathing Process Interaction

- Spend a few moments centering yourself to recognize your presence.
- Begin the session with intention to facilitate healing and peaceful deathing.

At the Beginning of the Deathing Process

- Encourage the patient and the family/significant others as the caregiver(s) in the following:
    1. Set realistic goals.
    2. Identify different behaviors that have surfaced in their interactions.
    3. Gather a healing team and honor the patient's personal needs and feelings in order to avoid more suffering.
    4. Accept current circumstances, and release things that are beyond their control.

5. Take frequent breaks, at least 20 minutes daily, to evoke quality quiet time with relaxation, imagery, music, meditation, prayer, journal keeping, or dreamwork to assist in the letting go process.
6. Exercise, take long hot baths or showers, eat nutritious foods, eliminate excess caffeine or junk food, and ask other people for relief.

- Encourage the client and caregivers to tell themselves over and over what a good job they are doing. Repeating it helps in releasing guilt, anger, and frustration.

During the Deathing Process

- Consider the one who is dying, as this person is usually the best teacher about what is right. The place of death is not as important as the care, trust, compassion, acceptance, and love that is provided and shared in deathing.
- Determine the care needed. Will the dying person receive better care in a hospital, in a hospice, or at home? What kind of medical treatment, technology, and equipment is needed? Can a hospice nurse or health care professional assist with treatments and medication? What expenses will be involved? What expenses will be covered by insurance? Is the patient eligible for state or federal disability payments, veteran's or Social Security benefits, or Medicaid or Medicare? Who will assume the care 24 hours a day? Who will provide respite care? Are there children at home who also need continuous care? Can the care of the dying person and young children both be managed? Will organs be donated?
- Explore the advantages of the home for dying. The patient and the family are free to do anything they wish because they have control to change or alter routines and schedules, for example. In addition, the continuous support of family and friends is available; meals are prepared fresh and served with specific attention to details; less stress is incurred from traveling to and from the hospital or hospice; there is a unique beauty in familiar surroundings; there is quality time available to focus on inner work for the moment of death; feelings and emotions are experienced in a different way because of closeness with fewer interruptions. Finally, the patient and family can make most of the decisions regarding care, medication, and treatments and can ask advice from professionals when needed.
- Integrate therapies. Does the dying person believe that medical and nonmedical modalities are complementary? How motivated is he or

she to try nonmedical resources (e.g., acupuncture, touch therapies). What nonmedical resources are available? Does the dying person really want to try different modalities, or is he or she receiving so much advice about therapies that the response is passive rather than active?

- Incorporate the senses in rituals.
    1. *Touching*. Lovingly, freely, and joyfully convey through your hands what your heart is feeling. Touching is a powerful way to break the illusion of separateness, loneliness, fear; it may evoke laughter, calmness, or tears. Create times to give and get hugs.
    2. *Smelling*. Use lotions and colognes with mild fragrances, remembering that illness will probably change the types of fragrances that can be tolerated.
    3. *Tasting*. Remember that tasting varies with degrees of illness, but stays with us until the end of life.
    4. *Seeing*. Arrange in a pleasing manner healing objects and different touchstones that have special meaning and symbolize people, places, and events in the patient's life. Because of an increased sensitivity to light, a room that receives soft, subdued rays from the sun can bring balance to surroundings. Lighter colors are usually more soothing.
    5. *Hearing*. Sharp to the end of life, so special words at death can be heard. Remember being present in silence, sitting or holding one another.
- Practice sitting quietly with relaxation, meditation, or prayer. Gentle sounds from wind chimes or audio tapes of environmental recordings of ocean waves, wind, rain, birds, and music (e.g., harp, flute, stringed instruments) can offer a sense of peace. Music thanatology, referred to as sung prayer, indicates that the human voice, when chanting or singing, brings balance to the dying—dissolving fears and lessening the burden, sorrows, and wounds[7]; using words ending in "ing" such as releasing, floating, softening, or words ending in "ness" such as openness, beingness, awareness, vastness, help the patient to relax.
- Recognize the patient's going in and out of spaces. The moment of death itself has no pain, but is a reflex last breath. It opens up very special exchanges of intention, intimacy, and bonding where the patient may share the dying spaces. The patient's eyes can take on a staring, a glazing, a spaciness so different that the patient appears

to be going somewhere else, to another realm of knowing, or to be focusing on something that the caregiver cannot see; the dying person can return with a smile and possibly share that he or she was in a space of peace.

- Learn about changes in the body during deathing. Knowing what body changes to expect as death approaches helps family anticipate personal healing rituals and removes the fear, shock, and mystery from the moment of death.
- Understand and accept the body's shutting down. The conscious dying person knows that the physical body is shutting down, that it is time to leave the physical body, and can consciously choose to shut physical life down. The caregiver and family/significant others journey with the dying person as far as possible and then tell the person it is all right to leave; this can evoke the purest, most special moments for all involved.

At the Moment of Death

- Prepare rituals for the moment of death. The dying person usually has serenity and inner calm, particularly if healing rituals have been involved during deathing. Before the dying person's eyes close, tight brow muscles may become relaxed; the peace in the face or within the room is often palpable.
- Trust inner wisdom of touching, holding, talking, and how to be with the dying one; deepen hope and faith for a peaceful crossing into death and beyond.
- Surround yourself and the dying person with the peace and the light of love, taking the energy of love and light in with each breath; imagine and experience literally going inside the breath, flowing inside the breath with co-meditation (p. 446) into the death of each moment.
- Talk to the dying loved one as restlessness or agitation moves to unresponsiveness; give gentle love squeezes, touches, and hugs; play favorite music; read poems, or say mantras and prayers. Shut the half-closed eyes, stroke and hug the physical body, and adjust the loved one's head on the pillow for the last time. Give permission for this special person to be free, to soar, to meet others who have died before. Say all you need to say, and share your own kind of blessings for the smooth transition.
- Use the patient outcomes (see Table 17–1) that were established before the deathing process and the family's/significant other's subjective experience (Exhibit 17–1) to evaluate the intervention.

- Schedule follow-up session/visit with family/significant others if appropriate.

Specific Interventions

Planning an Ideal Death (Basic to Advanced). To help patients and families experience peace in the dying process, it is important to engage them in planning. To be of maximum assistance to someone else in the deathing journey, it is helpful for the nurse to explore this journey as well. The following reflective questions provide enormous insight about death myths, beliefs, problem solving, loving, and forgiving:

- What would an ideal death be like?
- When are you going to die?
- Where are you going to die?
- Who do you want to be with you, or do you want to be alone?
- What legal matters, relationships, or other personal business must be finished?
- What have been and what are the most precious events in your life?
- Who are the important people in your life?
- Have you told them why they are important?
- Are there family or friends who need to be told special things that you have never shared?
- Do you need to forgive or be forgiven?
- Have you written your obituary or your epitaph?
- Have you completed a living will?
- What are your assets?
- What treasures do you wish to leave to specific family members or friends?
- What person/s have you appointed to be in charge of your medical decisions?
- Have you planned rituals for your burial, or a funeral, memorial service, or cremation?
- If to be buried, what do you want to be buried in?
- What kind of a coffin or container do you want for your body?
- Who will perform your burial ceremony?
- What kind of a ceremony do you want?
- Do you prefer a wake or another form of ceremony?

- What prayers, passages, poems, or music do you want to have read or spoken?
- Who will direct the ceremony? Or do you want a deathday celebration?

Part of confronting death is deciding how to use medical care and technology. As part of their right to die, individuals can decide whether they want medical treatment; what kind of treatment; and under what circumstances to start, continue, or stop treatment. The American Medical Association has created a document called the medical directive,[8] a three-page form on which an individual can record his or her wishes for four different life situations: (1) mental incompetence, (2) terminal illness, (3) irreversible coma, or (4) persistent vegetative state. It also has a place for the appointment of someone to make medical decisions for the individual, should that become necessary, and a place for information about organ donation. Since states vary in the legislative details of such documents, it is necessary to call the office of the state attorney general or consult an attorney. Furthermore, because these wishes often reflect philosophic, personal, religious, and spiritual desires, individuals should discuss these matters with the family and friends who will function on their behalf should they become incompetent.

Learning Forgiveness (Basic). Borysenko describes the steps to forgiving self and others as a parallel six-step process.[9] The six steps to forgiving ourselves are (1) taking responsibility for what we have done; (2) confessing the nature of the wrongs to ourselves, another human being, or God; (3) looking for the good points in ourselves; (4) being willing to make amends where possible, as long as we can do this without harm to ourselves or other people; (5) looking to God for help; and (6) inquiring about what we have learned.

The six steps to forgiving others are (1) recognizing that we are responsible for what we are holding onto; (2) confessing our story to ourselves, another person, and God; (3) looking for the good points in ourselves and the other person; (4) considering whether any specific action needs to be taken; (5) looking to God for help; and (6) reflecting on what we have done. These steps take time to complete. As the awareness of forgiving self and others is developed, the more we recognize unconditional love. Because it helps us connect more with our source of joy, not focusing on loss, sadness, or pain, unconditional love helps release us from fear.

Deathing in Peace: Relaxation and Imagery Scripts (Basic to Advanced). To learn how to let go of attachments, what is right and wrong, what is good and bad requires practice. Nurses encourage patients to hear their inner voice of judging and to release the judging, just to listen and be ready for the next moment of listening, and to be in the present moment. It is essential to practice opening and releasing ordinary fears in order to emerge with awareness in the healing moment. This skill assists a person to be more present when assisting another during death.

Patients and their caregivers may set aside 20 minutes or more several times a day to practice opening to the moment. It may be helpful to create a special relaxation and imagery tape as part of a personal ritual to practice releasing and letting go. The breathing, relaxation, imagery, and music scripts that follow are important experiential exercises to help self and others learn the letting go experience of calming the mind and creating a sense of spaciousness within the body (see also Chapters 22 and 23). Recording one or several of these scripts, after a 5- to 10-minute relaxation exercise, allows the dying patient and caregivers to use them repeatedly, even when professionals are not present. The following scripts are adapted from the work of Stephen Levine, and Anees and Katrina Sheikh.[10–12]

Script: **Introduction.** *(Name), as your mind becomes clearer and clearer, feel it becoming more and more alert. Somewhere deep inside of you, a brilliant light begins to glow. Sense this happening. The light grows brighter and more intense. Breathe into it. Energize it with your breath. The light is powerful and penetrating, and a beam begins to grow out from it. The beam shines into the core of your spirit.*

Script: **Letting Go.** *Notice the rhythm of the breath . . . becoming more aware of all the sensations that arise from the breath. Watching . . . noticing . . . feeling . . . as the breath begins to breathe you. As you become more aware of the breath, let your conscious awareness release the notion of breathing . . . becoming more and more aware as the breath arises in each moment. As interfering thoughts arise, let them float on . . . dissolving into awareness . . . quieting the constant chatter of the ego. . . .*

Script: **Opening the Heart.** *Relax into the moment of the awareness of the breath. . . . Let the rhythm of the breath just breathe you. Allow a fearful image to emerge in thought . . . noticing where it is in the body . . . letting the feelings of fear be in the body. In a way that seems right for you . . . let the fear move to the center of your chest . . . to the center of your heart. There is space within your heart to let the fear be . . . noticing the sensations of fear as they rest in the spaciousness of your heart center . . . opening* *and softening . . . opening and releasing denial . . . letting the fears become what they need to be . . . opening and accepting. Within the center of your heart . . . your love and compassion are present to let the fear(s) be present.*

Script: **Forgiving Self and Others.** *Relax into the moment of the awareness of the breath. . . . Let the breath just begin to breathe you. Allow yourself to let an image emerge of a person . . . alive or dead . . . who brings forth feelings of resentment. As that image is forming, . . . notice the spaciousness of your heart . . . and the openness of your heart center. Send the image of the person who causes you to feel resentment into your heart center. From the spaciousness of the center of your heart . . . hold the image of this person as you repeat, "I forgive you for anything you may have done in the past . . . in thoughts, words, or actions that may have caused you or me pain. I forgive you."*

As you do this, . . . notice any change in the feelings of resentment . . . opening and softening to the moment. If any feelings such as pain . . . tightness . . . or any other body sensation arise . . . just let them be . . . watching . . . noticing . . . all changes . . . opening into the moment. Just continue to focus on the image of this person . . . speaking from your heart . . . releasing resentment . . . pain . . . forgiving yourself . . . forgiving others.

Script: **Releasing Grief and Pain.** *With one or both thumbs or the palms of your hands, locate the point just at the base of your sternum, and press into this area; feel the point of maximum pressure for you. Notice any sensations of tension, pain, or aches that result from sadness, grief, and loss. Continue to hold the thoughts, feelings of yourself, the loved one you have lost, or any other person or issues that cause you loss. If it seems right, as often as needed, return yourself to the power of the awareness of your own breath as it breathes you.*

Relax into the moment of the awareness of the breath. . . . Let the breath just begin to breathe you. Within your heart just now may be grief and pain . . . the feelings of loss . . . the heaviness of sadness. With your thumb(s) or palm(s) of your hand(s) . . . press into the area below your sternum . . . become aware of any sensations of pressure, pain, or any aches. Continue to hold the pressure. As you notice the pressure in this area . . . breathe slowly into the sensations as they arise . . . emerging through the many levels of protection. Let yourself open into the pain . . . being with the feelings that come . . . not holding back . . . not pushing away . . . opening . . . softening.

Observing and experiencing . . . allowing the pain . . . the fear . . . the sadness . . . the loss . . . just to be . . . not evaluating. Continuing to hold the pressure . . . releasing control . . . become aware of the fear . . . all fears that come as you feel the fear of losing your loved one . . . all loved ones. And become aware of your fear of your own death . . . any pain, fear . . . anger . . . sadness.

Let all your feeling now penetrate to the center of your heart . . . opening to the moment . . . receiving the love . . . the caring . . . the warmth . . . coming from the center of your heart. And now . . . let yourself release the physical pressure . . . continuing to receive the love and caring from your heart center.

While consciously living, it is possible to experience conscious dying. It is helpful to use a relaxation or imagery technique in order to become grounded before the exercise. After the exercise, this same technique can facilitate the return to full alertness and readiness to proceed with daily activities. *These scripts are intended to be a rehearsal, not an actual shutting down and leaving of the physical body.*

Learning to confront our own death helps us be more present to assist others in facing their death. It reaffirms that we really need to do nothing but be present with another and speak with our hearts in dying time. The nurse may begin with an extended head to toe general relaxation or other breathing exercise (see Chapter 22 or the previous scripts). Because the experience of dying can be described as melting or dissolving away at the moment of death, the words *dissolving* and *melting* are used in the script. To continue this script, the four elements of the body described by the ancients—earth, water, fire, and air—are used to represent decomposition as the body dissolves.

Script: **Conscious Dying.** *Relax into the moment of the awareness of the breath. Let the breath just continue to breathe you. As you focus on the breath, . . . begin to notice how the breath lets you move from heavy sensations in the body to the lighter . . . subtle body of awareness . . . all awareness on the breath . . . the breath in . . . and the breath out. . . . Let yourself be in the heavy body . . . and now all awareness on being in the light body. . . . The breath is all that there is . . . just breathing . . . let each thought dissolve into the breath . . . melting into the* *breath . . . awareness of the light body . . . and now letting the breath go . . . this is the final breath . . . let the breath in . . . and the breath out . . . dissolving . . . opening to death . . . and let yourself die.*

Script: **Earth.** *The body . . . solid . . . heavy . . . mass . . . compact . . . all changing as death comes . . . the vital body losing its form . . . weakening and dissolving . . . becoming thinner like the elements of earth . . . changing . . . dissolving . . . all parts dissolving . . . organs . . . extremities . . . muscles . . . all senses dissolving . . . fading away . . . melting away. . . .*

Script: **Water.** *All feelings becoming one . . . dissolving . . . all sensations dissolving . . . body fluids that flow through you . . . drying up . . . all body organs closing down . . . dissolving. . . .*

Script: **Fire.** *The fire of life within you . . . going out . . . all body warmth and heat leaving . . . all organs ceasing to function . . . your body becoming cooler and cooler . . . your sense of boundary is dissolving . . . all senses dissolving . . . breath is dissolving. . . .*

Script: **Air.** *Your body is without function . . . the air is the element of consciousness . . . dissolving . . . all sensation . . . all feeling . . . all senses have gone . . . body boundaries are no more . . . light . . . melting . . . dissolving . . . no separate body . . . no separate mind . . . all separateness dissolving . . . all in the vastness of oneness. . . .*

Take a few slow, energizing breaths and, as you come back to this awareness, know that whatever is right for you at this point in time is unfolding just as it should and that you have done your best, regardless of the outcome.

Script: **Moving into the Light.** Adapted from Levine's work, the following script is useful for someone who is preparing for the death moment or for a family member or friend whose loved one has just died.[13] It can be expanded as needed. The four elements part of the imagery script may also be used to assist one whose death is imminent.

Fill yourself with an awareness of brilliance of clear light . . . a pure light within you and surrounding you . . . go forward . . . releasing anything that keeps you separate . . . pushing away nothing . . . spaciousness . . . releasing . . . dissolving . . . all body . . . dissolving into consciousness itself. . . . Let go of all distractions. . . . Listen and be with the transition . . . what is called death has arrived. . . . You are not alone . . . many have gone before you . . . let yourself go . . . into the clear light.

The dying person may move in and out of sleep or comatose states after this script or the conscious dying script. The nurse or family member sits with the person as long as necessary to bring closure to this time. If the person lingers a while longer, the nurse or family member may close with the following phrases.

Script: **Closure.** *Take a few slow, energizing breaths and, as you come back to this awareness, know that whatever is right for you at this point in time is unfolding just as it should, and that you have done your best, regardless of the outcome.*

The Pain Process (Basic). In 90 to 99 percent of cases, pain can be managed. Pain medication should be evaluated at least every 72 hours. When giving the medication, the nurse reminds the patient that the pain medication is in the body and working.

Although the physical body can experience pain, the mind's fear of the pain is often more intense. Acute pain has qualities of suddenness and surprise that can evoke anxiety and fear. The best thing to do with this suddenness is to encourage the dying person to breathe rhythmically and soften into the pain to decrease the resistance to the experience. Relaxation, imagery, or acupressure may be combined with pain medication. Even the worst of pain can be shifted in many ways. For example, shifting the pain experience by calling it sensations rather than pain often reduces discomfort. It also helps to encourage the person to make decisions over which he or she has control, such as decisions about medications, treatments, and daily routines.

When guiding the person in pain, the nurse may suggest allowing pain images and the different felt experiences to emerge. Each person enters pain in a way that opens in the moment, and each person will know how far to go in exploring the pain. Common expressions an individual may have about the pain (e.g., "pain attacks," "it has a grip on me and takes my breath away," "it has a loud and deafening pulsation," "it is violent and unrelenting") create negative images that may interfere with the emergence of healing images. These negative images may become positive if the person focuses on "the grip of pain being released and a deep belly breath coming forth evenly and effortlessly" or "the pulsating sound becoming like the falling of gentle raindrops or falling snowflakes." Different relaxation and imagery exercises help the person practice "letting go of this solidness" of the physical body. Not only does this letting go help ease both physical and emotional pain, but also it helps the person get through difficult procedures and conflicts, and experience death with peace and dignity.

With continued gentle exploration of opening and releasing into the pain, the person may begin to see the pain floating and diminishing. This is also a way of expanding one's sense of time. Another suggestion is to have the patient step aside in the mind and "watch the pain to see how it might be changed to release some of the pressure, resistance, and holding on to the pain." Such guidance and presence over time will help the person to stay with a focused attention to open and soften into the pain.

Blending Breaths and Co-Meditation (Basic). The simple release of the breath and the ah-h-h-h sound is an ancient ritual for dying into peace. The practice of sharing the breath with another is called "co-meditation" or "cross-breathing."[14] Co-meditation is based on the principle that respiration evokes a particular state of mind and serves as a direct link into the nervous system. There is a direct correlation between breathing and thinking. At first, the ah-h-h-h sounds may be like an echoing of words, but staying with the sounds allows the release of tension, fears, and pain. Following are the steps for co-meditation:

- Position yourself comfortably close to the person in dying time. A session may last 20 to 30 minutes or longer. Obtain whatever is necessary to make you and the person comfortable, such as pillows or a light blanket.
- Suggest to the person that watching the breath is an ancient method of calming the body and the mind. Let the person first begin noticing the rise and fall of his or her abdomen with each breath in and each breath out.
- Sitting at the person's midsection, focus on the rise and fall of the abdomen with each inhalation and each exhalation. Focus your attention on the person's lower chest area, and observe closely for the natural flow of the exhalation from the person. With this focused attention, you can begin breathing in unison with the person. At the beginning of the exhalation, begin softly and out loud the sound ah-h-h-h, matching the respiration of the person.
- Simple, powerful phrases such as "peaceful heart" or "releasing into the breath," may be said occasionally. However, the fewer words spoken, the more powerful is the breath work. If the person should fall asleep, you may wish to sit with the person for a while or sit until he or she awakes.

Mantras and Prayers (Basic). A mantra is the repetition of a word or sound; a prayer may be special phrases or repeated words. There is considerable evidence for the effectiveness of at least two forms of prayer, the "directed" and the "nondirected."[15,16] In direct prayer, the individual has a specific goal or outcome in mind. In the nondirected form, the individual takes an open-ended, nonspecific, non-goal approach.

Mantras and prayers can decrease many lonely hours at home, as well as in the hospital. They also serve as an affirmation of a deeper faith. In asking the dying person about wishes for prayers or repeated phrases, we may encourage him or her to select phrases that are short, easy to remember, and rhythmic. The personal selection of focus words enhances the faith factor.[17] It may be helpful to pray for the highest good for the dying one or ourselves rather than for what we want. If we are praying for another, we need to hold the person in our conscious thought, thereby keeping our ego out of the way and causing ourselves less grief, frustration, and fear.

Reminiscing and Life Review (Basic). A process basic to human existence is reminiscing and recounting past events, either alone or with friends. Much of our life is spent talking, thinking, or writing about plans, goals, resources, successes, disappointments, and failures. This is especially true when facing death. Life review is a process that involves reviewing present and past experiences and imaging events to come, based on previous events. (See Chapter 14 for details.)

Leavetaking Rituals (Basic). A nurse who works with survivors must remember that their grief period is unique for them. Furthermore, grief has no timetable. Healing grief requires a commitment to imagine a fulfilling life without a loved one. Action steps toward continued self-discovery after the death of a loved one include dreamwork, meditation, movement, drawing, journal keeping, crying, sighing, drumming, chanting, singing, and music, as well as the following rituals.[18]

Celebrating Holidays. Special holidays, birthdays, anniversaries, and other important dates can be a time for creating rituals to ease pain and acknowledge feelings. For example, a widow fixed a place at the Christmas dinner table for her deceased husband. She and her six children gave him a farewell toast and shared special memories of him before they ate. A young couple who had a stillborn child asked several of the nurses and the attending physician to a memorial service in the hospital chapel before the baby was taken to the funeral home. After her mother died, a woman chose to have her healing team of eight friends with her at a memorial service by the sea. The family of a teen-aged girl who died in an automobile accident had a gathering for her class and gave each person an opportunity to say special things about the girl. Her favorite music was played while dancing and singing began in her honor.

Rearranging and Giving Away. If a loved one has died at home, the family member who shared the bedroom must decide what is best to do. Some wish to rearrange the room and remove hospital beds and other equipment quickly after death. Giving away a loved one's possessions, such as special mementos of jewelry, clothes, shoes, makeup, shaving equipment, and other personal possessions, is healing.

Letting Grief Be Present. There are periods after death when a person appears brave, in control, or strong to others. Grief will come, however. It is important to share with the grieving person that there is no special way to grieve. When pain, fear, and anger can dissipate, the body-mind-spirit knows the best way to grieve. Grieving allows love to heal the loss one feels for self and the person who has died.

Sustaining Faith and Hope. There are many ways to sustain faith and awareness toward life, meaning, and purpose during grieving time. For example, survivors sometimes have a sense of talking to deceased loved ones, being enveloped in their love, and feeling their presence. People have described experiences such as having a faith in oneness, feeling an energy, vaguely sensing the presence of the deceased person, hearing the voice of the deceased giving guidance, or working on the same problem at different energy levels. For example, one woman said, "My [deceased] husband told me how to finish this business deal." Another woman created a healing ritual after the death of her husband. When the weather permitted, she would get in her truck in the evening and drive to her husband's favorite hill on their big Texas ranch. As she looked out over the prairie and gazed into the Milky Way, she would choose a bright star and carry on a dialogue with the star, experiencing a sense of unity with her deceased husband somewhere in infinity. This provided her with calmness, wisdom, and clarity of thought.

Releasing Anger and Tears. The release of anger, sadness, and tears is a cleansing process of the human spirit that makes a person more open to experience living in the moment. Holding grief in increases the suffering, fear, and separation.

Healing Memories. It is not necessary to stop thinking about the person who has died. Often, a grieving person who feels that the grief process is over finds that a memory, a song, or a meal suddenly evokes a sense of loss so deep that it seems as though it will never heal. The person needs to stay with the pain, sadness, guilt, anger, fear, or loneliness. Love and joy will begin to fill the heart again. The wisdom is to let pain in and to stay open to it, to let the pain penetrate every cell in your body, to trust pain, to know that what emerges from the pain is a new level of healing awareness.

Getting Unstuck. Grieving can bring on suffering; therefore, it may be helpful for survivors to ask for assistance from friends, family, or a health care professional to help them move past the blocks. Some people think, "It's been 6 months since my mother died [or a year since my husband, son, or wife died], why am I still depressed and cry so frequently?"

Case Studies

Case Study No. 1

Setting: Critical care unit where visiting schedule was one visitor every 2 hours.

Patient: S.R., a 30-year-old mother of three children

Nursing Diagnoses:
1. Decreased cardiac output related to end-stage heart failure.
2. Grieving related to imminent death
3. Spiritual strength related to dynamic belief systems and family/friend support

S.R. said to the nurse, "I feel death over my right shoulder. Call my husband. I need him to come and bring my children, my parents and my three friends. Tell them to come as soon as possible." The nurse also had an inner felt sense of the presence of death and began calling S.'s family. Four hours before her death, all her family was present. Her friends sang her favorite songs as one played a guitar.

Case Study No. 2

Setting: Writing thoughts about healthy grief in a letter, 4 years after son's death

Client: V.D.J., a 45-year-old professional and mother

Nursing Diagnosis: Spiritual strength related to ability to deliberate the meaning of life, death, grief, and suffering

There is a holy purpose in grief and nothing should stand in its path. Grief begins with so few words. Sounds take shape traveling from a great distance. Within, a reserve is sensed. Something sacred that holds a luminous darkness which stills the mind even as the heart shudders with waves of deep sorrow.

The natural quality of grief is ancient and bone bare. It tolerates nothing false. Grief is unrestrained; conscious effort is not required.

A mother who has lost a child learns what true freedom is. It is being cut free from the knot of habit, customs, rules. It is not being bound by considerations or even fear, for the worst has happened. Your child is dead and you live. A mother's lament begins.

Your heartbeat creates a tone for your body to hear. It drums and moves you slowly forward with your family even as you weep and prepare to say your last goodbye.

Now is not the time to be a bystander. It is crucial that you support and include your other children and family in the vigil, the wake, the funeral and burial or cremation ceremonies. They, too, are in shock and disbelief. And it doesn't end there.

Let nothing be left undone, unsaid, unwritten or unsung in this farewell. This is not the place to lose courage or even your humor, for you will need both to sustain the intense suffering you have yet to bear.

Nature provides the exact dosage for dealing with the constant strikes of pain experienced. Usually there is no real need for outside medication. Your body in its perfect wisdom gauges your requirements and numbs you accordingly. You will feel cold, but your mind/body will not allow more pain than you can tolerate. To disrupt the natural safeguards may only postpone the initial pain in your mourning process.

During the vigil and the wake your only thought is to do everything you can do to console your children and other family members. You realize they have the same concern for you. Plan the funeral ceremonies together. In the process, some small consolation may be experienced.

The Path of Grief leads inward when you watch and listen. Didn't you bring this spirit child into the world, flesh of your flesh? This last goodbye may enable you to complete the circle; keeping a vigil through the night allows you to be closer to your child.

The vigil with your child provides a place to begin to say goodbye, the goodbye you were both denied, by sudden, unexpected death. You hear yourself talking and reassuring your son.

You must now help your child to take the first steps into the Great Mystery, by talking aloud and guiding, much as you did when he was very young. Empty your mind and your heart and give him all your love and spiritual strength for his journey.

The week following the funeral I moved everything from my bedroom except basic essentials. I felt driven to sleep on a mat and to make a low altar which I filled with family photographs, mementos, and childhood treasures belonging to Sean and my children, family poetry, drawings, vigil candles, prayer fans, fresh flowers and ceremonial sage.

Prayers became conversations and chants and death songs for the son who had no time to create them for himself. Forty-nine days of talking-prayer asking the angelic beings to guide my son on his journey.

Each member of the immediate family scattered Sean's ashes in places special to him. A spirit bundle was placed and kept before the altar for him.

Always the moving between worlds; letting go of the loneliness through weeping, sound and moving prayer—to returning to repose, listening, and sitting. A year goes by.

You find it difficult to speak. Your breathing habits are changing. You become aware of differences in your breath. You sense your heart breathing, your brain breathing. You notice that when you breathe out, you see thought. Some days you don't remember breathing at all.

You keep a journal as an on-going discussion with your child, seeking solace. You somehow deal with daily life, guilt, illness, helplessness, and the grief of your other children.

Four more years go by; four years of dreams, voices and mourning. I begin to understand the innate usefulness of creative work and humor as an antidote to loneliness and pain. My children need me and continually pull me onto the more solid ground where they stand.

Dream walks, drumming, chanting, and round dancing lead me to my tribal traditions.

My children personify the creative weaving of compassion, intelligence and courage and remind me of how precious each

Exhibit 17–1 Evaluating the Patient's (Family's/Significant Other's) Subjective Experience with Deathing Interventions*

1. Can you continue to be aware of ways to recognize your anxiety, fear, and grief at this time?
2. Which of your strengths can best serve you as you move through this difficult time?
3. What are the things that you will do to take care of yourself at this time?
4. Do you have any questions that I can help you with just now?
5. Whom can you ask for help?
6. Will you call on others to help you?
7. Were the imagery exercises helpful for you?
8. Are there images, feelings, or emotions that surfaced during the imagery exercises that I can help you with?
9. Can I help you with anything just now?
10. Are there rituals that you can begin to create to help you heal your grief?

*These subjective experiences may be used in helping a patient/family/significant others during the deathing process or with the family/significant others during the grieving process.

individual life is and the miracle of being together with Sean and with each other in this life and in this time and in this place.

My son Sean has taught me that the true object of death is life. I have learned that a dream can be shaped by the dreamer; that in the act of sacrifice, the sacred is manifested through surrender of all that is.[19]

Evaluation

With the patient (family/significant others), the nurse determines whether the patient outcomes for deathing in peace (see Table 17–1) were successfully achieved. To evaluate the session further, the nurse may again explore the subjective effects of the experience with the patient (family/significant others) (Exhibit 17–1).

Caring and counseling a dying person and the family/significant others is an art, and the art of peaceful living and peaceful deathing are the same. Deathing can be a series of conscious, spirit-filled, light-filled moments that lead to the ultimate peaceful moment of death. True healing and deathing in peace come from integrating the creative process and art of healing into our daily lives. The paradox is that, although this healing awareness may appear at first to be rare, it is a very ordinary and natural event that is available to each of us at all times. The more we integrate solitude, inward-focused practice, and conscious awareness into daily life, the more peaceful is the deathing process and the moment of death.

DIRECTIONS FOR FUTURE RESEARCH

1. Evaluate the attitudes and stress levels of nurses who work with deathing and death; compare those of nurses who routinely use self-regulation nursing interventions with nurses who do not use self-regulation interventions.
2. Determine the relationship of scripts, physiologic response, near death awareness, and peaceful deathing.

NURSE HEALER REFLECTIONS

After reading this chapter, the nurse healer will be able to answer or begin a process of answering the following questions:

- Do I feel a greater sense of healing intention when I include relaxation, imagery, or music in my life every day?
- What are the effects on me when I guide others in healing modalities to facilitate peace in deathing?
- How do I know that I am actively listening?
- What new death mythologies and skills can assist me in releasing attachment to my physical body, possessions, and people?

NOTES

1. A. Foos-Graber, *Deathing: An Intelligent Alternative for the Final Moments of Life* (York Beach, ME: Nicolas-Hays, 1992).
2. L. Dossey, *Meaning and Medicine* (New York: Bantam Books, 1991).
3. D. Feinstein and P.E. Mayo, *Rituals for Living and Dying* (San Francisco: Harper San Francisco, 1990).
4. G. Luce, *Your Second Life: The SAGE Experience* (New York: Delacorte Press, 1979).
5. M. Callanan and P. Kelly, *Final Gifts: Understanding the Special Awareness, Needs, and Communication of the Dying* (New York: Bantam Books, 1993).
6. Feinstein and Mayo, *Rituals for Living and Dying.*
7. T. Schrodeder-Sheker, Music for the Dying: A Personal Account of the New Field of Music—Thanatology—History, Theories, and Clinical Narratives, *Journal of Holistic Nursing* 12, no. 1 (1994):83–99.

8. L.L. Emanuel and E.J. Emanuel, The Medical Directive: A New Comprehensive Advance Care Document, *Journal of the American Medical Association* 261(1989):3288–3293.
9. J. Borysenko, *Guilt Is the Teacher, Love Is the Lesson* (New York: Warner Books, 1990).
10. S. Levine, *A Gradual Awakening* (New York: Anchor Press, 1979).
11. S. Levine, *Healing into Life and Death* (New York: Doubleday, 1989).
12. A. Sheikh and K. Sheikh, *Death Imagery* (Milwaukee, WI: American Imagery Institute, 1991).
13. S. Levine, *Who Dies?* (New York: Anchor Press, 1982).
14. R. Boerstler, *Letting Go* (Watertown, MA: Associates in Thanatology, 1982).
15. L. Dossey, *Healing Words: The Power of Prayer and the Practice of Medicine* (San Francisco: Harper San Francisco, 1993).
16. L. Dossey, *Recovering the Soul* (New York: Bantam Books, 1989).
17. H. Benson, *Beyond the Relaxation Response* (New York: Times Books, 1984).
18. J. Achterberg, et al., *Rituals of Healing* (New York: Bantam Books, 1994).
19. V. Durling Jones, personal communication, 1991; used with permission.

UNIT IV

LIFESTYLE ALTERATION

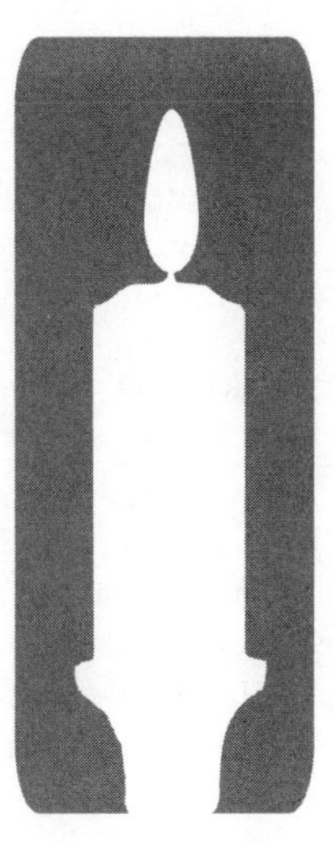

VISION OF HEALING

Nourishing Wisdom

Our hurried meals often reflect our hurried lives. Explore for a few minutes how we can experience food as nourishing wisdom. David refers to this awareness as principles of ordered eating.[1]

When we eat with conscious awareness, the true meaning of nourishing wisdom of food deepens. It is an awareness of the food (e.g., its color, texture, aroma), the process of eating (e.g., chewing, swallowing, and feeling food in our stomach), and all aspects of the atmosphere and environment (e.g., temperature of the room, the colors and shapes within the room, the table setting).

If we are sharing a meal with others, we are aware of the company and enjoyment of these people. We recognize that the presence of others can be nourishing to us, as well as to them. If we are eating alone, this awareness may provide an intimate experience of being alone, calm, relaxed, and present with each morsel of food. If we smile while we eat, we may experience more joyfulness in the moment of eating. As we reflect on the way that food feels within us and satisfies us, we deepen the experience of the art and ritual of eating.

We acknowledge our connection with the food by recognizing the origin of the food (e.g., the earth, animals, plants, trees) and being thankful for the sun, rain, water, and soil; for the farmers who cultivate the growing, flowering, and harvesting of the food; and for the packaging and delivery of the foods to the store or marketplace. Our awareness of being connected to the food source can also help us to eat in moderation and to eat balanced, healthy foods. This wisdom encourages us to choose from a variety of foods grown locally and to receive the benefit and nourishment of seasonal foods. Then, as we prepare the food, adding our own personalized taste with herbs and spices, we experience the joy of composing a meal of different foods, tastes, and textures that we believe to be right for us—not what another imposes on us as a correct combination of foods.

Nourishing wisdom of food also helps us to increase our awareness of the synergy of the food by combining food with exercise, rest and sleep cycles, relaxed breathing, and our other healing rhythms.

The more we are aware of body-mind-spirit connections while choosing, preparing, eating, and finishing the eating of foods, the greater is our potential for inner satisfaction and personal unfolding in relationship to food.

NOTE

1. M. David, *Nourishing Wisdom: A New Understanding of Eating* (New York: Bell Tower, 1991), 170–173.

Chapter 18

Weight Management: Eating More, Weighing Less

Barbara Montgomery Dossey

NURSE HEALER OBJECTIVES

Theoretical

- Analyze the setpoint theory of weight management.
- Exaine the way in which ultradian rhythms can help four types of overeaters achieve and maintain an ideal weight.

Clinical

- Develop a tape about healthy eating and guide a colleague in an experiential session.
- Explore with clients the effect of a healthy body image on healthy eating awareness.

Personal

- Examine ways to enhance your current nutrition plan for increased well-being.
- Compare and contrast your stress levels, moods, and healthy versus unhealthy eating.

DEFINITIONS

Basal Metabolic Rate (BMR): the amount of calories that the body burns just to stay alive.

Resting Metabolic Rate (RMR): the daily rate at which calories are burned.

Specific Dynamic Affect (SDA): the body's enhanced metabolic efficiency determined by the quality of food and the time of day the food is ingested.

THEORY AND RESEARCH

Raising the Resting Metabolic Rate

Frequent crash dieting seriously depresses a person's metabolic rate. The basal metabolic rate (BMR) is the amount of calories that the body burns just to stay alive. The resting metabolic rate (RMR) is the rate at which calories are burned during a day's activities. These rates are not set; rather, they are influenced by food patterns, eating patterns, and exercise patterns.[1]

Breakfast is an important part of weight management because the specific dynamic affect (SDA), the increase in metabolic rate immediately after eating, is highest in the morning after breakfast and decreases throughout the day.[2] Breakfast "revs up" the metabolic pump; it acts as the body's primer for the day. After establishing the habit of eating breakfast, people find that they are hungry around lunch time. This means that the metabolic pump is working on schedule; it is time to break for a nutritious meal to continue the efficiency of the SDA.

Fasting leads to weight gain. Animal studies have shown that animals that are intermittently placed on a fast (2 days per week) convert a higher percentage of food to fat.[3] Animals that are permitted to eat for only 2 hours in the evening are 30 percent heavier than if they had eaten several small meals throughout the day. Also, the weight and size of the stomach and intestines are higher than normal in animals that are fed according to these patterns. So, dieting does not decrease the size of the stomach. Behaviors that we should promote are to avoid dieting and to eat small frequent meals during the day.

Scientific studies show that the best nutrition and food benefits come from a high-fiber diet (complex carbohydrates—whole grains, vegetables, fruits, and legumes).[4] This diet increases the metabolic rate and accelerates intestinal motility. A diet lower in fat reduces the body's production of what are called free radicals. Free radicals are the by-product of normal metabolism and also the body's response to sunlight, X-rays, and air pollution.[5] Free radicals are molecules that accumulate in the body that can cause damage to normal cells. They hasten aging and contribute to cancer, heart disease, and a variety of illnesses. When we reduce free radical formation by a low-fat, high-fiber diet, we decrease aging and decrease chances of illness. The food guide pyramid (see Figure 11–1) is also high in antioxidants—vitamins A (beta-carotene), C, and E, the scavengers that help the body remove free radical molecules.[6] High-fiber, low-fat diets have also proven effective in reversing coronary artery disease and certain forms of cancer.[7,8] With such a diet, people may find that they develop a natural tendency to eat small portions throughout the day or to graze. They feel full faster, and they are able to eat more food without gaining weight. Grazing on high-fiber foods is healthy,[9] as fiber prevents certain fat from being absorbed. In fact, an increased intake of high-fiber snacks and at least two high-fiber servings at each meal prevent 10 percent or more of total fat intake from being absorbed.[10] Furthermore, an increase in complex carbohydrates in the diet correlates directly with a decrease in mood disorders.[11]

Setpoint Theory

An increased intake of fat affects metabolism. It is easier to get fat on a high-fat diet than on a diet in which excess calories come from complex carbohydrates and protein. Metabolism uses four or five times more thermic energy to convert carbohydrates and protein for storage into fat cells than it uses to convert dietary fat for fat storage.[12]

Recent evidence suggests that the weight-regulating mechanism or the fat thermostat plays a key role in determining a person's body weight. Many weight management researchers believe that people have an individual "setpoint" for weight.[13] They believe that a combination of largely genetic factors, including the number of fat cells in the body and the metabolic rate, go together to "set" a level of weight that is natural for each person.

The fat thermostat is a basic survival mechanism located in the region of the hypothalamus. It controls appetite, food intake, and the use of food energy from consumed calories. Once this setpoint has been established, the body will defend it. For example, when a person whose ideal weight is 130 pounds has weighed 150 pounds for some time, the body will fight to stay at 150 pounds despite any attempt to lose the 20 pounds by fasting or significantly reducing calories, because it cannot tell the difference between a decrease in calories and starvation. The body changes metabolically and conserves fuel by burning fewer calories. Although the person loses weight temporarily, he or she soon gains it back unless there has been a change in eating and exercise patterns. In fact, the person not only gains back the same weight, but also has an enhanced ability to store fat and adds an extra few pounds in the body's anticipation of another starvation. The only way to stay at the new weight level is to ingest fewer fat calories, increase complex carbohydrate intake, and exercise regularly.

Ultradian Healing Response and Balanced Food Intake

Biologic rhythms and the ultradian healing response (see Chapter 4) are important in weight management. The following four classic types of overeaters can be helped with the ultradian approach[14]:

1. Stress overeaters overeat and oversnack in response to stress.

   Ultradian Solution: Recognize stress limits and learn to say no to stress eating before reaching for unhealthy snacks; use the ultradian healing response to break the stress syndrome.
2. Fatigue overeaters snack between 3:00 and 4:00 P.M., even after a full meal and until bedtime.

   Ultradian Solution: Establish a pace throughout the day that allows two or three ultradian healing periods; experiment with healthy snacks of complex carbohydrates before an ultradian break so that food energy is assimilated in a way that reduces fatigue.
3. Addictive overeaters use foods that are especially high in sugars for their mood-altering effects in an effort to stave off depression throughout the day.

   Ultradian Solution: Study the ultradian pattern of the addiction, noticing how long it is between the time of overindulgence and time of withdrawal symptoms. Using the ultradian healing response before or just as soon as the withdrawal craving is recognized begins to maximize a person's bodymind capacity to heal the withdrawal symptoms with natural beta-endorphins and other messenger molecules for comfort and rejuvenation.
4. Escapist overeaters eat alone to escape unpleasant realities and to avoid uncomfortable situations.

   Ultradian Solution: Use the time that is spent in escape eating to do a life inventory and what is needed from food. Ask questions from the inner self that may be answered in relaxation and imagery sessions during an ultradian healing break.

NURSING PROCESS

Assessment

In preparing to use weight management interventions, the nurse assesses the following parameters:

- the client's fat style eating patterns
  1. skipping meals, especially breakfast
  2. dieting frequently
  3. fasting (i.e., frequent 24-hour periods without eating)
  4. eating the majority of calories in the evening
  5. consuming more high-fat foods, alcohol, and sugar foods than fresh vegetables and fruit
  6. consuming more highly processed foods than whole foods
  7. what is actually eaten in a week
- the client's attitudes, beliefs, and motivation for learning new life style patterns for maintaining ideal weight
- the client's exercise routine

Nursing Diagnoses

The following nursing diagnoses compatible with weight management interventions and that are related to the human response patterns of Unitary Person (see Chapter 7) are as follows:

- Exchanging: Altered nutrition (more than body requirements)
- Valuing: Spiritual distress
- Choosing: Ineffective individual coping
- Moving: Decreased physical mobility
- Perceiving: Disturbance in body image
Disturbance in self-esteem
Hopelessness
- Knowing: Knowledge deficit
- Feeling: Anxiety

Client Outcomes

Table 18–1 guides the nurse in client outcomes, nursing prescriptions, and evaluation to help clients achieve their ideal weight.

Table 18–1 Nursing Interventions: Weight Management

Client Outcomes	*Nursing Prescriptions*	*Evaluation*
The client will demonstrate attitudes, beliefs, and behaviors that indicate a desire to reduce body weight and learn new life style patterns.	Determine the client's desire to reduce weight.	The client demonstrated attitudes, beliefs, behaviors, and desire to reduce weight and learn new life style patterns.
	Assist the client in setting a realistic plan to lose 1–2 pounds per week by • exercising 3–5 times/week • using food guide pyramid (see Figure 11–1) • keeping a food diary daily • practicing relaxation/imagery daily • integrating behavioral changes • deciding rewards for attaining goals • joining support groups	The client set a realistic plan and lost 1–2 pounds per week. The client • exercised 3–5 times/week • used food guide pyramid • kept a food diary daily • practiced relaxation/imagery daily • integrated behavioral change daily • rewarded self for attaining goals • attended a weekly support group

Plan and Interventions

Before the Session

- Spend a few moments centering yourself to recognize your presence and to begin the session with the intention to facilitate healing.
- Create an environment in which the client will be encouraged to share his or her story.

At the Beginning of the Session

- Have the client identify stress signals. If stress leads to overeating, emphasize that eating to relieve the negative emotions associated with stressful situations adds many pounds. Troubles can be drowned in a hot fudge sundae or almost any food that has special significance, because sugars and carbohydrates change the biochemicals in the brain and may produce brief euphoria and relief of depression; these effects are only temporary, however. Moreover, the physiologic activity required to digest large amounts of food can make one drowsy, warm, and less anxious, resulting in less exercise and increasing weight gain. The key is to find less fattening ways to relieve the stress so that the stress-and-eat cycle can be interrupted.

- Teach the client about the BMR, the SDA, and the importance of eating breakfast. Compare the SDA to starting a car. It will not start in the morning without gasoline. With the wrong kind of gas, the car knocks, jerks, and does not run smoothly. Similarly, the body requires breakfast in the morning.
- Teach the client about the setpoint theory. Compare the fat thermostat to the thermostat in the client's home, which is set at a point to maintain a certain temperature. Explain that the fat thermostat is set to keep the client at a certain weight. Ask the client to think about his or her setpoint.
- Reinforce that the setpoint of the fat thermostat is not fixed, but varies with the client's daily activities. Assist the client in learning to change the patterns that keep him or her above or below ideal weight and create life style patterns to maintain ideal weight.

During the Session

- Teach the client to change his or her body image by using daily affirmations, relaxation, and imagery skills. Encourage the client to locate a special quiet place to become separated from the events of the busy day. Explain the steps that will be included in the weight management program.
- Teach the client to create specific imagery patterns (see Chapter 23):
  1. active imagery: experiences of walking, talking, and being at an ideal body weight; frequent repetition of these images throughout the day to create present moment experiences of living that ideal image.
  2. process imagery: distinction between hunger and anxiety or boredom; rehearsal of situations in which the client would normally be eating, but is using healthy eating patterns instead of overeating.
- Have the client learn to listen, while eating, to internal cues of comfort and feeling satisfied.

- Encourage the client to create time to eat. Emphasize the importance of starting with breakfast and turning on the fat-burning system so that the body can operate with efficiency.
- Encourage the client to eat away from the workplace because a break in the day is a stress manager. Reinforce the suggestion to eat slowly, relax with each bite, and drink a glass of water with each meal.
- Explore with client the food guide pyramid (see Figure 11–1).
- Have the client decide in advance what foods to eat each day in order to eliminate junk foods that put on the pounds. Encourage the client to record in a diary daily food groups eaten, including snacks, as well as to keep a running list in his or her head.
- Have the client establish new healthy eating patterns that will be useful for the rest of his or her life.
    1. eating at home in a quiet place sitting down
    2. placing food on a small plate and eating small bites, always finishing each bite before the next
    3. eating slowly, relaxed and at ease; putting the fork down between bites; appreciating the texture, taste, and satisfaction of every bite; removing the plate to prevent eating more, even at a restaurant
- Encourage the client to drink six or more 8-ounce glasses of fluid throughout the day, which slows down eating.
- Help the client release the "clear-your-plate syndrome." Reinforce the idea that eating the extra food on a plate becomes a "waist" and is "wasted" in the form of excess fat deposits and excess cholesterol. Suggest that the client get a food container bag and save that good food for the next meal or the next day.
- Teach the client to create an enjoyable exercise pattern to raise his or her overall metabolism and, thus, lower the fat thermostat.

At the End of the Session

- Explain that, as clients near their ideal weight, they can
    1. reduce the number of times that they listen to a relaxation and imagery tape, but need to continue rehearsal of new eating and exercise patterns
    2. decrease diary keeping, but they need to continue keeping an image of the food guide pyramid and new eating patterns in conscious awareness

3. distinguish hunger from anxiety and boredom

- Reinforce the idea that the client can outwit relapse by being ready to avoid unnecessary eating temptations. The best strategies can be decided on in advance, because the client has learned new healthy life style skills. If slipping occurs, however, the client should once again keep some form of record of recognized hunger, foods eaten (fiber, fat grams), stopping eating when comfortable, practicing stress management strategies, listening to relaxation and imagery tape, paticipating in fat-burning exercise.
- In the first session discuss contracting with the client and have the client sign a contract (Exhibit 18–1). In repeat sessions, review the contract and add any specifics needed.
- Give teaching sheets as needed to reinforce new behaviors.
- Use the client outcomes (see Table 18–1) that were established before the session and the client's subjective experience (Exhibit 18–2) to evaluate the session.
- Schedule a follow-up session.

Specific Interventions

Fat Reduction (Basic). It is essential for weight management to reduce the amount of fat in the diet. Fats do count, and prepared foods have much hidden fat. To determine how much fat, we need only to read labels listing total calories, grams of fat, and percentage of U.S. recommended dietary allowance (RDA) for the ingredients. The average American diet contains 40 percent fat. Currently, the American Heart Association recommends that 30 percent or less of the total daily calories come from fat.[15] Of this 30 percent, less than 10 percent should be saturated; 10 percent, monosaturated; and 10 percent, polyunsaturated. Many researchers, however, are beginning to suggest that foods are acceptable if the total calories are closer to 10 percent fat or less.[16] Each gram of fat contains 9 calories, and the client can calculate fat in the diet as follows:

$$\frac{\text{grams fat} \times 9}{\text{calories}} \times 100 = \text{percent fat calories}$$

Fat sneaks into a diet so easily. For example, advertising leads clients to believe that a breakfast snack bar is nutritious. The label indicates that there are 140 calories and 6 grams of fat in the snack bar. According to the formula given, the percent fat in that bar is 39 percent.

Exhibit 18–1 Weight Management Contract

Starting today, *(date)* __________, my weight management program begins and will continue until I reach my ideal weight. I will

- record in my diary all the food that I eat
- drink a minimum of 6 glasses of water daily
- walk 20 minutes 3 to 5 times a week, gradually building up to 45 minutes of exercise 3 to 5 times a week
- practice relaxation each day at least once for 20 minutes
- create active, process, end-stage and general healing imagery of being at my ideal weight

Signed ______________________ Date: ________________

Signed ______________________ Date: ________________

$$\frac{6 \times 9}{140} \times 100 = 39\%$$

If the client instead ate a slice of whole wheat bread, which is 110 calories with 2 grams of fat, the percent fat of that slice is only 16 percent; furthermore, the latter is more nutritious.

$$\frac{2 \times 9}{110} \times 100 = 16\%$$

Reading food labels is educational and allows a client to see eating patterns. Descriptive labels such as *dietetic*, *light*, or *natural* sell a lot of products, but caution is necessary. The products frequently contain fat, such as "dietetic" fruit bars made with a palm oil that is high in saturated fat. An important guide is the knowledge that ingredients are listed in the order of weight in a product. If the first four ingredients are acceptable, the food product is usually acceptable.

Food Guide Pyramid (Basic). There are five essential food groups: (1) milk, (2) meat (meat alternative), (3) grain, (4) fruit, and (5) vegetables. A client may find it easier to obtain a balance of these five food groups by using the food guide pyramid (see Figure 11–1).[17] By eating the recommended number of servings from each food group and choosing a variety of foods, the client consumes all the essential vitamins and nutrients needed for daily balanced nutrition. The basics of each group are as follows:

1. milk group: preferably nonfat or low-fat milk, nonfat or low-fat yogurt, cheese made from skim milk (e.g., mozzarella, Swiss, sapsago)
2. meat or meat alternative group: chicken (skin removed), turkey, lean beef, fish; legumes (e.g., split peas, pinto beans, kidney beans)
3. grain groups: whole grain cereals, breads, muffins, pasta, rice, bulgur, corn tortilla, pita bread
4. fruit and vegetable group: preferably raw and unpeeled, or steamed

A client who wants a 10 percent fat diet does not need a calculator, but does need to read labels and follow these guidelines.[18]

- four food groups
  1. beans/legumes
  2. fruit
  3. grains
  4. vegetables
- foods to be eaten in moderation: nonfat dairy products, nonfat or very low-fat commercially available products
- foods to be avoided: meats, oils, avocados, olives, nuts, seeds, whole milk, butter, cheese, egg yolks, sugar/sugar derivatives, alcohol, *any commercial product with more than 2 grams of fat per serving*

A key to success with nutritious snacks is having a variety of foods readily available. Clients may create a ritual for preparing food; they may wash and store fruits/vegetables in small servings ready to eat. Conscious eating of snacks is healthy because it prevents hunger. Knowledge about basic foods also has natural "hunger-busting" properties.

Snacks should be dense foods, which means that each mouthful should provide the highest nutritional value possible. These foods should be high in vitamins, minerals, and fiber with minimal processing; low in fat, sodium, and cholesterol. New snack behaviors may begin with fruits and the alternatives, such as low-fat yogurt and low-fat cottage cheese. The natural, water-soluble fiber found in fruit will curb the appetite. "Just fruit" spreads or mashed fresh strawberries or other berries can substitute for sugar-filled jams.

There are no forbidden foods on a weight management program. If the client says "No chocolate chip cookies, no ice cream," images of these food items will persist all day long. The client can eat anything; the purpose of the intervention is just to learn how to eat correctly. The client can eat one scoop of ice cream slowly, which is satisfying and, thus, keeps the client from eating three scoops fast and in an unconscious manner.

Clients should be aware of the restraint theory.[19] A person who rigidly restrains himself or herself from eating certain foods has a tendency to overeat when a *disinhibitor* comes along. A disinhibitor is a situation or event that makes a person give in to eating certain foods. For example, the client says, "I'm not going to eat a cookie." Then, if the client eats one cookie, guilty feelings may cause the client to rationalize that the whole box of cookies should be eaten to eliminate temptation.

Moods, Hunger, and Eating Satisfaction (Basic). Roughly 50 percent of first slips with new eating patterns occur when a client experiences a negative mood, such as anxiety, boredom, or depression.[20] Clients should learn to recognize moods, hunger, and eating satisfaction. They can record moods in a diary before and after eaten and answer the following questions:

- Are you happy, sad, depressed, or anxious?
- Do you see a pattern?
- Are you coping with your emotion by turning to food?
- What are your bodymind signals of feeling satisfied before, during, and after eating?
- Before eating what is your hunger/fullness level on a scale of 1 to 10, where 1 is extreme, ravenous hunger; 5 is comfort; and 10 is an uncomfortable, extremely stuffed sensation?

Clients should try to establish a habit of stretching meals over 10 to 20 minutes and learn to register feelings of satiety. People do best when they do not eat on the run, but in this fast-paced society it sometimes occurs. The old phrase "I don't have time to fix a meal" is foolish. In 1 to 3 minutes a client can pop a piece of whole wheat toast in the toaster while pouring a glass of orange juice and a glass of skim milk for breakfast.

Integration of Exercise (Basic). An exercise program is essential if clients are to reach and maintain their ideal weight. Exercise helps to achieve the "after burn," boosting metabolism so that calories are used up for hours after a workout. The client should incorporate warm-up exercises prior to exercise. The most effective exercise is slow and moderate, such as walking.[21,22]

While exercising, clients can repeat positive statements. Believing and actually experiencing the positive self-talk increase exercise time usually. Positive statements are as follows:

- I am getting slimmer and slimmer.
- My body is getting better and better.
- My flexibility is increasing.
- I am losing the fat on my thighs.

Assertion of Bill of Rights (Basic). Clients may find it helpful to recite a Bill of Rights throughout the day, particularly before meals. They can be creative and add to this list.

I have a right to

- eat what I need on food plan and not necessarily what my family or friends are eating.
- call a host or hostess and let my special food needs be known.
- refuse sweet desserts.
- ask how foods are prepared when I eat out.
- ask for my salad dressing to be placed in a side dish.
- send my food back if it is not prepared the way I requested.
- bring my own nutrition kit to restaurants (e.g., butter substitute, diet dressing, sodium-free herbs, spice shaker).
- call the restaurant ahead and have food prepared a special way.
- ask for a food container to carry uneaten food home with me.

Image Change (Basic). There is no magic formula to melt away the pounds; the magic resides in learning relaxation and imagery skills.[23] The imagination has an unending supply of seeds for motivation and determination that can be planted and cultivated into new, healthy life style patterns. It is essential that clients change the image of their bodies. Through years of being over or under their ideal weight, they have stored many negative statements in their memories.

Affirmations and imagery for body parts help clients begin to love their bodies. Taking the time each day to say the following affirmations and to picture these positive statements as the words are read helps them to accept a new body image.

Face:	My face is beautiful and the right size and shape.
Neck:	My neck is beautiful and relaxed.
Shoulders:	My shoulders are relaxed and upright.
Arms:	My upper arms are firm, toned, and beautiful.
	My lower arms are firm, toned, and beautiful.
Back:	My back is strong, flexible, and beautiful.
Chest:	My chest is defined just the way I want it to be.
Breasts:	My breasts are beautiful just the way they are.
Midriff:	My midriff is toned, strong, and flexible.
Waist:	My waist is perfect, toned, smooth, and flexible.
Abdomen:	My abdomen is toned, strong, and beautiful.
Hips:	My hips are toned, shapely, and flexible.
Buttocks:	My buttocks are toned, shapely, and firm.
Thighs:	My thighs are toned, shapely, and firm.
Calves:	My calves are toned, shapely, and firm.
Ankles:	My ankles are toned, strong, and flexible.

Maintaining the ideal body weight requires an image change of the internal self as well as the external self. Clients shoud learn to think about what happens when they are at their ideal weight; for example, they may think, "My stomach is flat; my arms are strong; my thighs are firm." To reinforce the power of the imagination and its influence on body responses, clients can imagine what happens when they are over their ideal weight by 10 to 15 pounds and feel the experience. Frequent comments by clients when creating these images are "I feel sluggish," "I waddle when I walk," and "I get out of breath just doing simple tasks."

With relaxation and imagery, a client can learn to be a conscious eater and avoid eating amnesia.[24] It is necessary to integrate a feeling of inner calm throughout the day because, when stressed, a person eats unconsciously and does not remember the "mouthful of this and the handful of that." In addition, when one eats quickly, the brain does not register the feeling of satisfaction until the overeating feeling is present. It takes the brain approximately 20 minutes to send the message to the stomach to register feeling full. The person who eats slowly and becomes conscious of the full feeling is satisfied with less food. When a client is stressed and not sure that he or she is hungry, the client may drink water. If hunger is present after 20 minutes, the client may eat a healthy snack.

Healthy Weight: Imagery Scripts. To assist a client in reaching his or her ideal weight, the nurse can make a personalized relaxation and imagery tape that includes such specifics as features of eating environments, shopping, and labels. The following scripts are to be integrated into the imagery tape after determining what is best for the client. These scripts help the client form correct biologic and end state process images of being at his or her ideal weight because he or she integrates healthy eating and exercise patterns to reach and maintain that desired weight. A relaxation exercise from Chapter 22 may be recorded for 5 to 10 minutes. Then, the script for healthy weight may be recorded for 15 minutes or longer.

Script: **Introduction.** *(Name), as your mind becomes clearer and clearer, feel it becoming more and more alert. Somewhere deep inside of you . . . a brilliant light begins to glow. Sense this happening. . . . The light grows brighter and more intense. This is the bodymind communication center. Breathe into it. . . . Energize it with your breath. This light is powerful and penetrating, and a beam begins to grow from it. The beam shines into your body now as you prepare yourself for reaching your ideal weight.*

Just continue in your relaxed manner . . . feel the deep relaxation from the top of your head all the way to your feet. Receive the inner message "I am calm and I am relaxed. I am excited about being consciously aware of healthy eating." With this inner feeling . . . you will feel good about yourself, just flowing with the challenges of each day. You will take this same feeling into your healthy eating. You will eat slowly and feel inner calmness.

Script: **Imaging Self at Ideal Weight.** *Take a few moments to see yourself at your ideal weight. You are standing in front of the mirror. Look at each part of your body. Your face looks just the way you want. And now looking at your whole body . . . part by part . . . your face . . . neck . . . arms . . . chest . . . waist . . . abdomen . . . hips . . . buttocks . . . and legs. Your body is at the ideal size for you. All parts of your body are taking on a new shape* *with your new eating and exercise program. Experience the way that this feels. Hear positive compliments about the new you from family . . . friends . . . and business associates. . . . How does this feel? You have the knowledge . . . skills . . . and insight to be at this healthy weight . . . feeling alive with energy and wisdom with your new way of being.*

Script: **Affirmations.** *Choose the affirmation that you want to give yourself at this new weight. Affirm to yourself that you are very wise and have the right to be at your ideal weight. You have the skills . . . and the knowledge . . . and you can listen to your inner wisdom that knows how to eat healthy . . . and how to maintain this new weight.* (Add specific affirmations that the client wants to maintain new life style eating awareness.)

Script: **Food Guide Pyramid and Food Diary.** *Imagine your food guide pyramid. Mentally plan which foods you will eat today. Now you are writing your food plan in your diary. As you keep your food diary . . . new awareness about your eating patterns comes to you. Your goals is to lose weight slowly, only a pound or two each week. You select healthy foods. You make time to eat. As you shop for food, . . . see yourself reading food labels and checking for fat content. As you eat, . . . you know correct food groups . . . you know exactly how to create your nutritious eating plan.*

Anytime that you want high-calorie, rich, fat foods . . . these sensations will pass. If the thoughts of addictive candies, cookies, pies, and cakes come . . . remember you have many choices. . . . You may say, "Stop!" You will remember to drink water and wait 20 minutes. If you are still hungry, eat a healthy snack or fruit . . . and be satisfied. But if those thoughts of a cookie are still present, let yourself savor the taste of the cookie . . . slowly . . . enjoying every bit.

Script: **Recognizing Hunger.** *Become aware of your signals of feeling hungry. With this awareness you are able to recognize true hunger and can eat healthy foods. Sometimes you may feel hungry with daily hassles or a tight time schedule. Remember . . . you can satisfy your mouth in a lot of ways that won't involve a lot of calories. You may need just a drink of water or to suck . . . munch . . . or crunch something nutritious.*

Script: **Imagine Yourself at Home.** *You feel hungry . . . and are excited, for you have recognized your true hunger signals. You go* *to the refrigerator . . . and it is full of special, nutritious foods that you have bought and prepared. You choose a healthy snack and go and sit down to enjoy every bite. It feels so good to be using your conscious eating skills.*

Script: **Eating Slowly.** *You are learning to recognize feelings within yourself about true hunger as different from stress. You will not be hungry . . . the food intake that you have decided on will satisfy your hunger needs. You notice that there is plenty of time to chew each bite. As you eat slowly, enjoying every bite you take, . . . you will recognize a full feeling sooner than usual. And with your new awareness, you now put your fork down and are pleased that you have recognized this full feeling. As you continue to move toward your ideal weight, . . . you are proud of every pound that you lose. You will continue your new eating patterns and will keep the weight off.*

Script: **Eating Out.** *In your mind take yourself to your favorite restaurant. . . . See yourself ordering from the menu. Imagine your food guide pyramid. What do you need to eat? What can you eat that will satisfy you . . . and will also make you feel good about yourself? Practice using your Bill of Rights. You have a right to eat just what you need . . . and to ask that your food be prepared just as you wish. Imagine that you are relaxed and at ease as you eat. If you are alone, . . . you are enjoying yourself. If with friends, . . . you are enjoying their company. You have now recognized that you are full and you still have half of your food left. At this point, you ask the waiter to take the food away and place it in a container for you to take home. You continue to sip on a nice beverage . . . and are thrilled at your new eating patterns.*

Script: **Exercising.** *In your mind rehearse your exercise routine. Notice how you are enjoying exercise. . . . Your body is stretching and gliding with every move you make. You feel light and energetic. As you increase your exercise, you speed up your body's metabolism and reset your fat thermostat to be more efficient. Many hours after exercising, you are still receiving the benefits of your exercise.*

Take a few slow, energizing breaths and, as you come back to full awareness of the room, know that whatever is right for you at this point in time is unfolding just as it should and that you have done your best, regardless of the outcome. . . .

Case Studies

Case Study No. 1

Setting:	Afternoon session in a clinic weight management program
Client:	A.W., a 44-year-old professional woman, mother of two children, aged 9 and 11
Nursing Diagnosis:	Health maintenance related to new strategies to achieve ideal weight

A.W. joined the weight management program to become more educated about reaching and maintaining her ideal weight, as well as to obtain professional counseling and group support. After 12 weeks in the program, she shared the following: "I've been on and off diets since I was 12 years old. I've put on 50 pounds over the last 2 years, which started with my new administrative position. I've lost 15 pounds over the last 12 weeks, with 35 more to go before I'm at my ideal weight.

"I can't remember feeling more proud of myself in 20 years. I've just got so much stress in my life. However, I don't see an end to it, so I've decided that I might as well start taking care of myself for the rest of my life. I've never really honored myself. I've always taken care of the kids, my husband, and my chronically ill mother.

"I'll have to confess how I got here. Three months ago, the kids and my husband headed to a movie. After they left, I got a bag of chocolate chip cookies, went to the bathtub with the plans of eating cookies while I took a long, hot bubble bath. Well, here I am in this wonderful warm bubble bath, eating my cookies, when I hear the children's and my husband's voices coming down the hall. The movie was sold out, so they rented movies and came home.

"I don't know what came over me, except a lot of guilt. I was feeling so guilty about my obesity, and the family had been asking me to lose weight. Here I was, eating again. I quickly closed the bag of cookies securely and sat on them in this tub of water, thinking that I could get the family to go into the family room. Much to my dismay, both children came to the bath to chat, and so did my husband. All of a sudden, the sack of cookies, which I thought were sealed tightly in the sack, began to surface one by one. Need I say more? I'll never live that story down." The group roared with laughter, which prompted A. to continue the story. Other group members began to tell their personal stories.

Different group members offered new insights about eating and the healthy new behaviors that they had learned. A. revealed the following insights about keeping her food journal, food patterns, and exercise patterns: "At first, I resented the diary and approached it as a waste of time, something else to do on my overloaded daily schedule. I also resented having to come to a class twice a week for the first 2 weeks, but I realized after several weeks how much I was learning. The group support here, along with the support of my family, has been a huge factor in my success and good feeling about myself.

"I begin each day with quiet time to affirm to myself my clear intentions for the day with relaxation, imagery, and planning what I will eat for the day ahead of time. This planning is essential. I take 30 minutes after the kids leave for school to do this.

"What I have learned about my food patterns and food plans over the last 12 weeks is how I was eating all the time and my food plan was nonexistent. Sure, I ate, but it was eating unconsciously. It was like a fear of not being able to get food when I was anxious, which was all the time. I never let food get out of my sight. I had food in the car, in my desk drawer, in the bathroom; I ate a full meal while preparing dinner for the family and always ate another full meal of snacks right before bedtime. Sometimes, I would raid the icebox at 2:00 A.M.

"The relaxation and imagery work has been most helpful. I recognize for the first time in my life feeling full before I finish eating. I understand how to eat and maintain my ideal weight. My new rituals around eating, exercise, and new self-image I will use the rest of my life. I'm so proud of myself for pushing away from the table, removing the remaining food as soon as I feel full. I've never exercised in my life, and now I actually feel cheated if I don't get my 45-minute walk at least 3 to 5 times a week.

"Before I started this program, I literally repressed, ignored, and misinterpreted anxiety and fear as hunger. The other marvelous breakthrough for me is to experience feeling smaller in my mind when I lost the first 10 pounds and also to have people tell me I look better. I've felt fat all my life. I really didn't believe I could ever do it. I've learned about healthy ways to reward myself without food. (See example of weight management contract in Exhibit 18–1). There is a big birthday party for my husband at work, and I have all the confidence of going to the party and sticking with my meal plan. It will work because I'm planning for my success."

Case Study No. 2

Setting:	Support group of Overeaters Anonymous
Client:	J.R., a 45-year-old professional, sharing her personal story

Nursing Diagnosis: Health maintenance related to strategies to maintain ideal weight and overcome eating addiction behaviors

It's the deepest, darkest secret I ever had to keep—a secret that isolated me further and further from family, friends, and worst of all, from myself. What I needed, but didn't understand, was an inner acceptance, an uncompromising "I'm okay," "I'm unique," "I'm precious." My life is dedicated to deepening that understanding for myself and others.

I'm a recovering bulimic. Bulimia is a disease that progresses from emotional food bingeing to a cycle of bingeing and purging everything you eat. This is how I lived my life from age 18 to age 40. Why did I do this? Every addict has his story of unbearable pain which he stuffs down with food, drugs, sex, gambling, alcohol, overworking, etc. It boils down to "I didn't know *how* to do it differently." And I was too ashamed to admit how desperate I really was.

My disease began when, as a child, I was praised for stuffing my real feelings. If I wanted praise, I had to express only what was pleasant. My belief was there were good and bad emotions. Good emotions are shared—unpleasant ones are hidden and disregarded. The problem here is that we all experience a broad range of emotions, but we are taught only to acknowledge the positive ones. When life becomes difficult, this belief system will leave you unprepared to cope. But we find other ways, don't we?

Today I am in the process of recovery. It took me over 2 years to accept that it is a process, not an event I could put behind me. This process evolves and changes but is never under my total control.

How did I get here? The overeating and subsequent bulimia began in 1960 while living through the Cuban revolution. My family and I moved to Havana, Cuba, during Premier Batista's heyday—a time of extravagance and excess. When Fidel Castro and his army stormed the city on New Year's Day 1959, nothing remained the same. My family and I had been shot at several times; we witnessed the murder of our neighbors; we experienced the dissolution of our family as we had known it. We fled from Cuba in 1961. My brothers and I were sent to private schools until my parents could relocate—although we never lived together again as a complete family.

I learned to cope with all this upheaval by suppressing my fears and anxieties. Instead of feeling all those negative emotions, I used food to comfort me. Once I gained 50 lbs. I became ashamed of my appearance—I didn't look perfect, so it occurred to me to purge all those unnecessary calories. I was hooked into the binge-purge cycle for over 20 years.

At age 40, I had a spiritual awakening, which coincided with my decision to follow the dictates of my heart rather than the reasoning of my mind. It was a turning point because, for the first time, I surrendered to a Higher Power; I acknowledged my disease and shame, but was still too frightened to ask anyone but God for help. Prayer became my medication; spiritual community became my sole support; but I still wasn't talking about my disease, and I certainly wasn't learning new ways to cope. By this time, my spiritual practices had brought me some rewards: I had overcome my intense shyness and had achieved significant respect in my professional field. One day, after a weekend of intense despair, a friend called, and I confessed my secret. With that single act of surrender, the recovery process began. I took her advice and committed to medical treatment and aftercare programs. In so doing, I exposed my shame, confronted my family with the truth, and removed many obstacles to healing. I was like a child, learning how to eat, how to recognize feelings, how to reach out to others. At the foundation of my recovery was the ability to integrate what I had discovered about my body, mind, and spirit. Each operated separately, but together created the wholeness I was searching for. This understanding created a consciousness in which progress and achievement had nothing to do with my efforting. In fact, today when I try to do everything right, I usually stumble in my recovery.

Recovery for me means loving and accepting myself as I am today. It means loving my body for what it really is—by feeding it, exercising it, and giving it rest. It means loving my mind for what it really is—by teaching it discipline and keeping it active. It means loving my spirit by recognizing what it really is—by meeting my needs for friendship, beauty, music, service, and play.

At this point, I still have to work at loving myself—maybe not all the time, but it still isn't effortless, especially at times of intense change or stress. One technique that has helped more than any other is talking to my inner child, listening to her

> needs, and being willing to act on them. I ask myself how I *really* feel (that means my inner child). It took me a while before I trusted myself enough to answer honestly. That trust was the basis for a friendship which I nourish each and every day. When I was a child, no one wanted to know how I felt because they didn't know what to do with their *own* feelings. Today I at least recognize that my inner child is the key to my intuition and wisdom, to my creativity and playfulness. These are aspects of myself well worth nourishing. And interestingly enough, with that kind of nourishment, I feel no compulsion to overeat.

Counseling a client such as J.R. should be based on the principles of addiction counseling (see Chapter 20) and participation in group support meetings with other clients recovering from bulimia. Researchers at Boston University Medical Center narrowed a list of 112 questions to 2 questions that are a fast screen for bulimia and should be included in routine histories: Are you satisfied with your eating patterns? and Do you ever eat in secret? Since women with bulimia appear healthy, have a normal weight, and do not talk about their eating behaviors, the disorder frequently goes undetected.[25]

Evaluation

With the client, the nurse determines whether the client outcomes for weight management (see Table 18–1) were successfully achieved. To

Exhibit 18-2 Evaluating the Client's Subjective Experience with Weight Management Interventions

1. Did you gain any new insight today about your eating patterns?
2. Do you have any questions about the food guide pyramid?
3. How does the concept of grazing appeal to you?
4. Do you have any questions about keeping a food diary?
5. What will be your exercise program?
6. Do you have any questions about the active and process imagery exercises you experienced today?
7. Did you like the imagery exercises?
8. Did you gain any new insight about your self-talk of achieving your ideal weight?
9. What are three affirmations that will help you create an image change of being at your ideal weight?
10. Are you aware of your bodymind signals of feeling full after eating?
11. What is your next step?

evaluate the sesson further, the nurse may again explore the subjective effects of the experience with the client (Exhibit 18–2).

The most important message that a nurse can give a client is to begin to stop dieting. Dieting only tampers with the body's ability to regulate its food intake. Obesity involves more than just overeating. It is usually due to nutritionally poor diets, fat- and alcohol-rich diets, a sedentary life style, and chronic dieting. The achievement and maintenance of ideal weight require (1) consistently healthy eating patterns, (2) exercise, and (3) behavior modification. The integration of these three areas helps clients to achieve a new awareness of healthy life style patterns.

DIRECTIONS FOR FUTURE RESEARCH

1. Compare and contrast various strategies for motivating clients to change their life style.
2. Determine whether nurses who model healthy life style behaviors are more effective teachers with clients who want to learn new health behaviors.

NURSE HEALER REFLECTIONS

After reading this chapter, the nurse healer will be able to answer or begin a process of answering the following questions:

- What are the best healthy foods for me to eat each day?
- What sensations accompany my physical and emotional well-being as I improve my nutrition?
- What insights can I gain from keeping a food diary?
- How do I feel when I consistently integrate exercise into my life?

NOTES

1. K.D. Brownell et al., The Effects of Repeated Weight Loss and Regain in Rats, *Physiology and Behavior* 38, no. 4 (1986):459–464.
2. D. Schlundt et al., The Role of Breakfast in the Treatment of Obesity: A Randomized Clinical Trial, *American Journal of Clinical Nutrition* 55, no. 3 (1992):645–651.
3. Brownell et al., Effects of Repeated Weight Loss, 459.
4. D. Ornish, *Eat More, Weigh Less* (New York: HarperCollins, 1993).
5. Ibid., 24.
6. Government Gives New Shape to Eating Right, *Tufts University Diet and Nutrition Letter*, no. 4 (1992):2.
7. D. Ornish et al., Can Lifestyle Changes Reverse Coronary Heart Disease? The Lifestyle Heart Trial, *Lancet* 336(1990):129.

8. D. Ornish, *Dr. Dean Ornish's Program for Reversing Heart Disease* (New York: Random House, 1990).
9. J. Jenkins et al., Nibbling versus Gorging: Metabolic Advantages of Increased Meal Frequency, *New England Journal of Medicine* 321, no. 14 (1989):929–934.
10. A. Lissner et al., Weight Loss on a Low-Fat Diet: Consequences of the Imprecision of the Control of Food Intake in Humans, *American Journal of Clinical Nutrition* 53, no. 5 (1991):1124–1129.
11. J. Wurtman, Carbohydrated Craving: Relationship between Carbohydrated Intake and Disorders of Mood, *Drugs* 39, suppl. 3 (1990):49–52.
12. J. Lisser, et al. Variability of Body Weight and Health Outcomes in the Framingham Population, *New England Journal of Medicine* 324, no. 26 (1991):1839–1844.
13. Ibid., 1839.
14. E. Rossi, *The 20 Minute Break* (Los Angeles: Jeremy P. Tarcher, 1991).
15. American Heart Association, *Dietary Guidelines for Healthy American Adults* (Dallas: American Heart Association National Center, 1989).
16. Ornish, *Eat More, Weigh Less,* 24.
17. Government Gives New Shape to Eating Right, 2.
18. Ornish, *Eat More, Weigh Less,* 24.
19. J. Gurin, Leaner Not Lighter, *Psychology Today* (July 1989), 32.
20. Ibid., 32–36.
21. S. Blair et al., Physical Fitness and All-Cause Mortality: A Prospective Study of Healthy Men and Women, *Journal of the American Medical Association* 262, no. 17 (1989):2395–2401.
22. J. Duncan et al., Women Walking for Fitness. How Much Is Enough? *Journal of the American Medical Association* 266, no. 23 (1991):3295–3299.
23. J. Achterberg et al., *Rituals of Healing* (New York: Bantam Books, 1994).
24. C. Simon, The Triumphant Dieter, *Psychology Today* (June 1989), 50–54.
25. K. Freund, Detection of Bulimia in a Primary Care Setting, *Journal of General Internal Medicine* 8, no. 5 (1993):236–242.

RESOURCES

Nutritional Guidelines
American Holistic Medical Association
4101 Lake Boone Trail #204
Raleigh, North Carolina 27607
(919) 787-5181

Self Care: A Program To Improve Your Life
(Audiocassette, 100-page book, and 47 affirmations)
Bodymind systems
910 Dakota Drive
Temple, Texas 76504
(817) 773-2337

Positive Harmonic Imagery: Weight Management
(videocassette)
New Era Media
P.O. Box 410685-BT
San Francisco, California 94141
(415) 863-3555

Supermarket Savvy (videocassette)
Supermarket Savvy
P.O. Box 7069
Reston, Virginia 22091
(703) 742-3364

VISION OF HEALING

Acknowledging Fear

What is fear, and where does it come from? Fear can surface as we contemplate changes in life style patterns. For example, a person who wishes to stop smoking fears not being able to stop, gaining weight, experiencing nicotine withdrawal, offending other people by asking them not to smoke, among other things. Fear comes only in relation to something else. If this is so, how can we gain freedom from fear? This is the healing journey—learning more about the fear in relationship with all things.

Fear somehow can attach itself to the spirit and lodge somewhere within the physical body. Fear makes us feel separate and alone, but it can become a path that will lead deeper into the present moment. It does not have to be a barrier to the moment. Although fear always creates more fear, its every occurrence can become a moment to learn more about another level of life's journey. Fear is useful in that it alerts us to areas in which we have some resistance. Releasing the fear returns us to our unconditional core of love so that we release the "shoulds." Approaching an event with the notion that we "should" behave in a certain way further distances us from our core of being present in the moment. The basic human fears—fear of failure, fear of rejection, fear of the unknown, fear of isolation, fear of dying, and fear of loss of self-control—are closely related and may overlap. Any kind of fear is related to our level of self-esteem. When our self-esteem is low, our fears even increase. The negative self-talk intensifies the lack of self-confidence and takes us further from the resolution of the fear. It is helpful to identify our stressors and determine the fears that they evoke. We need to reflect on the following questions:

- *How do you usually deal with your fears? Are you the type of person who hopes that circumstances surrounding these fears will go away?*
- *Does one of these basic human fears tend to dominate your list of stressors? If so, why do you suppose that is the case?*
- *What are some ways to deal with some of these major fears?*

Chapter 19

Smoking Cessation: Breathing Free

Barbara Montgomery Dossey

NURSE HEALER OBJECTIVES

Theoretical

- Examine the eight stages of successful smoking cessation.
- Analyze the bodymind responses to nicotine.

Clinical

- Interview a client who smokes and listen to the reasons that the client gives for smoking. Ask if the client has ever tried to quit smoking or will attempt smoking cessation again.
- Give the Smoking Profile Questionnaire to a client. Discuss the score with the client to gain insight into the meaning of smoking and explore ways to teach smoking cessation.

Personal

- Examine the effect of passive smoking on you.
- If you are a smoker, identify habit breakers to become a successful nonsmoker.

DEFINITIONS

Focused Smoking: smoking reduction technique done under supervision.

Habit Breakers: new action behaviors that replace old "smoke signals."

Nicotine Fading: gradual reduction of the nicotine level in the body to avoid withdrawal symptoms.

THEORY AND RESEARCH

Prevalence and Stages for Smoking Cessation

There are 1.3 million U.S. citizens who quit smoking every year. The prevalence of cigarette smoking among adults in the United States has declined from 40 percent in 1965 to 29 percent in 1987.[1] In 1986, more than 30 percent of persons (approximately 17 million) who had smoked during the preceding year reported that they had tried to quit during that period. If the 1.3 million new ex-smokers are representative of the 17 million who attempt cessation, it seems that less than 10 percent who try to quit are successful each year.[2] The major reason that people find it so difficult to quit smoking is that they do not take the time to learn new behaviors for sustained change. There are two interesting trends associated with the increase in the number of health-concerned smokers. They are tired of feeling guilty about the health risk they incur for themselves, their family, friends, and other passive smokers. They are also increasingly more sensitive to the rights of nonsmokers.

To become a successful ex-smoker is a gradual step-by-step process that requires preparation and planning. It involves the following eight stages[3]:

1. Stage 1: The client identifies himself or herself as a concerned smoker and becomes educated about quitting, explores alternatives to smoking, and begins to monitor smoking patterns without changing anything.
2. Stage 2: Once aware of the patterns, the client takes steps to reduce nicotine intake by changing brands, cutting down, or just stopping—going "cold turkey," which means Stage 3 has begun.
3. Stage 3: The client makes a firm commitment to quit and decides on a quit date.
4. Stage 4: The client smokes the last cigarette and spends his or her first 24 hours smoke-free. All traces of cigarettes are removed from the body and environment.
5. Stage 5: The first week is smoke-free.

6. Stage 6: The second week is smoke-free.
7. Stage 7: The third week is smoke-free.
8. Stage 8: The fourth week is completed smoke-free.

Fiore and colleagues have shown that more than 90 percent of successful quitters do so on their own, without participating in an organized smoking cessation program.[4] They defined quit rates as smoking abstinence for more than 1 year and noted that quit rates are twice as high for those who quit on their own as for those who participate in a cessation program. Smokers who quit "cold turkey" are more likely to remain abstinent than are those who gradually decrease their daily consumption of cigarettes, switch to cigarettes with lower tar or nicotine, or use special filters or holders. Smokers who receive nonsmoking advice from their physicians are nearly twice as likely to quit than are those who are not advised to quit. Heavy (25 cigarettes a day), more addicted smokers are much more likely to participate in an organized cessation program than are people who smoke less.

Smoking is indeed a major health hazard and has been called the chief preventable cause of death in our society. Lung cancer remains the Number 1 cause of death attributed to carcinoma in the United States and is likely to be responsible for 153,000 deaths in 1994.[5] The American Cancer Society predicts that the risks of dying from lung cancer are 22 times higher in male smokers and 12 times higher for female smokers than for people who have never smoked; and in 1994, there were more than 419,000 tobacco-related deaths.[6]

The marketing strategies of the tobacco companies imply that cigarettes with less tar, less nicotine, and less carbon monoxide are safer for smokers. These strategies seem to have proven particularly successful among women, who make up the largest proportion of low-yield cigarette smokers. Low-tar, low-nicotine cigarettes are equally hazardous to the health of the heart, however, according to epidemiologists at the Boston University School of Medicine.[7] In addition, while the percentage of men who smoke dropped from 51 percent in 1964 to 29 percent in 1986, the proportion of women who smoke only fell from 33 percent to 24 percent. In a comparison of 910 women under 65 years of age who had suffered a first heart attack with 2,375 women who had been hospitalized for other reasons, it was found that women who smoked ran 4 times the overall risk of suffering a nonfatal heart attack than did nonsmokers and ex-smokers. Furthermore, the risk for women who smoked cigarettes that yielded the lowest amount of nicotine and carbon monoxide was the same as that for women who smoked cigarettes that yielded the highest amounts. Women who smoked fewer than four cigarettes a day ran 2.5 times the risk of heart attack compared with nonsmokers; women who smoked more than 45 cigarettes a day, regardless of nicotine content, had 22 times the risk.[8]

In the United States, approximately 70 percent of children live in homes where at least one adult smokes. Because mothers usually spend more time in the home and more time with their children than do fathers, maternal smoking has been linked with childhood respiratory problems. Data available on 4,331 children aged 0 to 5 years who were included in the 1981 National Health Interview Survey show that young children whose mothers smoke more than ten cigarettes a day are twice as likely to develop asthma than are children of nonsmokers.[9,10] These same youngsters are 2.5 times more likely to develop asthma in their first year of life and 4.5 times more likely to need medicine to control asthma attacks. Maternal smoking remains an indicator of childhood asthma even after variables such as gender, race, presence of both biologic parents in the household, and number of rooms in the house were taken into account.[11] Investigators caution, however, that their information is based on parents' reports of smoking habits and asthma symptoms, not on objective clinical data. In addition, investigators found no information on the mothers' respiratory symptoms, which can influence both their children's symptoms and the parents' reports of these symptoms. One study has linked exposure to environmental tobacco smoke as reported by parents to diminished pulmonary function and more frequent exacerbation of asthma in children. Measurement of urine cotinine levels provided evidence of an association between exposure to environmental tobacco smoke and pulmonary morbidity in children with asthma.[12]

Body Response

Over time, smoking severely harms the body, stripping the lungs of natural defenses and completely paralyzing the natural cleansing process. The early morning cough associated with smoking results from the bronchial cilia's attempt to clear from air passages the mucus that accumulated because toxic cigarette smoke the day before had interfered with the cilia's normal function. This cleansing action results in thick, yellow or yellow-green mucus, which triggers the cough reflex. As exposure continues, the bronchi begin to thicken, which predisposes the person to bacterial and viral infections, asthma, emphysema, and cancer. The smoker's heart rate speeds up an extra 10 to 25 beats per minutes, with a predisposition to dysrhythmias. The blood pressure increases by 10 to 15 percent, thus predisposing the person to myocardial infarction, stroke, and vascular disease.

Within seconds after the smoke is inhaled, irritating gases, such as formaldehyde, hydrogen sulfide, and ammonia, begin to affect the eyes, nose, and throat. With each inhaled breath of smoke, carbon monoxide enters the bloodstream, and its concentration eventually rises to a level 4 to 15 times as high as that of a nonsmoker. The carbon monoxide passes immediately to the bloodstream, binding to the oxygen receptor sites and, thus, depleting the cells of oxygen. Hemoglobin, which normally carries oxygen throughout the body, becomes bound to the carbon monoxide and is converted to carboxyhemoglobin, which is unable to deliver oxygen to the cells. Smoking also makes the blood clot more easily.

The constriction of the tiny blood vessels decreases the delivery of oxygen to the skin and contributes to the "smoker's face," where deep lines appear around the mouth, eyes, and center of the brow. There is an established link between nicotine and erection problems in male smokers, and smoking is believed to be the leading cause of impotence in the United States today. Smoking also adversely affects fertility by decreasing the sperm count and sperm motility. Female smokers are three times more likely than are nonsmoking females to be infertile, and female heavy smokers have a 43 percent decline in fertility.[13]

Brain/Mind Response

Nicotine quickly reaches the smoker's brain. Since it has been estimated that the average smoker makes ten puffs per cigarette, a pack-a-day smoker gets about 200 puffs per day.[14] Each nicotine "hit" goes directly to the lungs, and the nicotine-rich blood travels to the brain in approximately 7 seconds. This time is twice as fast as that of an intravenous injection of heroin, which must pass through the body's systemic circulatory system before reaching the brain.

As nicotine enters the brain, it acts as a "mood thermostat" and appears to mimic acetylcholine (ACh), a powerful neurotransmitter that is involved with learning memory, pain control, and alertness.[15] Nicotine sets the general level of arousal within the reticular formation center in the brain. Because ACh mediates the neurotransmitters through which most nerve impulses are transmitted within the brain's reticular formation center, nicotine has the ability to modify nerve transmission involving ACh and other neurotransmitters at the junction between nerve cells. Thus, the general level of arousal is adjusted up or down due to presence or absence of nicotine levels that allow the smoker to feel stimulated or relaxed.

Acetylcholine also can stimulate powerful neurotransmitters for dealing with environmental stimuli.[16] These neurotransmitters are norepinephrine, beta-endorphin, dopamine, epinephrine (adrenaline), arginine, and vasopressin. Norepinephrine controls arousal and alertness. Beta-endorphin, referred to as the "brain's natural analgesic," can decrease pain and anxiety. Dopamine is part of the brain's pleasure center and is able to decrease pain and anxiety. The smoker's "attention thermostat" effect is mediated through the brain's limbic system, where the major neurotransmitters are adrenaline and dopamine, both of which are influenced by nicotine. It appears that nicotine helps the smoker concentrate by promoting selective attention to important tasks, which increases learning and memory. Smoking also prevents the unpleasant side effects of nicotine withdrawal—irritability; irrational mood changes; low energy levels; lack of ability to feel stimulated; and increased sensitivity to light, touch, and sound.

The overall effect of smoking is a shift in brain chemistry that creates the mood needed for the situation at hand—more relaxation, alertness, increased pleasure, or decreased pain or anxiety. (Refer to Chapter 4 for ultradian stress response and ultradian healing response.) Even though this is true, concerned smokers can create and sustain new behaviors to achieve the same positive effects without the health risk to themselves or to passive smokers. Success in smoking cessation requires a plan of action. Moreover, smoking cessation is a process, not something that occurs in a week or so. (Refer to Chapter 5 for stages of change.)

Prevention Programs and Strategies

Physicians and nurses have considerable opportunity to reach all demographic subgroups of the population. Seventy percent of smokers see a physician at least once a year. Although the impact of physician advice varies, 70 percent of smokers say that they would quit if urged to do so by a physician.[17] For smoking intervention to become a routine part of medical practice, however, medical education must integrate smoking cessation strategies into the curriculum. Since 1990, the National Cancer Institute has worked to train practicing physicians nationwide in tobacco use prevention and intervention techniques.[18] Its goal is to train 100,000 practicing physicians in these techniques. This must also be emphasized in nursing education. Follow-up can be most effective if done by a physician-nurse team.

In a telephone survey of 24,296 Californians, Gilpin and colleagues found that 9,796 current smokers, including 5,559 daily smokers, had visited a physician in the preceding year.[19] Thus, the simple intervention by a physician of advising every smoker to quit at every visit can have an impact. For patients who already have cancer, heart disease, or other tobacco-related diseases, education in smoking cessation is essential. For example, patients with small cell lung cancer who survive cancer-free for more than 2 years, but continue to smoke, have a significantly increased risk for developing a second primary smoking-related cancer; smoking cessation after successful therapy was associated with a decrease in this risk.[20]

Physicians can offer smokers nicotine replacement therapy (NRT) by gum, transdermal patch, intranasal spray, or inhalation—in addition to smoking cessation programs. Although NRTs are expensive, they can be helpful.[21] In one study, nicotine patch therapy combined with physician interventions, nurse counseling follow-up, and relapse intervention showed clinical significance.[22] Smokers with lower baseline nicotine and cotinine levels had better cessation rates, which provides indirect evidence that this fixed dose of transdermal nicotine may have been less satisfactory for those smokers with higher baseline levels.

Another study identified predictors of smoking cessation success or failure with and without transdermal patch treatment.[23] Smoking status (abstinent or smoking) during the first 2 weeks of nicotine patch therapy, particularly week 2, was highly correlated with clinical outcome and can serve as a powerful predictor of smoking cessation. Smoking behavior early in the treatment also predicted outcome among placebo patch users. Traditional measures of dependence are not consistently predictive of cessation success. Clinicians are advised to emphasize the importance of total abstinence after a quit attempt and to follow up with patients within the first 2 weeks of quitting. Smoking during this critical time should be assessed and treatment altered as appropriate.

Prevention should focus strongly on the youth. Currently, there are as many as 2.2 million U.S. teen-aged smokers.[24] The American Heart Association, using figures for the population group aged 12 through 17 years, cited estimates that as many as 3,000 youngsters each day start smoking in this country.[25] As many as 9 million U.S. children younger than 5 live with at least one smoker and are exposed to second-hand smoke regularly.[26] Most first-time smoking in the United States is among teen-agers, although there is concern about perceived efforts to attract women to smoking.

In one study implemented in 11 junior high schools in San Diego County, California, researchers used a psychosocial intervention that combined refusal skills training; contingency management; and other tobacco use prevention methodologies, such as telephone and direct mail brochures.[27] Eleven other junior high schools served as controls. At the end of the third year, the prevalence of tobacco use was 14.2 percent among the intervention students and 22.5 percent among the controls. It was concluded by college undergraduates serving as change agents that direct one-to-one telephone interventions appear to provide cost-effective tobacco-related behavior modification.

Studies have documented an excessive rate of cigarette smoking among black men.[28] However, a survey conducted in two urban areas of South Carolina documented a high rate of smoking among young white men with fewer than 12 years of education.[29] Differences in smoking rates by educational level were significant only for those younger than 40.

The advertising campaigns targeting women, which were launched in 1967, were associated with a major increase in smoking among girls younger than the legal age for purchasing cigarettes.[30] Most teen-aged girls who smoke want to quit, and 77 percent of them have tried.[31] More than half have reported a quit attempt within 6 months preceding the Teenage Attitudes and Practices Survey, a National Center for Health Statistics survey of adolescents about their use of tobacco.[32] Sadly, 92 percent of teen-aged girls who smoke do not expect to be smoking in 1 year, revealing a dangerous naiveté about the addictiveness of tobacco. Getting teen-agers who smoke to quit is difficult; only 1.5 percent are successful. For the 16 percent of female teen-agers who smoke regularly and the additional 28 percent who experiment, time is of the essence.[33]

There is also a movement to discourage smoking through effective role models on television, in magazines, and in all public advertising. In addition, athletes, particularly baseball players, are being urged to stop the use of smokeless tobacco. The American College of Sports Medicine notes that athletes and others will not only set good examples by not using smokeless tobacco products, but also may avoid serious problems for themselves.[34]

NURSING PROCESS

Assessment

In preparing to use smoking cessation interventions, the nurse assesses the following parameters:

- the client's addiction to cigarettes, as determined by the smoking profile (Exhibit 19–1)
- the client's motivation to learn interventions to become a permanent nonsmoker

Exhibit 19–1 Smoking Profile

Are you addicted to cigarettes, or is your smoking "just a habit"? Answer the following questions to learn more about your smoking behavior:

1. How soon after you wake up do you smoke your first cigarette?
   a. after thirty minutes (0)
   b. within thirty minutes (1)
2. Do you find it difficult to refrain from smoking in places where it is forbidden, such as the library, theater, or doctor's office?
   a. yes (1)
   b. no (0)
3. Which of all the cigarettes you smoke in a day is the most satisfying one?
   a. any other than the first one in the morning (0)
   b. the first one in the morning (1)
4. How many cigarettes a day do you smoke?
   a. 1–15 (0)
   b. 16–25 (1)
   c. 26 or more (2)
5. Do you smoke more during the morning than during the rest of the day?
   a. yes (1)
   b. no (0)
6. Do you smoke when you are so ill that you are in bed most of the day?
   a. yes (1)
   b. no (0)
7. Does the brand you smoke have a low, medium, or high nicotine content? (Refer to your cigarette pack.)
   a. low (0.9 mg or less) (0)
   b. medium (1.0–1.2 mg) (1)
   c. high (1.3 mg or more) (2)
8. How often do you inhale the smoke from your cigarette?
   a. never (0)
   b. sometimes (1)
   c. always (2)

To get your score, add the points (found in parentheses) beside each of your responses. The questions are scored so that the higher points are given for answers that reflect a higher level of addiction to cigarettes. A total score of 6 or greater reflects a significant probability of nicotine dependence.

Smoking behaviors are typically a complex combination of nicotine dependence and habituation. Nicotine is a highly addictive drug and is considered by some physicians to be more addictive than alcohol or cocaine. Smoking occurs mostly due to automatic behaviors in response to feelings or to situations which are often stressful.

Source: Reprinted from Clinical Opportunities for Smoking Intervention, U.S. Department of Health and Human Services, 1986.

- the client's eating patterns and exercise program
- the client's existing stress management strategies
- the client's attitudes and beliefs about successful and sustained smoking cessation
- the client's support and encouragement from family and friends

Nursing Diagnoses

The following nursing diagnoses compatible with the interventions for smoking cessation and that are related to the nine human response patterns of Unitary Person (see Chapter 7) are as follows:

- Exchanging: Altered circulation
  Altered oxygenation
- Valuing: Spiritual distress
  Spiritual well-being
- Choosing: Ineffective individual coping
  Effective individual coping
- Moving: Self-care deficit
- Perceiving: Disturbance in body image
  Disturbance in self-esteem
  Hopelessness
- Knowing: Knowledge deficit
- Feeling: Anxiety
  Fear

Client Outcomes

Table 19–1 guides the nurse in client outcomes, nursing prescriptions, and evaluation for successful smoking cessation.

Plan and Interventions

Before the Session

- Spend a few moments centering yourself to recognize your presence and to begin the session with the intention to facilitate healing.
- Gather teaching sheets to be used during the session.
- Create a quiet place to begin guiding the client in smoking cessation strategies.

Table 19–1 Nursing Interventions: Smoking Cessation

Client Outcomes	*Nursing Prescriptions*	*Evaluation*
The client will demonstrate attitudes, beliefs, and behaviors that indicate the desire to be a nonsmoker.	Determine the client's desire to be a nonsmoker.	The client demonstrated attitudes, beliefs, behaviors, and the desire to be a nonsmoker.
	Assist the client in setting realistic plans for being a nonsmoker by	The client set a realistic plan and became a nonsmoker over 1 week as follows:
	• establishing quit date	• focused on quit date goal
	• drawing up a nicotine withdrawal schedule	• went "cold turkey"
	• cleansing self and environment of nicotine	• cleansed body/ environment of nicotine
	• developing habit-breaker strategies	• adhered to habit-breaker strategies
	• keeping a smoking diary	• kept a smoking, exercise, food diary
	• practicing relaxation and imagery	• practiced relaxation/ imagery daily
	• integrating behavior changes	• integrated behavior changes daily
	• deciding on rewards for attaining goals	• rewarded self for attaining goals

At the Beginning of the Session

- Go over the results of the smoking profile, and explore the meaning of these patterns with the client. Elicit insight into changing behaviors.
- Instruct the client in the importance of keeping a smoking diary.
- Establish pre-quitting strategies. Suggest that the client be patient and identify and combine the methods that can work best.
- Encourage the client to take a few days before the quit date to rid the body of toxins and to clean the house, office, and car of any evidence of cigarettes or odors.

- Have the client establish the quit date and sign a contract that specifies the quit date.
- Encourage the client to call on family and friends on the first smoke-free days, particularly when confidence is low.

During the Session

- Reinforce the quit date and have the client imagine being smoke-free in 5 days.
- Teach basic relaxation and imagery skills to shape bodymind changes for internal and external smoke-free images. These new images also create a new felt sense and are a major source of the client's success. Rhythmic breathing and muscle relaxation are most helpful in teaching body-centered awareness and effective coping. Relaxation and imagery help the client to recognize and block smoke signals. Combine this practice with a stop smoking video once or twice a day.
- Teach the client to create specific imagery patterns (see Chapter 23).
  1. active images—cleansing the body of nicotine and other toxins; finding a safe place that establishes a feeling of security and comfort; envisioning a protective bubble that receives what is needed from others and blocks out negative images, such as smoke signals.
  2. process images—people, events, and situations that make the client smoke. Have the client rehearse being in a situation where smoking normally occurs, but now using a new behavior, such as reaching for a glass of water.
  3. end-state images—being smoke-free; accessing one's inner healer.
- Have the client create strategies to break smoke signals and become smoke-free—waking up and having a glass of water; reading the morning paper in a different room; taking a break and drinking water or juice; talking on the phone and practicing relaxation and rhythmic breathing.
- Encourage the client to be patient in making this major life style change and to remember that smoking is about self-protective control. The old unhealthy control must be replaced with a new, healthy control. Identify internal and external experiences as new health behaviors are being shaped. Some are easy to change; others take longer.

- Ask the client to become aware of new opportunities for being with family, friends, and self while being smoke-free.

At the End of the Session

- Suggest that the client create a personal reward after 5 smoke-free days.
- Evaluate with the client the goals of behavior changes—reduction of smoking urges and development of new habit patterns.
- Encourage the client to make a list of anticipated high-risk situations and decide in advance steps to prevent a relapse. The most frequent high-risk situations are social situations, emotional upsets, home or work frustration, interpersonal conflict, and relaxation after a meal.
- Reinforce the fact that the client can avoid relapse. Having learned to recognize high-risk situations for relapse, the client can be ready to act quickly in using strategies to resist smoking temptations. Successful coping strategies must honor internal responses (bodymind feelings and thoughts) and action-oriented responses (action steps).
- Suggest that the client become a support person for someone else who is trying to become smoke-free to decrease chances of relapse.
- Use the client outcomes (see Table 19–1) that were established before the session and the client's subjective experience (Exhibit 19–2) to evaluate the session.
- Schedule a follow-up session.

Specific Interventions

Recording Habits (Basic). Smoking is such a pervasive, automatic habit that it is essential to keep a smoking diary of when, where, how often, and what moods are associated with smoking. The client records the feelings associated with smoking and begins to think about new habits to replace these urges. Keeping such a record for several weeks before the quit date allows the client to identify patterns, and knowing the smoke triggers leads to permanent changes. To strengthen the new awareness, the client may record thoughts, feelings, urges, and observations about smoking. With each cigarette that is smoked, for example, the client should consider the following questions:

1. What internal cues made me think that I needed a cigarette (e.g., breathing patterns, mouth watering, tense muscles, fidgety hands)?

2. What external cues made me think that I needed a cigarette (e.g., talking on the phone, watching television, finishing eating, sitting down with friends)?
3. Now that I've smoked that cigarette, did I enjoy it?

Preparation for Quit Date (Basic). The desire to be a nonsmoker should build. Becoming smoke-free requires preparation. The client should take the time to identify personal reasons for quitting, such as to reduce the risk of heart, lung, or circulatory disease; to increase endurance and productivity; to improve sense of smell and taste; to increase self-esteem; to be in control; or to decrease the risk to family health from passive smoking. Once certain that it is time to quit, the client's goal is to be a nonsmoker in 5 days. The nurse may encourage the client to identify family members, friends, or a specific person who may want to join the effort as a quit-smoking partner. The client should tell significant people the quit date.

Preparation for Nicotine Withdrawal (Basic to Advanced). There is no one best way to quit smoking. Some people are successful at just quitting "cold turkey" and going through the nicotine withdrawal, with the worst part usually lasting 5 days or less. Others require a gradual decrease of nicotine with the use of NRT. The client must decide which way is best for him or her.

If the client does not wish to use NRT, nicotine fading is a way to reduce the nicotine level in the body gradually and avoid withdrawal symptoms (e.g., irritability, lack of energy, increased cough). Each week for 3 weeks, the client buys a different brand of cigarette, each containing progressively less nicotine. By the end of the 3 weeks, the level of nicotine in the body has been substantially reduced. While using nicotine fading, it is important to record smoking habits accurately; the nicotine amount, time smoked, place smoked, alone or with others, and mood or feeling. The client should continue to smoke the same number of cigarettes and maintain the same manner of inhaling, because changes here defeat the purpose of this technique.

Another way to quit smoking is called focused smoking or rapid smoking. Clients should try this technique only under supervision, particularly those with heart disease or diabetes. Since this technique is not a pleasant experience, many researchers believe that it should be a last resort. The client needs cigarettes, matches, ashtray, candle and candle holder, wastepaper basket, paper to record responses, and pen or pencil. During a session, the smoker goes to his or her place and arranges the supplies. The wastepaper basket is placed to one side to be available in case vomiting occurs. The smoker lights a candle, then lights a cigarette from the candle flame, and takes a puff every 6 seconds. Immediately upon finishing one cigarette, the client lights the next cigarette. This is continued until the client is nauseated, three cigarettes have been smoked, and more smoking is impossible due to unpleasant body responses. The process is recorded and then repeated.

The client should record unpleasant body responses, such as hot lips, hot mouth, hot tongue, burning throat, burning lungs, dizzy feeling, pounding heart, tingling hands and legs, flushed face, watering eyes, nausea, or headache. The responses should be rated on a scale of 1 (not at all unpleasant) to 10 (extremely unpleasant).

Acupuncture programs that include the use of citrate compound are another means of reducing the body's nicotine level and are a rapid way to quit smoking, but, for sustained success, it is necessary to plan and learn new behavior strategies to bring about new health behaviors to replace smoking habits. This kind of program involves a single acupuncture session and the oral administration of a citrate compound, which causes the urine to become alkaline and retards the urinary excretion of nicotine. This process prevents a sudden fall of nicotine blood level, which reduces the craving for nicotine and the withdrawal symptoms.

Smoke-Free Body and Environment (Basic). During the first few nonsmoking days, the client rids the body of toxic waste left from the cigarettes by bathing, brushing teeth, drinking water, exercise, relaxation, imagery, rest, and good nutrition. A fresh nonsmoking living environment can be accomplished by placing clean filters in heating and cooling units and cleaning carpets, drapes, clothes, office, and car. Signs may be placed on the office door: "Thank you for not smoking." The more energy that the client puts into these activities, the more likely that the client will quit on the target date and become a permanent nonsmoker. The client should become aware of how quickly the senses of smell and taste increase and how disgusting the smell and taste of cigarettes become.

Identification of Habit Breakers (Basic). Becoming smoke-free is directly related to minor changes in daily routines, referred to as habit breakers. Many ex-smokers report that the first 5 days of being smoke-free are the hardest. Minor or major changes in daily activities can be less stressful if accompanied by a healing state of awareness. If the client should slip and fall back into old routines, these relapses can become learning situations. The client can identify negative self-talk or a stressful situation in which a new habit breaker may not have been used soon enough. The following events are the times when smoking is most likely:

before starting the day:
- getting out of bed
- taking a bath or shower
- eating breakfast
- reading the newspaper
- starting work or driving to work

morning:
- telephone calls
- office or housework
- meetings
- morning breaks
- before, during, and after lunch

afternoons:
- telephone calls
- office or housework
- meetings
- afternoon breaks
- completing and organizing your work for the next day
- driving home or resting in late afternoon

evenings:
- before, during, and after dinner
- relaxing, watching television, or out with family or friends
- preparing for bed

It is helpful to create habit breakers for each of these events. Success with habit breakers requires commitment to identifying them, writing them down, and finding ways to personalize this list. For example, the client can take this list, divide a piece of paper into two columns, and write down new habit breakers.

Routine	*Habit Breaker*
Turning to radio news on awakening	Play relaxing music
Five cups of coffee at breakfast	Hot tea instead of coffee
Frequent lighting of cigarettes	Keep hard candy nearby
Get energy from morning smoke	Eat an apple; drink water

Integration of Exercise (Basic). To the person becoming smoke-free, an exercise program serves as a stress manager (as an alternative to smoking), helps with weight management, and increases energy levels. If the client does not have an exercise program, the nurse offers assistance and helps the client decide what life style patterns to approach first. It usually takes about 3 months for an exercise program to become a regular part of life, so the client may look for an exercise partner who is as serious about exercising or being a nonsmoker.

Weight gain can be avoided. It occurs because the nonsmoker eats too much, lacks aerobic exercise, and consumes too much alcohol. If weight management is a challenge, it is helpful to set a target date for establishing and following an exercise program 3 months or longer before the quit date. (Refer to Chapter 18 for specific strategies to maintain healthy weight.) Then, as the client commits to quitting smoking, one component of an effective stress management program has already begun.

Assertion of Bill of Rights (Basic). Clients may find it helpful to recite their Bill of Rights. They can be creative and add to this list.

I have a right to

- be smoke-free in any situation.
- review my list of reasons to stop smoking frequently, particularly before any social gathering.
- ask others not to smoke in my home, office, or car.
- sit in nonsmoking sections.
- remind myself that cigarettes actually taste bad and leave toxic substances in my body.
- throw away all objects associated with smoking.
- keep sugarless gum and hard candy close at hand.
- practice my relaxation, imagery, and coping skills anywhere and at any time.
- keep liquids close by at work and at home.
- support legislation to protect nonsmokers from the dangers of passive smoking in public places.

Integration of Rewards (Basic). The client should plan a reward at least every 5 to 7 days for having a smoke-free life style. These rewards should continue as long as the client needs to be aware of new life style habits. The client is considered smoke-free when his or her habits are indeed nonsmoking behaviors. Continued use of the listed habit breakers always helps a client anticipate when smoke signals can surface and, thus, quickly take actions to prevent relapse. (Refer to Chapters 10 and 14 for more on rewards.)

Reinforcement of Positive Self-Talk (Basic). Feelings, moods, behaviors, and motivation affect physiologic changes. As the client learns to recognize the self-talk that sabotages his or her positive outlook, it is possible for the client to remain in control and not give in to the urge to smoke. Negative rationalization must be recognized, because it can gradually lead to doubt about the ability to change. The client may change "I've become more nervous since I quit smoking" to "I am noticing a change in my moods since quitting and replacing it with relaxation and imagery practice. This makes me feel much better than the short burst of nicotine energy." Similarly, negative thoughts must be identified and replaced with positive thoughts. For example, "I'll never get over this urge to smoke; I'll never be successful at breaking the habit" may be reframed as "Of course, I can get over this urge. I am learning new coping strategies, and I can really imagine myself smoke-free."

Smoking Cessation: Imagery Scripts (Basic). To enhance the client's success at becoming smoke-free, the nurse can create a relaxation and imagery tape or provide the following script/s to the client to make his or her own tape. The following scripts help the client form correct biologic images of being smoke-free. They can be modified or expanded, depending on present habits and which new skills the client wishes to develop in order to break the nicotine habit. A relaxation exercise from Chapter 22 may be recorded for 5 to 10 minutes; then the script for smoking cessation is recorded for 15 minutes. The nurse should encourage the client to listen to the tape for 20 minutes several times a day.

Script: **Introduction.** *(Name), as your mind becomes clearer and clearer, feel it becoming more and more alert. Somewhere deep inside of you, a brilliant light begins to glow. Sense this happening. . . . The light grows brighter and more intense. . . . This is your bodymind communication center. Breathe into it. . . . Energize it with your breath. The light is powerful and penetrating, and a beam begins to grow from it. The beam shines into your body now as you prepare to focus on being smoke-free. . . .*

In your relaxed state . . . affirm to yourself at your deep level of inner strength and knowing . . . that you can stop smoking. Say it over and over as you begin to see the words and feelings in every cell in your body. Feel your relaxed state deepen. You can get to this space anytime you wish . . . all you have to do is give yourself the suggestion and stay with the suggestion as you move into your relaxed state. This is a skill that you will use repeatedly as you move into being smoke-free.

Script: **Quit Date.** *Congratulate yourself for setting your quit date. You are aware of all your resources to quit. With your mind's eye now . . . see your calendar and experience yourself reading your quit date. With full intention to quit, mark your quit date on the calendar. Enlist the help of your family or a friend as you set your quit date.*

Script: **Cleansing Your Body and Environment.** *It is now time to rid your body of toxins left from the cigarettes. Begin to cleanse your body. . . . Feel the toxins flowing out of your body as you increase the liquids you drink. Practice your deep breathing exercises, remembering to exhale completely . . . enjoying this new awareness of how healthy your lungs will become with the cleansing and clearing of toxins. Experience your breath, skin, hair . . . fresh as a spring breeze. See yourself making your surroundings smoke-free day by day. Notice the pleasant changes in your new, nonsmoking environment. . . . First, begin to notice how you are becoming more sensitive to smells . . . enjoy the freshness of your clothes, home, office, and car being free of smoke.*

As you keep your records, become aware of your progress. Reward yourself regularly. Imagine you have had 5 smoke-free days. The worst of any withdrawal is over. What is your first reward going to be? Give yourself a big reward!

As you continue to deepen your relaxation, repeat to yourself the words "I am calm." Let your body experience these words in your own unique way. Register this feeling throughout your body. Begin to increase your awareness of feeling good about being alive, to be conscious of beginning new habits . . . free of smoking.

Script: **Smoke Signals.** *Starting now, reflect on your wonderful decision to release the habit of smoking . . . a habit that could cause illness and take away your energy and vitality. Get in touch with your smoke signals. Is it a certain time of day, a person, a place, or social gathering? As you bring them into awareness, . . . rehearse in your mind the healthy behaviors you will use to replace the urges. . . . Is it drinking a glass of water . . . chewing sugar-free gum, going for a walk, listening to music, chewing on a toothpick, or taking a hot shower or bath. And as you think* *about smoking urges . . . those foolish habits . . . you can hear your powerful inner voice repeating clear affirmations, . . . "I have stopped smoking . . . I am free of smoking . . . I feel strong and healthy . . . I can taste, and smell fragrances. My cough has gone."*

Hear your own voice saying, "I no longer crave a habit negatively affecting my health. This habit is diminishing steadily, and I can envision being completely free of this addiction. My mind is functioning in such a manner that I no longer crave tobacco . . . a habit that has affected my lungs and heart. I no longer place unnecessary strain on these organs so vital to life."

When you feel the urge to smoke, hear yourself saying, "Stop! I don't need to smoke any more. I am free." These words will become more powerful the more you say them. Remember this message is always with you . . . and you are no longer a smoker. That is behind you.

Script: **Nutritious Eating and Exercise.** *"As I stop smoking, I will not be excessively hungry or eat excessively. Because of the power of my unconscious mind, I am free of my addiction. I am conscious of increasing my exercise to three or four times a week for 20 minutes or longer. I am increasing my fluid intake and chewing sugar-free gum. I am sleeping soundly at night. I am free of smoking . . . I am free." You can reach this inner wisdom any time that you wish . . . all you have to do is take the time.*

Script: **Closure.** *Take a few slow, energizing breaths and, as you come back to full awareness of the room, know that whatever is right for you at this point in time is unfolding just as it should and that you have done your best, regardless of the outcome. . . .*

Case Study

Setting: Nurse-based wellness clinic smoking cessation program

Client: J.N., a 48-year-old interior designer, telling her story to the new clients after she has been smoke-free for 5 years.

Nursing Diagnosis: Health maintenance related to engagement in strategies to remain smoke-free

"You can call it midlife crisis or whatever; I just happened to wake up and tell myself that I'm worth a better state of health and mind. How did I do it—lots of determination and reprogramming my mind with successful images. I never dreamed that I could be so successful at quitting smoking. I'd tried to quit on many occasions, but the reason I never was able to sustain change is that I had tried to quit before I really was ready to do so.

"I'd been smoking for 27 years, and I just got tired of my chronic cough and feeling tired. Other things began to happen also. My family and friends began to ask for nonsmoking sections in restaurants and gave me 3 months before they declared the house a nonsmoking house. They also placed a disgusting, ugly series of pictures of me smoking with a title on it saying, 'We Love You—Quit Smoking!' The first time I looked at the pictures, I burst into tears and heard their message loud and clear. I got in touch with why I began smoking in the first place as a teenager—I thought I looked important and glamorous. Those pictures certainly didn't convey that image.

"The last straw that really got my attention was when a friend and I were driving along with our windows down on a nice spring day. My friend said to me, 'Who do you think is smoking?' We could see no person smoking, but my friend could smell it. It turned out that our lane of traffic started moving before the one next to us. Sure enough, there was a smoker three cars in front of us in the left lane to us. I was driving, and, as we passed the car, smoke came in our window. I couldn't smell it even though I could see the smoke coming in the window. My friend was able to smell it long after we passed the smoker. I was astounded that I couldn't smell it.

"I really planned a ritual for my quit date for ending smoking—which has changed my life in many ways. I have now been smoke-free for 5 years. Let me begin by saying that, in the previous 15 years, I had tried to quit smoking seven times; each time I was successful for 1 month at the longest, so I knew that it was possible. As I look back on it now, the reason that I didn't have any sustained change was that I didn't shape any new behaviors or thoughts.

"Let me share with you my rituals. I planned a 5-day period to be by myself to focus on shaping new behaviors. The reason I chose to stay at home was the importance of preparation and concentration of new thoughts and behaviors prior to my quit date.

"Prior to that special week, I began my 'detox' process. I decided to buy a new bright blue toothbrush, which I placed in a beautiful small wicker basket. I also placed this on the opposite side of where I usually kept my toothbrush. It just seemed important to change all of my bathing habits. When brushing my teeth gently, frequently followed by a mouthwash, I was aware of repeating words to myself about cleansing and purifying. I used these same thoughts when I bathed. I would stand in the shower and concentrate on the water washing the toxins from my skin. For the internal removal of toxins, I increased my fluid intake of water and herb teas to 6 to 8 glasses a day. Exercise also became part of my ritual. I would get up each day and start my morning with a 30-minute walk. On the walk, I used the time to see myself smoke-free. When I came in from my walks, I would watch a 20-minute video of beautiful images and healing statements about successfully breaking the smoke habit and being free. [See resource list.]

"Well, my home environment reeked of smoke and staleness. My drapes and fabric chairs and couches had not been cleaned in 16 years; my carpets, in 8. I allowed myself the luxury of having them professionally cleaned. Not only did the house smell fresh, but all the colors were very fresh and seemed new. Air conditioning filters were changed. I cleaned clothes that were well overdue. I aired the house.

"The biggest task was to gather all the cigarette packages throughout the house. They were in every room, and I had about three full cartons when I finally gathered them all up. This was really scary for me, because when I saw them all together, the thought that came to me was, 'I'm really addicted. There is no way I can break this habit.' Out of nowhere, this very loud, powerful voice blurted out, 'Yes, you can, and you have already begun.' I have never heard such volume from my own voice. It was as if it was a voice other than my own. Prior to that, I also removed all of the ashtrays and bought a beautiful door sign which read, THANK YOU FOR NOT SMOKING. When I placed it above the door bell, I felt this inner sensation of glee and energy. It was very affirming to me, and, from that moment on, there was no stopping my success. I really believed for the first time that I was going to be successful, and I felt an inner strength that I had never experienced before. I also received so much encouragement from my husband and two children when they came home that evening. I cleaned my car as well as I had the house. Now it was time to sign my contract with the family.

"During this period of 1 week of cleaning my body, house, and car, I recorded my internal and external cues of why I smoked. It was when I was hungry, talking on the phone, when I was putting on my makeup in the morning, and after meals. During this time, I let myself smoke no more than three cigarettes a day—outside standing up. I concentrated on what a disgusting habit smoking was. As I focused on these messages to myself, I not only slowed down the smoking, I also didn't enjoy the cigarettes and found that it was really not as pleasant as in the past. I had tried this before, but my thoughts were also on how much I was going to miss the smoking and pleasure of the buzz from smoking. I was so aware of not really enjoying it as much as I used to.

"I well remember my quit date 5 years ago. It is so clear; it is as if I planned it just yesterday. The reason it seems so recent is that my preparation and commitment to stopping smoking has spilled over into other areas in my life. Do I miss smoking? Frankly, I'll say yes. I have those urges on occasions. However, as I've integrated relaxation, imagery, and positive affirmations in my life, my commitment to being smoke-free is stronger. I honor that inner voice that says, 'Light Up.' For me, what works best is to hear the message, honor that I heard it, but to replace smoking with something that is always with me—the power of relaxed breathing. I also use a saying a friend taught me, which is Avoid H.A.L.T.—avoid becoming too *h*ungry, too *a*ngry, too *l*onely, or too *t*ired. Time, commitment, and believing in my success is part of every day for me. Quitting smoking is one of the hardest things I've ever done. I can't remember planning so well for any event in my life. I believed I could do it, and that is exactly what continued to happen."

Evaluation

With the client, the nurse determines whether the client outcomes for smoking cessation (see Table 19–1) were successfully achieved. To evaluate the session further, the nurse may again explore the subjective effects of the experience with the client (Exhibit 19–2).

Exhibit 19–2 Evaluating the Client's Subjective Experience with Smoking Cessation Interventions

1. Did you gain any new insight today about your smoking patterns?
2. Do you have any questions about preparing for a quit date?
3. Do you have any questions about recording your habits?
4. Can you identify two new habit breakers right now to be smoke-free?
5. Are you aware of your bodymind signals of wanting to smoke?
6. What relaxation exercises are most helpful to you in replacing smoking habits?
7. What will be your exercise program?
8. Do you have any questions about the active, process imagery and end-state imagery exercises you experienced today?
9. Did you like the imagery exercises?
10. Did you gain any new insight about your self-talk of being smoke-free?
11. What are three affirmations to help you just now create an image change of being smoke-free?
12. What is your next step?

To become an ex-smoker, a client must understand that it is a gradual step-by-step process that requires learning new skills. Smoking cessation involves (1) recognizing smoking habits, (2) establishing habit breakers, (3) preparing for detoxification of body and environment, (4) following a good nutrition and exercise program, and (5) modifying behavior. The integration of these five areas helps clients achieve new awareness about being smoke-free with new life style patterns and improved relationships with people at work and at home.

DIRECTIONS FOR FUTURE RESEARCH

1. Determine the nursing interventions that most effectively minimize stress as clients begin a smoking cessation program.
2. Evaluate combinations of smoking cessation content and teaching methods to determine which are most effective in assisting a client in sustained smoking cessation.
3. Identify the nursing interventions that are most useful in helping a client cope with fears regarding relapse.

NURSE HEALER REFLECTIONS

After reading this chapter, the nurse healer will be able to answer or begin a process of answering the following questions:

- What rituals can I create or assist others in creating to detoxify and cleanse the body and environment of all traces of nicotine?
- What are my internal cues of reacting to smoke?
- What are my external cues of reacting to smoke?
- What are specific process, end-state, and general healing images for teaching myself or others about releasing attachments to smoking and moving forward in being smoke-free?

NOTES

1. M.C. Fiore et al., Methods Used To Quit Smoking in the United States: Do Cessation Programs Help? *Journal of the American Medical Association* 263, no. 20 (1990):2760–2765.
2. Ibid., 2760.

3. T. Ferguson, *The No-Nag, No-Guilt, Do-It-Your-Own-Way Guide to Quitting Smoking* (New York: Ballantine Books, 1987), 18–29.
4. Fiore et al., Methods Used To Quit Smoking, 2761.
5. P. Gunby, Legal Challenge to Medically Correct Smoking Bans, *Journal of the American Medical Association* 271, no. 8 (1994):577.
6. Ibid.
7. J.R. Palmer, et al., Low Yield Cigarettes and the Risk of Nonfatal Myocardial Infarction in Women, *New England Journal of Medicine* 320, no. 24 (1989):1569–1573.
8. Ibid., 1571.
9. M. Weitzman, et al., Maternal Smoking and Childhood Asthma, *Pediatrics* 85, no. 4 (1990):505–511.
10. Ibid., 512.
11. Ibid., 513.
12. B. Chilmonezyk, Association between Exposure to Environmental Tobacco Smoke and Exacerbation of Asthma in Children, *New England Journal of Medicine* 328, no. 21 (1993):1665–1669.
13. Ferguson, *Guide to Quitting Smoking*, 20–25.
14. Ibid., 14–16.
15. H. Aston and R. Stepney, Smoking as a Psychological Tool, in *Smoking: Psychology and Pharmacology*, ed. H. Aston and R. Stepney (London: Tavistock Publications, 1982), 91–119.
16. Ferguson, *Guide to Quitting Smoking*, 20.
17. M. Fiore et al., A Missed Opportunity: Teaching Medical Students To Help Patients Successfully Quit Smoking, *Journal of the American Medical Association* 271, no. 8 (1994):624–626.
18. Ibid.
19. E. Gilpin, Physician Advice To Quit Smoking: Results from the 1990 California Tobacco Survey, *Journal of General Internal Medicine* 8(1993):549–553.
20. G. Richardson et al., Smoking Cessation after Successful Treatment of Small-Cell Lung Cancer, *Annals of Internal Medicine* 119, no. 21 (1993):383–390.
21. C. Silagy et al., Meta-Analysis on Efficacy of Nicotine Replacement Therapies in Smoking Cessation, *Lancet* 343 (1994):139–142.
22. R. Hurt et al., Nicotine Patch Therapy for Smoking Cessation Combined with Physician Advice and Nurse Follow-Up, *Journal of the American Medical Association* 271, no. 8 (1994):595–600.
23. S. Kenford et al., Predicting Smoking Cessation: Who Will Quit with and without the Nicotine Patch, *Journal of the American Medical Association* 271, no. 8 (1994):589–594.
24. P. Gunby, Health Experts to Youth: Don't Give Tobacco a Start, *Journal of the American Medical Association* 271, no. 8 (1994):580.
25. Ibid.
26. Ibid.
27. J. Elder et al., The Long-Term Prevention of Tobacco Use among Junior High School Students: Classroom and Telephone Interventions, *American Journal of Public*

Health 83 (1993):1239–1244.

28. D. Sheridan et al., Demographic and Education Differences in Smoking in a Tobacco-Growing State, *American Journal of Preventive Medicine* 9 (1993):155–159.
29. Ibid.
30. J. Pierce, Smoking Initiation by Adolescent Girls, 1944 through 1988: An Association with Target Advertising, *Journal of the American Medical Association* 271, no. 8 (1994):608–611.
31. N. Kaufman, Smoking and Young Women, *Journal of the American Medical Association* 271, no. 8 (1994):629–630.
32. Ibid.
33. Ibid.
34. P. Gunby, Sports, Medical Officials Call 'Spit' Tobacco 'Out,' *Journal of the American Medical Association* 271, no. 8 (1994):580.

RESOURCE

Positive Harmonic Imagery: Stop Smoking Program (video)
New Era Media
P.O. Box 410685-BT
San Francisco, California 94141
(415) 863-3555

VISION OF HEALING

Changing One's World View

Each of us holds a world view, a set of beliefs about how the world operates, why things happen the way that they do, and what rules they follow. We seldom give a thought to our world view, but it is a powerful, guiding force in all our lives. We cannot escape the effects of our world view. It begins to operate the very moment that we begin each day. The moment we walk into work or into a social gathering, we put our world view into action. Do we have control over our lives, or do things happen by accident? Do people with addictions have any control over their illness, or is illness only a function of the physiologic processes that are occurring in the body? Does choice exist in health and illness, or is the body entirely "on automatic"? Our world view gives us answers to difficult questions like these. The more conscious we become of the assumptions we make in our world view, the more effective we will become in our interactions with self and others.

To be present for ourselves and others, we must honor our personal needs. It is necessary to accept the current circumstances of our lives and release our attempts to control things over which we have no control. We can honor ourselves each day with relaxation, imagery, music, meditation, or prayer. We can create an exercise program; take long, hot baths or showers; eat nutritional foods; eliminate excess caffeine or junk food; and ask other people for help, if needed. We need to tell ourselves over and over, until we believe it, what a good job we are doing.

Caring for ourselves each day requires simple things. When waking up in the morning and before getting out of bed, we can say to ourselves, "The part of me that is most in need of healing right now is . . ." and "The things that I can do to bring about my healing are. . . ." The answers are usually simple, such as "I need to take a morning break and a lunch break, have a massage, or ask a friend to meet me for a chat." Repeating such statements as often as necessary during the day increases our awareness of basic assumptions and life choices. By honoring ourselves, we release fear, depression, loneliness, suffering, feelings of discouragement, crisis, or tragic moments so that being with ourselves or another is quality time. Recognizing our world view and learning to care for ourselves make it possible for us to help a person with addictions move toward healing and spiritual transformation.

Chapter 20

Overcoming Addictions: Recovering through Life

Barbara Montgomery Dossey

NURSE HEALER OBJECTIVES

Theoretical

- Discuss fragmented families, origins, and recurrent themes of addiction.
- Analyze the concepts of context and validation as major keys to spiritual transformation for overcoming addiction.

Clinical

- Develop your interview style of assessing clients' awareness of substance abuse.
- Identify addictions counselors and specific addiction support groups in your community to which clients can be referred.
- Provide support staff, qualified counselors, and a mechanism to obtain treatment, if required, for any clients and colleagues who have a substance abuse problem.

Personal

- Take the Problem Drinker Self-Assessment, and determine if drinking is a problem in your life.
- Compare and contrast your stress levels, moods, and use of substances (e.g., alcohol) and learn more effective stress management strategies.

DEFINITIONS

Addiction: a physiologic or psychologic dependence upon a substance (e.g., alcohol, cocaine) or behavior (e.g., gambling, sex, eating).

Co-dependence: a dysfunctional relationship between two or more people in which an individual is as dependent on an alcoholic as the alcoholic is on alcohol or others for addictive substances or sources.

Spiritual Emergency: a crisis that an addicted person goes through in learning about the spiritual self.

Spiritual Transformation: the insights gained by the addicted person when breaking through addiction/s.

THEORY AND RESEARCH

Addiction As an Illness

Addiction is literally a disconnection from the human spirit in which a person develops a dependence on various aspects of the external world—a substance, a person, a situation, or a behavior—as the major source of satisfaction. It often leads to dysfunctional relationships in which the participants are co-dependent. The American Medical Association and the World Health Organization have both recognized addiction as an illness, not a lack of willpower. There are many types of addictions, but alcohol is the most prevalent addiction problem in the United States.

Prevalence of Alcoholics and Social Drinkers

Alcoholism afflicts at least 11 million people in the United States. It leads to approximately 200,000 premature deaths a year; disrupts the lives of some 40 million family members; and costs an estimated $117 billion a year in medical bills, property damage, and lost time and productivity.[1] In the United States today, there are 90 million social drinkers who enjoy alcohol and have a habit of using it.[2] As part of the health revolution, many people have decreased their intake of fat, sugar, caffeine, and cholesterol. They have started exercise and weight management programs, and they are becoming more educated about decreasing alcohol consumption as part of improving their health. There are many theories about the amount that someone can drink and remain healthy. For the majority of people, alcohol seems to be a relatively safe relaxant. For the minority who cannot control their drinking or ingestion of drugs or other substances, alcohol has an enormous price. To help these people, it is necessary to collect and understand information about their present life patterns and family history through self-assessment and advice from a physician, member of the clergy, or a health care professional who specializes in addiction counseling.

Fragmented Families

Addiction is indeed a family disease. It narrows the family's vision so that the family does not grow.[3,4] Instead, the family is always trying to maintain balance and stability. When one family member introduces an unhealthy element, such as alcohol or drugs, the whole system becomes unhealthy in order to maintain its balance. The family that once supported the addicted person now supports the disease, often denying the problems of alcohol or drugs, hiding from the evidence, and covering up the addicted family member's behaviors (referred to as enabling behaviors). The spouse of an alcoholic is at higher risk for physical and emotional problems than is the spouse of a nonalcoholic. Children of alcoholics are at increased risk of behavioral problems, depression, and child abuse. There is also an increased likelihood that the children of alcoholics will themselves develop alcoholism or marry into another family with alcoholism, which perpetuates the high-risk situation.

The only way to break an addiction is to learn new life style patterns. Regardless of how fragmented an individual, a family member, or friend has become, the addicted person and the family can obtain access to their inner resources. The dynamic nature of the human energy system is such that it always has the possibility for healing. Individuals who learn to replenish vitality and develop a sense of self-control are less likely to become dependent on alcohol or drugs to "unwind" or to energize them.

Story Themes of Addictions

As addicted clients or their families and friends tell their personal stories, recurring themes appear. Old behaviors are unconsciously repeated, and past behaviors become present life style. These clients become attached to the external sources of alcohol, drugs, food, people, events, and material possessions as a way to maintain their self-image or ego. They have feelings of suffering or victimization as they seek satisfaction outside themselves. Along the way, they may feel a deeper anxiety and fear that, without the attachment, the self will totally disintegrate.[5]

In spite of the spiritual emptiness that addicted individuals experience, most are unaware of this as an issue at the time that they seek treatment. The dominant feelings of addicted clients are chaos, pain, and suffering associated with problems in relationships at home and at work. Desperation and disgust with themselves often make them feel that they may die or wish that they could die. Prior to treatment, they usually deny the spiritual issues. The longer a person holds onto destructive behavior patterns, however, the more emotional pain and suffering arise. Regardless of the struggle to find satisfaction in external sources, no genuine happiness can be sustained unless one connects with the healing core—the spiritual nature.

Origin of Addiction

Confusion, turmoil, and fragmentation in health, work, and relationships are frequent experiences for people with addictions. They often describe their early childhood in terms of parental rejection, neglect, or overindulgence. Their perception of events may not be accurate, but it is their frame of reference. The sense of rejection may lie in their memory of parents' saying that they were never good enough or could never be as good as their siblings. The absence of parental supervision, maybe being left alone at night or with intoxicated parents, may be a reflection of neglect. Overindulgence may have been originated in a smothering relationship, such as being a "favorite child" that evoked a tremendous guilt in the person toward siblings.

The most successful approaches to healing a client from addiction encourage the client to heal the origins of trauma in the old life and to release the intellectual explanations of his or her identity. Moving into emotional recovery (e.g., by inner child work) is the first step. The work of addicted persons who awaken to their spiritual resources occurs long into the recovery process. Alcoholics and other addicts describe declining into the depths of addiction as filling the hole (spiritual bankruptcy) or meeting a need (soul sickness) and their recovery as healing their impoverished soul or being reborn.[6] The way for a person to achieve this breakthrough is to learn healing strategies that help create inner peace and harmony in life. The resulting state of transcendence is beyond the day-to-day ordinary state of awareness.

Spiritual Development and Transformation

Spiritual development is an innate evolutionary capacity of all people. With the addiction process in a client's life, self-care and support groups are important because of their goal of helping the client develop spiritually. As shown in Chapter 1, spirituality is not a concept, but a process of learning about love, caring, empathy, and meaning in life. This process leads a person to connect with his or her psyche—soul, spirit—and to have a lived experience of inner peace and harmony that allows access to inner wisdom, the healer that always resides within. Addicted people are often totally out of touch with their feelings; when they are in touch with their feelings, they have no reference point that allows them to recognize a normal emotional response. The substance has served as an emotional anesthesia, and their emotional development may have ceased when they started using substances, which is often adolescence. Addicted people are in touch only with a "chemical high" and devoid of the transcendent experience.

Most treatment centers focus on helping clients get in touch with their feelings. Currently, there is much interest in recovery from addictions through transpersonal exploration. By engaging the addicted individuals' imagination and memory, transpersonal interventions may evoke a state of spiritual awakening as they enter into the pain that they have denied and learn about their spiritual self. Spiritual transformation requires investigation of one's addiction and learning skills to once again reconnect with a life of purpose and direction. It takes a long time and comes late in recovery. When it comes, there are two major keys for transformation of the spirit: context and validation.[7] Support programs based on 12-step work are effective because they provide a context within which the addicted person can explore many experiences, including mystical or religious questions and events, and new insight about the validation for these human processes. This is the healing journey of learning about the dark side of the soul in order to return to the source of wholeness that is always present.[8] As suggested in the founding principle of Alcoholics Anonymous (AA), *spiritus contra spiritum*, it takes the core qualities of a spiritual approach to heal a disorder.

Bodymind Responses

In a study of 1,862 persons, Benson and Wallace found that those who used prescription and illicit drugs began reducing their intake of drugs as they learned to experience a deep state of relaxation.[9] After 21 months of regular meditation, most had stopped using drugs completely. The investigators also looked closely at alcohol use in these same subjects. They classified drinkers as light users (three times a month or less), medium users (once to six times a week), and heavy users (once a day or more). After 21 months of meditation, heavy use of illicit drugs had dropped from 2.7 to 0.6 percent, medium use from 15.8 to 3.7 percent, and light use from 41.4 to 25.8 percent. The percent of nonusers of alcohol rose from 40.1 to 69.9 percent. Most participants in this study, 61.1 percent, reported that meditation was "extremely important" in helping to reduce their alcohol consumption. The more these people meditated, the less they drank.

In another study, 20 male drug users between the ages of 21 and 38 began a meditation program.[10] Over several months, the men reported that they were no longer taking drugs because drug-induced feelings became extremely distasteful when compared to those experienced during the practice of meditation.

At the University of Washington in Seattle, Marlett and Marques found that college students who were heavy drinkers were able to reduce their alcohol use by 50 to 60 percent when they exercised and meditated regularly.[11] Exercise and meditation are effective because they offer an alternative method of reducing daily stress, confusion, discomfort, and fear. Brainwave biofeedback is also important in that it assists clients in getting in touch with feelings of tension and then learning to recognize the deep relaxation that replaces the chemical high from addicted substances.[12]

Researchers at Seattle's Harborview Medical Center tested 2,378 trauma patients for intoxication on admission (blood alcohol count higher than 100 mg/dL) and chronic alcohol abuse (abnormal levels of the liver enzyme gamma-glutamyltransferase) and followed the patients for an average of 28 months after discharge.[13] Even after other factors had been accounted for, patients who were drunk at the time of the trauma or chronic abusers were 50 to 60 percent more likely than others to return. Trauma centers have largely ignored alcohol abuse; nearly half do not screen for alcohol abuse, and those that do only rarely refer patients known to be alcoholic to treatment programs. Yet the research just cited from Harborview suggests that trauma can be used to motivate the patient and his or her family to confront the alcohol problem.

Ultradian Approach to Addictions

The bio-psycho-social-spiritual factors behind addictive behaviors are complex and vary from person to person. The ultradian stress syndrome (see Chapter 4) suggests that binge behavior of any sort becomes an addiction when it interferes with an individual's normal ultradian and circadian rhythms. The substances of abuse in all behavior addictions are the body's own natural mind-body messenger molecules poured out to excess. When individuals chronically override the normal ultradian/circadian rest periods, they become addicted to an emotional high from the body's own stress-released hormonal messenger molecules.

The ultradian healing response (the 20-minute period of rest and rejuvenation out of every 90- to 120-minute ultradian cycle) works in three ways to help people avoid and overcome addictions.[14] First, ultradian breaks sensitize people to the natural mind-body signals for a period of rest and recovery, and they reduce the risk of the ultradian stress syndrome that sets the stage for substance abuse. Second, ultradian healing responses throughout the day keep every day's stressors from building to a point at which recovering abusers are tempted to relapse and allow them to move through the stages of change and maintain the termination stage (see Chapter 5). Third, the consistent use of ultradian healing responses throughout the day can facilitate recovery from emotional dysphoria (depression) and anhedonia (lack of pleasure) during the withdrawal period and afterward.

Individuals can learn that the feeling or desire for a drug is a prime cue that they are beginning to experience the ultradian stress syndrome and that the best thing for them to do is to take a breather to get in touch with their inner experiences. It is also important to link binges with the ultradian stress response and physiologic events. For example, research suggests a link between alcoholism and hypoglycemia.[15] Thus, as addicted individuals learn to eat nutritious foods, they are more likely to recognize the ultradian stress syndrome and take a break for a high-fiber, low-fat snack. Rather than indulging in the usual addiction, this can be an opportunity to heal tension through the natural ultradian healing response.

NURSING PROCESS

Assessment

As mentioned earlier, the most prevalent addiction in the United States is alcoholism. In preparing to use strategies to assist clients in overcoming alcoholism, the nurse assesses the following parameters:

- the client's characteristics that may suggest alcoholism
    1. restlessness, impulsiveness, anxiety
    2. selfishness, self-centeredness, lack of consideration
    3. stubbornness, irritability, anger, rage, ill humor
    4. physical cruelty, brawling, child/spouse abuse

5. depression, isolation, self-destructiveness
6. aggressive sexuality, often accompanied by infidelity, which may give way to sexual disinterest or impotence
7. arrogance that may lead to aggression, coldness, or withdrawal
8. low self-esteem, shame, guilt, remorse, loneliness
9. reduced mental and physical function; eventual blackouts
10. susceptibility to other disease
11. lying, deceit, broken promises
12. denial that there is a drinking problem
13. projection of blame onto people, places, and things

- the client's current drinking patterns (Exhibit 20–1 provides a self-scoring test that can be taken by a client or by a family member or friend concerned about the client's drinking.[16])
- the client's attitudes, beliefs, and motivation to learn interventions to become nonaddicted
- the client's available family and friends
- the client's eating and exercise patterns
- the client's existing stress management strategies
- the client's willingness to join a support group

Nursing Diagnoses

The following nursing diagnoses compatible with interventions for addictions and that are related to the human response patterns of Unitary Person (see Chapter 7) are as follows:

• Exchanging:	Altered nutrition (more/less than body requirements)
• Communicating:	Impaired verbal communication
• Relating:	Altered social interaction
	Altered family processes
• Valuing:	Spiritual distress
• Choosing:	Ineffective individual/family coping
• Moving:	Decreased physical mobility
• Perceiving:	Disturbance in self-esteem
	Disturbance in personal identity
	Hopelessness
	Powerlessness

Exhibit 20–1 Are You a Problem Drinker?

1. Have you ever tried to stop drinking for a week (or longer), only to fall short of your goal?
2. Do you resent the advice of others who try to get you to stop drinking?
3. Have you ever tried to control your drinking by switching from one alcoholic beverage to another?
4. Have you taken a morning drink during the past year?
5. Do you envy people who can drink without getting into trouble?
6. Has your drinking problem become progressively more serious during the past year?
7. Has your drinking created problems at home?
8. At social affairs where drinking is limited, do you try to obtain "extra" drinks?
9. Despite evidence to the contrary, have you continued to assert that you can stop drinking "on your own" whenever you wish?
10. During the past year, have you missed time from work as a result of drinking?
11. Have you ever "blacked out" (loss of memory) during your drinking?
12. Have you ever felt you could do more with your life if you did not drink?

Did you answer YES four or more times? If so, chances are you have a serious drinking problem, or may have one in the future.

Source: Courtesy of Alcoholics Anonymous World Services, Inc.

- Knowing: Knowledge deficit
  Altered thought processes
- Feeling: Anxiety
  Potential for violence
  Fear

Client Outcomes

Table 20–1 guides the nurse in client outcomes, nursing prescriptions, and evaluation for overcoming addictions.

Plan and Interventions

Before the Session

- Spend a few moments centering yourself to recognize your presence and to begin the session with intention to facilitate healing.

Table 20–1 Nursing Interventions: Overcoming Addictions

Client Outcomes	*Nursing Prescriptions*	*Evaluation*
The client will demonstrate attitudes, beliefs, and behaviors that indicate a desire to overcome addiction.	Determine the client's desire to overcome addiction.	The client demonstrated attitudes, beliefs, and behaviors that indicate a desire to overcome addiction.
	Assist the client in setting realistic plans for overcoming addiction by: • seeking support of family • attending AA meetings • seeking support of a sponsor • detoxifying self and environment of alcohol • practicing relaxation and imagery • integrating behavior changes • deciding rewards for attaining goals	The client set realistic plans for overcoming addiction as shown by: • accepted family support • attended AA meeting weekly • met with AA sponsor weekly • detoxified self and environment of alcohol • practiced relaxation/imagery daily • integrated behavior changes daily • rewarded self for attaining goals

AA, Alcoholics Anonymous

- Create a quiet place to begin guiding the client in strategies to overcome addiction/s.

At the Beginning of the Session

- Review the results of the self-assessment.
- Reinforce the concept that overcoming addictions is a process requiring commitment, new behavioral skills, and support from family and friends.
- Get the client to tell his or her personal story.
- Assist the client in identifying the steps necessary for overcoming addictions. The experiences for breaking addiction are unique to each client, but ***detoxification is absolutely essential*** for everyone. Assist the client in going through detoxification and being sober, as sobriety is prerequisite to any meaningful healing journey. Detoxifi-

cation may or may not require hospitalization. The client's healing team, family and friends, support group, or the treatment center staff can offer hope and insight about trusting self and others. Programs for all types of addictions, including those for pregnant addicts and newborns, are now offering acupuncture for detoxification.[17]

During the Session

- Teach the client general relaxation and imagery exercises with a focus on body-centered awareness of body responses to feelings.
- Teach the client how to create specific imagery patterns (see Chapter 23) and to practice and integrate the following:
  1. active images—cleansing the body of impurities, such as by a gentle waterfall; creating a safe place where the client can feel secure and comfortable; using a protective shield to let the client receive what is needed from others and to block out negative images, such as drink or drug signals, places, or events.
  2. end-state images—quality life of health, accomplishment of the important things in life with the assistance of supportive family and friends.
  3. healing images—inner healer and ways to connect with spiritual resources.
  4. process images—overcoming drink or drug signals that increase desire to drink or take drugs, such as places, people, times of day, smells.
- Teach the client to reframe current situations and problems. For example, instead of the client saying, "I can't admit publicly that I'm an alcoholic," help the client rehearse being at a 12-step meeting and saying, "Thank you for letting me share my story with you. I have been an alcoholic for 10 years, and I am ready to quit." Similarly, the client can rehearse being with friends at a party and refusing a drink or choosing a nonalcoholic beverage.
- Encourage the development of creative skills as a means of working with strong emotions and experiences. Some of these areas are actively working with dreams, journal keeping, letter writing (see Chapter 14); using artistic expressions by drawing, painting, sculpting with clay (see Chapter 23); playing evocative music to enhance images or to dance with the emotions (see Chapter 24).
- Have the client assert his or her Bill of Rights (see Chapters 18 and 19).

- Have the client identify his or her habit breakers (see Chapter 19).
- Have the client learn forgiveness (see Chapter 17).

At the End of the Session

- Encourage the client to explore the value of a 12-step program as an adjunct to treatment, to select a sponsor, and to be in daily contact with this person.
- Encourage the client to contract for health (see Chapter 10), for example, by co-signing a written contract with a nurse, a sponsor, a family member, or a friend to attend a 12-step meeting regularly. As the client progresses, extend the contract to include healthy nutrition, regular exercise, practice of relaxation and imagery techniques, and healthy recreational activities. Creating natural highs with new life style patterns requires planning to set aside time each day. The majority of people who start an exercise program stop because of time constraints. Exercise, relaxation, and imagery must become values, not just beliefs (see Chapter 5).
- Emphasize the importance of a support person who can be called at any time for help and involvement in a long-term support group to increase the likelihood of continued sobriety.
- Reinforce the idea that the client can outwit relapse by learning how to recognize high-risk situations (e.g., social situations, emotional upset, home or work frustration, interpersonal conflict) and being ready to act quickly to resist drinking or taking drugs. Successful coping strategies must honor internal responses (bodymind feelings and thoughts) and action-oriented responses (action steps). Encourage the client to make a list of the high-risk situations that can be anticipated and decide in advance quick action steps to prevent relapse.
- Use the client outcomes (see Table 20–1) that were established before the session and the client's subjective experience (Exhibit 20–2) to evaluate the session.
- Schedule a follow-up session.

Specific Interventions

Support from Family and Friends (Basic). The most special gift that a family can give an addicted member is to affirm that the person is loved unconditionally, but that the addicted behavior can no longer be tolerated. The family must decide the best approach to help that member and the whole family with recovery. Each family is unique. It is helpful for the spouse to get professional help, as many husbands and wives blame themselves for a spouse's addiction. Professional counseling for the family is advisable even if the addicted person chooses to join a support group. If the addicted person's behavior is unmanageable, a team of people will be necessary to get the addicted person admitted into a residential treatment program. For the team to be successful, intervention must be well planned; moreover, it usually involves a professional skilled in intervention.

Support Groups and Professional Help (Basic). The client needs continually to assess personal and work life and stressors. Because group support is vital to success, the client should become actively involved in a local support group for those with his or her specific addiction. Group support programs based on the 12-step programs—Alcoholics Anonymous (AA), Narcotics Anonymous (NA), OverEaters Anonymous (OA), CoDependency Anonymous (CODA), for example—are helpful. These groups are listed under the specific types of addiction in the telephone directory (see also Resource List). Alcoholics Anonymous is the best known support program, with a success rate that studies show is on a par with or better than expensive inpatient programs. The client should also seek out a professional who specializes in addictions counseling.

Few individuals successfully achieve freedom from addiction on their own. Addictive behaviors have been established and repeated over many years. Even if a client stays free of alcohol and drugs or stops the binge-purge cycle of bulimia or other addictions without help, the data show that the odds of relapse are high, because the person has not learned any new attitudes or health behaviors. Those who stop an addictive behavior on their own usually replace it with a new addiction, develop physical symptoms or illness, or begin other destructive behaviors that lead to further dysfunctional patterns. As reflected in the AA phrase, "The further you are from the last drink, the closer you are to the next one," AA views sobriety as a lifelong issue. The addicted person must be "working with the program," according to AA terminology, which means that the individual must explore inner psychologic work. Any resistance to working with the program is seen as a danger signal in the abstainer's recovering process. If the abstainer continues to be resistant to attitudinal and behavioral transformations, the abstainer is considered a "dry drunk," that is, someone who is not currently drinking (or using other substances), but who retains all the self-defeating attitudes of the active alcoholic.

Learning To Tell a Personal Story (Basic). Support groups provide clients with an opportunity to tell their unique stories and to listen to other people's stories, which help them reach their inner resources (see Chapters 14 and 15). A client's continuous inner dialogue creates stories and assigns meaning to experiences in life and perceptions of the world. The client can develop new awareness skills while listening as well as sharing stories.

Listening to other individuals' stories, as well as being listened to while telling a personal story, allows the client more opportunities to restore positive self-esteem, meaning, and purpose in life, and to develop a deeper insight into what is wrong or right. In 12-step work, a person takes a realistic look at one's self by reviewing life's journey and making amends to people who have been involved in the addiction process. One of the most painful parts of reviewing life's journey is learning to forgive oneself and others. The major factors that determine releasing attachments from addictions most often depend on how high the stakes are. Loss of health, family, or job may have enough impact to change behaviors. The point at which the stakes are so high that surrender with acceptance occurs is referred to as "hitting bottom."

Resistance to Spirituality (Basic to Advanced). There is much cynicism and discouragement in addictions treatment because professionals in private practice and in rehabilitation and treatment centers often see the "revolving door syndrome." Unlike so many other conditions with which nurses deal, an addiction is completely reversible. There is the possibility of a person's dramatic transformation. As nurses and other health care professionals interested in addictions counseling explore their own spirituality, they can serve as role models of grounding spirituality in real, human terms.[18] Furthermore, it is genuinely difficult for spiritually repressed nurses or psychotherapists to assist clients who are working through AA's 12-step program.[19]

Because of their compatibility with 12-step program and AA philosophy, spiritually oriented therapies and psychotherapy are important. Nurses and other professionals need to recognize that they cannot be available to the client 24 hours a day, and they cannot control the client's behavior. No single nurse or therapist can provide enough support and reinforcement for the recovering process. Thus, the nurse must be aware of the client's degree of participation in AA and any resistance to the AA spirituality dimensions in each of the AA meetings. If there is any such resistance, the nurse can help the person work through it, because an addicted person who rejects the spiritual components of AA is unlikely to participate in AA meetings.

When the spiritual discomfort is identified, the nurse or therapist can consider various cultural forms and expressions of spirituality.[20] Some individuals hear the word God in meetings and begin to reject AA's "God talk." If this is the case, the nurse can facilitate a more general approach to spirituality. For example, a woman who believes that God has not heard her prayers for protection from sexual abuse in adolescence may perceive AA meetings as confused and full of new age jargon. She feels desperate because she has been using alcohol and drugs for the second time. The nurse may then introduce the client to the possibility of spirituality without God, such as the approach of Buddhists, who have no concept of a personal God, but have a strong belief in the power of prayers to evoke healing. Thus, the client may develop a more open view of spirituality (see Chapter 10).

Relaxation and Imagery (Basic to Advanced). As previously noted, addicted individuals are not in touch with their bodies or feelings. Basic relaxation and imagery training can help them break the same old repetitive addiction habits that can create the spiral of hopelessness, depression, and despair. Not only does the daily practice of relaxation and imagery exercises reverse stress and depression, but also, immediately following the practice, the client is usually in a state to recognize inner knowledge and resources. Stopping the noisy chatter of negative self-talk, thoughts, and emotions helps the person to listen to the "voice of healing silence" and consciously choose to draw on inner strengths to begin and deepen the recovery process.

The client must become aware of body responses to stress—muscle tightness, headaches, stomachaches, for example. The abuse of alcohol, drugs, food, or other substances or behaviors numbs the body responses, literally anesthetizing the bodymind. Learning body and inner awareness becomes the touchstone for healing. With increased periods of inner calm, the client can shift to internal and external images of being without drugs or alcohol. Trusting this new feeling of calmness is the key to going beyond addiction and consistently integrating spiritual resources.

The client must learn to practice stress management skills daily rather than waiting until anxiousness occurs. Rhythmic breathing and progressive muscle relaxation exercises are very helpful in relearning body awareness. They also become a means of coping with anxiety in stressful situations. Learning to be in control without alcohol, drugs, or overeating, the client begins to anchor new feelings about trusting self in experience. Relaxation assists the person in "letting go" of attachments and overcoming barriers to recovery. As the client continues to practice deep relaxation and achieve active, process, and end-state images of breaking addiction signals, the client's own endorphin production creates states of "natural highs" without alcohol or drugs. These natural healthy states have a multiplier effect; they reduce not only substance abuse, but also coffee drinking, cigarette smoking, and junk food consumption.

The mind responds best when it is given positive images about new ideas and new behavior patterns. For example, an old alcohol addiction image is that of always having an alcoholic drink in hand at a party. Instead, the client can imagine drinking sparkling water at a party and learning to get in touch with the body sensations that might accompany this new behavior, such as natural feelings of confidence and energy without drugs. These new thinking patterns and events are novel stimuli with high informational value, and the bodymind responds. These new thought patterns create new life style patterns that become challenging and intriguing. When the mind receives new information, a person can begin to break addictions. As the client chooses more effective coping styles and strategies, sustained new behaviors emerge.

Daily relaxation and imagery practice provide quality time for clients to assess their current state and develop a willingness to let go of old life style patterns. As a result, attachments to things outside of self lose their strength. Creating process images and practicing these images so that they become integrated into bodymind patterns can block drink or drug signals, because the client can more easily recognize body sensations leading to addiction patterns. For example, a nurse may guide clients in a rhythmic breathing exercise, telling them to bring in images of being sober and clean and mentally to rehearse a walk down the street where they went to drink or use drugs with friends. These new process images, with practice, create new patterns. Clients can experience all the details and notice all the sensations in depth. Such rehearsals can help decrease anxiety about support meetings, as well as help the clients be open to receiving new insight.

Overcoming Addictions: Imagery Script (Basic to Advanced). To speed up the client's recovering process, the nurse can take time to create a special relaxation and imagery tape or provide the following scripts to the client to make a personal tape. The client should listen to a tape for 20 minutes several times a day. The following five scripts focus on substance abuse, but they can be modified for other addictions. A relaxation exercise from Chapter 22 may be recorded for 5 to 10 minutes; then one or several of the scripts for overcoming addictions may be recorded for 15 minutes or longer.

Script: **Introduction.** *(Name), as your mind becomes clearer and clearer, feel it becoming more and more alert. Somewhere deep inside of you, a brilliant light begins to glow. Sense this happening. The light grows brighter and more intense. This is the* *bodymind communication center. Breathe into it. Energize it with your breath. The light is powerful and penetrating, and a beam begins to grow out of it. The beam shines into the core of your spirit.*

Script: **Affirming Strengths.** *In your relaxed state . . . affirm to yourself at your deep level of inner strength and knowing . . . that you can stop drinking [or taking drugs]. Say it over and over as you begin to image the words and feelings in every cell in your body. Feel your relaxed state deepen. You can get to this space anytime that you wish . . . all you have to do is give yourself the suggestion and stay with the suggestion as you move into your relaxed state. This is a skill that you will use repeatedly as you move into your new healthy life patterns.*

You have gone through detox . . . you are sober. Notice what you are feeling. Increase your awareness of deepening your relaxation. You have come a long way and are on your path toward healing.

Have the client provide affirmations, and repeat them several times. For example, "I am at peace" . . . "I am totally relaxed" . . . "I feel safe and calm" . . . "I can drink water or other kinds of liquids that will satisfy my oral needs" . . . "I am secure in my inner knowledge that I have the strength for recovering."

Script: **Overcoming Drink/Drug Signals.** *Get in touch with your drink [or drug] signals. Is it a building, a time of day, a certain person, a social gathering? As you bring them in to awareness, rehearse in your mind changing one of those signals. For example, if a certain bar is your signal, . . . imagine you are walking down the street and you approach that favorite bar. But see yourself doing something different . . . as you pass by, you take a deep relaxed breath . . . and on the exhale . . . you have walked by the front door of the bar. Consciously affirm to yourself the choice that you have made. You feel confident, excited, pleased with your new patterns.*

Imagine that you are with people who are drinking at a party. You have water or another nonalcoholic beverage in your hand. You are enjoying your friends, but in a new way. Experience how well you can talk and share some stories without alcohol [or drugs]. If any tension arises, . . . once again, access your skills of relaxation and images of confidence . . . in control of your life and free of addiction. Notice these new, sensation-rich images of awareness and responsibility.

Script: **AA Meeting Rehearsal.** *See yourself attending an AA meeting. You have opened your body and mind to receive many positive messages and support from others about being sober. Imagine now that you have entered the meeting room and are pleased with yourself for being there. Look around the room. Is there any one person that you might like to meet? If yes, see yourself going over to meet this person, and hear your voice as you introduce yourself. If there is no one you wish to meet, that is okay. See yourself finding a place to sit, and continue to focus on your relaxed breathing. With your relaxation you are able to be more present during the meeting . . . to be open to hear other people share their stories.*

Imagine that you are ready to share part of your story. Remember there are many ways to share your story . . . sharing with a friend . . . a counselor . . . or your AA sponsor. Listen to your inner wisdom . . . you will know what is right for you. Can you imagine sharing something special about your journey? What would it be? How would you like to feel? The meeting is now over. Is there anyone that you wish to greet? If so, see yourself doing so.

Script: **Learning To Trust and Forgive.** *Be with some essential steps for giving power back to yourself . . . the steps of learning to trust and forgive yourself and others. What comes forth for you as you imagine forgiving yourself? What would this be like for you? Relive another aspect of your life's journey for a moment. Choose one person who has let you down or caused you turmoil in the past. Create your own healing images for loving yourself and this person. What are the new images? Gather your family and friends in a healing image. What do you want to tell them? Listen to what they have to say. Listen to what you say in return. Know that, as you continue to be aware of your special images, . . . very healing images will continue to be present for you.*

Script: **Releasing Old Patterns.** *Allow the experience of letting old life programs emerge in consciousness, and then release them one by one. . . . Release your intellectual level of being . . . and open to your Higher Power. Let yourself glimpse a space of your basic good self . . . it must occur . . . and every time it does . . . you open more of yourself . . . and your spirit sings its song. Remember it is one day at a time toward recovery. Over time, bring other people and other situations that need healing into your* *imagination. Let yourself continue to rehearse trust and forgiveness . . . your special touchstones on your healing journey.*

Script: **Closure.** *Take a few slow, energizing breaths and, as you come back to full awareness of the room, know that whatever is right for you at this point in time is unfolding just as it should and that you have done your best, regardless of the outcome.*

Case Study

Setting:	AA meeting
Client:	S.W., a successful, married professional with two children, sharing his story to illustrate the experience of nongrowth. At the time he told us his story, he had been free of alcohol and amphetamines for 3 months and had begun his path toward recovery.
Nursing Diagnosis:	Health maintenance related to engagement in strategies to remain free of addiction

"My healing began when I finally admitted to myself, family and friends I was addicted to alcohol and drugs. I began to explore and own my dark side. I've created some wonderful healing rituals, which include getting the nerve up to attend my first AA meeting—which gave me the opportunity to hear other people tell their story. I've been regularly attending AA meetings and have a sponsor who I've called several times when I felt myself slipping. I realized I didn't know how to do anything to relax except drink. If I needed energy, I didn't know any way to get it but to take speed. So I've learned relaxation and imagery skills, started an exercise program, and am taking time for myself.

"Here I was at 45 feeling lost and wondering if this was all life had to offer. How could I feel lost? I had so much. My career was going well. I had good kids, a loving and supportive wife, good looks, and I was involved in several civic projects. Everyone was always telling me how wonderful I was and stressing my contributions to the community. But I was searching for more to fulfill my life. I had been a secret drinker and had taken speed off and on since college in order to do all that I needed to accomplish. Everybody saw me as perfect, but I could feel my world falling apart. I got scared.

"For the past 5 years or so my wife had said that she thought I was drinking too much—which had recently become a source of tension between us. I told my wife to take the kids and go on a holiday while I worked at home alone. As soon as they left, I got drunk. When I fractured my ankle from a fall in my own house the first day they were gone, I really began to look at my life. I had a month of deep depression. During that time, my inner voice was screaming at me about all the abuse I was into. It was as if I was having a conversation with a part of myself that I had never heard. The message was so clear I couldn't turn it off.

"I'm not like many addicts who lose family, money, jobs, and friends. During a month of struggling to perform and continuing to hear my inner dialogue, one day my depression lifted enough for me to find a local AA meeting and hear myself say, "I've had it; I need help." I finally admitted in public that I was addicted to alcohol and drugs and used them to be successful. I began educating myself about addictions. I asked for help. What I recognized was that previously I sought ways to connect with sources outside of myself to make me feel good. The real healing came when I learned to connect with the core of my spirit, which awakened my inner resources for feelings of wholeness."

Evaluation

With the client, the nurse determines whether the client outcomes for overcoming addictions (see Table 20–1) were successfully achieved. To evaluate the session further, the nurse may again explore the subjective effects of the experience with the client (Exhibit 20–2).

Exhibit 20–2 Evaluating the Client's Subjective Experience with Overcoming Addictions

1. Did you gain any new insight today about overcoming addictions?
2. Do you have any questions about preparing for a quit date?
3. Do you have any questions about how to record your habits?
4. Can you identify two new habit breakers right now to overcome your addiction?
5. Are you aware of your bodymind signals of wanting to drink?
6. What relaxation exercises are the most helpful to replace your addictions?
7. What will be your exercise program?
8. Do you have any questions about the active, process, end-state, and general healing imagery exercises you experienced today?
9. Did you like the imagery exercises?
10. Did you gain any new insight through your self-talk of overcoming addictions?
11. What are three affirmations to help you just now create an image change of being addiction-free?
12. What is your next step?

In order to overcome addictions, the client must first admit that the addiction exists. This is a time of anger, pain, and emotional distress on many levels. The client's best chance for recovery lies in joining a support group, finding a sponsor, and learning habit breakers to change old behaviors. The client must acknowledge that he or she is not alone in the struggle. The new skill power required for overcoming addictions includes (1) learning when and where the drink or drug signals occur, (2) knowing what other behaviors and options are available, (3) evaluating each option, (4) using discipline to integrate the best behaviors and options, and (5) reaching spiritual transformation and acceptance.

DIRECTIONS FOR FUTURE RESEARCH

1. Determine the nursing interventions that support clients most effectively as detoxification begins.
2. Compare various combinations of content and teaching methods for their effectiveness in helping clients sustain sobriety.
3. Determine which nursing interventions are most useful in helping clients cope with fears regarding relapse.

NURSE HEALER REFLECTIONS

After reading this chapter, the nurse healer will be able to answer or begin a process of answering the following questions:

- What rituals can I create for detoxification and cleansing myself, if any addictions are present in my life?
- What specific process, end-state, and general healing images for releasing attachments and moving forward in my recovery can I practice each day?
- How can I achieve a natural high?
- Can I allow an image to emerge that represents my wise spirit?
- Can I identify times when I disconnect from my wise spirit?
- As I tell myself or another person my special life stories, can I imagine spinning healing threads to and from the core of my healing spirit?

NOTES

1. K. Blum and J. Payne, *Alcohol and Addictive Brain* (New York: Free Press/Maxwell Macmillan, 1991).
2. A. Luks and J. Barbato, *You Are What You Drink* (New York: Villard Books, 1989), 146.

3. S. Wegscheider, *Another Chance* (Palo Alto, CA: Science and Behavior Books, 1981).
4. J. Small, Awakening in Time: The Journey from Co-Dependency to Co-Creation (New York: Bantam Books, 1991).
5. S. Grof, Spirituality, Addiction, and Western Science, *Revision* 10, no. 2 (1987):5–18.
6. C. Grof and S. Grof, *The Stormy Search for the Self* (Los Angeles: Jeremy P. Tarcher, 1990).
7. Ibid., 74–75.
8. J. Small, Spiritual Emergence and Addiction: A Transpersonal Approach to Alcoholism and Drug Abuse Counseling, *Revision* 10, no. 2 (1987):23–35.
9. H. Benson and K. Wallace, Decreasing Drug Abuse with Transcendental Meditation, *Drug Abuse—Proceedings of the International Drug Abuse Conference* (Boston: 1972), 369–375.
10. Ibid., 371–373.
11. G.A. Marlett and J.K. Marques, Meditation, Self-Control and Alcohol Use, in *Behavioral Self-Management: Strategies, Techniques, and Outcomes*, eds. R. Stuart and B. Stuart (New York: Brunner/Mazel, 1977), 117–153.
12. K. Blum and J. Payne, *Alcohol and the Addictive Brain* (New York: Free Press/Maxwell Macmillan, 1991).
13. Ibid.
14. E. Rossi, *The 20 Minute Break* (Los Angeles: Jeremy P. Tarcher, 1991), 137–139.
15. M. Judge, Alcohol's Deadly Sweet Tooth, *Common Boundary* (1993):53–57.
16. Do You Drink Too Much? *The University of Texas Lifetime Health Letter* 1, no. 8 (1989):1.
17. Blum and Payne, *Alcohol and the Addictive Brain.*
18. B. Schaub and R. Schaub, Alcoholics Anonymous and Psychosynthesis, in *Readings in Psychosynthesis: Theory, Process, and Practice*, Vol. 2, eds. J. Weiser and T. Yeomans (Toronto: Ontario Institute for Studies in Education, 1988), 55–59.
19. Ibid.
20. Ibid.

RESOURCES

Gamblers Anonymous
National Service Office
PO Box 17173
Los Angeles, CA 90017
1-213-386-8789

Narcotics Anonymous
World Service Office
PO Box 9999
Van Nuys, CA 91409
1-818-780-3951

Overeaters Anonymous
4025 Spencer #203
Torrance, CA 90503
1-310-618-8835

Sexaholics Anonymous
International Central Office
PO Box 300
Simi Valley, CA 93062
1-818-704-9854
or
PO Box 1542
New York, NY 10001
1-212-570-7292

Sex and Love Addicts Anonymous
PO Box 1964
Boston, MA 02105
1-617-625-7961

Shopaholics Unlimited
15 West 18th St., 4th floor
New York, NY 10011
1-212-675-4342

Survivors of Incest Anonymous (SIA)
SIA World Service Office
PO Box 21817
Baltimore, MD 21222-6817
1-410-433-2365

Workaholics Anonymous (WA)
511 Sir Francis Drake Blvd.
C-170
Greenbrae, CA 94904
1-510-273-9253

UNIT V

HOLISTIC NURSING INTERVENTIONS

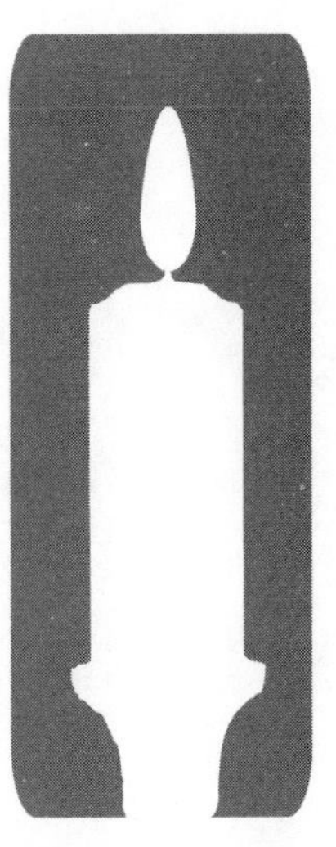

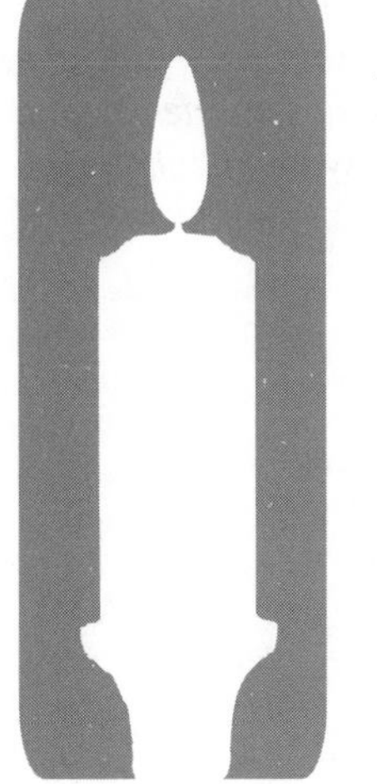

VISION OF HEALING

Using Our Healing Hands

Imagine being transported into a dimension that bathes your entire being in a delicious sensation that stimulates and/or relaxes all of your physical sensory receptors and then taps into your mental and spiritual domains. Many people report that this is what happens to them when they experience hands on healing for the first time. Subsequent sessions build upon and augment the initial effect.

Stroking and enfolding, kneading manipulation, light touch, pressure point, and working within an energy field are just some of the phrases that come to mind when thinking about the modality of touch. Within a single generation the phenomena of touch as a nursing intervention has evolved from the basic bedside backrub into an expansive variety of full body hands on techniques.

Many practitioners and recipients of the growing plethora of touch modalities believe that the end result is more beneficial than the obvious advantageous physical effect. Numerous hands on therapies are designed to engage the recipient's psyche and heighten spiritual awareness while producing both overt and covert physical changes. The setting where the therapy is practiced, the centeredness of the practitioner, the specific modality selected, and the receptivity of the client all contribute to an experience that has the power to embrace both psyche and soma and result in a positive alteration of body, mind, and spirit.

Nurses refer to the "hands on" phenomena of nursing as touch therapy, therapeutic touch, healing touch, therapeutic massage, body work, or a variety of other labels. Despite the different names, the intent is always the same: to care for another through some mode of physical touch or energy field manipulation. Although the techniques vary among practitioners, the objective of the various therapies are similar: to relax, soothe, stimulate, relieve physical, mental, emotional, and/or spiritual discomfort, or aid in the transition of the client to a heightened plateau of being. Those who use touch as a therapeutic modality do so from a calm, centered place and believe that focused intention facilitates the transference of healing energy. However, it is important to note that just as all nurses do not relate well to the technical nature of an intensive care unit or operating room, not all nurses have the ability or desire to use the medium of touch. Generally people know after a few encounters if this approach works for them. If it does, the nurse who develops hands on therapeutic skills can become a practitioner of a whole new array of powerful healing modalities.

Chapter 21

Touch: Connecting with the Healing Power

Lynn Keegan

NURSE HEALER OBJECTIVES

Theoretical

- Learn the definitions and various types of touch techniques.
- Compare and contrast the various touch therapies.
- Observe subjective and objective changes in the client after the touch therapy session.
- Compare and contrast your responses to touch therapy with the published descriptions of other nurses

Clinical

- Develop your abilities to center and become calm before you use touch therapies in your practice.
- Learn to calm, soften, and steady your voice as you use it as an adjunct to touch therapy.
- Experiment with soothing music or guided imagery (spoken or from cassette tapes) as an adjunct to the touch session.
- Create opportunities to practice the touch therapies in your clinical area.
- Notice whether you have any changes in your emotions during or after you use touch therapy.
- Notice any change in your sense of time when you use touch. Does it slow down or speed up?

Personal

- Become aware of how you utilize touch in your everyday life.
- Examine the significance of touch in your personal and professional relationships.

DEFINITIONS

Acupressure: the application of finger and/or thumb pressure to specific sites along the body's energy meridians for the purpose of relieving tension and re-establishing the flow of energy along the meridian lines.

Body Therapy and/or Touch Therapy: the broad range of techniques that a practitioner uses with the hands on or near the body to assist the recipient toward optimal function.

Caring Touch: touch done with a genuine interest in the other person, as well as empathy and concern.

Centering: a sense of self-relatedness that can be thought of as a place of inner being, a place of quietude within oneself where one can feel truly integrated, unified, and focused.[1]

Energy Meridian: an energy circuit or line of force. Eastern theories describe meridian lines flowing vertically through the body with culminating points on the feet, hands, and ears.

Foot Reflexology: the application of pressure to points on the feet that correspond to other parts of the body.

Intention: the motivation or reason for touching.

Procedural Touch: touch done to diagnose, monitor, or treat the illness itself; touch that focuses on the end result of curing the illness or preventing further complications.

Shiatzu: the use of the thumb and/or heel of the hand for deep pressure work along the energy meridian lines.

Therapeutic Massage: the use of the hands to apply pressure and motion on the skin and underlying muscle of the recipient for the purposes of physical and psychologic relaxation, improvement of circulation, relief of sore muscles, and other therapeutic effects.

Therapeutic Touch: a specific technique of centering intention used while the practitioner moves the hands through a recipient's energy field for the purpose of assessment and treatment of energy field imbalance.

THEORY AND RESEARCH

Touch in Ancient Times

Healing through touch is as old as civilization itself. Practiced extensively in all ancient cultures, this oldest form of treatment was to "rub it if it hurts."[2] The Egyptians used bandages, poultices, touch, and manipulation. The oldest written documentation of the use of body touch to enhance healing comes from the Orient. The *Huang Ti Nei Ching* is a classic work of internal medicine that was written 5,000 years ago. The *Nei Ching*, a 3,000- to 4,000-year-old Chinese book of health and medicine, records a system of touch based on acupuncture points and energy circuits. The ancient Indian Vedas also described healing massage, as did the Polynesian Lomi and the native American Indians.

During the height of Greek civilization, Hippocrates wrote of the therapeutic effects of massage and manipulation; he also gave instructions for carrying them out. He wrote at the time of the great healing centers—the Aesclepions—at which many whole body therapies included touch. Touch therapies were also employed at the healing centers to assist individuals who wished to make the transition to a higher level of function. Massage was used as a mode of preparation for dream work, which was a significant part of therapy in the healing rites. Following the Greek era, the Roman historian Plutarch wrote of Julius Caesar being treated for epilepsy by being pinched over his entire body every day.

Both shamans and traditional practitioners used touch widely until the rise of the Puritan culture during the 1600s and the shift from primitive healing practices to modern scientific medicine.[3,4] Puritan culture equated touch with sex, which was associated with original sin. During the late nineteenth and early twentieth centuries, the movement away from anything associated with superstition and primitive healing and toward the new miracle maker—scientific medicine—began. Because touch had always been associated with primitive healing and because of the strong Puritan ethic, all unnecessary touch was discouraged. Consequently, touch as a therapeutic intervention in U.S. health care remained undeveloped until the research into its benefits that began in the 1950s.

Cultural Variations

The fact that all cultures, both ancient and modern, have developed some form of touch therapy tells us that rubbing, pressing, massaging, and holding are natural manifestations of the desire to heal and care for one another. Yet, attitudes toward touch vary from culture to culture.[5] One society may view touch as necessary, whereas another may view it as taboo. The nurse must be aware of personal and cultural views and reactions to touch.

Philosophic and cultural differences have influenced the development of touch in various areas of the world. The Oriental world view is founded on energy, whereas the Western world view is based on reductionism of matter. This basic cultural difference has resulted in the evolution of widely differing approaches to touch. The Oriental world view holds that Qi, also described as chi energy or vital force, is the center of body function. A meridian is an energy circuit or line of force that runs vertically through the body.[6] Magnetic or bioelectrical patterns flow through the microcosm of our bodies in the same way that magnetic patterns flow through the planet and the universe. Meridian lines and zones are influenced by pressure placed on points along those lines. Expert practitioners in acupuncture or Shiatzu purport to direct healing energy to the recipient via an energy flow through the body and out through their hands.[7] In contrast, the Western world view holds that it is the physical effect of cellular changes that influences healing. For example, massage stimulates the cells to aid in waste discharge, promotes the dilation of the vascular system, and encourages lymphatic drainage. Swedish and therapeutic massage were developed to produce these physical changes.

A blending of Eastern and Western techniques has resulted in an explosion of new and widely practiced modalities. The modern day renaissance of body therapies is probably a response to the fast-paced technologic revolution that has swept our culture. This revolution has left little room for the practice of the art of touch.

Modern Concepts of Touch

Research is finally beginning to document what healers have always intuitively known. Some of the first studies documenting the significance of touch involved baby monkeys and surrogate mothers.[8] In the 1950s, Harlow caged one group of monkeys with a monkey-shaped wire form and a second group with a soft cloth mother surrogate. When frightened, the monkeys housed with the wire form reacted by running and cowering in a corner. The other group reacted to the same stimuli by running and clinging to the soft cloth surrogate for protection. These baby monkeys even preferred clinging to an unheated cloth surrogate mother to sitting on a warm heating pad. Even though the cloth surrogate was unresponsive, the offspring raised with it developed basically "normal" behavioral outcomes. This and other classic studies conclusively documented the significance of touch in normal animal growth and development.

Studies of human development soon followed. One study of abandoned infants and infants whose mothers were in prison found that the babies whom the nurses held and cuddled thrived, but those who were left alone became ill and died.[9] Other studies have shown that touch has a positive effect on the immune system.[10]

These early studies in the 1950s and 1960s awakened scientific interest in the phenomena of healing touch. Grad, a biochemist at McGill University, was one of the first to investigate healing by the laying on of hands. He conducted a series of double-blind experiments with the renowned healer Oskar Estebany.[11] These studies divided wounded mice and damaged barley seeds into control and experimental groups. After Estebany used healing touch in their energy fields, the experimental groups demonstrated a significantly accelerated healing rate in comparison to the control groups. In a subsequent study, an enzymologist worked with Grad in using the enzyme trypsin in double-blind studies.[12] After exposure to Estebany's treatments, the activity of trypsin was significantly increased in the experimental groups.

Nursing Studies

Although touch therapy is as old as civilization, documentation of how, why, and where it works is relatively new in the nursing literature. Hand holding has been described as a positive means of communication that seems to break down barriers.[13] Through the mechanism of touch, a nurse can convey feelings of caring and understanding to the client.[14] One study of 52 hospitalized patients addressed three universal questions regarding nonprocedural touch; it was found that 70 percent felt that touch was emotionally comforting, 87 percent agreed that the nurse's touch was soothing and comforting, and 75 percent agreed that the use of touch makes them feel valued and personalized their care.[15] In a proactive paper, Bottorff concludes that the dearth of studies on the subject reinforces the fact that little is known with certainty about nurse-patient touch.[16]

Critical Care

It is well-known that the anxiety level of myocardial infarction patients in coronary care units is high. The coronary care nurse is in a position to manipulate the client's environment to reduce or eliminate anxiety. Glick did a quasi-experimental study to determine the relationship between the type of touch and anxiety experienced by the myocardial infarction patients in the intermediate cardiac care unit.[17] Those receiving the greatest benefits from the caring touch of nurses were patients with preexisting coronary artery disease and men under the age of 60 years. Those experiencing the least benefit were women who were touched both by significant others as well as by the investigator.

McCorkle investigated the effects of touch as nonverbal communication on a group of seriously ill middle-aged adults and found that the nurse's touch increased the duration of verbal responses.[18] These findings support another study in which it was concluded that the use of touch increased verbal interactions between nurses and patients.[19] Still another study indicated that touch slows the heart rate, decreases diastolic blood pressure, and reduces anxiety.[20] The beneficial effects of touch have also been documented for the surgical patient in the perioperative area.[21] Despite the growing evidence that touch is beneficial, Schoenhofer, in a natural field observation study of 30 nurse-patient dyads in hospital critical care units found that touch is seldom used as a nursing comfort measure.[22]

Care of the Elderly

Our culture has been described as suffering from skin hunger, a form of malnutrition that has reached epidemic proportions in the United States.[23] Skin hunger or poverty of touch is often acute among the elderly. Rozema notes that the elderly need touch as much or more than any other age group, however.[24] First, they often have fewer family members or friends; second, touch functions as an effective communication channel at a time in life when the effectiveness of other communication channels is reduced.

A study of the utilization of touch by health care personnel found that patients in the age range of 66 to 100 received the least amount of touch.[25] Clients in geriatric institutions show not only their hunger for affection, but also the great value that they place on the smallest gesture, the simplest touch.[26] A study that used an experimental design to examine anger and hostility among nursing home residents found that the less mobile patients responded more positively to touch and were less angry than their more mobile counterparts when touched.[27,28]

Professionals must examine their own feelings about the meaning of touch before using it as a therapeutic tool. In a study of their perceptions of touch and their feelings about infants and nursing home residents, student nurses were asked to describe the tactile and affective sensations of touching in five words.[29] The students described the infants as cuddly, small, warm, soft, and smooth, but described the elderly as wrinkled, loose, flabby, bony, and cold. The students were more comfortable touching newborns than the geriatric patients. A nurse who reacts adversely to the skin changes of old people may find it difficult to touch an elderly client.[30] The nurse's reluctance may then communicate a negative message to the elderly person. Relatively little expressive touch actually takes place between nurses and elderly patients.[31]

Not all clients want to be touched. Analysis of 24 nursing home residents with high agitation and severe cognitive impairment found that touch was related to an increase in aggressive behaviors. The researchers believe that the cognitively impaired elderly may view touch as a violation of their personal space.[32] It has also been reported that 2 percent of nursing home patients are uncomfortable with touching.[33] Two factors were associated with the discomfort: the gender of the nurse and the part of the body that was touched. Female patients were not comfortable being touched by older male nurses. Hand or arm holding did not evoke a negative reaction, but many patients reported feeling discomfort or pain when the nurse placed an arm around their shoulders. An older female nurse's touch to the face was well accepted by almost all the patients, however.

The art of touch, as well as when to and when not to touch, can be a learned behavior. Nursing students can and should be taught the importance of touch as therapy. They need exposure and experience to overcome their cultural conditioning against touching adults, especially unfamiliar ones, to increase their ease in initiating this intervention.

Care of Children

In a study to compare the effectiveness of therapeutic touch and casual touch for stress reduction in hospitalized children aged 2 weeks to 2 years, it was demonstrated that therapeutic touch reduced the time needed to calm children after stressful experiences.[34]

Obstetrics

Thirty women who experienced a normal spontaneous vaginal birth attended by a nurse-midwife were interviewed during the immediate postpartal period. They perceived touch as therapeutic most frequently during the transition phase of labor. Hand holding was the type of touch most consistently valued throughout labor. The finding showed that touch helped the woman in labor cope with the experience.[35]

Touching Styles

Data collected by in-depth interviews with eight experienced intensive care nurses revealed two substantive processes, the touching process itself and the acquisition of a touching style, neither of which has been previously reported in the literature. Estabrooks and Morse note that the touching process is more than skin-to-skin contact; it involves entering the patient's space, connecting, talking, following nonverbal cues, and, eventually, touching. Nurses learn about touch from cultural background, family, street learning, personal experience, and nursing school.[36]

Effects of Therapeutic Touch

Therapeutic touch, a movement of the practitioner's hands through the recipient's energy field without body contact, has gained increasing attention during the past decade. A controlled study of 90 subjects in a cardiovascular unit of a large medical center showed a significant decrease in anxiety in those patients who received therapeutic touch, compared with those who received only casual touch or no touch at all.[37] Another study revealed an average 70 percent reduction of tension headache pain over 4 hours after therapeutic touch, more than twice the average pain reduction following placebo touch.[38] Krieger and others continue to document the importance of therapeutic touch and encourage its investigation using controlled studies.[39,40]

TOUCH TECHNIQUES

A variety of techniques fall under the umbrella heading of body therapies. Except for therapeutic touch, all the body therapies involved actual physical contact. The contact usually consists of the practitioner touching, pushing, kneading, or rubbing the recipient's skin and underlying fascia tissue. Each of the therapies has its own body of knowledge, history, and technique.

Bodymind Communication

Touch is perhaps one of the most highly used, yet least applauded of the five recognized senses. It is the first sense to develop in the human embryo and the one most vital to survival. Literal descriptions of touch vary from subtle fleeting brush strokes to violent physical attacks. Touch evokes the full range of emotions from hatred to the most intimate love relationship. Figuratively, touch is used in literature and even daily conversation to describe emotions. For example, "That speech really touched me," or "This workshop will allow you to touch one another heart to heart." These figurative expressions signify the deep importance and value of touch.

As the largest and most ancient sense organ of the body, the skin enables us to experience and learn about the environment.[41] Through the skin, we perceive the external world. The skin, particularly the face, not only communicates to the brain the knowledge about the external world, but also conveys to others information about the state of an individual's body, mind, and spirit.

A piece of skin the size of a quarter contains more than 3 million cells, 12 feet of nerves, 100 sweat glands, 50 nerve endings, and 3 feet of blood vessels. It is estimated that there are approximately 50 receptors per 100 square centimeters, a total of 900,000 sensory receptors.[42] Viewed from this perspective, the skin is a giant communication system that, through the sense of touch, brings the messages from the external environment to the attention of the internal environment—the bodymind.

Because care is increasingly being delivered in very complicated technologic settings, nurses are concerned with ensuring that the human spiritual and social needs of patients are not overlooked.[43] Yet, nurses must take into account social contexts and cultural differences before engaging in energetic efforts to provide touch therapy. A nurse should never assume that a client will find touch comforting, but should always ask before touching. If the suggestion evokes no response or a pained expression, the nurse may try a tentative touch and observe the client's response carefully. In order to be truly effective, touch must be authentically given by a warm, genuine, caring individual to another who is willing to receive it. It cannot and should not be packaged and dispensed. Phony touching may be more upsetting than none at all.

Like any other nursing intervention, hugging and touching demand careful assessment. Nurses need to recognize their own feelings, as well as consider the client's age, sex, and ethnic background.[44] A few key questions (e.g., Would a back massage help you relax? Would it help if I held your hand?) can help the client clarify his or her own beliefs and values regarding different types, locations, and intensities of touch.

There are many variations and names for the touch therapies available for use as nursing interventions. Some are basic human contacts, such as hand holding and hugging. Others are more complex. The following four touch therapies are used by holistic practitioners who often advocate and teach healthy life style behavior patterns to their clients to augment well-being during the course of the touch therapy treatments. The addition of guided imagery and/or music before and during treatment may heighten the relaxation response elicited during touch therapies. The setting, be it acute care, long-term, home care, rehabilitation center, or wellness center, will also affect the focus and length of the treatment.

Therapeutic Massage

As a nursing intervention, therapeutic massage has a twofold purpose. First, clients who are on bedrest or immobilized in a wheelchair require the circulatory stimulation that massage brings. Second, it is a means of relaxation.

During this century, nurses have used therapeutic massage primarily on the backs of their clients. Back care is not new; for decades, it has been incorporated into the standard bathing and evening care routine of most hospitals. Because of time constraints and traditional neglect of the body therapies in institutions, these patients receive only a portion of the complete range of touch therapies.

Learning full body massage greatly augments and expands the basic massage techniques. Most practitioners learn these techniques in continuing education classes, but there are also books on massage available that illustrate the techniques.

Because no two clients will have the same needs, either within or outside the institutional setting, the nurse must become skilled at adapting the therapy to the setting and the time permitted. Learning massage techniques that can be done quickly—for example, for the hands, feet, or neck and shoulders—may have equally beneficial results in similar short time periods.

Therapeutic Touch

A healing modality that involves touching with the conscious intent to help or heal, therapeutic touch decreases anxiety, relieves pain, and facilitates the healing process.[45] The process of therapeutic touch has four phases:

1. centering oneself physically and psychologically, that is, finding within oneself an inner reference of stability
2. exercising the natural sensitivity of the hand to assess the energy field of the client for clues to differentiate the quality of energy flow
3. mobilizing areas in the client's energy field that appear to be nonflowing (i.e., sluggish, congested, or static)
4. directing one's excess body energies to assist the client to repattern his or her own energies[46]

Several factors ensure the safe and successful practice of therapeutic touch: intentional motivation, personal recognition, and acceptance by the practitioner of the reason that he or she has chosen to act in the role of healer.[47] Krieger describes these qualities.

> Intention connotes a clear formulation of a goal; it suggests that the TT [therapeutic touch] practitioner should have a lucid concept of how to help heal as well as the mere desire to do so. The practitioner's motivation provides the psychodynamic thrust toward the direction that this healing/helping act will take and, therefore, it colors the emotional tone of the dyadic relationship between healer and healee. Finally it is important for the practitioner to understand his/her own drives in wanting to play the role of healer. It does not matter what these drives are; what is important is that the practitioner willingly recognizes the personal foundations for his/her involvement in this highly personalized interaction.[48]

Therapeutic touch is taught at beginning, intermediate, and advanced levels in continuing education programs, graduate nursing education, and summer intensive workshops.

Healing Touch

Defined as an energy-based therapeutic approach, healing touch influences the energy field and energy centers, thus affecting physical, emotional, mental, and spiritual health and healing.[49] Within the past 5 years, an enormous network of healing touch practitioners has emerged. Four levels of healing touch programs have been developed to prepare nurses from beginners to instructors in a combination of healing touch philosophies and techniques. In 1993, it became a certificate program of the American Holistic Nurses' Association (AHNA). Practitioners from the healing touch center (headquartered in Lakewood, Colorado) offer primarily weekend workshops designed to prepare nurses to practice.[50] The most recent addition to this growing body of knowledge is Hover's book, *Healing Touch*.[51]

Acupressure and Shiatzu

The Oriental energy system of meridian lines and points is the foundation of acupressure and Shiatzu. The application of finger and/or thumb pressure to energy points along the meridians releases congestion and allows energy flow.

There are 657 designated points on the human body that can be stimulated or treated with acupuncture, acupressure, or Shiatzu.[52] These points run along 12 pathways, or meridians, that connect the points on each half of the body. In addition to the 12 pairs of body meridians, there are two coordinating meridians that bisect the body. Acupressure is concerned primarily with the 12-organ meridian system.

The word *shiatzu* comes from the Japanese *shi* (finger) and *atzu* (pressure).[53] The technique is a product of 4,000 years of Oriental medicine and philosophy. Although widely known and practiced in Japan, it was virtually unknown in the West until acupuncture began receiving widespread public attention. Shiatzu is based on the same points that are used in acupuncture. Instead of inserting needles, however, the practitioner applies pressure on the points with thumbs, fingers, and heel of the hand. Another difference between acupuncture and Shiatzu is that Shiatzu's main function is to maintain health and well-being rather than to treat illness.

Reflexology

In the early 1900s, Dr. William FitzGerald noted that pressure applied on certain points on the hands caused anesthesia in other parts of the body.[54] Another physician, Dr. Edwin Bowers, learned of FitzGerald's work and joined him in the exploration and development of this zone therapy. The technique became more specific as it evolved into reflexology, which encompasses many more pressure points.

Reflexology is based on the theory that there are ten equal, longitudinal zones running the length of the body from the top of the head to the tips of the toes.[55] This number corresponds to the number of fingers and toes. Each big toe matches to a line up the medial aspect of the body through the center of the face and culminating at the top of the head. The reflex points pass all the way through the body within the same zones. Congestion or tension in any part of a zone affects the entire zone running laterally throughout the body. More than 72,000 nerves in the body terminate in the feet.[56] A problem or disease in the body often manifests itself by forming deposits of calcium and acids on the corresponding part of the foot.

The purpose of this therapy is twofold.[57] First, relaxation alone is an important goal. Good health is dependent on one's ability to return to homeostasis after injury, disease, or stress. From this perspective, reflexology is effective in helping the bodymind restore and maintain its natural state of health because foot manipulation triggers deep relaxation. The second goal of this therapy is to release congestion or tension along the longitudinal and lateral zones by pressure manipulation at the precise end point of the zones. This pressure stimulates the reflexes in the feet to cause a corresponding release. All skeletal, muscular, vascular, nervous, and organ systems are believed to be affected. Manuals with specific diagrams are used to instruct the therapist.

At this time, there is no documented scientific research to validate the effectiveness of reflexology, although it relaxes muscles and causes a simultaneous bodymind connection that results in the relaxation response. This affects the autonomic response, which is tied into the endocrine, immune, and neuropeptide systems.

NURSING PROCESS

Assessment

In preparing to use touch interventions, the nurse assesses the following parameters:

- the client's perception of his or her bodymind problem.
- the client's potential pathophysiologic problems that may require referral to a physician for evaluation.
- the client's history of psychiatric disorders. The nurse must modify the approach with clients with present or past psychiatric disorders. Touch itself may present a problem and the deeply relaxed semihypnotic state that a balanced person finds enjoyable may actually frighten or alarm an unbalanced individual.
- the client's cultural beliefs and values about touch.
- the client's past experience with body therapies. There is a wide variation in the knowledge level of clients. The approach will differ markedly depending on the client's previous experience. Assisting a client in transferring prior learning, such as from childbirth preparation classes, to a new situation is a valuable nursing intervention.

Nursing Diagnoses

The following nursing diagnoses compatible with touch interventions and that are related to the human response patterns of the Unitary Person (see Chapter 7) are as follows:

- Exchanging: Altered circulation
  Impairment in skin integrity
- Relating: Social isolation
- Valuing: Altered spiritual state
- Moving: Physical mobility impaired
- Perceiving: Altered meaningfulness
- Feeling: Altered comfort
  Anxiety
  Grieving
  Fear

Client Outcome

Table 21–1 guides the nurse in client outcomes, nursing prescriptions, and evaluation for the use of touch as a nursing intervention.

Plan and Interventions

Before the Session

- Wash your hands.
- Wear loose-fitting, comfortable clothing. If you have on street clothes, cover them with a laboratory coat.
- Have the client empty the bladder for comfort.
- Prepare the hospital bed, therapy table, or surface on which you will be working. If you will be using a therapy table, drape it with a cotton blanket and place a sheet over the top. Lay out a large towel for the client to use as a cover when he or she lies on the table. Adjust the height of the table/bed for optimal use of your body mechanics.
- Have small pillows or towel rolls available for supporting the head, back, or lower legs.
- Control the room environment to be warm, dimly lit, and quiet. If you are in a client's hospital room, draw the curtain and turn off the television. A radio or cassette tape player may be left on for soothing music.
- Use relaxation and breathing techniques, imagery, or music to elicit the relaxation response.
- After you have talked with the client, spend a few moments to quiet and center yourself, focus on your healing intention, and then begin.

Table 21-1 Nursing Intervention: Touch

Client Outcomes	*Nursing Prescriptions*	*Evaluation*
The client is relaxed following a touch therapy session.	Encourage the client to receive touch therapy in order to evoke the relaxation response.	The client willingly accepted touch therapy.
	During the touch therapy session, help the client • decrease anxiety and fear • decrease pulse and respiratory rate • recognize a feeling of bodymind relaxation • develop a sense of general well-being • increase effectiveness in individual coping skills • increase a sense of belonging and lessened loneliness • feel less alone and express that feeling	The client • exhibited decreased anxiety and fear • demonstrated a decrease in pulse and respiratory rate • reported muscle relaxation • exhibited satisfied facial expression and expressed inner calmness • reported greater satisfaction in individual coping patterns
The client has improved circulation.	Provide the client with information about how touch therapies improve circulation and tissue perfusion	Clients with white skin had a reddened color in the area where the nurse had used effleurage and petrosauge massage strokes. Skin in the massage area will be warmer than before the therapy.
The client receives touch therapy to maintain and enhance health.	Encourage the client to ask for touch therapy. Suggest that the client seek out the nurse. Recommend that the client accept touch when offered by the nurse	The client asked for touch therapy.

At the Beginning of the Session

- Explain to the client the steps in the touch process to be used. The first session always takes the most time because of the needed explanations and adjustment. The length of the remaining sessions may be from 15 to 60 minutes.
- As you progress through the intervention, explain what you are about to do before you actually begin.
- Position the head comfortable. If the client has long hair, pull it up and away from the neckline.
- If working on the client's entire physical body, have the client disrobe completely and cover up with a towel from the chest to the thighs. The client lies on a padded therapy table or hospital bed that is covered with a cotton blanket and sheet. The sides of the sheet and blanket are then wrapped over the client so that he or she feels protected and warm. (This procedure is done for the physical touch therapies and is not needed with therapeutic touch.)
- Unwrap only the body area that is being massaged or pressed as the therapy proceeds.
- In most cases, begin with the client lying on the back. When therapy on the medial aspect and limbs of the body is complete, lift the wraps and reapply them after the client turns over.
- Encourage the client to take slow, deep, releasing breaths. When he or she lets go of tension through breath, affirm in a soft tone, "Ah, feel the release of tension."
- During the turning process, slide the towel around the client's body, thereby ensuring that the client will not be exposed. As the client lies prone, continue the therapy on the dorsal aspect of the body.

During the Session

- Be attuned to the client's responses to therapy. This will help the client build trust and achieve optimal relaxation.
- In initial sessions, continue to explain what the client can expect to happen so that he or she may feel comfortable with the continued direction of the touch sessions. After trust has been established and the relaxation response learned, the client will relax more quickly and move to deeper levels in subsequent sessions.
- In subsequent sessions, proceed the same as in the initial session. Explanations may be shorter, however.

- Remember to use your voice in a soft, soothing manner that enables the client to relax.
- Reassess the client's responses as you proceed.

At the End of the Session

- When you have finished the touch therapy session, verbally let the client know that it is time to return gradually to the here and now, begin to move around slowly, and fully awaken.
- Anticipate that the client will take a few minutes to reorient to time and place because of deep states of relaxation.
- All periods of silence for the client to appreciate fully the wisdom of his or her relaxed bodymind.
- Stay in the room while the client rouses and sits up. Give necessary assistance to ensure a safe transfer to an ambulatory position.
- Allow time to receive the client's verbal feedback about the meaning of the session, if this need to talk surfaces. If this does not occur spontaneously, ask for feedback. The insight gained provides guidelines for further sessions or specific ideas that the client can follow up in daily life.
- When the touch therapy is used for relaxation or sleep induction for hospitalized patients, close the session by softly pulling the bed covers up over the patient's back and quietly turning off the light as the patient moves into sleep.
- Use the client outcomes (see Table 21–1) that were established before the session and the client's subjective experience (Exhibit 21–1) to evaluate the session.
- Schedule a follow-up session.

Specific Interventions

General Touch (Basic). Each of the therapies discussed in the text has basic, intermediate, or advanced levels. The complexity of each type depends on the amount of time spent studying the multiple variations of the therapy and whether it is used in conjunction with another therapy, such as music and imagery. Anyone who begins with the basic level and likes this approach will probably study or take continuing education courses to learn the intermediate and advanced levels.

Therapeutic Massage (Basic to Advanced). Although called by different names (massage, Swedish massage, massotherapy), the techniques of therapeutic massage are all essentially the same. They involve the use of effleurage, petrosauge, and tapotement: all the classic nursing back rub strokes. These strokes are designed to enhance the circulation of both blood and lymph. Therapeutic massage increases the dispersion of nutrients to promote the removal of metabolic wastes by increasing both lymphatic and blood flow.

Therapeutic Touch (Advanced). Therapeutic touch (TT) is generally taught by experienced practitioners in continuing education seminars. The courses include all or part of the following elements: assessment, hand scan, intuition, energy field reading mapping—recording, pattern comparison, verbal information, stress levels, relaxation levels, meditation experience.

In a therapeutic touch session, the practitioner may ask the client to visualize clearly the part of the body that is to be influenced with the intent of enhancing contact with that body part's energy field. The practitioner's goal is to ascertain the degree of blockage in the energy field of the muscles or viscera. In order for practitioners to come in contact with these energies, they must develop an awareness of events that normally occur below the level of consciousness. The imagery and visualization process is one way of tuning into this unconscious process. Therapists can use synergistically the effect of one modality (imagery) to affect another (touch).

Figure 21–1 illustrates a 5-year-old child's use of imagery and drawing to describe her self-perception before and after the use of therapeutic touch to treat an asthmatic episode. When she has an asthma attack, the child says that she "feels bald headed and sad." In drawing A, the disconnected arm is moving up to wipe away her tears. The figure lacks sturdy legs to support it. At the completion of the 15-minute therapeutic touch session, the child feels well and happy and is free of respiratory distress. In drawing B, the child increased the figure size, strengthened the lines, and added long hair that symbolizes strength to the child.

It is time to stop the therapeutic touch process when there are no longer any differences in body symmetry relative to density or temperature variation. Four commonly seen responses are (1) flushed skin, (2) deep sighs, (3) physical relaxation, and (4) verbalized relaxation. A caution in therapeutic touch is to limit the amount of time and/or energy sent to the very young, the old, and the infirm. When the client's energy field is full, the energy pushes the nurse away.

Healing Touch (Advanced). An energy-based therapeutic approach, healing touch combines philosophy with a way of caring and considers

A

B

Figure 21–1 Self-Perception of a 5-Year-Old Girl with Asthma before **(A)** and after **(B)** Therapeutic Touch Session.

healing a sacred art. It uses a collection of noninvasive, energy-based treatment modalities with the purpose of restoring wholeness through harmony and balance. The healing is done through the centered heart, thus establishing a spiritual process.[58] Specific uses of healing touch are cited as

- acceleration of wound healing
- relief of pain and increased relaxation
- reduction of anxiety and stress
- energizing the field
- prevention of illness
- enhancement of spiritual development
- aid in prevention for and follow-up of complications after medical treatments and procedures
- support for the dying process[59]

Acupressure and Shiatzu (Basic to Advanced). There is a broad range and depth of technique involved in acupressure and Shiatzu. Most practitioners receive continuing education in this area; some spend years perfecting these techniques.

Reflexology (Basic to Advanced). The primary purpose of reflexology is to evoke bodymind relaxation. Some practitioners believe that the areas shown in Figure 21–2 represent the nerve or meridian endings for the specific vital body parts. When a therapist works these specific areas, there is a corresponding energy release or relaxation in the internal body system.

Nurses who have not studied reflexology can still use general massage on the client's feet to elicit relaxation. The primary caution in this, as well as other body therapies, is to stop massage in any area that provokes pain. Additional touch therapies not discussed in this chapter are noted in Table 21–2.

Case Studies

Case Study No. 1

Setting: Oncology unit in a general hospital

Patient: E.S., a 58-year-old single male

Nursing Diagnoses:
1. Anxiety
2. Altered comfort
3. Social isolation: all related to terminal cancer

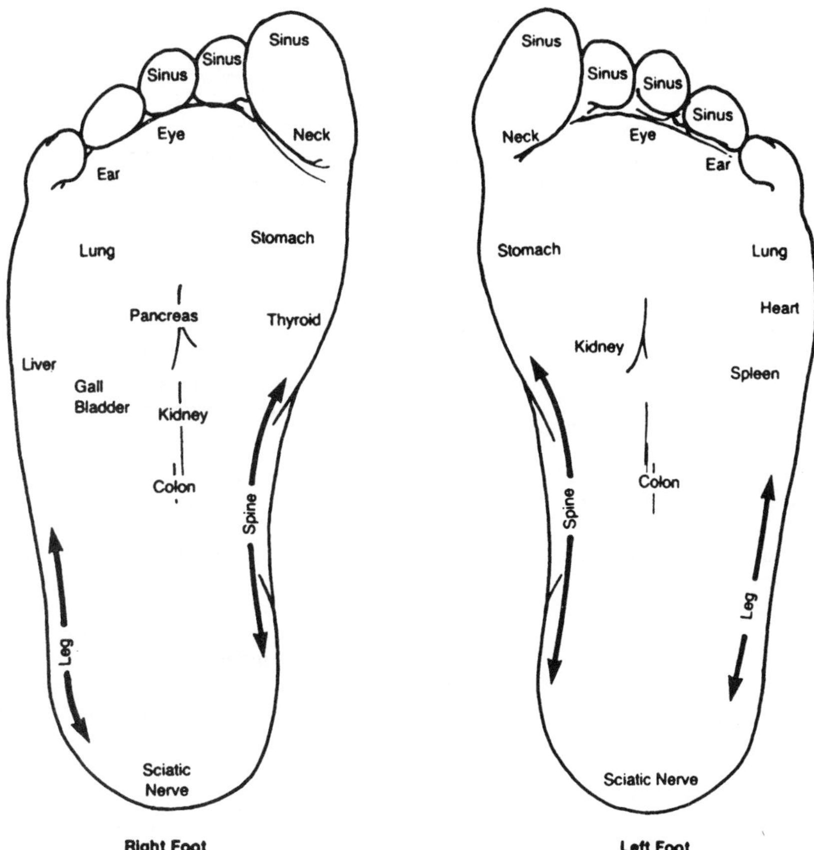

Figure 21–2 Foot Reflexology Chart.

E.S. knew that he was in the terminal stage of cancer, yet he was ambulatory and in basic good humor. E.S. had grown up in the city in which he now found himself hospitalized. He had never married and had no remaining living family.

A nurse who was knowledgeable about touch therapy and felt comfortable using this modality worked evenings on the unit where E.S. was assigned. After assessing his condition, she felt that E.S. needed touch to increase comfort and to allay apprehension. Because the unit was continually short-staffed and little time was available for lengthy one-on-one interventions with clients, this intervention had to become a priority

Table 21–2 Additional Touch Therapies

Therapy	*Originator*	*Primary Purpose and Function*
Applied Kinesiology	George Goodheart	Focuses on the relationship of muscle strength and energy flow. The theory is that if muscles are strong, then circulation and other vital functions are also strong.
Chiropractic	D.D. Palmer	Based on alignment of spinal vertebrae. This therapy involves manipulations to restore natural alignment.
Feldenkrais	Moshe Feldenkrais	Purpose is to give the client gentle manipulations to heighten awareness of the body. As awareness increases, clients can make more informed choices about how to move the body in daily situations.
Jin shin Jyutsy	Master Jiro Murai of Japan in early 1900s	A milder form of acupressure that involves pressure along eight extra energy meridians.
Kofutu Touch Healing	Frank Homan	System developed in the early 1970s when a series of symbols for use in touch came to the originator during meditation. It is called "Kofutu" for the symbols and "touch" healing because the auras of the healer and recipient must touch. This therapy uses higher consciousness energy symbols for the purpose of self-development and spiritual healing.
Lomi	R.K. Hall, R.K. Heckler	Directs attention to current muscle tension to aid learning of postural alignment to enhance free flow of the body's physical and emotional energies.
Polarity	Randolph Stone	Repattern energy flow in the individual by rebalancing positive and negative charges. The practitioner places finger or whole hand on parts of the client's body of opposite charge for the purpose of facilitating energy balancing where it is needed. Through these contacts, with the help of pressure and rocking movements, energy can reorganize and reorder itself.
MaríEL	Ethel Lombardi	A 1980s variation of Reiki.
Neuromuscular Release		Practitioner moves the limbs into and away from the body to assist the client in learning to "let go" for the purpose of enhanced circulation and emotional release.

continues

Table 21-2 continued

Therapy	*Originator*	*Primary Purpose and Function*
Reiki	2,500-year-old Buddhist practice lost and rediscovered in late 1800s	Term means universal life energy. A touch technique in which the practitioner places hands in one of 12 positions on the recipient's body to direct healing energy to those sites.
Rolfing	Ida P. Rolf	Purpose is to help the client establish deep structural relationships within the body that manifest themselves via a symmetry and balanced function when the body is in an upright position. Technique involves deep muscle manipulation.
Trager	Milton Trager	Limbs and often the whole body are rocked rhythmically to aid relaxation of the muscles to promote an optimal flow of blood, lymph, nerve impulses, and energy.

item in E.S.'s care. Evening back care was entered on his care plan and, despite sometimes hectic assignments, was never omitted when this particular nurse was on duty.

Back care became so important to E.S. that he eagerly greeted the nurse when she came on shift and was ready when she arrived at the appointed time. The touch he received from this nurse was the high point of his hospital stay. During the sessions, he relaxed so deeply that his breathing rate became slowed; he stated that his perception of pain decreased and that he felt the pleasure of closeness to another caring human being. When the nurse was about to have a few days off after 10 consecutive days, E.S. was profoundly saddened that he might have to go without this daily anticipated ritual. The nurse assured him that she had left specific orders for his back care for the oncoming nurse for the next evening. The next evening, however, the regular nurse called in sick, a float nurse was assigned to the unit, and E.S. received no special attention. He unexpectedly died in his sleep during the night shift.

At this point, we do not have the sophisticated tools needed to measure relationships between such deaths and the omission of certain nursing interventions. Consequently, we cannot make any direct correlations. We can only begin to ask research questions and gather anecdotal data about whether the omission of a nursing intervention such as back care can so grieve a client that the resulting physiologic changes can lead to death.

Case Study No. 2

Setting:	Wellness center
Client:	J.S., a 36-year-old married woman
Nursing Diagnoses:	1. Anxiety related to personal and family stress 2. Altered self-image related to obesity

A psychologist referred J.S. to a nurse in a wellness center for weight management. In addition to the weekly counseling program, this client elected to follow each counseling session with a therapeutic massage. She also continued to work with the psychologist for resolution of personality disorder problems. Both the psychologist and the nurse saw this client regularly for more than a year until her move away from the area terminated the relationship.

The counseling sessions with the nurse focused on J.S.'s eating disorders, nutritional education, and ways to institute life style changes that would change the overweight pattern. These sessions were sometimes emotional, but for the most part were straightforward and did not evoke emotional, spiritual, or attitudinal change. In contrast, the elective therapeutic massage elicited a response that allowed this client to make connections with a deeper level of herself and finally understand the true nature of her physical problems. While using touch, the nurse also played relaxation music and/or guided the client in imagery. In addition, the nurse did foot reflexology and concluded the sessions with therapeutic touch.

When work with this client first began, the client complained of a feeling of a knot in her stomach that had not abated for 15 years. The only time her stomach felt better was after eating. After a few sessions of therapeutic massage, she stated that this stomach pain was relieved during the time that she received the touch therapies.

As the client became more trusting of the nurse, she gradually began divulging more of her feelings while in the deeply relaxed state that she experienced during the session. She revealed that she was physically distant from her husband and her 14-year-old daughter. After receiving the massage for approximately 6 weeks, she learned to relax immediately upon reclining on the table—which dissolved her stomach knot. By 8 weeks, the pain stayed away for 2 to 3 days after a session, and weight loss became possible. By the fourth month, she began to hug and touch her daughter at home to dissolve the discomfort she had with their relationship.

The power of touch became so important to her that, by the eighth month, she brought her daughter to the nurse so that her daughter could experience massage firsthand. The daughter, of course, did not have the emotional response or release felt by the mother, for she had not experienced the years of holding tension and withdrawal. The daughter was happy to see how massage was done, however, as she and her mother planned to exchange massage sessions at home between visits to the nurse. Touch had initiated a healing bond between mother and daughter.

Case Study No. 3

Setting:	Wellness center
Client:	A.R., a 50-year-old woman
Nursing Diagnoses:	1. Altered spiritual state related to death of her husband 2. Grieving related to death of her husband

A.R. had visited the wellness center three to four times a month over a period of 18 months before the unexpected death of her husband. Her initial reason for coming to the center was for therapeutic massage, but the nurse also used therapeutic touch, acupressure, reflexology, guided imagery, and music. The combination of all of these modalities enhanced the overall therapeutic value of the sessions, which A.R. found particularly effective in maintaining her own high-level wellness. Thus, there was a strong therapeutic relationship between the nurse and the client.

The private individual sessions at the wellness center were her opportunity to relax completely, unwind, and say whatever she felt as she simultaneously allowed her physical body to receive healing touch. Initially, she struggled with letting go and allowing the deep relaxation to come. After only three or four sessions, however, she was able to move into the relaxation mode immediately so that she was able to use her time most effectively. Over the months, she had various muscle stresses and strains that were addressed with extra attention. The nurse recommended exercises to strengthen those areas. As her trust in the nurse increased, A.R. came to view these sessions as a safe place where she could be completely herself. She received nurturance and empowerment to increase peak performance in her demanding executive position and prominent social position that required national travel and being in the public eye.

In addition to the weekly individual sessions, A.R. attended two separate series of group classes that the nurse conducted at the center. One series was on stress management, and the other was on high-level wellness. She learned all she could from the classes and continued regular individual sessions whenever she was in town.

The unexpected sudden death of her husband was an emotional blow with which she was unprepared to cope. Because of her husband's prominence, she was overwhelmed with the condolences, the demands of decision making, and the attempts of well-meaning friends to cheer her up. Her friends' diversionary tactics and inability to allow her to grieve only deepened her sadness and masked her true feelings of despair.

Within a week of the funeral, as soon as the relatives had departed, she was back at the wellness center. Here she had already established a therapeutic relationship, and thus the healing could proceed. During these sessions, touch and the therapeutic relationship were the channels that opened her release of grieving. Here, in the safe environment of the wellness center, the power of the music, the touch of the hand, and the guiding by the nurse's voice allowed her to let go completely. She no longer had any of the neck or shoulder pain that she often came in with because, as she said, "My body is limp."

At this point, muscle release was no longer the primary goal; the therapy that had achieved a physical release was now used for emotional release. She learned to use her breath in conjunction with the effleurage massage strokes to release the sorrow and permit the tears. The sessions were always concluded with her lying prone and wrapped cocoon-like in a sheet and blanket as the nurse did therapeutic touch and guided imagery.

During the 3-month bereavement period, she occasionally came for sessions as often as twice a week. She symbolically and literally left her reality of worldly demands and shed the clothing of literal and figurative protection to allow release and healing. Through the modality of touch, she sought spiritual answers and was able to begin a transformation process that will affect her and those she interacts with for years to come.

Case Study No. 4

Setting:	School nurse's office
Client:	7-year-old second-grade student
Nursing Diagnoses:	1. Altered respiration related to asthma 2. Fear related to difficulty breathing

A teacher's aide brought a 7-year-old second-grade student to the nurse's office. The child was coughing and apprehensive. The school nurse listened for and heard bronchial wheezes. She had the child sit upright in a chair and spoke soothingly to her as she used therapeutic touch. The nurse spent approximately 7 minutes quietly talking and moving her hands over the child's chest area. The child stopped wheezing, her apprehension disappeared, her facial textures relaxed, and her color returned to normal. The nurse then called the child's mother to explain what had happened. The mother was amazed at her daughter's quick recovery because, on every previous occasion, the child had to be taken to the hospital or doctor's office for intravenous medication and respiratory treatments. The mother asked the nurse to teach her the technique so she could use it at home when the asthma occurred there.

Evaluation

With the client, the nurse determines whether the client outcomes for touch therapies (see Table 21–1) were successfully achieved. To evaluate the session further, the nurse may again explore the subjective effects of the experience with the client (Exhibit 21–1).

Exhibit 21–1 Evaluating the Client's Subjective Experiences of Touch Therapies

1. Was this a new kind of experience for you? Can you describe it?
2. Did this feel like a comforting, stimulating, or both tactile sensation?
3. Was it pleasurable on all planes—physical, mental, emotional, and spiritual—or more focused in one area than another?
4. Were you aware of your surroundings during the experience, or did you sink into a sense of timelessness?
5. Did emotions surface during the experience? If so, what were they? Can you focus on them now?
6. Did you experience any imagery during the touch session?
7. Did you feel comfortable with the therapist? Is there anything that you want to do to increase your comfort level with the touch therapist?
8. Did you feel relaxed and refreshed after the experience?
9. Would you like to try this again?
10. What would be helpful to make this a better experience for you?
11. Can you develop a plan or strategy to integrate more of the touch therapies into your life on a regular basis?

Nurses who work in institutional settings should chart the use, type, location, and duration of the touch therapy and its subjective and objective effects on the patient. When sessions are effective, they should be reported in writing, as well as orally, at change of shift report. Other nurses need to be apprised of the effectiveness of this independent nursing intervention.

Nurses who work in wellness centers, independent practice, or other areas in which the touch therapies are done as the primary care modality should keep records on their clients stating the nursing diagnosis, touch therapy employed, and the effectiveness of each session.

DIRECTIONS FOR FUTURE RESEARCH

1. Investigate the effects of therapeutic massage on relaxation, on pain relief, sleep induction, stress management, sensory deprivation, apprehension, and a host of other parameters.
2. Examine the effects of reflexology on pain relief, relaxation, and/or specific physiologic parameters.
3. Develop valid and reliable tools to measure the effects of touch.
4. Formulate studies to examine the relationship among guided imagery, music, smell, color, taste, and touch.
5. Determine if clients can be taught relaxation techniques by using images of the sensations and emotions evoked during the touch therapy session.
6. Conduct qualitative studies that investigate the meanings of nonprocedural touch throughout the life cycle.
7. Investigate if periodic touch therapy sessions increase work or performance productivity.
8. Examine the relationship between the touch therapies and healing.
9. Ask how the results of therapeutic touch on a child at rest compare to the results of therapeutic touch on a child in stress.
10. Question how the age of the child influences the outcome of therapeutic touch.
11. Investigate how touch can be effectively taught in nursing schools and what methods are best suited to accomplish this.
12. Ask how the nurse's cultural learning, acquired prior to entering nursing school, affects subsequent learning in school.

NURSE HEALER REFLECTIONS

After reading this chapter, the nurse healer will be able to answer or begin a process of answering the following questions:

- How do I feel about using touch as an intervention?
- What do I experience with touch therapy when I touch a client from a place of being centered?
- When I touch with intention, what is my inner experience?
- When I use touch, what happens to my sense of time?
- How does my touch as a nurse affect the recipient?
- Whom do I know who can be my mentor for helping me increase skills with touch?
- What other modalities can be used concurrently to heighten the effectiveness of touch?

NOTES

1. D. Krieger, *The Therapeutic Touch* (Englewood Cliffs, NJ: Prentice-Hall, 1979), 36.
2. Quest for Healing: Massage, Manipulation, Movement. The Discovery Channel, May 14, 1987.
3. R. Jahnke, The Body Therapies, *Journal of Holistic Nursing* (1985):7–14.
4. L. Baldwin, The Therapeutic Use of Touch with the Elderly, *Physical and Occupational Therapy in Geriatrics* 4(Summer 1986):45–50.
5. C. Guzzetta and B. Dossey, *Cardiovascular Nursing: Holistic Practice* (St. Louis: Mosby Year Book, 1992), 586–587.
6. R. Jahnke, Body Therapies, *Venture Inward* (March/April 1986):41–45.
7. S. Burnham, Healing Hands, *New Woman* (March 1986):72–77.
8. H. Harlow, Love in Infant Monkeys, *Scientific American* 200 (1958):68–74.
9. R. Spitz. *The First Year of Life* (New York: International Universities Press, 1965).
10. L.L. Roth and J.S. Rosenblatt, Mammary Glands of Pregnant Rats: Development Stimulated by Tickling, *Science* 151(1965):1403–1404.
11. B. Grad, Some Biological Effects of the Laying on of Hands: A Review of Experiments with Animals and Plants, *Journal of the American Society for Psychical Research* 59(1965):95–127.
12. M.J. Smith. Enzymes Are Activated by the Laying on of Hands, *Human Dimensions* (February 1973):46–48.
13. J. Khable, Handholding: One Means of Transcending Barriers of Communication, *Heart and Lung* 10(1981):1106.
14. C. Schmahl, Ritualism in Nursing Practice, *Nursing Forum* 11(1964):74.
15. L. Fisher and D. Hunt Joseph, A Scale To Measure Attitudes about Nonprocedural

Touch, *Canadian Journal of Nursing Research* 21, no. 2 (1989):5–14.

16. J. Bottorff. A Methodological Review and Evaluation of Research on Nurse-Patient Touch, In *Anthology on Caring*, ed. P.L. Chin, NLN Publications 15-2392 (1991):303–343.
17. M. Glick, Caring Touch and Anxiety in Myocardial Infarction Patients in the Intermediate Cardiac Care Unit, *Intensive Care Nursing* (February 1986):61–66.
18. R. McCorkle, Effects of Touch on Seriously Ill Patients, *Nursing Research* (1974):125–132.
19. D.C. Aguilera, Relationship between Physical Contact and Verbal Interaction between Nurses and Patients, *Journal of Psychiatric Nursing* 5, no. 1 (1967):5–21.
20. S.J. Weiss. Effects of Differential Touch on Nervous System Arousal of Patients Recovering from Cardiac Disease, *Heart and Lung* 19, no. 5 (1990):474–480.
21. M. Tovar and V. Cassmeyer, Touch: The Beneficial Effects for the Surgical Patient. *AORN Journal* 49 no. 5 (1989):1356–1361.
22. S. Schoenhofer, Affectional Touch in Critical Care Nursing: A Descriptive Study, *Heart and Lung* 18, no. 2 (1989):146–154.
23. S. Simon, Please Touch! How To Combat Skin Hunger in Our Schools, *Scholastic Teacher* (October 1974):22–25.
24. H. Rozema, Touch Needs of the Elderly, *Nursing Homes* (September/October 1986):42–43.
25. K. Barnett, A Survey of the Current Utilization of Touch by Health Team Personnel with Hospitalized Patients, *International Journal of Nursing Studies* 9 (1972):195–209.
26. I.M. Burnside, Touching Is Talking, *American Journal of Nursing* (1973):2060–2066.
27. E. Duffy, An Exploratory Study: The Effects of Touch on the Elderly in a Nursing Home (Master's thesis, Rutgers State University, 1982).
28. E. Steuding, Selected Psychosocial Effects of Touch on the Elderly in a Nursing Home (Master's thesis, Rutgers State University, 1984).
29. S.J. Tobiason, Touching Is for Everyone, *American Journal of Nursing* 4(1981):728–730.
30. A Yurick et al., *The Aged Person and the Nursing Process* (New York: Appleton-Century-Crofts, 1980), 298.
31. S. Oliver and S.J. Redrern, Interpersonal Communication between Nurses and Elderly Patients: Refinement of an Observational Schedule, *Journal of Advanced Nursing* 16, no. 1 (1991):30–38.
32. M. Marx and P. Werner, Agitation and Touch in the Nursing Home, *Psychological Reports* 64(1989):1019–1026.
33. M. DeWever, Nursing Home Patients' Perceptions of Nurses' Affective Touching, *Journal of Psychology* 96 (1977):163–171.
34. N. Kramer, Comparison of Therapeutic Touch and Casual Touch in Stress Reduction of Hospitalized Children, *Pediatric Nursing* 16, no. 5 (1990):483–485.
35. E. Birch, The Experience of Touch Received during Labor: Postpartum Perceptions of Therapeutic Value, *Journal of Nurse-Midwifery* 31, no. 6 (1986):270–276.
36. C.A. Estabrooks and J.M. Morse, Toward a Theory of Touch: The Touching Process and Acquiring a Touching Style, *Journal of Advanced Nursing* 17(1992):448–456.

37. P. Heidt, Effect of Therapeutic Touch in Anxiety Levels of Hospitalized Patients, *Nursing Research* 30(1981):32.

38. E. Keller and V. Bzdek, Effects of Therapeutic Touch on Tension Headache Pain, *Nursing Research* 35(1986):101–106.

39. Krieger, *The Therapeutic Touch*, 36.

40. J. Quinn, One Nurse's Evolution as Healer, *American Journal of Nursing* 79 (1979):662.

41. A. Montagu and F. Matson, *The Human Connection* (New York: McGraw-Hill, 1979), 89.

42. Ibid., 90.

43. S. Smoyak, High Tech, High Touch, *Nursing Success Today* 3, no. 11 (1986):88.

44. S. Hartman, Hug a Patient, P.R.N., *Nursing 86* 16, no. 8 (1986):88.

45. M. Bogusalawski, The Use of Therapeutic Touch in Nursing, *Journal of Continuing Education in Nursing* (October 1979):9–15.

46. D. Krieger, *Foundations for Holistic Health Nursing Practices: The Renaissance Nurse* (Philadelphia: J.B. Lippincott, 1981), 46.

47. M. Boreli and P. Heidt, *Therapeutic Touch: A Book of Readings* (New York: Springer Publishing Co.), v.

48. Ibid.

49. J. Mentgen and M.J. Trapp Bulbrook, *Healing Touch* (Carrboro, NC: North Carolina Center for Healing Touch, 1994), 81.

50. Healing Touch, 198 Union Blvd., Suite 210, Lakewood, CO 80228, (303) 989-0581.

51. D. Hover, *Healing Touch* (New York: Delmar Publishing, 1995).

52. Y. Irwin, *Shiatzu* (Philadelphia: J.B. Lippincott, 1976), 15–19.

53. Ibid.

54. A. Bergson and V. Tuchak, *Zone Therapy* (New York: Pinnacle Books, 1974), 15.

55. K. Kunz and B. Kunz, *The Complete Guide to Foot Reflexology* (Englewood Cliffs, NJ: Prentice-Hall, 1980), 2–6.

56. Krieger, *Foundations for Holistic Health Nursing Practices*, 158.

57. Kunz and Kunz, *Complete Guide to Foot Reflexology*, 46.

58. J. Mentgen and M.J. Trapp Bulbrook, *Healing Touch: Level 1 Notebook* (Carrboro, NC: North Carolina Center for Healing Touch, 1994), 7.

59. Ibid., 1.

VISION OF HEALING

Creating Receptive Quiet

We as nurses experience and teach the steps in profound psychophysiologic relaxation. As we achieve and maintain a deeply relaxed state, we connect all bodymind systems. Relaxation is a learned skill that can become a familiar, integrated part of the spectrum of nursing interventions available to us and our clients.

To watch a healthy infant or toddler sleeping is to observe one of the earliest and deepest forms of relaxation. Unfortunately, as we grow up, we receive many verbal and nonverbal messages that relaxation is not to be one of our goals in life. We receive no positive reinforcement for releasing our muscle tension, taking our time, or watching the floating clouds. Thus, we lose our early ability to let go of physical and emotional tension and sink peacefully into a deeply relaxed state. Although relaxation is not a new skill for nurses and clients, we must relearn and practice it in order to use it successfully to increase wellness and support healing.

There are many definitions and descriptions of relaxation. The following quotations describe relaxation:

> *Be still and know that I am God.*
>
> Psalm 46
>
> *Sitting quietly and doing nothing,*
> *Spring comes*
> *and the grass grows by itself.*
>
> Zen saying
>
> *Meditation is a way in which we come to feel our basic inseparability from the whole universe. What that requires is that we shut up. We become interiorly silent and cease from the interminable chatter that goes on inside our skulls.*[1]
>
> A. Watts, *Meditation*
> (Millbrae, CA: Celestial Arts, 1974), 9.

Chapter 22

Relaxation: Opening the Door to Change

Leslie Gooding Kolkmeier

NURSE HEALER OBJECTIVES

Theoretical

- Learn the definitions of relaxation and self-regulation.
- Compare and contrast different relaxation exercises.
- List the psychophysiologic changes that accompany profound relaxation.

Clinical

- Describe three different types of relaxation exercises and their appropriate clinical application.
- Identify a commonly used piece of equipment in your practice, and describe how it could be used as a biofeedback device.
- Use breathing strategies with a client, and record the subjective and clinical changes that occur with relaxed breathing.

Personal

- Pick one or a combination of breathing techniques and apply them to the stressful moments in your day.
- Identify through focused awareness and body scanning the places where you accumulate muscle tension most often.
- Identify three personally meaningful relaxation cues, and use them as reminders to perform a body scan and relax.

DEFINITIONS

Autogenic Training: self-generated therapy that includes repetition of phrases about the desired state of the body (e.g., heaviness and warmth).

Biofeedback: the use of instrumentation to mirror psychophysiologic processes of which the individual is not normally aware and which may be brought under voluntary control; allows the person to be an active participant in health maintenance.[1]

Body Scanning: the focus of conscious awareness on various parts of the body for the purpose of detecting early levels of accumulating tension.

Hypnosis: a technique for achieving an altered state of consciousness, sometimes induced in a cooperative individual by a facilitator for the purpose of changing perception, memory, or sensations.

Mantra: a word or short phrase that is repeated silently or aloud as a focusing device during the practice of meditation.

Meditation: a process of focusing and concentrating one's attention while maintaining a passive attitude; a discipline that requires concentrated practice.

Open Focus: an intervention to establish permissive conditions for a state of attention that is nonexclusive, tension-diffusing, nonjudgmental, and self-integrating.[2]

Pain (Medical Definition): localized sensation of hurt or an unpleasant sensory and emotional experience associated with actual or potential tissue damage, or described in terms of such damage.

Pain (Nursing Definition): whatever the experiencing person says it is, existing whenever he or she says it does, including both verbal and nonverbal behavior.[3]

Progressive Muscle Relaxation: the process of alternately tensing and relaxing muscle groups in order to become aware of subtle degrees of tension.

Relaxation: a psychophysiologic state characterized by parasympathetic dominance involving multiple visceral and somatic systems; the absence of physical, mental, and emotional tension; the opposite of Cannon's "fight or flight" response.[4]

Relaxation Response: an alert, hypometabolic state of decreased sympathetic nervous system arousal that may be achieved in a number of ways, including breathing exercises, relaxation and imagery exercises, biofeedback, and prayer. A degree of discipline is required to evoke this response, which increases mental and physical well-being.

Self-Hypnosis: a technique for achieving an altered state of consciousness voluntarily for the purpose of changing one's perception, memory, or sensations.

Self-Regulation: conscious control of various functions of the sympathetic nervous system.

Stress: the felt effect of overactivity of the sympathetic nervous system.

Transpersonal: transcending or going beyond personal, individual identity and meaning to include purpose, meaning, values, and identification with universal principles; spiritual.

THEORY AND RESEARCH

Relaxation makes it possible to quiet the bodymind and focus inward. One learns to retreat mentally from one's surroundings, still thoughts, relax muscles, and maintain the state of relaxation for a sufficient amount of time to reap the benefits of decreased tension, anxiety, and pain. Regardless of the approach, the end result is a movement of the person toward balance and healing.

This activity of retreating from one's surroundings is seen in the use of sweat lodges; vision quests; spiritual withdrawal to deserts, monasteries, or caves; or the mental equivalent attained through prayer or concentrative/restrictive meditation. Retreats—either physically to a different location or psychophysiologically to a different mental state through music, repetitive exercise (e.g., jogging), daydreams, naps, deep concentration, prayer, hypnosis, and other practices—are necessary to our health and not merely escapism. This ability to separate oneself from one's surroundings, or sensory deprivation, has been called "an effective way of turning toward reality, of increasing our sensitivity to and awareness of the world as it is."[5]

Relaxation interventions are useful with people in all stages of health and illness: intubated intensive care unit (ICU) patients, the critically ill (Figure 22–1), expectant parents attending childbirth preparation classes, or bus drivers learning to regulate blood pressure while weaving through city traffic. Even in the acute phase of recovery from a myocardial infarction or while undergoing an examination in an emergency room after an accident, patients can learn basic breathing and muscle relaxation exercises. Nurses on all shifts can reinforce this self-care strategy, allowing patients to be actively involved in the healing process. Nurses can also intervene in the tension-anxiety cycle that family members and friends of the patient, particularly those keeping vigil in emergency rooms, surgery waiting rooms, and ICU family areas, are experiencing.

Relaxation training has the following benefits:[6]

- decreasing the anxiety associated with painful situations, such as débridement or dressing changes
- easing the muscle tension pain of skeletal muscle contractions
- decreasing fatigue by interrupting the fight or flight response
- providing a period of rest as beneficial as a nap
- helping the client fall asleep quickly
- increasing the effect of pain medications
- helping the client dissociate from pain

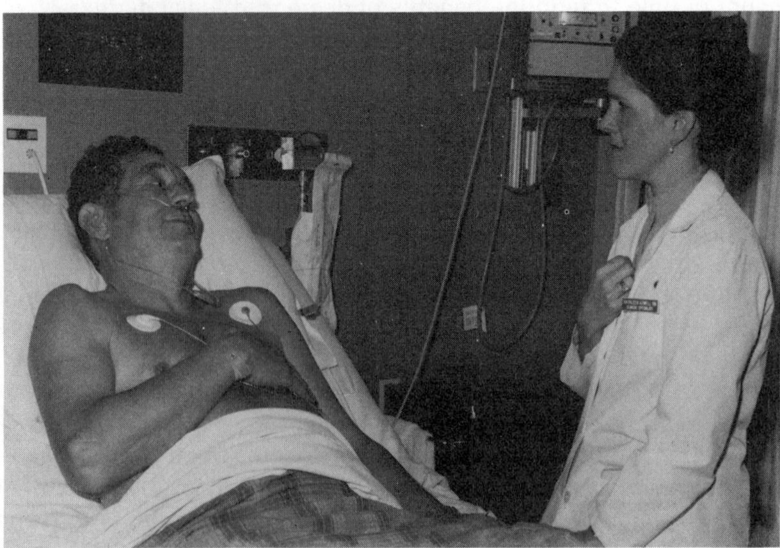

Figure 22-1 Relaxation Intervention during the Acute Phase of Recovery from a Myocardial Infarction. *Source:* Reproduced by permission from *Cardiovascular Nursing: Bodymind Tapestry* by C. Guzzetta and B. Dossey, The C.V. Mosby Company, St. Louis, © 1984.

Meditation

The practice of meditation has been recorded for many centuries in a variety of forms, either practical or religious. Practical meditation is "essentially nonstriving and relatively goal-less."[7] Meditation as a nursing intervention is almost always practical meditation. The four major routes to the meditative state are (1) through the intellect, (2) through the emotions, (3) through the body, and (4) through action.[8]

Meditation does not necessarily indicate total body relaxation. In fact, several meditative practices require the maintenance of a particular body posture over a period of time, which can become uncomfortable. Other forms of active meditation, such as Sufi dancing, require a great deal of physical energy and activity. If seeking relaxation of the body through meditation, a client must select a form of meditation that requires a relaxed body position, perhaps documenting the relaxation with the use of biofeedback.

In one study, when presented with a choice of 40 different words to use for mantra meditation, more than 15 percent of the respondents chose the word *love*. Next in order of choice were *OM*, *SHIRIM* (Sanskrit mantras), *lum* (a nonsense word), *fly*, and *relax*. Forty percent chose words ending in *M* or *N*, apparently for the resonance created in the mind and body by the sound of those consonants when spoken aloud.[9] Campbell describes *om* or *aum* as "a word that represents to our ears that sound of the energy of the universe of which all things are manifestations. . . . AUM is a symbolic sound that puts you in touch with that resounding being that is the universe."[10]

Progressive Muscle Relaxation

In 1935, Jacobson detailed a strategy leading to deep muscle relaxation.[11] The body responds to anxious thoughts and stressful events with increased muscle tension. This physiologic tension further provokes the subjective sensations of anxiety. By deliberately tensing muscle groups, focusing on the sensations of tightness and discomfort, and then slowly releasing that tension, the client can control the levels of muscle tension. Thus, the technique of progressive muscle relaxation allows the client to remain comfortable.

Several studies have shown that progressive muscle relaxation reduces the subjective feelings of anxiety and increases peak expiratory flow rates in asthmatic clients. Progressive relaxation has also been used successfully with patients who are hypertensive and those who are undergoing invasive diagnostic tests. Significant positive results have been documented through use of the State Trait Anxiety Inventory and Internal-External Locus of Control.[12] Progressive muscle relaxation is considered most effective with moderate to high panic–fear levels.[13]

Autogenics

Schultz, in 1932, developed a series of brief phrases designed to focus attention on various parts of the body and induce change in those parts.[14] The phrases are called autogenic because of their ability to assist a person in changing from within—a rather new approach to health care in the 1930s. Similar to self-hypnosis, autogenic strategies are a means of gaining access to the natural homeostatic recuperative mechanisms of the brain and are effective with disorders in which cognitive involvement is prominent.[15]

Hypnosis and Self-Hypnosis

Hypnosis, the process of quieting the muscles in order to attend mentally to positive statements, has been used with varying degrees of success for centuries. In the late 1950s, the American Medical Association endorsed it as a part of medical education.[16] Since that time, hypnosis has been integrated into medical, dental, and psychologic practices, and it is now becoming a part of holistic nursing practices. Nurses wishing to use hypnosis with clients should receive formal training and should be aware of their state's position on hypnosis, as indicated in the state nursing practice act.

Although hypnosis is used for general relaxation, it is used more frequently in an active role: to help a patient obtain relief from pain, as in childbirth and surgery; to enhance patient cooperation; to alter physiologic processes; to promote healing; or to assist in changing behaviors, such as smoking or eating behaviors.[17–19] Hypnosis is most successful when it is tailored to a client's individual mode of processing information (e.g., visual, auditory, kinesthetic). Holistic hypnosis is a tool used within a psychophysiologic, interactive, and interpersonal process designed to provide therapy by integrating mental and physiologic processes.[20]

Both hypnosis and self-hypnosis enhance a client's ability to form images because of the purposeful use of suggestion and guiding the client within an altered state of consciousness. Furthermore, self-hypnosis is a valuable tool for nurses as well. Nurses on an oncology unit who were taught to use self-hypnosis reported an increase in their ability to cope with both external and internal stressors.[21] Being able to employ self-hypnosis increases one's credibility and effectiveness when teaching such skills to patients and clients.

Biofeedback

Without feedback, nothing can be learned.[22] With appropriate feedback, many skills can be learned much more easily and quickly. We are accustomed to employing conscious feedback, the type used when we learn to play darts or to drive a car. Through training and technology, we can also gain access to many previously unconscious sources of feedback, such as heart rate, peripheral skin temperature, blood pressure, and muscle tension.

Green and Green are pioneers in the field of biofeedback. Arriving at the Menninger Clinic in 1964, they began to explore the realm of self-regulation as demonstrated by autogenic training. Their research, encouragement, and interest over the years led to the development of devices and strategies that enable clients to learn increasingly sophisticated control over autonomic events previously thought to be beyond the reach of the conscious mind. As Green and Green state, "Biofeedback isn't the panacea—it is the power within the human being to self-regulate, self-heal, re-balance. Biofeedback does nothing to the person; it is a tool for releasing that potential."[23]

Biofeedback research and clinical application have centered on the management of vascular and tension headaches, cardiovascular control (i.e., of cardiac rate, rhythm, hypertension), temporomandibular joint disorders and bruxism, disorders of motor function, gastrointestinal disorders, chronic pain, and Raynaud's syndrome.[24] Electroencephalographic (EEG) biofeedback is being used successfully to help patients with attention deficit–hyperactivity disorder and addictions. Biofeedback has also been used to teach relaxation skills to type A individuals.[25] Their type A characteristics (e.g., perfectionism, sense of time-pressure, competitiveness), when combined with feedback of physiologic information, assisted them in learning relaxation skills. The implication is that coronary disease–prone individuals can be challenged through their own character traits to modify their symptoms.

Open Focus

In the early 1970s, Fehmi developed Open Focus as an adjunct to biofeedback training, particularly EEG biofeedback. Through the use of phrases that are felt to expand an individual's awareness to include all perceptible events simultaneously, the client learns to increase the production of large amplitude and synchronous alpha waves, which signify deep levels of relaxation.[26] The intervention is especially suited to those who approach the biofeedback task with a striving, goal-oriented attitude. It is particularly effective in treating pain and anxiety. According to Fehmi,

> As the positive effects of Open Focus become manifest, the imagery of space pervading and permeating all sensory, perceptual, emotional, and mental experience can be maintained and deepened. As a result, many negative sensations or experiences which have intruded into and doggedly persisted in consciousness begin to diffuse. For example, various types of pain can and often have quickly diffused and disappeared to the considerable surprise of long-suffering bearers of pain.[27]

Relaxation Response

We are all familiar with the intense internal reaction that we experience when faced with an emergency: a truck cuts in front of us on the highway, a "code 99" comes over the loudspeaker, a child darts into the street. What some researchers refer to as an "adrenaline rush," the familiar "fight or flight response," is actually a complex series of psychophysiologic processes that prepare us to deal with the real or perceived emergency. It is important to note that people respond in an identical manner to an imagined threat as to an actual threat to their well-being.

The work of Benson and colleagues with a nonreligious form of meditation that is similar to transcendental meditation has been applied in health care settings and been validated in a variety of studies.[28,29] Their strategy consists of 20 minutes a day of focused, passive concentration on a neutral word, such as *one*. Slow repetition of the word, repeated with each exhalation, has been shown to bring about the same psychophysiologic responses as other deep relaxation processes. Further studies have documented deep relaxation when the client focuses on a short, personally meaningful religious statement or quotation.

The changes that occur when an individual reaches a deep level of relaxation are exactly opposite to those of the "fight or flight" response. Changes occur in the autonomic, endocrine, immune, and neuropeptide systems as follows:

- increases in:
    1. peripheral blood flow
    2. electrical resistance of the skin
    3. production of slow alpha waves
    4. activity of natural killer cells
- decreases in
    1. oxygen consumption
    2. carbon dioxide elimination
    3. blood lactate levels
    4. respiratory rate and volume
    5. heart rate
    6. skeletal muscle tension
    7. epinephrine level
    8. gastric acidity and motility
    9. sweat gland activity
    10. blood pressure, especially in the hypertensive individual[30]

Relaxation: Commonalities

Mindfulness

To succeed in using any of the interventions, one must cultivate the ability to focus only on one thing, that which one is presently doing. This activity may be meditation, dancing, breathing, or any other single, focused activity. Mindfulness is an attitude of remaining present, watchful, and aware of what is happening without becoming emotionally involved or captured by the images or sensations. Being truly present implies the absence of either anticipating or ruminating.[31]

Time

All of the interventions take time to learn and to do. Many may be used when there is an emergency or when the amount of time available is limited, but to be most effective, they must be practiced until they are almost automatic. The discipline and self-responsibility involved in learning a relaxation intervention must be communicated to the client early in the training.

Timelessness

One goal of all the interventions is a decrease in muscle tension and its accomplice, anxiety. The sense of timelessness that accompanies the achievement of real relaxation makes it possible to eliminate anxiety, manipulate pain, and gain voluntary regulation of physiologic change. This state of timelessness is the condition through which one goes even more deeply into the transpersonal and transcendental levels of creative insights and deeply meditative states.

Mental Aikido: Passive Volition

One element that all the interventions share is passive attention or passive volition, which is the opposite of trying to make or making a change happen. Like experts in the Japanese martial art of Aikido, individuals allow the energy of the thought or image of relaxation to carry them with it to the state of calmness. This is in direct contrast to the most familiar way of problem solving or learning a new skill, which is to try harder if the first attempts do not succeed. When attempting to lower muscle tension, for example, clients may find that they are not succeeding. They immediately begin to try harder, which further increases tension and makes them realize that their old coping skill is no longer valid. In order to be successful, they must step aside mentally; adopt an expectant, but nonstriving, attitude; and allow the bodymind to let go of tension. Documenting this phenomenon with biofeedback is the only objective way of validating this experience.

Compassionate Guide

A major factor in the success of any intervention is the building of rapport, openness, and trust between guide and client. Nurses come into the profession with a large measure of compassion and empathy, but may need to reevaluate their motives, particularly when dealing with "difficult" patients or clients. A nurse must be open to possibilities; be accepting of the other person's responses; and be able to adjust to that person's needs, likes, and dislikes as they appear during a relaxation teaching session. It is essential to approach the client and the teaching of the relaxation skill with an attitude of loving acceptance.

Relaxation: Caveats

Control

Some people resist the idea of passively "letting go," feeling that doing so would somehow cause them to lose control of themselves, their thoughts, their environment, or their actions. This resistance often occurs in clients who have endured much pain or many surgical procedures and have a need to be in complete control of their schedules, medications, dressing changes, and so forth. These clients require reassurance that they will remain in control throughout the exercise and reminders that they may test this control at any time by opening their eyes or moving a hand at will. Knowing that the interventions will indeed give them increased control over such previously overwhelming concerns as pain or insomnia will encourage and comfort them.

Other clients fear losing their competitive edge, going so far as to describe themselves as "adrenaline addicts." They must be reassured that relaxation will allow them to regulate their tension levels more appropriately and, therefore, more finely tune their "edge."

Clients may resist the idea of practicing relaxation on the grounds that it seems like a waste of time or makes them feel lazy. These clients must learn to perceive relaxation as an active, creative, and dynamic process. It is far from "doing nothing"; it involves intention and practice, and it influences all other coping skills. Relaxation is not the same process as sleeping. Biofeedback studies have shown that some people actually increase their muscle tension levels when they sleep, a direct contrast to conscious relaxation.

Lack of Time

A common protest of clients is, "I can't find the time to do this." Assurances that the time invested in relaxation will be multiplied in such benefits as increased energy, efficiency, and comfort will help clients be creative in the ways that they incorporate these skills into their daily activities. Clients can find time in their busy lives for relaxation exercises by trading household responsibilities with a housemate or spouse, taking public transportation and relaxing on the way to and from work, taking a few extra moments in the bathroom, relaxing while young children nap or in the evening after children are in bed, getting up 15 minutes early, or learning to let repetitive tasks (e.g., washing dishes, pulling weeds, chopping wood, painting walls) become moving meditations. Relaxation can be incorporated into all activities. Clients may need guidance in order to avoid the trap of allowing relaxation exercises to become an additional stressor. Chapters 14 and 23 describe the use of diaries and other means of increasing compliance and documenting the change achieved through relaxation training.

Choices

There is no formula to determine which relaxation intervention is best for which client. It is necessary to tailor the approach to the individual based on his or her condition, personal preferences, and time available.

A few clients may resist the idea of relaxation in spite of the nurse's best efforts to present it in a positive manner. In this situation, there is no need to force the issue, for the client may accept the intervention at a later time. Taking some time to explore the roots of a client's resistance may reveal misconceptions or myths that further dialogue can dispel. The use of tapes that present relaxation instructions in a nonthreatening, gentle manner, often accompanied by soothing music, may hasten acceptance of the intervention. Relaxation video tapes of calming scenes may be left playing on a television set or tranquil music played on the home or business audio system as gentle background to daily activities. One client noticed that sales increased in his store when he played relaxation music because people stayed longer and felt more relaxed. Following are guidelines for the introduction and use of relaxation tapes:

1. Listen to an exercise at least once a day, preferably twice a day.
2. Never listen to a tape when you are driving or doing any other activity.
3. Arrange to have uninterrupted privacy while you listen to your tape.
4. Listen with headphones to help block out distracting noises from the environment.
5. Listen to your tape in a relaxing position, one in which you will not have to support your body.

Medications

As clients become more adept at the relaxation process, their need for certain medications may decrease. Close monitoring and modification of dosages of antihypertensives, insulin, tranquilizers, antidepressants, and sleeping pills are essential. If the client chooses to discontinue the relaxation practice and return to old habits, however, the medications in their original dosages may again be necessary.

Body Scans and Cueing

It has been estimated that we spend 40 minutes a day, or at least 2 years of our lives, waiting.[32] We can choose to spend this time simply waiting (and probably growing impatient, thus adding to our tension burden), or we can use it to scan our bodies for muscle tension. Body scanning is taking a moment to inventory all parts of the body mentally and identify areas that are full of tension. The client who has perfected relaxation skills can then allow relaxation to replace tension.

One of the main causes of increasing levels of tension in the body is a lack of awareness. We live in our heads—thinking, seeing, hearing, and talking our way through our daily activities. We become oblivious to the signals that the body sends concerning tension, tight muscles, maladaptive body positions, restricted breathing, and other clues to our state of well-being.

Linking a body scan to another frequently performed activity makes it easier to remember to do a body scan. With these cues, one can monitor muscle tension levels and modify them before they have progressed to painfully tight muscles, headaches, or other stress-accentuated problems. Some cues around which to build a body scan habit are hearing a telephone ringing, seeing an amber or red light, being on "hold" on the telephone, taking a bathroom break, getting a drink of water, seeing a colored dot or gold star placed strategically in the environment, or entering a client's room.

Supplying a client with a small counting device, similar to those used to keep track of golf scores, provides both an incentive and a means of record keeping. Clients affix more importance to an activity if there is a "thing" or toy involved rather than just verbal instructions to practice. Each time the client takes a moment to recognize a personal cue and perform a body scan, he or she records that activity on the counter. Doing 20 to 30 scans a day can provide not only insight into tension-producing events, but also several minutes of relaxation time. This practice may be increased with the use of contracts, as described in Chapter 10.

NURSING PROCESS

Assessment

In preparing to use relaxation interventions, the nurse assesses the following parameters:

- the client's perception of personal tension levels and need to relax
- the client's readiness and motivation to learn relaxation strategies, as relaxation is a very subjective and personal endeavor
- the client's past experience with the process of relaxation, hypnosis, or meditation
- the client's personal definition of what it means to be relaxed
- the client's ability to remain comfortably in one position for 15 to 30 minutes
- the client's hearing acuity so that you can speak at an appropriate level while guiding the client in relaxation exercises

- the client's religious beliefs so that you can present the relaxation process in a way that will meld comfortably with the client's belief system
- the client's level of pain or discomfort, anxiety, fear, or boredom
- the client's perception of reality, history of depersonalization states, and locus of control, as deep relaxation may exacerbate the symptoms of psychotic and prepsychotic individuals
- the client's medication intake, particularly medications that may alter response to relaxation or may need to be altered as relaxation progresses

A questionnaire may be used to complete the assessment. The information gathered in the questionnaire provides starting points for discussion and further exploration.

Nursing Diagnoses

The following nursing diagnoses compatible with relaxation interventions and that are related to the human response patterns of the Unitary Person (see Chapter 7) are as follows:

- Relating: Social isolation
- Choosing: Coping, ineffective individual and family
- Moving: Activity intolerance: actual or potential
  Diversional activity, deficit
- Perceiving: Powerlessness
  Self-concept: disturbance in self-esteem, role performance, personal identity
  Altered sensory perception: visual, auditory, kinesthetic, gustatory, tactile, olfactory
- Knowing: Altered thought processes
- Feeling: Anxiety
  Altered comfort, pain
  Fear
  Violence, potential for: self-directed or directed at others

Client Outcomes

Table 22–1 guides the nurse in client outcomes, nursing prescriptions, and evaluation for the use of relaxation as a nursing intervention.

Table 22-1 Nursing Interventions: Relaxation

Client Outcomes	*Nursing Prescriptions*	*Evaluation*
The client will demonstrate decreased anxiety, tension, and other manifestations of the stress response as a result of the relaxation intervention.	Guide the client in the relaxation exercise. Evaluate for decrease in anxiety, tension, and other manifestations of the stress response as evidenced by heart rate within normal limits, decreased respiratory rate, return of blood pressure toward normal, resolution of anxious behaviors such as anxious facial expressions and mannerisms, repetitious talking or behavior, inability to sleep or restlessness.	The client exhibited decreased anxiety, tension, and other manifestations of the stress response as evidenced by normal vital signs; a slow, deep breathing pattern; and decreased anxious behaviors.
The client will demonstrate a stabilization or decrease in pain as a result of the relaxation intervention.	Evaluate for decrease in pain as evidenced by reduction or elimination of pain control medication and increase in activities or mobility.	The client's intake of pain medication stabilized and then decreased with relaxation skills practice. The client began to participate in activities previously limited by pain.
The client will link breathing awareness to a commonly occurring cue and use this combination to reduce tension.	Teach awareness of breathing patterns and habitual linking of relaxing breathing to a cue in the environment.	The client used turning in bed as a cue to take a slow, deep breath and relax jaw muscles.

Plan and Interventions

Before the Session

- Become personally familiar with the experience of the intervention before approaching the client.
- If the client has previous positive experience with a particular relax-

ation intervention, encourage further practice and use of that intervention.

- Review with the client or gather information from the chart, diaries, and/or verbal self-report concerning pain, anxiety, and activity levels since last session.
- Arrange medical and nursing care to allow for 15 to 45 minutes of uninterrupted time.
- Shut the door or otherwise decrease extraneous noise and distraction. Place a note on the door indicating a need for privacy until a designated time.
- Unplug the telephone, or ask a family member or roommate to answer the telephone should it ring during the relaxation training session.
- Reduce the lighting to a low level; be aware that rheostats may interfere with biofeedback equipment.
- Use incandescent lighting if possible; fluorescent lighting interferes with biofeedback equipment.
- Have the client empty his or her bladder before starting the intervention.
- Help the client find a comfortable sitting or reclining position with hands resting by the sides or on the thighs.
- Ensure the client's comfort by providing a blanket or by adjusting the thermostat to a comfortably warm setting; have small, soft pillows available for positioning.
- Hold the training session before meals or more than 2 hours after the last meal. A full stomach coupled with relaxation may lead to sleep.
- Have available music tapes and a tape recorder.
- If the session is to be followed by drawing, have paper, crayons, or markers available.
- Tell the client that you may be asking simple "yes" or "no" questions during the session to check the comfort level of the music or to confirm the client's understanding of the verbal instructions. The client may answer these questions by raising a finger or nodding the head. Tell the client that, if there is no response, the question will be repeated.

At the Beginning of the Session

- Review briefly the potential benefits of the relaxation intervention and enlist the client's cooperation.

- Explain to the client that relaxation may be easier if practiced with the eyes closed. Rather than causing the client to drift off to sleep, this position allows the client to focus attention inward while remaining wide awake.
- Explain that the purpose of breathing and relaxation exercises is to experience inward relaxation and become aware of the bodymind connections associated with relaxation.
- Emphasize that you are merely a guide and that any results obtained from the session are because of the client's involvement, interest, and practice.
- Reduce the opportunity for self-blame if sessions go poorly. There is an ebb and flow to the learning experience; there are no guarantees that pain, disease, or death will be held at arm's length forever.
- Arrive at mutually agreeable goals for the session, such as reduction of pain, decreased time to sleep onset, or reduction of anxiety.
- Have the client quantify the level of the parameter to be changed; for example, "My pain or anxiety level right now is a 7 on a 1 (none) to 10 (extreme pain) scale." Record the level.
- Record baseline vital signs; if using biofeedback equipment, record baseline physiologic parameters.
- Assure the client that sensations of heaviness, warmth, floating, or spinning are naturally occurring indications of deep relaxation; explain that, if such sensations become uncomfortable, opening the eyes will reorient the client, decrease or eliminate the sensations, and enable the exercise to continue.
- Begin soft background music. (See Chapter 24 for suggestions about music selections.)
- Guide the client through a basic breathing relaxation exercise. Each of the following breathing exercises may be repeated slowly for several minutes as an introduction to deeper relaxation:

—simply attending to the breath, counting ONE on each exhalation

—counting the breaths sequentially up to four and starting over

—imagining the body as hollow and allowing each breath to fill the hollow body slowly with relaxation

—in the mind's eye, seeing the breath as a soft relaxing color and breathing that color into all parts of the body

—breathing the relaxation up one side of the body and down the other, breathing the relaxation up the front of the body and down the back, breathing the relaxation up through the soles of the feet and relaxing the inside of the body, breathing the relaxation down from the top of the head, over the skin, and back into the feet

- Start the sessions with short breathing or relaxation exercises; lengthen the exercises as the client becomes better able to relax and attend to inner thoughts and feelings.

During the Session

- Phrase all suggestions and self-statements in a positive form; for example, "I am aware of warmth moving into my fingertips each time I exhale, leaving my head cool and calm," rather than "My head does not hurt." These suggestions enhance the imagery process, and the unconscious mind may not hear the "not."
- Speaking in a relaxed manner, ask the client for feedback concerning the appropriateness of the imagery and his or her ability to hear the background music and instructions. Have the client respond with a finger movement or nod of the head, and make adjustments as necessary.
- Pace your instructions according to the following visual cues from the client:
  —a change in breathing pattern: slower, deeper breaths progressing to slow, somewhat shallower breathing as relaxation deepens
  —more audible breathing
  —fluttering of eyelids
  —blanching of the skin around the nose and mouth
  —easing of jaw tightness, sometimes to the extent that the lips part and jaw drops slightly
  —if client is supine, toes point outward, rather than straight up
  —complete lack of muscle holding—ask client's permission to lift arm gently by the wrist; you should feel no resistance and arm should move as easily as any other object of similar weight.
- Modify your instructions and strategies to fit the situation. Encourage an intubated and ventilated patient who cannot control respiratory rate or volume to drop the jaw and allow the rhythm of the ventilator to soothe tight muscles, for example. Gently placing your hand over the clavicle as you speak increases the human bond for relaxation—despite the machinery.
- Intersperse your instructions with short phrases of encouragement that the client can use after the session as triggers to recapture a

part of the relaxation experience. Examples of such phrases are

—*Let go* of your tension.

—Feel the tightness *melting away*.

—*Loosen and soften* around your muscles.

—*Smooth out* your muscle tightness.

—Allow the tension to *drift away*.

—Gather up your tension and *throw it away*.

- As clients relax, they may experience a release of emotional life issues, which then surface in the conscious mind. Be alert for signs of emotional discomfort or letting go, such as tears, vomiting, or a change in breathing to deeper, faster breaths. If these occur, ask gentle questions (e.g., Can you put words on those feelings?) and allow time for the client to express and deal with the material before continuing with or concluding the session. Refer to Chapter 16 for information on helping clients stay grounded if they tap into emotion-laden material. Often, clients in a deeply relaxed state gain insight into ways to resolve problems or directions to take in their lives.

At the End of the Session

- Bring the client back gradually into a wakeful state by suggesting that he or she take deep, re-energizing breaths, begin to move hands and feet, and stretch.
- Have the client reevaluate, on the same scale of 1 to 10, the level of severity of the previously selected parameter to be changed. Record the level.
- Allow time for a discussion of the experience, including the techniques that seemed especially effective, the distractions that became apparent, and the physical and emotional sensations.
- Ensure that medication changes, if indicated, are appropriately monitored.
- Engage the client's cooperation in continuing practice on an individually assigned basis until the next session. See Chapter 23 for ideas to increase compliance with a practice regimen.
- Help the client choose cues with which to associate practicing the relaxation skill.
- Review the log or journal in which the client records symptoms, medications, practice, time, and results. See Chapter 14 for examples.

- Use the client outcomes (see Table 22–1) that were established before the session and the client's subjective experience (Exhibit 22–1) to evaluate the session.
- Schedule a follow-up session.

Specific Interventions

Relaxation interventions should not be used to remove symptoms without knowing the cause of the symptoms. They are not meant to replace diagnosis and treatment, but to enhance healing and well-being.

Tension Awareness: Progressive Muscle Relaxation (Basic). The purpose of a tension awareness exercise is to help the client identify subtle levels of mental tension and anxiety and the accompanying physical tension. The client who is aware of the internal differences induced by this exercise can move to threshold levels of tension, holding just enough tightness in the muscle group to be aware of beginning tension and then relaxing the group. By moving from strong contractions to very subtle ones, the client becomes aware of the ability to fine tune the relaxation process. The exercise requires 10 to 30 minutes.

Script: *First take a few moments to focus on your breathing. This will help you to focus better on internal cues of muscle tension and then relaxation. I will guide you as we begin to move through the muscles in your body. Become aware of how you can gain control over the tension found in those muscles. This process involves alternately tightening and relaxing muscle groups. Let yourself tighten each muscle group, hold the tension for 5 to 10 seconds or until mild fatigue is felt in the area, and then release the tension. . . . Begin with the muscles in your feet and calves; tighten that area as much as you can. Pull your toes up toward your head, and become aware that as the muscles tighten and as you continue to hold that tightness, they will perhaps tremble or shake a bit as they fatigue. . . . Now, let the tension slowly dissolve and feel the difference in your lower legs and feet. . . . Let your attention move up to your knees and thighs; tense those muscles by pressing your legs into the surface of the bed [couch, floor, or chair]. . . . When you are aware of how they feel, then allow the tension to drift away as you exhale.*

The exercise then proceeds to the following areas: hips and buttocks, abdomen and lower back, chest and upper back, shoulders and biceps, forearms and hands, neck and shoulders, jaw and tongue, and finally facial muscles. If the client is experiencing pain or difficulty with a particular part of the body, the exercise should begin as far away from the involved area as possible and conclude with the primary area of difficulty.

Clients should be coached to breathe throughout the session, thereby avoiding the temptation to hold their breath as they tighten their muscles. Clients may learn to exhale as they tighten muscle groups. Tension in muscles should be held short of true discomfort.

Progressive muscle relaxation is particularly effective for clients who are feeling physically tense, anxious, and perhaps agitated. Because it is an active intervention, it may be preferable to other passive exercises, especially early in client training. It should be used with caution for clients with hypertension and back pain, however.

Return to Balance: Autogenic Training (Basic). To help consciously rebalance the internal homeostatic mechanisms of the cardiovascular and respiratory systems, which simultaneously affect the autonomic, endocrine, immune, and neuropeptide systems, clients may find autogenic training helpful. The exercise generally lasts 10 to 20 minutes.

Script: *Slowly and silently repeat the following phrases to yourself as I say them out loud to you* [repeat each phrase two to four times, pausing a few seconds between each repetition]: *"I am beginning to feel quite quiet. . . . I am beginning to feel relaxed. . . . My feet, knees, and hips feel heavy. . . . Heaviness and warmth are flowing through my feet and legs. . . . My hands, arms, and shoulders feel heavy. . . . Warmth and heaviness are flowing through my hands and arms. . . . My neck, jaw, tongue, and forehead feel relaxed and smooth. . . . My whole body feels quiet, heavy, and comfortable. . . . I am comfortably relaxed. . . . Warmth and heaviness flow into my arms, hands, and fingertips. . . . My breathing is slow and regular. . . . I am aware of my calm, regular heartbeat. . . . My mind is becoming quieter as I focus inward. . . . I feel still. . . . Deep in my mind I experience myself as relaxed, comfortable, and still. . . . I am alert in a quiet, inward way." As I finish my relaxation, I take in several deep, re-energizing breaths, bringing light and energy into every cell of my body.*

Autogenic training should begin in a warm (75° to 80° Fahrenheit) room to facilitate sensations of warmth. Clients can then progress to cooler environments to generalize their training. The use of the phrases while the mind is relaxed and receptive allows the peripheral circulation to increase and cardiac and respiratory rates and rhythms to slow and stabilize. It may take several weeks for the client to feel sensations of heaviness and warmth, although the client usually achieves heart rate and respiratory control much sooner.

The Golden Moment: Quieting Response (Basic). It is helpful for clients to become aware, on a frequent basis, of external stressors and their internal responses to these stressors. With the quieting response, clients can learn to control their internal responses and continue with daily activities.

An abbreviated version of a quieting response that can be done frequently during the day takes only 5 to 10 seconds.

Script: *Check your breathing. Notice what is bothering you at this moment. Smile at yourself and say to yourself, "What a silly thing to do to my body!" Take a slow deep breath to a count of 1–2–3–4, and breathe out slowly to a count of 1–2–3–4. Again, slowly breathe in and, as you breathe out, let your body go as limp as possible, particularly your lips and jaw. Imagine warmth and heaviness flowing down your body to your toes. Allow your eyes to dance and inwardly smile. Go on with your activities, alert and relaxed.*

Developed by Stroebel, this intervention is an eclectic combination of stressor identification skills, breathing techniques, progressive relaxation, changing self-talk, and autogenics. The strategy has been modified into a program called "QR for Kids" to help children identify their body responses to stressors and replace them with relaxation.[33] Children learn to identify what is bothering them, let their eyes sparkle, breathe in through imaginary holes in their feet, and allow their bodies to become warm and relaxed as they exhale. This intervention is reinforced with a variety of imagery exercises.[34]

Expanding Awareness: Open Focus (Advanced). To diffuse a client's attention, rather than focus it narrowly on one point, it is helpful to expand awareness. The open focus exercise asks the client a series of questions relating to his or her imagination of something other than a concrete object or experience. Distance, no-thing-ness, and spaces between points and objects form the basis of the script. The exercise takes 45 minutes. (The following contains excerpts from the complete script.[35])

Script: Begin each phrase with *Is it possible for you to imagine . . .* or *Can you imagine . . . the space between your eyes . . . the space between your ears . . . the space inside your throat . . . that the space inside your throat expands to fill your whole neck as you inhale . . . that your feet and toes are filled with space . . . that the region between your arches and your ankles is filled with space . . . that your buttocks and the region between your hips and your legs and feet and toes are simultaneously filled with space . . . the space inside your lungs as you inhale and exhale . . . that the boundaries between the space inside and the space outside are dissolving and that the space inside and the space outside become one continuous and unified space.*

The entire series of exercises consists of 95 statements that expand and open the attention and awareness of the client, leading to a deeply relaxed state. After repeated practice, clients can often return to the state of open focus simply by repeating a cue word or phrase to themselves.

Quiet Heart: Relaxation Response (Basic). Clients can achieve a relaxed, alert, hypometabolic state in 15 to 20 minutes by means of the relaxation response.

Script: *As you exhale, mentally repeat the word ONE with each breath out. As thoughts interfere with the single focus of breathing out to the count of ONE, let the thoughts go and come back to the activity of breathing and counting. Focus on your breathing and the word ONE.* After 20 minutes, the client may stretch, take a deep breath, and continue with normal activities.

As the length of hospital stays in acute care have been reduced, the relaxation response is an increasingly valuable intervention because it can be taught in a short time period. Clients involved in an outpatient wellness practice, long-term care, or a hospice situation are able to learn the more involved disciplines of meditation.

Quiet Heart: Meditation (Basic to Advanced). Meditation makes it possible to gain access to more of our human potential, to increase our ability to function in reality more effectively. In general, 10 to 15 minutes should be available for meditation.

Script [after making sure client is comfortable with water image]: *Picture yourself sitting comfortably on the floor of a beautiful clear lake. Each time you experience a thought, feeling, or perception, picture it as a bubble rising slowly to the surface of the lake. Take 5 to 10 seconds to observe each thought, feeling, or perception rising until it passes from your sight. Do not explore or associate with any of the bubbles; simply notice them with a background of "oh, that's what I'm thinking (or feeling, or sens-*

ing) now. How interesting." As each bubble disappears, wait calmly for the next one.[36]

This is a single example of a meditation strategy. There are many variations, and no one is any better than another. Each provides a different means to the same end: a voluntarily achieved, relaxed, hypometabolic state, accompanied by a quiet bodymind. Most teachers recommend staying with a particular meditation path for a minimum of 1 month before contemplating a change. Individuals should follow what intuitively feels right, should "be" with the feelings experienced after a period of meditation, and should know that, if they feel better and less fragmented than they did before, they are on the right path.[37]

Quiet Heart: Prayer (Basic to Advanced). Prayer is a way of eliciting the relaxation response in the context of a client's deeply held personal, religious, or philosophic beliefs. Benson refers to this as incorporating the "Faith Factor" into relaxation.[38] Many clients are comfortable with prayer as a meditative strategy, and it requires only seconds to minutes. The nurse should strive to accommodate the client's spiritual needs, either by calling on his or her personal backgrounds and resources or by enlisting the help of appropriate family, clergy, or chaplaincy staff.

Utilizing Inner Awareness: Biofeedback (Advanced). Biofeedback involves the use of instrumentation to show clients alterations in their physiologic function in a way that allows them to intervene and change their own internal activity. Biofeedback devices do not do anything to the client; they simply record information about the client. For example, a very simple biofeedback device is the common bathroom scale. One steps on the scale, sees one's weight, and according to that information chooses whether to change one's eating habits. A thermometer and mirror are other good examples.

Clinical biofeedback devices are electronically sophisticated, sometimes portable, instruments that present information in a variety of engaging fashions. Through skin electrodes or thermistors, they monitor subtle changes in temperature, muscle activity, brain waves, sweat gland activity, blood pressure, and cardiac rate and rhythm. This information, in combination with other relaxation interventions, allows the client to make internal adjustments toward a relaxed state and receive immediate rewards for having done so. The equipment provides an external validation of the internal changes, thus greatly speeding up the learning and reinforcement of those changes.

The most frequent use of biofeedback is to help clients learn to prevent overactivity of the sympathetic nervous system. Biofeedback is also used for neuromuscular retraining, such as to increase muscle activity after stroke or spinal cord injury. Local or national workshops, training courses, seminars, and resources at the end of this chapter offer further information on biofeedback training and certification.

Door to the Inner Mind: Hypnosis (Advanced). As the bodymind becomes alert, but relaxed, self-talk decreases, and one is able to communicate with the subconscious. Hypnosis has the features of motivation, relaxation, and concentration in common with other relaxation interventions, but it has the added feature of direction by a person trained in hypnosis. The altered state of consciousness achieved through hypnosis is similar to, and at times indistinguishable from, guided imagery. Clients may use the hypnotic trance to rehearse new coping skills, open new possibilities, and gain self-regulatory mastery over various aspects of the sympathetic nervous system.

There are four basic stages of hypnosis:

1. induction: the initial stage of the trance, achieved through gazing at a point; staring upward; or fixating on a monotonous action, such as a clock pendulum or waves on a beach
2. deepening: increasing the depth of the trance through spiral images, moving down a staircase or elevator, counting breaths, etc.
3. plateau: that stage of the trance in which one embeds suggestions for positive change or reinforces previously decided, mutually agreed on behaviors or goals
4. reversing: a return through the process followed in deepening to a state of relaxed alertness[39]

Hypnosis, particularly the hypnotic trance, may have negative connotations to some clients and should be presented in a positive framework. To frame the hypnotic state in familiar terms, the nurse can remind clients of times that they have become completely engrossed in a movie or a book. Assurances that they will always remain in control and can only enter a hypnotic state voluntarily will help ease clients' misgivings.

Door to the Inner Mind: Self-Hypnosis (Basic). Hypnotic strategies can give clients and patients a powerful tool in dealing with anxieties, behavior patterns, or pain. In addition to the immediate benefits, there is a long-term increase in self-esteem as clients learn to apply the methods successfully to a variety of situations.

Self-hypnosis instruction is most helpful, and safest, when it is coordinated with the recommendations of the client's physician and other health care providers. Clients' willingness to understand the cause of their symptoms, as well as to change their programming, mental attitudes, and life style, are essential to letting go of their symptoms.[40] (See Chapter 9 for affirmations and Chapter 23 for self-talk and imagery strategies to incorporate into the self-hypnosis experience.)

Yoga (Basic to Advanced). Yoga is a philosophy of living that attempts to unite physical, mental, and spiritual health. When practiced for the purpose of relaxation, it involves breathing and stretching exercises and postures called asanas. Because the exercises vary greatly in difficulty, starting with very gentle stretches and breathing techniques, yoga is ideally suited for clients with stiff muscles and decreased activity levels who are attempting to begin an active relaxation and exercise program. Clients need not embrace the philosophy to benefit from the activity.

Case Studies

Case Study No. 1

Setting:	Pediatric pulmonary care unit; biofeedback-mediated relaxation
Client:	A.B., an 11-year-old boy
Nursing Diagnoses:	1. Altered oxygenation, impaired gas exchange, ineffective breathing pattern, ineffective airway clearance 2. Social isolation 3. Ineffective individual coping 4. Activity intolerance 5. Disturbance in body image 6. Powerlessness 7. Pain 8. Anxiety 9. Fear: all related to end-stage cystic fibrosis

A.B. had been diagnosed with cystic fibrosis at the age of 7 months. Since that time, he had spent much of his life in the hospital. He had seen most of his older friends die. His parents had divorced when he was 5 years old; when not hospitalized, he lived with his mother and 13-year-old sister. His pediatrician felt that A.'s present admission would likely be his last. His pulmonary infections were not responding to the antibiotics administered intravenously; he was losing weight; and he required continuous oxygen by cannula. In order to decrease A.'s fear and anxiety, which was interfering with his ability to sleep and further compromising his pulmonary status, the pediatrician asked that the biofeedback nurse therapist work with the patient.

With the aid of relaxation exercises, imagery, and electromyographic biofeedback devices, A. learned, over the space of five daily sessions, to decrease the activity of his accessory breathing muscles and increase the excursion of his diaphragm. He began to use his relaxation skills to help him sleep. He also discovered that he was better able to clear accumulated pulmonary secretions after a biofeedback session, further increasing his oxygenation and comfort level.

Knowing that the physical and emotional states achieved with relaxation are often difficult to communicate, the nurse asked A. to draw how he felt before a relaxation-biofeedback session. In Figure 22–2, the difficulty that A. was having in breathing is graphically illustrated by the heavy bands around his neck and chest. His self-concept was communicated through the unhappy face, stunted size, and presence of only three fingers on each hand.

After 20 minutes of biofeedback-mediated deep relaxation, he drew the picture shown in Figure 22–3. Now, A. depicted himself as well-proportioned; with a happy face, five fingers on each hand, and powerful muscles in his arms; and able to breathe freely. When asked to comment on the lines coming from the surface of his body, he explained, "Those are the warm, tingly feelings I get when I relax."

A. died 2 weeks later, sleeping quietly in his mother's arms. He practiced his new skills up until his last hours.

Figure 22–2 Drawing Done before Relaxation-Biofeedback Session.

Figure 22–3 Drawing Done after 20 Minutes of Relaxation.

Case Study No. 2

Setting:	Preoperative visit to physician's office
Client:	C.D., a 38-year-old female secretary
Nursing Diagnoses:	1. Altered physical regulation (rheumatoid, autoimmune disorder) 2. Altered physical mobility (right wrist, degeneration/dysfunction both knees) 3. Anxiety 4. Coping, ineffective individual 5. Fear 6. Powerlessness: all related to rheumatoid arthritis

The immediate problem was scheduled surgery to remove three displaced bones from C.'s right wrist that were causing radial nerve impairment. In addition to her long-term concern about whether she would be able to continue working as a secretary, C. confided to her nurse her fear associated with the time period just before surgery. She had undergone arthroscopic knee surgery several years before and still had vivid, unpleasant memories of lying in a preoperative area and hearing the voices of the nurses on the other side of the curtain. She had felt abandoned and frightened and had wondered if anyone even knew she was there. Postoperatively, she had experienced several hours of nausea and vomiting.

In addition to providing C. with the usual preoperative information the week before her scheduled surgery, the nurse taught her relaxation and imagery exercises. She was asked to relax for a few moments in a comfortable position so that she could begin to rehearse in her imagination the following week's procedure. After guiding C. through a few moments of breathing relaxation, the nurse asked C. to close her eyes and begin to imagine waking up on the day of her surgery. The nurse took her step-by-step through the morning routine of getting dressed, being driven through the early morning sunrise to the hospital, going through the outpatient admission process, going to her room, putting on a hospital gown, getting a preoperative injection, and waiting calmly while holding her husband's hand until the orderly came to take her to the surgery waiting area.

At this point in the relaxation imagery, the nurse directed C. to imagine being wheeled down the long corridor to the surgery doors, watching the ceiling lights passing above her. Each time she saw a light in the ceiling, she was to use that as a cue to take a deep breath and release all the tension from her bodymind. C. was instructed to rehearse this three times a day until the day of surgery. The nurse recorded this voice instruction so C. had her own personalized tape for healing before, during, and after surgery. (Even if a nurse has only a short time for teaching before surgery, there is time to teach rhythmic breathing exercises.)

At her first postoperative visit, C. enthusiastically reported the positive results of her mental rehearsal and relaxation. She vividly remembered her mental relaxation and imagery as she had rehearsed, her confidence increasing as she was wheeled under each light. The surgery waiting area seemed calm and safe to her this time, and she had no postoperative nausea. At this visit, the nurse taught her imagery of healing and increasing mobility in the same format as her visit before surgery. Her success with using cues to help her remember to relax encouraged C. to use the intervention whenever she was faced with an unpleasant or frightening experience.

Exhibit 22–1 Evaluating the Client's Subjective Experience of Relaxation

1. Was this a new experience for you? Can you describe it?
2. Did you have any physical or emotional responses to the relaxation exercise? If so, can you describe them?
3. Do you feel different after this experience? How?
4. How does your bodymind communicate with you when your stress level is at an uncomfortable point?
5. Would you like to try this again?
6. Were there any distractions to your relaxation?
7. What would make this a more pleasant experience for you?
8. How do you see yourself integrating relaxation skills into your daily life?

Evaluation

With the client, the nurse determines whether the client outcomes for relaxation interventions (see Table 22–1) were successfully achieved. To evaluate the session further, the nurse may again explore the subjective effects of the experience with the client (Exhibit 22–1). Because the accomplishment of these interventions may take place over a period of days or weeks, they must be reviewed and reevaluated periodically. Continuing support and encouragement are necessary.

Relaxation exercises can be taught to clients under almost any circumstances. They not only reduce the fear and anxiety associated with many medical and nursing interventions, but, once learned, they may also be used in all aspects of a client's life. They increase the overall movement toward wholeness and balance for both client and nurse, and they facilitate other interventions by allowing the client to move toward learning and participating in his or her health.

DIRECTIONS FOR FUTURE RESEARCH

1. Correlate the changes in psychophysiology with the specific interventions used in order to determine the most effective interventions and their presentation.
2. Conduct tightly structured studies that use control groups to validate changes brought about by relaxation exercises.
3. Monitor and validate the effect of the "compassionate guide" in the relaxation process.

NURSE HEALER REFLECTIONS

After reading this chapter, the nurse healer will be able to answer or begin a process of answering the following questions:

- How does my inner experience of tension or anxiety shift when I release my muscle tightness?
- How do I model relaxation to my family, friends, colleagues, and clients?
- What is my kinesthetic experience of letting go of tension, concerns, and physical and emotional stresses?
- What cues about my inner states of tension or relaxation do I receive from my breathing pattern?
- What peace of mind do I experience as I move through my potentially stressful job activities?
- Am I aware that my attitudes toward my tasks are contagious to my clients?

NOTES

1. G. Fuller, *Biofeedback: Methods and Procedures in Clinical Practice* (San Francisco: The Biofeedback Institute of San Francisco, 1977), 1.
2. L. Fehmi, Paper presented at the Council Grove Conference on Voluntary Control of Internal States, Council Grove, Iowa, 1975.
3. N. Meinhart and M. McCaffery, *Pain: A Nursing Approach to Assessment and Analysis* (East Norwalk, CT: Appleton-Century-Crofts, 1983), 377.
4. K. Phillips, Biofeedback as an Aid to Autogenic Training, in *Mind and Cancer Prognosis*, ed. B. Stoll (New York: John Wiley & Sons, 1979), 153.
5. M. Hutchinson, *The Book of Floating* (New York: William Morrow and Company, 1984), 25.
6. M. McCaffery, Relieving Pain with Noninvasive Techniques, *Nursing 80*, 10, no. 12 (1980):57.
7. D. Sutterly and G. Donnelly, *Coping with Stress: A Nursing Perspective* (Gaithersburg, MD: Aspen Publishers, 1982), 190.
8. L. LeShan, *How To Meditate* (New York: Bantam Books, 1975), 32.
9. D. Morse and M. Furst, *Women under Stress* (New York: Van Nostrand Reinhold, 1982), 381.
10. J. Campbell, *The Power of Myth* (New York: Doubleday, 1988), 230–231.
11. E. Jacobson, *Progressive Relaxation* (Chicago: University of Chicago Press, 1938).
12. P. Freeberg et al., Effect of Progressive Muscle Relaxation on the Objective Symptoms and Subjective Responses Associated with Asthma, *Heart and Lung* 16, no. 1 (1987):24–30.

13. N. Pender, Effects of Progressive Muscle Relaxation Training on Anxiety and Health Locus of Control among Hypertensive Adults, *Research in Nursing and Health* 8 (1985):67–72.
14. J. Schultz and W. Luthe, Autogenic Training: A Psychophysiologic Approach in Psychotherapy (New York: Grune & Stratton, 1959).
15. J. Stoyva and W. Luther, In Memoriam, *Biofeedback and Self-Regulation* 11, no. 2 (1986):91.
16. V. Moss, Beating the Stress Connection, *Association of Operating Room Nurses* 41, no. 4 (1985):720.
17. W. Kroger and W. Fezler, *Hypnosis and Behavior Modification* (Philadelphia: J.B. Lippincott, 1976), 179–221.
18. H. Crasilneck and J. Hall, *Clinical Hypnosis* (New York: Grune & Stratton, 1985), 147–176.
19. R. Zahorek, Clinical Hypnosis in Holistic Nursing, *Holistic Nursing Practice* 2, no. 1 (1987):22.
20. Ibid., 17.
21. G. Boyne, ed. *Hypnosis: New Tool in Nursing Practice* (Glendale, CA: Westwood Publishing Co., 1982), 8.
22. E. Green and A. Green, *Beyond Biofeedback* (Ft. Wayne, IN: Knoll Publishing Co., 1977), 24.
23. Ibid., 116.
24. J. Hatch et al., eds. *Biofeedback: Studies in Clinical Efficacy* (New York: Plenum Press, 1987).
25. C. Moreno, Concepts of Stress Management in Cardiac Rehabilitation, *Focus on Critical Care* 14, no. 5 (1987):17.
26. L. Fehmi, Paper presented at the Council Grove Conference on Voluntary Control of Internal States, Council Grove, Iowa, 1975, 2.
27. Ibid., 9.
28. H. Benson et al., Decreased Premature Ventricular Contraction through the Use of the Relaxation Response in Patients with Stable Ischemic Heart Disease, *Lancet* 2, no. 7931 (1975):380.
29. M. Frenn et al., Reducing the Stress of Cardiac Catheterization by Teaching Relaxation, *Dimensions of Critical Care Nursing* 5, no. 2 (1986):108–116.
30. H. Benson, *Beyond the Relaxation Response* (New York: Times Books, 1984).
31. E. Peper and E. Williams, *From the Inside Out* (New York: Plenum Press, 1981), 76.
32. E. Charlesworth and R. Nathan, *Stress Management* (New York: Atheneum, 1984), 75.
33. E. Stroebel, *Kiddie QR* (Wethesfield, CT: QR Publications, 1987), audiotape and workbooks.
34. Stroebel, *Kiddie QR*.
35. L. Fehmi, Paper presented at the Council Grove Conference on Voluntary Control of Internal States, Council Grove, Iowa, 1975.
36. LeShan, *How To Meditate*, 60.
37. Ibid., 33.
38. Benson, *Beyond the Relaxation Response*, 3.

39. Moss, *Beating the Stress Connection*, 722.
40. Boyne, *Hypnosis*, 10.

SUGGESTED READING

Benson, H., and Proctor, W. *Your Maximum Mind* (New York: Random House, 1987).

Csikszentmihalyi, M., *Flow: The Psychology of Optimal Experience* (New York: Harper & Row, 1990).

Curtis, J., et al., *Teaching Stress Management and Relaxation Skills: An Instructor's Guide* (LaCrosse, WI: Coulee Press, 1985).

Dossey, L., *Healing Words: The Power of Prayer and the Practice of Medicine* (New York: HarperCollins, 1993).

Green, J., and Shellenberger, R., *The Dynamics of Health and Wellness* (Fort Worth, TX: Holt, Rinehart and Winston, 1991).

Harmon, W., and Reinhold, H., *Higher Creativity* (Los Angeles: Jeremy P. Tarcher, 1984).

Sethi, A., *Meditation as an Intervention in Stress Reactivity* (New York: AMS Press, 1989).

Zahorek, R.P., ed., *Relaxation and Imagery: Tools for Therapeutic Communication and Intervention* (Philadelphia: W.B. Saunders, 1988).

Zahorek, R.P., ed., *Clinical Hypnosis and Therapeutic Suggestion in Nursing* (Orlando, FL: Grune & Stratton, 1985).

RESOURCES

Biofeedback Workshops:
Association for Applied Psychophysiology and Biofeedback
10200 West 44th Ave., #304
Wheat Ridge, CO 80033-2840

Hypnosis Workshops:
American Society of Clinical Hypnosis
2250 East Devon Ave., Suite 336
Des Plaines, IL 60018

VISION OF HEALING

Modeling a Wellness Life Style

Nurses must identify their own state of wellness and model a wellness life style if they are to be effective teachers. Wellness is an evolving process. It does not just happen, but requires ongoing self-assessments in all areas of human potential, as well as an investigation of one's values and beliefs. We need to pause for a moment and reflect on these questions about our state of wellness:

- *Do we see wellness as a fluctuating state that we can continuously participate in creating?*
- *Do we see our health as affected and determined by family, friends, job, and environment?*
- *Can we learn new wellness behaviors?*
- *Is the responsibility for staying well ours or somebody else's?*

Self-responsibility for wellness resides within each of us. What are the key elements in our wellness program? Do these elements include all areas of the circle of human potential as discussed in Chapter 9? It is through these areas that we focus on maximizing wellness. In planning a wellness program, we must develop and incorporate four basic and critical factors: (1) a positive self-image, (2) a positive attitude, (3) self-discipline, and (4) integration of body-mind-spirit. Each person will develop and incorporate these factors in his or her own unique way.

Our self-image is positive when we view ourselves as worthy human beings. We must continue to develop all our senses and see ourselves as well in all respects—physical, mental, emotional, social, and spiritual. A positive attitude means that we like and respect ourselves. To thrive in this life, we have to learn to respect our body-mind-spirit and to discipline ourselves. Self-discipline embodies the idea of being calm and consistently following positive wellness patterns, such as relaxation, exercise, play, and good nutrition. Body-mind-spirit integration means that we see ourselves as a whole. We learn to "walk our talk" of integration in the personal and professional aspects of our lives. We must learn to be more humane to ourselves. We are part of a whole universe, and, as we are interacting wholes, the universe is different from the sum of the parts. We must feel a keen sense of balance and relatedness between who we are, where we are, and how we interact with everyone.

Application of the wellness model to our own lives can assist us in feeling whole and inspired about life. To apply the model, we need to take the following steps:

- *Search for patterns and antecedents or precipitants of stress and anxiety.*
- *Identify positive feelings and emotions.*
- *Emphasize our human values.*
- *Assess any pain and disease as valuable signals of internal conflict, not as totally negative events.*
- *Place emphasis on achieving maximal body-mind-spirit wellness.*
- *View our own body-mind-spirit as equal factors, with one element never more important than the others.*

Chapter 23

Imagery: Awakening the Inner Healer

Barbara Montgomery Dossey

NURSE HEALER OBJECTIVES

Theoretical

- Define and contrast the different types of imagery.
- Discuss the different theories of imagery.
- Explain different imagery interventions.

Clinical

- Incorporate imagery interventions into your clinical practice.
- Learn techniques to empower your spoken words.
- Train your voice so that your tone of voice and the pacing of selected word phrases convey the qualities of calmness, reassurance, openness, and trust.

Personal

- Choose a special healing image to focus on throughout the day.
- Learn to trust and interpret the meaning of your images.
- Experience the internal change of "lightening your personal load" with the imagery process.

DEFINITIONS [1]

Active Imagery: conscious formation of an image/s that is directed to a body area or activity that requires attention.

Correct Biologic Imagery: biologically accurate images that appear as real life as if seen under a microscope.
Customized Imagery: images that contain personalized, unique information.
End-State Imagery: images of final healed state.
General Healing Imagery: image of an event, healing light, forgiveness, opening, and so forth.
Guided Imagery: access to the imagination through a guide.
Imagery: internal experiences of memories, dreams, fantasies, and visions—sometimes involving one, several, or all the senses—that serve as the bridge for connecting body, mind, and spirit.
Packaged Imagery: commercial tapes that have general images.
Process Imagery: step-by-step goal to be achieved.
Receptive Imagery: unexpected reception of an image, as if it "bubbled up" or entered the stream of consciousness.
Symbolic Imagery: metamorphosis of personal symbols from a person's unconscious and conscious awareness; part of the person's own hero's journey or personal mythology.
Transpersonal Imagery: imagery that is not confined to a single person's bodymind, but serves as a mode of communication from one person to another, through an unknown, invisible pathway. For example, transpersonal images evoked in prayer are petitions that are relayed appropriately by a divine switchboard.

THEORY AND RESEARCH

Imagery is a nonverbal modality and a rich source about a person's life processes. Powerful, noninvasive, and cost-effective, imagery interventions can be done by the client alone or with guidance. Imagery connects the complex phenomenon of mind modulation with the unlimited capabilities of the body-mind-spirit. Awareness of imagery processes is a more satisfying way to interact with self and others. As more nurses gain an understanding of the effectiveness of imagery and use it to complement traditional nursing interventions, it will revolutionize the practice of nursing. It will change nursing primarily because it engages the nurse and the client/patient at a higher level than traditional nursing does. Nurses play a key role in contributing to the scientific basis for imagery. Research-based protocols for nursing practice can be the outcome of quantitative and qualitative studies.

Effects of Imagery on Physiology and the Senses

People can learn to produce positive healing results through the imagery process. Messages—feelings, attitudes, beliefs, emotions, purpose, and meaning—have to be translated by the right hemisphere of the brain into nonverbal terminology before they are comprehensible to the involuntary or autonomic nervous system. The images so intimately connected with physiology, health, and disease are preverbal (i.e., without a language base), except through their physiologic connection with the left hemisphere. If connections between the right and left hemispheres were severed, untranslated images would continue to affect emotions and alter physiology, but there would be no intellectual interpretation. Research findings on imagery and physiology include the following[2]:

- Images relate to physiologic states.
- Images may either precede or follow physiologic changes, indicating that they have both a causative and a reactive role.
- Images can originate in conscious, deliberate behaviors, as well as in subconscious acts (e.g., electrical stimulation of the brain, reverie, dreaming, and brain wave biofeedback).
- Images can be the hypothetical bridge between conscious processing of information and physiologic change.
- Images can influence the voluntary (peripheral) nervous system, as well as the involuntary (autonomic) nervous system.

Imagery is not about mental pictures, but is a resource for gaining access to the imagination and more subtle aspects of inner experience. It may involve all sensory modalities: visual, olfactory, tactile, gustatory, auditory, and kinesthetic. Each of the known senses has many different, extremely complex functions that are separate from and parallel to the functions of the other senses. More than 17 senses have been identified. Among the more recent sensory findings are

- the vomeronasal system, which is capable of detecting pheromones, the chemicals that are given off to indicate intraspecific messages, such as sexual receptivity and identification
- nocioception, a separate sensory organ for pain, distinct from touch and temperature sensing
- a parallel, but separate sensory system for experiencing thermal and tactile sensations
- parallel separate systems that detect the visual contour/contrast of an object and its colors

- a functional pineal gland that responds to light and synchronizes internal body rhythms of night and day[3]

Imagery and State-Dependent Learning

Because memory is dependent on and limited to the state in which it was acquired, it is referred to as state-bound information.[4] For example, how can a person hang onto a painful memory from childhood, such as being reprimanded in front of friends? At the time of the experience (state-dependent), the person's body-mind-spirit remembers at many different levels being severely embarrassed, angry, or shamed (state-bound information). These emotions of the body-mind-spirit experience become embedded in the memory. Therefore, what is learned and remembered is dependent on the person's psychologic state at the time of the experience.

The dramatic psychophysiologic changes that occur in imagery and hypnosis result from gaining access to state-dependent memory, learning, and behavior systems and making their encoded information available for problem solving.[5] Every time the client gains access to such information, he or she has an opportunity to reframe experiences and develop new health behaviors/thoughts. Painful state-dependent memory, thus, can be reassociated, reorganized, or reframed in a manner that resolves the negative memory and evokes new patterns of wellness and healing.

State-dependent learning and memory are the basis for all imagery interventions. As the nurse engages with the client in assessing life stressors, developing problem-solving skills, and choosing healthy life style behaviors, a three-step imagery process occurs. First, the nurse and client initiate a communication process together. Second, they engage in some sort of therapeutic work. Third, they develop some criteria for problem resolution so that they know when to discontinue the interaction.

Imagery Theories

Eidetic Psychotherapy

Ahsen's eidetic psychotherapy has three unitary, interactive modes of awareness: (1) image—I, (2) somatic response—S, and (3) meaning—M.[6] The image is the aroused sensation, the response to external reality and the objects around a person. Simultaneously, there is an "as if" image, an internal reality that, in its own way, is as real as the external image. The person's seeing the image produces a somatic response, or a neurophysiologic response. The meaning ascribed to the image results from the left hemisphere's trying to make verbal sense of a globally perceived experience. Some images create meaning that is superficial, incomplete, or unclear. The behavior in some images may be seen as defensive and self-limiting. A person can have a fixed, frozen image of past events that disrupts thought processes and obstructs the development of more effective behaviors in the present experience. The opposite is also true. A person can have very vivid images that provide profound insight about life processes.

Lexical and Enactive Modes of Imagery

According to Horowitz,[7] imagery is encoded, retrieved, and expressed, and it flows among patterns of thoughts, physical responses, and a person's world view. Images form, express, and evoke emotions that directly affect physiologic response. Information enters the central nervous system, is encoded into images, and is stored in two modes: lexical and enactive. The lexical mode is that type of logical and analytical thinking that occurs in the left hemisphere. The enactive mode of thinking occurs in the right hemisphere, where emotions and kinesthetic experiences evolve.

A person has the ability to learn a new solution or develop new, sensation-rich imagery patterns for different memories in life. If taught to suspend negative images, a person has a basis for a new experience. Using this approach, a client confronts memory-images that are having a negative consequence on health and well-being in order to associate more healthy, adaptive imagery with new meaning and new somatic responses.

Psychosynthesis

Assagioli's psychosynthesis model has three parts.[8] The first part, the lower unconscious, represents the past in the form of forgotten memories and repressed events; it includes the "fight or flight" survival mechanism. The second part, the middle unconscious, involves the personal self, that is, the levels of social awareness (e.g., role expectation, approval of behaviors). The middle unconscious is the day-to-day processing of logical and intuitive information and daily functioning. The third part is the higher unconsciousness or the superconscious, the drive and pursuit for meaning and purpose. In the superconscious, individuals touch the higher possibilities and challenges for living through inspiration, intuition, philosophy, and contemplation. The superconscious is the connection with the Higher Self and is referred to as the Transpersonal

Self because it transcends the personal self. The Higher Self is a synthesis of individual and universal connectedness. Transpersonal imagery allows for connections with the Transpersonal Self.

Training in psychosynthesis focuses on three elements: (1) the patterns of thought, feelings, or attitudes of a person, which may be conscious or unconscious; (2) the manifestations of these patterns in the person's daily *life* through behaviors, values, beliefs, and relationships; and (3) the imagery that continually occurs in life. When a person is in pain or is suffering with illness, something in life is out of balance. Often, such situations evoke negative imagery. The client can be taught to bring about healing imagery to decrease worry, fear, and stress. The rich symbolism of knowledge of a person's unconscious realm can be brought into full awareness. The information that comes forward in this way is enormously powerful in providing insight into changing unwanted behavior.

Types of Imagery

Individuals unconsciously and consciously create images of well-being. They also create images of their disease, disability, and a reversal or stabilization of that dysfunction. Although it is important for the nurse to understand the various types of imagery, it is even more important to understand individual variations. These differences include images, colors, shapes, symbols, and meanings in relation to the cultural diversity of individuals. As the nurse learns to recognize these different types of imagery, his or her guidance in the imagery process becomes much more effective because it helps clients discover the unique inner healing capability of their own imagery patterns. The nurse is aware of the point at which a client is ready to engage in imagery of more depth and can avoid flooding the client with too many imagery suggestions.

Receptive Imagery. Common when a person is daydreaming, falling asleep (hypnagogic), and just awakening (hypnopompic), receptive imagery is experienced as an inner knowing acquired without effort. Images seem to "bubble up" in conscious thought. Common imagery expressions in regard to tension, for example, are tightness, tingling, warmth, or knots. With this kind of imagery, it is important for nurses to trust the client's imagery process and stay out of the way as the person tells the story and explores the images.

Active Imagery. When a person focuses on the conscious formation of an image, the imagery is active. Common expressions that come from persons who are developing active images of tension are popping or grinding of muscles, or knots in muscles. A person can literally "speak to a body part" by sending a message to see, feel, hear, or touch smooth muscles and release the tension. One man with hypertension whose blood pressure averaged 160/90 mm Hg expressed his active images as "tight as a spring and a sense of blood vessels very tight with high pressure," "hands ice cold," and "feeling like a firecracker getting ready to explode." As he learned bodymind awareness of his elevated blood pressure and began to integrate relaxation and imagery, he shifted his images of his blood vessels to being relaxed and those of his tension to dripping out through his fingertips. He had consistent success at becoming normotensive within 3 weeks.

Correct Biologic Imagery. Clients need to be educated in the increased effectiveness of correct biologic images (i.e., images seen as if looking under a microscope), because inaccurate images often block a person's inner healing resources. The person with hypertension who was previously discussed, for example, was able to make positive changes only after he had learned the first step in self-regulation. As he began to notice his body and inner awareness, he became aware of the impact of his negative images on his physiology. By recognizing the negative images, he was able to create positive correct biologic images of normal blood flow to his hands and feet. Since we communicate with the body through our images, the importance of correct biologic imagery in our natural imagery process cannot be overemphasized.

Symbolic Imagery. An unfolding process that clients cannot force, symbolic imagery is unique to each client. As a client enters into and deepens relaxation, his or her innate inner wisdom is likely to release symbolic images that may or may not have healing qualities. For each individual, the nurse must assess the kinds of images that emerge. The nurse can then help the individual explore the meaning of any negative images and continue to guide the person in developing positive healing images. Individuals often wonder about the origin of the images. These images emerge from both the unconscious and the conscious, and they shape attitudes, belief systems, and cultural experiences. People with illness often have mythic symbols emerge. The storytelling-therapy process can help nurses use fables as a therapeutic tool and as a method to explain symbolism of mythic characters.[9,10]

One 46-year-old man with supraventricular tachycardia developed his images and his meaningful symbols from his work as an engineer. He chose a huge computer to symbolize his bodymind communication center. At work, he was under very tight deadlines and frequently became angry, which often began his tachycardia. He became aware of his irregular breathing patterns and the tightness in his chest prior to his tachycardia, and he learned to use a simple breathing exercise. In his mind, he imagined his heart as a computer that contained many programs and files that he could use to help him control his anger and his aggressive, competitive nature toward life. He imaged in his mind's eye an elaborate sinoatrial control panel where he could push a button to start the program that sent impulses correctly down his heart's conduction pathways. Thus, he was able to integrate the correct biologic images of conduction with his own symbolic images of the computer. Both types of images are important. Symbolic images are more powerful, however, because a person's engagement in the process makes the symbolism personally relevant and usually facilitates its integration into the healing imagery.

Process Imagery. A nurse may use process imagery to help a person rehearse step-by-step any procedures, treatment, surgery, or other events related to health problems prior to the event. This type of imagery also involves helping the individual integrate correct biologic images of healing in his or her imagination. For example, in teaching patients about their heart healing after an acute myocardial infarction, a nurse would use process imagery that focuses on the normal evolution from damage to building collateral blood flow to healthy scar formation. The nurse would also include information on medication, rest, and other specific aspects of cardiac rehabilitation. With process imagery, clients/patients can also increase their inner healing resources of self-esteem, independence, and commitment to healthy living and decrease emotions such as fear or anxiety prior to tests or surgery. Patients feel powerful to the extent that they are actively participating in their recovery.

End-State Imagery. A person often finds it helpful to rehearse being in a final, healed state. End-state images for a person recovering from an acute myocardial infarction are to focus on a healed heart along with exercising, returning to work, and engaging in healthy sexual activity and other activities of normal life.

General Healing Imagery. Because general healing images are events rather than a process, they frequently appear as colors, sounds, or as an inner guide (e.g., a wise person, animal, or totem). These images may also come in the form of a felt sense of unity, universal power, spirit, or God. General images emerge for each person and have a personal healing significance. One post–myocardial infarction patient described "being bathed with relaxation and the warmth of the sun, and being surrounded by a gold bubble." In expressing other general healing images, one post–open heart surgery patient said, "I experienced an 'OM' sound and light blue color [general image] as penetrating down to the core of my being with a smiling angel [symbolic image] hovering over my right shoulder."

Packaged Imagery. Another person's images, such as those found on self-hypnosis, relaxation, and imagery scripts recorded on commercial tapes, are sometimes helpful. Commercial tapes or tapes prepared by the nurse can be therapeutic and serve as general guides. They can facilitate a client's healing and learning of the skills when a nurse cannot be present. The nurse can also assist a client in recording specific imagery scripts in his or her own voice for later replay.

Customized Imagery. Images that are specific to an individual are customized. For example, prior to open heart surgery, a woman used a commercial tape that had general images. Following her surgery, she customized her images and saw her new jump grafts as violet cylinders through which blood flowed without obstruction. As she continued to integrate her relaxation and imagery practice, she learned to let the healing violet color fill her whole body. She said, "As I take time to experience inner peace, my softer nature is part of my total healing. I am learning how not to be so hard on myself and to ask others for help."

Imagery with Disease/Illness

Much emphasis is placed on treating disease, the pathologic changes in organic form either observed or validated by laboratory tests, rather than illness, the personal experience of the problem or one's general state of being. The nurse using guided imagery can promote a sense of well-being in clients and help them change their perceptions about their disease, treatment, and their healing ability. Relaxation and imagery interventions affect a person's attitudes, behaviors, tension, and anxiety that may lead to a devastating spiral of hopelessness.[11] Fear and negative imagery are not unusual in an individual with an undiagnosed or even a known illness. For example, it is very common for a woman who discovers a palpable breast lump to conjure up frightening images before any tests or diagnoses. These images may include cancer, mastectomy, chemotherapy, radiation, hair loss, nausea/vomiting, severe pain, metastatic disease, the deathing process, funeral, and the actual moment of dying. This process may be conscious or preverbal, or it may be noticed in a person's body as a felt sense/shift (see Chapter 15).

Imagery education for specific diseases/illness is important. Often, this education begins the cure. Many studies have demonstrated that it is possible to decrease the psychophysiologic arousal that increases stress, that individuals can begin to understand the connection between symptoms and behaviors, and that thoughts affect the course of the process.[12–20] Nurses must be creative in teaching patients about helpful images. Available sources include drug advertisements, anatomy coloring books, or education information pamphlets from professional organizations such as the American Heart Association, the American Lung Association, or other organizations that focus on specific disease/health problems. Teaching materials that are one to two pages in length are effective, because clients tend to take the time to read brief informational material.

Concrete Objective Information

The most promising nursing research into the imagery domain has been conducted over the last 20 years in the area of concrete objective information, formerly called preparatory sensory information.[21] This concept has a theoretical-empirical foundation supported by self-regulation theory (see Chapter 4). Concrete objective information describes both the client's subjective and the client's objective experience of health care events, such as procedures or recovery. For example, a surgical patient's subjective experience may be what is felt, heard, seen, smelled, or tasted before, during, or after a procedure. It may also include the sensory experiences of a postsurgical healing incision (e.g., pressure, smarting, tingling), as well as sensations over time (e.g., fleeting sharp sensations from the incisional area when turning in bed or when coughing). Objective experiences can be observed and verified by someone other than the person going through the procedure (e.g., information about the visits, the timing of the event, the environment of the procedure). For the surgical patient, an objective experience may include the time and place of the presurgical nurse's visit, the information to be discussed in the visit, the preoperative preparation of the skin, placement on the stretcher to go to surgery, awakening in the recovery room, and expected sensations.

Clients who receive information about both the subjective and the objective components of tests, procedures, and surgery recover quicker and are able to use more effective coping strategies than are those individuals who receive only one of the components. When the nurse conveys a clear picture of both the subjective and the objective experience and the sensations that the person may anticipate from a particular procedure, more effective coping naturally follows. Table 23–1 describes sensations evoked by selected procedures as documented in the literature. The following procedural points related to the use of concrete objective information originate in science-based nursing practice:

- Identify the sensory features of the procedure to be used.
- Determine the individual's perception of the procedure/treatment/test to be experienced.
- Choose words that have meaning for the person.
- Use synonyms that have less emotional impact, such as "discomfort" instead of "pain."
- Select specific experiences when giving examples rather than abstract experiences (see Table 23–1).
- Help individuals reframe any negative imagery.

Techniques for Empowering Imagery Scripts and Spoken Words

Teaching sessions and imagery scripts are more effective when the nurse learns the speaking skills of voice modulation, specific word emphasis, and the use of pauses. Truisms, embedded commands, linkages, reframings, metaphors, therapeutic double-binds, synesthesia, and interspersals are techniques that, when used correctly, satisfy both brain hemispheres.[22,23]

A ***truism*** is a statement that the client believes or accepts to be true. It may precede a suggestion and be connected to another truism. When this occurs, the analytical left hemisphere of the brain is satisfied that a fact is logical. It does not analyze or negate, and it leaves the right hemisphere free to accept the suggestion. To a person learning relaxation and imagery for hypertension, for example, the nurse may say, "As you take your next breath in, become aware that you are breathing air into your lungs [truism] and that the oxygen from the air moves from your lungs into your bloodstream [truism], . . . let yourself imagine that your blood vessels are very relaxed as you continue into this deep state of relaxation." The two truisms are followed by suggestions for physiologic changes of relaxed blood vessels while the person is in a deep state of relaxation. The left hemisphere is occupied with the truisms, leaving the right hemisphere free to go with the suggestions of deep relaxation and to experience what happens when the blood vessels relax.

Embedded commands are separate messages for the right hemisphere. They are usually in short phrases that stand out because of the pauses around them. The guide uses a change in voice, such as intonation, pitch,

Table 23–1 Documented Subjective Experience Descriptors by Stressful Health Care Event

Stressful Event	*Descriptors*
Gastroendoscopic examination	Intravenous medication; feel needle stick, drowsiness As air is pumped into stomach, feeling of fullness like after eating a large meal Feel physician's finger in mouth to guide tube insertion
Nasogastric tube insertion	Feeling passage of tube Tearing Gagging Discomfort in nose, throat, mouth Limited mobility
Cast removal	Hear buzz of saw Feel vibrations or tingling See chalky dust Feel warmth on arm or leg as saw cuts cast; will not hurt or burn Skin under padding looks and feels scaly and dirty Arm or leg may feel a little stiff when first trying to move it Arm or leg may feel light because cast was heavy
Barium enema	Lying on hard table Table feels hard Feel fullness Feel pressure Feel bloating Feel uncomfortable Feel as if might have a bowel movement
Abdominal surgery	Preoperative medications: feel sleepy, light-headed, relaxed, free from worry, not bothered by most things, dryness of mouth Feel incision: tenderness, sensitivity, pressure, smarting, burning, aching, sore Sensations might become sharp and feel like they are traveling along incision when moving Arm with intravenous tube feels awkward and restricted but not painful Feel tired after physical effort Feel bloating in abdomen Cramping due to gas pains Pulling and pinching when stitches are removed
Tracheostomy	When moving about, swallowing, or during suctioning: feel hurting, pressure, choking
Mastectomy—mean of 5.5 years postoperative	Arm or chest wall pain, "pins and needles," numbness, weakness, increased skin sensitivity, heaviness Phantom breast sensations, such as twinges, itching
4-vessel arteriography	Before contrast, medium: table is hard, head taping is uncomfortable, cleansing solution is cold After contrast, medium: hot, burning sensation in face, neck, chest, or shoulders

Source: Adapted from *Nursing Interventions: Essential Nursing Treatments*, 2nd ed., by G. Bulechek and J. McCloskey, p. 145, with permission of W.B. Saunders Company, © 1992.

volume, speed, and textural quality, and a change in normal grammatical structure to deepen suggestions. This confuses the left hemisphere and causes the embedded command to stand out. When the nurse uses the client's name, the right hemisphere may comprehend the short message much easier. For example, "You don't have to . . . cry, Susan . . . if you don't want to." The pause before and after the phrase " . . . cry, Susan . . ." gives the client permission to be more present with emotions and feelings if she needs to cry. When the nurse uses (1) changes in the quality of the voice, (2) pauses, and (3) the person's name, the right hemisphere hears the suggestion "cry, Susan" in one or all three of the ways listed.

Linkages are conditional statements that connect behaviors or actions with a suggestion. They are best used with a truism as a distraction to satisfy the brain's left hemisphere. A linkage may be appropriate for a client who is lying flat on a stretcher and is about to undergo a procedure. The nurse says, "Let yourself relax into the surface under your body [linkage]. As you are moving down the hall [linkage], you will see overhead lights on the ceiling. Each time you pass under a light, let it remind you to take a deep breath, and let oxygen fill your lungs [truism] and relax more deeply [linkage]."

Reframing helps a person contact the part of a behavior that is keeping him or her blocked or that is preventing the occurrence of a certain behavior. For example, a client with migraine headaches has hand temperatures averaging 70° Fahrenheit even in a warm room or outside on a hot day. Intellectually, she understands that she can abort her severe headaches by increasing her hand temperatures. She does not think that she can learn the skills, however, because she has had cold hands since her teenage years. She believes that her hands are always cold and that there is no way to change her physiology. Reframing involves having this client say repeatedly and feel the experience as she says the words, "Anytime I want to . . . all I have to do is allow the feelings of warmth and heaviness to flow into my hands." Reframing suspends a person from the old or current belief systems. It provides an opportunity to reassociate and reorganize a problem or experience in a manner that establishes a healthier state.

A ***metaphor*** is a figure of speech that contains an implied comparison in that a word or phrase ordinarily and primarily used for one thing is applied to another. In imagery scripts for healing and teaching purposes, metaphors are effective because they leave the right brain free to deepen the images that the spoken words evoke. For example, "Imagine the relaxation flowing down through your body like a gentle warm waterfall." Such words as warming, cooling, releasing, and sinking can be expanded upon to enhance right brain activity.

The ***therapeutic double-bind*** is a technique of giving an individual several different suggestions from which to choose. It is effective because the person's left hemisphere is occupied, involved, and participating in making a choice. For example, "As you are stretched out in the chair, . . . you may find that you can change your position . . . maybe adjust your head . . . or your arms . . . your legs or other parts of your body . . . even more . . . as you get ready to go deeper into relaxation . . . just scan your body to see if you can get more comfortable until you find just the right position."

Synesthesia is a technique that involves several senses simultaneously. It is also referred to as cross-sensing. Through this technique, the client becomes more aware of the different sense modalities that are present. For example, "Can you hear the color of the wind?" or "Can you see the sounds around you?"

Interspersal is a technique of making specific words or phrases within a script stand out as separate suggestions. This is accomplished by changing the volume or tone of the voice more dramatically than with embedded commands. For example, "Allow yourself to . . . relax into the pain with the next breath. . . . Feel . . . as you . . . breathe into that pain now." The words that would change with tonal inflection would be "relax into the pain," and "feel," and "breathe into that pain now."

NURSING PROCESS

Assessment

In preparing to use imagery as a nursing intervention, the nurse assesses the following parameters:

- the client's potential for organic brain syndrome or psychosis in order to determine if general relaxation techniques should be used instead of imagery techniques.
- the client's anxiety/tension levels in order to determine which types of relaxation inductions will be most effective.
- the client's homework assignments or tasks that were to be completed before the session, if any.
- the client's expected gains from the session, reason for seeking help, and hoped for changes.
- the client's wants, needs, desires, or recurrent/dominant themes.
- the client's understanding that it is not necessary to hear, see, feel, touch, and taste literally when working with guided imagery—only to experience what the image might be like.

- the client's primary sensory modalities.
- the client's understanding that imagery is basically a way in which we talk to ourselves and make friends with our body systems.
- the client's experience with the imagery process.
- the client's ability to work with the eyes closed in order to establish states of internal awareness and achieve profound imagery as fast as possible. If clients have contact lenses or are reluctant to close their eyes, have them gaze at a fixed point approximately 1 or 2 feet in front of them. Their peripheral vision will blur, and their eyelids usually get heavy. They then have no trouble closing their eyes. Clients begin to trust their relaxation process because they are experiencing a natural phenomenon.
- the client's knowledge of relaxation skills. If the client is not skilled in relaxation, explain what the normal sensations will be. Allow time for the client to shift to the "letting go" state. Once clients learn physiologic control with the phrases used in relaxation induction, they usually choose a word or two to gain the relaxed state.
- the client's ability to avoid falling asleep in the session.

Nursing Diagnoses

The following nursing diagnoses compatible with imagery interventions and that are related to the nine human response patterns of Unitary Person (see Chapter 7) are as follows:

- Exchanging: All diagnoses
- Relating Social isolation
Role performance
- Valuing: Spiritual well-being
Spiritual distress
- Choosing: Altered effective coping
- Moving: Sleep pattern disturbance
- Perceiving: Altered self-concept
Disturbance in body image
Disturbance in self-image
Potential hopelessness
Potential powerlessness
- Feeling: Pain
Anxiety
Fear
Post-trauma response

Client Outcomes

Table 23–2 guides the nurse in client outcomes, nursing prescriptions, and evaluation for the use of imagery as a nursing intervention.

Plan and Interventions

Before the Session

- Become calm and centered. Let your bodymind release any tension and tightness. Prepare to guide the client with relaxation and imagery scripts.
- Focus on the client's baseline feelings/emotions as revealed during the assessment process.
- Prepare the room to ensure quietness and the client's comfort.
- Have the client empty the bladder before the session begins.
- Place a sign on the door stating that the session is in progress in order to avoid interruptions.
- Have the client sit, recline, or lie down, depending on client preference and clinical situation.
- Have a selection of music tapes available from which the client can choose (see Chapter 24).
- Have a light blanket available in case the client should feel cool.
- Have blank paper, crayons, and colored markers available should the client wish to draw before or after the session.

At the Beginning of the Session

- Give the client a general definition of imagery: "Imagery is a natural way to connect body-mind-spirit by quieting the busy mind and body. This helps you tap into the power of the imagination."
- Have the client develop a positive expectation of what is to occur. Process and end-state imagery directed toward a successful outcome reinforces what the client wants to happen; it helps the client to focus and organize healing efforts and to move in the direction of hoped for outcomes.
- Assist the client in experiencing the imagery process and making friends with one's wise self. This process is a key to the creative process.
- Have the client focus on the present moment in order to facilitate the best imagery process.

Table 23–2 Nursing Interventions: Imagery

Client Outcomes	*Nursing Prescriptions*	*Evaluation*
The client will demonstrate skills in imagery.	Following an assessment, guide the client in an imagery exercise.	The client participated in imagery exercise by choice.
	Assess the client's levels of anxiety with this new process.	The client demonstrated no signs of anxiety with imagery process.
	After the imagery process experience, assess effectiveness through client dialogue.	The client stated that the imagery experience was helpful.
	Encourage the client to recognize daily self-talk and the images that lead to balance and inner peace.	The client reported constant self-dialogue with imagery.
	Help the client to create images of desired health habits, feelings, desires for daily living.	The client reported creating images of desired health habits, feelings, and desires for daily living.
	Teach the client coping, power over daily events, ability to move toward healthy life style.	The client reported increased coping with daily stressors.
	Teach the client to recognize images leading to self-defeating life style habits.	The client reported recognition of negative images leading to self-defeating behavior; the client creates positive images.
The client will participate in drawing, if appropriate.	Encourage the client to draw images and symbols as a communication process with self.	The client used drawing as a communication process with self.

- Instruct the client to let spontaneous images emerge from the inner self without analyzing them. If the client begins to analyze the images, suggest that the images are just floating on. Release any expectation of logically working the images through to resolving conflicts, establishing goals, and so forth. These steps will come in the images, but not in a logical manner.

- Tell the client that, in following guided relaxation and imagery scripts, different images will appear. If any images appear that the client is unwilling or unready to deal with, the inner self (ego) will block those images. Then instruct the client to go with the next imagery process that appears.
- Remind the client that changing to positive imagery can evoke healing and healthy expectations.
- After giving the client the preceding information, begin a relaxation exercise to assist the client in deep relaxation. The nurse may begin, "Let your eyes close to be fully awake." After a state of deep relaxation is demonstrated, the nurse can suggest that the client "allow the images to emerge from this relaxed state."

During the Session

- With your guidance, let the client create his or her own images.
- Assess the state of relaxation throughout the session. Notice decreased tension in the face, chest, torso, and legs. The changes can range from subtle to dramatic. Respirations become deeper, with more space between the breaths. The eyelids may flicker (especially with very vivid imagers), and the lips and face may change to a paler color.
- Determine if the client is following the imagery process. The nurse may instruct the client, "If you are following the imagery, raise a finger to indicate yes." Similarly, the nurse may ask if the client finds the imagery satisfactory, needs a slower pace, or would like to get more comfortable. Clients who are used to working with inner imagery states can usually clear their minds of distracting thoughts more easily than novices. If the client cannot clear the mind, increase the length of the relaxation induction, or suggest that the client focus once again on the image or on the breathing pattern.
- Determine the length of the session based on the client's needs, body responses, and session outcomes. The sessions can last from 10 or 15 minutes to an hour or longer.
- Allow your personal intuition to emerge while guiding. It helps you to recognize subtle cues from the client that something special is present in the imagery process.
- Continually assess the client's body language and facial expressions for resistance to the imagery process. If there is resistance, the

imagery should be kept simple and more directed: "Focus on your right hand . . . and notice sensations in your right hand. . . ." At other times, a less direct, guided imagery approach is needed, such as "At your own pace, . . ." "In your own way. . . ." Resistance or blocking on the experience is not failure, but becomes a tool for the client to recognize that the body-mind-spirit needs some healing. Refer to Chapter 15, Figure 15–1 on Focusing. Carefully selected phrases and voice tone modulation help the client stay with the imagery process and to strengthen the imagery experience.

At the End of the Session

- Bring the client to an alert state gradually by allowing time for silence before the discussion. Observe and take cues from the client as to the appropriate time to begin the discussion. The moments following a session can be a time for deep personal insight; this opportunity may be lost if talking begins too soon. Both the client and the guide need to be immersed in the healing of silence, even if only for 20 to 30 seconds.
- If appropriate, have the client finish the session by drawing or writing down some thoughts.
- Discuss the experience with the client, and encourage the client to interpret the imagery. The nurse can facilitate the interpretation by weaving imagery questions into conversational interaction and asking open-ended questions that guide the client in further contemplation.
- Provide the client with appropriate educational materials. Give written guidelines for integrating imagery skills and bodymind communication into daily life.
- Encourage the client to integrate relaxation and imagery daily. Instruct the client to notice patterns of tension at different times during the day. Then show the client how to replace tension patterns with relaxation and different types of imagery.
- Encourage the client to notice constant self-talk. Help the client to focus on creating positive images that lead to healthy outcomes.
- Introduce the idea of "constant instant practice," that is, using some frequent activity of daily life (e.g., telephone calls) as a reminder to practice imagery, thereby integrating the practice into daily life.
- Have the client use the images that come forth from inner awareness as guides for practice. Suggest the use of a journal or diary for recording images and their interpretation.

- Emphasize to the client that practice is the key to developing deep levels of insight from this process. Have the client establish a scheduled time to practice imagery, just as he or she takes medication on a schedule.
- Have the client alternate between short and long practice sessions.
- Encourage the client to chart daily, weekly, and monthly progress.
- Experiment with different exercises.
- Use the client outcomes (see Table 23–2) that were established before the imagery session and the client's subjective experience with imagery (Exhibit 23–1) to evaluate the session.
- Schedule a follow-up session.

Specific Interventions

Facilitation and Interpretation of the Imagery Process

It is essential that nurses become aware of their own imagery process and familiarize themselves with the rich variety and individuality of imagery experiences. When nurses come together in a group to listen and share personal and professional stories, they hear many perspectives and can train themselves to listen to the use of metaphors, images, and different types of imagers.

In order to facilitate the imagery process, the nurse serves as a guide. There is absolutely no way to predict what will surface in a client's imagination, however, for every experience is different—even when the same script is used. Nurses who are unfamiliar with imagery and guiding should learn a few basic relaxation and imagery scripts and use them repeatedly while gaining experience and confidence with the intervention. Once they trust and understand the value of the process, they may use many different scripts. It is helpful to learn a variety of scripts that pertain to common problems in clinical practice, such as preoperative anxiety, recovery from surgery, postoperative coughing, effective wound healing, fear, anxiety, pain, and relationship problems. For scripts not frequently used, some nurses keep a notebook or reference book where they highlight key script phrases for quick reference.

Each individual is the best interpreter of his or her own imagery process.[24] Symbolic information that surfaces in the imagination is rich with personal meaning. Many people close themselves off from their rich imagination. Nurses should encourage clients to record these images in a diary or journal for further exploration, however, because it is easy to lose symbolic imagery in the conscious thoughts that dominate the individual's attention during a busy day.

There are two basic factors to remember in teaching imagery. Listening to the way that a client tells his or her story will indicate if the client has a materialistic, concrete outlook or if the client has a vivid, spontaneous outlook. For the logical, concrete thinker, written information is useful. When teaching clients to warm the hands, for example, suggested content on an imagery teaching sheet may include (1) an explanation of normal blood flow physiology, (2) a drawing of blood flow to the hands via radial and ulnar arteries that branch into intricate blood vessel networks of the hands and the fingers, and (3) examples of images that warm the hands. If clients have vivid, spontaneous images, the nurse encourages them to use their images for hand warming first. The teaching sheets can serve as a supplement to what the vivid imager already knows.

Teaching sheets do not require an individual to follow them explicitly. Suggested images are to be adapted to fit with what feels right to the client. Teaching sheets refresh and reinforce the teaching-learning session and provide additional information to be mastered. Clients can add their own notes about specific images and personalize their skills. The nurse can guide a client in revamping weak or erroneous imagery toward health outcomes so that the client is in a better position to strengthen the body's own defense mechanisms and normal processes. For example, images should focus on weak, confused cancer cells and a strong immune system instead of vice versa.

Nurses can be most effective in teaching a client the imagery process if they follow these guidelines:

- Assist client in identifying the problem, disease, or goal of imagery.
- Have a basic understanding of the physiology involved in the normal healing process.
- Begin with several minutes of relaxing, meditating, or paying attention to the breath.
- Help client develop images of the following:
  1. problem/disease
  2. inner healing resources (e.g., strengths, belief systems, coping strategies)
  3. external healing resources (e.g., treatments, medications, tests, surgery)
- End with images of the desired state of well-being.

Guided Imagery Scripts

The guidelines that follow will help the nurse use imagery scripts as nursing interventions:

- Do not talk to the client during the imagery process unless the client has a question that must be answered at the time. Because it is a logical process, talking disrupts the free flow of images.
- Precede all these scripts with a general relaxation script; close the session with a general relaxation script (see Chapter 22).
- Insert the client's name at the beginning of each script and, occasionally, in the middle of the script.
- To lengthen the scripts, pick up cues from the client's behavior and insert key words, such as "good . . . and relax even more."
- Repeat key words that increase the client's relaxation response.
- Speak slowly and pace the script as you watch the client's breathing patterns and other body responses.
- Use phrases to enhance the power of the spoken word as previously discussed.
- Let yourself relax as you guide the client. This increases your being very present in the moment with the client.
- Provide continuous encouragement and guidance for novices and less vivid imagers. Clients who are vivid imagers do not need continuous encouragement and may find it distracting or intrusive. The extremely vivid imager may need to keep the eyes partially open so as not to feel overwhelmed.
- Scripts have ". . ." to indicate a pause. Increase the length of the pauses or add more depending on the observed cues from the client.
- Feel free to invent and create new scripts based on the special information gathered before the session, as well as the insight that comes from intuition during the session.

Special/Safe Place (Basic). Clients need to identify a special place that is a safe retreat. This is an easy place for novices to start. It takes 10 to 20 minutes. Several different approaches can be useful.

Scripts:

- *Let your imagination choose a place that is safe and comfortable . . . a place where you can retreat at any time. This is a healthy technique for you to learn . . . this place will help you survive your daily stressors.* [If the client is in the hospital, . . .] *This safe and special place is very important, particularly while you are in the hospital . . . any time that there are interruptions, just let yourself go to this place in your mind.*

- *Form a clear image of a pleasant outdoor scene, using all of your senses. Smell . . . smell the fragrance of flowers or the breeze. Feel . . . feel the texture of the surface under your feet. Hear . . . hear all the sounds in nature, birds singing, wind blowing. See . . . see all the different sights around as you let yourself turn in a slow circle to get a full view of this special space.* [Include taste, if appropriate.]
- *Let a beam of light, such as the rays of the sun, shine on you for comfort and healing. Allow yourself to experience the warmth and relaxation.*
- *Form an image of a meadow. Imagine that you are in the meadow. . . . The meadow is full of beautiful grass and flowers. In the meadow, see yourself sitting by a stream . . . watching the water . . . flowing by . . . slowly and gently.*
- *Imagine a mountain scene. See yourself walking on a path toward the mountain. You hear the sound of your shoes on the path . . . smell the pine trees and feel the cool breeze as you approach your campsite. You have now reached the foothills of the mountain. You are now higher up the mountain . . . resting in your campsite. Look around at the beauty of this place.*
- *Imagine yourself in a bamboo forest. . . . You are walking in a large bamboo forest. The bamboo is very tall. . . . You lean against a strong cluster of bamboo . . . hear the swaying . . . and hear the rustling of the bamboo leaves, gently moving in the wind.*
- *Look into the sky of your mind . . . see the fluffy clouds. A cloud gently comes your way, . . . and the cloud surrounds your body. You climb up on the cloud and lie down. Feel yourself begin to float off gently in a gentle breeze.*

Protective Shield/Space (Basic). To create an imaginary personal space where the client feels protected from outside pressures, the nurse may use a special script. It generally requires 10 to 20 minutes.

Script: *In your imagination, let yourself begin to create a protective shield/space or protective bubble around yourself. This will serve as a filter to accept what you want to receive and protect you from those things that you wish to keep out. The shield is invisible, and only you know where it is around your body and how close it is to you.*

Let yourself begin to move this shield. Experience it now as you move the shield close to your body. . . . Now let yourself move it out away from the skin. Imagine that you wish to protect yourself from an event or person. In whatever way that feels right for you, become aware of your protective shield. Place your shield where you wish now . . . close to your skin or further out from your body. This is your special way of receiving what you wish for yourself and a way of staying relaxed and calm.

Worry and Fear (Basic). Some images can help clients change the internal experience of worry and fear. Clients should set aside 10 to 20 minutes a day to worry, preferably in the morning before they start their daily routines. This approach satisfies the subconscious that it has worried, and the person has a greater success at stopping the habitual worry during the rest of the day.

Script: *Let worries come one by one . . . just watching as one replaces the other. As you do this for a short period of time, feel the experience that occurs with each of those worries and fears. Notice how just having a worry or fear changes your state right now.*

Stop the images. Focus on your breathing . . . in . . . and out. . . . Allow yourself to have three complete cycles of breathing before continuing. . . . In your relaxed state, become aware of these feelings of relaxed bodymind. This time, take your relaxed state with you into your imagination. Let one worry come to your mind right now. See and feel it . . . see yourself in that situation relaxed and at ease.

Right now, just say to yourself, "I can stop this worry." Imagine yourself functioning without that worry or fear. See yourself waving good-bye to that worry and fear. See yourself completely free of that worry and fear. Look at the decisions that you can make for your life that will lead you in new directions. Feel your energy as you breathe in. As you exhale, let go of all of the worry, fear, tension, and tightness.

Experience your comfortable bodymind. Know that you can work with many of your worries and fears that surface daily. Whenever they come, let the dominant worry surface . . . then feel what it is like as you gradually give up portions of the worry . . . til it is completely gone. If that seems impossible right now, decide which part of that worry and fear you need to keep and which part you can let go. And now, see yourself waving good-bye to the part that you can let go.

Now, feel what it is like in your mind with part of that worry or fear gone. Experience that and feel the changes within the body. Assess the part of the worry or fear that remains. Again, allow a portion of that worry or fear to move away. See yourself waving good-bye. Feel the change inside as more is released.

Let yourself now be in a place where the worry and fear are diminished. Assess what part remains and see if you can now begin to give up that part. Pay attention to the experiences inside your body as you do this.

This script has many variations: writing worries/fears on a seashell and watching a seagull pick up the shell and drop it into the sea; running along a road, dropping the worries/fears by the road, and watching the wind blow them away; letting a picture of worries and fears flow forward in a moving stream. This basic script can also be individualized by putting into words what the client revealed before the session.

Inner Guide (Basic). The nurse can assist the client in creating purposeful self-dialogue that gains access to inner wisdom and personal truth that always resides within one's being. It is advisable to allow 10 to 20 minutes for this exercise.

Script: *As you begin to feel even more relaxed now . . . going to a greater depth of inner being . . . more relaxed . . . more secure and safe . . . let yourself become aware of the presence of not being alone. With you right now is a guide . . . who is wise and concerned with your well-being. Let yourself begin to see this wise being with whom you can share your fears or your joys. You have a trust in this wise guide.*

If you do not see anyone, let yourself be aware of hearing or feeling this wise being, noticing the presence of care and concern. In whatever way seems best for you . . . proceed to make contact with this wise inner guide. Let yourself establish contact with your guide now . . . in any way that comes. Your guide may appear to you in any form, such as a person, an animal, or inner presence/peace . . . or as an image of the very wisest part of you.

Notice the love and wisdom with which you are surrounded. This wisdom and love are present for you now. . . . Let yourself ask for advice . . . about anything that is important for you just now. Be receptive to what emerges. . . . Let yourself receive some new information. This inner guide may have a special message to share with you. . . . Listen with openness and pure intention to receive.

Allow yourself to look at any issue in your life. It may be a symptom, a choice, or decision. . . . Tell your wise guide anything that you wish. . . . Listen to the answers that emerge. Imagine yourself acting on the answers and directions that you received. . . . Imagine yourself calling upon the wisdom and love of this wise guide to help you in the days to come. Now in whatever way is best for you . . . bring closure to the visit with this inner guide. You can come back here any time that you wish. All you have to do is take the time.

This script helps clients gain an awareness of their own inner wisdom. It is best to introduce this exercise after a client has done several imagery sessions. Word choices should take into account the client's dominant sense. If a client prefers the visual, for example, the nurse uses the word "see"; if the client prefers the auditory, "hears"; if the client prefers the kinesthetic, "feels." Seeking an inner guide can be done over many sessions. The client should be aware that many different guides (also referred to as advisors, presence of energy, angels, or spirits) will surface over time. There are many versions to this script, so the nurse can add, invent, and explore. Much detail can be added to this imagery script to lengthen the session. When time is extended, a wealth of insight can emerge for the client. The nurse should pause frequently and let a few seconds to a full minute pass in silence during the guiding, as indicated by his or her intuition.

White Light of Healing Energy (Basic). General healing images focus awareness within for health and balance. Such imagery requires 10 to 20 minutes.

Script: *Begin to imagine that there is a sphere of white light of healing energy about 4 inches above your head. The white light is now touching the top of your head. Begin to feel this light as it flows from the top of your head and allow it to flow down through the entire inside of the body.*

The healing light has filled the inside of your head, . . . and it now flows down your shoulders, back, down your arms, and into your fingertips. The white light is now flowing into your chest . . . around your sides . . . into your middle and lower back . . . below your waist . . . around your sides flowing into your abdomen . . . into your buttocks . . . and into your pelvis. The light now flows down your thighs . . . to your lower legs . . . and to your feet.

The white light has completely filled the inside of your body. There is now a wonderful abundance of this healing light, . . . and it begins to bubble up and flow back out through the top of your head . . . down the outside of your body . . . coating the entire outside of your body. The more you allow it to flow throughout your body, . . . the more abundant it is. Send the healing white light to specific areas that need extra attention, such as places of discomfort or disease.

The nurse gives the client specific details about the major problem areas. The color of the light can be any color that the client wishes.

Red Ball of Pain (Basic). To decrease psychophysiologic pain, clients can learn to use distraction. This kind of imagery is good for both acute and chronic pain, as well as for the discomfort or pain of procedures. It takes 10 to 20 minutes.

Script: *Scan your body . . . gather any pains, aches, or other symptoms up into a ball. Begin to change its size . . . allow it to get bigger . . . just imagine how big you can make it. Now make it smaller. . . . See how small you can make it. . . . Is it possible to make it the size of a grain of sand? Now allow it to move slowly out of your body, moving further away each time you exhale. . . . Notice the experience with each exhale . . . as the pain moves away.*

Give suggestions to the client to change the size of the ball several times in both directions. This serves as a distraction how to manipulate the pain experience rather than being trapped or overwhelmed by the pain. It provides a tremendous sense of control as well as pain relief for the client. Watching the person's body cues indicates how many times to go in each of the opposite directions.

Pain Assessment (Basic). Imagery helps access and control both acute and chronic psychophysiologic pain. The following exercise can be done in 10 to 20 minutes.

Script: *Close your eyes and let yourself relax. . . . Begin to describe the pain in silence to yourself. Be present with the pain. . . . Know that the pain may be either physical sensations . . . or worries and fears. Let your pain take on a shape . . . any shape that comes to your mind. Become aware of the dimensions of the pain. . . . What is the height of your pain? . . . the width of the pain? . . . and the depth of the pain? Where in the body is it located? . . . Give it color . . . a shape . . . feel the texture. Does it make any sound?*

And now with your eyes still closed, . . . let your hands come together with palms turned upward as if forming a cup. Put your pain object in your hands. [Once again, the nurse asks these questions about the pain, preceding each question with this phrase, "How would you change the size, etc.?"]

Let yourself decide what you would like to do with the pain. There is no right way to finish the experience . . . just accept what feels right to you. You can throw the pain away . . . or place it back where you found it . . . or move it somewhere else. Let yourself become aware . . . of how pain can be changed. . . . By your focusing with intention, the pain changes.

It is not unusual for the pain to go completely away or at least lessen after this exercise. The client also learns to manipulate the pain so that it is not the controlling factor of his or her life. The exercise is also effective with severe pain. After giving pain medication, the nurse can have the client relax during the imagery process.

Correct Biologic Imagery Teaching Sheets and Scripts

Clients who are given specific information about the role of bodymind connections, correct biologic healing images, and stress management strategies have fewer complications and shorter recovery time.[25–27] The nurse elicits from the client/patient images and symbols that have special healing meaning and value, then makes an audiocassette for the client/patient that includes correct biologic images, specific concrete objective information, specific symbols, and specific types of imagery (see Chapter 24 for guidelines on making an audiocassette tape and establishing an audio/video library).

It may seem that the following scripts may appear suitable for well-educated, sophisticated individuals, but this is not the case. It is necessary, however, for the nurse to assess the individual's education level and adapt these scripts to fit the person's needs, cultural beliefs, and symbols. Imagery is an important tool, particularly, for those clients who do not read.

Bone Healing[28] (Basic). An imagery exercise for bone healing may be done in 20 to 30 minutes. Prior to imagery, to teach basic biologic imagery of bone healing, the nurse explains

- reaction (cellular proliferation). Within the hematoma surrounding the fracture, cells and tissues proliferate and develop into a random structure (Figure 23–1A).
- regeneration (callus formation). At 10 to 14 days after the fracture, the cells within the hematoma become organized in a fibrous lattice. With sufficient organization, the callus becomes clinically stable.

The callus obliterates the medullary canal and surrounds the two ends of bone by irregularly surrounding the fracture defect (Figure 23–1B).

- remodeling (new bone formation). Approximately 25 to 40 days after the fracture, calcium is laid down within bone that has spicules perpendicular to the cortical surface (Figure 23–1C). Osteonal bone gradually replaces and remodels fiber bone. The fracture has been bridged over by new bone (Figure 23–1D). Conversion and remodeling continue up to 3 years following an acute fracture.

Script[29]: *In your relaxed state, (name), allow yourself to imagine a natural process that is occurring within your body. . . . New cells are gathering very fast at the site of your fracture* [cellular proliferation]. *This is an important process as it lays the foundation for your bone healing. With your next breath in . . . become aware of the fact . . . that right now your body is allowing those new cells to multiply rapidly* [truism]. *Your blood cells . . . at the site of your fracture, are arranging themselves in a special healing pattern* [reaction]. *You can relax . . . even more . . . if you want to . . . as you continue with this very natural healing process* [embedded command].

In a few days . . . your wise body will begin to create a strong lattice network of new bone [regeneration]. *This will allow your bone to become stable, bridging the new bone that is forming. As you focus in a relaxed way, . . . you help in your healing . . . for relaxation increases this natural process* [linkage]. *Imagine your relaxation to be like a gentle breeze of wind that flows over and throughout your body* [metaphor].

In a few more weeks, your new bone will be formed . . . natural deposits of calcium from your body will be taken into the place of healing [remodeling]. *Allow an image to come to your mind now of beautiful, healed bone. In about 6 weeks, you will have a beautiful bridge where the calcium has formed new bone* [remodeling]. *Can you imagine the healing colors that are within you right now, and seeing sounds* [synesthesia]? *Just for a few minutes more . . . allow yourself . . . to relax into the healing process . . . feel . . . as you breathe into this healing movement* [interspersal].

Burn Graft Healing*[30] *(Basic). In 20 to 30 minutes, the nurse can teach patients about the normal burn graft healing process with correct biologic images (Figure 23-2A).

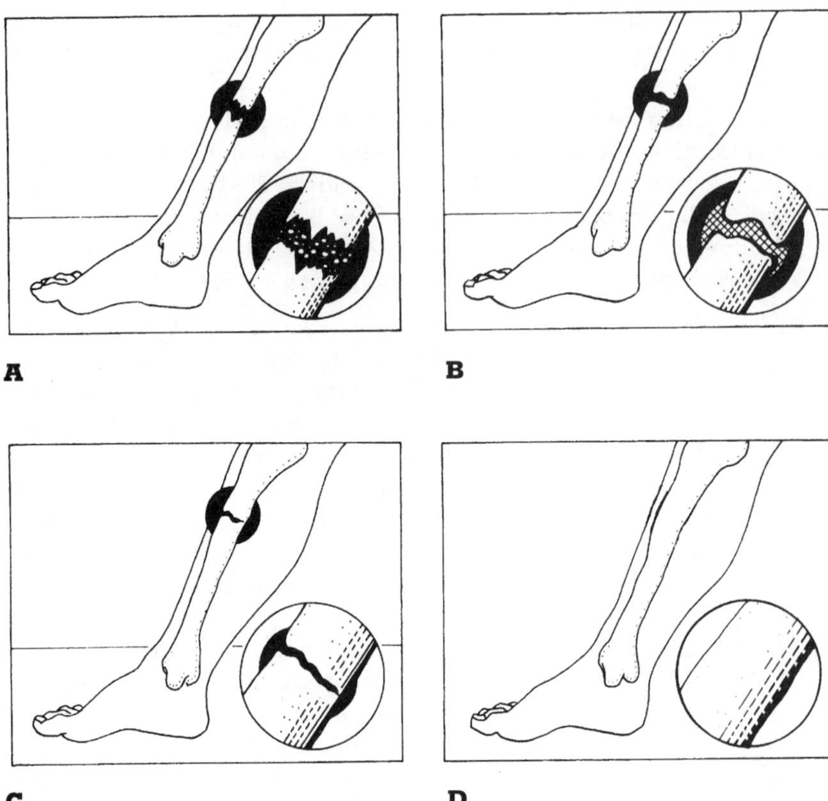

Figure 23–1 A, Reaction: hematoma and cellular proliferation. **B**, regeneration. **C**, Remodeling: calcium ossification. **D**, healed bone. *Source:* Reprinted from *Rituals of Healing* by Jeanne Achterberg, Barbara Dossey, and Leslie Kolkmeier, Bantam Books, with permission of the authors, © 1994.

- Day 1: the adhesion of surfaces and the bridging of the space between the graft bed and the graft (Figure 23–2B).
- Day 2: the vessels from the patient grow into the graft (Figure 23–2C).
- Day 3: the vessels establish vascular continuity (Figure 23–2D).

Script[31]: *In your relaxed state now, . . . let's begin on a journey into your body. . . . Begin to identify the capacity that you have to work with the healing process with your new graft. In your mind, go to the area where you have been burned. I am going to de-*

scribe the healing process . . . that is taking place with your new graft. In your mind, . . . go to the area of your body where you have received your new graft. If you begin to feel any tension . . . just take a deep breath, and know that you can let yourself relax and release any tension at this time. . . . Notice how you can deepen your state of relaxation [embedded command] . . . *release the tension as you breathe out* [truism]. *Your relaxation is like a still mountain lake. Imagine that the gentle wind has formed ripples on the surface of the lake . . . and as the ripples spread out, they are the ripples of relaxation that move into your body and mind* [metaphor]. *Before your graft, the area where you were burned was cleaned very, very well. In this clean area, the graft was gently placed and covered with a thick layer of dressings.*

In your mind, begin to imagine the healing process. On Day 1, imagine that your own skin secretes a kind of glue. This glue is very important, because it will allow your new graft to stick and hold in a healthy way. Just take several relaxing breaths now . . . in, and out . . . feeling the pause between each of those breaths. As you increase your relaxation, . . . allow yourself . . . to relax . . . [interspersal] *into the natural healing process . . . your skin secreting a glue, and your new graft sticking to it and becoming part of your body and part of the healing* [linkage]. *During this first day, you will also remember to move gently and work with the nurses as they help you with your comfort, your healing, and your recovery.*

Now begin to move to Day 2. On this day, after receiving your graft, your body continues the healing process. Your own body now . . . sends nutrients to the graft, and small blood vessels begin to sprout out . . . just like little hands moving out, sending nutrients to every cell in this area for healthy survival. Remember to stay as still as possible and let the nurses help you move. [Adapt this phrase as needed if working with a small child.] *This is important, . . . for it also helps those tiny blood vessels grow in a very healthy manner. During this time, you will continue to increase your relaxation to that particular area where your grafts will take hold. And as you exhale, let go of any tension and tightness.*

Now move to Day 3 of your recovery process. By Day 3, the blood vessels from your own body . . . and the blood vessels from your graft actually grow together. You might even imag-

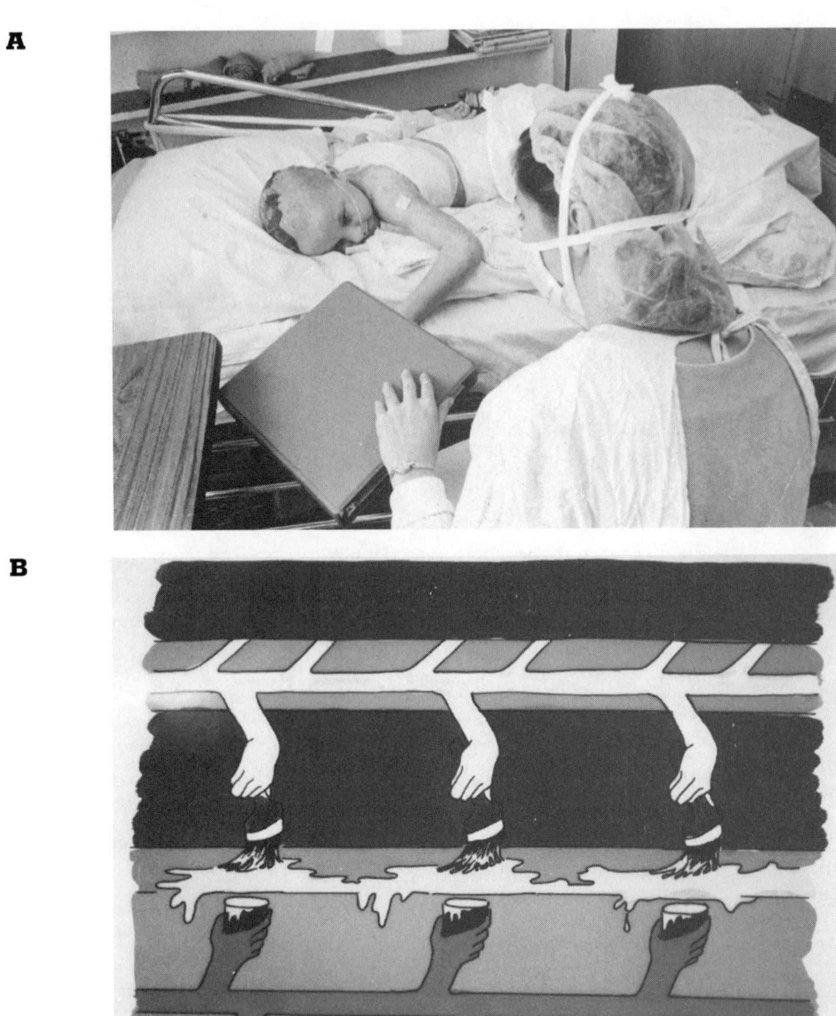

Figure 23-2 A, A child who has been severely burned is provided process images just prior to his surgery. **B**, Skin grafts, using the boy's own healthy skin, will be placed over the burned areas. He is shown these pictures and told that, on the first day, something like glue will come out of his body to stick on the graft. *Source:* Reprinted from *Rituals of Healing* by Jeanne Achterberg, Barbara Dossey, and Leslie Kolkmeier, Bantam Books, with permission of the authors, © 1994.

C

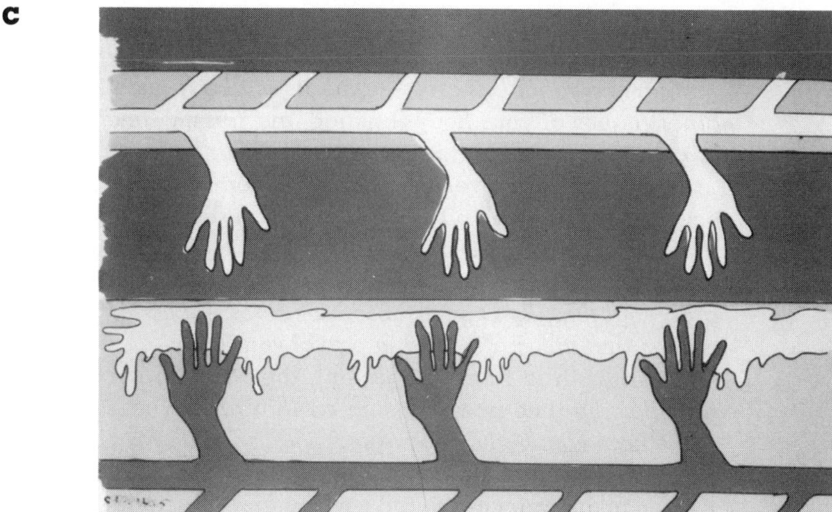

D

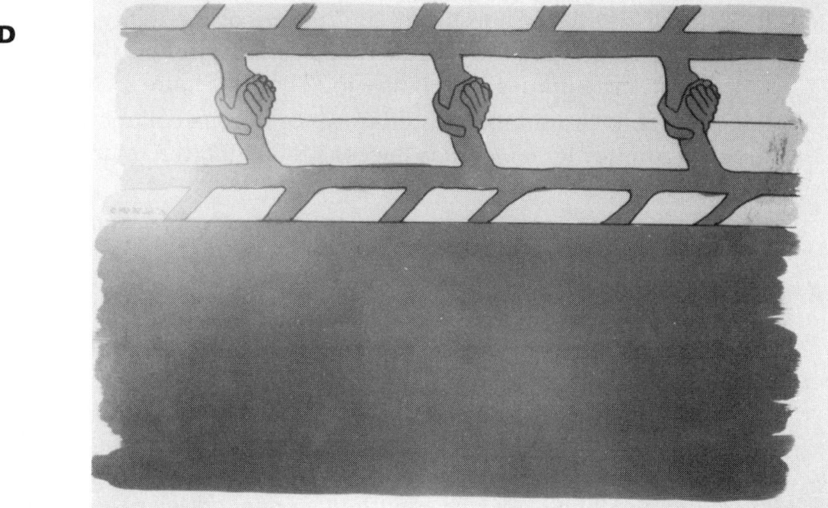

Figure 23–2 continued. C, On the second day, blood vessels (like hands) will reach out toward each other. **D**, Finally, if all goes well, on the third day, his skin graft will be complete. *Source:* Reprinted from *Rituals of Healing* by Jeanne Achterberg, Barbara Dossey, and Leslie Kolkmeier, Bantam Books, with permission of the authors, © 1994.

ine this as those blood vessels join hands [metaphor]. . . *As you feel this experience of your blood vessels joining hands, just imagine now that this graft is part of your body just like all the other tissues of your body* [linkage and truism]. *Imagine that happening . . . the graft is now a part of your body.*

Again, let us go over these three important areas that will occur after your graft. On Day 1, your skin secretes a glue, and the glue sticks to your own skin. On Day 2, blood vessels from your own skin and the blood vessels from the graft begin to grow together. By Day 3, those blood vessels have joined together, and this graft is now a part of your body.

[If the graft is from the patient, the nurse may continue.] *Spend some time now focusing on that area where the graft came from your body. The natural healing ability is also occurring there, with the new skin now being formed.* [Repeat information in the script on wound healing, but substitute the words "new skin" for "graft."]

Wound Healing[32] ***(Basic).*** To teach the normal wound healing process with correct biologic images, the nurse explains

- Reaction. Fluid leaks into tissue at the time of the injury, causing swelling and inflammation; white blood cells migrate to the wound. Inflammation continues from injury to 72 hours (Figure 23–3A).
- Regeneration. Granulation and deposit of fibrous collagen protein tissue continues for as long as 3 weeks following the injury (Figure 23–3B).
- Remodeling. Healing of a wound takes 3 weeks to 2 years for severe wound (Figure 23–3C).

A wound healing intervention may last 20 to 30 minutes.

Script[33]: *Focus on calmness and rhythmic breathing . . . and become aware of your ritual . . . for cleansing your wound. Let it be done slowly . . . without hurry. To avoid holding your breath, . . . take several rhythmic breaths prior to cleansing your wound. When you are ready to begin the cleansing of your wound . . . take a breath in . . . and, on the exhale, place the hydrogen peroxide or other solutions on the wound and surrounding area or along suture lines. Next, on the area that has been cleaned and patted dry, place the ointment in the same area to help speed the healing process. Now is the time to place a clean dressing on the wound.*

Allow yourself to imagine a natural process that is occurring within your body. . . . New cells are being made in the open skin area . . . to allow a stable place for repair and new growth. Now your blood flow is surging to this area. . . . Special white blood cells, your macrophages, are recognizing any foreign material and carrying it away. Remember . . . be with the special healing process of your wound. . . . If your wound is superficial, it heals from the edges toward the center. . . . A deep wound will heal from the inside to the outside.

A beautiful area is now forming . . . you might imagine it like looking down into a lovely shallow bowl. Within this area . . . your body now places soft, healthy, delicate fibrous protein tissue . . . like a network of beautiful lights . . . the beginning of a strong scar that starts below the surface of the skin.

Become more aware . . . of the fact . . . that your own special cells, the fibroblasts, are producing this collagen protein. Many small buds of new tissue continue to be laid down and grow stronger and fuller, creating healthy new skin and scar tissue. The opening shrinks and becomes smaller as healing occurs.

Let an image or feeling of the new healed skin surface emerge. . . . Your skin has healed from the inside to the outside. See, hear, and feel your healed, smooth, new skin that is strong and healthy.

Immune System Odyssey*[34] *(Basic). Patients can be taught correct biologic images of the normal process of the immune system. (For more details, refer to Chapter 4 on mind modulation of the immune system and Figure 4–4.) The nurse may explain the following:

- neutrophils. The most numerous cells, billions of neutrophils swim in the bloodstream; when they sense unhealthy tissue, they pass through the blood vessel, move to the unhealthy tissue or cells, surround it, shoot caustic chemicals, and destroy the unhealthy tissue or cells (Figure 23–4).
- macrophages. Moving throughout the body, ever ready to eat, macrophages travel in hoards, each one swells up, moves to the enemy (e.g., bacteria, viruses, yeast, and cancer cells).
- T-cells. Born in the bone marrow, millions of T-cells go from infancy to adolescence each minute. They go to the thymus gland where they get a special imprint; some are designated killer cells, while others become helpers or suppressors. All these specialized cells keep a watchful vigil in the lymph nodes and tissue until needed.

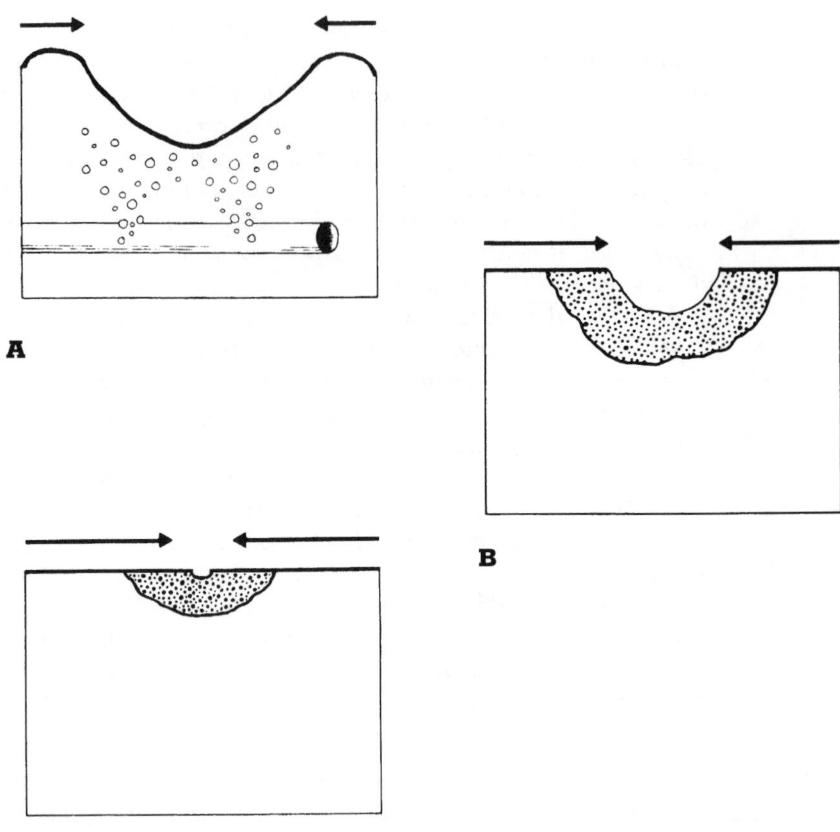

Figure 23–3 **A**, Reaction: inflammation and stabilization of wound (injury to 72 hours). **B**, Regeneration: granulation and deposit of fibrous collagen protein tissue (up to 3 weeks). **C**, Remodeling: healed wound (3 weeks to 2 years). *Source:* Reprinted from *Rituals of Healing* by Jeanne Achterberg, Barbara Dossey, and Leslie Kolkmeier, Bantam Books, with permission of the authors, © 1994.

- B-cells. For years, B-cells wait and mature in the bone marrow until needed. They can change like cocoons to butterflies, becoming plasma cells that manufacture magic bullets, the protein called antibodies. Operating like a guided missile, they can shoot the target, paralyze the enemy, shoot caustic chemicals, and explode the bad cells and tissue. B-cells can clone themselves and create whatever number it takes to do the battle.

In 20 to 30 minutes, the nurse can modify the script as needed and guide the client through an intervention such as this.

Script[35]: *You are about to embark on the most incredible journey imaginable, a journey through your own immune system, touching your body's healing forces with your mind; you will sense, feel, envision a miracle. A miracle of defense and protection, a miracle of the billions of honorable, persistent warriors within that have but one mission: to guard you from disease and injury and invasion.*

To fully appreciate this odyssey, which is as complex as it is magnificent, it is important to clear and focus your mind, to relax your body. The bridge between your mind and body is easily crossed when distractions are released, when a sense of peace and calm spreads warmly from the top of your head to your toes. As you let go of stress, your immune system is activated. Relax, now, as you participate and observe your own healing process.

As your mind becomes clearer and clearer, feel it becoming more and more alert. Somewhere deep inside of you, a brilliant light begins to glow. Sense this happening. . . . The light grows brighter and brighter and more intense. . . . This is your bodymind communication center. Breathe into it. . . . Energize it with your breath. The light is powerful and penetrating, and the beam begins to grow from it. The beam shines into your body into any area you wish. It is your searchlight, your bridge into the glorious mysteries about to unfold. Practice shining it into your body. Sometimes this is easier to do than other times. Just allow it to happen.

The immune journey begins inside your bones. So take this most intelligent beam of light and shine it into a long bone—a leg bone perhaps. Penetrate deeply into the marrow. This is the birthing center for all your blood cells. Just imagine if you can, feel if you can, billions of young cells being born . . . many kinds, each with a task to nurture and protect you. As we go through this exercise, we will focus on a few types of cells that are vital to defending you. They have names: neutrophils, macrophages, T-cells, B-cells, natural killer cells. One by one, we'll shine the light on them, watching them work to guard and protect and remove cells that no longer serve you.

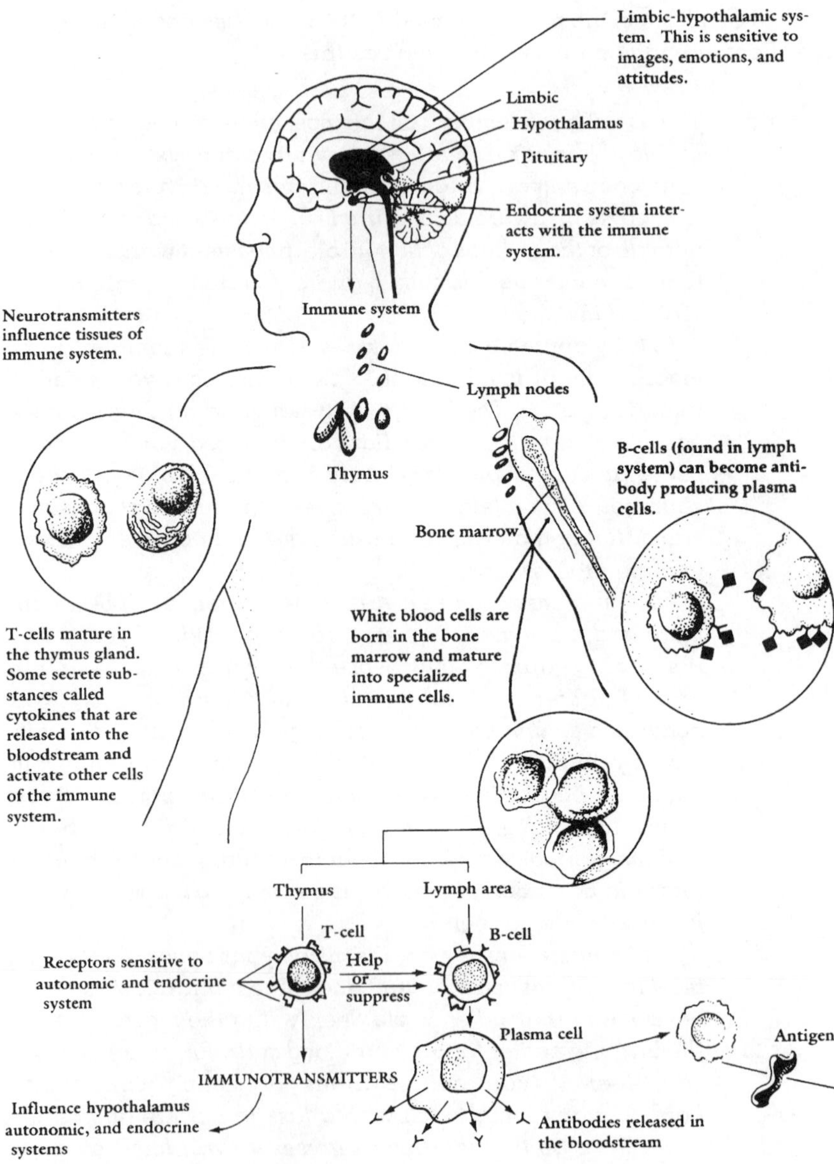

Figure 23–4 Immune system components. *Source:* Reprinted from *Rituals of Healing* by Jeanne Achterberg, Barbara Dossey, and Leslie Kolkmeier, Bantam Books, with permission of the authors, © 1994.

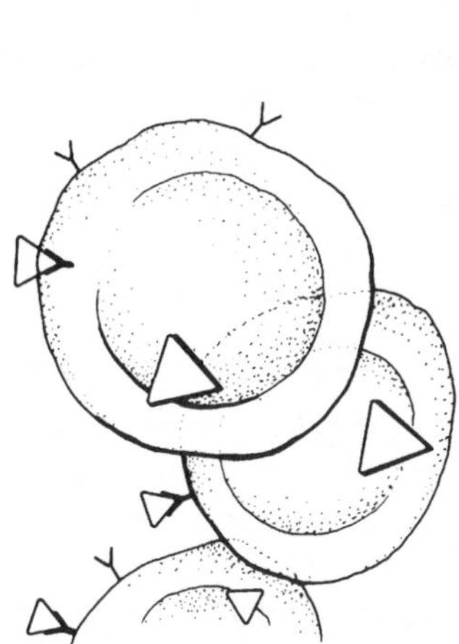

Neuropeptides produced in the brain lock onto specific receptors of immune cells.

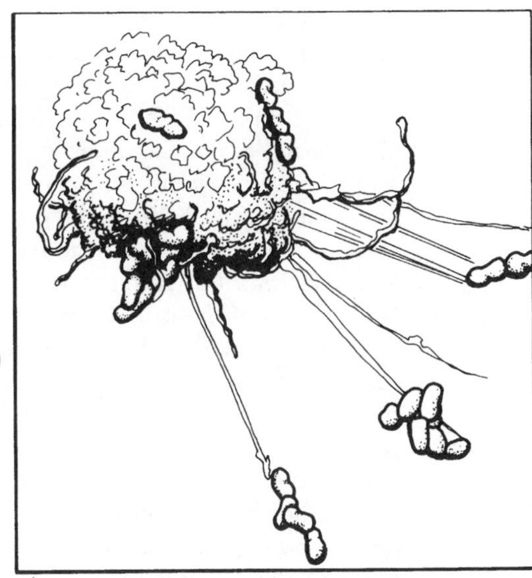

Phagocytes, such as neutrophils and the macrophage pictured here literally eat bacteria, viruses, cancer cells, and other foreign particles or destroyed tissue and contain chemicals that break down and destroy the invaders.

The immune system produces memory cells when exposed to an antigen, and the immune system then remembers that encounter and becomes more efficient against it the next time it gets invaded by microorganisms that produce antigens.

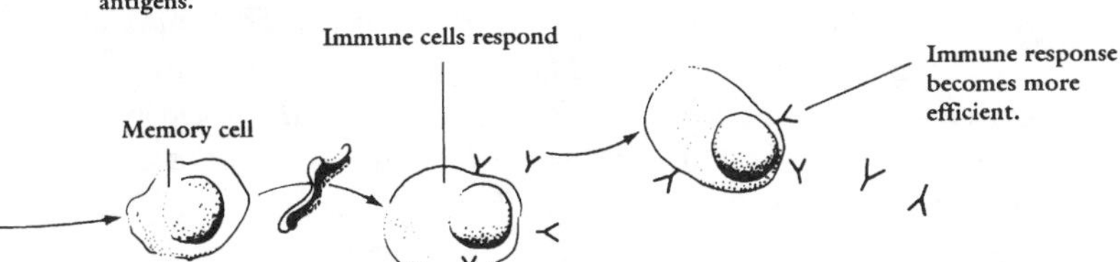

Figure 23-4 continued

The most numerous cells are called neutrophils. They eat and engulf the invaders in a most ingenious way. Imagine them maturing, moving into your bloodstream, floating, ever alert for a call to work in your defense. As a call warns them of an invader, they become exceedingly alert. No longer swimming freely, millions, billions of them sense the danger and move methodically, directly, preparing for attack. The blood vessels become sticky, attracting the neutrophils to their surface. The small opening in the blood vessel walls dilates in the vicinity of the attack. Imagine the neutrophils being attracted to the walls. They move quickly along the vessel walls until they know with absolute certainty that the invader is near. Now, they extend a small foot, a pseudopod, into the walls, and changing shape, they slither through, entering your tissues. Moving forward now, as they approach the invader, they send another small foot out, surrounding the enemy, shooting caustic chemicals into it, wearing it thin. The enemy is halted, destroyed, may even explode into harmless bits. Imagine this happening, constantly, protecting you from the dangers of living in a hostile world. Billions and billions of neutrophils are born every day.

Now, shining the beam of light back into the bone marrow, imagine the macrophages, or the giant eaters. Fewer of them, but long-lived with many talents. As they mature, watch them move into tissues and organs and blood. They line the walls of the lungs and liver. Waiting, surveying, watching, ever ready to move. Bacteria, viruses, yeast cells, even cancer cells trigger the alarm. As the warning of an invader sounds, the macrophages swell up, becoming large and powerful. They may even mesh together with the other macrophages, moving rapidly in a powerful, connecting flank. They reach out for the enemy; lasso it with their arm-like extensions, and bring the invader into their bodies, injecting it with potent enzymes. With lightning speed, they consume an enemy. What they can't destroy, they encircle and preserve, protecting you from its dangerous acts. The macrophages are also your scavengers. They can and will digest anything and everything in your body that you no longer have use for. Imagine this happening for a moment.

The macrophages and neutrophils are nonspecific, nondiscriminating in their attack and clean up activities. Other cells, the lymphocytes, or the T-cells and the B-cells, have an assigned function, a target that they spend their entire lives stalking. It might be a special virus, or bacteria, or cancer cell or other foreign tissue. Let's look at these cells in action.

Shining the beam, again, into the bone marrow, observe the T-cells being born. Millions—more than you could possibly count—move from infancy to adolescence each minute. The T-cells will each be given a special task as they are processed in the thymus gland. Shine your imagery light into the middle of your chest—here is the thymus gland. Feel it pulsating with energy. Watch, now, as the adolescent T-cells flow in rapidly, each touched with a spark of wisdom, each challenged with a mission. Some will be killers, assassins with a single target. Others will be helpers for your B-cells, still others will be suppressors, signaling that the battle is over, protecting your body from excessive immune activity. Imagine these, the killers, the helpers, the suppressors, maturing quickly and with glorious specificity in your thymus. When each has been imprinted, they leave the thymus to go about their tasks. The T-cells keep a wakeful vigil in your lymph nodes, your spleen, other lymph tissue. Think of this for a time. . . .

Back in the bone marrow once again, the B-cells are highlighted by the beam. They mature and move into the lymph tissues and blood, waiting for the encounter. Each has a specific enemy to protect you from, and they can wait patiently for years, patrolling, waiting, and watching. When the encounter finally takes place, the B-cells change, like cocoons into butterflies, becoming a plasma cell. The plasma cells manufacture magic bullets, which are proteins called antibodies. Each antibody is like a guided missile—it moves directly for its target and hooks on to it, like a key in a lock. The enemy is paralyzed and its surface damaged. Other chemicals are liberated in the blood by this action, and they burn holes in the wall of the enemy, causing an explosion. The B-cells also clone themselves, creating whatever number is needed to do pure and perfect battle in your defense.

One last time, peering into the birthing center of the immune system, the light shines onto natural killer cells. The natural killers are wondrous defenses against cancer. Like viruses and bacteria, cancer cells are not especially unusual in the human body. The body simply recognizes them as invaders and sends out the forces of defense. Only in the most un-

usual circumstances (e.g., when cancer cells wear a disguise), does the immune system fail to find them. Watch now, as the natural killer cells are born and move into the bloodstream. Take the light and shine it on one cell, and watch its action. Ever alert, it senses a cancer cell in the vicinity. Moving at lightning speed, it collides with the cancer cell. Its mere touch paralyzes the cell. Fingers of the natural killer cell reach into the cancer cell, oozing in its power and might. Then a small cannon-like structure within the natural killer cell tilts, aims, and fires deadly chemicals into the cancer cell. Already paralyzed, the cancer cell develops blisters, peels like an orange. Its cellular matter dissolves, leaving only harmless skeletal remains. The natural killer cell, alive and well, continues its alert patrol of your body.

Before you end this exercise, go over the immune process once more, sensing all the immune cells working in a superbly coordinated team of defense. In the bone marrow, billions of cells are being born each minute, in exactly the number and combinations that you need to stay healthy. As the white blood cells mature, each develops a remarkable intelligence. Each has a dedicated task. Witness them moving out of the bone marrow, into blood tissue, watching and waiting for the opportunity to protect and cleanse you. Feel the presence of these magnificent guardians, and sense their power. These dedicated warriors, this system of defense has a universe of its own—that universe is you. By relaxing, as you have just done, and concentrating on this process, you have actively participated in keeping yourself healthy.

Drawing

In the imagery process, drawing is an effective way to open up communication with the self and others. It externalizes previously internal mental images and emotions. The emphasis in this intervention is not on how well the client can draw, but on the client's ability to get in touch with feelings and healing potential through drawing. When clients are overwhelmed with emotions, drawing images of the feelings can be therapeutic. Drawing is also helpful with children who are not verbally sophisticated. Tremendous insight can be gained in this process with both adults and children who are going through painful procedures or are experiencing certain concerns, fears, or problems in daily life. This intervention becomes advanced when in-depth psychologic explanations of the drawing are explored. When using drawing as an intervention, the nurse can suggest the following general ideas:

- Express yourself with a few images. There is no one best way to draw. Drawings can be realistic or symbolic. The most important thing is that you express yourself in a nonlogical way. This can bring new awareness and understanding into your life.
- If you find that you are too focused on the result of the drawing exercise, use your nondominant hand. With your eyes closed, allow yourself to get into the expressive quality of drawing.
- Do not judge your drawing. Allow your body, mind, and spirit to connect as you begin simply to be with the paper and crayons in the present moment.
- Notice the energy flow from you. Let your body energy resonate with your imagery/spirit energy. Let the energies slowly begin to resonate together. Do not try to control the process, because this inner quality comes from being immersed in the imagery and drawing experience.
- On the blank piece of paper, allow an image to begin to form that represents your feelings and thoughts in this moment. Choose colors that speak to you. If you wish to change the color that you started working with, feel free to do so.
- After you have drawn, you might want to write some details of your images. Often, what you felt or heard during the imagery drawing may surface into conscious awareness and provide new insights about your important images.

Frequently, after the client has been guided through an imagery exercise or is listening to an imagery tape or music alone, drawing can bring tremendous insight. The creativity that is evoked is different from the logical mode of explaining the felt experience in words. Drawing works very well when a client is crying and is unable to talk easily, but wants to express what he or she is experiencing.

Symptom/Disease Drawing. Symptoms or disease can keep a person from attaining a quality life or moving toward accomplishment of life goals. When working with a client's specific disease/symptoms, the nurse encourages the client to become more aware of the normal body process; the disease/symptoms and its medication, treatments, and associated procedures; and his or her personal belief systems. Asking the client to draw the disease/symptoms in the way that has self-meaning often reveals a client's constricted view of healing possibilities or misunderstanding of the disease/symptoms, either of which may impair recovery. The drawing process helps the client recognize that the disease need not control his or her life. Insight from drawing helps the client learn how to join the disease process, to let go of the inner struggle, and to end the resistance in order to achieve desired outcomes.

The challenge for nurses is to develop innovative teaching worksheets, booklets, and verbal descriptions of bodymind healing; to integrate imagery as part of each nursing interaction and intervention; and to develop assessment tools.[36,37] The nurse and client should identify the following elements for the best outcome:

- disease or disability: the vividness of the client's view of the disease, illness, or disability and, if the process is ongoing, the strength of the disease/illness to decrease health or the client's focus on the reverse—the vividness and the strength of the ability of the client to stabilize the disease/illness or stop the process.
- internal healing resources: the vividness of the client's perception of his or her healing ability and the effectiveness of this ability/action to combat the disease.
- external healing resources: the vividness of the treatment description and the effectiveness of some positive mechanism of action.

Family and Group Drawing. In many cases, drawing can play an important role in family therapy sessions. It is most effective when the nurse facilitates in-depth interpretation of drawings and uses family therapy interventions. For example, family members may draw at the same time, but on separate sheets of paper, their main concern or problem, their suggestion for a solution, and the steps that they see from problem to solution. Each family member may draw a variation of the same problem, or someone may identify something that has never been shared with the other members. The dynamics of the family unit and the various viewpoints come out in ways that words may not express. During the interpretation of the drawings, family members can be asked to list positive and negative events in the family and then to discuss the importance of the events listed. The light and shadow of each situation is usually revealing to each individual, as well as to the family.

With groups, a nurse can use a 4-foot long paper on a large roll, stretching it out on the floor or a table. The nurse may ask the group members to draw simultaneously in a realistic or symbolic way, all the things for which they are thankful or that excite them in life. Each person then takes a turn and shares with the group what his or her drawing represents. The healing that occurs in listening and sharing personal stories is profound.

When everyone has had a turn, the person who started the sharing draws a line to and circles an object or several objects that were drawn by other people, but have personal meaning for him or her. By the time everyone has had a chance to share, the drawings and symbols are connected by many lines, showing the group members' interconnectedness. This exercise is very effective in rehabilitation groups, such as classes for cardiac, cancer, and diabetic patients, because the focus can shift to drawing or listing worries, fears, or problems as related to health problems. This exercise reminds clients of many important perceptions and events in their own lives, and ways to cope effectively. When people share their joy or sadness, it often evokes deep feelings in others of forgotten memories or current life events.

Drawing is a very helpful intervention with people who are at high risk for burnout.[38] Their drawings often reveal symptoms throughout the body and reveal a disconnection from feelings. Images of the self may be very small and may lack detail. The absence of color or empty space on the paper is usually indicative of high stress. The goal with drawing for these individuals is to begin to find potential solutions to the current stressors. Drawing often helps them establish the problem, the solutions, and effective ways of coping.

Another way to approach group work is to ask everyone to contribute to a mural on clear plexiglass. Half of the group is on one side and the other half is on the opposite side. In a different exercise, group members may choose partners and have half the group lie down on a large piece of paper. The person lying down takes a position of fear on the paper, and the other person traces around the body of the person in a fear position. Next, the person on the paper assumes a relaxed, free position while the partner traces this body position. Then the people switch places. After both people have experienced the positions of fear and relaxation, they share the experiences with each other.

Symbolism, Colors, and Associations. People should be encouraged to experiment with free-style drawings that elicit a multitude of images. Tables 23–3, 23–4, and 23–5 give very general explanations for common symbols, colors, associations, and feelings that people either draw or choose to emphasize. Images experienced throughout life, such as paintings, recognized universal symbols, television, movies, and advertisement, influence a person's imagery process. As nurses use imagery, it is extremely important for them to be sensitive to the cultural context within which a client is experiencing symptoms. Cultural diversity shapes the attitudes, beliefs, and meaning regarding the individual's expression of symptoms, disease, illness, and the symbols, colors, and association.[39–41]

Table 23-3 Common Symbols

Air	Activity, male principle, primary element, creativity, breath, light, freedom, liberty, movement
Fire	Ability to transform, love, life, health, control, spiritual energy, regeneration, sun, God, passion
Water	Passive, feminine, abysmal, liquid
Earth	Passive, feminine, receptive, solid
Ascent	Height, transcendence, inward journey, increasing intensity
Descent	Unconscious, potentialities of being, animal nature
Duality	Opposites, complements, pairing, away from unity, male-female, life-death, positive-negative, is-is not
Unity	Spirit, oneness, wholeness, centering, transcendence, the source, harmony, revelation, active principle, a point, a dot, supreme power, completeness in itself, light, the divinity
Center	Thought, unity, timelessness, spacelessness, paradise, creator, infinity, neutralizing opposites
Cross	Tree of life, axis of the world, ladder, struggle, martyrdom, orientation in space
Dark	Matter, germ, before existence, chaos
Light	Spirit, morality, All, creative force, the direction East, spiritual thought
Mountain	Height, mass, loftiness, center of the world, ambition, goals
Lake	Mystery, depth, unconscious
Moon	Master of women, vegetation, fecundity
Eye	Understanding, intelligence, sacred fire, creative
Image	Highest form of knowing, thought as a form
Sun	Hero, son of heaven, knowledge, the Divine eye, fire, life force, creative-guiding force, brightness, splendor, active principle, awakening, healing, resurrection, ultimate wholeness

Source: From *Seeing with the Mind's Eye* by Mike Samuels and Nancy Samuels. Copyright © 1975 by Mike Samuels and Nancy Samuels. Reprinted by permission of Random House, Inc.

Drawing Mandalas. A mandala is a circular design containing concentric geometric forms and images. Often drawn or painted to symbolize the universe, totality, or wholeness, mandalas can become very complex. Some are symmetric; others have shapes and colors that are different in each quarter. These shapes represent conscious and unconscious materials that surfaces over time. Mandalas may be used for psychologic evaluation and treatment.

The client needs general information about the process of drawing a mandala before picking up the supplies. The nurse may explain as follows:

- A mandala is an ancient symbol of wholeness that has been recorded throughout time. It can serve as a vehicle for self-expression.

Table 23-4 Color Symbolism, Association, and Effects

Red	Sunrise, birth, blood, fire, emotion, wounds, death, passion, sentiment, mother, the planet Mars, the musical note "C," anger, chakras #1, excitement, heat, physical stimulation and strengthening the blood, iron, alcohol, oxygen, treatment of paralysis and exhaustion
Orange	Fire, pride, ambition, egoism, the planet Venus, the musical note "D," chakra #2, stimulation of the nervous system, treatment as emetic and laxative
Yellow	Sun, light, intuition, illumination, air, intellect, royalty, the planet Mercury, the musical note "E," luminosity
Green	Earth, fertility, sensation, vegetation, death, water, nature, sympathy, adaptability, growth, the planets Jupiter and Venus, the musical note "G"
Blue	Clear sky, thinking, the day, the sea, height, depth, heaven, religious feeling, devotion, innocence, truth, psychic ability, spirituality, the planet Jupiter, the musical note "F," the chakra #5, physical soothing and cooling, treatment as a sedative, anti-inflammatory, cure for headache
Violet	Water, nostalgia, memory, advanced spirituality, the planet Neptune, the musical note "B," a treatment for madness

Note: Chakras (a Sanskrit word meaning wheel or disk-like spinning vortex of energy; 7 major energy centers in Eastern medicine)
#1 Root Center (located at base of spine and perineal floor)
#2 Social Center (located midsacral lower abdomen, below navel)
#3 Solar Plexus (located at solar plexus)
#4 Heart Center (located between shoulder blades at the heart level)
#5 Throat Center (located at the center and base of throat)
#6 Brow Center (located between eyebrows at the center of the brows)
#7 Crown Center (located at the top of the head)

Source: From *Seeing with the Mind's Eye* by Mike Samuels and Nancy Samuels. Copyright © 1975 by Mike Samuels and Nancy Samuels. Reprinted by permission of Random House, Inc.

- The effectiveness of mandalas has nothing to do with how well they are drawn. Their value is in helping an individual reflect on inner wisdom and self-awareness.
- Each person has many different levels of the self. These different levels come into conscious awareness as voices or images and can be thought of as advisors (see Inner Guide script). Listen to the constant self-talk as you draw your mandala.
- Reflect on mandalas in art museums or books.
- The purpose of drawing mandalas is to have a creative experience that facilitates self-reflection.

Table 23–5 Shapes: Symbolism and Associations

Circle	Heaven, ether, intellect, thought, sun, the number ten, unity, perfection, eternity, oneness, the masculine-active principle, celestial realm, hearing, sound
Triangle	Communication, between heaven and earth, fire, the number three, trinity, aspiration, movement upward, return to origins, gas, sight, light
Square	Pluralism, earth, feminine-receptive principle, firmness, stability, construction, material, solidity, the number four
Rectangle	Most rational, most secure, used in grounding objects such as houses and desks
Spiral	Evolution of the universe, orbit, growth, deepening, cosmic motion, relationship between unity and multiplicity, macrocosm, breath, spirit, water

Source: From *Seeing with the Mind's Eye* by Mike Samuels and Nancy Samuels. Copyright © 1975 by Mike Samuels and Nancy Samuels. Reprinted by permission of Random House, Inc.

- Listen to your inner wisdom. Experience your ability to free-associate and to use symbols that have meaning for you.
- This drawing experience reveals enormous resources to your conscious awareness.

The necessary supplies for drawing mandalas include different-colored crayons, felt-tip markers, or oil pastel crayons. White, newspaper quality paper in a variety of sizes, such as 10 × 12 and 14 × 17 inches, is advisable. A paper dinner plate or some other object measuring 10 inches in diameter should be available to be traced onto the blank sheet. This size and shape are recommended because it is roughly the size of the human head and serves as a mirroring device for contemplation.

Drawing a mandala can take from 20 minutes to 1 hour and can be an effective intervention in individual or group sessions. Listening to music can enhance the activity, and several different selections should be on hand. Before drawing, clients should sit in silence, invite the music into their conscious awareness, and watch the thoughts as they flow through their minds. Another way is to reflect on the emptiness within the circle while listening to the music (see Chapter 24 for music selections). If it feels right, the guide may leave the room after all the materials are set up and the client is comfortable. Frequently, this allows the client more space and time for self-reflection. Mandalas can be drawn at a desk or while sitting on the floor. The nurse can instruct the client as follows:

- You may start in the center of the circle and work outward, or you may draw within or outside of the circle. The circle is merely a possible starting place. Reflect on the first mark and the color(s) chosen, and continue to draw.

- Think of the space within the mandala as sacred space. It is waiting for a part of the unexpressed self to be revealed. Although a certain idea may have initiated the drawing process, the mandala may begin to take on a life of its own if one lets inner wisdom flow. It is as if one awaits a revelation to the conscious mind, "Pick up purple, and draw circles in a clockwise manner."
- The content of the mandala reflects one's personal journey at the moment. During the session, many emotions can come forward, such as happiness, sadness, excitement, or anger. Throughout the drawing process, just be present in the moment and invite the music into conscious awareness to enhance your images. It will help release any blocks that may occur.
- The drawing can take the form of either abstract or familiar designs. It may literally contain symbols that have specific significance, such as objects, people, or animals.

The nurse can also make some general closure remarks at the end of the mandala exercise:

- Each of us is a living mandala that changes moment by moment. When we are alive with ideas, the mandalas seem to flow freely.
- During periods of illness or extreme emotional turmoil, we often forget to use our creative selves. We use only conscious awareness and forget about the wisdom in the subconscious. Mandalas can facilitate the release of creativity, however. Through mandalas, we acknowledge the enormous reservoirs of wisdom and strengths in the subconscious.
- The patterns and processes that a person produces in a mandala may lead to important insights that ordinary states of consciousness may block.
- It is wise to place a date on the mandala and to keep it. A series of mandalas are very helpful in revealing life patterns and processes.

Because they reflect a person's consciousness and subconscious thoughts and images, mandalas are best interpreted first by the person who produced them. There may be times when an individual does not like the drawing or does not want to describe the process, and it is important to honor the person's wish.

It is necessary for nurses to draw mandalas in order to understand the process. Furthermore, it is helpful to study mandalas drawn by healthy, well functioning people in order to learn to recognize the work of clients with chronic illness or depressed states. When a healthy person is drawing, mandalas change in response to the person's state; however, mandalas of chronically ill people are usually repetitive.

Case Study

Setting:	Coronary care unit (CCU), followed by outpatient cardiac rehabilitation program
Patient:	J.D., a 48-year-old male, with acute myocardial infarction complicated by congestive heart failure and pericarditis secondary to the infarction
Nursing Diagnoses:	1. Decreased cardiac output related to mechanical factors (congestive heart failure) 2. Altered comfort related to inflammation (pericarditis) 3. Anxiety related to acute illness and fear of death.

The nurse asked J. several questions in order to explore with him his psychospiritual state. Following the interaction, the nurse felt that further exploration of the meaning and negative images that he conveyed was essential to his recovery. She asked him if he wanted to pursue some new ideas that might help him access his inner healing resources and strengths. He said that he would.

Nurse: "In your recovery now with your heart healing, how do you experience your healing?"

J.D.: "There is this sac around my heart and every time I take a deep breath, my breath is cut off by the pain [pericarditis]. My heart is like a broken vase. I don't think it is healing."

Nurse: "I can understand why you are discouraged. However, some important things that are present right now show that you are better than when you first came to the CCU. Your chest pain is gone, and your heartbeats are now regular. If you focus on what is going right, you can help your heart and lift your spirits. Let me help you learn how to think of some positive things."

J.D.: "I don't know if I can."

Nurse: "I would like to show you how to breathe more comfortably. Place your right hand on your upper chest, and your left hand on your belly. I want to show you how to do relaxed abdominal breathing. With your next breath in, through your nose, let the breath fill your belly with air. And as you exhale, through your mouth, let your stomach fall back to your spine. As you focus on this way of breathing, notice how still your chest is."

J.D. *(after three complete breaths):* "This is the easiest breathing I've done today."

Nurse: "As you focused on breathing with your belly, you let go of fearing the discomfort with your breathing. Can you tell me more about the image you have of your heart as a broken vase?"

J.D.: "I saw this crack down the front of my heart right after the doctor told me about my big artery that is blocked, that runs down the front of my heart, that caused my heart attack."

Nurse *(taking a small plastic bag full of crayons out of her pocket and picking up a piece of paper):* "Is it possible for you to choose a few crayons and draw your broken heart using those images you just talked about?"

J.D.: "I can't draw."

Nurse: "This exercise has nothing to do with drawing, but something usually happens when you draw an image of your words."

J.D.: "Do you mean the image of a broken vase?" *(When halfway through with the drawing)* "I know this sounds crazy, but my father had a heart attack when he was 55. I was visiting my parents. Dad hadn't been feeling well, even complained of his stomach hurting that morning. He was in the living room, and as he fell, he knocked over a large Chinese porcelain vase that broke in two pieces. I can remember so clearly running to his side. I can see that vase now, cracked in a jagged edge down the front. He made it to the hospital, but died 2 days later. You know, I think that might be where that image of a broken heart came from" (Figure 23–5A).

Nurse: "Your story contains a lot of meaning. Remembering this event can be very helpful to you in your healing. What are some of the things that you are most worried about just now?"

J.D. *(tears in his eyes):* "Dying young. I have this funny feeling in my stomach just now. I don't want to die. I'm too young. I have so much to contribute to life. I've been driving myself to excess as far as work. I need to learn to relax and manage my stress, even drop some weight, start exercising, and change my life."

Nurse: "J., each day you are getting stronger. You might even consider that this time of rest after your heart attack can be a time for you to reflect on what are the most important things in life for you. Whenever you feel discouraged, let images come to you of a beautiful vase that has a healed crack in it. This is exactly what your heart is doing right now. Even as we are talking, the area that has been damaged is healing. As it heals, there will be a solid scar that will be very strong, just in the same way that a vase can be mended and become strong again. New blood supplies also come into the surrounding area of your heart to help it heal. Positive images can help you heal, because you send a different message from your mind to your body when you are relaxed and thinking about becoming strong and well. You help your body, mind, and spirit function at their highest level. Let yourself once again draw an image of your heart as a healed vase, and notice any difference in your feelings when you do this."

With a smile, he picked up several crayons and began to draw a healing image to encourage hope and healing (Figure 23–5B).

When J. entered the outpatient cardiac rehabilitation program following his acute myocardial infarction, he was motivated to lower his cholesterol, lose weight, learn stress management skills, and express his emotions. Two weeks into the program, J. did not appear to be his usual extroverted self. The cardiac rehabilitation nurse engaged him in conversation, and before long, he had tears in his eyes. He stated that he was very discouraged about having heart disease. He said, "It just has a grip on me." The nurse took him into her office, and they continued the dialogue. After listening to his story, she asked J. if he would like to explore his feelings further. He very shyly nodded yes.

In order to facilitate the healing process, she thought it might be helpful to have J. get in touch with his images and their locations in his body. She began by saying, "If it seems right to you, close your eyes and begin to focus on your breathing just now." She guided him in a general exercise of head-to-toe relaxation, accompanied by an audiocassette music selection of sounds in nature. As his breathing patterns became more relaxed and deeper, indicating relaxation, she began to guide him in exploring "the grip" in his imagination.

Nurse: "Focus on where you experience the grip. Give it a size . . . , a shape . . . , a sound . . . , a texture . . . , a width . . . , and a depth."

J.D.: "It's in my chest, but not like chest pain. It's dull, deep, and blocks my knowing what I need to think or feel about living. I can't be-

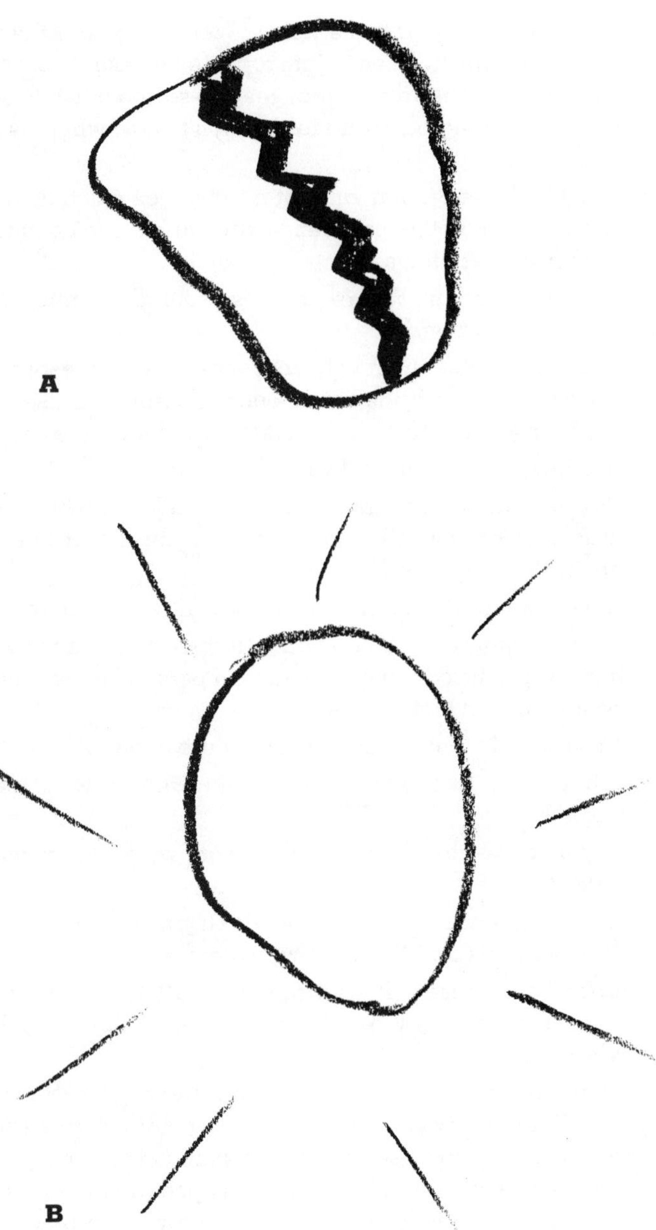

Figure 23–5 **A**, J.D.'s drawing of his broken heart. **B**, J.D.'s drawing of his healed heart.

lieve that I'm using these words. Well, it's bigger than I thought. It's very rough, like heavy jute rope tied in a knot across my chest. It has a sound like a rope that keeps a sailboat tied to a boat dock. I'm now rocking back and forth. I don't know why this is happening."

Nurse: "Stay with the feeling, and let it fill you as much as it can. If you need to change the experience, all you have to do is take a deep breath several times."

J.D.: "It's filling me up. Where are these sounds, feelings, and sensations coming from?"

Nurse: "From your wise inner self, your inner healing resources. Just let yourself stay with the experience. Continue to use as many of your senses as you can to describe and feel these experiences."

J.D.: "Nothing is happening. I've gone blank."

Nurse: "Focus again on your breath in . . . , and feel the breath as you let it go. . . . Can you allow an image of your heart to come to you under that tight grip?"

J.D.: "It is so small I can hardly see it. It's all wrapped up."

Nurse: "In your imagination, can you introduce yourself to your heart as if you were introducing yourself to a person for the first time? Ask your heart if it has a name?"

J.D.: "It said hello, but it was with a gesture of hello, no words."

Nurse: "That is fine. Just say nice to meet you, and see what the response might be."

J.D.: "My heart seems like an old soul, very wise. This feels very comfortable."

Nurse: "Ask your heart a question for which you would like an answer? Stay with this and listen for what comes."

J.D. *(after long pause):* "It said practice patience, that I was on the right track, that my heart disease has a message, don't know what it is."

Nurse: "Just stay with your calmness and inner quiet. Notice how the grip changed for you. There are many more answers to come for you. This is your wise self that has much to offer you. Whenever you want, you can get back to this special kind of knowing. All you have to do is take the time. When you set aside time to be quiet with your rich images, you will get more information. You might also find special music to assist you in this process . . . your skills with this way of knowing will increase each time you use this process. . . . Know that whatever is right for you in this moment is unfolding, just as it should.

"In a few moments, I will invite you back into a wakeful state. On five be ready to come back into the room, wide awake and relaxed. One . . . two . . . three . . . four . . . , eyelids lighter, taking a deep breath . . . and five, back into the room, awake and alert, ready to go about your day."

J.D.: "Where did all that come from? I've never done that before."

Nurse: "These are your inner healing resources that you possess to help you recognize quality and purpose in living each day. In our future classes, we will teach and share more of these skills."

Evaluation

With the client, the nurse determines whether the client outcomes for imagery (see Table 23–2) were successfully achieved. To evaluate the session further, the nurse may again explore the subjective effects of the experience with the client (Exhibit 23–1).

Imagery is a tool for connecting with the unlimited capabilities of bodymind because it is a nonverbal modality and a rich resource for information about all life processes. Using imagery, a nurse can help a client make changes in perception and behavioral attitudes that can

Exhibit 23–1 Evaluating the Client's Subjective Experience with Imagery

1. Was this a new kind of imagery experience for you? Can you describe it?
2. Did you have a visual experience? Of people, places, or objects? Can you describe them?
3. Did you see colors while being guided? Did the colors change as the guided imagery continued?
4. Were you aware of your surroundings? Were you able to let the imagery flow?
5. Did you like the imagery?
6. Did the imagery produce any feelings or emotions?
7. Did you notice any textures, smells, movements, or taste while experiencing the imagery?
8. Was the experience pleasant?
9. Did you feel relaxed and refreshed after the experience?
10. Would you like to try this again?
11. What would make this a better experience for you?
12. What is your next step (or your plan) to integrate this on a daily basis?

promote healing. The client experiences more self-awareness, self-acceptance, self-love, and self-worth. Nurses and clients come to know themselves in a new way as they create and communicate in a symbolic language.

DIRECTIONS FOR FUTURE RESEARCH

1. Determine whether a client's specific images increase the client's psychophysiologic healing.
2. Develop valid and reliable tools that measure imagery.
3. Compare the stress level, attitudes, and work spirit of nurses who routinely use imagery as a nursing intervention to those of nurses who do not use imagery.
4. Evaluate the relationship of imagery scripts, physiologic response, and healing in different clinical settings.
5. Determine if subjects can learn through manipulation of both imagery scripts and their verbal reports to eliminate or modify negative psychophysiologic responses.
6. Examine cultural diversity through specific types of imagery and symbols.

NURSE HEALER REFLECTIONS

After reading this chapter, the nurse healer will be able to answer or begin a process of answering the following questions:

- How do I feel about my imagination?
- When I work with imagery, what inner resources can assist me in my life processes?
- How am I able to remove the barriers to my imagery process?
- In what way do I recognize the nonrational part of myself?
- Can I allow my clients to interpret their own imagery to facilitate their own healing?

NOTES

1. J. Achterberg et al., *Rituals of Healing* (New York: Bantam Books, 1994), 37–53.
2. J. Achterberg, *Imagery in Healing* (Boston: Shambhala Publications, 1985), 115–116.
3. R. Rivlin and K. Gravelle, *Deciphering the Senses: The Expanding World of Human Perception* (New York: Simon & Shuster, 1984), 16–18.

4. E. Rossi, *The Psychobiology of Mind-Body Healing: New Concepts of Therapeutic Hypnosis*, Rev. ed. (New York: W.W. Norton, 1993), 47–68.
5. Ibid., 51–54.
6. A. Ahsen, Imagery, Dreams, and Transformation, *Journal of Mental Imagery* 8 (1984):53–78.
7. M. Horowitz, *Image Formation and Cognition* (New York: Meredith Corp., 1970), 73–79.
8. R. Assagioli, *Psychosynthesis: A Manual of Principles and Techniques* (New York: Hobbs, Doorman and Co., 1965), 17–18.
9. G.F. Lawlis, *The Cure: The Hero's Journey with Cancer* (San Jose, CA: Resources Publications, Inc., 1994).
10. G.F. Lawlis, *The Caregiver's Guide to the Cure: The Hero's Journey with Cancer* (San Jose, CA: Resources Publications, Inc., 1994).
11. H. Benson and E. Stuart, *The Wellness Book* (New York: Birch Lane Press Publishing, 1992), 58–59.
12. J. Achterberg and G.F. Lawlis, *Imagery and Disease* (Champaign, IL: Institute for Personality and Ability Testing, 1978).
13. D. Ornish, Can Lifestyle Changes Reverse Coronary Heart Disease? *Lancet* 336(1990):129–135.
14. B. Gruber et al., Immune System and Psychological Changes in Metastatic Cancer Patients Using Relaxation and Guided Imagery: A Pilot Study, *Scandinavian Journal of Behavior Therapy* 17(1988):25–46.
15. B. Dossey et al., Body-Mind-Spirit, in *Critical Care Nursing: Body-Mind-Spirit*, 3rd ed., ed. B. Dossey et al. (Philadelphia: J.B. Lippincott, 1992), 1–30.
16. E. Barrett, Innovative Imagery: A Health-Patterning Modality for Nursing Practice, *Journal of Holistic Nursing* 10, no. 2 (1992):154–165.
17. P. Salmon, Healing Images, *Journal of Holistic Nursing* 11, no. 1 (1993):21–41.
18. B. Rees, An Exploratory Study of the Effectiveness of a Relaxation with Guided Imagery Protocol, *Journal of Holistic Nursing* 11, no. 3 (1993):271–276.
19. M. Thompson and N. Coppens, The Effects of Guided Imagery on Anxiety Levels and Movement of Clients Undergoing Magnetic Resonance Imaging, *Holistic Nursing Practice* 8, no. 2 (1994):59–69.
20. H. Wadeson et al., *Advances in Art Therapy* (New York: John Wiley & Sons, 1989).
21. N. Christman et al., Concrete Objective Information, in *Nursing Interventions: Essential Nursing Treatments*, 2nd ed., ed. G. Bulechek and J. McCloskey (Philadelphia: W.B. Saunders, 1992), 140–149.
22. G. Peterson and L. Mehl, *Pregnancy As Healing: A Holistic Philosophy for Prenatal Care* (Berkeley, CA: Mindbody Communications, 1984), 214–222.
23. Achterberg et al., *Rituals of Healing*, 72–77.
24. Ibid., 77–78.
25. Achterberg, *Imagery in Healing*.
26. Achterberg and Lawlis, *Imagery and Disease*.
27. Achterberg et al., *Rituals of Healing*, 142–160.
28. Ibid., 129–130.

29. Ibid., 131–132.
30. Ibid., 44–45.
31. B. Dossey et al., Psychophysiologic Self-Regulation, in *Critical Care Nursing: Body-Mind-Spirit*, 3rd ed., ed. B. Dossey et al. (Philadelphia: J.B. Lippincott, 1992), 37–38.
32. Achterberg et al., *Rituals of Healing*, 124–125.
33. Ibid., 126–127.
34. Ibid., 317–328.
35. Ibid., 243–245.
36. Achterberg and Lawlis, *Imagery and Disease*.
37. Achterberg et al., *Rituals of Healing*, 77–78.
38. M. Haack and J. Jones, Diagnosing Burnout: Using Projective Drawings, *Journal of Psychosocial Nursing and Mental Health Services* 21(1983):9–16.
39. B. Schaub et al., Clinical Imagery: Holistic Nursing Perspectives, in *Mental Imagery*, ed. R.G. Kunzendorf (New York: Plenum Press, 1991), 207–213.
40. J. Arguelles and M. Arguelles, *Mandala* (Boulder, CO: Shambhala Publications, 1972).
41. J. Cornell, *Drawing the Light from Within* (Englewood Cliffs, NJ: Prentice-Hall, 1990).

RESOURCES

Bodymind Tape Series from Bodymind Audio Tapes
New Era Media
425 Alabama Street
San Francisco, CA 95070
(415) 863-3555

Tapes for Children with Leukemia
Dawn Rivera
980 Royal Palm Court
Orlando, FL 32808
(407) 896-1857

Video on Children with Cancer
No Fears, No Tears
British Cancer Society
955 W. Broadway
Vancouver, British Columbia
Canada V52 3X8
(604) 877-6000

Audio tapes:
The Art of Caring: Holistic Healing with Imagery, Relaxation, Touch, and Music
(set of 4 tapes)—a companion to *Holistic Nursing: A Handbook for Practice, Second Edition.*
Aspen Publishers, Inc.
7201 McKinney Circle
Frederick, Maryland 21701
(800) 638-8437
ISBN: 1-56455-302-7

VISION OF HEALING

Composing the Harmony

Grown-ups love figures. When you tell them that you have made a new friend, they never ask you any questions about essential matters. They never say to you, "What does his voice sound like? What game does he love best? Does he collect butterflies?"

Instead they demand: "How old is he? How many brothers has he? How much does he weigh? How much money does his father make?" Only from figures do they think they have learned anything about him.[1]

And we must learn that to know a man is not to know his name but to know his melody.[2]

Moisture from the drops of music nurtures and supplies vital nutrients to our physical and emotional well-being. We become healthy. We flourish as species. We prosper. We grow. We laugh. We cry. We dance. We sing. We love. We live. We become one.[3]

Music therapy is personal power made manifest. It's a map to the place where strength and well-being and love lie buried deep inside us all. It is a force to create change from within, to find the healer in all of us.[4]

The ancients knew it; our bodies know it. The emerging physician, the new doctor of balance, fullness, and resonance, rests on a new understanding of the physics of harmonics and the powers in sound. The overture is sounding for the twenty-first century. The ancient healers are calling forth our deeper senses. Orpheus, Apollo, Tubal-cain, Aesculapius, David, St. Gregory, St. Francis, Saraswati, and St. Cecilia are sounding their calls. How soon will we be able to use the beauty of musical sound to compose ourselves into perfect octaves of harmony in mind, body, and spirit?[5]

NOTES

1. A. De Saint Exupery, *The Little Prince* (New York: Harcourt, Brace, & World, 1971), 16.

2. Unknown Oriental Philosopher.
3. B.J. Crowe, Music—The Ultimate Physician, in *Music: Physician for Times To Come*, ed. D. Campbell (Wheaton, IL: Quest Books, 1991), 118.
4. Ibid.
5. D. Campbell, Introduction: The Curative Potential of Sound, in *Music: Physician for Times To Come*, ed. D. Campbell (Wheaton, IL: Quest Books, 1991), 8.

Chapter 24

Music Therapy: Hearing the Melody of the Soul

Cathie E. Guzzetta

NURSE HEALER OBJECTIVES

Theoretical

- Evaluate the principles of sound.
- Analyze the psychophysiologic theories that explain why music therapy works as a bodymind modality.

Clinical

- List the factors to be considered in choosing music selections that are relaxing for clients.
- Develop a music library for use with clients.
- Develop several different music therapy techniques and use them in clinical practice.
- Explore with clients their internal responses when listening to music in a relaxed state.

Personal

- Participate in "experimental listening."
- Record your responses to various types of music in a music notebook.
- In a music log, record your most intimate memories associated with music.
- Participate in a music bath each day.

- Participate in a toning and groaning exercise before listening to music.
- Practice focused and conscious hearing each day to recognize subtle differences in sound.

DEFINITIONS

Cymatics: the study of patterns of shape evoked by sound.
Frequencies: the number of vibrations or cycles per unit of time.
Music Therapy: behavioral science concerned with the systematic application of music to produce relaxation and desired changes in emotions, behavior, and physiology.
Oscillation: fluctuation or variation between minimum and maximum values.
Resonance: the vibration of a structure at a frequency that is natural to it and most easily sustained by it.
Sonic: of or having to do with sound.
Sound: that which is produced when some object is vibrating in a random or periodic repeated motion.
Sympathetic Resonance: the reinforced vibration of an object exposed to the vibration at about the same frequency as another object.

THEORY AND RESEARCH

Music and medicine have been linked throughout history. According to Greek mythology, Orpheus was given a lyre by the God Apollo and was instructed in its use by the muses; hence, the word *music*. Apollo was the god of music, and his son Aesculapius was the god of healing and medicine. The Greeks believed music had the power to help heal the body and soul.

Music has been a vital part of all societies and cultures, no matter how primitive or advanced. It is used in spiritual ceremonies and in celebrations. Armies march to battle with music, and mothers lull their infants to sleep with song. Music is played during rites of initiation, during funeral ceremonies, and on harvest and feast days. There is something about the power of music that cannot be expressed in verbal language. It is of no surprise then that music is currently being applied as an alternative therapy in health care.

Origin of Sound

It is necessary to appreciate the principles and theories of sound to understand fully its tremendous capacity to achieve therapeutic psychophysiologic outcomes. Sound is produced when some object is vibrating in a random or periodic repeated motion. It can be heard by the human ear when it ranges from 16 to 25,000 cycles per second. Within this vibratory range, we can hear, 1,378 different tones.[1] We also hear and perceive sound by skin and bone conduction. Our other senses, such as sight, smell, and touch, allow us to perceive an even wider range of vibrations than those sensed by hearing. Thus, we are sensitive to sounds in ways that most people do not even consider.

The interrelationship between wave forms and matter can be understood by rendering vibrations into physical forms. When scattered liquids, powders, metal filings, or sand are placed on a disk with a vibrating crystal, repeatable patterns form on the disk. As the pitch is changed, the harmonic pattern formed on the disk also changes. Thus, matter assumes certain shapes or patterns based on the vibrations or frequency of the sound to which it is exposed. The study of patterns of shapes evoked by sound is called cymatics.[2] The forms of snowflakes and faces of flowers may take on their shape because they are responding to some sounds in nature.[3] Likewise, it is possible that crystals, plants, and even human beings are, in some way, music that has taken on visible form.

The human body also vibrates. The ejection of blood from the left ventricle during systole distends the aorta with blood. The pressure produced by aortic distension causes a pressure wave to travel down the aorta to the arterial branches. The pressure wave travels faster than the flow of blood and creates a palpable pulse called the pressure pulse wave.[4]

Waves are a series of advancing impulses set up by a vibration or impulse. The pressure pulse wave is composed of a series of waves that have differing frequencies (i.e., number of vibrations per unit of time) and amplitude. In the arterial branches, there is one fundamental frequency and a number of harmonics that usually have a smaller amplitude than the fundamental frequency. The arterial vessels resonate at certain frequencies (fundamental frequency), thereby intensifying some waves while other waves are damped and disappear. This phenomenon is called resonance.[5]

The human body vibrates, from its large structures, such as the aorta and arterial system, down to the genetically preprogrammed vibrations coded into our molecular cells. Our atoms and molecules, cells, glands, and organs all have a characteristic vibrational frequency that absorb and emit sound. Thus, the human body is a system of vibrating atomic particles acting as a vibratory transformer that gives off and takes in sound.

Because our bodies absorb sound, the concept of resonance has implications for all of us. Sympathetic vibration, or sympathetic resonance, refers to the reinforced vibration of an object exposed to the vibration at about the same frequency as another object.[6] For example, if two tuning forks are designed to vibrate at approximately the same pitch, striking one of the tuning forks produces a sound that spontaneously causes the second tuning fork to vibrate and produce the same sound—even though the second fork was not physically struck. Actually, the sound wave from the first fork does physically strike the second fork, causing the second to resonate responsively to the tune of the first. This sympathetic resonance occurs because the vibratory characteristics of the two forks allow energy transfer from one to the other. When two objects have similar vibratory characteristics that allow them to resonate at the same frequency, they form a resonant system.

The atomic structure of our molecular system is also a resonant system. Nuclei vibrate and the electrons in their orbit vibrate in resonance with their nucleus. Moreover, as long as the atom, cell, or organ contains an appropriate vibrational pattern, it can be "played" by outside stimuli in harmony with its vibrational makeup.[7] The phenomenon of sympathetic vibration depends on pitch. Thus, environmental sounds, such as those emitted from a dishwasher or television, may be capable of stimulating or producing sympathetic vibrations in the molecules and cells of our body.

Our entire body vibrates at an inaudible fundamental frequency of approximately 8 cycles per second when it is in a relaxed state. During relaxed meditation, the frequency of brain waves produced is also about 8 cycles per second. Furthermore, the earth vibrates at this same fundamental frequency of 8 cycles per second. This phenomenon, called Schumann's resonance, is a function of electromagnetic radiation and the earth's circumference. Thus, there is a sympathetic resonance between the electrically charged layers of the earth's atmosphere and the human body, and, therefore, "being in harmony with oneself and the universe" may be more than a poetic concept.[8]

Purposes of Music Therapy

Defined as a behavioral science that is concerned with the use of specific kinds of music to affect changes in behavior, emotions, and physiology,[9] music therapy can reduce psychophysiologic stress, pain, anxiety, and isolation. It also is useful in helping clients achieve a state of deep relaxation, develop self-awareness and creativity, improve learning, clarify personal values, and cope with a variety of psychophysiologic dysfunctions.[10,11] Music therapy complements traditional therapy, providing clients with integrated bodymind experiences and encouraging them to become active participants in their own health care.

Appropriate music is an important vehicle in achieving the relaxation response; it removes a person's inner restlessness and quiets ceaseless thinking. It can be used as a healing ritual to stop the mind from running away and to achieve inner quietness. The healing capabilities of music are intimately bound to the personal experience of inner relaxation.[12]

Shifting States of Consciousness

When appropriately used, music can serve as a vehicle for reaching nonordinary levels of human consciousness.[13] Music makes it possible to alter ordinary states of consciousness to achieve the mind's fullest potential. With music therapy, individuals are able to shift their perception of time from virtual time, which is perceived in a left brain mode and is characterized by hours, minutes, and seconds, to experiential time, which is perceived through the memory.[14]

Experiential time exists because we experience both a state of tension and a state of resolution.[15] Our memory perceives tensions and resolutions in a linear sequence that is called a disturbance or an event. An emotion or a sound, for example, is a disturbance that can produce tension (i.e., psychophysiologic effects), which is followed by a return to equilibrium or resolution. The rate of these linear sequences or events influences our perception of time. Slow-moving music lengthens our perception of time because our memory has more time to experience the events (tensions and resolutions) and the spaces between the events. Thus, clock time becomes distorted, and clients can actually lose track of time for extended periods, enabling them to reduce anxiety, fear, and pain.

Music can assist the individual in moving through the six states of consciousness: (1) normal waking state, (2) expanded sensory threshold, (3) daydreaming, (4) trance, (5) meditative states, and (6) rapture.[16] During relaxation, music is first perceived in a normal wakeful state. Continued relaxation reduces sensory thresholds, and expanded awareness states predominate. The individual can then continue to move through the daydreaming, trance, and meditative states and progress to rapture, depending on the level of involvement with the music and relaxation.

Psychophysiologic Responses

Music alters a person's psychophysiology. The goal of music therapy and the type of music played (i.e., soothing or stimulating) determine the direction of the psychophysiologic changes. Soothing music can produce a hypometabolic response characteristic of relaxation in which autonomic, immune, endocrine, and neuropeptide systems are altered. Similarly, music therapy produces desired psychologic responses, such as reductions in anxiety and fear.

Effects of Music Therapy on Hemispheric Functioning

Right brain functioning is concerned with the intuitive, creative, and imaging way of processing information. The right hemisphere is employed differently in the musical process than is the left. The right "metaphoric" hemisphere is responsible for the major aspects of musical perception and music behavior (i.e., the recognition of pitch, a Gestalt sense of melody, rhythm, style, and musical memory). The commonalities between the components of speech and music are a basis for the perceptual processes of the right hemisphere that influence language functions and behavior. The left hemisphere is predominantly involved with analytic thinking, especially in verbal and mathematical functions.[17] It has been suggested that, when we ignore or do not listen to our right brain because we are busy, rushed, and stressed, the right brain probably sends foggy messages to the left brain. Such messages of imbalance may conflict with the logic of the moment in our left brain, and physical illness may result.[18] Music may activate the flow of stored memory material across the corpus callosum so that the right and left hemispheres work in harmony rather than conflict.

As one's musical knowledge grows, the brain's response to music shifts from a holistic to a more sequential and linear experience.[19] Music students and musicians tend to analyze the music to which they listen, classify the instruments, and critique the compositional techniques. Instead of integrating right and left brain functioning while listening to music in a relaxed state, such individuals tend to remain in or change to the left brain mode. With practice, however, they can let go of these conditioned responses to integrate the functioning of both hemispheres.[20]

Because music is nonverbal in nature, it appeals to the right hemisphere, whereas the traditional verbalization that the nurse uses in therapy with a client has its primary effect on the logical left brain. Music therapy, therefore, establishes a means of communication between the right and left brain.[21] The more connections that can be made in the brain, the more integrated the experience is within memory[22] (Figure 24–1).

Music, even more than the spoken word, "lends itself as a therapy because it meets with little or no intellectual resistance and does not need to appeal to logic to initiate its action . . . is more subtle and primitive, and therefore its appeal is wider and greater."[23] In a relaxed state, individuals can let go of preconceived ideas about listening to music and its

Figure 24–1 Melodic memories. Courtesy of Alexandra Lavie.

patterns, instruments, and rhythm and shift their thinking to the right side of the brain to alter their states of consciousness.[24]

Effects of Music Therapy on the Limbic System

Music therapy evokes psychophysiologic responses through the influence of musical pitch and rhythm on the limbic system.[25] Our emotional reactions to music may occur because the limbic system is the seat of emotions, feelings, and sensations. The quieting and calming effect of music can also produce other desired autonomic, immunologic, endocrine, and neuropeptide changes (see Chapter 4). Thus, the immediate influence of music therapy is on the mind state, which, in turn, influences the body state, producing a psychophysiologic response and a balance of body-mind-spirit.

Effects of Music Therapy on Our Bodies

Our entire body responds to sound, whether we consciously hear the sound or not. Even though our minds can tune out the sounds of airplane or automobile traffic, our bodies cannot. Many sounds assault our body because they are not in harmony with our fundamental vibratory pattern. On the other hand, musical vibrations that are in tune with our fundamental vibratory pattern may have a profound healing effect on the entire human body and mind, affecting changes in emotions and in organs, enzymes, hormones, cells, and atoms. Theoretically, musical vibrations may help restore regulatory function to a body out of tune (i.e., during times of stress and illness) and help maintain and enhance regulatory function to a body in tune. The therapeutic appeal of music may lie in its vibrational language and ability to align the body-mind-spirit with its own fundamental frequency.[26]

Effects of Music Therapy on Imagery, Emotions, and the Senses

Music elicits a variety of different experiences in individuals. Clients reaching an altered state of consciousness during relaxation and music therapy may visualize settings, peaceful scenes, or images, or they may experience various sensations or moods.[27] Music passages can evoke scenes from fantasy to real life. Melodic patterns can evoke love, joy, and deep peace.

During relaxation and music therapy, individuals can be guided in experiencing synesthesia, or a mingling of senses.[28] Musical tones can evoke color and movement, or tastes can evoke shapes. Many children spontaneously "see" sounds and "taste" textures.[29]

Music and color can be expressed in terms of vibrations. When color is translated into musical vibrations, the harmonies of color are 40 octaves higher than the ear can hear. A piano spans approximately 7 octaves. If the piano keyboard could be extended another 50 octaves higher, the keys played at these higher octaves would produce color rather than audible sound.[30]

The musical selection entitled "Spectrum Suite" (see Steve Halpern Sound Rx in Resources at the end of chapter) is designed to evoke colors. While listening to this selection, clients are guided in focusing on seven main energy centers known to exist in the body. In Eastern culture, these centers are called chakras. Each energy level is then associated with a specific musical tone and a specific color. For example, while focusing on the spine (the first energy center), the client is guided to hear and feel the keynote of C resonating in the spinal area and to visualize the vibrations of red bathing this area of the body.[31]

Music Therapy Applications

Music has been used to foster a variety of desired outcomes.[32] For example, it enhances creativity, the development of new ways of association. The manner in which a person approaches and considers things rather than that person's education or professional qualifications determines creativity.[33] It incorporates the unexpected, the unknown, and the peculiar. It can be enhanced by relaxation wherein the busy mind settles into a more quiet and receptive state. Through visualization, the mind can envision new ideas and ways of thinking. The playing of appropriate music produces alpha and theta brain waves, which are known to stimulate creativity.[34]

Music and movement and/or tonal exercises help clients become aware of their bodies and the energies released in them. Such techniques are employed to achieve bodymind balance and release blocked energies. Therapists have used musical instruments in another form of music therapy, particularly with disabled individuals. Clients play various instruments during the therapy to develop the qualities of perseverance, perceptiveness, concentration, and initiative and to promote perceptual-motor coordination and group interaction.[35]

Music has been used to improve learning. High psychophysiologic stress levels inhibit or block learning. When music and relaxation are combined, students learn better. Their learning can become more fun, and they become more fully involved in the experience. Music also has been used as a catalyst during the process of accelerated learning.

Audiotapes are now available in the marketplace to correct and reprogram unhealthy unconscious thought patterns. Music enhances such tapes, as their aim is to put the listener in a relaxed and balanced state.

During relaxation, the reprogramming message reaches the deeper unconscious mind where the new thought pattern will ultimately reside. Such self-help tapes frequently include desired affirmations or suggestions, combined with meditative music or white noise.[36]

Similarly, music has been used to facilitate reframing of past memories and experiences.[37] In achieving an altered state of consciousness, the unconscious mind can remember details of an individual's past experiences that the conscious mind may have forgotten. When the conscious mind remembers such experiences, the nurse can help the client reframe or reorganize them to produce a more healthy and positive experience.[38]

To enhance learning and facilitate self-help, music has been combined with subliminal suggestions. The subliminal technique delivers verbal messages to the individual at a volume so low or through a change in speed or frequency so fast that the conscious mind cannot perceive them. The conscious mind responds to the music while the unconscious mind absorbs and responds to the verbal suggestion.[39]

Music has been used to evoke imagery for a number of therapeutic ends (see Chapter 23). Clients who have difficulty with the imagery process may find relaxing background music helpful. Appropriately selected music can activate right hemisphere functioning and release a flow of images.[40] Bonny has developed an innovative approach called guided imagery and music, which is the conscious use of imagery that is evoked by relaxation and music.[41–43] It is a method of self-exploration, self-understanding, growth, healing, and transformation. In this approach, the client listens to classical music in a relaxed state, allowing the imagination to come to conscious awareness and sharing these experiences with a guide. The guide helps integrate the experience into the client's life.

Lastly, music thanatology is a new field of music therapy that is used to address the complex needs of the dying. The primary focus of the music is to help the person complete the transition between life and death. It helps patients let go of the physical body during the last hours before death by enhancing peace, acceptance, and a calm anticipation of death. Specially trained therapists, using the media of harp and voice, implement music thanatology.[44]

Music Therapy in Clinical Settings

Music can act as a catalyst to facilitate mental suggestion and enhance a client's own self-healing capacities. Thus, music has potential usefulness in the treatment of many health problems,[45] such as cardiovascular disease,[46–51] hypertension, migraine headaches, gastrointestinal ulcers, Raynaud's disease, acquired immunodeficiency syndrome (AIDS),[52] cancer (e.g., during chemotherapy to reduce nausea and vomiting and to induce distraction),[53–55] and pain.[56,57] It has also been shown to be effective for brain-damaged patients following head trauma,[58] for elderly and demented patients,[59] for patients with Alzheimer's disease,[60] and for patients undergoing general anesthesia.[61,62]

Several hospitals are using relaxation music to reduce stress and pain in hospitalized patients.[63] Music has been used in birthing, counseling, and massage rooms; during physical therapy; with multiply handicapped children; and in psychiatric hospitals, addiction treatment centers, and prisons.

Selection of Appropriate Music

It is an important and challenging task to select appropriate music for use in music therapy. The selections can influence the outcomes of music therapy.[64] Most music, however, is not composed for the purposes of relaxation and healing. Individuals often associate events in their lives, both pleasing and displeasing, with certain kinds of music.[65] This conditioned learning response influences music preferences and perceptions. Thus, it is necessary to choose the appropriate music for the particular individual.

No one musical selection or any one type of music works best for all people in all situations. A variety of soothing selections should be available for working with clients (i.e., popular, classical, country, operatic, folk, jazz, choral hymns), because it is difficult to predict a client's music preference and response to a particular selection. Musical selections that are relaxing and meditative to one client can be disruptive and annoying to another. Moreover, the music that some individuals identify as relaxing may not be physiologically relaxing at all.[66] Although music experts tend to agree that rock music does not evoke psychophysiologic relaxation (even if the individual thinks it does), classical, spiritual, or popular music may not be relaxing or soothing either.[67] Musical selections without words are preferable, as clients may concentrate on the words, their messages, and their meaning rather than allowing themselves to concentrate and flow with the music.[68]

New Age Music

Most traditional musical selections are based on tension and release. Such music is designed to create a sense of anticipation, followed by a sense of relief. The sense of anticipation is used most in popular and classical music. The tension-release music may be emotionally exciting and helpful in eliciting imagery, but it is not designed to relax most individuals.[69]

A new type of music has evolved for the purposes of orchestrating human instruments. The goal of therapy with this music is to allow the bodymind to choose whatever response mode that it needs in order to operate at a higher level of efficiency. Called nontraditional, meditative, or New Age, this music potentially has a wide appeal, because it is actually designed to transcend personal taste. There is no recognizable melody and no harmonic progressions; frequently, there is no central rhythm or natural beat. Nontraditional music requires neither intellectual analysis nor emotional involvement. It is a vibrational language that helps the bodymind attune itself with its own pattern or resonance. The music tends to flow endlessly and serves as a vehicle for relaxation, self-absorption, and contemplation.[70] A world of caution is necessary, however. Not all music labeled New Age is relaxing and meditative. Each selection must be evaluated before its use to determine its soothing and meditative qualities.

Hospital Music

Several companies and individuals have developed relaxing musical selections for use in the clinical setting (see Resources at the end of the chapter). For example, Halpern has created nontraditional long-playing musical selections that provide up to 8 hours of continuous relaxing music.[71] These tapes are designed for patient use in hospitals during surgery, childbirth, and postoperative recovery.

Bonny has also developed a set of music tapes, called Music Rx, for use in various hospital settings. The tapes consist of classical selections designed to reduce stress, provide a pleasant diversion, and quiet mood states. Music Rx was tested with intensive care and surgical patients at two hospitals. Patients participating in the Music Rx program had reduced heart rates, greater relief from pain, and positive psychologic ratings.[72] Music Rx is recommended for patients in the critical care units and operating and recovery rooms, as well as other inpatient and outpatient settings. As we learn more about how vibratory frequencies and patterns affect our bodymind, healing music will be composed to strengthen our altered vibratory patterns and bring them back to balance.[73]

Individual Musical Preference

Individuals need to evaluate their responses to various types of music. Although different musical selections can produce various effects, the fullest effect occurs when the listener is appropriately prepared to experience the sounds. The therapeutic effect of music is lessened when the listener is angry, distracted, critical, analytic, or resistant. With a relaxed and receptive bodymind, however, music has the potential to enter the body and play through it rather than around it. Thus, some form of relaxation exercise is recommended before the music experience.

Depending on the individual's physiology, mind state, and mood, music can produce different feelings at different times. An important rule to follow when listening to music is the iso-principle,[74] which states that matching the individual's mood to the appropriate music helps achieve an altered state of consciousness. When the mind and feelings are vibrating at a certain frequency, the music should be in resonance with that frequency.

Individuals can create their own tapes to match their moods and musical preference. If their mood is tense or angry and a quiet outcome is desired, they may start out with a short selection (3 minutes or less) of music that resonates with the mood and then add selections that increasingly move to a relaxed state.

Before creating a personal tape, an individual should spend some time experimenting with music—trying a variety of musical selections and learning what happens when listening to specific selections. "Experimental listening" involves listening to various types of music at different times of the day and week.[75] For example, spend 20 minutes listening to each type of music and then systematically evaluate your response to the selection, according to the following procedure:

1. Set aside 20 minutes of relaxation time.
2. Find a comfortable position.
3. Find a quiet place where you will not be interrupted.
4. Check your pulse rate.
5. Observe your breathing pattern (fast, slow, normal).
6. Assess your muscular tension (pain, muscle tightness, shoulder stiffness, jaw and neck tension). Are you loose, limp, sleepy?
7. Evaluate your mood state (angry, happy, sad).
8. Listen to the music for 20 minutes. Let your body respond to the music as it wishes: loosen muscles, lie down, dance, clap, hum.
9. Following the session, assess your breathing pattern.
10. Assess your muscular tension (more relaxed? more stimulated? tighter? tenser? calmer?).
11. Evaluate your mood state.
12. Record the name of the music selection and your before-and-after

responses in a music notebook for use when developing your own therapeutic tapes.

13. On a separate page in your notebook, recall and write down the many ways that music has empowered your life psychologically, physically, and spiritually. Include your most dramatic, intimate, and emotional memories associated with music. You will begin to realize the importance of sound in your life and recognize its healing potential.

Based on your response, create your own relaxation music tape of 20 to 30 minutes in length. The more regularly you use the tape, the more effective it will become.

Listening to music can be a holistic experience. As more individuals come to realize that music can be a principal source of healing and stress reduction, they will take great care to select their music. Music therapy may be incorporated into daily living activities, such as taking a "music bath" after a morning shower as a means of balancing the bodymind for the events of the day.[76]

NURSING PROCESS

Assessment

In preparing to use music therapy interventions, the nurse assesses the following parameters:

- the client's music history and the types of music that the client prefers (e.g., classical, popular, country, folk, hymns, jazz, rock, blues, other)
- the client's ability to identify types of music that make him or her happy, excited, sad, or relaxed
- the client's ability to identify types of music that are distasteful and make him or her tense
- the client's awareness of the importance of music in life: Is music played at home? In the car? At work? For relaxation? For excitement? For enjoyment? During times of stress? As a means of coping with stress?
- the client's frequency of music listening (per day or per week)
- the client's preference of music listening, such as radio, phonograph, or cassette recordings
- the client's previous participation in relaxation/imagery techniques combined with music: How long? How regularly?

- the client's use of some type of music for relaxation purposes; if so, ask the client to describe the bodymind responses evoked by music
- the client's insight into the use of music to produce psychophysiologic alterations
- the client's mood (iso-principle) that will determine the type of music to choose and the goals of the session.

(Assessment parameters outlined in Chapter 22, Relaxation, and Chapter 23, Imagery, should also be included, because relaxation, imagery, and music cannot be separated.)

Nursing Diagnoses

The following nursing diagnoses compatible with music therapy interventions and that are related to the nine human response patterns of Unitary Person (see Chapter 7) are as follows:

- Exchanging: All diagnoses
- Relating: Social isolation
- Valuing: Spiritual distress
- Choosing: Ineffective individual coping
Noncompliance
- Moving: Sleep pattern disturbance
- Perceiving: Altered self-concept
Disturbance in body-image
Disturbance in self-esteem
Hopelessness
Powerlessness
- Feeling: Altered comfort: pain
Anxiety
Fear

Client Outcomes

Table 24–1 guides the nurse in client outcomes, nursing prescriptions, and evaluation for the use of music therapy as a nursing intervention.

Plan and Interventions

Before the Session

- Establish the goals for the session with the client.
- Discuss how music therapy relaxes the bodymind and facilitates relaxation and self-healing.

Table 24–1 Nursing Interventions: Music Therapy

Client Outcomes	*Nursing Prescriptions*	*Evaluation*
The client will select music of choice and will participate in music therapy sessions to achieve a relaxed response and facilitate healing.	Provide the client with various musical taped selections to facilitate selecting music of choice. Guide the client in music therapy sessions and help the client to establish the routine of listening to music once or twice a day.	The client chose music of choice for listening and reported enjoying the music. The client participated in music therapy sessions twice a day to facilitate healing.
The client will demonstrate positive physiologic outcomes in response to the music therapy session, such as: • decreased respiratory rate • decreased heart rate • decreased blood pressure • decreased muscle tension • decreased fatigue	Assess the client's physiologic outcomes in response to music therapy before and immediately after the session. Evaluate the client's: • respiratory rate • heart rate • blood pressure • muscle tension • level of fatigue	The client demonstrated: • decreased respiratory rate from 28 to 18 per minute • decreased heart rate from 120 to 90 beats per minute • decreased blood pressure from 160/100 to 130/70 • decreased muscle tension • decreased fatigue
The client will demonstrate positive psychologic outcomes in response to the music therapy session such as: • positive emotions and relaxed feeling • decreased restlessness and agitation • decreased anxiety/depression • increased motivation • increased nonverbal expression of feelings • increased positive imagery • decreased isolation	Assess the client's psychologic outcomes in response to music therapy before and immediately after the session. Evaluate the client's: • emotions and level of relaxation • level of restlessness and agitation • level of anxiety/depression • level of motivation • ability to express feelings nonverbally • type of imagery experienced • level of social isolation	The client demonstrated: • positive emotions and more relaxed feeling • reduced restless and agitated behaviors • decreased levels of anxiety (or depression) • increased motivation to accomplish life's daily tasks • increased nonverbal expression of feelings • increased positive imagery • decreased feelings of social isolation

- Discuss the length of the session, usually 20 to 30 minutes.
- Ask the client to urinate, if necessary.
- Dim the lights.
- Close the drapes.
- Ask the client to remove eyeglasses or contact lenses.
- Ask the client to sit or lie in a comfortable position. It is sometimes helpful to place a small pillow under the knees to relieve lower back strain. Have a light blanket available for warmth, if needed.
- Spend a few moments centering yourself to be fully present with the client.

At the Beginning of the Session

Script: *The purpose of the session is to relax in a wakeful state and have a quiet experience listening to music. First, I will guide you in a few exercises to relax. Then I will guide you in how to listen to music (of your choice). Then try to let the music relax your body-mind-spirit even more as you listen to the music for 20 minutes. Now close your eyes if you wish. Find a comfortable position with your hands at the side of your chest or on your body—whatever is most comfortable. At any time, you may change positions, scratch, or swallow. There may be noises around, but these will not be important if you concentrate on my voice.*

Guide the client in a general relaxation or imagery script (see Chapters 22 and 23).

During the Session

Script: *Now, as you continue to relax, I will turn on the music. Listen to the music. Tell yourself that you would like to go wherever the music takes you. Allow yourself to follow the music. Let the music suggest to you what to think and what to feel. Do not try to analyze the music or the melody. If you find distracting thoughts occurring, simply let go of them and come back to concentrating on the music. Allow the music to relax you even more than you are now. The music will play for 20 minutes, and I will leave the room. I will quietly come back into the room before the music is over. Now continue to relax your body-mind-spirit; let the music help you.*

At the End of the Session

Script: *Now that the music is over, I will guide you in counting from 5 to 1. You will come back into the room easily and quietly. You will feel very relaxed, calm, and peaceful. You will remember the pathway that led you to this new experience, and you will be able to find it quickly whenever you wish to return.*

Close the session as follows:

- While the client is in a self-reflective state, lead him or her in further guided imagery exercises, or journal entries, if desired.
- Use the client outcomes (see Table 24–1) that were established before the session and the client's subjective experience (Exhibit 24–1) to evaluate the session.
- Schedule a follow-up session.

Specific Interventions

Development of Audio/Video Cassette Library

Nurses can develop an audio/video cassette library on each clinical unit or in each practice area. Relaxation, imagery, and music therapy audio and video tapes are recommended for use in all clinical settings from the birthing to the dying process. Audio and video tapes can be developed and collected that are of specific benefit to the particular client/patient population with which the nurse is working. Following are suggestions for building a successful audio/video tape library:

1. Equipment
    - Have several tape recorders with comfortable headsets per unit.
    - Place all equipment in a safe and convenient location.
    - Have a variety of music tapes available. Commercial tapes are relatively inexpensive and readily available. A complete tape library will include music, relaxation, imagery, stress management tapes, and specific tapes for smoking cessation, pre- and postsurgery, weight reduction, pain management, insomnia, self-esteem, subliminal learning, and so on. Consider different types of music, such as easy listening, light and heavy classical, popular, jazz, operatic, folk, country, hymns, choral, and nontraditional selections.
    - Ask staff members to donate one favorite relaxation tape to the library.

- Write different companies (see Resources at the end of the chapter) and request a catalogue of their selections.
- Encourage nurses to develop tapes for specific client/patient problems that can help with procedures, tests, and treatments. The tapes may or may not have soothing background music.
- Have brochures and catalogues of recording companies available upon request from the patient.
- Encourage use of different tapes for further relaxation, imagery, and stress management training.

2. Procedures
   - If tapes are checked out on an outpatient basis, have the client make a deposit for the tape. It is suggested that the deposit cover the cost of the tape in case it is not returned.
   - Establish who will have authority to check out the tapes and equipment. If in the hospital, a volunteer could assist in checking out the equipment for the patient after the nurse has assessed the patient's needs and selected the appropriate tape.
   - Prepare a sign-out log that records the patient's name, room, date, and check-out time.
   - Instruct the patient in the use of the equipment and tapes, if necessary.
   - Allow 20 to 30 minutes of listening without interruption twice a day. Place a sign on the patient's door stating, "Relaxation Session in Progress—Please Do Not Disturb."
   - Following the listening session, evaluate the patient's response to the tape and answer any questions.
   - Chart the patient's specific response to the therapy. For example, were the desired outcomes achieved (e.g., lowered respiratory rate, decreased heart rate and blood pressure, decreased muscle tension and anxiety)? Identify the client's subjective evaluation of the experience (e.g., found the experience relaxing, helped with sleep, assisted in coping with pain, assisted with painful procedure).
   - Return the equipment and tapes to the library and record the check-in information in the log.

Music Therapy Scripts

Taking a Music Bath (Basic). Listening to music for 20 minutes can help clients to prepare for a balanced day, prevent stress, and reduce stress.

The nurse first explains the purpose of the session to the client. It is also important to conduct a general relaxation session with the client before proceeding with the script. After turning on the music, the nurse begins slowly, pacing the words with the client's increased relaxation.

Script: *As the music begins, you will begin a music bath. Allow the sound to wash over you, letting the music touch every surface of your body. Permit the sound to rinse off any tension, unpleasant emotions, and any sound pollution to prepare for the day. . . .*

Allow yourself to be immersed in the musical sounds as if you were in a warm, relaxing tub of water or standing under the warm water in a shower. Imagine the water filled with soothing, relaxing sounds. The sounds are cleansing your body and calming your emotions. . . .

As you allow your entire body to become immersed in the sounds, notice how the music resonates in different parts of your body. As you become more relaxed, notice how much more you are enjoying the music. . . .

As the music rinses away your tension, permit yourself to feel refreshed. The music bath has reached every part of your body. You have renewed and refreshed energy. . . .

Allow any remaining tension to be washed away, permitting you to feel balanced, calm, and refreshed.

Continue listening to the music now for 20 minutes. As the music ends, gradually come back into a wakeful, relaxed, and refreshed state.

Expanding the Senses (Basic). Listening to music for 10 to 20 minutes can help clients to expand awareness, open up the senses, and participate in a mingling of the senses. The nurse (1) explains the purpose of the session to the client, (2) conducts a general relaxation session with the client, (3) turns on the music, and (4) begins slowly, pacing the words with the client's increased relaxation.

Script: *Let the music take you to a soothing peaceful place that is filled with various textures, sights, colors, and sounds. . . . Take a moment to find this place. . . . You feel comfortable and relaxed in this peaceful place. Slowly begin to explore the surface and texture of your surroundings. Permit the music to help you experience softness, smoothness, and gentleness. . . .*

As you continue to explore, discover the colors associated with the shape, texture, and feelings of things. Let the music suggest the sound of the colors and textures.

Touch the things in your environment. Let your fingers, tongue, and cheeks experience the textures. Take time to enjoy each feeling. Do not feel rushed as you explore. . . .

As you touch each thing in your surroundings, take time to investigate its source. Where did it come from? Why does it feel as it does? And why is it here?

With each surface, explore its color, its sound. The deeper you travel into the essence of your surroundings, the richer the experience will be. . . .

Continue this experience for another 10 to 20 minutes. Gradually come back into the room awake, alert, and ready to continue the day.

Merging the Bodymind with Music (Basic). A quiet listening experience that mingles the senses and induces relaxation may last 20 minutes. Nontraditional music, with nonmetered beat and periods of silence between sounds is suggested. (See Steve Halpern Sound Rx for nontraditional selections in Resources at the end of this chapter.) After conducting a general relaxation session with the client, the nurse turns on the music and begins, pacing the words with the client's increased relaxation.

Script: *Visualize your ears. Explore your ears. Feel your ears expanding and becoming larger. Permit your ears to become channels in the sides of your head that open and lengthen throughout your body and into your feet. Allow these channels to hear all parts of your body.*

Think of the sounds you are hearing as something more than a pleasant hearing sensation. The sounds are nourishment and energy for your body—your mind—your spirit. . . . Let the sound of the music move in you, around you, above you, below you. The sound is everywhere, and you can hear it throughout your body. . . .

See the sound, taste it, feel it, smell it, hear it. Turn the sound into light and color and see it. Concentrate your attention on the sounds and the silence between the sounds. . . .

Open your ears. You have beautiful, big ears—channels throughout your body. Let the sounds pass through these channels to totally experience the event. Merge with the music. There will no longer be music and a listener, rather a state of total experiencing of the sound. Total concentration of the sound . . . moment-by-moment and on the silence between . . . You can go beyond. . . . You will experience the soundless sound, the state where sound becomes silence, silence becomes sound, and they merge together.

Continue the experience for another 10 to 20 minutes. Gradually come back into the room awake, alert, and ready to continue the day.

Toning and Groaning (Basic). By listening to music for 10 to 20 minutes, clients can prepare for meditation, release intensive emotions, or induce an altered state of consciousness.

Script: *Lie comfortably on your back. Begin with an audible groan such as "Oh-h-h" or "Ah-h-h." Let the groan be as deep as possible without forcing it. Let it give you a feeling of release, of emptying out any tension. Feel your skin and bones vibrate with the sound.*

Many people spontaneously groan when they have taken off a tight belt or tight shoes. Your groaning should be a comparable release of and freedom from constraint. Let it be loud and natural without forcing the sound. . . . You might even feel a bit silly about groaning. You might giggle or laugh. That's okay. Just let it out. . . .

Stretch your arms and legs now. Then let your body relax and groan again. Notice the sound becoming effortless, relaxing, and deeper. . . . Be sure to let the groan come from deep down in your feet. Notice the vibrations starting up your body. As you continue to groan, feel a weight being lifted from you. Heaviness is being lifted while a sense of lightness sets in. . . . Groaning is a healing process. Allow it to happen. Enjoy the feeling of release. . . .

You will notice a tendency for your voice to rise as your tensions are allowed to leave. Let your voice do what it wants as you continue to groan. It will find its natural place. When your body reaches its tone, it will be satisfied, and you will sigh a deep satisfying sigh.

At this point you are toning. You have found your tone. You are sounding your tone. You are resonating with your body. This is your own music.

The nurse ends the session or prepares for imagery scripts, meditation, or music listening.

Training for Skillful Listening (Basic). Music therapy sessions of 15 minutes may help clients improve the art of listening and train them consciously to hear sounds clearly.

Script: *Concentrate on the sounds around you. Let your ears hear every possible sound. Explore the subtle sounds, breathing, distant cars, wind blowing, hum of the lights. . . . Limit your sensations. Keep your eyes closed. Avoid touching. Heighten and isolate your perception of sound. Listen to the parts of sound. Listen to a sound. Imagine the sound makes a line. Bend the line that the sound makes. Does it go up? Does it go down? Does it curve or have humps? The word* bend *itself has a bend. Notice the height of the bend. Imagine the top and bottom of the bend. . . .*

Image the grain of the sound. Is it rough or smooth? Rough like sandpaper or smooth like silk or something in between? What is the volume? High/low? What is the intensity? Loud or soft? What color do you associate with the sound? What emotions do you notice as you listen to this sound?

Now use your voice to imitate sound. Imitate the sound of a jet flying high through the air. . . . Now imitate the sound of a helicopter flying through the air. . . . Imitate the sound of a soft wind. . . . Imitate the sound of an autumn leaf falling. The point of this exercise is not to become an expert jet imitator, but to realize there is more to the art of listening and hearing than we think. When you practice focused and conscious hearing, you will recognize subtle differences in sound. You will expand your skills in the art of listening.

Case Study

Setting: Coronary care unit (CCU)

Patient: W.R., a 62-year-old man who was admitted at 3:00 A.M. with the presumptive diagnosis of acute myocardial infarction

Nursing Diagnoses:
1. Altered comfort: chest pain related to acute myocardial infarction
2. Anxiety related to cardiovascular stressors and hospitalization

Prior to admission, W. had experienced severe, substernal chest pain that radiated to the left shoulder, arm, and hand and was associated with nausea, vomiting, and shortness of breath. The chief of military police at a local military base, he stated that he worked 10 to 12 hours every day and was a hard-driving individual. He had been in excellent health before this episode and denied any previous hospitalization.

W. was on bedrest, attached to a cardiac monitor; he was receiving nasal oxygen and an intravenous nitroglycerin drip. He had no current chest pain, and his vital signs and cardiac rhythm were stable. However, he was assessed to be highly anxious, with clenched fists and jaw, obvious muscle tension, startle reactions to minor noise, and flight of ideas with constant talking.

When asked by the nurse if he wanted to participate in a relaxation exercise that would help him cope better with his admission to the CCU and his illness, W. was reluctant, but agreed because he said he did not have much else to do.

After providing a music history, the patient selected a soothing classical music tape from the CCU's audiocassette library. The patient was supplied with a tape recorder and comfortable headsets. The music was checked for the appropriate volume and turned off, and the headset was placed beside the patient's pillow. A small finger thermistor was taped to the patient's left index finger, and his apical heart rate and peripheral temperature were recorded. The nurse guided the patient with a head-to-toe relaxation script and continued with the "Merging the Bodymind with Music" script. The headsets were then placed on the patient, and he continued the relaxation exercise while listening to music for 20 minutes.

Following the first session, W. said that he was sure he was not doing it "right" and that he did not wish to try it again. The nurse said she understood. She also explained that there is no "right" way to experience relaxation and that everyone experiences it a little differently. She added that relaxation is a skill to be learned, like riding a bike, and that the more people practice the technique, the better and richer is their response. She encouraged W. to try one more session, and he agreed. The nurse observed that there had been no change in W.'s finger temperature or heart rate following this first session.

Following the second session, W. was noticeably quiet. When the nurse inquired how he perceived the session, W. said, "It was okay—see you tomorrow." Following the third session, the nurse identified an 8-degree increase in finger temperature and a 10 beat/minute decline in heart rate from pre-session readings. W. had a small grin on his face and stated, "I can't believe what just happened to me. This stuff really works. I felt really relaxed. You know, I have a tough job. I work 10 hours a day. For me, relaxing means having a beer after work or going on a vacation 1 week a year. I have been walking around for 62 years with a stiff neck, and I never knew it. No one ever told me how to really relax. After this [session], I know now that, when I thought I was relaxing, I really wasn't. I have never felt like this in 62 years."

W. was transferred out of the CCU to the telemetry unit that afternoon. He stated that he planned to continue his music therapy sessions twice a day during the remainder of his hospitalization and after his return home. He was given catalogues on relaxation music tapes and informed that such tapes could also be purchased from the hospital's gift shop.

Evaluation

With the client, the nurse determines whether the client outcomes of music therapy (see Table 24–1) were successfully achieved. To evaluate the session further, the nurse may again explore the subjective effects of the experience with the client (Exhibit 24–1).

It is important to ask clients to share their experiences, as the sharing helps evaluate the experience and clarify any misconceptions. Some people may report that their experiences were totally different from any previous experience and they discovered previously unknown mind spaces. Others may not perceive any beneficial effects of the therapy after the first or second session. They may worry if they cannot image, see colors, or feel relaxed. These clients need reassurance that there is no right response and that not everyone experiences the same type of sensations, feelings, sights, or sounds in the same way. They also need encouragement to continue to practice the technique a few more times before

Exhibit 24–1 Evaluating the Client's Subjective Experience with Music Therapy

1. Was this a new kind of music listening experience for you? Can you describe it?
2. Did you have any visual experiences? Of people, places, or objects? Can you describe them?
3. Did you see any colors while listening? Did the colors change as the music changed?
4. Did you notice any textures, smells, movements, or taste while experiencing the music?
5. Were you less aware of your surroundings? Were you able to flow with the music?
6. Did you like the music?
7. Did the music produce any feelings or emotions?
8. Was the experience pleasant?
9. Did you feel relaxed and refreshed after the experience?
10. Would you like to try this again?
11. What would be helpful to make this a better experience for you?

drawing any conclusions regarding its effectiveness. The desired outcomes of music therapy are relaxation and a psychophysiologic quieting of body-mind-spirit. Clients should understand that relaxation is an acquired skill and the effectiveness of such therapy is usually a function of practice. The more they practice relaxation skills, the better they become in producing changes in their psychophysiology.

Some people may feel that they need "two or three more" sessions with the nurse before they have acquired the skills to practice the technique themselves. In reality, no guide can teach the client relaxation skills. Any changes happen because of the individual's motivation, involvement, and skill—not because a guide is present. As soon as clients realize that they can make similar suggestions to themselves to induce relaxation, they are ready to continue the technique alone. Some people may wish to make an audiocassette of the guide's voice during the session or record their own script. The audiocassette then serves as the guide.

DIRECTIONS FOR FUTURE RESEARCH

1. Pre-test and post-test various types of "relaxing" music to validate that clients perceive such music as relaxing.
2. Create a sound-and-color healing room within a hospital setting and evaluate its effects on patient recovery.
3. Evaluate several music scripts to determine whether one script is more effective than another in achieving specified outcomes.
4. Compare the effectiveness of music therapy with that of other relaxation techniques in various client groups to determine which technique is the most effective for which type of clients.
5. Develop valid and reliable evaluation tools that assess a client's subjective response to music therapy.
6. Evaluate the effects of a music audiocassette library on hospitalized patients' length of stay, recovery, and complications.
7. Contrast the attitudes and stress levels of nurses who routinely use music as a nursing intervention with those of nurses who do not use music.

NURSE HEALER REFLECTIONS

After reading this chapter, the nurse healer will be able to answer or will begin a process of answering the following questions:

- How do I feel about music as a healing ritual?
- How and when do I sense my own rhythm?

- What is my melody?
- When I listen to music, how do I allow myself to let go into the music?
- Am I able to use music with my clients to facilitate the healing process?

NOTES

1. R. Leviton, Healing Vibrations, *Yoga Journal* (1994, January-February): 59–60.
2. H. Jenny, *The Structure and Dynamics of Waves and Vibrations* (Basel, Switzerland: Basilius Press, 1967).
3. S. Halpern and L. Savary, *Sound Health: Music and Sounds That Make Us Whole* (San Francisco: Harper & Row, 1985), 33.
4. C.E. Guzzetta, Physiology of the Heart and Circulation, in *Cardiovascular Nursing: Bodymind Tapestry*, ed. C.E. Guzzetta and B.M. Dossey (St. Louis: Mosby, 1984), 104–153.
5. Ibid., 115–116.
6. Halpern and Savary, *Sound Health*, 33–37.
7. Ibid., 37.
8. Ibid., 39.
9. C. Schulbert, *The Music Therapy Sourcebook* (New York: Human Sciences Press, 1981), 13.
10. P.M. Hamel, *Through Music to the Self* (Boulder, CO: Shambhala Press, 1979), 166.
11. H. Bonny and L. Savary, *Music and Your Mind* (New York: Harper & Row, 1973), 15.
12. Hamel, *Through Music to the Self*, 174.
13. Bonny and Savary, *Music and Your Mind*, 14.
14. R. McClellan, Music and Altered States of Consciousness, *Dromenon* 2(1979):3–5.
15. Ibid.
16. S. Krippner, *The Highest State of Consciousness* (New York: Doubleday, 1972), 1–5.
17. D.G. Campbell, *Introduction to the Musical Brain* (St. Louis: MMB Music, 1984), 14–65.
18. Ibid., 54.
19. Ibid., 45.
20. Bonny and Savary, *Music and Your Mind*, 90.
21. R. Beebe, Synesthesia with Music, *Dromenon* 2(1979):7.
22. Campbell, *Introduction to the Musical Brain*, 14.
23. I. Altshuler, A Psychiatrist's Experience with Music as a Therapeutic Agent, in *Music as Medicine*, ed. D. Schullian and M. Schoen (New York: Henry Schuman, 1948), 267.
24. McClellan, Music and Altered States of Consciousness, 4.
25. Campbell, *Introduction to the Musical Brain*, 20–22.
26. Halpern and Savary, *Sound Health*, 39–43.
27. Bonny and Savary, *Music and Your Mind*, 30.
28. J. Page, Roses Are Red, E-flat Is, Too, *Hippocrates* (1987, September-October):63–66.

29. J. Houston, *The Possible Human* (Los Angeles: Jeremy P. Tarcher, 1982), 47–48.
30. Halpern and Savary, *Sound Health*, 183.
31. Ibid., 185.
32. B.J. Crowe, Music—The Ultimate Physician, in *Music: Physician for Times To Come*, ed. D. Campbell (Wheaton, IL: Quest Books, 1991), 111.
33. Halpern and Savary, *Sound Health*, 115.
34. Campbell, *Introduction to the Musical Brain*, 62–63.
35. Schulbert, *The Music Therapy Sourcebook*, 104.
36. Halpern and Savary, *Sound Health*, 136.
37. Ibid., 129.
38. Bonny and Savary, *Music and Your Mind*, 31.
39. Halpern and Savary, *Sound Health*, 137.
40. Ibid., 96–97.
41. H. Bonny, Guided Imagery and Music Brochure (Port Townsend, WA: Institute for Music and Imagery, 1986).
42. S.J. Stokes, Letting the Sound Depths Arise, in *Music and Miracles*, ed. D. Campbell (Wheaton, IL: Quest Books, 1992), 187–188.
43. K. Bruscia, Visits from the Other Side: Healing Persons with AIDS through Guided Imagery and Music, in *Music and Miracles*, ed. D. Campbell (Wheaton, IL: Quest Books, 1992), 195–207.
44. T. Schroeder-Sheker, Music for the Dying: A Personal Account of the New Field of Music Thanatology—History, Theories, and Clinical Narratives, *Journal of Holistic Nursing* 12, no. 1 (1994):83–99.
45. D. Aldridge, The Music of the Body: Music Therapy in Medical Settings, *Advances* 9, no. 1 (1993):17–35.
46. C.E. Guzzetta, Effects of Relaxation and Music Therapy on Patients in a Coronary Care Unit with Presumptive Acute Myocardial Infarction, *Heart and Lung* 18(1989):609–616.
47. C.A. Bolwerk, Effects of Relaxing Music on State Anxiety in Myocardial Infarction Patients, *Critical Care Nurse Quarterly* 13, no. 2 (1990):63–72.
48. P. Updike, Music Therapy Results for ICU Patients, *Dimensions of Critical Care Nursing* 9, no. 1 (1990):39–45.
49. J.M. White, Music Therapy: An Intervention To Reduce Anxiety in the Myocardial Infarction Patient, *Clinical Nurse Specialist* 6(1992):58–63.
50. D. Elliott, The Effects of Music and Muscle Relaxation on Patient Anxiety in a Coronary Care Unit, *Heart and Lung* 23, no. 1 (1994):27–35.
51. L.M. Zimmermann et al., Effects of Music on Patient Anxiety in Coronary Care Units, *Heart and Lung* 17(1988):560–566.
52. Bruscia, Visits from the Other Side.
53. L. Kammrath, Music Therapy during Chemotherapy: Report on the Beginning of a Study, *Krakenpflege-Frankfurt* 43(1989):282–283.
54. G. Kerkvliet, Music Therapy May Help Control Cancer Pain, *Journal of the National Cancer Institute* 82(1990):350–352.
55. J. Frank, The Effects of Music Therapy and Guided Visual Imagery on Chemotherapy Induced Nausea and Vomiting, *Oncology Nursing Forum* 12(1985):47–52.

56. L.B. Zimmerman et al., Effects of Music in Patients Who Had Chronic Cancer Pain, *Western Journal of Nursing Research* 11(1989):298–309.
57. J.A. Schoor, Music and Pattern Change in Chronic Pain, *Advances in Nursing Science* 15, no. 4 (1993):27–36.
58. C.M. Lucia, Toward Developing a Model of Music Therapy Intervention in the Rehabilitation of Head Trauma Patients, *Music Therapy Perspectives* 4(1987):34–39.
59. D. Prinsley, Music Therapy in Geriatric Care, *Australian Nurses Journal* 15(1986): 48–49.
60. J. Tyson, Meeting the Needs of Dementia, *Nursing of the Elderly* 1(1989):18–19.
61. L. Keegan, Holistic Nursing, *Journal of Post Anesthesia Nursing* 4(1989):17–21.
62. W. Lehmann and D. Kirchner, Initial Experiences in the Combined Treatment of Aphasia Patients Following Cerebrovascular Insult by Speech Therapist and Music Therapists, *Zeitschrift Altenforschung* 41(1986):123–128.
63. Halpern and Savary, *Sound Health*, 58.
64. G.C. Mornhinweg, Effects of Music Preference and Selection on Stress Reduction, *Journal of Holistic Nursing* 10, no. 2 (1992):101–109.
65. Hamel, *Through Music to the Self*, 169.
66. Halpern and Savary, *Sound Health*, 46.
67. Hamel, *Through Music to the Self*, 169.
68. Halpern and Savary, *Sound Health*, 98.
69. Ibid., 142.
70. Hamel, *Through Music to the Self*, 142.
71. Halpern and Savary, *Sound Health*, 203.
72. H. Bonny, Sound Spaces: Music Rx Is Proven in the ICU, *ICM West Newsletter* 2, no. 4 (1982):.
73. Halpern and Savary, *Sound Health*, 104.
74. Bonny and Savary, *Music and Your Mind*, 43.
75. B. Wein, Body and Soul Music, *American Health* (1987, April):67–74.
76. Halpern and Savary, *Sound Health*, 150.

RESOURCES

Relaxation, Music and Imagery Tapes

Awakening Productions
4132 Tuller Avenue
Culver, CA 90230

Bodymind Systems
910 Dakota Drive
Temple, TX 76504
(817) 773-2337

Catalog Services
P.O. Box 1244
Boulder, CO 80306
(303) 443-8484

Conscious Living Foundation
P.O. Box 9
Drain, OR 97435
(1-800) 752-CALM

Steve Halpern Sound Rx
P.O. Box 1439
San Rafael, CA 94915
(415) 491-1930

Institute for Music, Health, and Education
Don G. Campbell, Director
P.O. Box 1244
Boulder, CO 80306
(303) 443-8484

Magna Music
10370 Page Industrial Blvd.
St. Louis, MO 63132
(800) 543-3771

Mind/Body Health Sciences
393 Dixon Road, Goldhill
Salina Star Route
Boulder, CO 80302
(303) 440-8460

Music Design
4650 N. Port Washington Road
Milwaukee, WI 53212
1-800-862-7232

New Era Media
425 Alabama Street
San Francisco, CA 94110
(415) 863-3555

Sources Cassette
Dept. 99, P.O. Box W
Stanford, CA 94305
(415) 328-7171

Windham Hill Records
P.O. Box 9388
Stanford, CA 94305

Music Therapy Tapes Designed for Hospital Use

Music RX
P.O. Box 173
Port Townsend, WA 98368
(206) 385-6160

Steven Halpern (Hospital Suite)
P.O. Box 1439
San Rafael, CA 94915
(415) 491-1930

Additional Resources

American Association of Music Therapy
P.O. Box 80012
Valley Forge, PA 19484
(215) 265-4006

Institute for Consciousness and Music
7027 Bellona Ave.
Baltimore, MD 21212

International Society for Music in Medicine
Dr. Ralph Springe, Executive Director
Sportkrankenhaus Hellersen
Paulmannshoher, Strasse 17
D-5880 Ludenscheid, Germany

Mid-Atlantic Institute for Guided Imagery and Music
Sara Jane Stokes, Director
Box 4655
Virginia Beach, VA 23454

National Association of Music Therapy
8455 Colesville Road, Suite 930
Silver Spring, MD 20910
(301) 589-3300

Index

B

C

E

F

G

I

J

N

S

Y

Z